Urban Emergency (Mis)Management and the Crisis of Neoliberalism

Studies in Critical Social Sciences Book Series

Haymarket Books is proud to be working with Brill Academic Publishers (www.brill.nl) to republish the *Studies in Critical Social Sciences* book series in paperback editions. This peer-reviewed book series offers insights into our current reality by exploring the content and consequences of power relationships under capitalism, and by considering the spaces of opposition and resistance to these changes that have been defining our new age. Our full catalog of *SCSS* volumes can be viewed at https://www.haymarketbooks.org/series_collections/4-studies-in-critical-social-sciences.

Urban Emergency (Mis)Management and the Crisis of Neoliberalism

Flint, MI in Context

Edited by
Terressa A. Benz
Graham Cassano

Haymarket Books
Chicago, IL

First published in 2021 by Brill Academic Publishers, The Netherlands

Published in paperback in 2022 by
Haymarket Books
P.O. Box 180165
Chicago, IL 60618
773-583-7884
www.haymarketbooks.org

ISBN: 978-1-64259-791-2

Distributed to the trade in the US through Consortium Book Sales and Distribution (www.cbsd.com) and internationally through Ingram Publisher Services International (www.ingramcontent.com).

This book was published with the generous support of Lannan Foundation and Wallace Action Fund.

Special discounts are available for bulk purchases by organizations and institutions. Please call 773-583-7884 or email info@haymarketbooks.org for more information.

Cover design by Jamie Kerry and Ragina Johnson.

Printed in the United States.

10 9 8 7 6 5 4 3 2 1

Library of Congress Cataloging-in-Publication data is available.

Contents

Figures and Tables

Figures

Tables

Notes on Contributors

Terressa A. Benz

currently lives in Detroit, Michigan and is Assistant Professor of Criminal Justice at Oakland University. She is a critical criminologist whose work lies at the intersection of law and society, urban sociology, and criminology. Dr. Benz has written about poverty fetishism, environmental racism, campus carry, and the socio-legal exclusion of undesirable populations in the postindustrial city.

Graham Cassano

is an Associate Professor of sociology at Oakland University. His most recent books include *A New Kind of Public: Community, Solidarity, Political Economy in New Deal Cinema, 1935-48* and *Eleanor Smith's Hull House Songs: The Music of Protest and Hope in Jane Addams's Chicago.*

Daniel Clark

teaches history at Oakland University, in Rochester, Michigan. He is the author of *Like Night and Day: Unionization in a Southern Mill Town* (University of North Carolina Press, 1997) and *Disruption in Detroit: Autoworkers and the Elusive Postwar Boom* (University of Illinois Press, 2018).

Jon W. Carroll

is an anthropological archaeologist with research interests in cultural transmission, social interaction and integration, political and economic organization, and the social science applications of Geographic Information Systems (GIS). Dr. Carroll is a Registered Professional Archaeologist (RPA) who specializes in the archaeology of the Eastern Woodlands of North America and is an FAA-licensed drone pilot. His latest research conducted in Africa, Europe, North America and the Near East uses aerial drones to collect multispectral aerial imagery for anthropological and archaeological computer modeling and simulation.

Katrinell Davis

is an Associate Professor of Sociology and African American Studies at Florida State University, where she teaches courses exploring race and gender relations, poverty and policy, as well as work and mobility trends within the American labor market. Dr. Davis is a stratification sociologist who specializes in race and class inequalities in urban areas, especially as they manifest within the workplace, schools, and within communities. Her recent work explores the limits to community organizing for improved essential services in low resource communities.

Michael D. Doan
is Associate Professor of Philosophy at Oakland University and a community-based activist in Detroit. He has worked with Detroiters Resisting Emergency Management (D-REM) and the Detroit Independent Freedom Schools Movement (DIFS) and is currently a board member of the James and Grace Lee Boggs Center to Nurture Community Leadership. He is the author of "Resisting Structural Epistemic Injustice," *Feminist Philosophical Quarterly* (2018), and the co-author (with Shea Howell and Ami Harbin) of "Detroit to Flint and Back Again: Solidarity Forever," *Critical Sociology* (2017).

David Fasenfest
is an Associate Professor of Sociology and Urban Affairs, College of Liberal Arts and Sciences, Wayne State University, the editor of *Critical Sociology* and edits the book series *Studies in Critical Social Science* and *New Scholarship in Political* Economy, both with Brill Academic Press. His research focuses on inequality, urban development and Marxism. He is the author of "Emergency Management in Michigan: A Misguided Policy Initiative" (2018) in Ashley Nickels and Jason Rivera (eds.) *Community Development and Public Administration Theory: Empowerment through the Enhancement of Democratic Principles*, London: Routledge; "A Neoliberal Response to an Urban Crisis: Emergency Management in Flint, MI" (2018) *Critical Sociology*; "Monsieur Le Capital and Madame La Terre on the Brink" (2017) in Molly Scott Cato and Peter North (eds.) *Towards Just and Sustainable Economies: Comparing Social and Solidarity Economy in the North and South*. Bristol: Policy Press; "The Cooperative City: Building Economic Democracy" (2015), in Michael Peter Smith and Lucas Owen Kirkpatrick (eds.), *Reinventing Detroit*, Volume 11, Comparative Urban and Community Research, Piscataway, NJ: Transaction Books. In addition, he is the editor of *Engaging Social Justice: Critical Studies of 21st Century Social Transformation* (Haymarket, 2010), and *Social Change, Resistance and Social Practice* (Haymarket, 2011).

A.E. Garrison
is an Assistant Professor of Sociology in Youth Studies at Central Michigan University. She earned her doctorate in Rural Sociology from the University of Missouri-Columbia in 2011, with an emphasis in community development and educational policy and analysis. The focus of her work has been the development of graphic sociological methodology for use in scholarship and pedagogy.

Previous scholarly work includes "Boneyards of the Sortatropolis Exploring a City of Industrial Secrets-Lansing, Michigan (Part 1)" (Garrison 2017).

Dr. Garrison's graphic work includes "Ghosts of Infertility: haunted by realities of reproductive death" (Garrison, 2016), and "Boneyard Quiet: a ghost story" (Garrison, 2020). Dr. Garrison's research interests also include social consequences that result from state resource management policies and practices, especially impacting urban infrastructure in Rust Belt cities of the United States, and rural communities.

Peter J. Hammer

was named the A. Alfred Taubman Professor of Law at Wayne State University Law School in fall 2018. Hammer is the director of the Damon J. Keith Center for Civil Rights at Wayne Law. The Keith Center is dedicated to promoting the educational, economic and political empowerment of under-represented communities in urban areas and to ensuring that the phrase "equal justice under law" applies to all members of society. Hammer has become a leading voice on the economic and social issues impacting the city of Detroit.

Ami Harbin

is Associate Professor of Philosophy and Women and Gender Studies at Oakland University. Her research is in the area of feminist philosophy, moral psychology, and bioethics. She is the author of *Disorientation and Moral Life* (Oxford University Press, 2016).

Shea Howell

is a community-based organizer in Detroit. She is a writer and speaker, working closely with the James and Grace Lee Boggs Center to Nurture Community Leadership. She is a cofounder of Detroit Summer and works extensively in areas of community power, democratic processes, and transformative relationships. She is a member of the Riverwise Magazine Collective and Detroit Independent Freedom Schools. She is a professor of communication at Oakland University.

Jacob Lederman

is Assistant Professor of sociology at the University of Michigan-Flint. His research examines the relationship between urban governance and expertise.

Raoul S. Liévanos

is an Associate Professor in the Department of Sociology at the University of Oregon. His research focuses primarily on the organizational, institutional, demographic, and spatial dynamics of environmental and housing market inequalities and on the social movements and policy processes that attempt to address such inequalities in the United States.

Benjamin J. Pauli
holds a Ph.D. in Political Science from Rutgers University and is an Assistant Professor of Social Science at Kettering University in Flint, Michigan. His research interests include political ideologies, social movements, environmental justice, water, and the interface between scientists and the public. He has been involved in the response to the Flint water crisis as a resident, activist, researcher, and a member of a multi-university scientific team. His *Flint Fights Back: Environmental Justice and Democracy in the Flint Water Crisis* (MIT Press 2019) takes an ethnographic look at local water activism. Dr. Pauli is President of the Board of Directors of the Environmental Transformation Movement of Flint (etmflint.org), which seeks to educate and advocate around environmental justice issues and help develop the next generation of environmental justice leaders. He also serves as a representative of the academic community on the Environmental Protection Agency's National Environmental Justice Advisory Council.

Julie Sze
is Professor and the Founding Chair of American Studies at the University of California at Davis. She has published three books (most recently, *Environmental Justice in Moment of Danger* in 2020), edited a collection on *Sustainability and Social Justice* (2018), and over 50 articles and book chapters. Her research is on environmental inequalities, the relationship between social movements and policy implementation and in the areas of public and environmental humanities.

INTRODUCTION

The Flint Sacrifice Zone

Terressa A. Benz and Graham Cassano

1 Where We Are Today

> This pandemic has not been the great leveler. It's been the great magnifier, as it were.
>
> DR. RIYAZ PATEL, University College London (MUELLER 2020)

Spring, 2020. How can we write about Flint when the world seems to be falling down? First, because we are in debt. What happened in Flint was not an allegory, not a metaphor for a broken America. It was a real event with all too real consequences for the people of Flint, for the people of Michigan. It cost lives, money, and futures. As scientists we understand that even if our first obligation is to objective reality, our next is to the people who suffered these crimes and made our science possible. However, we do not write simply for that debt, nor only to preserve the memory of the state's crimes, and of all those who struggled for justice. We write now, as the COVID-19 virus spreads through Michigan, because Flint was a signal, a template through which we will watch this latest catastrophe unfold. The same "disparities" that shaped outcomes in Flint, structure life-chances today. "Disparities" is the word that has gained currency now. It is a nice, solid, scientific term for capturing a moment. But scientific terms function as abbreviations that contain and conceal an entire world of data, politics, and economics. Our intentions here are thoroughly scientific. Nonetheless, it is difficult, as scientists—indeed, unscientific—to ignore the injustices embedded in these "disparities."

Writing in The Atlantic, Ibram X. Kendi sees the possibility of a national "racial pandemic" within the folds of this international viral pandemic.

> In Michigan, black Americans comprise 14.1 percent of the state population, but an ungodly 40 percent of coronavirus deaths. In Washtenaw County, home to Ann Arbor, 48 percent of residents hospitalized with the coronavirus are black, though black people make up only 11 percent of the county. In Illinois, the infection rate among black Americans is *twice* their percentage of the state population. In North Carolina's Mecklenburg County, which includes Charlotte, black people comprise 32.9 percent of the residents, but 43.9 of the confirmed coronavirus cases, as of March

> 30. In Milwaukee, black Americans make up 26 percent of the county, but nearly half of the infections and a maddening 81 percent of deaths as of Friday.
>
> KENDI 2020b

These numbers are still fresh, and, of course, after the pandemic passes, it may turn out that the African American and Latinx death rates are closer to the white death rate. But based upon national health data, that would be quite a surprise. In a hyper-racialized society, health and illness are, themselves, hyper-racialized outcomes.

Writing a few weeks before Kendi, and in a different cultural context, Giorgio Agamben offers an alternative analysis. After enumerating the "freedoms" lost by Europeans during the unfolding pandemic, Agamben takes the Foucauldian position that this disease has been constructed so as to solidify the power of a totalitarian state apparatus.

> The disproportionate reaction to what according to the CNR is something not too different from the normal flus that affect us every year is quite blatant. It is almost as if with terrorism exhausted as a cause for exceptional measures, the invention of an epidemic offered the ideal pretext for scaling them up beyond any limitation.
>
> AGAMBEN 2020

For Agamben, as for Foucault, the plague becomes an event precisely through the mechanisms of surveillance and control that it unleashes. Yet, in *Discipline and Punish*, that surveillance apparatus depended upon layers of expert inquiry, and epidemiological power, in order to conduct its work. With COVID-19, at least as it unfolds in the United States, a regime of expert knowledge seems to inhabit a world parallel to the state apparatus and the latter's willful ignorance. The epidemic has been present for nearly two months, yet, as Kendi points out in another contribution to *The Atlantic*, the collection of demographic data has been episodic, sparse, and un-systematized.

> Maybe there is only a class issue here ... Maybe I should listen to those post-racial Americans suggesting that class is *the* salient divider of the infected from the healthy, the recovering from the dying. That the irresponsible behavior of disproportionately poor people of color is the problem—not racism—as the post-racial conservatives believe. That the irresponsible policies of capitalism are the problem—not racism—as the post-racial progressives believe. That the malfunctions of poor people of

> color and capitalism are the problems—not racism—as the post-racial centrists believe. But no conservative, centrist, or progressive can say for sure whether race or class *or even their intersection* is the salient divider during the pandemic. We have data on neither the class nor the race of victims, let alone the intersectional data that would allow us to assess, say, whether poor Asian women are dying at higher or lower rates than poor white women; or whether white elites and Latino elites are being infected at similar or dissimilar rates. We just don't know.
>
> KENDI 2020a

States like Michigan, New York, and Illinois, started to collect demographic data, including racial identifications, in the weeks after Kendi published his piece. But data collection remained far from systematic, and Kendi's fear, that the virus will be a serious problem in Black and Latinx communities, has come to pass. The virus will be folded into the "territorial stigma" that already brands racially segregated urban environments as quarantine zones, as "sacrifice zones" (Waquant 2008; Lerner 2012).

According to Loic Waquant, post-industrial systems of stratification appear as spatial relations within urban geography. Stigmatized spaces house the city's precariat. In his description of this seemingly disposable population, Waquant describes the pandemic's "essential workers."

> Long-term joblessness and the proliferation of precarious and low-pay employment, the accumulation of multiple deprivations within the same lower-class households and neighborhoods, the curtailing of social networks and the slackening of personal ties, and finally the difficulty that established programmes of social insurance and public assistance have in remedying or checking hardship and isolation ...
>
> WAQUANT 2008: 162

These workers, stigmatized in normal times, become fodder for the anti-virus efforts. Their precarious employment means that, during this pandemic, they are available, and often eager, for jobs as delivery workers, warehouse staff, gas station attendants, convenience store clerks, while their partners, brothers, mothers, fathers, sisters, and friends work as nurses, nursing assistants, police, EMTs. At the same time, as this class process is racialized within urban boundaries, these city workers tend to be Black, Latinx, Asian, and Native American. This relationship between the "precariat" and the pandemic's "essential workers" provides the first key to understanding the overrepresentation of underrepresented minorities in the current death toll.

But Wacquant's argument takes us further. Many of these essential workers navigate the public space of civil society during their work hours, but, afterward, return to neighborhoods infected with "territorial stigma." Wacquant argues that a *"powerful stigma attached to residence in the bounded and segregated spaces*, the 'neighborhoods of exile' to which the population marginalized or condemned to redundancy by the post-Fordist reorganization of the economy and the post-Keynesian reconstructed of the welfare state are increasingly consigned" (Wacquant 2008: 169). Again, it is worth noting that this population, 'redundant' during normal times, become 'essential' during a pandemic. But even as they shift from redundant to essential, their spaces of residence remain stigmatized territory, and that stigma permanently brands those workers. And so we now find a second key to understanding current mortality rates. Even as it marginalizes and stigmatizes the urban population, the state makes that population more difficult to engage. "Territorial stigmatization affects interactions not only with employers but also with the police, the courts and street-level bureaucracies such as the state unemployment and welfare offices, all of which are especially prompt to modify their conduct and procedures based on residence in a degraded *cité*" (Waquant 2008: 174). The former precariat, now (temporary) essential workers, have weaker social networks, a rational distrust of state authorities, fewer connections to the health care system, more reliance upon public transportation, and a dire need for work. These forces combine to ensure that the workers most essential to our social and economic well-being also have the most precarious access to health information, health insurance, and health care.

Exposure to the disease and lack of access to regular health care surely has had an impact on mortality rates in the Black and Latinx communities. But public health officials argue that underlying conditions like cancer, asthma, emphysema, heart disease, and immune-comprising disorders also have a stark impact on COVID-19 mortality rates. The same economic, social, and cultural forces that construct certain urban neighborhoods as stigmatized territory also allow that stigma to shape policy and planning decisions. They become environmental "sacrifice zones," contaminated by the waste of the industrial and post-industrial worlds.

> Sacrifice zones are the result of many deeply rooted inequalities in our society. One of these inequalities takes the form of unwise (or biased) land use decisions dictated by local or state officials intent on attracting big industries to their town, county, or state in an effort to create jobs and raise tax revenues. When decisions are made about where to locate heavily polluting industries, they often end up sited in low-income

> communities of color where people are so busy trying to survive that they have little time to protest the building of a plant next door. Those who make the land use decisions that govern sacrifice zones typically designate these areas as residential/industrial areas, a particularly pernicious type of zoning ordinance. In these areas, industrial facilities and residential homes are built side by side, and few localities have adequate buffer zone regulations to providing breathing room between heavy industry and residential areas.
>
> LERNER 2012: 6

While the epidemiological investigations will be done after the pandemic passes, cities like Chicago, Detroit, and New Orleans, house much of their precariat in these sacrifice zones, and, in all likelihood, the high mortality rate among Black and Latinx workers has something to do with a high rate of underlying conditions, which in turn are the result of neighborhood environmental contamination (Benz 2019).

In the last decade or so, Michigan has gone through at least four social and economic crises, three of them intimately related. There was the financial crash of 2008, the Emergency Manager laws that disempowered local urban governments, the Flint water crisis, and now the COVID-19 outbreak. In this volume, we trace the connection between the financial crash, the Emergency Manager laws, and the Flint water crisis. However, it is worth connecting these crises to our current fight against COVID-19. In a racialized society, the same forces that produced the racialized outcomes for the water crisis in Flint are producing racialized outcomes during this pandemic. Territorial stigma, governmental indifference to the fate of the precariat, outright racism, and the construction of Flint as a sacrifice zone, both caused and prolonged the water crisis. These same forces seem to be shaping the unequal outcomes in this pandemic. Thus, even as Flint falls into the policy makers' and politicians' rearview, social scientists and citizens forget Flint's lessons at their own peril.

2 Stigmatizing Michigan's (Post-industrial) Sacrifice Zones[1]

In 2014, the City of Flint began sourcing its water from the Flint River (Figure 0.1). Within a few months residents were reporting skin rashes, foul odors and serious illnesses resulting from use of the water to the deaf ears of

1 The discussion in this section is adapted from Cassano and Benz 2019.

FIGURE 0.1 Flint River

their political representatives. Flint was under state appointed emergency management and the goal was to get Flint back into financial shape through "tough" decisions and austerity driven policy making—the concerns of citizens, who were majority poor and black, did not factor into the decision making process. The result was the mass poisoning of nearly 200,000 people. While water infrastructure crumbles across the country and children are regularly testing with elevated blood-lead levels, what makes the case of Flint especially troubling was that it was a state orchestrated crisis. The Flint water crisis was not inevitable. What happened in Flint was the direct result of punitive austerity driven neoliberal policy created and implemented by state actors.

The rise of neoliberal discourse and policy has created a neoliberal urbanism in which cities must become entrepreneurial, directing all energy towards pro-business goals (Leitner et al. 2007). In the neoliberal city decisions by state actors are driven by cost-benefit analysis rather concerns over social good, equity, or service to constituents (Leitner and Sheppard 2002; Fasenfest 2019; Fasenfest and Pride 2016). Further this type of urban environment is characterized by the steady replacement of state run social services by quasi-public agencies tasked not with social welfare agendas but rather targeted schemes to promote economic development and competition among agencies (Soss, Fording, and Schram 2011; Leitner et al. 2007). Under this neoliberal regime citizens are expected to behave, work hard, and take responsibility for their successes and failures (Larner 1997; Soss, Fording, and Schram 2011). By making inequality and any attendant poverty the consequence of an individual's choices or moral failings, government is released of any formal obligation to account for or change potential structural or institutional causes of these inequities. Neoliberal governance mandates citizens submit to the 'free market' and the mantra of 'individual responsibility' or suffer the punitive consequences of austerity (Wacquant 2009). Further compounding the troubles of the neoliberal city is that while neoliberalism is formally and intentionally colorblind, it is in fact saturated with race.

When L. Brooks Patterson agreed to defend Irene McCabe and the National Action Group (NAG) in their attempt to stop school integration in Pontiac, Michigan, it launched his political career. After taking *Milliken v. Bradley* to the US Supreme Court, Patterson served as Oakland County Prosecutor, until, in 1992 he was elected Oakland County Chief Executive, a position he held until his death in 2019. Oakland is an affluent, largely white, and largely suburban, county bordering Wayne County, the home of Detroit. In 2014, as Detroit was emerging from bankruptcy, a New Yorker journalist asked Patterson about Detroit's "financial problems." The Oakland County Chief Executive responded:

> I made a prediction a long time ago, and it's come to pass. I said, 'What we're gonna do is turn Detroit into an Indian reservation, where we herd all the Indians into the city, build a fence around it, and then throw in the blankets and corn.'
>
> WILLIAMS 2014

This notion that "we" need to fence or wall "them" in reappears often on the comment pages of local newspapers in the Metro Detroit area. "Them" usually refers to the residents of majority black cities like Detroit, Pontiac, and Flint. Not every white resident of the suburban counties share these racial attitudes. But apparently enough did to re-elect Patterson to another term as Oakland County chief executive in November, 2016.

In 1961, Flint City manager, Thomas Kay, in an attempt to increase the tax base and make the city more attractive to industrial development, proposed the annexation of several industrial and commercial areas bordering Flint. Suburban resistance was fierce. As historian Andrew Highsmith observes:

> Civic leaders looked to gain support for the annexation bid by appealing once again to a shared sense of purpose among city and suburban residents. City Manager Kay even invoked images of ancient cities surrounded by walls to make his case, claiming, "History books have stories and pictures of cities with walls, and in American history, there were forts. The walls and forts fell as we became more civilized." By employing the metaphor of the walled city, Kay hoped to … resuscitate the metropolitan sensibility that had driven GM's local growth strategy. Yet the response to his petition revealed that many suburbanites actually embraced the barriers that separated Flint from its neighbors.
>
> HIGHSMITH 2015: 142

The history of Twentieth Century Michigan, like the history of much of Twentieth Century US, emerges through the growing antagonism between suburbs and urban centers. As cities lost population, suburbs became more powerful. Urban planners and city officials like Kay attempted to circumvent these forces, but with little success. More often than not, new urban developments displaced lower income residents of Flint and Detroit, without, in turn, bringing the expected revenue and foot traffic to the city (Sugrue 2014; Highsmith 2015). Nor are such failures surprising. The economic decline of Michigan cities is the result of more than a century of administrative, legal, and social, policies that enforced the color-line and effectively racialized city boundaries. This was accompanied by systematic disinvestment by General Motors and other large automakers, as they relocated plants from urban centers to Michigan suburbs, to southern and western states, and, later, to overseas facilities.

By constructing Detroit as an "Indian reservation," Patterson builds an invisible fence that is probably more effective than any wall made of concrete and iron. This imaginary barrier is maintained and enforced through a web of words and everyday social practices. As Patterson puts it in the same interview:

> I used to say to my kids, 'First of all, there's no reason for you to go to Detroit. We've got restaurants out here.' They don't even have movie theatres in Detroit—not one. ... I can't imagine finding something in Detroit that we don't have in spades here. Except for live sports. We don't have baseball, football. For that, fine—get in and get out. But park right next to the venue—spend the extra twenty or thirty bucks. And, before you go to Detroit, you get your gas out here. You do not, *do not*, under any circumstances, stop in Detroit at a gas station! That's just a call for a carjacking.
>
> WILLIAMS 2014

Patterson's parenting practices are reproduced in scores of suburban homes in Michigan and throughout the United States. Cities like Flint and Detroit are stigmatized, racialized, and symbolically transformed into walled reservations, without parents necessarily invoking racial terminology.

All of this matters because the Flint water crisis was not simply the result of the deindustrialization of a company town, government incompetence, neoliberal state and urban policies, outright corruption, and the attempted disenfranchisement of citizens through emergency management. All of these factors mattered immensely (Campbell et al. 2016). But just as important, the malign neglect of Flint for so long, and the consequent governmental inaction when residents first became alarmed about their water supply, were also important results of white supremacy, and its legacy in the form of distorted perceptions of cities and urban residents.

Andrew Highsmith's history of Flint, *Demolition Means Progress*, provides much needed context for the current water crisis. Highsmith's narrative unfolds as a dialectic of perpetual economic decline and failed neoliberal attempts at renewal during the late Twentieth and early Twenty-First centuries. The decline of Flint results from some familiar factors: first, the impact of recession and deindustrialization upon a company town; second, the hyper-segregation of neighborhoods and communities as the result of federal lending policies and local zoning codes and covenants. To these familiar forces, Highsmith adds several other elements that have received less attention from historians and social scientists. In particular, he uncovers the administrative measures through which school segregation was maintained, even after the open housing movement ended rigid racial neighborhood boundaries inside Flint's city limits. And he studies the tensions between the city and its surrounding suburbs as the local governments fought over tax revenue and land distribution. As industry left Flint, residents inevitably followed, leaving the city with less revenue and no room for expansion. The suburbs were largely the beneficiaries of Flint's population and industrial losses. In various efforts to reverse this economic decline, city planners and private foundations (especially the Charles Stewart Mott foundation) made various attempts at "renewal." But these neoliberal attempts at restructuring and resurgence invariably ended in failure, including some spectacular disasters, like "Autoworld," the indoor theme park and shopping mall. Meant to be the center piece of the "Great Leap Forward" in Flint, funded by the Mott Foundation in partnership with public and other private institutions, the park was open for less than a year in 1984, and finally demolished in the late 1990s (Highsmith 2014: 259–261).

Highsmith calls the epilogue to his book "America is a thousand Flints." And in many respects this is undoubtedly a valuable metaphor. Most important, what Flint has in common with urban centers all over the United States is the history of enforced residential segregation. As Thomas Sugrue (2014) has done for Detroit, Highsmith excavates the public regulations and the private decisions that enforced the color line in Flint. Like urban centers in much of the rest of the country, early Twentieth Century Flint property deeds often had racially restrictive covenants enforced by realtors and homeowners. As General Motors built relatively low-cost housing for their blue and white collar workers, "the homes were not available to all buyers."

> Specifically, GM mandated that only single-family homes could be built in its new subdivisions and that occupants could not keep livestock, sell liquor, or construct outdoor cesspools or privies on their property. The covenants also required racial segregation, stipulating that homes "could not be leased to or occupied by any person or persons not wholly of the white or Caucasian race."
>
> HIGHSMITH 2014: 32

Even after such covenants were declared unconstitutional by the Supreme Court in 1948's *Shelley v. Kraemer*, rigid racial segregation was maintained by the legacy of federal and local redlining policies. The Federal Home Owner's Loan Corporation was established in 1933 in order to stabilize the mortgage markets and make home ownership available to working class and middle class Americans. But from the beginning,

> HOLC's policies also hardened the color line by enshrining a racially and socioeconomically biased calculus for measuring risk, value, and stability in residential neighborhoods. As part of its operations, the HOLC created "residential security maps" for Flint and 238 other American cities.
>
> HIGHSMITH 2014: 38

These maps infamously graded neighborhoods from A to D, with the least desirable areas graded C and D. On these maps, D graded neighborhoods were often shaded in red, hence the term "redlining." Highsmith continues:

> To measure the favorability of an area's social characteristics, the HOLC asked its agents to list the percentage of Negroes, foreign-born residents, and families on relief in each neighborhood and to assess the risk of "infiltration" by these undesirable social groups. By the government's explicit standards, then, racial, ethnic, and class segregation were essential components of neighborhood stability.
>
> HIGHSMITH 2014: 40

While the HOLC ended its loan acquisition programs in 1936 (p. 38), these residential security maps, now utilized by the Federal Housing Administration, continued to shape the geography of race in America. By 1947, even the FHA removed explicit references to race from its *Underwriting Manual* (p. 52). As Highsmith shows, however, real estate professionals, urban planners, and policy makers maintained rigid racial residential boundaries well into the late twentieth century. These real estate maps, and the assumptions they represented, led to systematic disinvestment in the Black community, and, more than that, disinvestment in any neighborhood seen as racially "transitional" (integrated).

But this emphasis upon the real estate market and the racial geography of Flint, as important as it is, can lead to the mistaken impression that school segregation in the city was the result of these residential boundaries. Highsmith, however, demolishes the myth of de facto school segregation. Or, put more correctly, using the concept of *administrative* segregation (p. 8), he deconstructs the opposition between de jure and de facto segregation. Into the late Twentieth Century, "the language of de facto segregation distorted analyses of the color line in Flint and many other American cities" (p. 225). Indeed, Highsmith shows that Flint city officials and school board members used a wide variety of administrative mechanisms to maintain rigid school segregation, even as the open housing movement increasingly integrated city neighborhoods. These mechanisms included separate classrooms for white and Black students, a rigid tracking system that sent white students toward professional jobs and Black students into the trades, and transfer policies that generally allowed white students to transfer out of majority Black schools, and rarely if ever allowed Black students to transfer to majority white schools. But school district "gerrymandering was … the most common and effective of all the methods used to maintain administrative segregation in Flint and other urban school systems" (p. 69). As the racial constituency of neighborhoods changed, the school board redrew district boundaries.

> In several cases, the board's districting decisions left neighbors from the same street attending different "neighborhood schools." "They drew boundaries around houses," Ruth Scott remembered, "down the middle of the street. … When blacks moved onto a street, they would change the boundaries."
>
> HIGHSMITH 2014: 69

These same forces of residential and educational segregation and inequality structured urban life across the Midwest and throughout much of the United States. In this sense, America is indeed a thousand Flints. At the same time, Highsmith notes particular characteristics that set Flint apart from some other cities like Chicago, or even Detroit. While Detroit may have been an *industry* town, Flint was much more a *company* town. As General Motors shuttered and relocated plants throughout the late 1960s and early 1970s, residents left the city, and Flint accordingly lost a significant portion of its former tax base. Throughout the late twentieth century, as much of its middle class population, Black and white, left the city, foundation money disappeared, state aide dried up, and Flint spiraled into bankruptcy. By 2011, with a deficit of $25.7 million, the Michigan governor disempowered Flint's locally elected representatives, and put in their place an Emergency Manager to supervise both financial and policy decisions in the city (Campbell et al. 2016: 26–27). In 2014, under Emergency Manager Ed Kurtz, Flint switched from Lake Huron (Detroit) water to water from the Flint River. When this change was made, it was made without chemical corrosion controls being added to Flint River water. As a result, the polluted, acidic river water leeched lead from galvanized pipes in city water system, in schools water systems, and in private homes.

Flint became a sacrifice zone. As Flint industrialized, the Black community was at first stigmatized, then segregated, until, at the end of the twentieth century, Flint became a majority Black city. At that point, the stigma that had been consistently imposed upon Flint's Black community fueled statewide indifference to the fate of the city. The territorial stigma that enveloped Flint created the conditions for the sacrifice of its residents. This book attempts to understand the social, political, and economic conditions that made that sacrifice possible. Contributors examine the relationship between neoliberal economic policy, social inequality, and environmental racism. But our aim isn't simply to examine the conditions of Flint's defilement. In addition, our contributors attend to the reaction of those residents, their protests and their diverse forms of resistance. As we said at the outset, our intentions are entirely scientific. Yet science always has goals and presuppositions. Our goal is a more just society. Our presuppositions are too numerous to enumerate here, but they included our working assumption that capitalism and racism interactively block the justice that we scientifically seek. However diverse they are in method, theory, and discipline, these contributions share both that goal, and that presupposition.

3 Prospectus of the Work

Neoliberal ideology dictates that competition, privatization, and deregulation are supposed to grease the wheels of capitalism, increasing productivity and efficiency, improving quality, while reducing overall costs. As part and parcel, individual freedoms are lauded as unimpeachable and as a result each individual is held responsible for their own successes and failures. It is this obsession with individual choice and responsibility, devoid of any context or consideration of structural disadvantage that fuels contemporary laissez-faire racism and inequality. The impact of which is felt most acutely in rust-belt cities, like Flint who are all too often being taught lesson's in "individual responsibility" with austerity-based policies.

The water crisis in Flint is the result of the unwavering pursuit of this political ideology and while Flint is a quintessential example of the failure of neoliberalism, it is not alone, it is but a warning of tragedies to come. In this volume we seek to not just explore the Flint Water Crisis, but other sites of neoliberal demolition. The volume is divided into two sections: *Structure in Context* and *Reaction and Resistance*. The first section examines the political and legal underpinnings of various sites of neoliberal demolition and their consequences. Whereas the second section provides a closer look at the role of activists and community involvement in combating and also contributing to neoliberal agendas. This is not a volume of hope, but rather a systematic and scientific examination of the driving forces behind and consequences of neoliberal policy making on human lives.

3.1 *Structure in Context*

In this section, *Structure in Context*, the contributors explore the Flint water crisis and other sites of neoliberal demolition through scientific excavation of the overlapping layers of policy, place, and profit. The volume open's with a piece from David Fasenfest, who hones in on the neoliberal mechanisms and consequences of Michigan's Emergency Management (EM) law. Specifically, he explores the application and use of the EM law in various cities struggling with municipal debt. The law, which gave unelected individuals unfettered power to overrule elected officials and institute austerity-based neoliberal policies with little to no regard for underlying structural issues elevated the interests of bondholders above the health and humanity of the residents of each city under its purview. The consequences of this shift in political priorities was most acutely felt in Flint, which is the focus of Fasenfest's analysis.

Next, Terressa Benz explores the impact of neoliberal colorblind policy making at two sites in Michigan; Flint and Southwest Detroit. Using a socio-legal framework, based on critical race theorist, Alan Freeman's victim and perpetrator perspectives she examines how the pursuit of formal court-instituted racial justice at either site is impossible. The history of Michigan's environmental legal decision making, which requires proof of racist intent on the part of the perpetrator is examined and revealed to support a racialized caste system of "worthiness" when it comes to environmental protections.

In Chapter 3, Raoul Liévanos and Julie Sze demonstrate how the consequences of neoliberalism are not unique to Michigan. They create a model of racialized crisis driven urbanization to examine recent neoliberally derived water crises in both Flint, Michigan and Stockton, California. Using spatial and historical-comparative analysis on neighborhood-level land use, housing valuations, demographic, and water quality data at both sites they demonstrate how each water crisis is constituted by different "racial projects" of crisis driven urbanization. They find that in each case the expansion of neoliberal regulatory regimes coupled with increases in privatization worked to erode formal democracy with devastating human consequences. Next, Katrinell Davis examines the relationships between blood lead levels, demographics, and neighborhood decline in the City of Flint between 2010 and 2015. She demonstrates that children who live near environmental hazards like elevated water lead levels, water main breaks, and brownfield sites are more likely to experience heightened blood lead levels.

Continuing in the vein of socio-spatial analysis, Graham Cassano, Jon Carroll, and Dan Clark explore the racialized history of public housing in Pontiac, Michigan. Specifically, they examine the case of the Lakeside Federal Housing Complex by tracing the racial, demographic, and labor-based shifts in the city and how these changes worked to create a narrative of territorial stigma that allowed the problems of the Lakeside Complex and the city at large to be blamed on Black residents. Through their analysis they demonstrate that these transformations had a direct impact on Pontiac's fiscal health, resulting in the same process of Emergency Management that had such disastrous results in Flint.

3.2 *Reaction and Resistance*

While the previous section examined the policies and legal hurdles created by neoliberal regimes, the following section explores how everyday citizens work to combat, resist, and even shape austerity-based policymaking. To begin, Jacob Lederman, explores the process by which urban administrators produce consensual political discourse and present it as the will of "the community." Using the recent Flint master city plan, Lederman navigates the reader through the neoliberal consensus making process, which requires the meeting of dueling goals: the political discourse being produced must be in accordance with market principles yet it also requires an element of civic participation as a source of legitimacy. The result is a symbolic community discourse that reduces the urban collectivity to a political monolith.

Chapter 7 by Michael Doan, Shea Howell, and Ami Harbin focuses on the variety of ways grassroots coalitions in Detroit, Michigan have worked to resist emergency management and advance the message of water as a human right. The authors analyze the ways community organizing has worked to confront the neoliberal state's control of water. They examine the impact of grassroots organizing on the use of the media and the creation of counternarratives that center on the experiences, needs, and collective power of the people directly affected by water insecurity. They argue that the experiences and struggles of Detroit water activists are intertwined with the interests of Flint water activists and can be understood as mutually empowering.

Next, A.E. Garrison, using a comic-type medium, examines the complicated relationship citizens have with water under a neoliberal state. She does so by analyzing the relationship to water in two different Michigan communities: Flint where clean water is scarce and Evart of Osceola and Mescota counties where clean water is abundant but privatized. Both communities have suffered under the failures of state policymakers in terms of water access, regulation, and control. She critically examines how in both communities, despite civilian resistance, water has become a vehicle for profit rather than public good.

In Chapter 9, and perhaps as a larger implicit yet sympathetic critique of the academic perspectives presented in this volume Benjamin Pauli, challenges the expert discourse that classifies the Flint water crisis as environmental racism using his ethnographic work with Flint's own resident-activists. He argues that the classifications made by experts and academics of the crisis as race-based often agreed with the sentiments of those most impacted, but that there were important disjunctures as well. Among Flint resident-activists, he found many who resisted and or completely rejected the crisis as race-based, opting for a more inclusive discourse. He finds that these "popular" perspectives are mostly if not entirely ignored by the media and academics alike, with coverage and discussion of the crisis instead focusing on "expert" perspectives.

Lastly, we wrap up the volume with an Afterword from Peter Hammer, Professor of Law and Director of the Damon J. Keith Center for Civil Rights at the Wayne State University Law School, whose testimony, included here in its entirety, was presented to the Michigan Civil Rights Commission hearings on the Flint water crisis. This piece provides a comprehensive look at the various dimensions of state action that led to the water crisis, centralizing the role of strategic and structural racism in creating the catastrophe. Hammer dissects Michigan's Emergency Management regime and Governor Snyder's approach to fiscal distress as a lesson in neoliberal paternalism that resulted in the poisoning of an entire city.

While the authors of this volume come from a diverse range of disciplinary and theoretical backgrounds, the contributions share some common features: they all examine neoliberal crises from the perspective of class conflict; each chapter explores some possibilities of community agency; and, as a whole, they serve as a collective indictment of neoliberal political decision-making, which ignores the structural roots of inequality and racism. The purpose of this volume is not to assign blame to any one individual for what has happened at these sites of neoliberal demolition, but rather as an indictment of the entire neoliberal apparatus as brutal, racist, and (hopefully) future-less. We hope that the chapters in this volume encourage readers to look beyond official explanations of poverty and crisis, to critically examine the causes and consequences of neoliberal capitalism.

References

Agamben, G. (2020). "The Invention of an Epidemic." In "Coronavirus and Philosophers," A Tribune in the *European Journal of Psychoanalysis*. Available at: http://www.journal-psychoanalysis.eu/coronavirus-and-philosophers/.

Benz, T.A. (2019). "Toxic Cities: Neoliberalism and Environmental Racism in Flint and Detroit Michigan." *Critical Sociology* 45(1):49–62.

Cassano, G. and Benz, T.A. (2019). "Introduction: Flint and the Racialized Geography of Indifference." *Critical Sociology* 45(1): 25–32.

Campbell, B., et al. (eds.). (2016). "Poison on Tap: How Government Failed Flint, and the Heroes Who Fought Back." *Bridge Magazine*. Traverse City, MI: Mission Point Press.

Highsmith, A. (2015). *Demolition Means Progress: Flint, Michigan, and the Fate of the American Metropolis*. Chicago, IL: University of Chicago Press.

Fasenfest, D. (2019). "A Neoliberal Response to an Urban Crisis: Emergency Management in Flint, MI." *Critical Sociology* 45(1): 33–47.

Fasenfest, D. and Pride, T. (2016). "Emergency Management in Michigan: Race, Class and the Limits of Liberal Democracy." *Critical Sociology* 42(3): 331–334.

Kendi, I.X. (2020a). "Why Don't We Know Who the Coronavirus Victims Are?" *The Atlantic*, April 1, 2020.

Kendi, I.X. (2020b). "What The Racial Data Show." *The Atlantic*, April 6, 2020.

Larner, W. (1997). "The Legacy of the Social: Market Governance and the Consumer." *Economy and Society* 26(2): 373–399.

Leitner, H. and Sheppard, E. (2002). "The City is Dead, Long Live the Network: Harnessing Networks for a Neoliberal Era." *Antipode* 31(3): 495–518.

Leitner, H., Sheppard, E., Sziarto, K. and Maringanti, A. (2007). "Contesting Urban Futures: Decentering Neoliberalism." In: Leitner, H., Peck, J. and Sheppard E.S. (eds.). *Contesting Neoliberalism*. New York, NY: The Guilford Press.

Lerner, S. (2012). *Sacrifice Zones: The Front Lines of Toxic Chemical Exposure in the United States*. Cambridge, MA: MIT Press.

Mueller, B. (2020). "Coronavirus Killing Black Britons at Twice the Rate of Whites." *New York Times*. May 7, 2020. Available at: https://www.nytimes.com/2020/05/07/world/europe/coronavirus-uk-black-britons.html.

Soss, J., Fording, R. and Schram, S. (2011). *Discipling the Poor: Neoliberal Paternalism and the Persistent Power of Race*. Chicago, IL: University of Chicago Press.

Sugrue, T. (2014). *The Origin of the Urban Crisis: Race and Inequality in Postwar Detroit*. Princeton, NJ: Princeton University Press.

Wacquant, L. (2008). *Urban Outcasts: A Comparative Sociology of Advanced Marginality*. Malden, MA: Polity Press.

Wacquant, L. (2009). *Punishing the Poor: The Neoliberal Government of Social Insecurity*. Durham, NC: Duke University Press.

Williams, P. (2014). "Drop Dead Detroit." *The New Yorker*, January 27, 2014.

PART 1

Structure in Context

CHAPTER 1

Neoliberalism, Urban Policy and Environmental Degradation

David Fasenfest

> ... the ability to define a set of circumstance as constituting a crisis creates a political opportunity for more substantial change than would otherwise happen.
>
> WALBY 2015: 16–17

∵

1 Introduction[1]

Since 2009, the State of Michigan has used various renditions of its financial emergency law to assume control of eight different municipalities—more than any state during that time (see Sugar Law Center, 2015). Under the control of the state appointed manager, their charge was to mitigate severe fiscal distress. In that capacity the governing powers of local officials are substantially reduced or, in many cases, removed all together. Michelle Anderson (2011), Professor of Law at University of California-Berkley, views Michigan's recent "municipal takeovers" as a form of what she calls "democratic dissolution," in that it eliminates a city's government without terminating the city's corporate form in contrast to true dissolution, which is the termination of a charter without local consent. In addition to uprooting the democratic processes governing cities, the complete disempowerment of local governing bodies by the state during receivership also works to deprive residents living in those political units of their legally protected political rights at the local and community level. This approach to managing municipal fiscal distress, according to Anderson, blindly assumes that sacrificing the rights of voters and the

1 This chapter is based in part on my keynote address at the Annual Meeting of the Association of Humanist Sociologists, 8 November 2018, and on material in Fasenfest 2019.

American democratic political process will inevitably rescue cities from self-inflicted financial implosion. Although it may be unintended, such political disenfranchisement at the local level has disproportionately impacted communities of color, as nearly half of the state's African American population was under emergency manager rule from 2009 to 2014.

Informed by assumptions of mismanagement rather than an analysis of structural challenges facing Michigan cities, legislators implemented management-centered policies as a method to anticipate and solve municipal fiscal problems (State of Michigan, 2011). The solutions tailored by state appointed Emergency Managers (EMs) tend to singularly focus on budgetary strategies to alleviate short-term problems, which may in the long run culminate in the reemergence and exacerbation of fiscal crises. Structural problems, like the loss of revenue through lower tax rates, a declining tax base from out-migration and declining property values, and changes in state revenue sharing, are ignored in favor of the costs incurred through public employee wages, post-employment benefits, and public services. For example, diverted funds earmarked for revenue sharing deprived many of the EM cities with much needed funds (Oosting 2016). This has led to cutback management tactics that adversely impact the financial well-being of public employees while protecting corporate investors and elite financial institutions. Moreover, because of the racial and class disparities associated with the EM process, poor, black and brown communities will seemingly bear the brunt of the deleterious outcomes caused by Michigan's EM laws.

The problems associated with Michigan's EM laws and tactics mentioned above have been well documented (Peck 2012; Stampfler 2013; see also Loh 2015; Anderson 2011; and Donald et al. 2014 on the abrogation of democratic rights and the imposition of neoliberal austerity; Clement and Kanai 2015 on the reliance on market mechanisms and the negative impact on communities of color; Kasdan 2015 on how EMs rely on cutbacks, consolidation and service reduction to address fiscal stress). A myriad of scholars, activists, and political leaders have brought into question its legal merit, effectiveness, and fairness. The imposition of EMs relies on a system of assessment and reviews to determine whether a community needs to have that form of oversight. Crosby and Robbins (2013) point out that this approach is reactive, not proactive as a way to avoid fiscal stress or anticipate and rectify situations that could lead to the kinds of stress EM designations are designed to solve, noting "… do local decision-makers use the system to monitor and plan for probable fiscal crises and does the State rely on its own scorecard method as evidence enough to appoint an emergency manager? In Michigan, the answer to these questions is no" (p. 523). Rather, state actors assume mismanagement of local governments in deciding to appoint EMs, but instead should strive to understand and address factors leading to fiscal distress before they materialize (Kasdan 2015). The decline of cities in Michigan, especially Detroit, should not have come as a surprise. As Neill (2015) has detailed, notice of the decline has come "at regular intervals for decades previously" (p. 3). Report after report, starting in the mid-1960s, has highlighted the problems faced by cities when regional considerations are ignored yet each time their recommendations were set aside allowing Detroit to fall further down the rabbit hole of decline and despair.

Furthermore, Crosby and Robbins raise serious doubts about a process that relies on measurements that, at best, are suspect. "In addition, we question the validity and reliability of the state's numbers because when we measure these indicators, we could not obtain the same results. Michigan's system ... is not explanatory, replicable, descriptive, or predictive" (2013: 532). This chapter adds to the discussion on state-controlled emergency management in Michigan[2] by taking a broad look at the EM process from 2009 to 2015. First, following a brief discussion of the conditions facing Black Americans living in urban areas this chapter reviews the roots of neoliberalism and how it changes the policy framework of urban development in times of fiscal crisis (see Fasenfest 2015). Cities must borrow in order to meet their regular obligations, with expectations that their periodic revenues (through property tax collection) will service that debt. However, with the advent of financialization of society,[3] the nature and structure of the debts hold a dominant place in public policy. As we shall see, the Emergency Management of cities like Flint adversely and disproportionately impact the State of Michigan's African American population, depriving them of democratic decision making, the ability to determine how to deal with their fiscal crisis, and ultimately creates an environmental and health crisis.[4] The chapter then summarizes Emergency Management as it is applied to several cities in Michigan, compares EM cities with two examples of cities that did not have external controls placed upon them, and reviews the policy choices implemented more generally to deal with municipal debt. The chapter

2 See Nickels (2019) for a discussion of the politics of municipal takeovers.

3 As Bill Tabb points out, "Financialization can be understood to denote the dominance of the financial sector in the totality of economic activity such that financial markets determine the state of the overall economy and financial sector demands dictate nonfinancial company behavior" (2012: 10).

4 It is beyond the focus of this chapter to explore all the actions of Flint residents as they struggle against the actions of the Emergency Managers. For a full discussion of the political mobilization and community response to the health crisis by the residents of Flint, MI, see Nickels 2019. Her book raises the important question of who benefits as a development agenda emerges and morphs into a development regime.

closes with a discussion of the impact on EM policies on institutional racism and environmental degradation in Flint, MI as a result of decisions taken by its Emergency Manager.

2 Racial Politics and Subjectivities of Michigan's EM Process

In the US, government policies, laws, and institutional practices have historically had a disproportionate negative impact on racial minorities. Explicit examples include Jim Crow laws, enacted after the Reconstruction period in the American South, which enforced racial segregation, and the Federal Housing Authority's redlining of predominately African American neighborhoods in the 1940s and 1950s, which assisted in the creation of disinvested and blighted inner city ghettos throughout the country, occupied by mostly people of color. However, racially discriminatory policies, those crafted by federal, state, and local governments, can operate far more subtly and covertly. For example, during the 1980s the Reagan administration implemented a series of social and economic policies that, while ostensibly non-racial in its purported intent, produced uneven negative racial outcomes, particularly for African Americans. The most notable of these policies were Reagan's "war on drugs" and New Federalism. Reagan's policy on drugs, which made non-violent drug offenses more punitive, has, as many studies have shown, led to the explosion of the prison population over the last four decades. A disproportionate number of racial minorities have consequently been incarcerated due to these drug laws. Statistics show that African Americans make up 50 percent of the state and local prisoners incarcerated for drug crimes. Reagan's New Federalist agenda sought to devolve power and governing responsibility from the federal level to the state level. This shifting of responsibility allowed Reagan to slash federal aid and funding for struggling cities and poor Americans as poverty reduction primarily became the duty of the state. Reagan cancelled 500 separate funding programs, and assistance to cities of over 300,000 people was reduced by thirty-five percent (Tabb 2015). Since prior racially discriminatory laws, like the FHA redlining, helped to create poor inner cities where a large percentage of African Americans lived, these cuts had extreme racially uneven consequences.

Being Black in urban America poses many challenges. Every 7 minutes a Black person dies because of gun violence, which still is not treated as a public health concern (Priest and Williams 2018). At the age of 25, Blacks have a shorter life expectancy than whites (73 versus 78), and that gap increases at lower levels of educational attainment. A white person with only a High School diploma has a longer life expectancy than a Black person with a college degree. Income levels segregate the population so that the poor live in the least expensive and most challenging environments. Racial segregation creates formal and informal systems that restrict the access of poor urban Blacks to a reasonable housing stock and neighborhoods. The intersection of race and poverty intensifies vulnerabilities and amplifies the challenges communities face in the best of times.[5] In any given urban setting, there is not a single instance where the living conditions of Black residents are equal to those of white residents. Furthermore, the worst predominantly white neighborhood is better on a wide range of measures than the best predominantly Black neighborhood. As a result, residential segregation by income and race both creates and perpetuates racial inequality through inferior education and employment opportunities, the poor quality of housing and limited access to quality healthcare.[6]

Michelle Alexander (2012), the author of *The New Jim Crow*, argues that the war on drugs, to a large degree, using a racially coded political discourse, helped to resituate structural racism into the American political apparatus as an obfuscated practice, making it more difficult to identify. Racially biased government policies do not currently operate with the same overtness as it has throughout much of American history. Rather, the racialized character of social and economic policies of today are constructed through a careful post-racial language and identity that employs new racial codes and hidden racist politics to attract public support based on the existing cultural and racial biases of society. Thus, as Alexander has pointed out, racially discriminatory government policies are now much harder to identify as they are, on the outside, presented as colorblind panaceas for deeply raced problems. These seemingly non-racial policies, which produce concrete racial outcomes, become entrenched in the normative workings of the political process to form new practices of institutional racism.

More directly, research Kirkpatrick and Breznau (2016) conducted on the EM processes in Michigan to address urban fiscal crisis, concludes that African Americans were disproportionately impacted. They question whether what they call emergency political intervention (essentially the EM) as is applied to non-White communities is simply an artifact of the reality that non-White

5 See Gee et al. (2019) for a discussion of the impact of racism on health over the life course. See also Williams and Cooper (2019).

6 The recent COVID-19 pandemic is full of references to the higher incidence of infection and death among non-White and immigrant populations in the US and UK. See for example, Stafford, Hoyer and Morrison, April 18, 2020, "Racial toll of virus grows even starker as more data emerges," APNews. https://bit.ly/3dJk8AR.

populations congregate in fiscally distressed communities. That is, are non-Whites impacted because their communities are poor, and not because they are African Americans? What they find, instead, is that the odds of intervention increase proportionately with the size of the local Black population.[7] In conclusion, they find that racial bias and segregation may have had a direct impact on EM assignment, and that what they refer to as the logic of emergency fiscal intervention is related to a post-crisis pattern of urban value extraction in the form of the financialization of urban policies. Such policies come about as a result of the loans and other forms of financing (for example, credit default swaps sold to municipalities as a hedge, only to result in greater debt obligations) used to offset revenue shortfalls in distressed cities. What cannot be proven is whether or not the Emergency Management policies were targeted at mainly those communities with large African American populations. A comparison with two other communities below offers some suggestions that this might have been a factor.

3 Roots of Neoliberalism

At the end of the Second World War, Europe was in shambles and the United States was scrambling to convert war efforts back to peace time production and to absorb millions of demobilized soldiers into the domestic labor force. Western governments turned to a Keynesian policy of generating full employment through increased spending by the government. Public investments to subsidize or build infrastructure like schools, hospitals, and highways (for example, the Federal Highway Act of 1956, under President Eisenhower, created the Interstate system of roads crisscrossing the country, and was one of the largest public works projects ever), investments to subsidize mass consumption through family allowances, reducing indirect taxation, and keeping down the prices of necessities, or a combination of both initiatives (for example, low interest incentives to build affordable homes while giving households tax breaks for mortgage interest and real estate taxes paid), rapidly expanded the national economy. To undertake these programs, and to avoid dampening consumer demand by increasing taxes, large deficits were incurred through

7 At the time, the population of Michigan was just under 10 million people, of which about 1.4 million were African American (or about 14 percent of the total). The combined population of the EM cities was just over 1 million people, of which about 732,000 were African American (over 70 percent). In the end, about 1 out of every 2 African Americans living in the State of Michigan was likely to be living in a city run by an Emergency Manager.

government borrowing. These government expenditures had the effect of increasing employment directly through funded projects, but also indirectly as rising incomes had multiplier effects on the general economy as consumer spending sustained increased employment on the part of small local businesses. Overall, the period from 1950 to 1970 witnessed government spending programs designed to build the national economy and spur growth while at the same time creating increased employment.

During this period, a tight labor market and government borrowing resulted in several systemic effects. Increased unionization and the need to retain workers during a period of expanding production drove up the wage bill. With expanded government borrowing to finance spending on programs, interest rates began to climb. A growing wage bill and the rising cost of capital squeezed corporate profits. At the same time, the social solidarity that comes with greater unionization and society's awakening to things like racial and gender inequality, workplace health and safety, environmental degradation and eventually opposition to the war being fought in Vietnam, led to periods of social unrest, mass demonstrations, and pressure on the national government to enact laws to address these issues. The climate for business was one of increasing regulation by an active Congress and shrinking profits. The only way capital had to generate and sustain profits was to raise prices of goods and services, but in a low unemployment environment with strong unions this led to raising wages, which were offset again by more price increases, and so on, driving an inflationary spiral (anticipated by Kalecki 1943).[8]

The political writing was on the wall as the business community sought political solutions to an increasingly unfriendly economic and social environment. To avoid the collapse of investment and profits they turned to more business-friendly political campaigns, expecting elected officials to rein in organized labor, dismantle government regulations, and provide a friendlier tax environment. This resulted in the election of Ronald Reagan in 1980 in the US and Margaret Thatcher in 1981 in the UK. Almost immediately practices and policies changed. In 1981 the Professional Air Traffic Controllers Organization,[9] or PATCO, initiated what was called an illegal strike for better working conditions and wages. President Reagan fired the striking workers, broke the strike, and oversaw the decertification of the union. Shortly after, in 1984 the National

---

8 By the end of 1979 the national inflation rate was 13.5 percent, the average 30-year mortgage rates reached 16.32 percent by April 1980, and corporations had to offer an average of 15.51% interest on bonds issued to generate investment capital by October 1981.

9 In a 1969 ruling by the US Civil Service Commission, PATCO was deemed no longer to be a professional association but a trade union.

Union of Mineworkers (NUM) struck to shut down the British coal industry in order to keep coal mines open and protect jobs. The National Coal Board, a government agency, backed by Margaret Thatcher's Conservative government, opposed the strike and broke the trade union. Taken together,[10] both actions by these business-friendly governments reduced the power of the trade unions going forward.

A new era of smaller government and increasing deregulation created the foundation for a neoliberal agenda. Shifting from a national based economy, production was increasingly globalized. Financial regulations were relaxed to facilitate the mobility of capital and pave the way for financialization and eventually policies of austerity to offset declining public revenues due to tax cuts. To further minimize the voices of workers and their communities, policy making increasingly shifted from government agencies and Congressional committees to technocrats and think tanks. The emerging neoliberal state developed in ways that were unanticipated. As Harvey (2005: 64) points out, "[t]he somewhat chaotic evolution and uneven geographical development of state institutions, powers and functions over the last thirty years suggests, furthermore, that the neoliberal state may be an unstable and contradictory political form."

Where once the national government played an active role in managing the liberal welfare economy, functions devolved to states and local governments hampered in their inability to generate the revenues necessary to fund essential government services (see Table 1.1 for a summary of the transition from pre- and post-1980). When the dust settled, a neoliberalism shift became the order of the day,[11] one which sees competition as defining social and economic relations, where citizens are redefined as consumers, democratic choices are exercised by market interactions which rewards merit and punishes inefficiency. Any intervention into the market (whether through taxation or regulation) is a threat to liberty, public services should be privatized, and inequality is a reward while efforts at creating a more equal society is counterproductive. In the end, according to Klein, the core principles of neoliberalism, "...

10 Burns (2011) reflects on how the failure of the PATCO strike and Reagan's actions initiated the long decline of the influence of labor unions in US political and economic life. Coldrick (2013) offers a similar reflection of the impact of Thatcher's breaking the miner's strike on unions, and especially the people of Yorkshire.

11 Increasingly, neoliberalism in its current manifestation has become the topic of research. See Leshem (2016) for a more traditional account of neoliberalism as the historical outgrowth of religion and market economies, and Becchio and Leghissa (2017) for neoliberalism as a theory of organization and a description of how neoliberalism transformed the political nature of economic activity, especially Chapter 4: Turning the World into a Firm.

TABLE 1.1 Social and political differences pre and post the rise of neoliberalism

Inflationary period (1950s–1970s) Good for debtors	Deflationary period (1980 to today) Good for creditors
Sustained inflation	Secular deflation or low interest rates
Labor's share of nation income at all-time high	Capital's share of national income at all-time high
Corporate profits at all-time low	Real wage stagnation
Unions strong	Unions weak
Low inequality	High inequality
National markets	Global markets
Financial institutions and central banks weak	Financial institutions and central banks strong
A strong Congress is writing regulations	A weak Congress is deregulating
Active role for national government	Shrinking public sector and privatization
Liberal welfare economy	Rise of neoliberal austerity

privatization, deregulation and cuts to government services—had laid the foundation for the breakdowns" that were to follow (2007: 444).

By the beginning of the 21st Century, into the now well-established neoliberal and austerity society,[12] local governments were dependent on financial markets and their ever more convoluted debt instruments to raise the funds needed to operate and provide services to their constituencies. Localities were in fiscal decline as their ability to generate revenues from local sources fell, whether because of a loss of employers, changes due to the shift from manufacturing to services and retail in the economy, to the proliferation of low-wage or unskilled work, or simply as a result of a declining population. In Michigan, budgetary constraints and some decisions to withhold revenue sharing obligations put further strains on local budgets. It is no surprise that the poorest cities experienced financial emergencies and the threat of default and insolvency. Into this environment, the State of Michigan introduced its Emergency Management laws.

12 For a general discussion of austerity, its roots and implications, see Blyth 2013a.

4 Michigan's Municipal Financial Emergency Laws

On March 16, 2011, Governor Rick Snyder signed into law the Local Government and School District Fiscal Accountability Act, also known as Public Act 4 (PA 4). In signing this act, Governor Snyder said, "For too long in this state, we've avoided making the tough decisions (Landon 2012)." Now the governor and the state officers can make those "tough decisions" where the state could appoint an EM without evidence of fiscal distress. That is, a state takeover of a municipality, which suspends the decision-making authority of a local government's elected leaders, could be initiated based on the sole discretion of the governor and other state officials. EMs will "act for and in the place and stead of the governing body and the office of chief administrative officer," further specifying that throughout the "receivership, the governing body and the chief administrative officer of the local government may not exercise any of the powers of those offices except as may be specifically authorized in writing by the emergency manager and are subject to any conditions required by the emergency manager."

This gave EMs power far beyond the normal legal capacity of local governing units.[13] These new powers included the ability to unilaterally enact new laws, disregard existing local law as contained in municipal charters and ordinances, terminate collective bargaining agreements and contracts, dismiss elected officials, privatize or sell public assets, and dissolve the local municipality all together. The expanded powers granted to EMs resulted in a public outcry. Michigan residents subsequently voted to repeal Public Act 4. But by December 2012, a bill was amended to reenact the bill, passing both the Michigan House and Senate on December 13, 2012, and on December 26th the new bill was signed into law as the Local Financial Stability and Choice Act or Public Act 436 (PA 436). The new version gave municipalities more latitude on how to address their financial situations; the municipality can choose: 1) a consent agreement, 2) an emergency manager, 3) neutral evaluation, or 4) chapter 9 bankruptcy. At this point Detroit, Hamtramck and Lincoln Park were added to Allen Park, Benton Harbor, Flint, and Ecorse as cities under EM management.

How the process of municipal selection and EM designation operated reveals defects and biases associated with state receivership as a response to fiscal stress. The result provides a better understanding of the objective and, more importantly, subjective dynamics of the EM process and undermines

---

13 Nickels scans the range of policy options states have to deal with municipal fiscal distress, and in her chapters 2 and 3 identifies what she calls a "new normal" (2019: 49) to deal with this situation.

the seemingly apolitical nature of state appointed EMs. When considering the disparate impact of state receivership on select communities and recognizing that African Americans and low-income residents have been disproportionately affected, a more complete analysis of the reasons why municipalities were targeted brings into focus the cultural subjectivities, racial politics, and class biases of decision-makers at the state level. The result is a very uneven landscape of democratic dissolution in the state of Michigan. Inconsistencies in the decision-making process of assigning EMs between localities of differing racial and class compositions provokes critical questions regarding the motives and possible racial politics undergirding the EM process.

An overview of the EM selection and designation process from 2009 to 2014 identifies the various "trigger conditions" for state intervention can tease out the demographic, political, and cultural factors which may have influenced the disparities in the state's EM selection process. The emergency manager process begins with a preliminary review of a municipality's finances by the State Treasurer to determine if a financial emergency exist. In order to conduct such a preliminary review of the municipality, one or more of the trigger conditions must exist.

Trigger conditions fall into four categories: 1) Internal/non-state requests for a preliminary review made by actors such as local officials, creditors, residents, beneficiaries of a local government pension fund, city employees, or bondholders; 2) Senate or House of Representatives make a request; 3) violation of state fiscal law after preliminary reviews because the municipality violates state laws regarding the issuance of bonds or notes; and 4) tax violations due to municipality delinquency in the distribution of tax revenues, or when a court has ordered an additional tax levy without the prior approval of the governing body of the local government.

PA 436 also expanded the criteria the state could use more generally to investigate municipalities for financial distress, and reveals a key aspect of both the motivation for intervention and the structure of the solutions arrived at by each EM:

- The local government is in breach of its obligations under a deficit elimination plan or an agreement entered into pursuant to a deficit elimination plan.
- The local government has been assigned a long-term debt rating within or below the BBB category or its equivalent by 1 or more nationally recognized credit rating agencies.
- The existence of other facts or circumstances that, in the state treasurer's sole discretion for a municipal government, are indicative of

> probable financial stress or that, in the state treasurer's or superintendent of public instruction's sole discretion for a school district, are indicative of probable financial stress.

Concerned with the State of Michigan's overall bond rating, which determines the cost of borrowing, the EM mandate was to rectify delinquent municipal bonds that had a negative impact on the state's rating. This last condition essentially gives the state virtually unlimited power to investigate a municipality for fiscal distress (now more accurately described as a danger of default on municipal obligations), and thereby unilaterally impose an Emergency Manager.

Flint was targeted by the state primarily for fund deficits and violations of budgetary guidelines; specifically, they failed to submit a proper deficit elimination plan. Are those conditions used in appointing an EM for Flint applied equally across all municipalities? If not, why not? The State of Michigan took action in Flint based on the criteria that the municipality either: 1) ended a fiscal year in a deficit condition, and/or 2) failed to file or institute a deficit elimination plan. Management decisions and actions taken by the EMs to improve the fiscal health to Flint primarily involved a combination of cost reduction and revenue enhancement, to the degree possible, including: 1) compensation and post-employment benefit reductions for city employees and retirees, 2) raising fees and rates for city services, 3) eliminating positions and departments, and as a last resort 4) securing emergency loans from the state (see Table 1.2 for a broad comparison of policies employed in each city).

5 A Tale of Two Frameworks[14]

A review of the financial records and state budget compliance status of each municipality in Michigan from 2008 to 2014 reveals two comparable municipalities that were not appointed an EM: Taylor and Dearborn Heights. The City of Taylor is a distant suburb of Detroit located in the southern region of Wayne County. Taylor, a township incorporated as a city in 1968, was at the time the

14 Municipal data for this section were culled from a review of the annual financial audit reports for the cities of Taylor and Dearborn, Wayne County, Michigan over the period from 2008 to 2014, The reports are available from the Michigan Department of Treasury, Local Audit and Finance Division, accessible at https://treas-secure.state.mi.us/LAFDocSearch/. The data and many of the findings in this chapter come from an unpublished report on the overall impact of Emergency Managers in Michigan (see Fasenfest and Pride 2015). Details on the results appearing in this chapter are available from the author.

TABLE 1.2 EM deficit reduction orders by city, 2008–2015

Order/City	Allen Park	Benton Harbor	Detroit	Ecorse	Flint	Lincoln Park	Hamtramck	Pontiac
Fee/fine increase	X	X	X	X	X	X		X
Tax increase (millage)	X	X			X			
Emergency/private loan	X	X	X	X	X		X	
Issue bonds/notes	X	X		X		X		X
Sale of City Property/Assets	X	X	X	X	X	X	X	X
Reduce wages for city employees	X	X		X	X		X	X
Reduce compensation for fire and/or police	X	X	X		X	X		X
Reduce workforce	X	X	X	X	X	X	X	X
Reduce pensions			X					
Eliminate/reduce post-employment benefits of retirees	X		X		X	X	X	X
Eliminate/reduce benefits of city employees	X	X	X	X	X			X
Eliminate services	X							X
Contract out city services		X	X	X		X	X	X
Consolidate services/departments		X		X		X	X	X

SOURCE: EMERGENCY MANAGER ANNUAL REPORTS

17th largest city in Michigan with approximately 61,594 residents. While financial problems in Taylor have not been widely publicized, from 2012 to 2014 Taylor had fiscal problems similar to those of Flint.

According to audits conducted by the Michigan Department of Treasury, Taylor ended the fiscal years of 2012 and 2013 with significant deficits in their general fund. The state's audit revealed that Taylor's deficit was due to significant decreases in revenue, which was caused by declines property values, cuts in state-revenue sharing, and declines in revenue generated by the 23rd District Court. The audit also highlighted public employee wages and fringe benefit expense as costly expenditures that could be contained to reduce further financial distress. It concluded that "recurring revenue is not sufficient to pay for all expenditures", and that "economic conditions continue to deteriorate" in Taylor.

In 2012, the state denied Taylor authorization to issue municipal bonds. Taylor ended the fiscal year with a fund deficit and failed submit an appropriate deficit elimination plan to the state. Taylor's financial problems persisted into 2013. Once again Taylor still ended the fiscal year with a deficit in its general fund and the audit report pointed to persisting problems with falling property values and Taylor's inability to increase revenue due to poor economic conditions in southeast Michigan. Taylor was not in compliance with state finance laws and was delinquent in transferring employee taxes withheld to the appropriate agency, transferring taxes collected as an agent for another taxing unit, or making all required pension, retirement, or benefit plan contributions. By 2014, the audit report stated its revenues were nowhere near what the City must maintain in order to be considered financially stable. As they did for EM cities like Flint, the state could have elected to conduct a review and determine that an EM assignment was appropriate to address a range of issues.

The second case is a commuter town, the City of Dearborn Heights, located in the western suburbs of Detroit. Similar to Taylor, Dearborn Heights has experienced some significant problems with their finances. In 2011 the audit report suggested that the deficit, like the one in Taylor, was partly due to declining property values and rising costs of public employees and city services. They recommended that cuts be made to wages and post-employment benefits to reduce city expenditures. That year, Dearborn Heights was also in violation for ending the fiscal year in deficit condition and not submitting an appropriate deficit elimination plan. While there were some marked improvements in the city finances of Dearborn Heights, the ballooning deficits accrued in 2012 and 2013, along with the failure to submit a deficit elimination plan in 2012, presented adequate financial conditions to trigger a preliminary review by the state.

For the purposes of this comparison, it helps to explore the relationship of key indicators for Dearborn Heights and Taylor relative to two EM cities with comparable populations and similar fiscal concerns (see Table 1.3), Flint and Pontiac. While Flint is larger, Pontiac has about the same population as Dearborn Heights and Taylor over the period 2008–2014; the main difference is that the population in Pontiac (like in Flint) hovers around 50 percent Black when compared to the roughly 17 percent Black in Taylor and only about 7 percent Black in Dearborn (note that as the fiscal distress indicator in Dearborn Heights grows over this period, the percent of the population that is Black increased from about 7 percent to over 9 percent).

For these two municipalities that did not receive preliminary reviews from 2007 to 2014, financial indicators could have triggered a preliminary review. Multiple years with fund deficits, declines in revenue, and failures to meet state accounting requirement, factors motivating actions taken against Flint, failed to motivate a similar response. While other factors certainly play a part in the identification of municipalities with financial emergencies and the initiation of a review of municipal finances, the legislation does contain language that allows for the initiation of the review process to be discretionary. Taylor and Dearborn Heights exhibit comparable levels of fiscal distress, yet no action was taken. What follows identifies various differences that may help to shed light on the subjective aspect of state receivership in Michigan.

The degree of financial distress—the size of deficits, the duration of revenue shortages, the amount of debt-to-income—may play a role in the state's preliminary review selection process when choosing among the various cities dealing with financial problems. This would be considered subjective within the state's review process because nowhere in the different EM laws does it specify levels or even measures of financial distress that should be taken into consideration when determining the need to a preliminary review. It may be that state prioritizes municipalities by level of financial distress. Thus, cities with higher deficits and debt may be more susceptible to being targeted by the state than cities with lower deficits and debt.

While the deficits for the EM cities were higher than these comparable cities, the debt-to-income ratio (or debt-to-revenue) for Flint was actually lower than that of Taylor. The debt-to-income ratio measures a city's ability to repay the debt, calculated by dividing revenue by debt. Higher ratios indicate higher debt payments, which anticipates the city having increasing difficulty in making such payments. Taylor's debt-to-income ratio was higher than Flint's every year from 2010 to 2014. A key measure that illustrates the fiscal health of a municipality is long term debt as a percent of taxable value (LDPTV). Large debt levels relative to the ability of a municipality to generate revenue (based

TABLE 1.3 Key indicators of select EM and non-EM cities, 2008–2014

Year	EM cities								Non-EM cities							
	Flint				*Pontiac*				*Dearborn Heights*				*Taylor*			
	POP	% BL	LtD/ Rev	Fiscal Distr	POP	% BL	LtD/ Rev	Fiscal Distr	POP	% BL	LtD/ Rev	Fiscal Distr	POP	% BL	LtD/ Rev	Fiscal Distr
2008	112,900	56.4	0.88	6	66,095	51.8	0.80	7	51,972	6.6	0.54	2	60,619	17.1	0.73	2
2009	111,475	56.4	0.79	8	66,247	51.8	1.11	7	50,820	6.6	0.48	3	59,308	17.1	0.72	2
2010	102,190	56.6	0.55	9	59,488	52.1	1.01	6	57,648	6.9	0.50	4	62,991	17.3	0.69	4
2011	101,376	53.9	0.40	7	59,627	49.9	0.57	4	57,389	7.6	0.31	6	62,636	16.4	0.56	4
2012	100,475	55.4	0.68	8	59,537	50.2	0.54	6	57,173	9.2	0.42	7	62,418	16.9	0.80	7
2013	99,791	54.8	0.57	7	59,856	51.0	0.03	6	56,744	8.3	0.40	7	61,955	17.3	0.64	7
2014	99,002	55.4	0.63	7	59,808	50.2	0.31	2	56,415	9.2	0.41	5	61,594	16.9	1.01	6

POP = POPULATION; % BL = PERCENT AFRICAN-AMERICAN; LTD/REV = LONG-TERM DEBT/REVENUE; FISCAL DISTR = FISCAL DISTRESS SCORE
SOURCE: MUNETRIX 2015

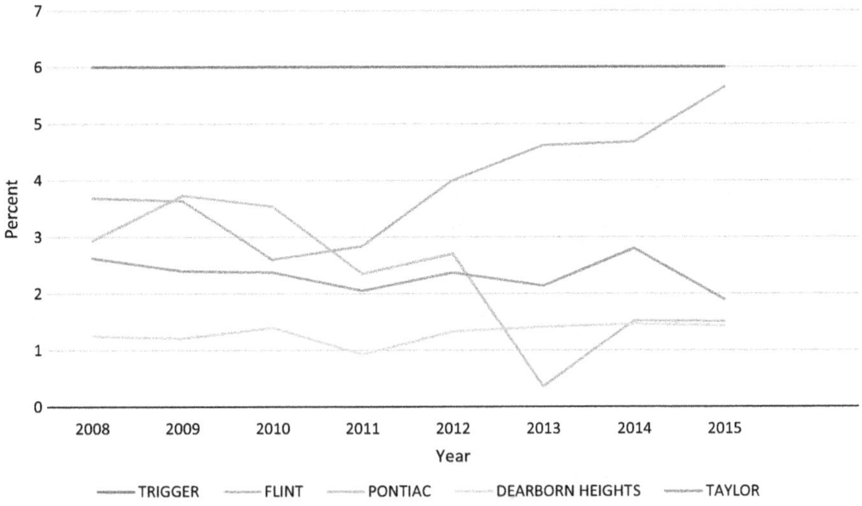

FIGURE 1.1 Long-term debt as a percent of taxable value for select cities, 2006 to 2015
SOURCE: MUNETRIX, 2015

on the city's taxable value) is a sign of fiscal distress. The Michigan Department of Treasury and Michigan State University developed a system that measures the financial stability (or instability) of a municipality, based on evaluations of several cities state-wide. Exceeding 6 percent on the LDPTV measure was a sign of fiscal distress. From 2006 to 2011 Flint's LDPTV was comparable to Taylor. As shown in Figure 1.1, by 2008 and 2009 Flint's LDPTV grows to 3.8 percent and then falls back down to 2.5 percent the following year.[15] During that time Taylor's LDPTV stays relative constant hovering between 2.0 and 2.5 percent.

In 2011, the year Flint underwent its preliminary review, its LDPTV was slightly higher than Taylor's. However, that first year Taylor reported general fund deficits and failed to submit a deficit elimination plan, and its LDPTV was only slightly lower than Flint's.

Flint's case was not so disparate; many of Flint's financial measures were either comparable or even better than that of Taylor and Dearborn Heights. Flint's general fund deficit was relatively close to each. Also, Flint's ability to make debt payments seemed to be slightly better than that of Taylor from 2010 to 2014. Lastly, Flint's ability (or inability) to pay off long-term debt seemed to be similar to that of Taylor up until 2011. Thus, Flint's financial health during

15 Figure 1.1 includes data for Pontiac to offer a comparison with an EM city with a comparable population.

the years leading up to it preliminary review in 2011 was essentially no different than the fiscal health of Taylor at the time Flint was appointed an Emergency Manager.

In conclusion, more work needs to be done to uncover the subjectivities used by the state in determining which city should undergo a preliminary financial review. The financial similarities between Flint and Taylor suggest that other factors besides the degree of fiscal distress motivated the state to take action against Flint and not Taylor. Local and municipal differences in racial composition, socioeconomic status, housing value, business investment, and political party control could provide interesting answers to this question.

6 What Did EMs Do?

There were three main tactics used in each of the EM cities to reduce expenditures in order to adjust revenues in line with debt service (see Kasdan 2014). Little regard was taken on how that might impact local residents, or whether those actions would lead to long-term viability and fiscal health. These were, in no particular order, cost cutting, revenue enhancements or taking emergency loans from the State, and the privatization of or outsourcing municipal services.

6.1 *Cost Cutting*

The wages and/or benefits of elected officials, city employees, and retirees were reduced and/or eliminated in every EM city except for Detroit. In Allen Park, Benton Harbor, Lincoln Park, and Pontiac, the salaries of the mayor and city council were reduced by 50 percent while in Ecorse the salaries of the mayor and city was reduced by 72 percent. In the cities where mayors and city council members' salaries were reduced their benefits were eliminated as well. The wages of city employees were reduced by up to 10 percent in most cities as well. In Allen Park, Benton Harbor, Detroit, Flint, Lincoln Park, and Pontiac, the wages and/or benefits of police officers and firefighters were cut. Typical compensation reductions for police officers and firefighters included reduced vacation and holiday pay, overtime, and the city pension contributions. The post-employment benefits of retirees were reduced or eliminated in every city except for Benton Harbor and Ecorse. In Lincoln Park, the post-employment benefits for all city retirees were eliminated. Post-employment alterations for most other cities involved health care plan changes that required retirees to pay higher fees. Lastly, the benefits of city employees were reduced or eliminated in every city except Lincoln Park and Hamtramck. Again, most of these benefit changes resulted in higher health care costs for employees.

To further reduce expenditures, the workforce was reduced and/or departments were eliminated/consolidated in every city. Several municipal employees were fired during the EM process. In Pontiac the number of city employees were amazingly reduced from 502 to 20. Pontiac's severe reduction of public sector employees was accomplished through the elimination of several departments including the police department, fire department, and public works. In Flint 16 percent of the workforce was cut, resulting in the loss of approximately 115 public sector jobs. Likewise, roughly 60 public sector jobs were eliminated in Benton Harbor. Other cities experienced small reductions in their workforce like Allen Park, losing 10 public sector jobs, and Ecorse, which lost 14 public sector jobs.

6.2 *Revenue Enhancement and Emergency Loans*

To increase revenue, the rates and fees for city services were increased in every city except for Hamtramck. In Allen Park the water rate increased from 2.634 per cubic feet to 2.774 per cubic feet and the sewer rate increased from 2.266 per cubic feet to 2.329 per cubic feet. Administrative, license, and permit fees were also increased in Allen Park. In Benton Harbor the rental fees for Klock Park were increased. In Ecorse the building fees, electrical fees, plumbing fees, and mechanical fees were increased. In Lincoln Park the water rates were increased by 15 percent and a booking fee for arrestees was established. In Detroit parking fines were increased.

Finally, to close fiscal shortfalls every city obtained an emergency loan from the state, or, in the case of Detroit, a private loan, except for Lincoln Park and Pontiac. The loans ranged from $2.3 million for Benton Harbor to $325 million for Detroit received (we should note that at the same time, the City of Detroit provided almost $250 million in loan guarantees to build a new privately-owned downtown hockey arena with a high value residential and commercial building complex for the Detroit Red Wings).[16]

6.3 *Privatization of Services*

Most of the EM cities saw much of their municipal services privatized or outsourced while under emergency management. Every city contracted out city

16 According to *Crain's Detroit Business* (September 21, 2014) the initial projected costs for the stadium was $450 million, guaranteed in part by $250 million Series A bonds back by property taxes captured by the Downtown Development Authority (https://bit.ly/3d5OMUn).

services or departmental functions except for Allen Park and Flint. While under emergency management, in February 2014, Detroit's city council approved the privatization of trash collection. The decision marked the largest privatization of services in Detroit's history. The deal was expected to save the city approximately $6 million a year, though little effort was made to study the impact this had on the community either through reduction of service or loss of municipal jobs.

7 Short Term Fixes, Long Term Viability and Local Austerity

As indicated above, there were a wide range of factors that resulted in cities facing serious budgetary deficits. Causes included failed investments, changes in the global economy that radically altered the local economic landscape, massive lay-offs and plant closings due to technological innovation, declining populations for a number of reasons, and a general erosion of the local tax base. In the end, cities were faced with debt burdens from past bond issues and unfunded pension contributions obligations. To address these issues, the State of Michigan implemented unprecedented control over local government by suspending (and at times removing) elected officials and wresting control over financial decision-making from the representatives of the residents of these cities.

Regardless of the causes for this fiscal crisis of cities, the responses by the EMs was strikingly similar. Their brief: find ways to impose austerity on the community to generate the resources needed to meet the existing bond obligations and debt service. The result: cut costs by cutting staffing salaries and personnel levels, enhance revenues by any means necessary, and when all else fails, take out loans to fill the gap. While the immediate objective of closing local deficits may be met, the long-term viability of these austerity strategies leaves much to be desired (Blyth 2013b). As Figure 1.2 clearly demonstrates, these communities generally saw declines in the taxable values of the communities and home prices (real estate taxes are a primary source of local revenues). Falling home values especially signals a decline in demand as these communities lose residents for a number of reasons lead by poor services, funding for their schools, lack of infrastructural repairs and improvements, and a continued absence of jobs in the communities in question. Curtailing of services resulted in massive cuts in local expenditures, but these communities also experienced continued declines in local revenues (Figure 1.3).

The EM's failure to address these underlying structural concerns, usually the task facing local elected officials, bodes poorly for the next decade or more.

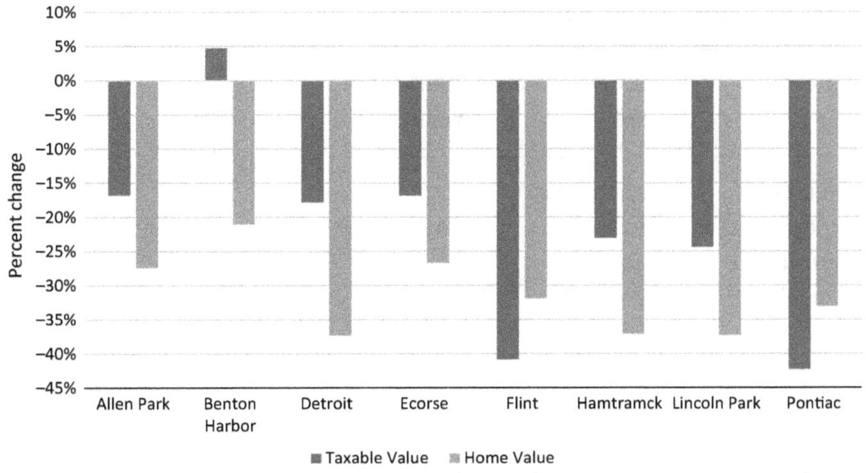

FIGURE 1.2 Percentage changes in taxable and home values, 2010–2013
SOURCE: MICHIGAN DEPARTMENT OF TREASURY, LOCAL AUDIT AND FINANCE DIVISION (HTTPS://TREAS-SECURE.STATE.MI.US/LAFDOCSEARCH/)

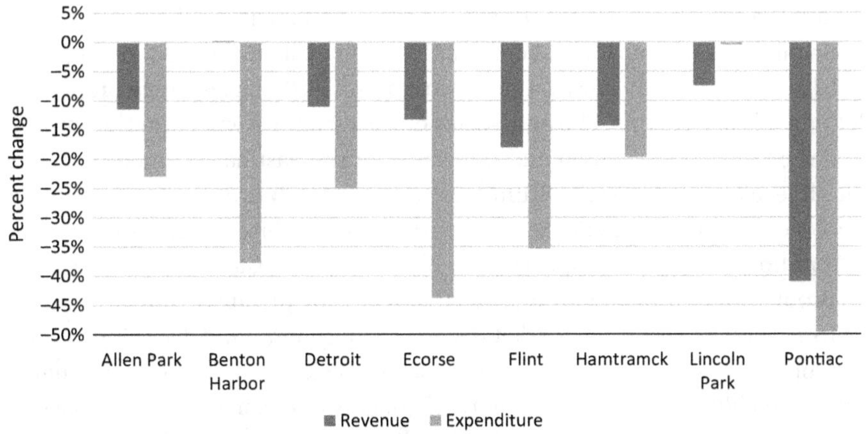

FIGURE 1.3 Percentage changes in revenues and expenditures, 2010–2013
SOURCE: MICHIGAN DEPARTMENT OF TREASURY, LOCAL AUDIT AND FINANCE DIVISION (HTTPS://TREAS-SECURE.STATE.MI.US/LAFDOCSEARCH/)

These communities will once again face rising debt payments as the new loans put pressure on community resources, and there is little reason to expect other than another situation of fiscal distress and budget shortfalls.

As shown in Table 1.4 below, the austerity measures implemented by state appointed EMs from 2009 to 2015 resulted in a significant cumulative

TABLE 1.4 Impact of EM orders: assets sold and jobs lost

EM city	Value of assets sold	Workforce reduction
Allen Park	$12,000,000	10
Benton Harbor	$102,000	60
Detroit	$405,000	
Ecorse	$200,000	14
Flint	$550,000	115
Hamtramck	$350,000	3
Lincoln Park	$911,464	1
Pontiac	$56,163,000	482
Total	**$70,681,464**	**685**

SOURCE: EMERGENCY MANAGER REPORTS

reduction of public assets, and public sector job loss. In total, approximately 1685 public sector jobs have been eliminated by EMs from 2009 to 2015. That job loss is particularly devastating for communities that have a high proportion of non-white residents. The only sector of steady improvement for the employment prospects for women and minorities in the past has been employment at all levels of government, from local to national. But the general shrinking of government services across the board has had a bigger impact on women (Abramovitz 2012), and especially on Blacks (Cooper, Gable and Austin 2012). A Brookings report on jobs indicates that while the private sector continues to hire, the public-sector job market is stagnant in general, and declining in some sectors (Harris et al. 2014). The public-sector is essential for the maintenance of a viable Black middle class, where "[R]oughly one in five black adults works for the government, teaching school, delivering mail, driving buses, processing criminal justice, and managing large staffs ... about 30 percent more likely to have a public sector job than non-Hispanic whites" (Cohen 2015; see also Public Works, 2015). The result is downward mobility (Wilson et al. 2013) that has a crushing impact on cities like Pontiac and Flint, which lost 482 and 115 jobs respectively.

And it is not just the loss of jobs in the city, it is the loss of futures for families living in a city with shrinking opportunities, it undermines the ability of formerly middle-class people of color to be able to afford their homes, pay taxes, and sustain the revenue base of the city. Other consequences of state-imposed austerity include higher costs for local residents through property tax and city service fee and fine increases. These budgetary and financial changes, as demonstrated throughout this report, typically occur in these low income and minority cities of Michigan. Thus, the overall negative impact of austerity is a disproportionate one and will decrease the social and economic well-being of most of Michigan's poor communities of color.

Reducing the workforce of a municipality can also lead to a decline in the quality of public service delivery for residents. In Allen Park, for example, curbside trash pick-up was eliminated. In this case the loss of waste disposal service creates an inconvenience for residents as they are forced to find alternative solutions, which may impose additional cost to residents. The loss of services may also make neighborhoods less attractive to homebuyers or lead to a loss in property values, which, again, imposes unwanted costs on residents in the form financial loss through depreciated home values. Furthermore, many of the jobs lost were public safety jobs—fire and police. In cities with high crime rates, like Flint and Detroit, a reduction in police officers presents serious public safety issues for residents.

In total, public assets were reduced by $70,681,464. However, this figure only represents the dollar amount received by the EM cities from the sale of city property/assets and not the "true" value of lost assets. Many of the city properties were sold under market value, thus the figure presented is an underestimation of the real value lost through the selling off of city owned assets by EMs. For example, in 2009, Pontiac's EM, Fred Leeb, auctioned the Pontiac Silverdome for $580,000 to investor Andreas Apostolopoulos of Triple Properties, Inc., which was significantly less than the $18 million bid for the property made in 2008 by United Assurance, or the assessed market value, which was around $7 million. While Pontiac more than likely would not have sold the Silverdome for its assessed market value, the decision by the EM to sell the Silverdome at all cost in order to eliminate the city's deficit led to a huge loss in potential value for Pontiac. Although unused and vacant property can be a financial burden to cash-strapped municipalities, through maintenance cost and tax revenue loss, the massive "fire sale" of city assets, which, in many cases, were far below fair market value, tends to unevenly benefit investors and corporations in the private sector. That is, the selling of public assets by EMs, like in the example above, produces disproportionate financial benefits for wealthy private investors.

The increased privatization of public space also impoverishes the social economy and diminishes the level of control local residents have over how the spaces and places in their communities are used. For example, in Benton Harbor, park land was sold to a private developer without requiring the purchaser to make concessions to provide replacement land for public consumption. Thus, Benton Harbor residents lost open green space for public use while the private developer, in this case, Geerlings Development Company, acquired cheap land that will be used to extract rent from Benton Harbor residents. The fiscal conditions of struggling cities with large low income and non-white populations have open the door for private investors to come in and assume more and more control over public space throughout Michigan, limiting the ability of poor and minority communities to shape and influence the process of place-making at the local level.

The austerity imposed on cities also creates direct higher costs for residents. To increase revenue, EMs raised property taxes and city fines and fees. Property taxes increased in Allen Park, Benton Harbor, and Flint. In Allen Park property taxes were raised 85.8 percent, in Benton Harbor they were raised 26.1 percent, and in Flint they were raised 2.71 percent. Fine and fee increases ranged from a 50 percent increase in parking fines in Detroit to an average 3.8 percent increase for water and sewer service in Allen Park. These cost increases essentially function to transfer the financial deficits of cities to local residents. That is, local residents are forced to bear the burden of municipal fiscal distress, a problem created, not by residents but, rather, and primarily, by structural forces largely outside of their control. Furthermore, this shift in cost also functions as a regressive tax on the poor as low income residents, already burden by falling wages and the rising cost of living, cannot afford the increases in city service fees, fines, and taxes.

8 The Environmental Impact of Strategic and Structural Racism

There is strong evidence that race, if not a direct factor in the decision to place an Emergency Manager in Flint, was important in understanding the well-rehearsed events which followed from that decision.[17] Ostensibly charged with bringing the city back to fiscal health, the focus was on clearing the problem debt. Among the various revenue enhancing or expense reducing strategies was the transition from Detroit City water to the Karegnondi Water Authority[18] pipeline. In the transition, a decision was taken that the city would draw its water from the Flint River, a well know polluted body of water because of

17 Soss et al. 2011, points out that what they refer to as neoliberal paternalism is used to discipline the poor through the power of racialized public policy.

18 See Hammer 2019, for a discussion of this decision.

decades of industrial activities that supported a previously prosperous city. Residents immediately saw problems with smell, color, taste and skin rashes due to water exposure, but citizen complaints were ignored or minimized. Instead, resident complaints were dismissed as a "typical" reaction of those unwilling to take responsibility and accept the need for necessary actions to resolve Flint's fiscal crisis. What is no longer in doubt is that this decision was calamitous for the residents of Flint, as lead in the water leached from old pipes as a result of the corrosive elements in the Flint River. The ensuing health crisis was slow to be recognized, even as the city's residence reported health problems and mobilized for a solution. State officials first denied there was a problem, then minimized the problem, but eventually acknowledged the problem after legal actions were brought against key individuals.

Racism, both manifest and latent, inform social, political and economic interactions in the US, and especially in the country's urban areas (as outlined to some degree above). Structural racism refers to a set of inter-institutional dynamics consistently producing and reproducing racially disparate outcomes over time. The concentration of poverty among urban African Americans has its roots in both the systematic constraints the limit the residential options. At the same time, the geography determines access to schools, healthcare, and jobs perpetuating that poverty. In essence there is both a spatialization of race and a racialization of space. What is missing in this frame is the intent to cause harm based on racist beliefs. In effect, this structural racism made it easier to assume that the fiscal problems in Flint was due to administrative mismanagement and there was little need to look at structural problems as the root cause. Once that was decided, the only solution was to replace—albeit temporarily—the city's leadership with an emergency manager.

At the same time, and somewhat cynically, strategic racism in the form of the manipulation of intentional, unconscious or structural racism, does not require an articulation of racist intent in action or purpose. Rather, actions can be taken that are detrimental to African Americans whether in the selection of those communities most in trouble financially or in the slow response to community concerns about health and safety. The people of Flint fought long and hard before their plight was taken seriously and they got the attention the problem warranted. As Benz points out, what happened in Flint was the response of "a system that systematically devalues the lives of black citizens and elevates the value of white lives when confronted with the 'need' for environmental protections" (2019: 50). Flint was emblematic of the structural inequality that resulted from a shrinking employment base due to technological change and plant closings, and from economic flight leaving behind the urban poor African Americans unable to afford to relocate. The consequences were declining property values and a shrinking tax base creating budget shortfalls increasing the city's debt burden. The combination of these two forces made Flint, and the other EM cities (not exclusively), increasingly unattractive because of reduced services and failing social and physical infrastructure. These, it would seem, were not matters of concern to the Emergency Manager in Flint. After all, to address the root causes of Flint's problems requires understanding that they are "more often a result of the legal, social, and economic practices and frameworks that surround these situations" (Thün, et al. 2015: 90).

The combination of structural and strategic racism created a perfect storm that informed the slow acknowledgement of residents' concerns over water quality and the subsequent harm lead in the water inflicted on residents and their children. The decision to approve the transition away from Detroit water was informed by the same logic that created incentives to hide or deny problems with the water in the first instance, and then to defend the actions of the EMs and subsequent State agencies. In effect, an implicit decision was taken to "wait out" the residents rather than come up with expensive remedial strategies. "Experts" from state agencies adopted flawed techniques and indefensible interpretations of test results thereby failing to protect public health in Flint. In short, structural racism created the problem, strategic racism empowered public officials to ignore Flint citizen concerns.

Citizens of Flint mobilized "... to protest against a plan or project approved by the public administration ... citizens mobilize to claim for better life conditions ..." (Cruz-Gallach and Solé-Figueras 2015: 143). Once the situation was taken seriously and residents were able to draw attention demanding action by the state to redress the problem, the decisions and behavior of key public officials were reviewed with serious charge were brought against them. Investigating how the water became contaminated, why the contamination was not properly uncovered, and how that contributed to an outbreak of Legionnaire's disease led to guilty pleas or court cases against staff from the Michigan Department of Environmental Quality, from the State's Department of Health and Human Services, from Flint's Department of Public Works, and two of the former Emergency Managers of the city. What is clear is that, in the end, urban neoliberalism's "colorblind policymaking" has created a situation whereby the interests of Michigan's African American residents are not considered (Benz 2019: 58).

9 Conclusion

Michigan cities have had a long history of economic hardships and social struggles over the past half-century, and the results have been the hollowing out of formerly industrial cities, population loss to accompany job loss, and for many parts of the state a persistent and severe downturn in both the quality of its infrastructure and pessimism over its outlook. Clearly, many cities have experienced stress, and as a result continue to deal with deficits as they try to balance the needs of their citizens by providing a range of services from public safety to city lights and snow removal with their inability to generate sufficient revenues to meet those needs. These problems have come about for many reasons, and for each city circumstances vary.

Cities have generally been left to fend for themselves on how to address their shortfalls, and most have resorted to a variety of financial instruments ranging from bond issues to credit default swaps to long- and short-term loans to balance budgets. However, over time the debt service on these instruments outpaced the community's ability to raise the funds necessary to cover costs. What has been absent has been any regional or state-wide effort to understand why cities faced these problems in the first instance, and how cities arrived at the situation of fiscal stress they now faced. There is no doubt that a concerted effort had to be made to resolve the fiscal crises facing some of Michigan's biggest cities.

The problem, however, is that the solutions created do not address the problem. Rather, broad assumptions are made about mismanagement without a careful examination of each city's circumstances. The result has been a broad application of one basic tool to solve all the various issues facing cities put under emergency management control. It is difficult to argue motivation for the cities selected, but as has been noted, some cities that might have qualified escaped the trauma of the loss of democratic rights while those chosen had, for the most part, large predominantly non-white populations. A reasonable question might have been raised as these actions unfolded as to why almost half of the state's African American population was now living under a form of political martial law.

We are left with the question: What did the EMs accomplish in Flint?[19] To resolve debt in danger of default they sold the city's assets, reduced staff and services, and suspended democratic processes. To "balance" Flint's budget, the EMs fired 20 percent of the city's workers, doubled water rates residents had to pay for service, and outsourced trash collection.[20] EMs did nothing to

19 Neoliberalism writ large has been identified as the root of financial, environmental and political problems across the board, and the cause of rising inequality (see Monbiot 2016).

20 The irony of these actions is that local government is often the only source of employment for unskilled workers, and public service in a city like Flint was a major employer after the departure of their GM facility. In an effort to resolve a revenue problem in the short term, these actions effectively intensified the problem going forward.

understand how the underlying structural racism had created the fiscal crisis in the first instance. These cuts in a range of social and economic supports made the city increasingly unsafe and undesirable. The people of Flint were the victims of strategic racism and as a result politically powerless to alter the course of action—first to have an Emergency Manager appointed, and then to challenge the logic and actions undertaken. In the end, the EMs replaced the current municipal debt with new debt, pushing the problem into the next decade and dictating future revenue streams, which left communities with a questionable.

The implementation of PA 426 and the subsequent assignment of Emergency Managers reflects a basic approach to society's ills; specifically, the application of market-based austerity policies that are based on a financial rather than a social solution to a community's ills. Austerity measures applied by EMs, broadly stated, achieve two objectives: a) they seek to preserve the financial interests of lenders and bond holders without exploring how those interests may have created the problem in the first instance, and b) the seek solutions that implicitly involve the privatization of public assets and explicitly turn to the very same financial instruments that are culpable in the first instance. Turning to government oversight to manage the needs of citizens through the market, in the context of neoliberalism, can be foolish and disappointing. As Mirowski points out, "[t]he prospect of the government serving as market-maker of last resort presumably cannot be extended indefinitely, which brings us to the final long game component of the full-spectrum brace of policies ... the policy consists more of unsubstantial promise than in demonstrated capabilities" (2013: 350).

Cities like Flint, unlike the other EM cities, did not request a preliminary review by state officials leading to an EM assignment. Rather, the state initiated this review based on provisions in PA 426 and imposed the EM on the community. Flint, now the victim of a neoliberal urban agenda, has become the posterchild representing what happens when resources are extracted, and when decisions are made, with apparently little regard for the health and safety for the people who live there (Fasenfest 2018). Recent revelations about how the city's residents have been subjected to environmental hazards as a result of decisions about its water system, driven solely by cost (and essentially market) considerations, exposes the EM process for what it ended up being. As Harvey (2005: 165) pointed out, "[t]o presume that markets and market signals can best determine all allocative decisions is to presume that everything can in principle be treated as a commodity." In the final analysis, one can make an argument that the residents of these communities (and other EM cities) were not the beneficiaries of actions purported to return the city to fiscal health.

Sadly, and to some degree ironically, most if not all of the EM cities have resolved their immediate financial problems without significant structural changes. In its place these cities manage the task of paying for services with new debt, but now face a long-run situation of declining revenues due to falling property values, an inability to attract new residents due to cuts in services, a greater burden of fees and costs on the remaining residents, and the prospect of a crippling debt service due to these new loans issued to meet current budgetary requirements. What gets forgotten is that municipalities should focus on "… securing government revenues to promote sustainable growth and avoiding an unnecessary default on basic public functions" (Tabb 2012: 247). The crisis faced by communities today will just be revisited upon them in the coming decades. This has been a problem delayed, not a problem solved.

References

Abramovitz, M. (2012). "The Feminization of Austerity." *New Labor Forum* 21: 32–41.

Alexander, M. (2012). *The New Jim Crow: Mass Incarceration in the Age of Colorblindness*. New York, NY: The New Press.

Anderson, M.W. (2011). "Democratic Dissolution: Radical Experimentation in State Takeovers of Local Governments." *Fordham Urban Law Journal* 39: 577–623.

Becchio, G. and Leghissa, G. (2017). *The Origins of Neoliberalism: Insights from Economics and Philosophy*. London, New York: Routledge.

Benz, T. (2019). "Toxic Cities: Neoliberalism and Environmental Racism in Flint and Detroit." *Critical Sociology* 45(1): 49–62.

Blyth, M. (2013a). *Austerity: The History of a Dangerous Idea*. New York, NY: Oxford University Press.

Blyth, M. (2013b). "The Austerity Delusion: Why a Bad Idea Won Over the West." *Foreign Affairs* May/June. Available at: https://www.foreignaffairs.com/articles/2013-04-03/austerity-delusion.

Burns, J. (2011). "The PATCO Strike, Reagan and the Roots of Labor's Decline." *In These Times*, November1, 2011. Available at: http://inthesetimes.com/working/entry/12208/the_patco_strike_reagan_and_the_roots_of_labors_decline.

Clement, D. and Kanai, M. (2015). "The Detroit Future City: How Pervasive Neoliberal Urbanism Exacerbates Racialized Spatial Injustice." *American Behavioral Scientists* 59(3): 369–385.

Cohen, P. (2015). "Public-Sector Jobs Vanish, Hitting Blacks Hard." *The New York Times*, May 24, 2015. Available at: http://www.nytimes.com/2015/05/25/business/public-sector-jobs-vanish-and-blacks-take-blow.html?login=email&_r=1 (consulted April 2, 2016).

Coldrick, M. (2013). "Margaret Thatcher and the Pit Strike in Yorkshire." *BBC News*. April 8, 2013. Available at: https://www.bbc.com/news/uk-england-22068640.

Cooper, D., Gable, M., and Austin, A. (2012). "The Public-Sector Jobs Crisis: Women and African Americans Hit Hardest by Job Losses in State and Local Governments." *EPI Briefing Paper*, #339, May 2, 2012. Washington, DC: Economic Policy Institute.

Crosby, A. and Robbins, D. (2013). "Mission Impossible: Monitoring Municipal Fiscal Sustainability and Stress in Michigan." *Journal of Public Budgeting, Accounting & Financial Management* 25(3): 522–555.

Cruz-Gallach, H. and Solé-Figueras, L. (2015). "Spatial Conflicts in Catalonia: An Overview of Social Struggles During the Last Decade." In: Gualini, E., Mourato, J.M., and Allegra, M. (eds.). *Conflict in the City*. Berlin: JOVIS Verlag.

Donald, B., Glasmeier, A., Gray, M., and Lobao, L. (2014). "Austerity in the City: Economic Crisis and Urban Service Decline." *Cambridge Journal of Regions, Economy and Society* 7: 3–15.

Fasenfest, D. (2015). "Social Sustainability and Urban Inequality: Detroit and the Ravages of Neoliberalism." In: Miraftab, F., Salo, K., and Wilson, D. (eds.). *Cities and Inequalities in a Global and Transnational World.* London: Routledge.

Fasenfest, D. (2018). "Emergency Management in Michigan: A Misguided Policy Initiative." In: Nickels, A. and Rivera, J. (eds.). *Community Development and Public Administration Theory: Empowerment through the Enhancement of Democratic Principles*. London: Routledge.

Fasenfest, D. (2019). "A Neoliberal Response to an Urban Crisis: Emergency Management in Flint, MI." *Critical Sociology* 45(1): 33–47.

Fasenfest, D. and Pride, T. (2016). *Unelected, Unaccountable: The Impact of Emergency Managers on Key Michigan Cities*. Unpublished report for the Michigan ACLU.

Gee, G., Hing, A., Selina, M., Tabor, D., and Williams, D. (2019). "Racism and the Life Course: Taking Time Seriously." *American Journal of Public Health*, January. Available at: https://ajph.aphapublications.org/doi/10.2105/AJPH.2018.304766 (consulted March 3, 2020).

Harris, B., Hershbein, B., and Kearney, M. (2014). "A Tale of Two Jobs Gaps: Private-Sector Recovery and Public-Sector Stagnation." September 5, Brookings on Job Numbers. Washington, DC: Brookings. Available at: http://www.brookings.edu/blogs/jobs/posts/2014/09/05-private-sector-recovery-public-sector-stagnation-jobs-gap (consulted April 2, 2016).

Harvey, D. (2005). *A Brief History of Neoliberalism.* Oxford: Oxford University Press.

Hammer, P. (2019). "The Flint Water Crisis, the Karegnondi Water Authority and Strategic-Structural Racism." *Critical Sociology* 45(1): 103–119.

Kalecki, M. (1943). "Political Aspects of Full Employment." *Political Quarterly* 14(4): 322–330.

Kasdan, D. (2014). "A Tale of Two Hatchet Men: Emergency Financial Management in Michigan." *Administration & Society* 46(9): 1092–1110.

Kasdan, D. (2015). "Emergency Management 2.0: This Time, It's Financial." *Urban Affairs Review* 52(5): 864–882.

Kirkpatrick, L.O. and Breznau, N. (2016). "The (Non)Politics of Emergency Political Intervention: The Racial Geography of Urban Crisis Management in Michigan." *Social Science Research Network.* March 24, 2016. Available at: http://papers.ssrn.com/sol3/papers.cfm?abstract_id=2754128 (consulted April 5, 2016).

Klein, N. (2007). *The Shock Doctrine.* New York, NY: Metropolitan Books.

Landon, S. (2012). "Public Act 4, Michigan Emergency Manager Law, Marks First Anniversary." *The Huffington Post.* March 16, 2012. Available at: https://www.huffpost.com/entry/public-act-4-michigan-emergency-manager-law-anniversary_n_1353510?guccounter=1 & guce_referrer= aHR0cHM6Ly93d3cuZ29vZ2xlLmNvbS8&guce_referrer_sig=AQAAAIAHsPmVBUAORYuOBV4B7tMMIyPwFhQogTN7eyopHeAPk7SiJj32oi5QGndiw-Zx4qJGppVDKYwm2pHX5qosB6qOrzYYEjrGl-TyDbuvcR7vq _-3cVt5DyQDfA__ 2zPY-1Dez1WzR8mqBrlLTTO4DRPniZOT4SkCoz_rwobxpsGb3e.

Leshem, D. (2016). *The Origins of Neoliberalism: Modeling the Economy from Jesus to Foucault.* New York, NY: Columbia University Press.

Loh, C. (2015). "The Everyday Emergency: Planning and Democracy Under Austerity Regimes." *Urban Affairs Review* 52(5): 832–863.

Mirowski, P. (2013). *Never Let a Serious Crisis Go to Waste: How Neoliberalism Survived the Financial Meltdown.* New York, London: Verso.

Monbiot, G. (2016). "Neoliberalism—The Ideology at the Root of All Our Problems." *The Guardian.* April 15, 2016. Available at: https://www.theguardian.com/books/2016/apr/15/neoliberalism-ideology-problem-george-monbiot.

Munetrix: Municipal Metrics. Available at: https://www.munetrix.com/page/site/static/municipals (consulted 2015).

Neill, W. (2015). "Carry on Shrinking?: The Bankruptcy of Urban Policy in Detroit." *Planning, Practice and Research* 30(1): 1–14.

Nickels, A. (2019). *Power, Participation and Protest in Flint, Michigan.* Philadelphia, PA: Temple University Press.

Oosting, J. (2016). "Michigan's $6.2B 'Raid' on Revenue Sharing? See How Much Local Communities Have Lost Since 2003." *MLIVE,* March 18, 2016. Available at: http://www.mlive.com/lansing-news/index.ssf/2014/03/michigan_revenue_sharing_strug.html (consulted April 5, 2016).

Peck, J. (2012). "Austerity Urbanism: American Cities Under Extreme Economy." *City* 16(6): 626–655.

Priest, N. and Williams, D.R. (2018). "Racial Discrimination and Racial Disparities in Health." In: Major, B., Dovidio, J.F., and Link, B.G. (eds.). *The Oxford Handbook of Stigma, Discrimination, and Health,* pp. 163–182. New York, NY: Oxford University Press.

Public Works. (2015). "Public Sector Job Cuts and the Black Middle Class." June 15, 2015. Available at: http://www.publicworks.org/publicsectorjobs/ (consulted April 7, 2016).

Soss, J., Fording, R.C., and Schram, S. (2011). *Disciplining the Poor: Neoliberal Paternalism and the Persistent Power of Race*. Chicago, IL: University of Chicago Press.

Stampfler, M.L. (2013). "Emergency Financial Management of Cities by the State: A Cure or Simply Kicking the Can down the Road." *The Journal of Law in Society* 14(1): 235–243.

State of Michigan Press Release. (2011). "Emergency Manager Legislation Will Give State Early Warning of Impending Trouble, Help Local Governments." Available at: http://www.michigan.gov/snyder/0,1607,7-277-57577_57657-252799--,00.html (consulted November 11, 2015).

Sugar Law Center. (2015). *Timeline and Historical Facts Regarding Municipal Financial Emergencies in Michigan*. Available at: http://sugarlaw.org/wp-content/uploads/2013/05/Emergency-Manager-Timeline-Background-Facts.pdf (consulted November 15, 2015).

Tabb, W.K. (2012) *The Restructuring of Capitalism in Our Time*. New York, NY: Columbia University Press.

Tabb, W.K. (2015). "If Detroit is Dead, Some Things Need to be Said at the Funeral." *Journal of Urban Affairs* 37(1): 1–12.

Thün, G., Velikov, K., Ripley, C., and McTavish, D. (2015). *Infra Eco Logi Urbanism*. Zurich: Park Books.

Walby, S. (2015). *Crisis*. Cambridge, MA: Polity Press.

Williams, D.R. and Cooper, L.A. (2019). "Reducing Racial Inequities in Health: Using What We Already Know to Take Action." *International Journal of Environmental Research and Public Health* 16(4): 606.

Wilson, G., Roscigno, V., and Huffman, M. (2013). "Public Sector Transformation, Racial Inequality and Downward Occupational Mobility." *Social Forces* 91(3): 975–1006.

CHAPTER 2

Colorblind Michigan

The Legal Impossibility of Environmental Justice in Flint and Southwest Detroit

Terressa A. Benz

1 Introduction[1]

Since the late-1970s the United States Supreme Court has hidden from the pursuit of real justice behind the discriminatory purpose doctrine, or the perpetrator perspective, which requires proof of individual intent to discriminate for a claim to be valid. A requirement that Ibram X. Kendi (2016) would say is rooted in a racist idea: that some groups are more worthy of equal protections than others. Essentially, the discriminatory purpose doctrine of the perpetrator perspective has legalized racial discrimination, except in extreme and rare circumstances where the racism of the perpetrator is overt and documented. The task here is to explore how this legal standard serves to perpetuate this racialized system of worthiness for equal protections under the law. In doing so the crisis of neoliberalism in Michigan as it relates to laws and legal decision making that both directly and indirectly promote environmental racism are examined in two communities: Flint during the water crisis and a neighborhood in Southwest Detroit whose attempts to be included in a housing buyout program have all been thwarted. It is argued that Michigan as a state, with the aid of the federal government, has institutionalized a racialized caste system of "worthiness" for environmental protections, which is created and enforced through neoliberal colorblind policies.

According to critical race theorist Alan Freeman (1995; 1998) the United States Supreme Court's treatment of racial discrimination claims can be viewed in terms of two perspectives, the short-lived victim perspective and the currently dominant perpetrator perspective. The victim perspective, embraced by the US Supreme Court briefly in the early 1970s, allowed evidence of disparate impact to be considered as evidence of unequal protection under the law.

1 The following chapter is an expanded version of the 2019 article by Terressa A. Benz entitled, "Toxic Cities: Neoliberalism and Environmental Racism in Flint and Detroit Michigan" that was published in *Critical Sociology* 45(1): 49–62.

The dominant perpetrator perspective, emerging only years later and largely in response to the advances made by the civil rights movement, requires proof of racist intent for a racial discrimination claim to be valid—a nearly impossible task as intent is rarely stated, much less documented. It is through strict adherence to the perpetrator perspective on the part of the state and the federal government that a racialized caste system of "worthiness" has become institutionalized: a system that systematically devalues the lives of Black citizens and elevates the value of white lives when confronted with the "need" for environmental protections.

In this chapter I integrate literatures on neoliberalism, socio-legal studies, environmental injustice, and critical race theory. It is only through this type of intellectual collaboration that the inhumanity of environmental racism by the neoliberal state can begin to be fully understood. The contribution this chapter makes is to draw parallels between the Flint water crisis and a lesser known case of environmental disregard for Black lives in southwest Detroit. In highlighting these parallels the "colorblind" legal steps that produce such racially disparate outcomes become legible. In the following pages the effects of neoliberalism on environmental justice are explored in terms of legal decision-making and treatment by regulatory agencies. In these sections, the literatures on environmental racism and neoliberalism are reviewed. Then, the victim and perpetrator perspectives are examined more closely, paying particular attention to the effects this shift in legal perspective has had on issues of racial justice. Next, the influence of the discriminatory purpose doctrine on environmental regulatory agencies and are discussed at the state and federal level. Then, the cases of the Flint water crisis and a home buyout program instituted by Marathon Oil in southwest Detroit are explored. Specifically, these examples examine the crisis of neoliberal governance and the attendant failure to protect poor people of color from discrimination while successfully instituting a government backed system of worthiness based on race first and class second. Rather than providing a narrative of environmental racism at these two sites, various bodies of literature are combined to provide an interdisciplinary examination of how specific laws and programs, in adherence to neoliberal ideals, have served to perpetuate environmental injustice.

2 Environmental Caste Systems

Numerous studies have found that race is the strongest predictor of exposure and proximity to environmental hazards (see Asch and Seneca 1978; Bullard 1983; USGAO 1995; UCC 1987; Mohai and Bryant 1992; Mohai, et al. 2009).

This reality is a direct result of environmental racism, or the "processes that resulted in minority and low-income communities facing disproportionate environmental harms and limited environmental benefits" (Taylor 2014: 2). Further there is considerable evidence that there are direct links between racial segregation, exposure to environmental hazards, and poor health outcomes (Crowder and Downey 2010; Downey 2006; Williams and Collins 2001).

A common objection to claims of environmental racism is that the disproportionate siting of hazardous facilities near or in minority communities is not the result of intentional discrimination, but rather a reflection of a natural sorting of individuals in response to neighborhood characteristics (Taylor 2014: 71). The veracity of the latter is up for social science debate; however, this paper eschews that line of questioning in favor of a consequentialist approach. The problem of environmental racism is not one of intent but impact. Contemporary American racial frames insist upon finding responsible actors on whom to place individual blame for racism's continued legacy. This insistence on having individuals to blame is orchestrated, as intent is nearly impossible to prove. Further this insistence allows the underlying racist idea, that some groups are more worthy of environmental protections than others to remain unaddressed. Insisting on proof of intent, as a legal requirement for discrimination claims limits the pursuit of justice to punitive frameworks and eliminates opportunities to pursue racial justice on a grander scale. By focusing only on intent we make what should be treated as an institutional issue the fault of individuals, whose racial intents remain elusive.

Flint and Detroit, Michigan are not unusual in their role as magnets for environmental hazards and toxic waste facilities. Rather they share social, political, legal, and economic history with other "rust-belt" cities that have experienced similar declines in industry. They are "sacrifice zones," areas that have been offered up as tribute to free-market ideology, which are opened up for exploitation in the name of profit, corporate capitalism, and "progress" (Hedges and Sacco 2012; Lerner 2010). All have long histories of racial segregation, all have suffered the flight of meaningful employment, businesses, and white people with their attendant capital. As such, any attempt to understand the various laws and practices that have led to the disproportionate impact of environmental hazards on these communities of color must begin with an understanding of institutional context and structural inequality. So while individual racists have most certainly been involved in this long history of disinvestment and discrimination, the search for individuals to blame is diversionary. Cole and Foster (2001) write, "The insistence on establishing a linear, causal connection between disproportionate outcomes and a "single bad actor" permeates our society's legal and social understanding of racism and injustice. This prevailing understanding obscures the forces at work in producing environmental racism" (p. 12–13). Even the briefest of looks at the history of race-based spatial segregation in the United States, including discriminatory redlining, zoning, and real estate practices reveals clear constructions of racial spaces, which in turn impact the distribution of social goods (Cole and Foster 2001).

3 Neoliberalism

Since the late 1970s, when the perpetrator perspective became dominant in the courts, there has been a shift in global economic thought towards a neoliberal agenda (Harvey 2005). According to Harvey (2005), neoliberalism is a theory of political economic practice that seeks a pure free market economy, with private property rights being paramount. Further, neoliberal ideals find that nearly everything can be run better as a business, including government. In this sense, a government run as a business focuses on returns on investments, rather than serving the needs of its constituents (Harvey 2005). The state's role under neoliberalism is to extend market logic to all realms of social and political relations (Soss et al. 2011).

Unfortunately, neoliberalism, despite claims to being colorblind, is "saturated with race" (Duggan 2003: xvi) in that it conceals racial inequality and racism behind the free-market ideology of a merit based system. The implication being that individual merit is valued above all else, including race. Race and neoliberalism are mutually constitutive and neoliberal discourse permits the circumvention of any consideration of institutionalized racism in favor of meritocracy and individual choice (Roberts and Mahtani 2010). This relocation of racial disadvantage to the private sphere absolves the state of its responsibility to correct for or intervene when racial disparity is apparent, leaving race and racism muted (Davis 2007). It is this way that we are left with a society saturated with racism, but one without racists (Bonilla-Silva 2014). The power of neoliberalism to mute race by deflecting attention away from racism and onto the individual is important to the discussion here regarding environmental racism and injustice. Under this regime any failure to succeed is attributed to personal flaws rather than structural barriers or institutionalized racism. All this has been done despite the fact that, "There is nothing in human history or human nature that supports the idea that sacrificing everything before the free market leads to a social good" (Hedges and Sacco 2012: xii). Despite this, to defend the "freedoms" so exulted by neoliberal philosophy the neoliberal state must pullback from its traditional role in providing social provisions such as environmental regulation, protections against discrimination in employment, and social welfare programs.

Often this retraction of social provisions, frequently embodied as austerity measures, has been interpreted as an abandonment of social programs. However, Soss, Fording, and Schram (2011) argue that instead of complete abandonment of social programs, the state comes to rely more on privatization and collaboration with market actors to handle these social provisions, making the state increasingly reliant on market actors to achieve public good. The result is that under neoliberalism the boundaries between the state and the free market become blurred as the state restructures itself around market principles (Soss et al. 2011). If social problems of the poor are due to individuals making bad choices, as neoliberalism dictates, then a paternalistic approach in which the government, through market actors and logics, works to bring discipline and morals to the poor makes sense. Out of this paternalistic turn, government policies are reconfigured to instill discipline in the unruly poor through aid being contingent on behavior, social programs that require significant supervision and direction, and increasingly punitive and invasive social control through the criminal justice apparatus (Soss et al. 2011; Wacquant 2009). Some examples of this shift are privatization of prisons and probation services and work requirements for food assistance.

According to the neoliberalist view, it is only through this step away from the traditional ways of providing social assistance that a true "colorblind" free-market can flourish in which "good" choices are rewarded and "bad" choices are disciplined. The goal of neoliberal paternalism then is to transform the unruly poor into contributing citizens through a carrot and "beat" with a stick approach. The reality is austerity-based intrusive policies like Michigan's Emergency Management law, explored here, which treats entire swaths of people as children in need of a strong hand to guide them. Once again while these neoliberal paternalistic policy changes are by all appearances colorblind, they in fact disproportionally impact poor people of color.

4 Equal Protection in Practice

The 1954 *Brown v. Topeka Board of Education* case, ending legal protection for school segregation, is often heralded as the beginning of the end of racism in America.[2] However, the reality of the decision-making process in this case

2 (1954) Brown v. Topeka Board of Education. 347 U.S. 483.

and the legal ramifications of the decision stand in opposition to this conclusion. Derrick Bell (1980; 2004) examines the *Brown* decision in terms of "interest convergence." He argues that the Court's decisions on occasion promote racial justice but not for noble cause. He points out that in those cases that do promote racial justice, the interests of white people happen to converge with those of people of color, as occurred in the *Brown* case. Bell finds that the Court, in service to the maintenance of capitalism, makes decisions that promote the economic and political health of the country and that sometimes the promotion of those interests aligns with issues of racial equality. In order to justify these decisions, the Court, under the guise of legal formalism, has developed standards and rhetoric that allows the side-stepping of racial equality when not in convergence with the needs of white elites.

In Alan Freeman's (1995; 1998) work on antidiscrimination law he examines US Supreme Court decisions from 1954 up until 1989. He argues that through a series of legal decisions the promise of equality embodied by the 1954 *Brown v. Topeka Board of Education* ruling, regardless of interest convergence, was never realized and further that promise was transformed by the civil rights cases of the 1980s which "enshrined the principle of 'unequal but irrelevant'" (1998: 284). Freeman explores this process and how the Court has shifted over time, often manipulating precedent, away from recognizing claims of racial discrimination based upon disparate impact to rejecting these same claims if they fail to prove individual racist intent. This shift has effectively rendered legal claims of racial discrimination virtually impossible to make. To understand this shift, Freeman offers what he calls the victim and perpetrator perspectives on legal decision-making.

The victim perspective recognizes that years of racial discrimination in education, housing, healthcare, politics, environmental protections, and employment have long term effects that need remedy. From this perspective historical experience must be factored into legal decision-making in order to best correct for past discrimination. Further, this perspective understands that racism does not go away simply because it is illegal, but rather it becomes subtler and more covert, yet ever-present. With this recognition a court using the victim perspective looks for disparate effects or outcomes of a particular law or policy as evidence of racial discrimination. Or as Charles Lawrence III writes "the injury of racial inequality exists irrespective of the decisionmakers' motives" (1995: 236). In other words, if the oppressive condition exists before and after an antidiscrimination law is implemented then the law is ineffective and needs to be changed, regardless of whether or not it was designed to discriminate. Legal remedies from this anti-racist perspective are more about deconstructing institutional mechanisms of racism as a social good rather than targeting racist actors.

On the other hand, the perpetrator perspective, ignoring the long-lasting effects of past discrimination, requires solid proof of individual racist intent for a discrimination claim to be valid. The perpetrator perspective is and has been the dominant approach used in our courts and politics since the late 1970s. From this perspective a law or practice is discriminatory if and only if specific intent to discriminate is proven. This perspective adheres to the belief that racism and racial discrimination vanished with the passage of various anti-discrimination laws, particularly the Civil Rights Act of 1964. Such a view ignores systemic or institutional forms of racism, and focuses at the individual or interpersonal level (Bonilla-Silva 2014; Haney López 2000; Feagin 2014; Feagin 2013). According to this microview, if racism exists, it is the result of a few bad apples. Violations of antidiscrimination law, then, cannot be found in unequal outcomes or impacts, but only in the clearly provable racist actions of individual perpetrators (Roberts 1991; 1997). In essence, "[T]he Court creates an imaginary world where discrimination does not exist unless it was consciously intended" (Lawrence III 1995: 239).

According to the Supreme Court in *Griggs v. Duke Power Co.* (1971), Title VII of the 1964 Civil Rights Act, which forbids racial discrimination in employment practices, requires the "removal of artificial, arbitrary, and unnecessary barriers to unemployment" and forbids "not only overt discrimination but also practices that are fair in form, but discriminatory in operation."[3] The Court goes on to address the issue of intent by stating that the absence of discriminatory intent does not matter when the employment procedures, testing for employment in this case, "are unrelated to measuring job capability." The Griggs decision is one of few SCOTUS rulings that fully embraced the victim perspective and had the potential for far-reaching consequences. However, the precedent set by this case was short lived as it was quickly manipulated and eventually discarded 5 years later by the Court in the 1976 case *Washington v. Davis,* which dealt similarly with testing in employment.[4] The Davis case replaced the use of disparate outcomes with a requirement for intent to discriminate (Lawrence III 1995). In the *Davis* case the doctrine of discriminatory purpose was established, shifting the burden of proof from the employer to prove the policy in question was necessary onto the victim who now would have to prove that the policy was intended to discriminate. While these cases dealt with employment they had far reaching consequences for all discrimination cases including those alleging environmental racism.

3 (1971) Griggs v. Duke Power Co. 401 U.S. 424.
4 (1976) Washington v. Davis. 426 U.S. 229.

Today, our courts have abandoned the promises of the victim perspective used in the late 1960s and have fully adopted the discriminatory purpose doctrine of the perpetrator perspective, as evidenced by our societal obsession with memos and emails that are capable of proving the racism and culpability of individuals. The shift in the courts from victim to perpetrator perspective aligns with the shift from Keynesian economic policies to neoliberal ones. This is not by accident. The focus on individual intent allows the courts to rule in ways considered pro-business and in accordance with neoliberal values. Today the discriminatory purpose doctrine is regarded as common sense. Meanwhile using disparate impact as proof of discrimination is considered radical and even anti-capitalist. Yet insisting on intent to prove any and all discrimination claims does nothing to address the pernicious racism that pervades our institutions, regulatory agencies, and the urgency with which government detects and responds to crises in communities of color such as Flint, Michigan and southwest Detroit. In the end, the people for which antidiscrimination law was created is co-opted by the powerful in the name of a so-called "colorblind" justice system (Gotanda 1995; Russell-Brown 2001).

The court's adherence to the perpetrator perspective leaves intact all of the institutionalized structures and practices of white domination under the guise of formal "colorblind" equality (Lawrence III 1998). Formal equality, then, allows those who benefit from white privilege to continue reaping all the usual advantages without any responsibility for the suffering of others. Accordingly, in today's "post-racial" colorblind society to take any note of race is not the place of law and is a violation of equal protection for all (Delgado and Stefancic 2012). The Court justifies this position with a fierce adherence to the ideals of meritocracy, that individuals should not be judged based upon the color of their skin, but rather according to their ability (Gotanda 1995). However, as Freeman (1995; 1998) notes the Court did for a time dabble in the victim perspective and a color conscious understanding of the law, but then shifted to the "colorblind" perpetrator perspective. Lawrence III (1995) argues that this shift was due in large part to the recognition that the true pursuit of equality would require a redistribution of opportunity. It is here that the interests of whites and people of color no longer converged and racial justice was halted (Bell 1980; 2004).

5 Environmental (Lack of) Regulation

Government, both state and federal, have at various times made attempts to remedy issues of environmental injustice and racism. Over the years, the state of Michigan has developed numerous environmental justice plans and initiatives, none of which have had enforcement powers, all of which over time have come to be understood as empty gestures. Michigan's Department of Environmental Quality (MDEQ) is the state body in charge of environmental regulation including early detection of health hazards. Over the years, like so many regulatory bodies, MDEQ has fallen victim to severe budget cuts due to neoliberal state policies aimed at reducing regulation in the name of free enterprise. According to a 2010 federal audit, MDEQ had been for years beset by budget cuts, staffing issues, and limited resources (Cadmus Group Inc. 2010). As a result of funding cuts and the expense of hiring and training new staff, old staff was shuffled around to fill vacancies, which the audit found "decreases the technical knowledge of staff." While MDEQ is regularly in the news for its failures, it is important to note that the agency has overtime been reduced by state policies so that it cannot function properly. To quote David Fasenfest and Theodore Pride (2016: 331): "Michigan has become the proving ground for neoliberal expansion and the taking of critically important social resources for private gain." When the state fails, the brunt of those environmental failures are born heavily and disproportionately on those who live in poor, working-class communities of color.

At the federal level attempts have been made to move towards environmental justice. One of the most discussed of these was President Bill Clinton's 1994 Executive Order 12898 (EO 12898), which required all federal agencies to "make achieving environmental justice part of its mission"" (Clinton 1994: section 1–101). EO 12898 was a considerable victory for many in the environmental justice community, however over time the victory proved hollow. EO 12898 was largely rhetorical, as it did not commit resources to its cause (for more on environmental justice claims in courts see Gross and Stretesky 2015). Additionally the order failed to create any system of accountability or standards of equity, while including limits on judicial review. In other words, EO 12898 gave no right to enforce the order, leaving individuals with environmental justice claims with no legal recourse as they are not allowed to sue for enforcement (Bertenthal 2018). Evaluations of the EPA and its actions in light of EO 12898 have found its implementation slow, inconsistent, and often nonexistent (NACA 2001; EPA 2004). These shortcomings are why scholars insist that the executive order was largely a symbolic political gesture (Cooper 2001; Konisky 2015).

While federal attention to environmental justice waned during the George W. Bush administration it was reinvigorated under President Barack Obama (Konisky 2015). In fact, President Obama created a presidential proclamation celebrating the 20th anniversary of EO 12898, which expressed a renewed commitment by the federal government to environmental justice (White House, 2014). Despite this, President Obama's administrative efforts made little difference when it came to the water crisis in Flint or the situation in the Boynton neighborhood of Detroit. The repeated failures of the EPA in its agency response in these two areas does not bode well for federal efforts aimed at achieving their promise of environmental justice.

Considering the doctrine of discriminatory purpose established by the Supreme Court in the late 1970s, many have given up on seeking legal remedies for discrimination claims in the court room and have instead looked into administrative redress. Title VI claims, which make it illegal for recipients of federal funds to engage in racial discrimination are heard through the EPA's Office of Civil Rights (OCR). Unfortunately, the complaints filed with the OCR do not seem to be taken seriously, despite proclamations by both Presidents Clinton and Obama to make environmental justice a priority. In fact, of the hundreds of Title VI complaints filed with the OCR *none* have been deemed valid enough to withdraw federal funding (the most severe punishment for violations) and the vast majority are rejected outright without even a formal investigation (Deloitte Consulting LLP. 2011; Hiar 2011; Qiu and Buford 2015). In the end, the commitment of the EPA to EO 12898 is for the most part non-existent (Gross and Stretesky 2015), and the policy itself is has become a non-enforcement policy (Hurwitz and Sullivan 2001). Considering the lack of action on the part of prior more progressive leadership little can be expected from the current GOP administration in terms of environmental justice or protecting the environment in general. In fact, based on the EPA's annual report, penalties assessed against corporate polluters in 2018 under the Trump administration were the lowest in over a decade (Cama and Green 2018; EPA 2018).

Hurwitz and Sullivan (2001) explore the influence of politics on the EPA and MDEQ through an examination of a 1998 Title VI complaint, *Select Steel.* In June of 1998 MDEQ granted a permit to Select Steel Corporation allowing the creation of a steel recycling plant in northern Flint, Michigan. The location of the plant was immediately adjacent to a largely African American neighborhood that was already subjected to exceptionally high levels of toxic environmental hazards. The residents of the community filed their Title VI administrative complaint without incident and in a timely manner, claiming disparate environmental impact on the community. The complaint was accepted by the EPA for investigation within a couple of months and then decided 74 days later, a decision-making window without precedent as most cases take years for processing (Hurwitz and Sullivan 2001). The EPA found in favor of MDEQ and subsequently Select Steel, allowing the corporation to build their recycling plant in the already overburdened area of northern Flint. It is unknown why the Select Steel complaint would be investigated prior to all the other pre-existing and pending complaints. Hurwitz and Sullivan suggest the political climate at the time in Michigan and federally was already very "pro-business" and that pressure, including explicit threats to dismantle the budget of the OCR, pressured the EPA to find a way to circumvent disparate impact claims in permitting applications (see also Moss 2000). The ruling in Select Steel set the federal standard that as long as the party seeking a permit was following national air quality standards, disparate impact claims were irrelevant and would not be heard, and with this decision the avenue for community members to seek administrative remedies for environmental injustice collapsed (Buford and Lombardi 2015).

6 The "State" of Michigan

In the following section two communities in Michigan are examined in order to highlight the consequences of reduced regulation in the name of free-market, colorblind, neoliberal paternalistic governance on people of color in terms of environmental toxic exposure. First, the water crisis in Flint is used to explore the emergency manager law that made way for the toxic switch of the community water supply to the highly corrosive Flint River. Second, the situation for residents of the Jefferies subdivision of Boynton, Michigan a neighborhood in southwest Detroit, who live in the shadow of Marathon Oil's tar sands refinery is examined. In this case the focus is placed on a home buyout project completed by the oil giant which bought the houses of white residents to help them relocate, but only a handful of Black residents.

6.1 *Flint, MI*

Flint, a majority Black city of about 100,000 residents, with some of the highest poverty rates in Michigan, had for years sourced its water from Lake Huron through the Detroit water system. In April 2014, it was decided under a state-appointed emergency manager in what was claimed to be a money saving move (Clark 2015), that the city would now source its water from the Flint River, a body of water so polluted it corroded the city's plumbing infrastructure, increasing lead levels in drinking water to exceed the EPA's standard of "toxic waste" (Craven and Tynes 2016). In an EPA memo sent in June 2015 lead levels in residential drinking water were as high as 13,200 parts per billion, an unthinkable 880 times the actionable federal level of 15 parts per billion (Craven and Tynes 2016). Residents immediately complained about the smell and taste of the water coming from their faucets and E.coli and other contaminants were detected within three months of the switch (Fonger 2014a). Despite repeated attempts by citizens-turned-activists, media members, and various agency officials to sound the alarm on the condition of the drinking water, local and state government continued to source the city's water from the toxic Flint River.

Perhaps the most blatant example of a government instituted system of worthiness is revealed by examining when and to whom access to clean water was granted amidst the crisis. In October of 2014, within six months of the switch to the Flint River, General Motors (GM) was permitted to cease the use of the toxic water in their plants. GM found that the high chloride levels in the Flint River water was corroding auto parts in their manufacturing plant (Flint Water Advisory Task Force 2016; Fonger 2014b). As a result the company reached an agreement with the city to purchase water from the Flint's previous Lake Huron source. The neoliberal city government was quick to accommodate the business concerns of GM, but remained deaf to the pleas of their plebeian constituents for an additional year.

Further, in January 2015 the state, while actively assuring residents that the water was safe to drink, began installing purified water coolers in all state-run office buildings in the City of Flint as well as giving bottled water to visitors (Egan 2016; Flint Water Advisory Task Force 2016). Even Flint's City Council voted in March 2015, 7–1 in favor of switching back to the Detroit-run system, a decision that was blocked by the latest State-appointed emergency manager over financial concerns (Mohai 2018). Meanwhile, activists reached out to scientists like Dr. Marc Edwards from Virginia Tech, who in response collected water samples from Flint households and found what he considered the "worst lead-in-water contamination that he had seen in more than twenty-five years" (Clark 2018: 110). State officials dismissed these findings as well as Dr. Hanna-Attisha's report, which showed using comparative data from before and after the switch, that Flint children had significantly elevated blood-lead levels after the switch (Clark 2018). It was not until local investigative reporters uncovered that Michigan's own data confirmed Dr. Hanna-Attisha's findings that the state government finally acknowledged problems with the water in Flint (Hanna-Attisha 2018; Tanner and Kaffer 2015).

In recent years more attention has been paid to the dangers of lead exposure, especially among children. Lead, even at low levels, is a neurotoxin that impairs cognitive and behavioral functioning (Rogan and Ware 2003; Bellinger et al. 1991) and has been linked to antisocial behavior (Needleman et al. 1996). Lead, once in the bloodstream disrupts cell functioning in terms of energy production and communication with the nervous system, this is especially disruptive in the body of a developing child (Denworth 2008; Hanna-Attisha 2018). Childhood exposures to lead has also been found to be disproportionately higher among Black people (Sampson and Winter

2016). Sampson and Winter, using blood tests from children living in Chicago from 1995–2013 in combination with geographical block matching, find that the racial ecology of lead exposure is an overlooked but significant form of health inequality. They find that Black and Hispanic neighborhoods showed extremely high rates of lead toxicity compared to white neighborhoods, and that Black people showed even higher levels than Hispanics for every year in the study. They argue that the situation in Flint is not unusual, and in fact reflects a form of biosocial stratification (Massey 2004) that reinforces racial inequality.

Lead also negatively impacts adults and causes anemia, hypertension, memory issues, kidney damage, fertility issues, miscarriages and stillbirths among other things (Denworth 2008). Further, lead collects in a person's body over the course of a lifetime. Like calcium, lead is collected and stored in teeth, bones, and soft tissue and just like calcium lead is released during pregnancy to the fetus. This released lead disrupts healthy fetal development, is linked to fetal death, premature birth, low birth weight, and prenatal growth abnormalities (Zhu et al. 2010; Edwards 2014; Taylor et al. 2015) and increased infant mortality rates (Troesken 2008; Clay et al. 2014). According to one study, the water switch in Flint correlates to a 12% drop in fertility accompanied by a decrease in overall health at birth (Grossman and Slusky 2018). So the massive lead exposure in Flint not only has had immediate impacts but will continue to haunt the victims throughout their lives and their future children's lives.

In the aftermath of the initial Flint water tragedy the pursuit of justice has taken shape according to a perpetrator perspective in that the focus is on finding individuals to blame, rather than finding targeted remedies for the neoliberal colorblind, pro-business policies that promoted fiscal austerity, emergency financial managers, housing segregation, and environmental deregulation. For example, recently Flint has been back in the news, not for progress made, but for who is allowed to be sued for the crisis. On April 1, 2019 a federal judge ruled that Rick Snyder, governor at the time of the water crisis, was not immune from prosecution (Oosting 2019), and just a few weeks later another ruling was handed down allowing the federal government, the EPA in particular, to be sued by the victims in Flint (Waldrop 2019). While these two rulings are in many ways' victories for the people of Flint, lawsuits such as these do nothing to remedy the neoliberal austerity driven politics that led to the crisis in the first place. By celebrating the ability to hold individuals and agencies responsible an over reliance on our punitive apparatus is created, which in turn perpetuates, rather than challenges, the free-market anti-regulation policies that led to the situation in the first place. So while the ability to sue may partially satisfy those in pursuit of justice or even vengeance, they also serve to distract people from the root causes of the crisis leaving us destined to repeat these same tragedies in the future.

The hegemony of neoliberal paternalism tells us that rust-belt cities like Flint, are unruly and in need of significant restructuring and discipline via fiscal austerity programs. Michigan has wholeheartedly adopted this approach. According to Minghine (2014) between 2003–2013 the state drastically cut funding to its municipalities. Flint, in particular, lost nearly 60 million dollars of state funding via revenue sharing from sales tax, which had actually increased over that same time period. Since 2002, Michigan state government appropriated over $6.2 billion in sales tax revenues from its cities and townships to balance its budget rather than adhering to the state Constitution that mandates a portion of this revenue sharing be returned to local municipalities (Fasenfest 2019). So while Michigan is disciplining its cities by pushing austerity measures and asking their cities to make due with nothing they are balancing their own budgets with revenues generated by their municipalities. In return the state has been able to paint cities like Flint and Detroit as mismanaged and living beyond their means, again resorting to the neoliberal paternalistic racially-coded language of individual choice and meritocracy. As a result, the appointment of emergency managers in majority Black cities has been seen by many adhering to the neoliberal austerity narrative to be well deserved, rather than a racist truncation of democracy.

The history of emergency management in Michigan is a tale of neoliberal paternalistic policy-making at its finest, in which the will of the people was not just ignored but overruled by the state legislature. Emergency management in Michigan began in 1988 with the passage of the state's first financial distress law, which simply authorized the state to get involved with local governments in distress (Conyers Jr. 2016). But after decades of a suffering economy and the growing political tide of neoliberal privatization the law was reconfigured. In 2011, Governor Rick Snyder and the Republican controlled legislature passed a new law (PA-4), which significantly expanded the role of the state when dealing with municipal financial crises. The new law gave the state the power to reign in unruly cities by granting the state the ability to renegotiate union contracts, change pension agreements, and sell private assets to pay municipal debts. The law was understood as government overreach and voters were able to repeal it in 2012 by referendum. However within a month, the Governor and state legislature passed another emergency manager law (PA-436), this one had a provision that it could not be repealed by the voters. By completely ignoring the will of the people the state government, through this law and the powers it granted, sent the message that it did not trust its constituents and further that they, or at least the majority Black cities to which this law would be used on, were in need of paternalistic guidance and discipline. The emergency manager (EM) law circumvents democracy by introducing a leader with nearly universal decision-making powers, who is only accountable to the governor,[5] and who was never elected by the people. Further, the standards to become an EM are appallingly low, "The emergency manager shall have a minimum of 5 years' experience and demonstrable expertise in business, financial, or local or state budgetary matters" (PA-436). Additionally, the EM need not have any experience with the city in question and they "shall serve at the pleasure of the governor" (PA-436). These requirements speak to the neoliberal understanding that government is to be run like a business, while completely ignoring the need for a leader to be accountable to the community they aim to serve. In the case of Flint, the decision to switch water supply demonstrates the hegemony of pro-business neoliberal thinking which considers costs and savings above all else.

The EM law is supposed to be "colorblind" but 52% of Michigan's Black population has lived in a city under emergency management (Fasenfest and Pride 2016; Clark 2018), and 16% of Latinos, while the same was true for only 2% of white Michiganders (Clark 2018; Conyers Jr. 2016). Emergency managers are most often assigned to cities with a majority African American population. However, the process of deciding which city is in need of a financial manager is supposed to be based upon neutral evaluations of financial circumstances and mismanagement, despite that numerous majority white cities in similar financial straits have not been taken over (Welburn and Seamster 2016). EMs engage in cutback management tactics that do nothing to address the structural issues that lead to financial distress in the first place, which adversely impacts community residents, public employees, and retirees while protecting the interests of corporate investors and financial institutions (Fasenfest and Pride 2016). Again we are confronted by glaring racially disparate impacts under a colorblind policy, which have no legal remedy under the discriminatory purpose doctrine. The disparate application of emergency management, including the consequences of such application, like the Flint water crisis, are clearly legible to those impacted as a government backed system of race-based worthiness.

6.2 *Jefferies Subdivision of Boynton, MI*

Southwest Detroit is home to 10 major polluting factories including a tar sands oil refinery run by Marathon Oil and manufacturing giants AK and US Steel. These factories spew literal tons of toxic chemicals into the air each year, yet

5 Michigan has had 49 governors all of whom have been white and male, aside from two white females, Jennifer Granholm (2003–2011) and current governor Gretchen Whitmer (2019–present).

they are for the most part considered in compliance with state and federal regulations. So while the plants remain in compliance the zip code, 48217, has been found to be the most toxic in the state, with high levels of air pollutants such as manganese, sulfuric acid, nickel, lead, trimethylbenzene, and chromium (Mohai et al. 2011). Pollutants that have been associated with increased risks of cancer, asthma, neurological disorders, cardiovascular disorders, and developmental disorders. The contradiction here, that these plants can be meeting emission standards yet are creating what amounts to toxic sludge for air, is explained by how Michigan's Department of Environmental Quality (MDEQ) evaluates emissions. MDEQ considers plants in isolation rather than considering the cumulative effect of emissions from multiple locations, a policy that seems to go against their proclaimed goal of protecting human health but agrees with state pressure to be pro-business. The result is that residents of southwest Detroit experience some of the highest air pollution levels in the state on a daily basis (Schlanger 2016; Mohai et al. 2011). This would be less concerning if nobody lived near this pollution, but thousands do and they are overwhelmingly poor and Black.

The zip code 48217 is home to two residential neighborhoods/census tracts, Boynton and Oakwood Heights. Boynton is a small community with a population of nearly 7,000 as of the 2010 census. Boynton ranges between 92 and 94% Black, 3–4% Hispanic, and less than 2% white. Oakwood Heights is adjacent to Boynton with a population of nearly 1,300 people. Oakwood Heights is 90% white and Hispanic and only 7% Black. Both neighborhoods are within the 48217 "dirtiest" zip code with pollution levels 45 times the state average (Oosting 2010; Mohai et al. 2011). Further, according to Michigan's Department of Public Health the 48217 zip code has consistently high rates of cancer and mortality rates from cancer (Lewis 2014). Both communities are exposed daily to extraordinary levels of pollutants, benzene in particular, a known human carcinogen. As such one community is not more exposed than the other. Despite this, in 2008 Marathon Oil announced plans for a $2.2 billion dollar expansion, part of this plan was to buy up homes in nearby Oakwood Heights to create a "100-acre green buffer zone" (Abbey-Lambertz 2012), this buffer zone included only 10 homes from the largely Black Jefferies subdivision[6] of the Boynton neighborhood (Lynch 2014). The media covered the plan, but barely touched on the glaring racialized aspects of the buyout.

The Jefferies subdivision is a small neighborhood located within the Boynton community, and immediately adjacent to the Marathon plant. Most

6 Jefferies subdivision includes homes within the boundaries of Schaefer Highway to Pleasant Street and from Fort Street to Bassett Street. The subdivision was named after the local elementary school in the area, which is now a large, several acre lead contaminated brownfield.

of these residents remember a time when the Marathon plant was a small factory that posed minimal threat to their health and wellbeing. Many have inherited their homes from their parents who bought the property during a time when Detroit, like many other places, was heavily engaged in redlining and restrictive housing covenants. However, overtime Marathon has gotten repeated permission from the City of Detroit and the state of Michigan to expand their operation, despite objections from the Boynton community. It is these Black residents whose living situation has greatly deteriorated as a result of the corporation's expansion and it is these Black residents that asked for and were denied home buyouts.

The buyout in Oakwood Heights, accepted by 266 of the 294 included property owners, provided residents with a minimum purchase price of $50,000 per home and some relocation expenses (Lynch 2014). So while the majority white residents of Oakwood Heights were able to have their homes purchased for tens of thousands above market value and move to areas with less toxic pollution the nearly exclusively Black Jefferies subdivision residents were left behind. Marathon has made no move to offer buyouts to these residents, stating the area qualifies for federal assistance under the Neighborhood Stabilization Program (NSP) for communities suffering from abandonment and foreclosures (Lynch 2014). According to the US Department of Housing and Urban Development (HUD) the goal of NSP is to aid in the purchase of foreclosed homes as well as to help rehabilitate or redevelop homes in order to stabilize neighborhoods and slow declining property values. However the mission of NSP is to target areas for *reinvestment*—Boynton has been labeled the most polluted zip code in Michigan with unusually elevated rates of cancer and deaths from cancer, as such it is not a community with reinvestment potential (Oosting 2010; Lewis 2014).

Since 2005 more than 1 out of 3 properties in Detroit have gone into foreclosure due to unpaid taxes or defaults on mortgages (Kurth and MacDonald 2015). As a result the competition among neighborhoods seeking NSP funding is extremely high. According to the Michigan Foreclosure Task Force the city of Detroit received $47.1 million in NSP funding and has had to engage in urban triage when distributing those funds. The city has identified target areas to try and revive with NSP funding, these are areas evaluated to have the greatest potential of bouncing back. Boynton, and Jefferies subdivision in particular, due to the high rate of pollution and resultant illnesses has been deemed unworthy of revival.[7] So while Boynton property values were

7 http://www.detroitmi.gov/How-Do-I/Obtain-Grant-Information/NSP-Maps.

already low, Marathon's expansion has decimated all remaining value to the point that the area is considered un-savable by the city of Detroit, with most homes estimated value at less than $15,000 and dropping steadily (Lewis 2014). A reality captured by the words of Emma Lockridge, a resident of the Jefferies subdivision and an environmental organizer, "I can't even give my house away."[8]

Marathon's justification for excluding the majority Black households of the Jefferies subdivision from the buyout, that they can get help elsewhere, allowed the corporation to easily circumvent racial discrimination claims from a perpetrator perspective. In effect Marathon has preempted any attempt by Jefferies residents to allege discrimination, by claiming their decision was made purely upon exit opportunities for each neighborhood rather than discrimination based upon race. Oakwood Heights, they claim, did not qualify for NSF funding while Jefferies Subdivision did. A claim that could not be verified or disproved. Regardless of which neighborhood theoretically could apply for NSP, the reality was that Jefferies subdivision, due to its proximity to Marathon Oil and other manufacturing giants will never receive NSP funds because of the dire need across all of Detroit coupled with the high levels of pollution in the area. Further, Marathon's positioning of the Jefferies residents as having the opportunity for government assistance places blame squarely on the resident's for not trying hard enough when the funds are not provided. In other words, failure to receive NSP funds indicates a failure among applicants rather than the reality of urban triage rooted in years of redlining and structural inequality. So even though the buyout disproportionately impacted Black Detroiters, any claim of racial discrimination would not hold up in court without concrete evidence that someone in charge of the program designed it specifically to exclude Black people.

To further compound the inferior treatment Jefferies residents have received they have repeatedly asked state and federal officials to provide the neighborhood with an evacuation plan in case of a serious malfunction at the refinery. All requests have been denied despite numerous serious chemical release incidents occurring at the refinery (Wilcox 2019). Most recently, around 3:00 am on February 3rd, 2019 residents of the Jefferies subdivision woke to poisonous air that induced immediate feelings of illness, dizziness, and vomiting (Feuer 2019). According to Feuer, those that could, packed up their families and fled their homes in the middle of the night to escape air that they could not breathe,

8 Emma Lockridge's quote is taken from a talk she gave at Oakland University on March 21, 2017 entitled "Picturing Pollution from the Hole."

the rest were left to breathe air that had people over 11 miles away calling 911.[9] The following day Marathon assured the public that no dangerous chemicals had been released and that the air was safe to breathe. The residents of Jefferies Subdivision know this is not true as humans do not have to flee healthy harmless air. But due to MDEQ's neoliberal pro-business policy of allowing industry giants like Marathon to self-report toxic chemical releases this statement is all Marathon has had to do regarding this situation (Feuer 2019).

The failure of the legal system on both a state and federal level to recognize the injustices occurring to the people of the Jefferies subdivision, whether in terms of a race-based housing buyout program or a failure to provide residents with an official evacuation plan, is an indictment of all environmental protections aimed at environmental justice. It reveals the hollowness of EO 12898 and the various attempts over the years by the state of Michigan to make environmental justice a priority. Without possibility of legal redress based upon disparate impact, programs like the Marathon buyout will be allowed to continue unabated and all attempts to prioritize environmental justice will remain toothless. Further, neoliberal discourse that attributes the inability to get government funding or programming to individual failings rather than the obstacles generated by systemic racism and destructive corporate behavior prevent the buyout and similar policies from ever being discussed in terms of race and racism.

7 Conclusion

Neoliberal colorblind policymaking has created an environment in which the interests of corporations, like General Motors and Marathon Oil, are considered more worthy of protection than the health and lives of Michigan residents, especially people of color who are disproportionately impacted by industrial pollution and environmental hazards statewide. Neoliberal paternalistic discourse silences claims of systemic racism through reliance on the racially-coded narrative of individual choice and intent, while cutting funding to state regulatory agencies in the name of the free market. The repeated budget cuts to the MDEQ and the EPA, institutions initially designed to protect and

9 On February 3, 2019 around 3am I called 911 to report "the air outside my house smells flammable." The air tasted sour and burned my eyes. I was concerned that my neighbors and I were at risk of being hurt or killed in a major explosion. The source of the odor was the cracked tower at Marathon refinery, which is over 11 miles from my house.

promote human health, have left both agencies crippled to the point that they are incapable of participating in any form of effective regulation. After the failures of MDEQ and the EPA in the Flint water crisis and the Jefferies subdivision of Boynton, it is clear that what remains of the regulatory functions of each is in service to neoliberal pro-business ideals rather than human health. MDEQ and the EPA, through their complacency and impotence serve to enforce and maintain a race-based system of worthiness in Michigan which places corporate business interests at the top and poor people of color at the bottom.

Contemporary American legal frames require the pursuit of individual actors on which to place blame for racism's continued legacy. However, such views limit the pursuit of justice to punitive frameworks and reduce opportunities to pursue racial justice on a grander scale. By focusing only on perpetrator intent we make what should be treated as an institutional issue the fault of individuals, whose racial intents remain elusive. The process of seeking out individuals to blame for the situations in Flint or southwest Detroit provides only temporary satisfaction to victims and the public, while producing nothing in terms of substantive change. While increasingly we see social unrest in reaction to the neoliberal arenas of criminal justice, policing, and employment we have not seen similar unrest regarding legal and administrative decision-making. We need to. Our courts and regulatory agencies need to be restructured, doing away with the illusion of legal formalism. Health opportunities and environmental protections must be redistributed so that no one group need carry the disproportionate burden of environmental toxic exposures. The state and federal governments must to do more than protect the conditions for capital accumulation, they must also protect the health and welfare of all its citizens, especially people of color who have been historically excluded from these protections. This cannot happen in our court rooms and regulatory agencies as long as the discriminatory purpose doctrine stands. However, not even the poisoning of children has been able to bring about these changes, which highlights the limited utility these types of pursuits may have when considered through the lens of Derrick Bell's (1980; 2004) concept of interest convergence.

With Bell's interest convergence in mind, one additional way to provoke changes in legal and administrative decision making may be to get the interests of white people to converge with those pursuing racial justice. Unfortunately, in terms of environmental equality this would in large part mean exposing more people, white people in particular, to lead and other environmental toxins in great enough levels to provoke action. The clearest arena that this type of interest convergence is happening in is in regards to gentrification. With the reinvigoration of cities nationwide young, highly-educated, middle-class white people are moving back to the city and being confronted with the environmental toxic exposures of the urban core that communities of color have long been accustomed to. It is on this front that we need more research. How does gentrification shape environmental regulations and protections? Does gentrification create interest convergence on a level significant enough to promote change for all people? And is there a way to harness this momentum to make it a tool of racial justice that can be more empowering than simply waiting for white people to care?

References

Abbey-Lambertz, K. (2012). "Marathon Petroleum Buyout Finds Support in Oakwood Heights." *The Huffington Post.* January 31, 2012. Availavble at: https://www.huffpost.com/entry/marathon-petroleum-buyout-oakwood-heights-detroit_n_1244351.

Asch, P. and Seneca, J.J. (1978). "Some Evidence on the Distribution of Air Quality." *Land Economics* 54(3): 278–297.

Bell, D.A. (1980). "Brown v. Board of Education and the Interest-Convergence Dilemma." *Harvard Law Review* 93(3): 518–533.

Bell, D.A. (2004). *Silent Covenants: Brown v. Board of Education and the Unfulfilled Hopes for Racial Reform.* New York, NY: Oxford University Press.

Bellinger, D., Leviton, A., Sloman, J., Rabinowitz, M., Needleman, H.L., and Waternaux, C. (1991). "Low-Level Lead Exposure and Children's Cognitive Function in the Preschool Years." *Pediatrics* 87(2): 219–227.

Bertenthal, A. (2018). "Environmental Justice in Context: Assumptions, Meanings, and Practices of Environmnetal Justice in U.S. Courts." *Environmental Justice* 11(6): 203–207.

Bonilla-Silva, E. (2014). *Racism without Racists: Color-Blind Racism and the Persistence of Racial Inequality in America.* Oxford: Rowman & Littlefield Publishers.

Buford, T. and Lombardi, K. (2015). "Environmental Justice Denied: Steel Mill that Never was 'Casts a Shadow' on EPA Office of Civil Rights." *The Center for Public Integrity.* Availabel at: https://publicintegrity.org/environment/steel-mill-that-never-was-casts-a-shadow-on-epa-office-of-civil-rights/.

Bullard, R.D. (1983). "Solid Waste Sites and the Black Houston Community." *Sociological Inquiry* 53(2–3): 273–288.

Cadmus Group Inc. (2010). "Program Review for the Michigan Department of Environmental Quality Water Bureau." *Environmental Protection Agency.* Available at: https://www.epa.gov/sites/production/files/2015-11/documents/program-review-mdeq-water-bureau-20100830-76pp_0.pdf.

Cama, T. and Green, M. (2018). "EPA Polluter Enforcement Hit Historic Lows in 2018." *The Hill.* February 8, 2018. Available at: https://thehill.com/policy/energy-environment/429184-epa-polluter-enforcement-hit-historic-lows-in-2018#:~:text=Penalties%20handed%20down%20to%20corporate,in%20its%20annual%20report%20Friday.

Clark, A. (2015). "How an Investigative Journalist Helped Prove a City was Being Poisoned by its own Water." *Columbia Journalism Review*. November 3, 2015. Available at: http://www.cjr.org/united_states_project/flint_water_lead_curt_guyette_aclu_michigan.php.

Clark, A. (2018). *The Poisoned City: Flint's Water Crisis and the American Urban Tragedy.* New York, NY: Metropolitan Books.

Clay, K., Troesken, W., and Haines, M. (2014). "Lead, Mortality, and Productivity." *Review of Economics and Statistics* 96(3): 458–470.

Clinton, W.J. (1994). *Memorandum on Environmental Justice: EO 12898.* Washington, DC: Executive Branch.

Cole, L.W. and Foster, S.R. (2001). *From the Ground Up.* New York, NY: New York University Press.

Conyers Jr., J. (2016). "Flint is the Predicted Outcome of Michigan's Long, Dangerous History with 'Emergency Managers'." *The Nation*. February 17, 2016. Available at: https://www.thenation.com/article/archive/flint-is-the-predicted-outcome-of-michigans-long-dangerous-history-with-emergency-managers/.

Cooper, P.J. (2001). ""The Law": Presidential Memoranda and Executive Orders of Patchwork Quilts, Trump Cards, and Shell Games." *Presidential Studies Quarterly* 31(1): 126–141.

Craven, J. and Tynes, T. (2016). "The Racist Roots of Flint's Water Crisis." *The Huffington Post*. February 3, 2016. Available at: http://www.huffingtonpost.com/entry/racist-roots-of-flints-water-crisis_us_56b12953e4b04f9b57d7b118.

Crowder, K. and Downey, L. (2010). "Interneighborhood Migration, Race, and Enviornmental Hazards: Modeling Microlevel Processes of Environmental Inequality." *American Journal of Sociology* 115(4): 1110–1149.

Davis, D. (2007). "Narrating the Mute: Racializing and Racism in a Neoliberal Moment." *Souls* 9(4): 346–360.

Delgado, R. and Stefancic, J. (2012). *Critical Race Theory: An Introduction.* New York, NY: New York University Press.

Deloitte Consulting LLP. (2011). "Evaluation of the EPA Office of Civil Rights." Available at: http://src.bna.com/gmK.

Denworth, L. (2008). *Toxic Truth: A Scientist, A Doctor, and th Battle over Lead.* Boston, MA: Beacon Press.

Downey, L. (2006). "Environmental Racial Inequality in Detroit." *Social Forces* 85(2): 771–796.

Duggan, L. (2003). *The Twilight of Equality? Neoliberalism, Cultural Politics, and the Attack on Democracy.* Boston, MA: Beacon Press.

Edwards, M. (2014). "Fetal Death and Reduced Birth Rates Associated with Exposure to Lead-Contaminated Drinking Water." *Environmental Science & Technology* 48(1): 739–746.

Egan, P. (2016). "Amid Denials, State Workers in Flint Got Clean Water." *Detroit Free Press.* January 28, 2016. Available at: https://www.freep.com/story/news/local/michigan/flint-water-crisis/2016/01/28/amid-denials-state-workers-flint-got-clean-water/79470650/.

Environmental Protection Agency. (2004). "EPA Needs to Consistently Implement the Intent of the Executive Order on Environmental Justice." *Office of the Inspector General.* Available at: https://www.epa.gov/office-inspector-general/report-epa-needs-consistently-implement-intent-executive-order.

Environmental Protection Agency. (2018). "EPA Enforcement Annual Results 2018." Available at: https://epa.maps.arcgis.com/apps/Cascade/index.html?appid=0b9d73f351d648698f63bba3f3b15114.

Fasenfest, D. (2019). "A Neoliberal Response to an Urban Crisis: Emergency Management in Flint, MI." *Critical Sociology* 45(1): 33–47.

Fasenfest, D. and Pride, T. (2016). "Emergency Management in Michigan: Race, Class and the Limits of Liberal Democracy." *Critical Sociology* 42(3): 331–334.

Feagin, J.R. (2013). *Systemic Racism: A Theory of Opression.* New York, NY: Routledge.

Feagin, J.R. (2014). *Racist America: Roots, Current Realities and Future Reparations.* New York, NY: Routledge.

Feuer, W. (2019). "Tlaib Joins Detroit Protest Against Marathon Oil Refinery Malfunction." *Detroit Metro Times.* February 4, 2019. Available at: https://www.metrotimes.com/news-hits/archives/2019/02/04/tlaib-joins-detroit-protest-against-marathon-oil-refinery-malfunction.

Flint Advisory Task Force. (2016). "Flint Advisory Task Force Final Report." Available at: https://www.michigan.gov/documents/snyder/FWATF_FINAL_REPORT_21March2016_517805_7.pdf.

Fonger, R. (2014a). "Second Positive Coliform Bacteria Test Means Flint's West Side Water Boil Notice Still in Effect." *MLive.* August 18, 2014. Available at: http://www.mlive.com/news/flint/index.ssf/2014/08/second_postivie_ecoli_test_mea.html.

Fonger, R. (2014b). "General Motors Shutting off Flint River Water at Engine Plant Over Corrosion Worries." *Mlive.* October 13, 2014. Available at: http://www.mlive.com/news/flint/index.ssf/2014/10/general_motors_wont_use_flint.html.

Freeman, A. (1995). "Legitimizing Racial Discrimination Through Antidiscrimination Law: A Critical Review of Supreme Court Doctrine." In: Crenshaw, K., Gotanda, N., Peller, G., and Thomas, K. (eds.). *Critical Race Theory: The Key Writings that Formed the Movement,* pp. 29–45. New York, NY: The New Press.

Freeman, A. (1998). "Anti-Discrimination Law from 1954 to 1989: Uncertainty, Contradiction, Rationalization, Denial." In: Kairys, D. (ed.). *The Politics of Law: A Progressive Critique,* pp. 285–311. New York, NY: Basic Books.

Gotanda, N. (1995). "A Critique of "Our Consititution is Color-Blind"." In: Crenshaw, K., Gotanda, N., Peller, G., and Thomas, K. (eds.). *Critical Race Theory: The Key Writings that Formed the Movement*, pp. 257–275. New York, NY: The New Press.

Gross, E. and Stretesky, P. (2015). "Environmental Justice in the Courts." In: Konisky, D.M. (ed.). *Failed Promises: Evaluating the Federal Government's Response to Environmental Justice*, pp. 205–231. London: The MIT Press.

Grossman, D.S. and Slusky, D.J.G. (2018). "The impact of the Flint water crisis on fertility." *Working paper*. Available at: https://www.irp.wisc.edu/newsevents/workshops/SRW/2018/participants/papers/2-GROSSMAN-SLUSKY-2018-06-10-wisconsin.pdf.

Haney-Lopez, I.F. (2000). "Institutional Racism: Judicial Conduct and a New Theory of Racial Discrimination." *The Yale Law Journal* 109(8): 1717–1884.

Hanna-Attisha, M. (2018). *What the Eyes Don't See: A Story of Crisis, Resistance, and Hope in an American City.* New York, NY: Random House.

Harvey, D. (2005). *A Brief History of Neoliberalism.* Oxford: Oxford University Press.

Hedges, C. and Sacco, J. (2012). *Days of Destruction Days of Revolt.* New York, NY: Nation Books.

Hiar, C. (2011). "Environmental Injustice: EPA Neglects Discrimination Claims from Polluted Communitites." *iWatch News: The Center for Public Integrity*. Available at: https://publicintegrity.org/environment/environmental-injustice-epa-neglects-discrimination-claims-from-polluted-communities/.

Hurwitz, J.H. and Sullivan, E.Q. (2001). "Using Civil Rights Laws to Challenge Environmental Racism: From Bean to Guardians to Chester to Sandoval." *The Journal of Law in Society* 2(5): 1–24.

Kendi, I.X. (2016). *Stamped from the Beginning: The Definitive History of Racist Ideas in America.* New York, NY: Nation Books.

Konisky, D.M. (2015). "The Federal Government's Response to Environmental Inequality." In: Konisky, D.M. (ed.). *Failed Promises: Evaluating the Federal Government's Response to Environmental Justice*, pp. 29–56. London: The MIT Press.

Kurth, J. and MacDonald, C. (2015). "Volume of Abandoned Homes 'Absolutely Terrifying'." *The Detroit News*. May 14, 2015. Available at: https://www.detroitnews.com/story/news/special-reports/2015/05/14/detroit-abandoned-homes-volume-terrifying/27237787/.

Lawrence III, C.R. (1995). "The Id, the Ego, and Equal Protection: Reckoning with Unconscious Racism." In: Crenshaw, K., Gotanda, N., Peller, G., and Thomas, K. (eds.). *Critical Race Theory: The Key Writings that Formed the Movement*, pp. 235–256. New York, NY: The New Press.

Lawrence III, C.R. (1998). "Race and Affirmative Action: A Critical Race Perspective." In: Kairys, D. (ed.). *The Politics of Law: A Progressive Critique*. 3rd ed., pp. 312–327. New York, NY: Basic Books.

Lerner, S. (2010). *Sacrifice Zones: The Front Lines of Toxic Chemical Exposure in the United States.* Cambridge, MA: The MIT Press.

Lewis, R. (2014). "Life in Michigan's Dirtiest Zip Code." *Aljazeera America.* March 3, 2014. Availabale at: http://america.aljazeera.com/articles/2014/3/3/michigan-tar-sandsindustryaccusedofactingwithimpunity.html#:~:text=According%20to%20the%20Michigan%20Department,the%20most%20polluted%20in%20Michigan.

Lynch, J. (2014). "Detroiters Left out of Marathon Buyouts Feel Neglected." *The Detroit News.* November 30, 2014. Available at: http://www.detroitnews.com/story/news/detroit-neighborhoods/2014/11/30/marathon-neighbors/19723939/.

Massey, D.S. (2004). "Segregation and Stratification: A Biosocial Perspective." *Du Bois Review: Social Science Research on Race* 1(1): 7–25.

Minghine, A. (2014). "The Great Revenue Sharing Heist." *Michigan Municipal League,* March/April. Available at: http://www.mml.org/advocacy/great-revenue-sharing-heist.html.

Mohai, P. (2018). "Keynote Address: Environmental Justice and the Flint Water Crisis." *Michigan Sociological Review* 32: 1–41.

Mohai, P. and Bryant, B. (1992). "Environmental Racism: Reviewing the Evidence." In: Bryant, B. and Mohai, P. (eds.). *Race and the Incidence of Environmental Hazards: A Time for Discourse,* pp. 163–176. Boulder, CO: Westview Press.

Mohai, P., Kweon, B-S., Lee, S., and Ard, K. (2011). "Air Pollution Around Schools is Linked to Poorer Student Health and Academic Performance." *Health Affairs* 30(5): 852–862.

Mohai, P., Lantz, P.M., Morenoff, J., House, J., and Mero, R. (2009). "Racial and Socioeconomic Disparities in Residential Proximity to Polluting Industrial Facilities: Evidence From the Americans' Changing Lives Study." *American Journal of Public Health* 99(3): 649–656.

Moss, K.L. (2000). "Environmental Justice at the Crossroads." *William & Mary Environmental Law and Policy Review* 24(1): 35–66.

National Academy of Public Administration. (2001). "Environmental Justice in EPA Permitting: Reducing Pollution in High-Risk Communities is Integral to the Agency's Mission." Washington, DC: Environmental Protection Agency. Avaialable at: https://www.epa.gov/environmentaljustice/napa-environmental-justice-epa-permitting-reducing-pollution-high-risk.

Needleman, H.L., Riess, J.A., Tobin, M.J., Biesecker, G.E., and Greenhouse, J.B. (1996). "Bone Lead Levels and Delinquent Behavior." *Journal of the American Medical Association* 275(5): 363–369.

Oosting, J. (2010). "Must-Read Report: Detroit's 48217 Zip Code is Michigan's Most Polluted." *MLive.* June 20, 2010. Available at: http://www.mlive.com/news/detroit/index.ssf/2010/06/must-read_report_detroits_4821.html.

Oosting, J. (2019). "Federal Judge: Flint Suit Against Snyder Can Advance." *The Detroit News*. April 1, 2019. Avaialble at: https://www.detroitnews.com/story/news/michigan/flint-water-crisis/2019/04/01/federal-judge-flint-suit-against-snyder-can-advance/3332102002/.

Qiu, Y. and Buford, T. (2015). "Decades of Inaction." *The Center for Public Integrity*. August 3, 2015. Available at: https://www.publicintegrity.org/2015/08/03/17726/decades-inaction.

Roberts, D.E. (1991). "Punishing Drug Addicts Who Have Babies: Women of Color, Equality, and the Right of Privacy." *Harvard Law Review* 104(7): 1419–1482.

Roberts, D.E. (1997). "Unshackling Black Motherhood." *Michigan Law Review* 95(4): 938–964.

Roberts, D.J. and Mahtani, M. (2010). "Neoliberalizing Race, Racing Neoliberalism: Placing "Race" in Neoliberal Discourses." *Antipode* 42(2): 248–257.

Rogan, W.J. and Ware, J.H. (2003). "Exposure to Lead in Children: How Low is Low Enough?" *The New England Journal of Medicine* 348(16): 1515–1516.

Russell-Brown, K. (2001). *The Color of Crime: Racial Hoaxes, White Fear, Black Protectionism, Police Harassment, and Other Microaggressions*. New York, NY: New York University Press.

Sampson, R.J. and Winter, A.S. (2016). "The Racial Ecology of Lead Poisioning." *Du Bois Review: Social Science Research on Race* 13(2): 261–283.

Schlanger, Z. (2016). "Choking to Death in Detroit: Flint Isn't Michigan's Only Disaster." *Newsweek*. March 30, 2016. Available at: https://www.newsweek.com/2016/04/08/michigan-air-pollution-poison-southwest-detroit-441914.html.

Soss, J., Fording, R.C., and Schram, S.F. (2011). *Discipling the Poor: Neoliberal Paternalism and the Persistent Power of Race*. Chicago, IL: University of Chicago Press.

Tanner, K. and Kaffer, N. (2015). "State Data Confirms Higher Blood-lead Levels in Flint Kids." *Detroit Free Press*. September 29, 2015. Available at: https://www.freep.com/story/opinion/columnists/nancy-kaffer/2015/09/26/state-data-flint-lead/72820798/.

Taylor, C., Golding, J., and Emond, A. (2015). "Adverse Effects of Maternal Lead Levels on Birth Outcomes in the ALSPAC Study: A Prospective Birth Cohort Study." *BJOG: An International Journal of Obstetrics & Gynaecology* 122(3): 322–328.

Taylor, D.E. (2014). *Toxic Communities: Environmental Racism, Industrial Pollution, and Residential Mobility*. New York, NY: New York University Press.

Troesken, W. (2008). "Lead Water Pipes and Infant Mortality at the Turn of the Twentieth Century." *Journal of Human Resources* 43(3): 553–575.

United Church of Christ. (1987). "Toxic Waste and Race in the United States: A National Report on the Racial and Socio-economic Characteristics of Communitites with Hazardous Waste Sites." Available at: https://www.nrc.gov/docs/ML1310/ML13109A339.pdf.

United States General Accounting Office. (1995). "Hazardous and Nonhazardous Waste: Demographics of People Living Near Waste Facilities." Report to Congressional Requesters United States. Available at: http://www.gao.gov/products/RCED-95-84.

Wacquant, L. (2009). *Punishing the Poor: The Neoliberal Government of Social Insecurity.* Durham, NC: Duke University Press.

Waldrop, T. (2019). "Flint Residents Can Sue the Federal Government Over Water Crisis, Judge Rules." *CNN.* April 19, 2019. Avaialble at: https://www.cnn.com/2019/04/19/us/flint-water-federal-lawsuit-ruling/index.html.

Welburn, J. and Seamster, L. (2016). "How A Racist System has Poisoned the Water in Flint, Mich." *The Root.* January 9, 2016. Available at: https://www.theroot.com/how-a-racist-system-has-poisoned-the-water-in-flint-mi-1790853824 (consulted May 17, 2016).

White House. (2011). "A Big Step for Environmental Justice." November 16, 2011. Available at: https://www.whitehouse.gov/blog/2011/11/16/big-step-forward-environmental-justice.

White House. (2014). "Presidential Proclamation—20th Anniversary of Executive Order 12898 on Environmental Justice." February 10, 2014. Available at: https://www.whitehouse.gov/the-press-office/2014/02/10/presidential-proclamation-20th-anniversary-executive-order-12898-environ.

Wilcox, M. (2019). "The "Original Sin" of Air Quality Regulations is Keeping Communities Polluted. But that is Changing." *Environmental Health News.* January 7, 2019. Available at: https://www.ehn.org/detroit-environmental-justice-toxic-48217-2624940172.html.

Williams, D.R. and Collins, C. (2001). "Racial Segregation: A Fundemental Cause of Racial Disparities in Health." *Public Health Report* 116(5): 404–416.

Zhu, M., Fitzgerald, E.F., Gelberg, K.H., Lin, S., and Druschel, C.M. (2010). "Maternal Low-Level Lead Exposure and Fetal Growth." *Environmental Health Perspectives* 118(10): 1471–1475.

CHAPTER 3

Stockton Isn't Flint, or Is It? Race and Space in Comparative Crisis Driven Urbanization

Raoul S. Liévanos and Julie Sze

1 Introduction

The Flint Water Crisis (FWC) refers to widespread exposures of the majority Black and low-income population of Flint, Michigan to toxic lead levels in the city's water supply. This poisoning followed a "cost-saving" drinking water supply switch to the Flint River from Lake Huron through the Detroit Water District in April 2014 by a state-appointed Emergency Manager (Fasenfest 2019). This manifestation of environmental racism was exacerbated through privatization, regulatory cover-ups and arguably criminal behavior, spearheaded by majority white elites working at the metropolitan and state levels (Benz 2019; Pulido 2016; Sadler and Highsmith 2016). In 2016, Flint initiated a contract with a transnational private company to assist with its water management. A private engineering firm promoted the treatability of the Flint River water in 2011 and consulted with officials after April 2014 and faced civil charges in June 2016 over their involvement in the FWC (Pauli 2019).

The FWC presents a sociological "enlightenment function" similar to the 2005 Hurricane Katrina disaster in New Orleans and the US Gulf Coast (Beck 2006; Picou and Marshall 2007). Similar to the case of New Orleans and Hurricane Katrina, in the FWC we see how environmental racism "works" and is embedded in the prevailing political and economic structures that produce some places and bodies as pollutable. Márquez (2014) and Pellow (2016; 2018) calls this status, "expendability," so that the status quo based on racism, profit, extraction, and violence can remain. In the FWC, we also see how water injustices are produced through the connections of racial segregation, urban disinvestment, neoliberalism, and political fragmentation that span public and private institutions (MCRC 2017; Ranganathan 2016; Sadler and Highsmith 2016).

Meanwhile, in California's San Joaquin Valley (SJV), tens of thousands of people of color and/or low-income people pay and use bottled water because they do not have access to clean drinking water systems (Balazs and Ray 2014; London et al. 2018; Ranganathan and Balazs 2015). Despite legislative measures that recognize water as a human right in California (London 2019), water service delivery has been historically structured to protect some geographic and political units, particularly cities, over the interests and wellbeing of less powerful, unincorporated locales (Pannu 2012). Contaminated tap water in areas of the SJV contains high levels of nitrates from harmful agricultural fertilizers, mega-dairy cow manure, pesticides and other toxic substances (Balazs et al. 2011; 2012). These water injustices are compounded by race- and class-based climate vulnerabilities (English et al. 2013) and unequal exposures to pesticides and other environmental health hazards in the air, land, and water environments (Harrison 2011; Huang and London 2012; Liévanos 2017, 2018a, 2018b; Liévanos et al. 2011; London et al. 2008; Sadd et al. 2014; Sadd et al. 2015). Water access and inequalities are seen as a rural problem, yet they range from the bodily, household, community, urban and county to the state (Balazs and Ray 2014).

In this chapter, we situate the FWC in a historical-comparative analysis with Stockton—a major urban center of the SJV. As in Flint (Highsmith 2015), racial segregation and uneven development intertwine throughout Stockton's history (Liévanos 2019a; Mabalon 2013; Ogbu 1974). Recent developments suggest Stockton offers a counterpoint to the rural drinking water injustices of the SJV following the high-stakes contract to privatize its drinking water in 2003 with OMI-Thames, a transnational corporation. A lawsuit from an anti-privatization coalition ended the contract in 2008, but the contract resulted in negative consequences (Robinson 2013: 4). Adverse impacts from this water privatization failure have more recently manifest in water quality concerns for Stockton's privileged and predominantly white Northside. According to one account, "Stockton is embroiled in controversy over a proposal to change the way it disinfects North Stockton's drinking water. (O)bservers ... charge that ... proposed switch from chlorine to chloramines poses a serious public health risk similar to that seen in Flint, Michigan ... *Stockton isn't Flint*." (emphasis added, Bagalayos 2016).

The suggestion here is that the local particularities of the Stockton case mean that it "isn't Flint." We treat this suggestion empirically: are Stockton and Flint comparable, and if so, why or why not? What is at stake in framing urban water crises comparatively? The answers to these questions have important implications for understanding how race, space, neoliberalism, and "crisis driven urbanization" unfold unevenly across Flint and Stockton, and the myriad of U.S. cities that "are potential crisis cities" (Gotham and Greenberg 2014: 16). Through a series of spatial, political and environmental crises, post war US cities limit the life chances and economic security of some, to the benefit of others, in the areas of wealth accumulation, housing, and education (Highsmith 2015).

First, we summarize our theoretical model of *racialized crisis driven urbanization*. We develop this model through engagement with Gotham and Greenberg's (2014) crisis cities framework, and a synthesis of urban and racial theory with environmental justice studies. We then present our historical-comparative analysis of racialized crisis driven urbanization in Flint and Stockton. We draw on original data collection of historical and multi-scalar spatial contexts, including an original analysis of land use and housing valuation data, longitudinal census data, and contemporary water quality data with geographic information systems.

We argue that the production of contemporary water crises in both Flint and Stockton is constituted by multiple "racial projects" of crisis driven urbanization. A racial project is "an interpretation, representation, or explanation of racial dynamics, and an effort to reorganize and redistribute resources along particular racial lines" (Omi and Winant 1994: 68). In Flint and Stockton, crisis driven urbanization is shaped by historically specific racial projects of (re-)organizing race and space in order to consolidate racial capitalism (Robinson 2000 [1983]), in particular, its hierarchical and historical order of "differential value" of racialized bodies and spaces, with non-white bodies variously stratified at the bottom of the social, economic and political order (Pulido 2016; 2017). We offer new empirical insights and show how racialized crisis driven urbanization unfolded consistently but unevenly from the 1930s New Deal era recovery from the Great Depression through crises that led to the contemporary water crisis in Flint and Stockton. Crisis driven urbanization in the United States is co-constituted by multi-scalar racialized dynamics of devaluation, dispossession, exclusion, and environmental hazard exposures grounded first in racist policy developments in housing and schools and transformed by neoliberalism.

2 Recasting Crisis Driven Urbanization: Race and Space

Scholars and activists have long been concerned with various urban crises. These include problems associated with the desertion of the city by the state; municipal fiscal insolvency; concentrated crime, poverty, unemployment; and the persistent segregation and devaluation of people of color amidst the urban renewal, gentrification, and predatory lending practices and home foreclosures (Du Bois 1996 [1899]; Hernandez 2009; Highsmith 2015; Immergluck 2009; Logan and Molotch 2007 [1987]; Massey and Denton 1993; Rugh and Massey 2010; Wacquant 2008; Wilson 1987, 1996; Smith 1996; Sugrue 1996).

Integrating disaster social science with critical urban studies, sociologists Kevin Fox Gotham and Miriam Greenberg (2014) argue the contemporary urban crisis manifests through "crisis-driven urbanization," as witnessed in the recovery from the September 11, 2001 terrorist attack on New York City and Hurricane Katrina in August 2005 in New Orleans. Within their framework, "crisis" is both "a historical moment of rupture and intervention and [a] framed event," while a disaster is "understood as a contingent event that under the proper conditions can trigger and be transformed into" crises (Gotham and Greenberg 2014: 6). They define "crisis-driven urbanization," as a "contested, market-oriented, and cyclical mode of urban redevelopment," centered on a dynamic whereby uneven development and "previous rounds of crisis and restructuring create the regulatory environment, public-private mode of governance, and socio-spatial inequalities and vulnerabilities that lay the ground for the crises and spatial politics of subsequent generations" (Gotham and Greenberg 2014: 11). They attend to dynamics of uneven (re)development that shape "uneven landscapes of risk and resilience," which are "landscape[s] ... conditioned by the existing degree of inequality and risk and the strengths or weaknesses of social and environmental protections" (Gotham and Greenberg 2014: 6). Neoliberal, crisis driven urbanization contributed to the spatial concentration of poverty, especially among Black people and youths. This uneven landscape of risk and resilience, exacerbated by neoliberal dynamics of uneven (re)development, "meant that marginalized communities [from the Lower Ninth Ward in New Orleans to Lower Manhattan in New York] ... would face the greatest risks to health and livelihood from disasters, no matter if the trigger was a hurricane or a terrorist strike" (Gotham and Greenberg 2014: 57).

We suggest that their notion of crisis-driven urbanization benefits through an explicit centralization and theorization of race and space. We use a socio-spatial, multi-scalar lens to examine how symbolic representations of social groups and physical spaces interact with political-economic dynamics of capital investment and state policy to produce uneven (re)development and landscapes of risk and resilience (Gottdiener and Hutchison 2006; Gotham 2002; Lefebvre 1991 [1974]). In so doing, we emphasize how racial and spatial relations are intricately interconnected social forces that shape our experiences of the biophysical world in the United States in ways that are irreducible to social class (see also Bonilla-Silva 1997; Omi and Winant 1994; Pellow 2007, 2016, 2018).

US urban history is defined by struggles over the articulation and extension of racial categories and hierarchies to bodies and communities in their socio-spatial spheres, such as racial segregation and unequal environmental health hazard exposure (Pulido 2000; Sze 2007; Taylor 2014; Zimring 2015). We also see it in the "white spatial imaginary" (Lipsitz 2011) or the valorization of whiteness and socially homogenous, controlled residential spaces. These racial and spatial logics are institutionalized in the US housing market through discriminatory regulatory regimes, school district policies, mortgage lending, real estate steering practices, and consumer preferences (Gotham 2002; Hernandez 2009; Highsmith 2015; Lipsitz 2011; Massey and Denton 1993; Charles 2006).

Historical and contemporary racial and spatial relations within the US are examples of the broader conditions of "racial capitalism," which is predicated on the use of race and racism to structure capital accumulation (Robinson 2000 [1983]). The articulation and rearticulation of racial inferiority and oppression toward "barbarians," "lower orders," and those marginalized within European feudal society was at the root of racial capitalism (Robinson 2000 [1983]). These racial logics were deployed through the devaluation, dispossession, colonization, enslavement, exploitation, and symbolic and material erasure of non-European peoples to produce a modern world system of capitalism (Bacon 2019; Du Bois 1999 [1920]; Fraser 2018; Márquez 2014; Mills 2001; Norgaard et al. 2018; Pellow 2016, 2018; Pulido 2015, 2016, 2017; Pulido and De Lara 2018; Robinson 2000 [1983]; Wolfe 1999).

Broader conditions contributing to water crises in Flint and Stockton illuminate complexities in this racial and spatial order. Pulido (2016) attributes the lead poisoning of Flint to white supremacy in Michigan, the neoliberal state's emergency management regime and prioritization of municipal fiscal solvency, and to the devaluation of the city's majority Black residents and their surplus status as "outcast," "underground," and "threat." Gilmore (2007) analyzes prisons and environmental pollution in California's SJV and the broader Central Valley, which encompasses Stockton. The prisons, which house overwhelmingly Black and Latinx urban populations from Los Angeles and the San Francisco Bay Area, function as a rural economic development and jobs program. The Southern half of the SJV, spanning Stockton to Bakersfield, is defined by a culture drawn from the Southern United States that shaped the racial and spatial politics of the region. Cotton farming from Georgia to Central California reproduced and materialized a deeply racist social order and politics of land development based on resource extraction and labor exploitation whereby Black people and places historically define the marginalized sphere of this racial and spatial order (Foley 1997; Gilmore 2007).

While differentiated by their local particularities, we examine how the Flint and Stockton cases share commonalities with the broader environmental racial formation and structuring through racial capitalism. That is, the contemporary environmental racial formation in the US is founded on the erasure of Indigenous peoples, followed by the devaluation, dispossession, and dispensability of Black and Latinx bodies and physical spaces whom are associated with filth, waste, uncleanliness, and logical deposits for environmental toxins (Pellow 2016, 2018; see also Márquez 2014; Mills 2001). White bodies and spaces are generally associated with purity, cleanliness, and relative environmental privilege (Lipsitz 2011; Park and Pellow 2011; Pulido 2000, 2015; Zimring 2015). Indeed, multiple forms of social disadvantage and exclusion are disproportionately concentrated in Indigenous, Black, and Latinx neighborhoods when compared to similarly marginalized whites and Asians and Pacific Islanders across the United States, with the multiply marginalized Latinx and Black urban-industrial neighborhoods bearing the brunt of life-threatening air pollution exposures (Liévanos 2019b).

2.1 *Racialized Crisis Driven Urbanization and Water Crisis Formation in Flint and Stockton*

Our model of racialized crisis driven urbanization anticipates that the production of environmental health hazards will disproportionately burden devalued Black and Latinx bodies and physical spaces. However, environmental racial inequality outcomes may not reproduce existing landscapes of uneven risk and resilience for at least three reasons. First, given the multiple and contradictory racial projects, environmental health hazards and crises have the potential to "boomerang" back upon those atop the racial and spatial hierarchy (e.g., white elites) (Pellow 2007; cf. Beck 2005 [1986], 1995). Second, environmental racial inequalities vary across US regions (Lievanos 2019b). These outcomes reflect regional racial formations, which are "place-specific processes of racial formation, in which locally accepted racial orders and hierarchies complicate and sometimes challenge hegemonic ideologies and facile notions of race" (Cheng 2013: 10). Third, our framework offers an intersectional view of environmental inequalities along the dimensions of race and class. Thus, rather than conceptualizing crisis driven urbanization as always "deepening risks and vulnerabilities" (Gotham and Greenberg 2014: 14), our model leaves open the possibility of contingent outcomes that can be more generally understood as *rearticulated* risks, resilience, and crisis frames across intersecting axes of social division.

We advance the following account. An uneven racialized and class-based landscape of risk and resilience characterized Flint and Stockton since before the economic disaster of the Great Depression of 1929 to 1939. New Deal housing policy and residential appraisal techniques deployed throughout the recovery from the Depression during "Crisis Period 1" of the 1930s institutionalized the devaluing and divesting in certain neighborhoods in Flint and Stockton through the explicit use of racist and class-inflected hierarchies of economic and social value. These hierarchies were inscribed in physical space through "concatenated crises" (i.e., a series of multiple and interacting crises) (Biggs et al. 2011; Gotham and Greenberg 2014), and material struggles reflected in uneven recovery, development, and redevelopment in both cities *and* their regions. Racialized crises of residential and school (de)segregation and urban renewal are fundamental to shaping US metropolitan areas (Highsmith 2015). We present our analysis of those concatenated crises over broad time scales: "Crisis Period 2," from 1940 to 1970, and "Crisis Period 3," from the 1970s to the 2010s. We end with an analysis of how racial hierarchies continue to pattern current water crises and their uneven landscapes of risk and resilience in Flint and Stockton, and we draw out the broader scholarly and practical implications of our comparative analysis.

3 Racialized Crisis Driven Urbanization

3.1 *Crisis Period 1: The Great Depression and New Deal Recovery, 1930s to 1940*

We begin our analysis of racialized crisis driven urbanization with the New Deal recovery following the Great Depression. The New Deal featured federal housing programs instituted in the 1930s that contributed to diverting resources and capital investments from non-white and devalued inner cities to the increasingly white and elite suburbs throughout the metropolis (Gotham 2002; Gottdiener and Hutchison 2006; Hernandez 2009). In 1933, Congress passed New Deal housing legislation that established the Home Owners' Loan Corporation (HOLC) to help distressed mortgage borrowers stay in their homes. The HOLC lent over 1 million mortgages during the Great Depression through its novel provision of long-term, low-interest, fully amortized loans (Highsmith 2015; Jackson 1985). The HOLC's "scientific basis" was firmly grounded in classic urban ecological theory drawn from the Chicago School of Urban Sociology (Gottdiener and Hutchison 2006). Resonant with segregationist worldviews held by the white real estate industry and dominant law and public policy (Gotham 2002; Light 2009), classic urban ecological theory held that neighborhood heterogeneity and "invasion and succession" of lower status groups in neighborhoods previously occupied by higher status groups contributed to "life cycles" of declining neighborhood values (Gotham 2002; Light 2009; Taylor 2014). The HOLC moved beyond its legal mandate to standardizing sophisticated residential appraisal methods throughout its confidential residential security surveys of 239 US cities (Hillier 2003; 2005). The HOLC survey, and later iterations used by the Federal Housing Administration

(FHA), used appraisal to forecast life cycles of neighborhood decline and devaluation to protect real estate investments increasingly coming from the state (Gotham 2002).

HOLC appraisals were influential in framing the ensuing crisis and recovery from the Great Depression in explicit racial and spatial terms. The 1940 US Census reported that the HOLC held 13.17 percent of the first mortgages in the Flint metropolitan area, 87.84 percent of which were concentrated in Flint City. In contrast, the HOLC held only 5.74 percent of the first mortgages in the Stockton metropolitan area with a smaller majority (59.84 percent) concentrated in Stockton City. As the HOLC moved beyond its original lending mandate, it *differentially* incorporated into its systematic neighborhood appraisals and the popular 1930s "national racial narrative" (Pulido 2006) regarding the racial threat of Black residents to the social stability and investment worthiness of a neighborhood (Jackson 1985). Through its incorporation of classic urban ecological theory and the "white spatial imaginary" (Lipsitz 2011), the HOLC valorized whiteness, social homogeneity, and controlled environments, and it devalued Black, mixed, and/or majority non-white areas.

The HOLC ordered neighborhood desirability by four grades. A ratings were given to the first grade, best areas; B ratings to second grade, still desirable areas; C ratings to third grade, "declining" areas; and D ratings to fourth grade, "hazardous" areas. The first grades were typically assigned to white and elite or middle-class enclaves that were protected by racially restrictive covenants and other exclusionary land use controls (Liévanos 2019a: 234). Often slightly older, less desirable, less homogeneous than the first grade areas, the second grade areas still received favorable mortgage lending terms. The HOLC assigned third- and fourth-grade ratings based on the extent of poor land use controls, devalued housing stock, and marginalized populations, especially Black residents (Jackson 1985; Liévanos 2019a; Taylor 2014). These lower two grades were given to neighborhoods because "they had already succumbed to 'decay' and the 'infiltration of subversive races' " (Liévanos 2019a: 234). The fourth grade, "hazardous" areas were represented with red color in the original HOLC map and later became associated with "redlining." These grades marked the highest investment risk and "were generally explained as having 'detrimental influences in a pronounced degree, undesirable population or infiltration of it' " (Liévanos 2019a: 234). Figures 3.1 and 3.2, respectively, present our digitized HOLC residential security survey maps for Flint and Stockton.

Higher-valued spaces are represented well in Figure 3.1 by the Woodcroft Estates and Woodland Park neighborhood (assigned first grade ratings) and the corporate housing subdivision (second grade rating) built by General Motors

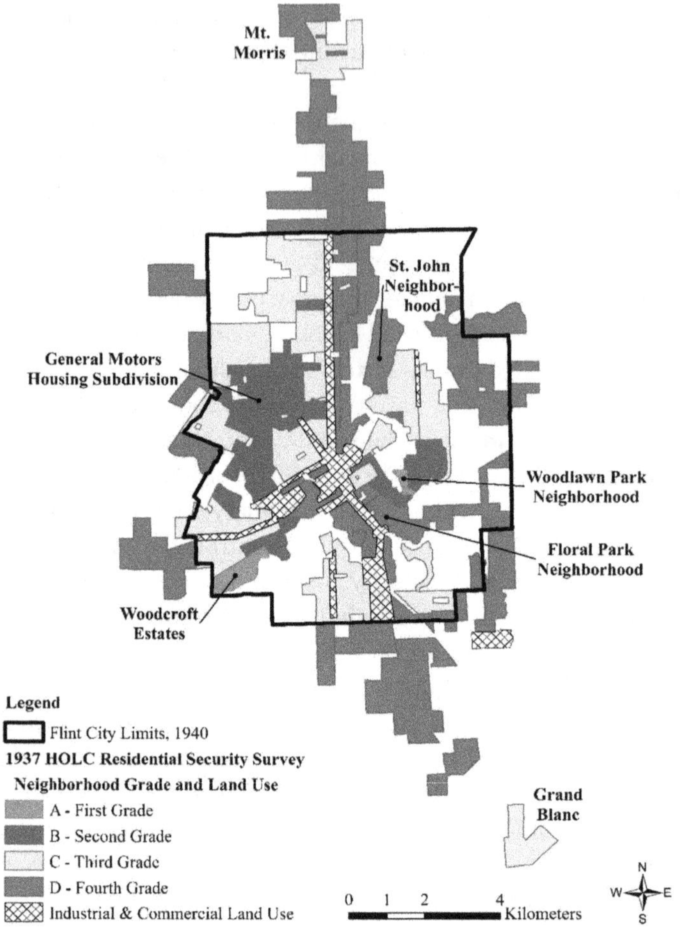

FIGURE 3.1 1937 Home Owners' Loan Corporation (HOLC) Residential Security Survey Map of Flint and vicinity
Note: Authors' original analysis of data from Manson et al. (2017) and Nelson et al. (2017).

(GM), who held considerable political-economic influence in Flint throughout its history (Highsmith 2015). Racially restrictive covenants and other exclusionary land use controls sought to maintain the racial homogeneous white spaces of Flint's first and second grade areas (Highsmith 2015: 33). In addition to GM discriminating against Black workers, GM similarly aimed "to protect home values and a high quality of life" by enforcing strict deed, building, and racial restrictions that made their new subdivisions exclusive for white single-family households (Highsmith 2015: 31–32).

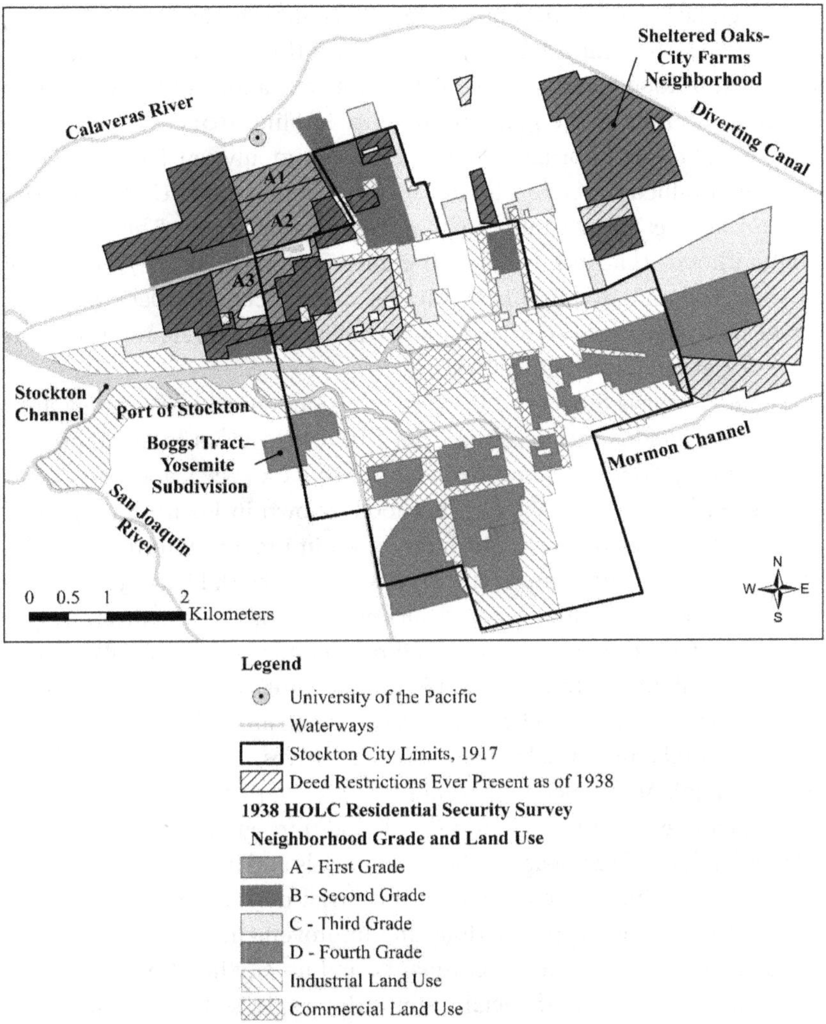

FIGURE 3.2 1938 Home Owners' Loan Corporation (HOLC) Residential Security Survey Map of Stockton
Note: Authors' original analysis of Stockton City boundaries from 1917 Sanborn Fire Insurance Maps and additional data from Marciano et al. (2010) and Liévanos (2019a).

The remaining areas in the HOLC's survey of Flint were seen as "declining" or already "hazardous." The third grade, "declining" ratings were applied to 18 neighborhoods defined by their immigrant composition—specifically, the presence of "Mexicans, Asians, and southern and eastern Europeans"—while the fourth grade ratings were applied in three instances to neighborhoods with Black residents (Highsmith 2015: 41). Among these three, Floral Park and the St. John's neighborhood contained the highest concentrations of Black residents and were the center of the Black community in Flint. HOLC appraisers and their local real estate informants nonetheless commonly saw Floral Park and St. Johns as devalued containers for low-income, laborers, and "Undesirables—aliens and negroes" (Highsmith 2015: 41; Nelson et al. 2017). The remaining 21 neighborhoods that received fourth grades (Nelson et al. 2017), including many that predominated in Flint's suburbs, did not contain Black residents. However, they were mostly devalued due to their lower class standing and limited municipal services (Highsmith 2015).

Figure 3.2 displays Stockton's forty-three residential security survey areas and the HOLC grades that resulted from HOLC field visits to Stockton. The Westmoor ("A1"), Oxford Manor–Avondale–Lake Park ("A2"), and Lake View–Lake Park–Park Terrace ("A3") neighborhoods shown in Figure 3.2 represent the first-grade spaces of North Stockton (often in proximity to the desirable University of the Pacific campus (UOP)) (Liévanos 2019a). Figure 3.2 also outlines all eighteen residential security survey areas that were entirely or partially deed-restricted by 1938. Those deed restrictions include racially restrictive covenants similar to those used in Flint. Like Flint's Woodcroft Estates and Woodland Park neighborhood, Stockton's first grade areas included a number of environmental amenities, businessmen, executives, and no people of color (Liévanos 2019a). As detailed in Liévanos (2019a), the HOLC assigned intermediary social and economic value to second- and third-grade areas. It assigned fourth grade, "hazardous" neighborhood appraisals and heightened real estate investment risk primarily to clusters of industrial neighborhoods with Black residents, "heterogeneous populations and improvements," limited mortgage financing and racially restrictive covenants, and no city flood protection services despite the history of racial animosities expressed toward Japanese, Chinese, Filipinx, Mexican, and Italian people in Stockton.

Anti-Black racial projects continued to organize Flint's crisis driven urbanization into the 1970s. Similar racial projects fused together to various extents with anti-Mexican racial projects that superseded the long-standing anti-Asian racial projects during Stockton's crisis driven urbanization over the same period.

3.2 *Crisis Period 2: Redevelopment and Concatenated Urban Crises, 1940 to 1970s*

Beginning with its founding in the 1930s, and continuing from the 1940s to the 1970s, the FHA coupled similar neighborhood risk-rating procedures as used by the HOLC with racist and anti-urban prerequisites for mortgage financing to restructure urban and suburban development in the United States (Gotham 2002; Hernandez 2009; Highsmith 2015; Light 2009). This prolonged period of federal redlining became an increasingly important way to maintain racial segregation following the 1948 *Shelley v. Kraemer* case in which the US Supreme Court declared racially restrictive covenants unenforceable (Gotham 2002; Lipsitz 2011).

The suburban housing boom during the 1940s and 1950s, fueled by FHA's racially-exclusive financing, was echoed within Flint's first and second-rated neighborhoods, like Woodlawn Park, Woodcroft Estates, and the remnants of GM's west-end Flint corporate housing subdivision. Throughout the broader expanse of Genesee County, "suburban capitalists worked to consolidate their independence from the city by blocking the New Flint plan, resisting annexation, and organizing numerous municipal incorporation campaigns" (Highsmith 2015: 147). Meanwhile, Black residents, particularly the thousands that came in the World War II period of industrial expansion, were mostly confined to Floral Park and the St. John's neighborhood where they experienced incredibly difficult living conditions. For example, St. John's was one of the most polluted and unlivable neighborhoods in the US and "contained the city's largest concentration of poverty" and second-most concentration of Black residents behind Floral Park (Highsmith 2015: 151). This spatial concentration compelled many Black residents and civil rights organizations advocating on their behalf for fair housing and better overall living conditions to support "urban renewal" and redevelopment in their neighborhoods—that is, before the realities of such discriminatory initiatives became manifest.

Urban renewal during the 1960s and 1970s included interstate freeway development that came ripping through Floral Park. It also featured the St. John Renewal Projects and the intensification of industrial land use. These redevelopments were aided by the passage of the Federal Housing Acts of 1949 and 1954 and the National Interstate and Defense Highways Act in 1956 (Gotham 2002; Hernandez 2009). Flint's white city leaders implemented a 1965 moratorium on building repairs that combined with discriminatory residential appraisals by white appraisers of Black-owned property in Flint. The moratorium and appraisals adversely impacted Black property owners by constraining their ability to improve their properties and aging housing stock, devaluing their property, compelling them into a situation where they had little choice but to sell properties to the city at a loss, and becoming dispossessed renters who were disproportionately relocated to racially segregated public housing (Highsmith 2015).

These conditions contributed to massive uprisings and a number of civil rights reforms, including a precedent-setting "open" housing law that boosters argued "made Flint one of the most progressive communities in the United States" (Highsmith 2015: 147). However, the multifaceted racial project of "urban renewal" devastated the Northside housing market where many Black people lived, exacerbated Black poverty, and contributed to new manifestations of residential segregation in Flint as whites and middle-class Black people increasingly fled to the suburbs (Highsmith 2015: 184). In suburban spaces like Davison Township and Grand Blanc, white residents met middle-class Black people seeking integration with violent opposition and exclusionary tactics from realtors and public officials. Concerted real estate "blockbusting" campaigns were waged in Flint, wherein realtors used middle-class Black people seeking integration to scare white homeowners into "panic selling" at low prices (Highsmith 2015). Further, racialized dynamics of deindustrialization became entrenched. Following the economic recession of 1973–1975, GM cut thousands of jobs and relocated production activities outside of Flint. The Black population was hit hardest, experiencing almost 50 percent unemployment (Highsmith 2015).

Figure 3.3 presents the percent of owner-occupied housing units that reached the census tract median value range of $17,499 or less as of 1970 (in 1970s USD) and that were owned by Black homeowners or Latinx homeowners in the Flint metropolis. In so doing, it visualizes racial segregation and devaluation in the Flint metropolis by 1970, which was influenced by Flint's discriminatory building moratorium and real estate appraisals and blockbusting practices of the 1960s (Highsmith 2015). Higher percentages of housing units at or below $17,499 were concentrated in Flint and in some devalued suburbs bordering Flint. When compared to Figure 3.1, the spatial patterns shown in Figure 3.3, Map A, suggest that lower-valued housing became spatially diffuse across neighborhoods that were given first-, second-, third-, *and* fourth-grade appraisals by the HOLC in the 1930s. Further, Figure 3.3, Map B, shows that the *majority* (62.15 to 89.54 percent) of the owner-occupied housing units concentrated in the North, centered on the St. John's neighborhood, and in the Southeast, centered on Floral Park, were held by Black homeowners and valued at or less than the tract median of $17,499. Comparing Figure 3.3, Map B, with Figure 3.1 indicates that devalued Black housing in 1970 was relatively contained in and around the primary Black, devalued spaces of Flint in the 1930s. Lastly, Figure 3.3, Map C, shows that detectable percentages of owner-occupied housing units, which were Latinx-owned and at or below the $17,499 median, bordered the St. John neighborhood. When compared to Figure 3.1, and its underlying data from the HOLC Flint survey, we see that Flint's spaces

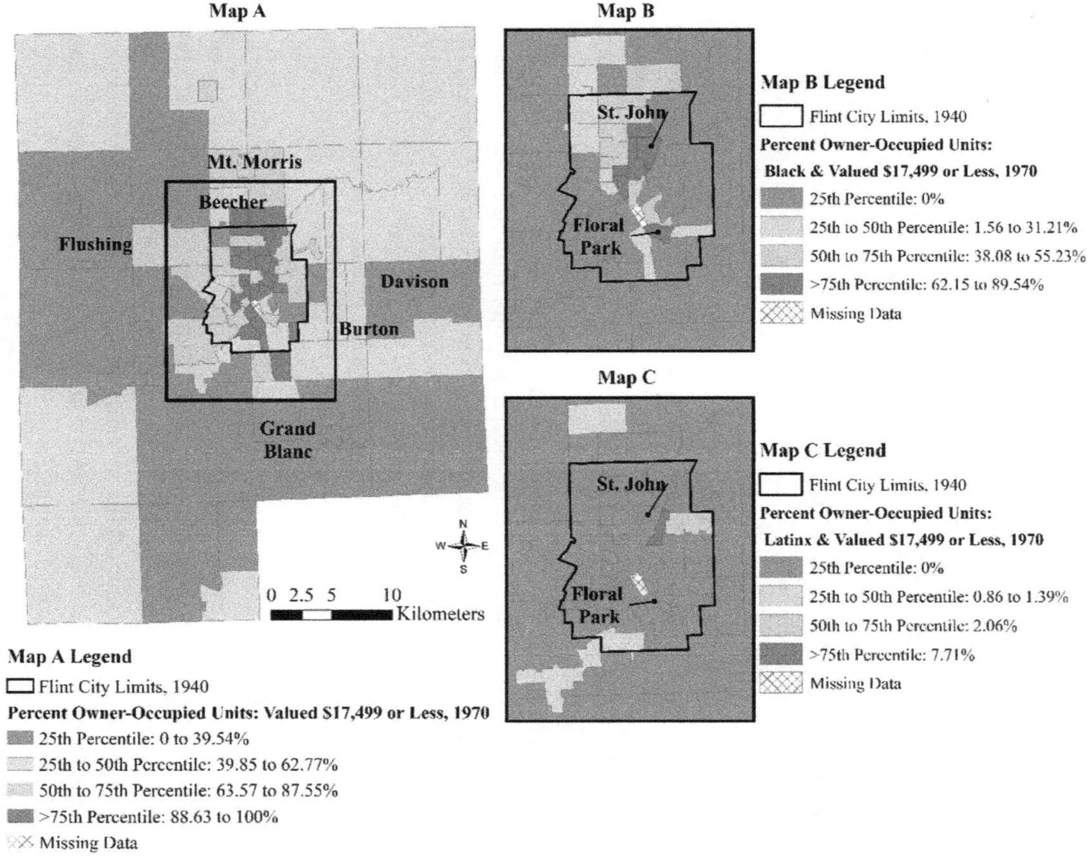

FIGURE 3.3 Percent owner-occupied housing units by value and Black and Latinx householders, 1970, in Flint and vicinity
Note: Authors' original analysis of data from Manson et al. (2017).

of lower-value Latinx housing in 1970 coincide with the HOLC's third grade ratings.

Stockton's Black and Latinx residents, as well as its large Filipinx population at the time (see Mabalon 2013), bore the brunt of harm from racialized crisis driven urbanization from the 1940s to the 1970s. Of the multiple racial projects occurring in Stockton during this period, we focus on those common between Flint and Stockton: urban renewal and freeway development from the 1950s to 1970s, "slum" clearance efforts between 1960 and 1970, and mortgage redlining.

Mabalon (2013) analyzes the fights over the Crosstown Freeway development and urban renewal in Stockton City from the 1950s to the 1970s. In the 1950s, California Highway Commissioners presented plans for Interstate-5 through Stockton's West End, including the Boggs Tract-Yosemite Subdivision that was redlined by the HOLC in the 1930s. Interstate-5 would then connect to the Crosstown Freeway and channel through other HOLC-redlined areas in downtown and Eastside Stockton to connect to State Route 99. While intended for "urban renewal"—after disinvestment from Stockton's devalued nonwhite urban spaces—these plans were predicated on crisis framing of those same spaces as "infested" and "cancer-like growth[s] ... that needed to be swept clean" (Mabalon 2013: 278). This context enabled a concerted effort for "slum clearance" by the Stockton City Council and its "urban blight committee," along with local real estate developers. In 1962, Stockton's Redevelopment Agency filed condemnation suits against property owners in the West End to clear the area. The Crosstown Freeway was finally finished in the 1990s, but had already caused considerable change to downtown Stockton and the West Side as it ultimately served as a wrecking ball through many of Stockton's low-income, Black, Latinx, and Filipinx neighborhoods that were previously redlined by the HOLC in the 1930s.

Racialized redlining and uneven development expanded throughout the Stockton metropolis from the 1940s to 1970s. FHA's discriminatory lending practices played a key role in these dynamics, contributing to (1) the disinvestment and devaluation of Stockton's predominantly nonwhite downtown, West End, Eastside, and Southside; and (2) the investment and valorization of Stockton's Northside, particularly around UOP and into the new exclusive suburban subdivision of Lincoln Village (Mabalon 2013). However, civil rights protests highlighted the importance of local and state lenders in contributing to redlining and uneven development throughout the Stockton metropolis. The California Department of Savings and Loan responded with hearings on annual "mortgage deficiency" rates from 1972 to 1976 (Hernandez 2009). In these hearings, mortgage deficient areas (MDAs) and their "low volume of loans" were equated with per capita loan volume at equal to or less than 25 percent of the county average in each respective year (CDSL 1977).

In Figure 3.4, we classify MDA tracts as such if they were mortgage deficient two or more years between 1972 and 1976. We find that 33 of 72 tracts (46 percent) in the Stockton metropolis were mortgage deficient during the 1970s (Figure 3.4, Map A). Their distribution in Stockton city nearly matched the fourth-grade and "hazardous" designations of the West End, Southside, and Eastside Stockton neighborhoods in the 1930s HOLC residential security survey (see Figure 3.2). However, Figure 3.4 displays the existence of MDAS in the neighboring city of Tracy, as well as in rural and suburban MDA tracts west, southwest, south, and southeast of Stockton. Figure 3.4, Map A, presents low housing values as of 1970 in relation to these MDAs. Elaborating on the visual associations between these tract conditions in Figure 3.4, Map A, we find that MDA tracts with valid housing value estimates (N=31) had an average of 81 percent of owner-occupied housing units that were valued at the tract-level median of $17,499 or less. In contrast, non-MDA tracts (N=37) had an average of 43 percent of owner-occupied housing units valued at $17,499 or less in 1970. The tract-level median housing values in the Stockton metropolis, their spatial distribution, and their association with redlining patterns from the 1930s to the 1970s appear to be consistent with comparable patterns we see in Flint (see Figure 3.3; Highsmith 2015).

As with Flint (Figure 3.3, Map B), Figure 3.4, Map B, shows that Stockton's Black homeowners with low-housing values were highly concentrated in particular marginalized neighborhoods (Boggs Tract, the Southside, and Eastside) at the close of this second crisis period. In addition, MDA tracts had, on average, 10 percent of the owner-occupied housing units held by Black homeowners and valued at or below $17,499. Non-MDA tracts had zero Black homeowners with property valued at or below that median level.

In contrast to Flint (Figure 3.3, Map C), the percent of owner-occupied housing units that were owned by Latinxs and equal to or below $17,499 were more prevalent and more spatially diffuse throughout the Stockton metropolis. Latinx low-housing values were also more prevalent in the metropolis's MDA tracts but also present in its non-MDA tracts. On average, 17 percent of the owner-occupied housing units were held by Latinx homeowners and were valued at or below $17,499. Non-MDA tracts had an average of 3 percent Latinx homeowners with property valued at or below $17,499.

The difference between Black and Latinx residential patterns and housing values reflects the "relational" way in which racial and spatial hierarchies manifest and rearticulate in Stockton overtime (Liévanos 2019a). Latinxs have a long history in Stockton dating back to before the city's incorporation (Liévanos

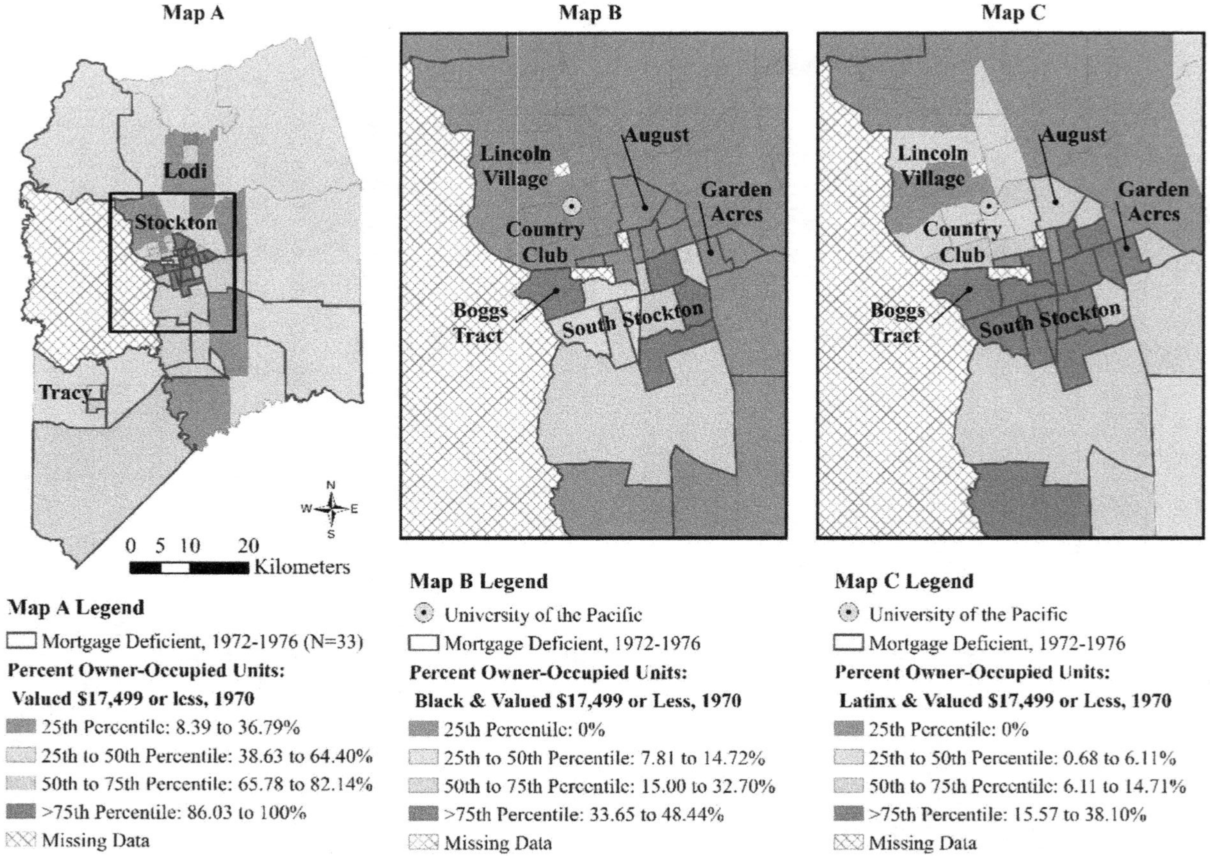

FIGURE 3.4 Redlining and percent owner-occupied housing units by value and Black and Latinx householders, 1970, in Stockton and vicinity

Note: Authors' original analysis of data from CDSL (1977) and Manson et al. (2017).

2019a). They are also highly diverse, including groups racialized as white and those mostly identified as "brown" and/or Mexican-American during this time (Ogbu 1974). It is likely that lighter-skinned Latinxs were able to cross the racial and spatial color lines to North Stockton. As Ogbu (1974: 42) elaborates, "most Mexican-Americans still live[d] in South Stockton," and "they constitute[d] the largest ethnic minority in the community but their political and economic power [was] quite small." By the late 1960s and into the 1970s, most Filipinxs lived in the Southside, and compromised similar economically and politically disadvantaged social locations as Black and Mexican Americans in Stockton (Mabalon 2013; Ogbu 1974). The degree of Black spatial confinement and devaluation likely reflects the legacy of anti-Black racism and exclusion characteristic of the national racial narrative of the time (Pulido 2006; Jackson 1985) and of Stockton's earlier real estate development (Liévanos 2019a). Further, as seen in Flint (Highsmith 2015), historical records suggest that state policy, discriminatory real estate practices, and white residents' general distaste for racial integration during this crisis period contributed to Black confinement and devaluation in Stockton (Fitzgerald 2001; Liévanos 2019a; Mabalon 2013; Meer and Freedman 1966; Ogbu 1974).

3.3 *Crisis Period 3: School Desegregation and Financial Instability, 1970s to 2010s*

Crisis driven urbanization prior to the 1970s across Flint and Stockton centered to varying degrees on the segregation and devaluation of Black and to a lesser extent, Mexican-American and Filipinx bodies and spaces. Those concatenated racialized crises were foundational for the fight over persistent school racial segregation and white resistance to desegregation in Flint and Stockton from the 1970s to 2010s. Building on the momentum of civil rights gains during the 1960s, school desegregation campaigns during the 1970s sought to break the "racial contract" (Mills 1997) of white domination in residential and learning environments. However, the civil rights battle for school racial desegregation devolved into debates over the efficacy of the "busing" experiment for school racial integration (Delmont 2016). Consensus seemed to emerge over the failure of that experiment.

Advocates of educational reform and "community education" endorsed segregation in order to build communal ties. Flint was site of a "40-year experiment" in which private philanthropy, spearheaded by the Mott Foundation, transformed the function of public schools through the community education program and its neighborhood-based system. Segregated schools and neighborhoods made one another, despite legal bans on both (Highsmith 2015: 54–77). Flint, and the creative ways in which white communities sought to avoid desegregation, is part of why regressive school movements and policies emerged in Michigan, from Pontiac mother and anti-busing activist Irene McCabe in the early 1970s, to the rise of privatization, philanthropy, and charter school "innovation" in the 1990s to the present.

Flint's school desegregation struggle followed federal officials' "discovery" of illegal school segregation in Flint and subsequent order for the Flint Board of Education to desegregate its schools in late 1975 (Highsmith 2015). Federal charges against Flint public schools fell "under three broad categories: discriminatory hiring and staff assignment policies, unequal educational opportunities for students, and racially biased pupil assignment procedures" (Highsmith 2015: 239). Those overseeing Flint's educational system dismissed the problem of school segregation in Flint with claims of "de facto" segregation in education caused by "housing patterns, economic factors and social mores once widely accepted" (quoted in Highsmith 2015: 230).

Meanwhile, the Stockton Unified School District (SUSD) attempted a voluntary busing program for its neighborhood-based segregated schools in 1968. However, it reached a larger scale after community and legal protests. California Rural Legal Assistance and Mexican American and Black students and parents filed a lawsuit to desegregate SUSD schools in 1970. In 1974, a judge declared that SUSD intentionally segregated schools, and another ordered the district to implement a school desegregation plan that included district-wide busing and magnet schools in 1978 (Tone 2004a). By 2002, a group of parents filed a lawsuit requesting a judge to declare the district racially integrated and end the desegregation plan. A 2003 judicial approval of the SUSD's desegregation phase out proposal followed with declaration that SUSD was now "unitary" (Tone 2004a).

School desegregation battles left a lasting impact on Flint (Highsmith 2015) and Stockton (Tone 2003; 2004a; 2004b). That influence is manifest in the degree of white flight and declining housing values during the 1970s to 2010s crisis period in both metropolitan areas. As shown in Figure 3.5, Map A, the tract-level percent of white residents in the north and west ends of the Flint Unified School District (FUSD)—as well as those in neighboring suburban settlement spaces northwest of the FUSD—changed considerably from 1970 to 2010. White composition dropped by 95-percentage points in some cases throughout the north and west portions of the FUSD. Figure 3.5, Map B, shows the corresponding change in aggregate housing values across census tracts within the Flint metropolis. The most drastic loss in aggregate housing values (-$140.91 to -$45.43 million) occurred within many of the North and West tracts that also experienced major decreases in their white population.

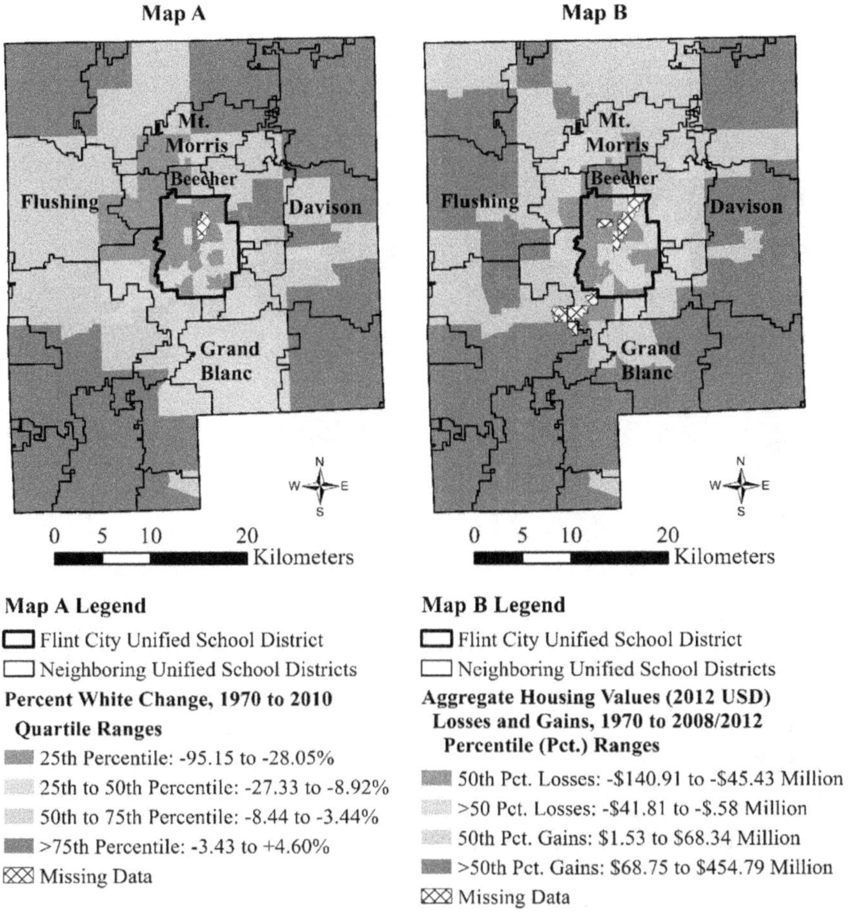

FIGURE 3.5 Unified school district boundaries and change in percent white, 1970 to 2010, and in housing values, 1970 to 2008–2012 (2012 USD) in the Flint metropolitan area
Note: Authors' original analysis of data from GeoLytics (2012) and Manson et al. (2017).

White flight and change in housing values operated differently in the Stockton metropolis during the 1970s to 2010s period. As shown in Figure 3.6, Map A, the tract-level percent of white residents in the north and east sides of the SUSD—as well as those southwest of Lodi, west of Tracy, and surrounding Manteca—declined between 77 and 45 percentage points from 1970 to 2010. Figure 3.6, Map B, displays the change in aggregate housing values across census tracts within the Stockton metropolis. In contrast to Flint, almost all of the

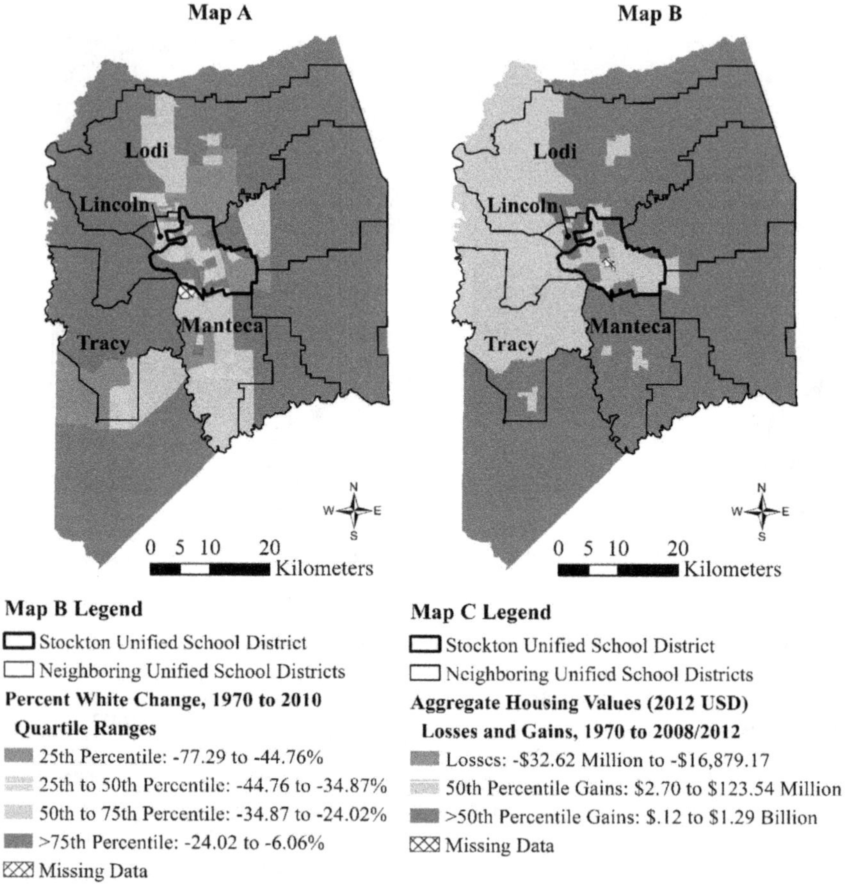

FIGURE 3.6 Unified school district boundaries and change in percent white, 1970 to 2010, and in housing values, 1970 to 2008–2012 (2012 USD) in the Stockton metropolitan area
Note: Authors' original analysis of data from GeoLytics (2012) and Manson et al. (2017).

census tracts within the Stockton metropolis *gained* aggregate housing values from 1970 to 2008–2012.[1]

---

1 In this discussion of housing values and similar data for the 2008–2012 period below, we use 5-year average estimates from the 2008–2012 American Community Survey (ACS) because that is where such data is now found given changes to the US Decennial Census after 2000. In using the ACS average estimates, we follow an emerging standard within the field of environmental health and inequality research to deal with ACS data reliability issues (Liévanos

3.4 *Race, Risk, and Resilience in the Current Water Crises*

Thus far, we have demonstrated how racialized crisis driven urbanization compares and contrasts between Flint and Stockton in ways that contribute to racial segregation and uneven development in both. We now examine how those histories contribute to uneven landscapes of risk and resilience with regard to the contemporary water crises affecting Flint and Stockton.

3.4.1 Flint

Flint residents were exposed to elevated levels of lead in their drinking water following the switch to the Flint River in April 25, 2014. The water drawn from the Flint River was more corrosive, incorrectly treated, and contributed to increased water lead levels (WLLs) and blood lead levels (BLLs) for many residents (Hanna-Attisha et al. 2016). Hanna-Attisha et al. (2016) found that census block groups in three contiguous city wards spanning west-to-east across the center of Flint had elevated BLLs and WLLs from before the drinking water source switch to after the switch. These three high-risk wards had significantly higher concentrations of Black residents, single-parent families, poverty, and low educational attainment than in other areas of Flint and the surrounding region. Figure 3.7 presents the high WLLs/BLLs wards that Hanna-Attisha et al. (2016) identified, along with other Flint wards, overlaid on census tract-level percent Black composition as of 2010. Figure 3.7 and the average 2010 racial composition indicators shown in Table 3.1 support patterns found in Hanna-Attisha et al. (2016) and related research (Sadler et al. 2017). Using a higher level of aggregation (i.e. census tract) in Figure 3.7 and Table 3.1, we see that wards with higher rates of lead exposure and poisoning during the FWC overlaid on "high-risk tracts" (N=14) with relatively high average concentrations of Black residents (70.49 percent) alongside a minority of white (27.25 percent), Latinx (3.07 percent), and Mexican-origin (2.21 percent) residents.

Table 3.1 also summarizes the average tract-level economic conditions and indicators of racialized uneven development in Flint by drinking water hazard exposure risk levels that we derive from Hanna-Attisha et al. (2016). As shown in Table 3.1, high-risk tracts differ from lower-risk tracts, and both types of at-risk tracts markedly differ from the unexposed tracts outside of Flint in their contemporary economic conditions and histories of racialized uneven development. On average, high- and lower-risk tracts had lower economic

2018a; 2019b) and use ACS estimates where the standard error of the estimate was less than half of the estimate. This medium-reliability level in the estimates minimizes measurement error from the ACS and small analytical samples that are associated with stricter reliability thresholds (Folch et al. 2016).

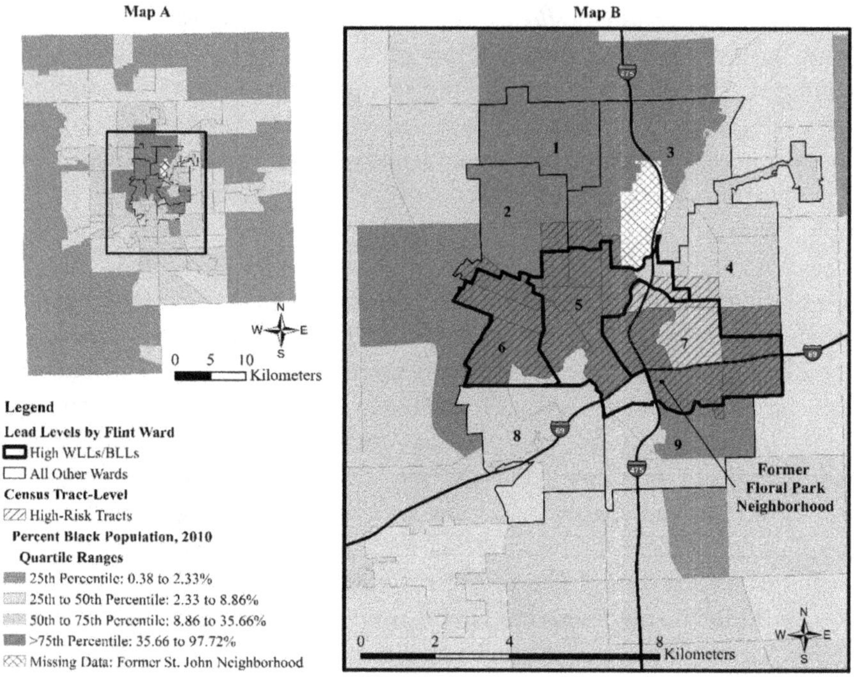

FIGURE 3.7 Ward-level estimated distribution of Water Lead Levels (WLLs) and Blood Lead Levels (BLLs) during the Flint Water Crisis and census tract-level percent Black population in 2010
Note: Authors' original analysis of documents and data from City of Flint (2018), Genesee County GIS Department (2012), Hanna-Attisha et al. (2016), and Manson et al. (2017).

resources (i.e., higher poverty rates and lower average aggregate housing values from 2008 to 2012), and they were primarily within the FUSD boundaries that are inscribed with a history of racialized struggles over school (de)segregation. However, Table 3.1 also shows that high-risk tracts had more of their area covered by moderately valued neighborhoods (i.e., HOLC second-grade appraisals), while lower-risk tracts had more of their area covered by lower HOLC grades (third and fourth grades) in 1937. Meanwhile, tracts outside of Flint were either not graded by the HOLC or had low average levels of their area covered by neighborhoods that received the HOLC's second-, third-, or fourth-grade designations.

Thus, racialized crisis driven urbanization following the New Deal involved the racialized devaluation of neighborhoods in or near Flint's Black spaces, as well as the working class suburbs outside of Flint. Racially exclusive suburbanization, urban renewal, and school desegregation followed and interacted with

TABLE 3.1 Average tract-level racial and economic conditions and racialized uneven development indicators by drinking water hazard exposure levels in the Flint metropolitan area

Variable	**Drinking water hazard exposure levels**		
	High-risk tract	**Lower-risk tract**	**Tracts outside of Flint**
Contemporary racial and economic conditions			
Racial composition, 2010			
Percent White	27.25	37.20	87.75
Percent Black	70.49	60.51	9.87
Percent Latinx	3.07	4.15	2.76
Percent Mexican origin	2.21	3.28	2.16
N	14	25	91
Average poverty levels, 2008–2012			
Percent with income below poverty	40.71	42.36	14.47
N	14	25	84
Average aggregate housing value, 2008–2012 (2012 USD in millions)	$40.61	$38.24	$142.45
N	13	23	90
Racialized uneven development			
Average HOLC grade coverage, 1937			
Percent tract assigned First/A grade	0.56	0.93	0.00
Percent tract assigned Second/B grade	28.02	4.14	0.03
Percent tract assigned Third/C grade	25.66	29.53	1.04
Percent tract assigned Fourth/D grade	14.65	16.98	4.9
Average percent tract intersection with Flint City unified school district	99.96	97.82	0.08
N	14	26	91

Note: "High-risk tracts" refer to the tracts with "50 percent areal containment" (Mohai and Saha 2007) in Flint wards with high WLLs and BLLs, while "lower-risk tracts" are those with 50 percent areal containment in other Flint wards that had lower levels of WLLs and BLLs as determined by Hanna-Attisha et al. (2016).

the "Fall of Flint" and its industrial base, which disproportionately affected its Black and working class residents (Highsmith 2015). These developments were foundational and productive in the consolidation of racial capitalism, as manifest in the devaluation and poisoning of Flint and its Black and diverse bodies and neighborhoods, and the racist and neoliberal response to the FWC.

3.4.2 Stockton

The City of Stockton spent a few years leading up to the commencement of its 2003 water privatization deal with the transnational corporation, OMI-Thames, studying the costs and benefits to various "capital improvements and asset management" options for its wastewater, water, and stormwater services that were normally held by the Stockton Municipal Utilities Department (SMUD). On February 19, 2003, Stockton's market-oriented, Republican mayor, Gary Podesto, called to order a city council meeting in which he and the six elected members of the council, representing districts throughout the city, would deliberate and vote on a resolution. The resolution was to approve (1) the wastewater, water, and stormwater service contract in the amount of $600 million over 20 years with OMI-Thames, and (2) a notice that the contract was exempt from review under procedures specified in the California Environmental Quality Act (CEQA).

Following staff reports and public comment, including from supporters and from the opposing anti-privatization coalition, Mayor Podesto and the six council members deliberated over the resolution. Stockton's city council initially had a 3-3 split vote regarding the privatization contract. However, Stockton's neoliberal and conservative mayor who was an active and visible supporter of the contract ultimately cast the decisive vote in favor of water privatization. Despite dissent and ambivalence from some council members, this vote and its outcome ultimately usurped an anti-privatization ballot initiative that was approved by city residents and activists soon after (Robinson 2013). It was not until 2008 that a successful lawsuit by the anti-privatization coalition halted the contract. The legal basis of their success rested in Stockton City Council's resolution to shield the privatization contract from systematic scrutiny through the environmental impact report mechanism of CEQA.

The anti-privatization coalition members, particularly those associated with the Concerned Citizens Coalition of Stockton, made clear the environmental stakes of the water privatization contract in the first phase of its implementation. In their December 2004 "Annual Service Contract Compliance Review," they attributed increasing water rates, unfulfilled customer service requests, staffing and personnel issues, use of unaccounted water, maintenance backlogs, and unauthorized water pollution by OMI to the water privatization deal

(Public Citizen 2005: 12). Robinson (2013: 4) summarizes the disastrous consequences of Stockton's water privatization initiative, noting that this five year water privatization experiment was "devastating, with major consequences for water treatment and delivery, including job losses at the [city] treatment plant, increased water rates, and lack of investment in … facility upgrades."

A subsequent Grand Jury investigation in 2014–2015 uncovered lasting effects that the privatization failure had on SMUD, who returned to managing Stockton's wastewater, water, and stormwater service after the OMI-Thames contract ended. The Grand Jury report noted the important role that the 2003–2008 water privatization had in degrading SMUD s financial conditions, institutional knowledge, and water service provision—independently from the Great Recession and Stockton's 2012 bankruptcy filing (San Joaquin County Grand Jury 2015).

Recent news reports show how Stockton grappled with local, regional, and statewide water quality and supply concerns while recovering from water privatization. As we note in the introduction to this chapter, these water quality concerns recently manifested in Stockton's racially and economically privileged Northside over a proposed water treatment switch. But, that is just part of the water quality concerns in Stockton and its surrounding Delta region. Concerns over local and regional drinking water supplies are linked to a number of federal and statewide water policy arenas. Some policies seek to ensure that the Delta region's extensive water resources support urban water users and agricultural interests throughout the state (Shilling et al. 2009; Sze et al. 2009). Other policies have as their goal improving water quality in the region's vast complex of polluted and federally designated, "impaired" water bodies for human consumption and endangered species protection (Liévanos 2017; 2018b).

In this context, local and regional water quality experts and advocates see similarities between Flint and Stockton loosely around the themes of drawing on distrust in government officials, " 'degraded bodies of water' for at least some of their drinking water supplies," using questionable water disinfectants, and on occasions violating federal water quality standards (Bagalayos 2016). However, they draw sharp distinctions between Stockton and Flint:

> Stockton isn't Flint. Because of both the privatization fiasco and ongoing Delta water issues, Stockton has a vibrant water watch-dog community that has decades of science-based knowledge and advocacy under its belt. Bill Loyko, chairman of the citizen Water Advisory Group, put it this way: "Where else do you have so many groups looking out for the water quality of their region?"
>
> BAGALAYOS 2016

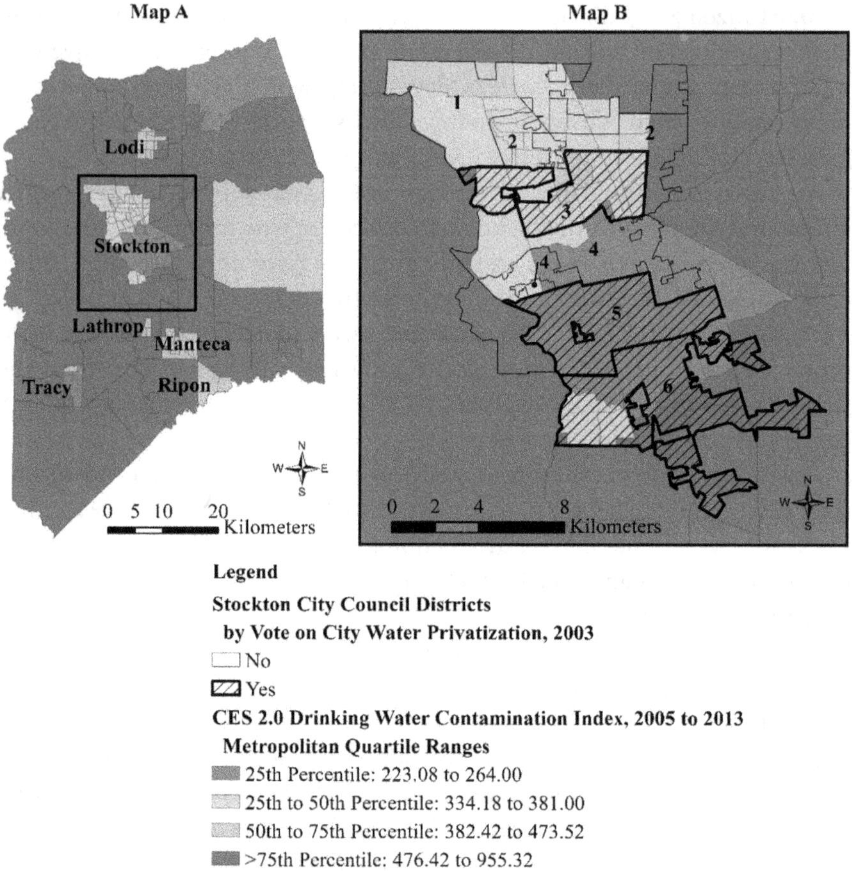

FIGURE 3.8 Stockton City Council votes on 2003 water privatization initiative and metropolitan quartile rankings of CalEnviroScreen (CES) 2.0 Drinking Water Contamination Index
Note: Authors' original analysis of data from Faust et al. (2014), City of Stockton (2019), and Manson et al. (2017).

Figure 3.8 and Table 3.2 shed light on the nature of Stockton's current water crisis and its relation to racialized crisis driven urbanization. In Figure 3.8 and Table 3.2, we use a tract-level drinking water contamination index (DWCI) in version 2 of the California Community Environmental Health Screening Tool, CalEnviroScreen. In summary, this indicator represents the average water contaminant concentrations or violation index (i.e., the sum of violations of the Maximum Contamination Level for any chemical contaminant and Total Coliform rule) from one compliance cycle of 2005 to 2013 for drinking water systems in California (Faust et al. 2014; Liévanos 2018a). Figure 3.8 overlays the

TABLE 3.2 Average tract-level racial and economic conditions, racialized uneven development indicators, and incorporation in Stockton City Council districts with 2003 water privatization vote by drinking water hazard exposure levels in the Stockton metropolitan area

Variable	Drinking water hazard exposures: quartiles of CalEnviroScreen 2.0 Drinking Water Contamination Index (DWCI)			
	High-risk tract	High-medium-risk tract	Medium-low-risk tract	Low-risk tract
Contemporary racial and economic conditions				
Racial composition, 2010				
Percent White	63.00	66.15	44.88	46.28
Percent Black	5.17	4.62	14.82	10.25
Percent Latinx	36.32	37.46	31.2	54.16
Percent Mexican origin	31.88	32.42	26.62	49.26
N	32	32	32	43
Average poverty levels, 2008–2012				
Percent with income below poverty	14.92	14.82	19.09	27.93
N	29	30	32	42
Average aggregate housing value, 2008–2012 (2012 USD in millions)	$423.66	$233.18	$203.35	$145.44
N	32	32	32	41
Racialized uneven development				
Average HOLC grade coverage, 1937				
Percent tract assigned First/A grade	0.00	0.00	0.00	1.81
Percent tract assigned Second/B grade	0.00	0.00	0.00	6.39
Percent tract assigned Third/C grade	0.00	0.00	0.00	6.22
Percent tract assigned Fourth/D grade	0.00	0.00	0.00	7.91

TABLE 3.2 Average tract-level racial and economic conditions, racialized uneven development indicators, and incorporation in Stockton City Council districts with 2003 water privatization vote by drinking water hazard exposure levels in the Stockton metropolitan area (*cont.*)

Variable	Drinking water hazard exposures: quartiles of CalEnviroScreen 2.0 Drinking Water Contamination Index (DWCI)			
	High-risk tract	High-medium-risk tract	Medium-low-risk tract	Low-risk tract
Average percent tract intersection with mortgage deficient areas, 1970	38.10	27.75	6.40	59.58
Average percent tract intersection with Stockton unified school district	6.30	3.39	33.13	73.89
Spatial distribution of water privatization vote				
Average percent intersection with Stockton City Council district by 2003 water privatization vote				
Percent tract in "No"-vote district	1.00	2.86	50.82	17.29
Percent tract in "Yes"-vote district	3.25	4.74	38.92	40.42
N	32	32	32	43

Note: "High-risk tracts" refer to tracts with > 75 percentile in the DWCI; "high-medium-risk tracts" refer to tracts in the 75-to-50 percentile range in the DWCI; "medium-low-risk tracts" refer to tracts in the 50-to-25 percentile range in the DWCI; "low-risk tracts" refer to tracts in the 25 percentile in the DWCI.

split "Yes" and "No" votes by the Stockton City Council members across the six council districts in Stockton on the drinking water contamination index for census tracts in the Stockton metropolis.[2]

2 Figure 3.8 displays current Stockton City council districts from City of Stockton (2019) to approximate the city council district boundaries at the time of the 2003 water privatization

Figure 3.8 provides two initial takeaways regarding the nature of the current water crisis in Stockton. First, the "Yes" votes for Stockton's 2003 water privatization came from two districts (5 and 6), which represent the historically racially segregated and marginalized West End, Southside, and Eastside, as well as another (District 3) in Stockton's Northside. The "No" votes for water privatization came from Stockton's Northside (Districts 1 and 2), as well as in Northcentral Stockton (District 4). Figure 3.8 also displays patterns that run counter to what we may expect in the crisis driven urbanization framework (Gotham and Greenberg 2014). That is, Stockton's Southside (and Northcentral) neighborhoods have some of the *best* water quality in the metropolis. In contrast, *lower* water quality is found throughout the rural spaces of the metropolis, as well as in the Stockton's racially and economically privileged Northside neighborhoods.

Table 3.2 elaborates these unexpected patterns. As shown in the table, high- and medium-high-risk tracts stand out for their average elevated concentrations of whites in 2010 and lower poverty levels and higher aggregate housing values from 2008 to 2012. The medium-low-risk tracts are those that predominantly reside in Stockton's Northside and find themselves being compared in public debate to the lead-poisoned neighborhoods of Flint. While they do not have similar drinking water hazard risks as seen in Flint, those tracts have the highest average share of Black residents in the Stockton metropolis. Table 3.2 also shows that only tracts in the low-risk percentile for the DWCI were appraised by the HOLC and most likely received fourth, third, and second grades in those 1930s appraisals. Likewise, the low-risk tracts had, on average, the greatest extent of their area covered by 1970 MDA tracts, the SUSD boundaries, and the boundaries of Stockton City Council districts that voted for Stockton's 2003 water privatization. In contrast, the high-risk tracts had, on average, relatively moderate levels of their area covered by 1970 MDA tracts, and low coverage by SUSD boundaries and the boundaries of Stockton City Council districts that voted for Stockton's 2003 water privatization. They also had the highest average increases in aggregate housing value from 1970 to 2008–2012. Whereas, the medium-low-risk tracts, predominantly located in Stockton's Northside, had the greatest share of their area covered by Stockton City Council Districts that voted "No" on Stockton's water privatization.

vote. Our preliminary comparison of City of Stockton (2019) council district boundaries and archived boundaries as of 2004 (Internet Archive 2019) indicate only slight changes that are inconsequential for the preliminary analysis we provide in this chapter.

4 Conclusion

In this chapter, we formulated a model of racialized crisis driven urbanization using as the fulcrum of our analysis the historical production of racialized, segregated, and differentially valued spaces in Flint and Stockton, which gave rise to the recent water crises in both cities. Too often, journalists and the general public use comparison to emphasize difference in order to make a particular situation seem relatively better or worse, or for political purposes. "Stockton isn't Flint" says one account (Bagalayos 2016), while another calls the regional home of Stockton—the SJV and its broader Central Valley—"the Flint of California" (Brown 2016). The politics of comparison are contested—in part because historians and policy analysts point to the endless differentiations between places, pollution, and politics. Yet, we find that comparative, interdisciplinary work is generative in part because comparison situates multiple crises and factors with one another. Urban crises are themselves fraught and interconnected, from water/blood lead levels and water contamination, to housing and school desegregation. To separate each "issue" or "problem" from one another is to deny the complexities in which "crises" are lived and racial capitalism is manifest. We see these dynamics unfold in the production and poisoning of communities of the poor and people of color in cases like Flint, or unexpectedly in Stockton's racially and economically privileged communities whose status as such was built through race- and class-based systems of devaluation and capital accumulation.

Consistent with previous research, we find that the FWC exacerbated previous racial and spatial inequalities in Flint by concentrating toxic water lead exposures in majority poor and Black neighborhoods. Our novel contribution is that we also find those elevated exposures occurred in those same neighborhoods, which had been moderately valued in Flint's real estate market during the Depression recovery of the 1930s but that were systematically devalued through racist strategies of capital accumulation and crisis driven urbanization in subsequent years. Similar to Flint, racist and racialized crisis driven urbanization created the conditions for Stockton's water privatization and recent drinking water quality concerns. That is, racialized crisis driven urbanization devalued Stockton's nonwhite urban core, particularly its West End, Southside, and Eastside. These dynamics subsequently legitimized a "cost-saving" switch—akin to what we saw in Flint—to privatize Stockton's water service provision.

Stockton contrasts with Flint, however, in that elevated drinking water hazard levels have recently bypassed Stockton's historically devalued and predominantly Black and Latinx neighborhoods for the historically white and elite North Stockton neighborhoods and rural and unincorporated spaces outside of Stockton. Stockton's "vibrant water watch-dog community" who claim "Stockton Isn't Flint" (Bagalayos 2016) come from these relatively privileged, white spaces, and they actively distance themselves and Stockton's water crisis from the FWC. These material and discursive dynamics speak to two important racialized and classed differences between Stockton and Flint, aside from Flint's far greater devastating racialized effects of deindustrialization. First, Stockton's privileged water watchdogs ignore the multi-scalar and cross-racial movements for community resilience against Flint's racist, neoliberal, and undemocratic order (Carrera et al. 2019; Pauli 2019). Second, the Stockton case illustrates the "boomerang" potential of "toxic" racism (Pellow 2007), whereby toxic risk accumulates among the racially marginalized but can "recoil" (Beck 2005 [1986]) to harm those atop the racial and spatial hierarchy. This boomerang effect appears to manifest in Stockton, but a resilient organizational infrastructure is in place to combat drinking water quality concerns in Stockton's affected (and privileged) neighborhoods. Yet, those neighborhoods are changing. Supplemental analyses indicate that Stockton's high-risk tracts became, on average, more Latinx (+17.52 percentage points), particularly more Mexican-origin (+24.30 percentage points), Black (+2.16 percentage points), and poor (+1.03 percentage points) over the last 40–50 years. A question thus remains as to whether Stockton will continue to represent the boomerang effect of toxic racism through the racial and spatial order in the future given these conditions.

Stockton and Flint are unique in their particular forms. They are also indelibly connected, which we illuminate through our new model of racialized crisis driven urbanization. We flesh out this comparative and interdisciplinary model vis-à-vis theories of urban crisis within sociology, racial theory and critical environmental justice studies. Using multiple methods—qualitative, semi-quantitative, and historical—we can get a stronger grasp on how crisis driven urbanization is shaped by racial projects of (re)organizing race and space in order to consolidate racial capitalism (Robinson 2000 [1983]).

As we illustrate in our analysis, the HOLC maps reflected the institutionalization of residential landscapes that conflated race and space and contained industrial hazards in "low-grade" neighborhoods. Then, economic value was consolidated in a hierarchical and historical order of "differential value." Civil rights initiatives to desegregate housing and schools re-triggered racialized discourses of "crisis" and environmental contagion that were reinscribed in patterns that reflect racially differentiated landscapes of risk in water crises (i.e., blood/water lead levels in Flint and drinking water contamination in Stockton). Our model of racialized crisis driven urbanization situates contemporary water crisis to show patterns over time, which manifest differentially in regional and racial contexts. Crisis generates further crises, dependent on racialized ideologies, past decisions, and institutional arrangements that shape the material realities of unfolding conflicts over race and space and their attendant environmental health vulnerabilities and impacts. The expansion of privatization and neoliberal regulatory regimes, and the erosion of formal democracy enabled capital to control discursive and material landscapes in both Flint and Stockton. In Flint, racialized and already politically vulnerable residents are made to bear the risk of environmental pollution with its concomitant health impacts (Grimmer 2017). In Stockton, the boomerang of toxic racism has sprung back upon historically white and elite neighborhoods that are becoming racially diverse and poorer.

Despite the insights and contributions afforded by our study, we note that it has important limitations. First, our model is limited, in that we do not show clear causal connections between racialized crisis driven urbanization and contemporary water crisis formation in Flint and Stockton. Our analysis is also limited in its attention to how social movements and civil rights organizations continually press and push against the hegemonic discourses of their particular historical times and in their regional and political contexts. We hope to investigate such dynamics in the future through comparative work on water injustice in Flint and Stockton—in both historical and contemporary manifestations. In the meantime, we maintain that our model of racialized crisis driven urbanization allows for productive comparisons between and beyond Flint and Stockton to the myriad of crisis cities in the waiting (Gotham and Greenberg 2014) and their racialized and devalued neighborhoods that occupy particularly vulnerable positionalities in the uneven landscape of risk and resilience of the metropolis.

References

Bacon, J.M. (2019). "Settler Colonialism as Eco-Social Structure and the Production of Colonial Ecological Violence." *Environmental Sociology* 5(1): 59–69.

Bagalayos, D. (2016). "Stockton Isn't Flint: Keeping Drinking Water Safe in the Delta." *KCET Redefine.* February 9, 2016. Available at: https://www.kcet.org/ redefine/stockton-isnt-flint-keeping-drinking-water-safe-in-the-delta (consulted May 6, 2019).

Balazs, C., Morello-Frosch, R., Hubbard, A., and Ray, I. (2011). "Social Disparities in Nitrate-Contaminated Drinking Water in California's San Joaquin Valley." *Environmental Health Perspectives* 119(9): 1272–1278.

Balazs, C., Morello-Frosch, R.., Hubbard, A., and Ray, I. (2012). "Environmental Justice Implications of Arsenic Contamination in California's San Joaquin Valley:

A Cross-Sectional, Cluster-Design Examining Exposure and Compliance in Community Drinking Water Systems." *Environmental Health* 11(1): 84. https://doi.org/10.1186/1476-069X-11-84.

Balazs, C. and Ray, I. (2014). "The Drinking Water Disparities Framework: On the Origins and Persistence of Inequities in Exposure." *American Journal of Public Health* 104(4): 603–611.

Beck, U. (2005 [1986]). *Risk Society: Towards a New Modernity*. Thousand Oaks, CA: Sage.

Beck, U. (1995). *Ecological Enlightenment: Essays on the Politics of the Risk Society*. New York, NY: Humanities Press.

Beck, U. (2006). "Living in the World Risk Society." *Economy and Society* 35(3): 329–345.

Benz, T.A. (2019). "Toxic Cities: Neoliberalism and Environmental Racism in Flint and Detroit Michigan." *Critical Sociology* 45(1): 49–62.

Biggs, D., Biggs, R., Dakos, V., Scholes, R.J., and Schoon, M. (2011). "Are We Entering an Era of Concatenated Global Crises?" *Ecology and Society* 16(2): 27.

Bonilla-Silva, E. (1997). "Rethinking Racism: Toward a Structural Interpretation." *American Sociological Review* 62(3): 465–480.

Brown, P.L. (2016). "The Flint of California." *Politico*. May 25, 2016. Available at: https://www.politico.com/agenda/story/2016/05/is-clean-drinking-water-a-right-000129 (consulted September 11, 2018).

Carrera, J.S., Key, K., Bailey, S., Hamm, J.A., Cuthbertson, C.A., Lewis, E.Y., Woolford, S.J., DeLoney, E.H., Greene-Moton, E., Wallace, K., Robinson, D.E., Byers, I., Piechowski, P., Evans, L., McKay, A., Vereen, D., Sparks, A., and Calhoun, K. (2019). "Community Science as a Pathway for Resilience in Response to a Public Health Crisis in Flint, Michigan." *Social Sciences* 8(3): 94. https://doi.org/10.3390/socsci8030094.

CDSL. (1977). *Fair Lending Report No. 1, Volume II*. Sacramento, CA: California Department of Savings and Loan.

Charles, C.Z. (2006). *Won't You Be My Neighbor? Race, Class, and Residence in Los Angeles*. New York, NY: Russell Sage Foundation.

Cheng, W. (2013). *The Changs Next Door to the Díazes: Remapping Race in Suburban California*. Minneapolis, MN: University of Minnesota Press.

City of Flint. (2018). "Ward Boundaries." Available at: https://www.cityofflint.com/wp-content/uploads/COFWard%20Boundariesreduced.pdf (consulted April 10, 2018).

City of Stockton. (2019). "Stockton City Council Districts." Stockton, CA: City of Stockton. Available at: http://www.stocktongov.com/files/CityCouncilDistricts.zip (consulted May 31, 2019).

Delmont, M.F. (2016). *Why Busing Failed: Race, Media, and the National Resistance to School Desegregation*. Berkeley, CA: University of California Press.

Du Bois, W.E.B. (1996 [1899]). *The Philadelphia Negro: A Social Study*. Philadelphia, pa: University of Pennsylvania Press.

Du Bois, W.E.B. (1999 [1920]). *Darkwater: Voices from Within the Veil.* New York, NY: Dover Publications.

English, P., Richardson, M., Morello-Frosch, R., Pastor, M., Sadd, J., King, G., Jesdale, W., and Jerrett, M. (2013). "Racial and Income Disparities in Relation to a Proposed Climate Change Vulnerability Screening Method for California." *International Journal of Climate Change: Impacts and Responses* 4(2): 1–18. https://doi.org/10.18848/1835-7156/CGP/v04i02/37156.

Fasenfest, D. (2019). "A Neoliberal Response to an Urban Crisis: Emergency Management in Flint, MI." *Critical Sociology* 45(1): 33–47.

Faust, J., August, L., Alexeeff, G., Bangia, K., Cendak, R., Cheung-Sutton, E., Cushing, L., Galaviz, V., Kadir, T., Leichty, J., Milanes, C., Randles, K., Slocombe, A., Welling, R., Wieland, W., and Zeise, L. (2014). *California Communities Environmental Health Screening Tool, Version 2.0 (CalEnviroScreen 2.0): Guidance and Screening Tool.* Sacramento, CA: Office of Environmental Health Hazard Assessment.

Fitzgerald, M. (2001). "Deep Roots of Stockton Segregation." *The Record.* April 27. 2001. Available at: http://www.recordnet.com (consulted October 10, 2012).

Folch, D.C., Arribas-Bel, D., Koschinsky, J., and Spielman, S.E. (2016). "Spatial Variation in the Quality of American Community Survey Estimates." *Demography* 53(5): 1535–1554.

Foley, N. (1997). *The White Scourge: Mexicans, Blacks, and Poor Whites in Texas Cotton Culture.* Berkeley, CA: University of California Press.

Fraser, N. (2018). "Roepke Lecture in Economic Geography—From Exploitation to Expropriation: Historic Geographies of Racialized Capitalism." *Economic Geography* 94(1): 1–17.

Genesee County GIS Department. (2012). "City of Flint Wards and Precincts." Available at: https://www.cityofflint.com/wad-map/ (consulted April 10, 2018).

GeoLytics. (2012). "Neighborhood Change Database (NCDB) 1970-2010." New Brunswick, NJ: GeoLytics, Inc.

Gilmore, R. (2007). *Golden Gulag: Prisons, Surplus, Crisis, and Opposition in Globalizing California.* Berkeley, CA: University of California Press.

Gotham, K.F. (2002). *Race, Real Estate, and Uneven Development: The Kansas City Experience, 1900-2000.* Albany, NY: State University of New York Press.

Gotham, K.F. and Greenberg, M. (2014). *Crisis Cities: Disaster and Redevelopment in New York and New Orleans.* New York, NY: Oxford University Press.

Gottdiener, M. and Hutchison, R. (2006). *The New Urban Sociology.* Boulder, CO: Westview Press.

Grimmer, C. (2017). "Racial Microbiopolitics: Flint Lead Poisoning, Detroit Water Shut Offs, and the "Matter" of Enfleshment." *The Comparatist* 41: 19–40.

Hanna-Attisha, M., LaChance, J., Sadler, R.C., and Schnepp, A.C. (2016). "Elevated Blood Lead Levels in Children Associated with the Flint Drinking Water Crisis: A Spatial

Analysis of Risk and Public Health Responses." *American Journal of Public Health* 106(2): 283–290.

Harrison, J.L. (2011). *Pesticide Drift and the Pursuit of Environmental Justice*. Cambridge, MA: Massachusetts Institute of Technology Press.

Hernandez, J. (2009). "Redlining Revisited: Mortgage Lending Patterns in Sacramento 1930-2004." *International Journal of Urban and Regional Research* 33(2): 291–313.

Hillier, A.E. (2003). "Redlining and the Home Owners' Loan Corporation." *Journal of Urban History* 29(4): 394–420.

Hillier, A.E. (2005). "Residential Security Maps and Neighborhood Appraisals: The Home Owner's Loan Corporation and the Case of Philadelphia." *Social Science History* 29(2): 207–233.

Highsmith, A.R. (2015). *Demolition Means Progress: Flint, Michigan, and the Fate of the American Metropolis*. Chicago, IL: University of Chicago Press.

Huang, G. and London, J.K. (2012). "Cumulative Environmental Vulnerability and Environmental Justice in California's San Joaquin Valley." *International Journal of Environmental Research and Public Health* 9(5): 1593–1608. https://doi.org/10.3390/ijerph9051593.

Immergluck, D. (2009). *Foreclosed: High-Risk Lending, Deregulation, and the Undermining of America's Mortgage Market*. Ithaca, NY: Cornell University Press.

Internet Archive. (2019). "Stockton City Council Districts, 14 October, 2004." Available at: https://web.archive.org/web/20041014180510if_/http://www.stocktongov.com:80/clerk/graphics/DistrictMaps/dist-map.GIF (consulted June 3, 2019).

Jackson, K. (1985). *Crabgrass Frontier: The Suburbanization of the United States*. New York, NY: Oxford University Press.

Lefebvre, H. (1991 [1974]). *The Production of Space*. Oxford: Blackwell.

Liévanos, R.S. (2017). "Sociospatial Dimensions of Water Injustice: The Distribution of Surface Water Toxic Releases in California's Bay-Delta." *Sociological Perspectives* 60(3): 575–599.

Liévanos, R.S. (2018a). "Retooling CalEnviroScreen: Cumulative Pollution Burden and Race-Based Environmental Health Vulnerabilities in California." *International Journal of Environmental Research and Public Health* 15(4): 762. https://doi.org/10.3390/ijerph15040762.

Liévanos, R.S. (2018b). "Impaired Water Hazard Zones: Mapping Intersecting Environmental Health Vulnerabilities and Polluter Disproportionality." *ISPRS International Journal of Geo-Information* 7(11): 433. https://doi.org/10.3390/ijgi7110433.

Liévanos, R.S. (2019a). "Green, Blue, Yellow, and Red: The Relational Racialization of Space in the Stockton Metropolitan Area." In: Molina, N., HoSang, D.M., and Gutiérrez, R.A. (eds.). *Relational Formations of Race: Theory, Method and Practice*, pp. 224–253. Berkeley, CA: University of California Press.

Liévanos, R.S. (2019b). "Air-Toxic Clusters Revisited: Intersectional Environmental Inequalities and Indigenous Deprivation in the U.S. Environmental Protection Agency Regions." *Race and Social Problems* 11(2): 161–184.

Liévanos, R.S., London, J.K., and Sze, J. (2011). "Uneven Transformations and Environmental Justice: Regulatory Science, Street Science, and Pesticide Regulation in California." In: Ottinger, G. and Cohen, B.R. (eds.). *Technoscience and Environmental Justice: Expert Cultures in a Grassroots Movement*, pp. 201–228. Cambridge, MA: Massachusetts Institute of Technology Press.

Light, J.S. (2009). *The Nature of Cities: Ecological Visions and the American Urban Professions, 1920-1960*. Baltimore, MD: Johns Hopkins University.

Lipsitz, G. (2011). *How Racism Takes Place*. Philadelphia, pa: Temple University Press.

Logan, J. and Molotch, H. (2007 [1987]) *Urban Fortunes: The Political Economy of Place*. Berkeley, CA: University of California Press.

London, J.K. (2019). "A Water Justice Victory." *Region Matters*. July 9. Available at: https://regionalchange.ucdavis.edu/blog/water-justice-victory (consulted July 9, 2019).

London, J., Fencl, A., Watterson, S., Jarin, J., Aranda, A., King, A., Pannu, C., Seaton, P., Firestone, L., Dawson, M., and Nguyen, P. (2018). *The Struggle for Water Justice in California's San Joaquin Valley: A Focus on Disadvantaged Unincorporated Communities*. Davis, CA: University of California Davis Center for Regional Change.

London, J.K., Sze, J., and Liévanos, R.S. (2008). "Problems, Promise, Progress, and Perils: Critical Reflections on Environmental Justice Policy Implementation in California." *UCLA Journal of Environmental Law and Policy* 26(2): 255–289. https://escholarship.org/uc/item/2hb823dd.

Mabalon, D.B. (2013). *Little Manila Is in the Heart: The Making of the Filipina/o American Community in Stockton, California*. Durham, NC: Duke University Press.

Manson, S., Schroeder, J., Van Riper, D., and Ruggles, S. (2017). "IPUMS National Historical Geographic Information Systems: Version 12.0 [Database]." Minneapolis, MN: University of Minnesota. http://doi.org/10.18128/D050.V12.0.

Márquez, J.R. (2014). *Black-Brown Solidarity: Racial Politics in the New Gulf South*. Austin, TX: University of Texas Press.

Marciano, R., Goldberg, D.T., and Hou, C.Y. (2010). "T-RACES: A Testbed for the Redlining Archives of California's Exclusionary Spaces." Chapel Hill, NC: The SALT Group. Available at: http://salt.unc.edu/T-RACES (consulted July 20, 2010).

Massey, D.S., and Denton, N.A. (1993). *American Apartheid: Segregation and the Making of the Underclass*. Cambridge, MA: Harvard University Press.

Meer, B. and Freedman, E. (1966). "The Impact of Negro Neighbors on White Home Owners." *Social Forces* 45(1): 11–19.

MCRC. (2017). *The Flint Water Crisis: Systemic Racism through the Lens of Flint*. Lansing, MI: Michigan Department of Civil Rights, Michigan Civil Rights Commission.

Mills, C.W. (1997). *The Racial Contract.* Ithaca, NY: Cornell University Press.

Mills, C.W. (2001). "Black Trash." In: Westra, L. and Lawson, B.E. (eds.). *Faces of Environmental Racism: Confronting Issues of Global Justice*, pp. 73–91. New York, NY: Roman & Littlefield Publishers.

Mohai, P. and Saha, R. (2007). "Racial Inequality in the Distribution of Hazardous Waste: A National-level Reassessment." *Social Problems* 54(3): 343–370.

Nelson, R.K., Winling, L., Marciano, R., Connoly, N., et al. (2017). "Mapping Inequality." In: Nelson, R.K. and Ayers, E.L. (eds.). *American Panorama.* Available at: https://dsl.richmond.edu/panorama/redlining/#loc=11/43.0175/-83.6920&opacity=0.8&city=-flint-mi (consulted October 27, 2017).

Norgaard, K.M., Reed, R., and Bacon, J.M. (2018). "How Environmental Decline Restructures Indigenous Gender Practices: What Happens to Karuk Masculinity When There Are No Fish?" *Sociology of Race and Ethnicity* 4(1): 98–113.

Ogbu, J.U. (1974). *The Next Generation: An Ethnography of Education in an Urban Neighborhood.* New York, NY: Academic Press.

Omi, M. and Winant, H. (1994). *Racial Formation in the United States: From the 1960's to the 1990's.* 2nd ed. New York, NY: Routledge.

Pannu, C. (2012). "Drinking Water and Exclusion: A Case Study from California's Central Valley." *California Law Review* 100(1): 223–268.

Park, L.S.H. and Pellow, D.N. (2011). *The Slums of Aspen: Immigrants vs. The Environment in America's Eden.* New York, NY: New York University Press.

Pauli, B.J. (2019). *Flint Fights Back: Environmental Justice and Democracy in the Flint Water Crisis.* Cambridge, MA: Massachusetts Institute of Technology Press.

Pellow, D.N. (2007). *Resisting Global Toxics: Transnational Movements for Environmental Justice.* Cambridge, MA: Massachusetts Institute of Technology Press.

Pellow, D.N. (2016). "Toward a Critical Environmental Justice Studies: Black Lives Matter as an Environmental Justice Challenge." *Du Bois Review* 13(2): 221–236.

Pellow, D.N. (2018). *What is Critical Environmental Justice?* Medford, MA: Polity Press.

Picou, J.S. and Marshall, B.K. (2007). "Introduction: Katrina as Paradigm Shift: Reflections on Disaster Research in the Twenty-First Century." In: Brunsma, D.L., Overfelt, D., and J. Steven Picou, J.S. (eds.). *The Sociology of Katrina: Perspectives on a Modern Catastrophe*, pp. 1–20. New York, NY: Rowman & Littlefield Publishers.

Public Citizen. (2005). *Waves of Regret: What Some Cities Have Learned and Other Cities Should Know About Water Privatization Fiascos in the United States.* Oakland, CA: Public Citizen.

Pulido, L. (2000). "Rethinking Environmental Racism: White Privilege and Urban Development in Southern California." *Annals of the American Association Geographers* 90(1): 12–40.

Pulido, L. (2006). *Black, Brown, Yellow, and Left: Radical Activism in Los Angeles.* Berkeley, CA: University of California Press.

Pulido, L. (2015). "Geographies of Race and Ethnicity I: White Supremacy vs. White Privilege in Environmental Racism Research." *Progress in Human Geography* 39(6): 809–817.

Pulido, L. (2016). "Flint, Environmental Racism, and Racial Capitalism." *Capitalism Nature Socialism* 27(3): 1–16.

Pulido, L. (2017). "Geographies of Race and Ethnicity II: Environmental Racism, Racial Capitalism and State-Sanctioned Violence." *Progress in Human Geography* 41(4): 524–533.

Pulido, L. and De Lara, J. (2018). "Reimagining 'Justice' in Environmental Justice: Radical Ecologies, Decolonial Thought, and the Black Radical Tradition." *Environment and Planning E: Nature and Space* 1(1–2): 76–98.

Ranganathan, M. (2016). "Thinking with Flint: Racial Liberalism and the Roots of an American Water Tragedy." *Capitalism Nature Socialism* 27(3): 17–33.

Ranganathan, M. and Balazs, C. (2015). "Water Marginalization at the Urban Fringe: Environmental Justice and Urban Political Ecology Across the North-South Divide." *Urban Geography* 36(3): 403–423.

Robinson, C.J. (2000 [1983]). *Black Marxism: The Making of the Black Radical Tradition.* Chapel Hill, NY: University of North Carolina Press.

Robinson, J.L. (2013). *Contested Water: The Struggle Against Water Privatization in the United States and Canada.* Cambridge, MA: Massachusetts Institute of Technology Press.

Rugh, J.S. and Massey, M. (2010). "Racial Segregation and the American Foreclosure Crisis." *American Sociological Review* 75(5): 629–651.

Sadd, J., Morello-Frosch, R., Pastor, M., Matsuoka, M., Prichard, M., and Carter, V. (2014). "The Truth, the Whole Truth, and Nothing but the Ground-Truth: Methods to Advance Environmental Justice and Researcher-Community Partnerships." *Health Education & Behavior* 41(3): 281–290.

Sadd, J.L., Hall, E.S., Pastor, M., Morello-Frosch, R.A., Lowe-Liang, D., Hayes, J.R., and Swanson, C. (2015). "Ground-Truthing Validation to Assess the Effect of Facility Locational Error on Cumulative Impacts Screening Tools." *Geography Journal* 2015: (324683). http://dx.doi.org/10.1155/2015/324683.

Sadler, R.C. and Highsmith, A.R. (2016). "Rethinking Tiebout: The Contribution of Political Fragmentation and Racial/Economic Segregation to the Flint Water Crisis." *Environmental Justice* 9(5): 143–151. https://doi.org/10.1089/env.2016.0015.

Sadler, R.C., LaChance, J., and Hanna-Attisha, M. (2017). "Social and Built Environmental Correlates of Predicted Blood Lead Levels in the Flint Water Crisis." *American Journal of Public Health* 107(5): 763–769.

San Joaquin County Grand Jury. (2015). "Stockton Municipal Utilities Department: Struggling in the MUD. 2014-2015 Case No. 1412." Stockton, CA: County of San Joaquin.

Shilling, F.M., London, J.K., and Liévanos, R.S. (2009). "Marginalization by Collaboration: Environmental Justice as a Third Party in and Beyond CALFED." *Environmental Science and Policy* 12(6): 694–709.

Smith, N. (1996). *The New Urban Frontier: Gentrification and the Revanchist City*. New York, NY: Routledge.

Sugrue, T.J. (1996). *The Origins of the Urban Crisis: Race and Inequality in Postwar Detroit*. Princeton. NJ: Princeton University Press.

Sze, J. (2007). *Noxious New York: The Racial Politics of Urban Health and Environmental Justice*. Cambridge, MA: Massachusetts Institute of Technology Press.

Sze, J., London, J., Shilling, F., Gambirazzio, G., Filan, T., and Cadenasso, M. (2009). "Defining and Contesting Environmental Justice: Socio-Natures and the Politics of Scale in the Delta." *Antipode* 41(4): 807–843.

Taylor, D. (2014). *Toxic Communities: Environmental Racism, Industrial Pollution, and Residential Mobility*. New York, NY: New York University Press.

Tone, J. (2003). "Stockton Unified Declared Integrated." *The Record*. May 1, 2003. Available at: http://www.recordnet.com (consulted October 10, 2012).

Tone, J. (2004a). "Parents Ask to Phase Out School Plan." *The Record*. March 31, 2004. Available at: http://www.recordnet.com (consulted October 10, 2012).

Tone, J. (2004b). "What We've Learned." *The Record*. May 16, 2004. Available at: http://www.recordnet.com (consulted October 10, 2012).

Wacquant, L. (2008). *Urban Outcasts: A Comparative Sociology of Advanced Marginality*. Malden, MA: Polity Press.

Wilson, W.J. (1987). *The Truly Disadvantaged: The Inner-City, the Underclass, and Public Policy*. Chicago, IL: University of Chicago Press.

Wilson, W.J. (1996). *When Work Disappears. The World of the New Urban Poor*. New York, NY: Alfred A. Knopf.

Wolfe, P. (1999). *Settler Colonialism and the Transformation of Anthropology: The Politics and Poetics of an Ethnographic Event*. London: Cassell.

Zimring, C.A. (2015). *Clean and White: A History of Environmental Racism in the United States*. New York. NY: New York University Press.

CHAPTER 4

Too Close to Home

The Incidence and Health Effects of Neighborhood Neglect in Flint, Michigan

Katrinell M. Davis

1 Introduction

For decades, many US communities have been fighting for environmental justice (Grant et al. 2010; Cable and Benson 1993). From the 1982 civil rights struggle in Warren County against building a Polychlorinated Biphenyls ("PCB") landfill to citizen-led efforts in Flint, Michigan, against overpriced and lead-contaminated drinking water, residents in predominately black and poor cities throughout America have been forced to utilize collective action and confrontation to express concerns regarding the various pollutants in their communities (Burwell and Cole 2007; Heard-Garris 2017; Mock 2016; Been 1995; Been and Gupta 1997).[1] Despite efforts by communities to address environmental hazards, these issues often persist because the regulation compliance norms and zoning ordinances that enable these inequities to persist often go unchanged (Glenn 2017; Beggs 1995).

Research illustrates that macrostructural adjustments to civil rights legislation and economic policies since the early 1980s significantly altered the conditions of major cities undergoing fiscal and population decline. Under neoliberalism, reductionist state interventions replaced the concept of public good with "personal responsibility" while dramatically undermining the regulatory authority of institutions and programs that were created to benefit the health and social welfare of residents. As a result, neoliberalism has contributed to a set of unique challenges for residents in low resource communities that are difficult to overcome. Discarded spaces within neoliberal cities wherein poor and black people predominately reside have been robbed of quality public services and, in many cases, sources of security that previously helped stabilize and empower the community (Lipman 2009; Brenner and Theodore 2002).

1 Mock, Brentin. (2016). Short Cuts Could Cause Permanent Damages: The water crisis in Flint, Mich., is the latest in a long history of African Americans being exposed to toxic poisoning. Crisis (15591573) 123, no. 1: 5.

Given the extensive decline in public infrastructure investments since the early 1980s, it is necessary to document how these neoliberal shifts in state action have shaped the quality of life in low resource spaces. While scholars have spent considerable time examining the extent to which neoliberal cities cater to capital through gentrification and privatization (Hanlon 2015; di Leonardo 2008; Niedt 2006; Harvey 2005), less focus has been devoted to examining the effects of benign neglect. To extend our knowledge about how postindustrial macrostructural policy changes have impacted the people within discarded spaces (LaChance et al. 2016), this analysis is designed to capture the health effects of neighborhood neglect by examining the relationship between blight and the prevalence of lead poisoning in Flint, Michigan, between 2010 and 2015.

Based on the events of the Flint water crisis and the area's extensive decline due to unresolved environmental hazards, neoliberal cost-cutting measures, and poverty, Flint, Michigan, serves as an optimal city for examining the effects of environmental injustice. According to the US Census, the City of Flint had a population of 102,434 in 2015, with black Americans and white Americans making up 56 percent and 37 percent of the city, respectively.[2] At Flint's peak population in the mid-1960s, the city boasted 200,000 residents, GM jobs were plentiful, and neighborhood stores and schools were considered among the best in the country. In recent years, the population has declined significantly due to a lack of jobs, decaying infrastructure, and macrostructural factors that have hindered the city from providing adequate essential services. Between 2012 and 2016, Flint's median household income was $25,650, with just over 40 percent of residents living in poverty.[3]

In this analysis, I set out to determine the effect of hazardous conditions, including but not limited to, distance from water main breaks, brownfields, and elevated water lead levels in Flint. Considering that brownfield sites are known for transferring lead and other heavy metals to vegetable crops (Attanayake 2014) and water main breaks result from widespread corrosion in aging pipeline systems, increasing the likelihood of water quality problems (Wood and Lence 2006), the effects of these forms of blight on blood lead levels may prove helpful in understanding racial disparities in health outcomes.

2 https://suburbanstats.org/population/michigan/how-many-people-live-in-flint.

3 https://www.census.gov/quickfacts/fact/table/flintcitymichigan/PST045216.

2 The Impact of Dwelling Characteristics and Socioeconomic Status on Lead Exposure

Many US cities experienced a significant decline in the late 20th century. Not only did these cities undergo a decrease in population, but many, such as Flint, also experienced disinvestment and depletion of resources (Dewar 2015; Anderson 2014; Dewar and Thomas 2013). Before the rise of neoliberal strategies in increasingly poor and depopulating black and brown spaces, the working class in the late 1970s experienced a period of significant decline precipitated by the exodus of middle class white and black families and the abandonment of low-skilled employers like General Motors in Flint or the steel industry in Youngstown, Ohio (Harvey 2005; Kruse 2005; Marable 1984).

Instead of implementing capacity building strategies and initiatives designed to invest in families and help sustain the social contract between employers and the working class, the federal government fundamentally altered its Keynesian stance. As private-sector restructuring blossomed and layoffs multiplied across the nation, the federal government began to disentangle the safety net previously available to the working class in ways that disproportionately impacted workers and families living in poor and black spaces (Hanlon 2015; Wacquant et al. 2014). Empowered by meritocratic and neoconservative rhetoric, the state and local levels of government gradually embraced a policy of benign neglect that manifested as a significant retreat from the provision of essential services cities previously provided residents (Slater 2009; Hackworth 2007; Marable 1984).

While state and city bureaucrats encouraged the atrophy of essential services in areas within cities that were predominately poor and black, efforts were made to salvage the spaces inhabited by higher income and status residents. In many cases, these residents are offered amenities ranging from subsidized garbage pick-up, tax easements and infrastructure improvements, to cheap land on which to build gated communities and mega shopping malls protected by private security hired to keep the poor away (Bridge et al. 2012; Lipman 2009; Atkinson 2000).

Research shows that efforts to address problems facing depopulating cities have been lacking, and the few policies implemented have been unsuccessful (Rosenman and Walker 2016; Dewar et al. 2015; Anderson 2014; Beauregard 2009). Rosenman and Walker (2016) note, for instance, that state actors have responded to declining cities by opting to demolish blighted or slum-like conditions instead of repairing existing infrastructure. As a result, cities like Flint have been surviving with limited resources and a diminished capacity to address the consequences of residing in a poverty-stricken community for decades (Bell and Ebisu 2012). Left to contend with depleted city resources (Dewar and Thomas 2013; Joassart-Marcelli et al. 2005), many urban dwellers in poor and blighted areas now grapple with poor quality grocery stores (Zenk et al. 2005), diminished medical and police response to emergencies (LeDuff 2013), and a disproportionate share of environmental toxins where they live (Sampson and Winter 2016; Bullard 2000).

To identify disparities in proximity to blight throughout the postindustrial era, scholars have examined socioeconomic and racial differences in exposure to environmental hazards primarily by engaging one of two approaches: pollution dispersion (Ash and Fetter 2004; Chakraborty and Armstrong 1997) and site proximity assessments (Maranville et al. 2009; Zhang et al. 2016; Lester, Allen, and Hill 2001; Ringquist 2005; Downey and Van Willigen 2005; Hipp 2010). In 1987, the Commission for Racial Justice Study for the United Church of Christ was the first among many studies to document the high concentration of hazardous waste facilities in or near minority populations. Subsequent research shows that, compared to high-income communities, poor areas persistently contend with elevated levels of environmental hazards (Campbell et al. 2010; Mohai and Saha 2006; Ringquist 2005; Pastor et al. 2001). For instance, research shows that poor neighborhoods are much more likely to suffer from lead poisoning than affluent communities (Belova et al. 2013; Winter and Sampson 2017; Pais et al. 2014; Nicholson, Schwirian, and Schwirian 2010; Quillian 2003). Poor communities face a disadvantage in part because these neighborhoods have diminished capacity to connect with the agencies responsible for intervening on these problems, making alleviating issues with lead much more complicated once they are recognized (Rajaram 2007; Carrel et al. 2017; Johnson and Arora 2017).

Accordingly, despite reductions of lead in paint, pipes, and gasoline between 1978 and 1995 (Akkus and Ozdenerol 2014), research illustrates that significant sources of lead exposure continue to stem from sources within deteriorating communities ranging from old paint and lead pipes to lead-contaminated soil (Edwards 2014; Brown and Margolis 2012; Edwards 2008; Bryant 2004; Lanphear et al. 1996). Roberts et al. (2003), for instance, associated age of housing stock data in Charleston County, South Carolina, to the distribution of lead poisoning prevalence ratios throughout the area. These researchers used three categories, pre-1950, 1950–1977, and post-1977, to make distinctions between the effects of housing stock age. They found that children who lived in homes built before 1950 were four times more likely to have elevated blood lead levels than children residing in a house built after 1950. Roberts et al. (2003) also found that, despite targeted lead prevention efforts in the area, many children residing in homes built before 1950 had never been screened for lead.

Vaidyanathan et al.'s (2009) study, which examines the effect of residing in old homes on lead exposure in Atlanta, Georgia, confirmed previous findings regarding lead screening rates. Vaidyanathan et al. (2009) found that over 90 percent of the homes in Atlanta were built before 1978 and that over 78 percent of children in Atlanta lived in homes built before 1950. Despite the use of targeted lead prevention efforts in areas with a significant percentage of older homes, these researchers also found that only 11.9 percent of children in Atlanta under three years old residing in pre-1950 homes received blood lead tests.

Relatedly, scholars have identified relationships between lead exposure, the racial composition of neighborhoods, and other compositional characteristics, including the ownership status of dwellings (White, Bonilha, and Ellis 2016; Jain 2016; Aelion et al. 2013). For instance, Macey et al. (2001) employed a multivariate analysis to ascertain whether there are racial and socioeconomic differences in exposure to environmental lead. Utilizing data from the EPA Toxics Release Inventory, Cumulative Exposure Project, and the Los Angeles County Department of Health Services' Hot Zone Census Tract Assessment, these authors conclude that race is associated with several cases of elevated blood lead. Moody et al. (2016) find that neighborhood characteristics correlate with blood lead levels among black and white children in metropolitan Detroit. They conclude that in Detroit, neighborhoods with lower socioeconomic characteristics and high racial residential segregation produce higher average childhood blood lead levels.

Researchers have also explored associations between proximity to small source polluters and lead exposure (Zhang et al. 2016). Yeh et al. (1996) found that the mean concentration of lead in the soil nearest to a storage battery processing plant was higher than the concentration of lead away from the plant. Further, Kim and Williams (2017) found a positive association between proximity to landfills and lead toxicity. According to these scholars, children residing near landfills were more likely than their counterparts to contend with adverse health outcomes, including encephalopathy and death.

While much of the analytic attention has been devoted to the siting procedures of hazardous facilities and related covariates, there have been minimal discussions of the relationship between the cleanup and redevelopment of hazardous neighborhood conditions and health (Eckerd and Keeler 2012). This study responds to gaps in research examining the effects of residential hazards known to pique blood lead levels in urban communities by taking into account the multiple sources of hazardous blight in the Flint community while examining the extent to which race and income level predict proximity to environmental hazards. This analysis attempts to build on existing scholarship by assessing the relationship between neighborhood blight, blood lead levels, and typical risk factors, including race and income level.

3 Data and Method

This study is designed to quantify the relationship between lead exposure and proximity to neighborhood blight in the City of Flint. By disaggregating the effects of neighborhood hazards, this study attempts to expand what we know about associations between lead exposure and different forms of neighborhood blight in Flint. The findings in this study stem from an analysis of private health data from the Lead Program, Medicaid, Children's Special Health Care Needs, and Vital records for Genesee County provided by the Michigan Department of Health and Human Services (MDHHS).

Brownfield site data derives from Michigan's Inventory of Facilities reported by local-level Brownfield Redevelopment Authorities (BRA) as authorized by the 1994 Natural Resources and Environmental Protection Act, PA 451, amended under Parts 201 and 213. Since owners are not required to inform the Department of Environmental Quality about contamination issues uncovered during land assessments, the Part 201 Projects Inventory does not account for all facilities subjected to Part 201 regulation. The Part 213 list includes facilities that have received corrective actions and documents why corrective action was issued. Duplicate addresses from Part 201 lists and Part 213 lists for Genesee County in 2016 were deleted from this analysis. Data was merged with demographic data from the US Census, water main break data from the City of Flint Water Department, and environmental indicators from the Environmental Protection Agency from 2010 to 2015. This research study was approved by the Florida State University and MDHHS Institutional Review Boards.

While assessing the association between key risk factors of lead exposure, including high water lead levels, water main breaks, and brownfields, I draw from geographic information systems (GIS) methods to examine the relationship between elevated blood lead levels and forms of water disorder in Flint. Various ecological studies examine the distribution of elevated blood lead levels and risk factors for childhood lead poisoning with GIS methods (Vaidyanathan et al. 2009; Roberts et al. 2003; Reissman et al. 2001). Procedures ranging from multivariate mapping of risk factors and blood lead screening data (Joseph et al. 2005) and proximity studies utilizing distance calculations (Garber et al. 2011) to spatial clustering (Oyana 2010; Oyana et al. 2007) and spatial autocorrelation (Haley and Talbot 2004; Griffith et al. 1998) have been used to interpret spatial patterns of lead poisoning and enhance intervention strategies designed to target vulnerable populations. GIS methods have been valuable in efforts to develop lead poisoning prevention strategies that identify sources of environmental lead and relate the distribution of lead-emitting sources to the distribution of lead exposure in the area (Kaplowitz et al. 2010;

Miranda and Dolinoy 2002). Since various pathways to lead exposure exist, GIS methods have been helpful with pinpointing where pockets of lead poisoning are located and have assisted attempts to determine which risk factors play a greater role in subjecting children to lead exposure (Miranda et al. 2011; Gonzalez et al. 2002; Griffith et al. 1998).

This study employs various GIS tools including geocoding, a buffer analysis, spatial autocorrelation (Moran's I and LISA) as well as kriging to illustrate spatial patterns of lead exposure in Flint (e.g., children with blood lead levels at and above 5 micrograms per deciliter). Variable width buffers were created to document the relationship between childhood lead poisoning and proximity to water main breaks to illustrate the relationship between elevated blood lead levels and water main breaks. With the assumption that lead exposure increases with proximity to a water main break, buffers were created 500 feet, 800 feet, 1,500 feet, and 3,000 feet away from water main breaks. Geocoded addresses for children with lead poisoning were then overlaid, as illustrated by red points.

Moran's I procedure was utilized to determine whether the spatial pattern of blood lead testing in the area was more clustered than random during the period of study. Additionally, local indicator of spatial association (LISA) statistics based on the Moran's I statistic and developed by Anselin (1995), were used to identify local clusters and outliers in the data. A LISA significance map was generated indicating four categories of spatial autocorrelation of lead poisoning prevalence rates: high-high cluster, high-low outlier, low-high cluster, and low-low outlier. Census blocks with high-high clusters represent areas with high lead poisoning prevalence rates that are near census blocks with lead poisoning rates. High-low categories are census blocks with high lead poisoning rates that are surrounded by neighborhoods with low prevalence rates. The low-high category represents blocks with low lead poisoning rates that are surrounded by blocks with high prevalence rates. In contrast, the low-low category displays neighborhoods with low lead poisoning rates that are surrounded by blocks with low lead poisoning rates.

Accordingly, based on blood lead data for the area between 2013 and 2015, I utilized kriging, a geostatistical interpolation technique commonly relied on to measure spatial variations in lead levels within human blood and soil, to analyze the spatial variability of lead poisoning among children in Flint under 12. While doing so, I took into account associated predictors of lead exposure, including year of housing stock, race, income, proximity to brownfield sites, and proximity to water main breaks. For the GIS analysis, I prepared the data to map in ArcGIS version 10.6 as points joined with different attributes to capture the spatial distribution of elevated blood lead levels in Flint. However, since only 3400 parcels could be mapped from over 52,000 parcels in Flint, the data were aggregated at the census tract level.

Employing descriptive and multivariate analyses, I identified priority areas needing further research by examining the associations between blood lead tests and key independent variables. T-Tests were used to calculate mean variations in neighborhood quality between children with and without lead poisoning. Associations between elevated water lead levels, brownfields, and water main breaks were further explored with a multivariate analysis.

To quantify factors predicting lead exposure among Michigan Medicaid-enrolled children under 11 years old residing in Genesee County between January 1, 2010, and December 31, 2015, I explored the level and variance of blood level concentration and identified population correlates of exposure. I calculated descriptive statistics, computed distributions, and determined whether any transformations are necessary for subsequent statistical analyses. I also performed bivariate analyses of the relationships between blood level concentration and potential exposure correlates. I compared the geometric means across the strata of covariates and explored the correlation among predictors.

Finally, I employed logistic regression to examine the associations between elevated blood lead concentrations, demographic indicators, and neighborhood blight in the City of Flint, while controlling for child and household characteristics (e.g., age, sex, high poverty at parcel level, sample type, percent black, percent vacant at zip code level, and those tested during the summer). The dependent variable is a binary indicator of elevated blood lead levels, which accounts for children with blood lead levels above 5 µg/dL. I included demographic variables used in past studies that examine the prevalence of lead poisoning among children (race, year housing stock constructed, and poverty status) as covariates. Associations were examined between levels of lead exposure (> 5 mg/dL), time (specimen year), demographic features (age, sex, race/ethnicity), and neighborhood/housing characteristics (median household income and year home built as well as distance from brownfield sites, water main breaks, and elevated water lead levels).

4 The Significance of Independent Variables

4.1 *Michigan's Treatment of Brownfield Sites*

Brownfield sites are the abandoned and underutilized factories, junkyards, gas stations, and other industrial/commercial facilities that contribute to urban blight. These properties sat vacant for years until the Reagan Administration began the process of identifying and redeveloping brownfield sites in 1980. With the passage of the Comprehensive Environmental Response, Compensation, and Liability Act (CERCLA) of 1980, a national program was launched to address this form of urban blight, and a protocol for assigning liability for the contamination clean-up and help needed to stimulate private enterprise in blighted areas was established. While providing lending institutions a statutory exclusion from liability, under CERCLA, previous owners of a property are considered responsible for the costs of the clean-up, even if they did not cause the contamination or undermine the environmental investigation of the ecological hazard (Opper 2005; Andrew 1996). CERCLA also grants a third-party the right to sue to recover cleanup costs (Collaton and Bartsch 1996).

Due to the liabilities, real estate developers often request a complete environmental investigation before securing the property. Further, when sites are deemed contaminated, prospective purchasers typically demand that property is remediated before purchasing or leasing it. The problem is that the remediation of brownfield sites is a complex process that usually snowballs into insurmountable technical and financial challenges (Opper 2005; Andrew 1996). As a result, since CERCLA was passed and amended throughout the years, research has demonstrated that this policy has caused more problems than it has solved (Goldfarb 2010; Powers et al. 2000).

Due to declines in the manufacturing industry that left many mid-Michigan cities with fewer family-sustaining jobs and more community disorder, including dilapidated buildings and abandoned businesses such as gas stations with leaking underground gas tanks, increased exposure to environmental hazards from blighted property has become an unfortunate norm. Many areas throughout Michigan have been substantially undermined by the presence of brownfields and require brownfield remediation and redevelopment. When brownfield redevelopment became an EPA initiative in the mid-1990s, states, including Michigan, began making efforts to assess, remediate, and redevelop brownfield sites. The number of state-implemented brownfield cleanup programs increased from 14 to 44 between 1993 and 1998 (United States General Accounting Office 1997; Hula 1999). While federal efforts to address brownfield cleanup grants autonomy to public authorities, states like Michigan opted to develop brownfield cleanup policy that gives more flexibility in developing cleanup efforts and imposes less owner liability. Regardless of contamination level, the State of Michigan also lists properties that are vacant and abandoned as brownfields. In Michigan, the 1996 Brownfield Redevelopment Financing Act, PA 381, and subsequent amendments empowered municipalities to develop a local BRA, responsible for creating and implementing brownfield projects. BRAs also help facilitate lending and mortgage activities related to brownfield properties.

Research illustrating relationships between socioeconomic factors and brownfield redevelopment trends in Michigan and other states has been mixed (Elliott and Frickel 2013; Lee and Mohai 2013). In the few studies that examine brownfield redevelopment, some argue that brownfields are typically located in poor spaces, compared to more affluent areas (McCarthy 2009). Meanwhile, other studies contend that redevelopment plans for brownfields are not related to race and class dynamics within the social spaces (Lee and Mohai 2013). With all the attention aimed at the politics and challenges of brownfield redevelopment, there has been no attempt to examine the health impacts of brownfields in communities. As environmental health and risk scholar, Michael Greenberg, put it in his analysis of brownfield redevelopment strategies, "environmental health scientists need to participate in brownfields redevelopment because, at best, a brownfield site is a neighborhood black eye, and, at worst, it becomes a neighborhood "cancer," spreading its disease to surrounding properties and causing people and businesses with any options to leave the neighborhood" (Greenberg 2003: A75). Indeed, the industrial histories of these many poor and black spaces should inspire this level of analysis, especially in cities like Flint.

4.2 *Problems with Gasoline in Flint*

During the mid to late 1980s, Flint residents began to report' problems with underground water pollution that came from leaking and abandoned gasoline tanks. During this time, almost daily, leaking or abandoned underground tanks were discovered in Flint. "It's getting way out of proportion," said local Department of Natural Resources specialist, Ben Hall. "Calls are coming daily now, where we get one or two tank removals; some are just upgrading their tanks, but others have a problem" (Braknis 1989). As a result of these discoveries, Genesee County began installing monitoring wells and digging up soil at corner gas stations and the sites of abandoned tanks to clean up the pollution problem that was overlooked by property owners and the Department of Natural Resources.

One of the most significant findings from the unpublished EPA report is that lead-contaminated soil was concentrated in residential areas. The study illustrated that nine Michigan cities averaged 1,339 parts per million in business districts and 2,372 in residential areas. While residential and business areas in cities like Flint were 3867 and 2689 parts per million, respectively (Lewis 1972), in other cities, the lead problem was concentrated in business areas. For instance, samples from Ann Arbor illustrated that lead-contaminated soil was more problematic in business areas since 1871 parts per million were detected in the residential soil samples while 4269 in commercial areas.

At this time in American history, lawmakers assumed that the lead problem in the soil came from gasoline from automobile exhausts. As noted in a letter to urge the EPA to strengthen its regulations of gasoline, Senator Phil Hart wrote that something needed to be done to protect children. "We conclude that neither cost nor competitive considerations provide a sufficient reason for abandoning a schedule of total lead removal by 1977 [because] ... if we do not adopt this schedule ... we will continue to expose the public, and particularly the inner-city poor, to substantial hazards" (as quoted by Lewis 1972).

Efforts to clean up the problems caused by leaking underground tanks increased once a federal program called LUST or leaking underground storage tanks was born in 1986. LUST was created in response to concerns about groundwater contamination, despite strong opposition from service station lobbyists who feared that the rise in regulations would put them out of business. Before 1986, few LUST violations were reported. After 1986, keeping up with the LUST violation workload began to become quite the task for the Department of Natural Resources. While it was estimated at the time that 35 percent of the underground storage tanks across the nation posed a threat to soil and groundwater, the problem was typical in large industrial areas that housed tanks stored by industry and gas stations. Nearly 400 underground tanks in the Flint area were removed in 1986, with 300 in 1987. By August 1988, 150 tanks were removed, and many more were expected to be discovered (Lewis 1972).

4.3 *Water Main Breaks*

The underlying infrastructure of underserved communities also tends to place them at disproportionate risk for unsafe water systems (Heaney et al. 2013). A water main is an underground pipe that carries water to customer service pipes (McGhee and Steel 1991). Often, especially in cold Michigan winters, holes or cracks develop in water mains that expand to the surface, creating extensive water flow at or near the site of the break until it is repaired (Rajani et al. 2012; Baker 2009). Water main breaks are typically caused by external corrosion of pipes during cold seasons when frost penetrates 3–5 feet into the ground (Miller 1976). Water main breaks can cause extensive property damage and usually contaminate the water supply (Baird 2011; Rose et al. 2000; O'Day 1989), even when the water appears to be clear (Livingston et al. 2016; Wood et al. 2007; Kaplan et al. 1984).

After a water main break is repaired, the drinking water may still be contaminated, especially in poor cities lacking funding to monitor the problem until the water is determined to be safe. Protecting residents from water main failures and minimizing the effects of water main breaks are primary challenges facing water utilities across the United States. In cities with severely deteriorated water distribution systems and a lack of funds to rehabilitate the infrastructure, such as Flint, water main breaks are infrequently repaired. Water main breaks also cause water contamination that remains until it has been flushed out of the pipes (Allen et al. 2018; Bradford et al. 2017). Various ailments can be caused by a water main break, including gastrointestinal disorders, disease outbreaks, and illness associated with exposure to unsafe toxins and chemicals, including lead, and dangerous microbial contaminants, including E coli (Thompson et al. 2013).

4.4 *Water Lead Levels above Action Level*

Accordingly, childhood lead poisoning has been associated with water treatment practices that cause high lead levels within public water systems. Previous research illustrates that changes in water chemistry influence how water interacts with lead pipes and lead-bearing plumbing parts (Miranda et al. 2007; Lytle and Schock 2005; Edwards and Dudi 2004). Once the water's aggressiveness increases and lead is leached into the water, water safety engineers have demonstrated that children consuming the water face an increased risk of lead poisoning. The Washington DC Lead Crisis is an example of how shifts in water treatment and chemistry impact community health. During 2001–2004, water chemistry changes were later associated with an increase in the incidence of children with elevated blood lead levels as well as adverse pregnancies in Washington, DC (Edwards 2014; Edwards et al. 2009).

This study examines the spatial distribution of lead exposure in Flint as the city attempted to rebound from increased water lead levels. This development stems from Flint's April 25, 2014, decision to discontinue drinking water service from the Detroit Water and Sewer Department and to begin supplying treated water from the Flint River, which had been a known polluted water source for decades (Michigan Civil Rights Commission 2017). Following the water source switch, residents reportedly observed aesthetic changes in the water and associated the rise in skin and gastrointestinal problems in the area with post-source water conditions. In response to residents' concerns, a research team led by Virginia Tech University Civil Engineer Marc Edwards in September 2015 later collected water samples in Flint and identified high lead levels in the public water system. At the 90th percentile, this research team found that the median water lead level for the 268 water tests conducted during the first sampling round was 26.8 micrograms per deciliter (μg/L), which is well over the federal action level (15 μg/L and over). (Pieper et al. 2018). Increased water lead levels during this time were also associated with a post-water switch rise in the incidence of childhood lead poisoning in the area (Hanna-Attisha et al. 2016; Olsen et al. 2017).

Drinking water infrastructure and housing conditions are also shaped by Lead and Copper Rule compliance norms (Renner 2010). When the Lead Action Level (an indicator of corrosion) is exceeded during testing for Lead and Copper Rule compliance, water officials must undertake a series of actions that include notifying and educating the public in addition to treating water to reduce corrosion. The motivation for addressing water quality issues may be influenced by the availability of resources, as well as the political power of the community. For instance, when the chemical treatment of water to reduce corrosion and lead levels fails, cities are required to begin replacing at least 7 percent of their lead lines per year (Guidotti et al. 2008). This standard creates a challenge for working-class communities, who may have fewer resources to implement costly remediation.

5 Hypotheses

Based on previous research concerning the health effects of brownfield sites, water main breaks, and high water lead levels, I expected there to be a robust association between elevated blood lead levels, and age of housing during the period of study. Consistent with previous research (Sadler et al. 2017), I expect to find that these neighborhood characteristics as well as demographic attributes, including race and class, will have independent and significant effects on the dependent variable, the natural logarithm of blood lead levels, in this analysis.[4] Additionally, scholars examining the distribution of lead exposure at the neighborhood level generally agree that urban communities with a large proportion of African American residents or individuals living under the poverty line, in addition to neighborhoods with high vacancy rates and low percentages of owner-occupied homes, are associated with greater risk of elevated blood lead levels (White et al. 2016; Lanphear et al. 1998).

Finally, even when taking into account neighborhood disorder/characteristics, I expect the relationship between race, class, and blood lead level to remain significant and robust. With few exceptions, scholars contend that race

4 There is only one blood lead test per child in this study. For children with more than one blood lead test during the period of study, their highest lead level was selected for this analysis. All other blood lead tests associated with children who have multiple test results were deleted.

and class indicators are critical to analyses of lead exposure, especially among children. Jones and colleagues (2009) assessed racial variations in lead exposure by comparing childhood blood lead levels in two cohorts, the first from 1988 to 1991 and the second from 1999 to 2004. They found that the percentage of children with elevated blood lead levels decreased from 8.6 percent in the first cohort to 1.4 percent in the second cohort (Jones et al. 2009). On average, according to Jones et al. (2009), blood lead levels in non-Hispanic black, Mexican-American, and non-Hispanic white children all declined over this period. However, despite the decline in the mean blood lead levels both overall and within each group, racial/ethnic disparities persist.

6 Results

Positive and significant Moran's I results were interpreted as evidence for clustering of lead poisoning in Flint. While Moran's I results do not illustrate where the clusters are and how lead exposure occurred, this spatial autocorrelation method verifies the existence of clustering of elevated blood lead levels. Based on estimates from the LISA procedure illustrated in Figure 4.1, there is evidence of statistically significant and positive spatial autocorrelation among high-risk neighborhoods in the city. These patterns confirm an uneven distribution of lead poisoning risk among children and identify pockets or clustering of lead poisoning that are located, primarily in Northwest Flint.

Furthermore, the map illustrating the relationship between elevated blood lead levels and water main breaks in Figure 4.2 shows a significant visual association between lead poisoning and proximity to water main breaks. This map captures the extent to which children with lead poisoning reside within fixed distances from water main breaks. It illustrates how the effect of living near water main breaks was more substantial for children within 800 feet and that this effect declined monotonically out to 3,000 feet. This spatial pattern suggests that lead exposure rates are highest among children residing closest to water main breaks.

Pediatric blood lead levels also appear to be associated with various other neighborhood characteristics. Figure 4.3 consists of a series of maps of Flint neighborhoods illustrating elevated blood lead levels aggregated at the census level in relation to water lead levels, brownfield sites, water main breaks, and the year housing structures were built. As seen in Figure 4.3, the highest concentrations of older homes and water main breaks are located in areas where the percentage of children with elevated blood lead levels are high. This figure not only shows that the highest concentration of children with elevated blood

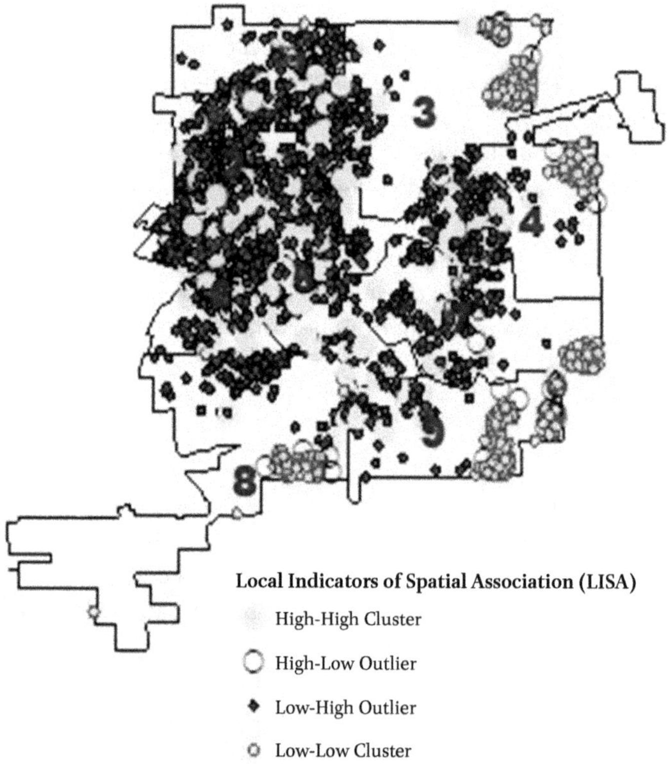

FIGURE 4.1 Childhood lead poisoning clusters and outliers in Flint
SOURCE: MDHHS CHILDHOOD LEAD POISONING PREVENTION PROGRAM

lead levels resided on the Northwest side of Flint, but that brownfield sites tend to border areas with the highest concentration of lead-exposed children.

Research suggests that there is a need to examine the relationship between brownfield sites, water main breaks, and lead contamination, given that pipe systems are not built to resist contaminated soils (USEPA 2012). Contaminated soil has been known to seep into pipes (e.g., cast iron, steel, and glass fiber reinforced plastic systems) where they are joined by natural or synthetic rubber gaskets (Glaza et al. 1992; Park et al. 1991; Holsen et al. 1991). Accordingly, in the long-term, cast iron and steel pipes, rust or crack, and provide additional opportunities for contaminated soil to compromise public water systems (USEPA 2012). Figure 4.4, which depicts the distribution of brownfields, water main breaks, and blood lead levels across Flint, illustrates an association between water main breaks and brownfield sites that confirms research on how contaminated soils compromise pipe systems. The map in Figure 4.4 also

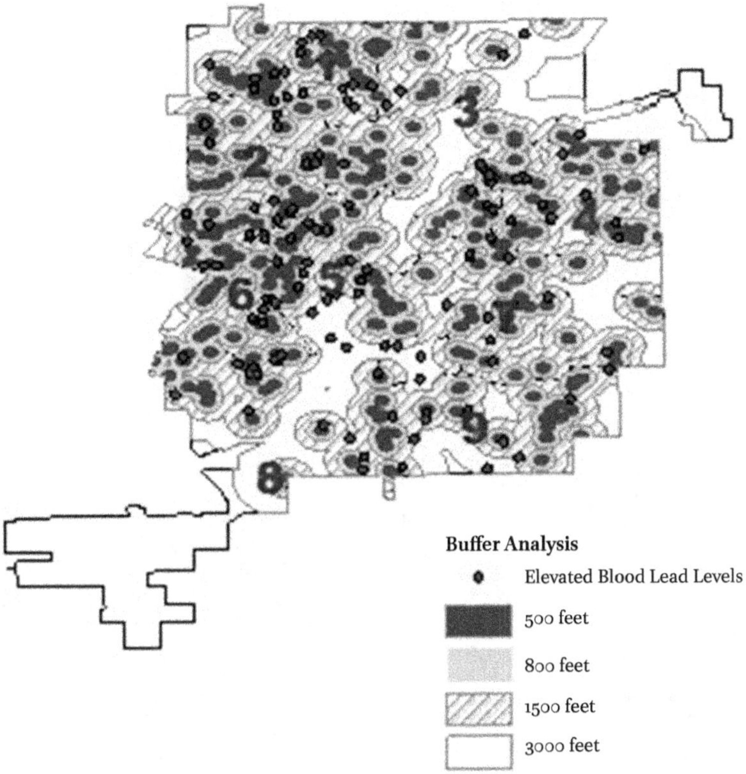

FIGURE 4.2 Spatial associations between childhood lead poisoning and water main breaks in Flint
SOURCE: MDHHS CHILDHOOD LEAD POISONING PREVENTION PROGRAM

locates the largest concentration of children with the highest blood lead levels in areas surrounded by water main breaks and brownfields.

Results from independent t-tests between water main breaks within 800 feet ($t(2056) = 2.7$, $p = .007$), brownfield sites within 800 feet ($t(1652) = 2.8$, $p = .006$), and blood lead levels further indicate a statistically significant difference between mean blood lead levels among children living closer to water main breaks (M=2.44, STD=2.31, N=1574) and brownfield sites (M=2.48, STD=2.81, N=1438), compared to children who reside farther away from water main breaks (M=2.27, STD=1.75, N=6212) and brownfield sites (M=2.27, STD=1.59, N=6348). Overall, t-test results suggest that children with higher blood lead levels tend to live closer to neighborhood hazards than children without lead poisoning, which indicates that blood lead levels are associated with these neighborhood conditions.

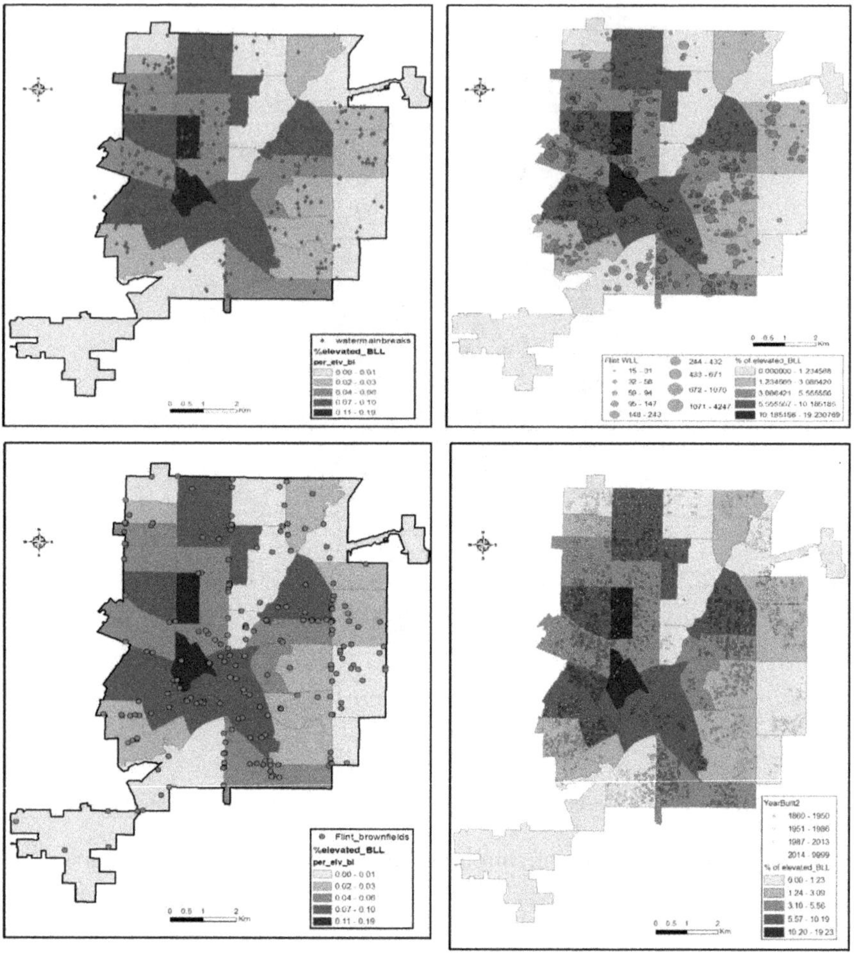

FIGURE 4.3 Select neighborhood characteristics and childhood lead poisoning in Flint
SOURCE: MDHHS CHILDHOOD LEAD POISONING PREVENTION PROGRAM, MICHIGAN BROWNFIELD REDEVELOPMENT PROGRAM, THE CITY OF FLINT WATER DEPARTMENT, AND GENESEE COUNTY TAX RECORDS

Table 4.1, which reports sample characteristics by period, demonstrates that the age of children tested for blood lead in Flint increased between 2010 and 2015. In 2010, just over 93 percent of the children tested for lead in Flint were age five and under, compared to nearly 86 percent of children five and under who were tested in 2015. Data in Table 4.1 further show that 80 to 90 percent of the lead screening population resides less than 3000 feet from some form of water blight in the community.

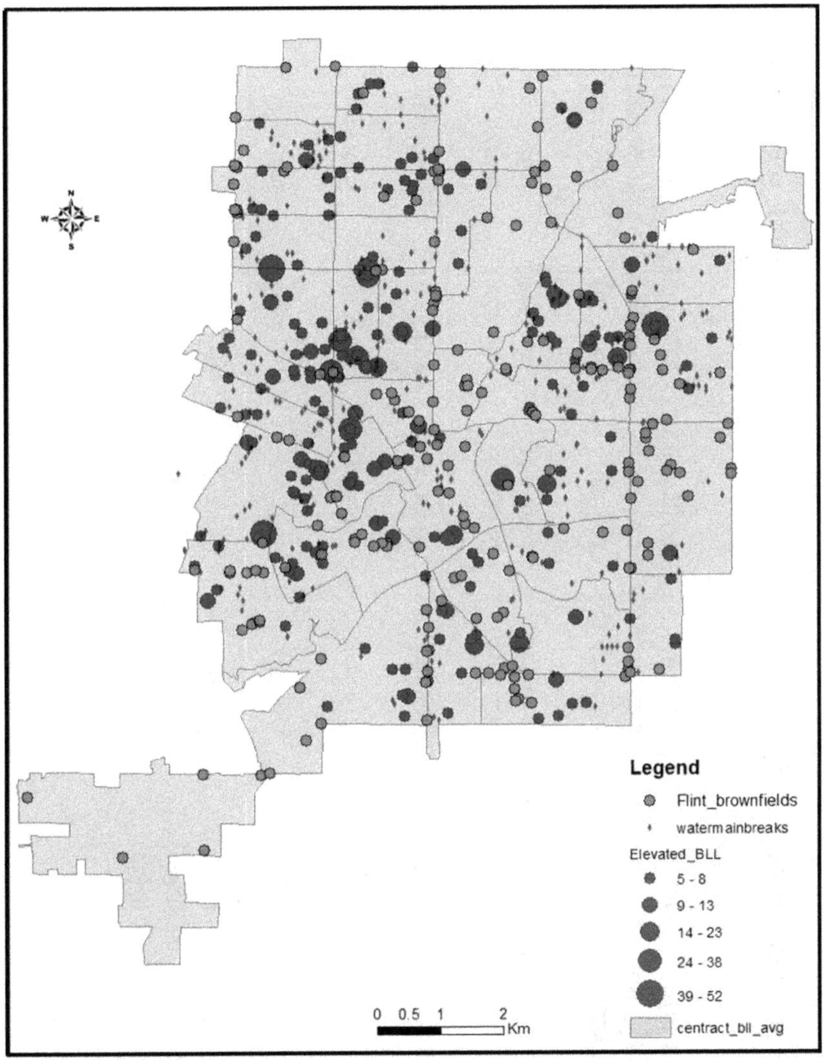

FIGURE 4.4 Spatial associations between water main breaks, brownfield sites, and childhood lead poisoning in Flint
SOURCE: MDHHS CHILDHOOD LEAD POISONING PREVENTION PROGRAM, MICHIGAN BROWNFIELD REDEVELOPMENT PROGRAM, AND THE CITY OF FLINT WATER DEPARTMENT

Table 4.2 reports the geometric means of lead levels in Flint disaggregated by various demographic indicators. As the independent effect of some indicators appeared to wane by 2013 (including income, percent African American, and percent vacant properties), these data reveal significant mean differences

TABLE 4.1 Sample characteristics by year

	2010 (n = 4235)	2011 (n = 3266)	2012 (n = 2847)	2013 (n = 2661)	2014 (n = 2461)	2015 (n = 2549)
Age						
Under 1	149(3.49)	198(6.01)	201(6.97)	217(8.04)	326(13.18)	369(14.12)
1–5	3844(89.96)	2749(83.38)	2357(81.76)	2214(82.03)	1992(80.52)	1878(71.87)
6–11	280(6.55)	350(10.62)	325(11.27)	268(9.93)	156(6.31)	366(14.01)
Sex						
Male	2152 (50.9)	1625(50.4)	1449(52.3)	1296(49.9)	1254(52.4)	1292(52)
Female	2073(49.1)	1601(49.6)	1377(48.7)	1303(50.1)	1138(47.6)	1191(48)
Race						
White	1058(33)	793(34.6)	396(45.1)	394(41.2)	403(38.0)	501(43.3)
Asian	7(0.2)	6(0.18)	*	*	*	8(0.7)
Black	2124(66.3)	1470(64.1)	463(52.7)	509(53.2)	540(51.0)	520(45.0)
Native American	8(0.2)	*	*	*	*	*
Mixed Race	9(0.3)	23(2.0)	17(0.59)	49(5.1)	114(10.8)	126(10.9)
Year residence built						
Before 1950	1578(56.2)	1111(51.6)	929(50.6)	862(50.4)	737(46.6)	874 (51.3)
Between 1951–1978	1174(41.8)	989(45.3)	854(46.5)	789(46.1)	785(49.7)	765(44.9)
Post 1978	56(2.0)	67(3.1)	54(2.9)	61(3.6)	58(3.7)	66(3.9)

Under 133 % of the FPL						
No	3203 (75.57)	2515(77.0)	2244(78.8)	2103 (79.0)	1948(79.1)	2032(79.7)
Yes	1032(24.43)	751(23.0)	603(21.2)	558(21.0)	514(20.9)	517(20.3)
Neighborhood Level						
Percent Black by zip code						
Under 10	722(17.04)	556 (17)	421(14.8)	466(17.5)	403(16.4)	420(16.5)
10–24	1688(39.9)	1442(44.2)	1341(47.1)	1216(45.7)	1152(46.8)	1254(49.2)
25–49	1825(43.1)	1268(38.8)	1085(38.1)	979(36.8)	907(36.8)	875(34.3)
Percent vacant at parcel level						
Under 10	645(15.2)	617 (18.9)	529 (18.6)	556 (20.9)	460 (18.7)	433 (17.0)
10–24	1836 (43.4)	1478 (45.3)	1340 (47.1)	1169(43.9)	1194(48.5)	1289(50.6)
25–49	1689 (39.9)	619(34.2)	937(32.9)	891(33.5)	768(31.2)	782(30.7)
over 50	65(1.5)	53 (1.6)	41 (1.4)	45(1.7)	40(1.6)	45(1.8)
Brownfields						
< 500	297(7.0)	225(6.9)	198(7.0)	186(7)	153(6.2)	209(8.2)
500–800	504(11.9)	368(11.3)	313(11.0)	284(10.7)	273(11.1)	304(11.9)
801–1500	1356(32.1)	1104(33.9)	935(32.9)	855(32.2)	794(32.3)	823(32.3)
1501–3000	1567(37.1)	1170(35.9)	1018(35.8)	975(36.7)	928(37.7)	923(36.2)
over 3000	503(11.9)	391(12.0)	379(13.3)	359(13.5)	313(12.7)	289(11.3)

TABLE 4.1 Sample characteristics by year (*cont.*)

	2010 (n = 4235)	2011 (n = 3266)	2012 (n = 2847)	2013 (n = 2661)	2014 (n = 2461)	2015 (n = 2549)
Watermains						
< 500	900(21.3)	655(20.1)	533(18.7)	510(19.2)	480(19.5)	554(21.8)
500–800	790(18.7)	559(17.1)	519(18.3)	467(17.6)	447(18.2)	456(17.9)
801–1500	1064(25.2)	835(25.6)	701(24.7)	666(25.1)	573(23.3)	648(25.5)
1501–3000	462(10.9)	356(10.9)	304(10.7)	264(9.9)	299(12.1)	312(12.3)
over 3000	1010(23.9)	857(26.3)	786(27.6)	750(28.2)	662(26.9)	576(22.6)
WLL						
< 500	1613(38.2)	1203(36.9)	1025(36.0)	957(36.0)	937(38.2)	1049(41.3)
500–800	706(16.7)	572(17.5)	481(16.9)	433(16.3)	374(15.2)	382(15.0)
801–1500	635(15.0)	465(14.2)	368(12.9)	366(13.8)	319(13.0)	366(14.4)
1501–3000	470(11.1)	323(9.9)	322(11.3)	269(10.1)	272(11.1)	274(10.8)
over 3000	804(19.1)	701(21.5)	649(22.8)	633(23.8)	553(22.5)	471(18.5)

SOURCE: MDHHS CHILDHOOD LEAD POISONING PREVENTION PROGRAM, MICHIGAN BROWNFIELD REDEVELOPMENT PROGRAM, AND THE CITY OF FLINT WATER DEPARTMENT

TABLE 4.2 Geometric mean blood lead by selected population characteristics by year, 2010–2015 (n=18020)

	Geometric mean Pb (95% CI)					
	2010 (n = 4235)	2011 (n = 3266)	2012 (n = 2847)	2013 (n = 2661)	2014 (n = 2462)	2015 (n = 2549)
Overall	1.94(1.9,1.97)	1.91(1.87,1.94)	1.74(1.71,1.78)	1.83(1.79,1.86)	2.1(2.05,2.14)	1.98(1.93,2.02)
Age						
Under 1	1.94(1.84,2.04)	1.96(1.85,2.08)	1.84(1.73,1.97)	1.79(1.68,1.91)	2.1(1.95,2.26)	1.94(1.81,2.09)
1–5	1.94(1.9,1.97)	1.9(1.87,1.95)	1.73(1.7,1.77)	1.83(1.79,1.87)	2.1(2.05,2.15)	2(1.95,2.05)
6–11	1.96(1.84,2.08)	1.88(1.75,2.01)	1.73(1.6,1.86)	1.82(1.7,1.95)	2.08(1.94,2.24)	1.83(1.71,1.96)
Sex						
Male	1.93(1.88,1.98)	1.96(1.91,2.02)	1.79(1.74,1.84)	1.84(1.79,1.9)	2.05(1.99,2.12)	1.99(1.93,2.05)
Female	1.94(1.9,1.99)	1.85(1.8,1.9)	1.68(1.64,1.73)	1.77(1.72,1.82)	2.1(2.03,2.17)	1.93(1.87,2)
Race						
White	1.84(1.78,1.91)	1.8(1.73,1.88)	1.64(1.54,1.74)	2.02(1.92,2.13)	2.43(2.31,2.55)	2.4(2.3,2.5)
Asian	1.64(1.11,2.42)	1.78(1.42,2.23)	2.29(1.76,2.98)	1.73(0.59,5.08)	1.73(0.59,5.08)	2.21(1.94,2.52)
Black	1.97(1.92,2.02)	1.87(1.82,1.93)	1.61(1.53,1.7)	2.06(1.96,2.17)	2.85(2.75,2.95)	2.77(2.68,2.86)
Native American	2.85(2.25,3.61)	1(1,1)	2.62(2.18,3.14)	1.41(0.72,2.79)	3(3,3)	3(3,3)
Mixed Race	1.96(1.49,2.59)	2.05(1.61,2.6)	1(1,1)	3.18(2.92,3.46)	3.28(3.13,3.43)	3.12(2.98,3.25)
Year residence built						
Before 1950	2.23(2.16,2.29)	2.16(2.09,2.24)	1.93(1.85,2)	1.99(1.91,2.07)	2.26(2.17,2.36)	2.11(2.03,2.2)
Between 1951–1978	1.82(1.76,1.88)	1.88(1.82,1.95)	1.64(1.58,1.7)	1.75(1.68,1.82)	2.09(2.01,2.17)	1.86(1.79,1.93)
Post 1978	1.69(1.49,1.92)	1.94(1.68,2.23)	1.82(1.61,2.05)	1.61(1.42,1.82)	2.18(1.91,2.49)	1.83(1.63,2.07)

TABLE 4.1 Geometric mean blood lead by selected population characteristics by year, 2010–2015 (n=18020) (*cont.*)

	Geometric mean Pb (95% CI)					
	2010 (n = 4235)	**2011 (n = 3266)**	**2012 (n = 2847)**	**2013 (n = 2661)**	**2014 (n = 2462)**	**2015 (n = 2549)**
Brownfields						
< 500	2.06(1.92,2.2)	1.83(1.71,1.97)	1.81(1.66,1.98)	1.91(1.74,2.1)	2.12(1.93,2.34)	2.03(1.87,2.21)
500–800	1.94(1.84,2.04)	1.97(1.86,2.08)	1.87(1.75,2)	1.88(1.76,2.01)	2.25(2.1,2.41)	1.98(1.86,2.11)
801–1500	1.94(1.88,2)	1.93(1.87,1.99)	1.75(1.69,1.82)	1.8(1.73,1.86)	2.08(2,2.17)	1.98(1.9,2.06)
1501–3000	1.95(1.89,2.01)	1.91(1.85,1.97)	1.69(1.63,1.74)	1.83(1.77,1.89)	2.08(2.01,2.16)	1.99(1.92,2.06)
over 3000	1.84(1.76,1.92)	1.84(1.75,1.94)	1.76(1.67,1.85)	1.79(1.7,1.89)	2.02(1.9,2.14)	1.9(1.79,2.01)
Watermains						
< 500	2.02(1.95,2.1)	2.02(1.94,2.1)	1.82(1.73,1.91)	1.94(1.85,2.04)	2.22(2.11,2.34)	1.98(1.89,2.08)
500–800	2.08(2,2.17)	2(1.91,2.1)	1.75(1.67,1.84)	1.94(1.84,2.04)	2.17(2.05,2.29)	2.03(1.92,2.14)
801–1500	2.04(1.97,2.11)	1.98(1.91,2.06)	1.75(1.68,1.82)	1.78(1.7,1.86)	2.03(1.94,2.13)	2.01(1.93,2.1)
1501–3000	1.87(1.78,1.97)	1.87(1.77,1.99)	1.75(1.64,1.87)	1.71(1.61,1.83)	2.07(1.94,2.2)	1.97(1.86,2.09)
over 3000	1.7(1.65,1.75)	1.72(1.66,1.78)	1.69(1.63,1.75)	1.77(1.7,1.83)	2.03(1.95,2.11)	1.9(1.82,1.98)

SOURCE: MDHHS CHILDHOOD LEAD POISONING PREVENTION PROGRAM, MICHIGAN BROWNFIELD REDEVELOPMENT PROGRAM, AND THE CITY OF FLINT WATER DEPARTMENT across racial groups. Compared to white children, children of color have higher mean lead levels, especially those who are members of indigenous groups (Native Americans). Further, children residing closer to water disorder have higher mean lead levels than children living farther from these hazards.

Additionally, as noted in Table 4.3, a higher percentage of lead-poisoned children reside in homes built before 1978 than in homes built after 1978. There is also a substantial difference in the percentage of children with lead poisoning living near water disorder compared to the percentage of children with lead poisoning residing farther from brownfields, water main breaks, and high-water lead levels. In 2013, while 2 percent of children living over 3000 feet away from brownfields and water main breaks had lead poisoning, nearly 5 percent of children living near Brownfields and 4percent of children living near water main breaks had lead poisoning. Also, Table 4.3 shows that by 2014, children residing near residences with high water lead levels had higher rates of lead poisoning than their counterparts living farther from sources of high-water lead levels.

Table 4.4 reports adjusted odds ratios for water blight in Flint, controlling for predictors such as sample type, tested during the summer, neighborhood-level effects, age, sex, and income level. Results from the logistic regression analysis confirm a positive but statistically insignificant relationship between blood lead levels and proximity to water disorder (from less than 500 feet to 3000 feet away, $p = .938$, .655, and .173, respectively). Results from this analysis also show that residing near brownfields (less than 500 feet away, Adjusted odds ratio=4.54, CI=0.92,22.54) more substantially affects blood lead level than living near residences with high water lead levels (less than 500 feet away, Adjusted odds ratio=0.92; CI=.12,7.00)

Finally, Table 4.5 illustrates variations in proximity to blight indicators among race and income groups, showing that regardless of race, poverty correlates with proximity to blight indicators. This table demonstrates that a higher proportion of African American residents with lower median household incomes live closer to blight indicators than similarly situated white residents. For instance, compared to white residents in Flint, a larger percentage of black residents live within 800 feet of a water main break as well as elevated water lead levels in the community.

7 Discussion and Conclusion

This research confirms findings from previous studies illustrating the relationship between demographic indicators (race and income) and proximity to

TABLE 4.3 Annual prevalence of lead poisoning by selected population characteristics (n=904)

	2010 (n=296)	2011 (n=197)	2012 (n=125)	2013 (n=103)	2014 (n=102)	2015 (n=81)
	%	%	%	%	%	%
Age						
Under 1	8.70	2.50	5.00	5.10	4.90	4.30
1–5	7.10	6.70	4.70	4.00	4.30	2.90
6–11	4.10	2.50	1.40	1.70	0.70	3.60
Sex						
Male	7.50	6.60	4.80	4.80	3.90	2.90
Female	6.50	5.60	4.10	3.10	4.70	3.60
Race						
White	6.10	5.80	4.50	3.80	5.00	4.60
Asian	*	*	*	*	*	*
Black	8.30	6.70	5.20	4.50	6.70	4.40
Native American	*	*	*	*	*	*
Mixed Race	*	*	*	10.20	8.80	4.80
Year residence built						
Before 1950	11.20	10.00	6.60	7.10	7.20	6.30
Between 1951–1978	4.50	4.60	2.50	2.50	3.60	1.40
Post 1978	*	*	*	*	*	*
Neighborhood level						
Brownfields						
< 500	9.80	7.00	7.10	5.40	6.50	5.70
500–800	7.50	4.40	6.70	5.60	6.20	3.00
801–1500	6.80	6.80	4.60	4.40	4.90	4.30
1501–3000	7.40	6.60	3.50	3.30	3.20	2.40
over 3000	4.20	6.20	2.90	1.90	1.60	*
Watermains						
< 500	8.8.	7.20	5.40	5.50	5.20	4.70
500–800	9.10	6.40	4.80	5.10	7.20	5.50
801–1500	7.90	7.80	5.00	4.10	3.80	2.30
1501–3000	6.50	6.20	5.30	2.70	3.70	2.60
over 3000	3.00	3.20	2.50	2.30	1.80	1.20

TABLE 4.3 Annual prevalence of lead poisoning by selected population characteristics (n=904) (*cont.*)

	2010 (n=296)	2011 (n=197)	2012 (n=125)	2013 (n=103)	2014 (n=102)	2015 (n=81)
	%	%	%	%	%	%
WLL						
< 500	9.10	7.50	5.30	4.50	5.20	4.40
500–800	9.80	7.30	5.20	5.80	6.40	4.20
801–1500	6.10	5.40	4.10	4.40	4.10	3.00
1501–3000	3.60	4.30	3.70	1.50	1.80	*
over 3000	2.90	3.70	2.90	2.20	2.00	1.50

SOURCE: MDHHS CHILDHOOD LEAD POISONING PREVENTION PROGRAM, MICHIGAN BROWNFIELD REDEVELOPMENT PROGRAM, AND THE CITY OF FLINT WATER DEPARTMENT

blight at the neighborhood level. The statistical results, based on race and class indicators, substantiate claims that race groups, namely Native Americans, African Americans, and mixed-race Americans in Flint, and especially those who are poor, are disproportionately burdened by toxins from neighborhood blight in the form of brownfields, corroded water, and water main breaks. Study results also indicate that as the percentage of African Americans relative to the number of whites increased, the incidence of neighborhood blight increases. The highest proportion of children with elevated blood lead levels in Flint is found in neighborhoods with the highest percentage of residents living near hazardous blight.

This study captures the conditions and effects of disparate exposure to neighborhood neglect in a neoliberal city. Rather than disproving claims of environmental racism, this research substantiates the previous scholarship illustrating the significance of context or ecological factors in determining health outcomes as well as the salience of intersecting race, class, and space tensions in urban America. While the findings in the study are persuasive, this study reflects a snapshot of data collected between 2010 and 2015 in Flint, Michigan, a city with considerable inequality that may not be representative of other cities with healthier local economies. A more detailed analysis of the conditions contributing to racial disparities in proximity to neighborhood blight, as reflected in this study, is necessary.

TABLE 4.4 Adjusted odds ratios comparing BLLs before and after the Flint Water Crisis (n=18020)

		Before FWC (n=13800)	During FWC (n=4193)
Race			
	African American	reference	2.42(1.616,3.618)*
Year residence built			
	Before 1950	reference	2.37(0.54,10.45
	Between 1951–1978	reference	0.858(0.191,3.86)
Under 133 % of the FPL			
	Yes	reference	1.52(0.964,2.402)
Neighborhood level			
	Brownfields		
	< 500	reference	4.54(0.92,22.54)
	500–800	reference	2.80(0.58,13.51)
	801–1500	reference	3.21(0.69,14.77)
	1501–3000	reference	2.43(.53, 11.22)
	Watermains		
	< 500	reference	0.81(.101,6.43)
	500–800	reference	1.103(0.137,8.86)
	801–1500	reference	0.616(0.076,4.99)
	1501–3000	reference	.643(0.076,5.41)
	WLL		
	< 500	reference	0.92(.12,7.00)
	500–800	reference	0.80(0.103,6.25)
	801–1500	reference	0.62(0.078,4.91)
	1501–3000	reference	0.171(0.04,2.18)

Predictors added simultaneously to the model.
Regression Controls: Sample type, tested during summer, percent black categories, percent vacant categories,
sex and age. * = $p < .05$

TABLE 4.5 Means for health and blight indicators by race and income

Health and blight indicators	White		Black	
	Low income	High income	Low income	High income
Resides within 800 ft. of Brownfield	0.27	0.08	0.10	0.09
Resides within 800 ft. of water main break	0.43	0.1	0.42	0.25
Resides within 800 ft. of WLL above AL	0.59	0.16	0.57	0.46
Resides within 5000 ft. of Genesee Power Station	0.01	0	0.05	0
BLL classified at elevated	0.06	0.02	0.06	0.04
Proportion within Flint	0.24	0.62	0.73	0.34
Proportion within other Genesee County cities	0.46	0.88	0.52	0.08

SOURCE: MDHHS CHILDHOOD LEAD POISONING PREVENTION PROGRAM, MICHIGAN BROWNFIELD REDEVELOPMENT PROGRAM, AND THE CITY OF FLINT WATER DEPARTMENT

Findings from this study support call by environmental justice proponents to correct race and income disparities in exposure to environmental hazards. Given that income and race predict proximity to hazardous blight, efforts to mitigate sources of blight are essential, particularly given the highly probable and dangerous association between blight and health. Provided that adverse health effects may derive from hazardous blight, including low birth weights and behavioral challenges among children, it can be argued that the cost of not cleaning up hazardous blight will likely be considerably more extensive in the long-term than in the short-term. Multiple forms of hazardous blight surround predominately African American and poor areas. If siting and pollution trends persist without adequate correction, the conditions of disparate exposure and the consequences of ignoring the challenge to clean up blighted communities may worsen.

As such, the need to determine a short and long-term strategy for cleaning up hazard-ridden communities is evident. Although the pace of cleaning up known hazards in Flint, including corroded water, has been slow, the challenge of restoring blighted communities cannot be avoided, particularly in poor and low resource communities inundated with pollution from a backlog of delayed or ignored public infrastructure repairs. Restoring blighted neighborhoods will require significant systemic and programmatic changes to current zoning ordinances that shortchange communities and to current state regulatory policies whose protections favor industry over public health. Relatedly, given that black, brown, and poor residents are more likely than higher-income residents to reside near hazardous neighborhood blight, these residents deserve an extended role in the process of crafting siting policies and determining the permit conditions of new hazardous and nonhazardous waste facilities.

Tackling racial disparities in health outcomes and embracing the task of restoring blighted communities due to the presence of life-threatening toxins is among America's most important civil rights challenges in the twenty-first century. Based on the findings of this study and the overwhelming majority of the environmental justice scholarship that precedes it, it is no longer a question of whether disparities exist. The important question facing society today is who should pay for the decades of neglect and pollution in urban areas. Will the costs of benign neglect continue to be paid by vulnerable populations within high-risk communities or the industries and pro-business state governments that help perpetuate these trends?

References

Aelion, C. M., Davis, H.T., Lawson, A.B., Cai, B., and McDermott, S. (2013). "Associations between Soil Lead Concentrations and Populations by Race/Ethnicity and Income-to-Poverty Ratio in Urban and Rural Areas." *Environmental Geochemistry and Health* 35(1): 1–12.

Akkus, C. and Ozdenerol, E. (2014). "Exploring Childhood Lead Exposure through gis: A Review of the Recent Literature." *International Journal of Environmental Research and Public Health* 11(6): 14–34.

Allen, M., Clark, R., Cotruvo, J.A., and Grigg, N. (2018). "Drinking Water and Public Health in an Era of Aging Distribution Infrastructure." *Public Works Management & Policy* 23(4): 301–309.

Andrew, A.S. (1996). "Brownfield Redevelopment: A State-Led Reform of Superfund Liability." *Natural Resources & Environment* 10(3): 27–31.

Anderson, M. (2014). "The New Minimal Cities." *The Yale Law Journal* 123(5): 1118–1227.

Anselin, L. (1995). "Local Indicators of Spatial Association—LISA." *Geogr. Anal* 27: 93–115.

Ash, M. and Fetter, T.R. (2004). "Who Lives on the Wrong Side of the Environmental Tracks? Evidence from the EPA's Risk-Screening Environmental Indicators Model." *Social Science Quarterly* 85: 441–462.

Atkinson, R. (2000). "The Hidden Costs of Gentrification, Displacement in Central London." *Journal of Housing and the Built Environment* 5(4): 307–326.

Attanayake, C.P., Hettiarachchi, G.M., Harms, A., Presley, D., Martin, S., and Pierzynski, G.M. (2014). "Field Evaluations on Soil Plant Transfer of Lead from an Urban Garden Soil." *Journal of Environmental Quality* 43: 475–487.

Baird, G. (2011). "Money Matters: Fasten Your Seat Belts: Main Breaks and the Issuance of Precautionary Boil-Water Notices." *Journal American Water Works Association* 103(3): 24–28.

Baker, L.A. (2009). *The Water Environment of Cities*. New York, NY: Springer Press.

Bearden, D.M. (2012). "Comprehensive Environmental Response, Compensation, and Liability Act: A Summary of Superfund Cleanup Authorities and Related Provisions of the Act." *Congressional Research Service*. June 14, 2012. Available at: https://fas.org/sgp/crs/misc/R41039.pdf (consulted April 2, 2019)

Beauregard, R.A. (2009). "Urban Population Loss in Historical Perspective: United States, 1820–2000." *Environment and Planning Journal* 41(3): 514–528.

Been, V. (1995). "Analyzing Evidence of Environmental Justice." *Journal of Land Use & Law* 11: 1–36.

Been, V. and Gupta, F. (1997). "Coming to the Nuisance or Going to the Barrios? A Longitudinal Analysis of Environmental Justice Claims." *Ecology Law Quarterly* 24(1): 1–56.

Beggs, J.J. (1995). "The Institutional Environment: Implications for Race and Gender Inequality in the U.S. Labor Market." *American Sociological Review* 60(4): 612–633.

Bell, M.L. and Ebisu, K. (2012). "Environmental Inequality in Exposures to Airborne Particulate Matter Components in the United States." *Environmental Health Perspectives* 120(12): 1699–1704.

Belova, A., Greco, S.L., Riederer, A.M., Olsho, L.E.W., and Corrales, M.A. (2013). "A Method to Screen U. S. Environmental Biomonitoring Data for Race/Ethnicity and Income-Related Disparity." *Environmental Health* 12: 114.

Bradford, L.E.A., Idowu, B., Zagozewski, R., and Bharadwaj, L.A. (2017). "There Is No Publicity like Word of Mouth … Lessons for Communicating Drinking Water Risks in the Urban Setting." *Sustainable Cities and Society* 29(1): 23–40.

Braknis, Greg. (1989). "Gasoline Leak? Family's Tainted Water Raises Health Concerns." *The Flint Journal*. March 16, 2989.

Brenner, N. and Theodore, N. (eds.). (2002). *Spaces of Neoliberalism: Urban Restructuring in Western Europe and North America*. Oxford: Blackwell Press.

Bridge, G., Butler, T., and Lees, L. (eds.). (2012). *Mixed Communities: Gentrification by Stealth*? Bristol: Policy.

Brown, M.J. and Margolis, S. (2012). "Lead in Drinking Water and Human Blood Lead Levels in the United States." *MMWR Supplements* 61(4): 1–9.

Bryant, S. D. (2004). "Lead-Contaminated Drinking Waters in the Public Schools of Philadelphia." *Journal of Toxicology-Clinical Toxicology* 42(3): 287–294.

Bullard, R.D., Mohai, P., Saha, R., and Wright, B. (2007). *Toxic Twenty 1987-2007: Grassroots Struggles to Dismantle Racism in the United States. A Report for the United Justice and Witness Ministries.* Cleveland, OH: United Church of Christ.

Bullard, R.D., Johnson, G.S., and Torres, A.O. (2000). *Sprawl City: Race, Politics, and Planning in Atlanta.* Washington, DC: Island Press.

Bullard, R.D. (1996). *Unequal Protection: Environmental Justice and Communities of Color.* San Francisco, CA: Sierra Club Books.

Bullard, R.D. (1990). *Dumping in Dixie: Race, Class, and Environmental Quality.* Boulder, CO: Westview Press.

Bullard, R.D. and Wright, B.H. (1986). "The Politics of Pollution: The Black Community." *Phylon* XLVII(l): 71–78.

Burris, H.H., Collins, J.W., and Wright, R.O. (2011). "Racial/Ethnic Disparities in Preterm Birth: Clues from Environmental Exposures." *Current Opinion in Pediatrics* 23(2): 227–232.

Burris, H.H. and Hacker, M.R. (2017). "Birth Outcome Racial Disparities: A Result of Intersecting Social and Environmental Factors." *Seminars in Perinatology* 41(6): 360–366.

Burwell, D. and Cole, L.W. (2007). "Environmental Justice Comes Full Circle: Warren County Before and After." *Environmental Law Journal* 1(1): 9–40.

Cable, S. and Benson, M. (1993). "Acting Locally: Environmental Injustice and the Emergence of Grass-Roots Environmental Organizations." *Social Problems* 40(4): 464–477.

Campbell, H., Peck, L., and Tschudi, M. (2010). "Justice for All? A Causal Analysis Toxics Release Inventory Facility Location." *Review of Policy Research* 27(1): 1–25.

Carrel, M., Zahrieh, D., Young, S.G., Oleson, J., Ryckman, K.K., Wels, B., Simmons, D.L., and Saftlas, A. (2017). "High Prevalence of Elevated Blood Lead Levels in Both Rural and Urban Iowa Newborns: Spatial Patterns and Area-Level Covariates." *Plos One* 12(5): 1–17.

Cassidy-Bushrow, A.E., Sitarik, A.R., Havstad, S., Park, S.K, Bielak, L.F., Austin, C., Johnson, C.C., and Arora, M. (2017). "Burden of Higher Lead Exposure in African Americans Starts in Utero and Persists into Childhood." *Environment International* 108: 221–227.

Chakraborty, J. and Armstrong, M.P. (1997). "Exploring the Use of Buffer Analysis for the Identification of Impacted Areas in Environmental Equity Assessment." *Cartography and Geographic Information Systems* 24: 145–157.

Collaton, E. and Bartsch, C. (1996). "Industrial Site Reuse and Urban Redevelopment—An Overview." *Cityscape* 2(3): 17–61.

Crowder, K.F. and Downey, L. (2010). "Interneighborhood Migration, Race, and Environmental Hazards: Modeling Microlevel Processes of Environmental Inequality." *American Journal of Sociology* 115(4): 1110–1149.

Dewar, M. (2015). "Reuse of Abandoned Property in Detroit and Flint." *Journal of Planning Education and Research* 35(3): 347–368.

Dewar, M., Seymour, E., and Druta, O. (2015). "Disinvesting in the City: The Role of Tax Foreclosure in Detroit." *Urban Affairs Review* 51(5): 587–615.

Dewar, M. and Thomas, J.M. (eds.). (2013). *The City After Abandonment.* Philadelphia, PA: University of Pennsylvania Press.

Dewilde, C. (2003). "A Life-Course Perspective on Social Exclusion and Poverty." *British Journal of Sociology* 54(1): 109–128.

di Leonardo, M. (2008). "Introduction: New Global and American Landscapes of Inequality." In: Collins, J., di Leonardo, M., and Williams, B. (eds.). *New Landscapes of Inequality: Neoliberalism and the Erosion of Democracy in America.* Santa Fe, NM: School of American Research Press.

Dixon, S. L., Gaitens, J.M., Jacobs, D.E., Strauss, W., Nagaraja, J., Pivetz, T., Wilson, J.W., and Ashley, P.J. (2009). "Exposure of US Children to Residential Dust Lead, 1999-2004: The Contribution of Lead-Contaminated Dust to Children's Blood Lead Levels." *Environmental Health Perspectives* 117(3): 468–474.

Downey, L. (2005). "The Unintended Significance of Race: Environmental Racial Inequality in Detroit." *Social Forces* 83(3): 971–1007.

Downey, L. and Van Willigen, M. (2005). "Environmental Stressors: The Living Near Industrial Activity." *Journal of Health and Social Behavior* 46(3): 289–305.

Eckerd, A. and Keeler, A.G. (2012). "Going Green Together? Brownfield Remediation and Environmental Justice." *Policy Sciences* 45(4): 293–314.

Edwards, M. (2014). "Fetal Death and Reduced Birth Rates Associated with Exposure to Lead-Contaminated Drinking Water." *Environmental Science and Technology* 48(1): 739–746.

Edwards, M., Triantafyllidou, S., and Best, D. (2009). "Elevated Blood Lead in Young Children Due to Lead-Contaminated Drinking Water: Washington, DC, 2001–2004." *Environmental Science and Technology* 43(5): 1618–1623.

Edwards, M. (2008). "Lead Poisoning: A Public Health Issue." *Primary Health Care* 18(3): 18–20.

Edwards, M and Dudi, A. (2004). "Role of Chlorine and Chloramine in Corrosion of Lead-Bearing Plumbing Materials." *Journal of American Water Works Association* 96(10): 69–81.

Elliott, J.R. and Frickel, S. (2013). "The Historical Nature of Cities: A Study of Urbanization and Hazardous Waste Accumulation." *American Sociological Review* 78(4): 521–543.

Enders, C.K. and Bandalos, D.L. (2001). "The Relative Performance of Full Likelihood Estimation for Missing Data in Structural Equation Models." *Structural* 8(3): 430–457.

Ezezika, O. (2007). "Frontlines of Global Environmental Justice: A Look at Inequality Worldwide." *Sage Magazine* 11(1): 12–15.

Garber, C.E., Blissmer B., Deschenes M.R., Franklin B.A., Lamonte M.J., Lee I.M., Swain, D.P. (2011). "Quantity and Quality of Exercise for Developing and Maintaining Cardiorespiratory, Musculoskeletal, and Neuromotor Fitness in Apparently Healthy Adults: Guidance for Prescribing Exercise." *Med Sci Sports Exerc* 43: 1334–1359.

Glaza, E.C. and Park, J.K. (1992). "Permeation of Organic Contaminants Through Gasketed Pipe Joints." *Journal AWWA* 84(7): 92–100.

Glenn, C. (2017). "Upholding Civil Rights in Environmental Law: The Case for Ex Ante Title vi Regulation and Enforcement." *Review of Law & Social Change* 41(1): 45.

Goldfarb, E. (2010). "Field Survey of HUD Site Contamination Policy." *Cityscape* 12(3): 71–83.

Gonzalez, E.J., Pham, P.G., Ericson, J.E., and Baker, D.B. (2002). "Tijuana Childhood Lead Risk Assessment Revisited: Validating a GIS Model with Environmental Data." *Environmental Management* 29: 559–565.

Graber, L.K., Asher, D., Anandaraja, N., Bopp, R.F., Merrill, K., Cullen, M.R., Luboga, S., and Trasande, L. (2010). "Childhood Lead Exposure After the Phaseout of Leaded Gasoline: An Ecological Study of School-Age Children in Kampala, Uganda." *Environmental Health Perspectives* 18(6): 884–889.

Graff, J.C., Murphy, L., Ekvall, S., and Gagnon, M. (2006). "In-Home Toxic Chemical Exposures and Children with Intellectual and Developmental Disabilities." *Pediatric Nursing* 32(6): 596–603.

Grant, D., Trautner, M.N., Downey, L., and Thiebaud, L. (2010). "Bringing the Polluters Back In: Environmental Inequality and the Organization of Chemical Production." *American Sociological Review* 75(4): 479–504.

Greenberg, M.R. (2003). "Guest Editorial: Reversing Urban Decay: Brownfield Redevelopment and Environmental Health." *Environmental Health Perspectives* 111(2): A74–A75.

Griffith, D.A., Doyle, P.G., Wheeler, D.C., and Johnson, D.L. (1998). "A Tale of Two Swaths: Urban Childhood Blood-Lead Levels Across Syracuse, New York." *Annals of the Association of American Geographers* 88(4): 640–665.

Guidotti, T., Moses, M., Goldsmith, D., and Ragain, L. (2008). "DC Water and Sewer Authority and Lead in Drinking Water: A Case Study in Environmental Health Risk Management'." *Journal of Public Health Management and Practice: JPHMP* 14(1): 33–41.

Haley, V.B. and Talbot, T.O. (2004). "Geographic Analysis of Blood Lead Levels in New York State Children Born 1994–1997." *Environmental Health Perspectives* 112(15): 1577–1582.

Hackworth, J. (2007). *The Neoliberal City: Governance, Ideology, and Development in American Urbanism*. Ithaca, New York: Cornell University Press.

Hanlon, B. (2015). "Beyond Sprawl: Social Sustainability and Reinvestment in the Baltimore Suburbs." In: Anaker, K.B. (ed.). *The New American Suburb: Poverty, Race, and the Economic Crisis*, pp. 133–152. Burlington, VT: Ashgate.

Hanna-Attisha, M., LaChance, J., Sadler, R.C., and Schnepp, A.C. (2016). "Elevated Blood Lead Levels in Children Associated with the Flint Drinking Water Crisis: A Spatial Analysis of Risk and Public Health Response." *American Journal of Public Health* 106(2): 283–290.

Harvey, D. (2005). *Brief History of Neoliberalism*. Oxford: Oxford University Press.

Heard-Garris, N.J., Roche, J., Carter, P., Abir, M., Walton, M., Zimmerman, M., and Cunningham, R. (2017). "Voices from Flint: Community Perceptions of the Flint Water Crisis." *Journal of Urban Health* 94(6): 776–779.

Heaney, Christopher D., Wing, S., Wilson, S.M., Campbell, R.L., Caldwell, D., Hopkins, B., O'Shea, S., and Yeatts, K. (2013). "Public Infrastructure Disparities and the Microbiological and Chemical Safety of Drinking and Surface Water Supplies in a Community Bordering a Landfill." *Journal of Environmental Health* 75(100): 24–36.

Hipp, J.R. and Lakon, C.M. (2010). "Social Disparities in Health: Disproportionate Toxicity Proximity in Minority Communities over a Decade." *Health & Place* 16(41): 674–683.

Hicken, M.T., Gee, G.C., Morenoff, J., Connell, C.M., Snow, R.C., and Hu, H. (2012). "A Novel Look at Racial Health Disparities: The Interaction between Social Disadvantage and Environmental Health." *American Journal of Public Health* 102(12): 2344–2351.

Holsen, T.M., Park, J.K., Bontoux, L., Jenkins, D., and Selleck, R.E. (1991). "The Effect of Soils on the Permeation of Plastic Pipes by Organic Chemicals." *Journal AWWA* 83(11): 85–91.

Hula, R.C. (1999). *An Assessment of Brownfield Redevelopment Policies: The Michigan Experience*. Ann Arbor: Department of Political Science and Urban Affairs, Michigan State University.

Hurley, A. (1997). "Fiasco at Wagner Electric: Environmental Justice and Urban Geography in St. Louis." *Environmental History* 2(4): 460–481.

Institute of Medicine. (1999). "Toward Environmental Justice: Research, Education, and Health Policy Needs." Washington, DC: National Academy Press.

Jain, R.B. (2016). "Trends and Variability in Blood Lead Concentrations among US Children and Adolescents." *Environmental Science and Pollution Research* 23(8): 7880–7889.

Johnson, G.S., Rainey, S.A., and Johnson, L.S. (2008). "Dickson, Tennessee and Toxic Wells: An Environmental Racism Case Study." *Race, Gender & Class* 15(3–4): 204–223.

Johnson, G.S. (2005). "Grassroots Activism in Louisiana." *Humanity and Society* 29(3–4): 285–304.

Jones, R., Homa, D., Meyer, P., Brody, D., Caldwell, K., Pirkle, J., and Brown, M.J. (2009). "Trends in Blood Lead Levels and Blood Lead Testing Among US Children Aged 1 to 5 Years, 1988-2004." *Pediatrics* 123: e376–e385.

Joseph, C.L.M., Havstad, S., Ownby, D.R., Peterson, E.L., Maliarik, M., McCabe, M.J., Barone, C., and Johnson, C.C. (2005). "Blood Lead Level and Risk of Asthma." *Environmental Health Perspectives* 113(7): 900–904.

Kaplan, M. and United States Congress. (1984). "Hard Choices." Joint Economic Committee. Subcommittee on Economic Goals and Intergovernmental Policy.

Kaplowitz, S.A., Perlstadt, H., and Post, L.A. (2010). "Comparing Lead Poisoning Risk Assessment Methods: Census Block Group Characteristics Vs. Zip Codes as Predictors." *Public Health Reports* 125(2): 234–245.

Kim, M.A. and Williams, K.A. (2017). "Lead Levels in Landfill Areas and Childhood Exposure: An Integrative Review." *Public Health Nursing* 34(1): 87–97.

Krieg, E.J. (1998). "The Two Faces of Toxic Waste: Trends in the Spread of Environmental Hazards." *Sociological Forum* 13(1): 3–20.

Kruse, K.M. (2005). *White Flight: Atlanta and the Making of Modern Conservatism*. Princeton, NJ: Princeton University Press.

LaChance, J., Sadler, R.C., and Champney Schnepp, A. (2016). "Elevated Blood Lead Levels in Children Associated with the Flint Drinking Water Crisis: A Spatial Analysis of Risk and Public Health Response." *American Journal of Public Health* 106: 283–290.

LeDuff, Charlie. (2013). *Detroit: An American Autopsy*. New York, NY: Penguin Press.

Lanphear, B.P., Weitzman, M., Winter, N.L., Eberly, S., Yakir, B., Tanner, M., Emond, M., and Matte, T.D. (1996). "Lead-Contaminated House Dust and Urban Children's Blood Lead Levels." *American Journal of Public Health* 86(10): 1416–1421.

Lanphear, B.P., Byrd, R.S., Auinger, P., and Schaffer, S.J. (1998). "Community Characteristics Associated with Elevated Blood Lead Levels in Children." *Pediatrics* 101(2): 264–271.

Lanphear, B.P., Hornung, R., and Ho, M. (2005). "Screening Housing to Prevent Lead Toxicity in Children." *Public Health Reports* 120(3): 305–310.

Lawson, L., and Miller, A. (2013). "Community Gardens and Urban Agriculture as Antithesis to Abandonment: Exploring a Citizenship-Land Model." In: Dewar, M. and Thomas, J.M. (eds.). *The City After Abandonment*, pp. 17–40. University of Pennsylvania Press. Available at: www.jstor.org/stable/j.ctt3fh93k.

Lee, S., and Mohai, P. (2013). "The Socioeconomic Dimensions of Brownfield Cleanup in the Detroit Region." *Population and Environment* 34(3): 420–429.

Leisering, L. and Walker, R. (1998). "New Realities: The Dynamics of Modernity." In: Leisering, L. and Walker, R. (eds.). *The Dynamics of Modern Society: Poverty, Policy and Welfare*, pp. 3–16. Bristol, UK: Polity Press.

Lester, J.P., Allen, D.W., and Hill, K.M. (2001). *Environmental Injustice in the United States: Myths and Realities*. Boulder, CO: Westview Press.

Levin, R., Brown, M.J., Kashtock, M.E., Jacobs, D.E, Whelan, E.A., Rodman, J., Schock, M.R., Padilla, A., and Sinks, T. (2008). "Lead Exposures in US Children, 2008: Implications for Prevention." *Environmental Health Perspectives* 116(10): 1285–1293.

Lewis, R. (1972). "Study Indicates High Lead Level in Flint's Soil." *The Flint Journal*. May 27, 1972.

Lipman, P. (2009). "The Cultural Politics of Mixed-Income Schools and Housing: A Racialized Discourse of Displacement, Exclusion, and Control." *Anthropology and Education Quarterly* 40(3): 215–236.

Livingston, B., Cate, C., Pridmore, A., Heidrick, J.W., and Geisbush, J. (eds.). (2016). *Pipelines 2016: Out of Sight, Out of Mind, Not Out of Risk*. [N.p.]: American Society of Civil Engineers.

Lytle, D. and Schock, M. (2005). "Formation of Pb (IV) Oxides in Chlorinated Water." *Journal AWWA* 97(11): 102–114.

Macey, G.P., Her, X., Reibling, E.T., and Ericson, J. (2001). "An Investigation of Environmental Racism Claims: Testing Environmental Management Approaches with a Geographic Information System." *Environmental Management* 27(6): 893–907.

Mallach, A. (2010). *Facing the Urban Challenge: The Federal Government and America's Older Distressed Cities*. Washington, DC: Brookings Institution.

Marable, M. (1984). *Race, Reform, and Rebellion: The Second Reconstruction in Black America, 1945-1982*. Jackson, MS: University Press of Mississippi.

Maranville, A.R., Ting, T., and Zhang, Y. (2009). "An Environmental Justice Analysis: Superfund Sites and Surrounding Communities in Illinois." *Environmental Justice* 2(2): 49–58.

Massey, A.R. and Steele, J.E. (2012). "Lead in Drinking Water: Sampling in Primary Schools and Preschools in South Central Kansas." *Journal of Environmental Health* 74(7): 16–20.

Massey, D.S. (2004). "Segregation and Stratification: A Biosocial Perspective." *Du Bois Review: Social Science Research on Race* 1(1): 7–25.

McCarthy, L. (2009). "Off the Mark?: Efficiency in Targeting the Most Marketable Sites Rather than Equity in Public Assistance for Brownfield Redevelopment." *Economic Development Quarterly* 23(3): 211–228.

McGhee, T.J. and Steel, E.W. (1991). *Water Supply and Sewerage*. 6th ed. New York, NY: McGraw-Hill Press.

Michigan Civil Rights Commission. (2017). "Flint Water Crisis Systemic Racism Through the Lens of Flint, Michigan Civil Rights Commission." February 17, 2017. Available at: https://www.michigan.gov/documents/mdcr/VFlintCrisisRep-F-Edited3-13-17_554317_7.pdf (consulted 12 November, 2019).

Mielke, H.W., Gonzales, C.R., Powell, E.T., and Mielke, P.W. (2013). "Environmental and Health Disparities in Residential Communities of New Orleans: The Need for Soil Lead Intervention to Advance Primary Prevention." *Environment International* 51: 73–81.

Miller, N.E. (1976). "Winter Water-Main-Break Operations in Milwaukee." *American Water Works Association* 68(1): 10–11.

Miranda, M.L., Anthopolos, R., and Hastings, D. (2011). "A Geospatial Analysis of the Effects of Aviation Gasoline on Childhood Blood Lead Levels." *Environmental Health Perspectives* 119: 1513–1516.

Miranda, M.L., Kim, D., Hull, A.P., Paul, C.J., and Galeano, M.A.O. (2007). "Changes in Blood Lead Levels Associated with Use of Chloramines in Water Treatment Systems." *Environmental Health Perspectives* 115: 221–225.

Miranda, M.L., Dolinoy, D.C., and Overstreet, M.A. (2002). "Mapping for Prevention: gis Models for Directing Childhood Lead Poisoning Prevention Programs." *Environmental Health Perspectives* 110: 947–953.

Mock, B. (2016). "Short Cuts Could Cause Permanent Damages: The Water Crisis in Flint, Mich., is the Latest in a Long History of African Americans being Exposed to Toxic Poisoning." *Crisis* (15591573) 123(1): 5.

Mohai, P. and Saha, R. (2007). "Racial Inequality in the Distribution of Hazardous Waste: A National-Level Reassessment." *Social Problems* 54(3): 343–370.

Mohai, P. and Saha, R. (2006). "Reasssessing Racial and Socioeconomic Disparities in Environmental Justice Research." *Demography* 43(2): 383–399.

Moody, H.A., Darden, J.T., and Pigozzi, B.W. (2016). "The Relationship of Neighborhood Socioeconomic Differences and Racial Residential Segregation to Childhood Blood Lead Levels in Metropolitan Detroit." *Journal of Urban Health* 93(5): 820–839.

Muldoon, S.B., Cauley, J.A., Kuller, L.H., Scott, J., and Rohay, J. (1994). "Life-Style and Sociodemographic Factors as Determinants of Blood Lead Levels in Elderly Women." *American Journal of Epidemiology* 139(6): 599–608.

Nicholson, L.M., Schwirian, K.P., and Schwirian, P.M. (2010). "Childhood Lead Poisoning Laws in New York City: Environment, Politics and Social Action." *Children, Youth and Environments* 20(1): 178–199.

Niedt, C. (2006). "Gentrification and the Grassroots: Popular Support in the Revanchist Suburb." *Journal of Urban Affairs* 28(2): 99–120.

Oakes, J.M., Anderton, D.L., and Anderson, A.B. (1996). "A Longitudinal Analysis of Environmental Equity in Communities with Hazardous Waste Facilities." *Social Science Research* 25: 125–148.

O'Day, D.K. (1989). "External Corrosion in Distribution Systems." *American Water Works Association* 81(10): 45–52.

Olson, T.M., Wax, M., Yonts, J., Heidecorn, K., Haig, S.J., Yeoman, D., Hayes, Z., Raskin, L., and Ellis, B.R. (2017). "Forensic Estimates of Lead Release from Lead Service Lines during the Water Crisis in Flint, Michigan." *Environ. Sci. Technol. Lett.* 4(9): 356–361.

Opper, Richard G. (2005). "The Brownfield Manifesto." *The Urban Lawyer* 37(1): 163–190.

Oyana, T.J. and Margai, F.M. (2010). "Spatial Patterns and Health Disparities in Pediatric Lead Exposure in Chicago: Characteristics and Profiles of High-Risk Neighborhoods." *Professional Geographer* 62(1): 46–65.

Oyana, T.J. and Margai, F.M. (2007). "Geographic Analysis of Health Risks of Pediatric Lead Exposure: A Golden Opportunity to Promote Healthy Neighborhoods." *Archives of Environmental & Occupational Health* 62(2): 93–104.

Pace, D. (2005). "More Blacks Live with Pollution: AP Analysis of U.S. Research Shows More Blacks Likely to Live with Dangerous Pollution." *The Associated Press.* December 13, 2005.

Pais, J., Crowder, K., and Downey, L. (2014). "Unequal Trajectories: Racial and Class Differences in Residential Exposure to Industrial Hazard." *Social Forces* 92(3): 1189–1215.

Park, J.K., Bontoux, L., Holsen, T.M., Jenkins, D., and Selleck, R.E. (1991). "Permeation of Polybutylene Pipe and Gasket Material by Organic Chemicals." *Journal AWWA* 83(10): 71–78.

Pastor, M., Sadd, J., and Hipp, J. (2001). "Which Came First? Toxic Facilities, Minority Move-In, and Environmental Justice." *Journal of Urban Affairs* 23(1): 1–21.

Phoenix, J. (1993) Get the Lead Out. *Race, Poverty & the Environment* 3/4(4/1): 9–26.

Pieper, K.J., Martin, R., Tang, M., Walters, L., Parks, J., Roy, S., Devine, C., and Edwards, M.A. (2018). "Evaluating Water Lead Levels During the Flint Water Crisis." *Environ. Sci. Technol.* 52(15): 8124–8132.

Powers, C.W., Hoffman, F.E., Brown, D.E., and Conner, C. (2000). *Great Experiment: Brownfields Pilots Catalyze Revitalization.* New Brunswick, NJ: Institute for Responsible Management.

Quillian, L. (2003). "How Long are Exposures to Poor Neighborhoods? The Long-Term Dynamics of Entry and Exit from Poor Neighborhoods." *Population Research and Policy Review* 22(3): 221–249.

Rabin, R. (2008). "The Lead Industry and Lead Water Pipes "A Modest Campaign"." *American Journal of Public Health* 98(9): 1584–1592.

Rajani, B., Kleiner, Y., and Sink, J. (2012). "Exploration of the Relationship between Water Main Breaks and Temperature Covariates." *Urban Water Journal* 9(2): 67–84.

Rajaram, S.S. (2007). "An Action-Research Project: Community Lead Poisoning Prevention." *Teaching Sociology* 35(2): 138–150.

Rainey, S. (2005). "Residents Speak Out: Sharing Concerns About Environmental Problems, Public Health, and Justice in Clarksville, Tennessee." *Humanity and Society* 29(3–4): 270–284.

Reddy, Y.S., Aparna, Y., Ramalaksmi, B.A., and Kumar, B.D. (2014). "Lead and Trace Element Levels in Placenta, Maternal, and Cord Blood: A Cross-Sectional Pilot Study." *Journal of Obstetrics and Gynecology Research* 40(12): 2184–2190.

Reissman, D.B., Staley, F., Curtis, G.B., and Kaufmann, R.B. (2001). "Use of Geographic Information System Technology to Aid Health Department Decision Making about Childhood Lead Poisoning Prevention Activities." *Environmental. Health Perspectives* 109(1): 89–94.

Renner, R. (2010). "Exposure on Tap: Drinking as an Overlooked Source of Lead." *Environmental Health Perspectives* 118(2): A69–A74.

Ringquist, E. (2005). "Assessing Evidence of Environmental Inequities: A Meta-Analysis." *Journal of Policy Analysis and Management* 24(2): 223–247.

Roberts, J.R., Hulsey, T.C., Curtis, G.B., and Reigart, J.R. (2003). "Using Geographic Information Systems to Assess Risk for Elevated Blood Lead Levels in Children." *Public Health Reports* 118(3): 221–229.

Rose, J.B., Daeschner, S., Easterling, D.R., Curriero, F.C., Lele, S., and Patz, J.A. (2000). "Climate and Waterborne Disease Outbreaks." *American Water Works Association* 92(9): 77–87.

Rosenman, E. and Walker, S. (2016). "Tearing Down the City to Save It? Back-door Regionalism and the Demolition Coalition in Cleveland, Ohio." *Environment and Planning* 48(2): 273–291.

Sadler, R.C., LaChance, J., and Hanna-Attisha, M. (2017). "Social and Built Environmental Correlates of Predicted Blood Lead Levels in the Flint Water Crisis." *American Journal of Public Health* 107(5): 763–769.

Sampson, R.J. and Winter, A. (2016). "The Racial Ecology of Lead Poisoning: Toxic Inequality in Chicago Neighborhoods, 1995-2013." *DuBois Review: Social Science Research on Race* 13(2): 261–283.

Schock, M.R. and Giani, R. (2004). *Oxidant/disinfectant Chemistry and Impacts on Lead Corrosion.* In the Proceedings of Water Quality and Technology Conference. AWWA: San Antonio, TX.

Slagter, L. (2017). "Traces of Petroleum, Lead Found in Water at Rover Pipeline Work Site." *Flint Journal/MLive.com.* Available at: https://www.mlive.com/news/ann-arbor/2017/11/deq_rover_pipeline_water_tests.html (consulted July 17, 2018).

Slater, T. and Anderson, N. (2012). "The Reputational Ghetto: Territorial Stigmatisation in St Paul's, Bristol." *Transactions of the Institute of British Geographers* 37(4): 530–546.

Slater, T. (2009). "Missing Marcuse: On Gentrification and Displacement." *City* 13(2): 292–311.

Sze, J. (2006). *Noxious New York: The Racial Politics of Urban Health and Environmental Justice.* Cambridge, MA: The MIT Press.

The United Stated Environmental Protection Agency (USEPA). (2012). *Permeation and Leaching.* April 15, 2002. Office of Ground Water and Drinking Water Distribution System Issue Paper. Available at: https://www.epa.gov/sites/production/files/2015-09/documents/permeationandleaching.pdf (consulted 15 November, 2019).

Thompson, K.C., Gray, J., and Borchers, U. (2013). *Water Contamination Emergencies: Managing the Threats.* Cambridge, MA: Royal Society of Chemistry.

Turner, R. (2016). "The Slow Poisoning of Black Bodies: A Lesson in Environmental Racism and Hidden Violence." *Meridians* 15(1): 189–204.

Vaidyanathan, A., Staley, F., Shire, J., Muthukumar, S., Kennedy, C., Meyer, P.A., and Brown, M.J. (2009). "Screening for Lead Poisoning: A Geospatial Approach to Determine Testing of Children in At-Risk Neighborhoods." *Journal of Pediatrics* 154(3): 409–414.

Wacquant, L., Slater, T., and Pereira, V.B. (2014). "Territorial Stigmatisation in Action." *Environment and Planning* 46(6): 1270–1280.

White, B.M., Bonilha, H.S., and Ellis, C., Jr. (2016). "Racial/Ethnic Differences in Childhood Blood Lead Levels Among Children <72 Months of Age in the United States: A Systematic Review of the Literature." *Journal of Racial & Ethnic Health Disparities* 3(1): 145–153.

Whitehead, L., Johnson, G., Boone, W., and Grant, H. (2012). "An Effective Environmental Justice Partnership: Centers for Disease Control and Prevention and Citizens for Environmental Justice." *Race, Gender & Class* 19(3–4): 241–265.

Winter, A.S. and Sampson, R.J. (2017). "From Lead Exposure in Early Childhood to Adolescent Health: A Chicago Birth Cohort." *American Journal of Public Health* 107(9): 1496–1501.

Wood, A. and Lence, B.J. (2006). "Assessment of Water Main Break Data for Asset Management." *American Water Works Association* 98(7): 76–86.

Wood, A., Lence, B.J., and Liu, W. (2007). "Constructing Water Main Break Databases for Asset Management." *American Water Works Association* 99(1): 52–65.

Yeh, C.Y., Chiou, H.Y., Chen, R.Y., Yeh, K.H., Jeng, W.L., and Han, B.C. (1996). "Monitoring Lead Pollution Near a Storage Battery Recycling Plant in Taiwan, Republic of China." *Archives of Environmental Contamination & Toxicology* 30(2): 227–234.

Zenk, S.N., et al. (2005). "Neighborhood Racial Composition, Neighborhood Poverty, and the Spatial Accessibility of Supermarkets in Metropolitan Detroit." *American Journal of Public Health* 95: 660–667.

Zhang, F., Liu, Y., Zhang, H., Ban, Y., Wang, J., Liu, J., Zhong, L., Chen, X., and Zhu, B. (2016). "Investigation and Evaluation of Children's Blood Lead Levels around a Lead Battery Factory and Influencing Factors." *International Journal of Environmental Research & Public Health* 13(6): 541.

CHAPTER 5

Housing Waste

The Lakeside Public Housing Complex, Pontiac, Michigan

Graham Cassano, Jon Carroll and Daniel J. Clark

1 Introduction[1]

In 2014, the completion of Elliott Tower—the carillon clock tower at Oakland University—was cause for celebration on the campus where the authors of this chapter practice their respective disciplines (see Figure 5.1). Elliott Tower serves multiple functions including acting as a rallying point for gatherings, as a place for the community to enjoy weekly performances by the University Carillonneur, and as a means to help students and faculty get to class on time. However, Elliott Tower is also a marker that defines space and place on the landscape, establishing and reinforcing social identities in observable and powerful ways. Through its placement in the center of campus, the tower serves as a symbol of the university itself, and as a spatial marker of the social status affiliated with the university. In that sense, it signals the transformation of place (as a geographical location) into a certain kind of social space, with certain attendant norms and interaction patterns. These patterns, through which people use the landscape, define who they are, and who they are not. Embedded within this binary tension is the notion that different social subjects have differential privileges when accessing the landscape, based upon normatively created identities and socially generated perceptions of other-ness. Some social subjects are allowed access to some spaces (students on a campus), some social subjects are forbidden from entering some spaces (protesters outside a police station), some social subjects

1 The authors would like to thank Oakland County Pioneer and Historical Society volunteers, Barbara Frye, Dave Decker, and Geoff Breiger, and the OCPHS executive director, Mike McGuinness, for their generous assistance with research. Emma Boyhtari proved invaluable as a research assistant throughout this project. David Carroll, Payton Orr, and Jacob Hopp, provided important research assistance as the project was nearing completion. In addition, we would like to thank Jo Reger and the Oakland University Department of Sociology, Anthropology, Social Work, and Criminal Justice for the research grant that allowed us to reproduce some of the historical images in this chapter. Professor Jacqueline Scherer's previous work on Pontiac has served as both source and inspiration. Brian Broughton, of Camera Exchange in Waterford, Michigan, provided technical advice and camera repair. Finally, we would like to thank Bia Cassano for her tireless and diligent editorial assistance.

are confined to certain spaces (prisoners in maximum security), etc. In each case, symbolic geography mediates social interaction and, thus, contributes to shaping the social identities of those interacting with, and within, the space. Some spaces are sanctified, complete with official rules and taboos that carefully govern interaction, while others are stigmatized, with a consequently quite different set of (often more informal, though no less constraining) rules and taboos. Stigmatized space (Lavin 2014) may exist within a single building, or, may exist as part of a larger geography of negative perceptions associated with select portions of the landscape and its inhabitants, as "territorial stigma" (Wacquant 2008). Since social constructions of race are based upon invidious standards that arbitrarily valorize some groups, while sanctioning others, stigmatized space, and territorial stigma, represent vital conceptual instruments for excavating contemporary racialized geographies. Using these tools, and the methods of our disciplines (sociology, archaeology, history), this chapter maps the racialized geography of late twentieth century Pontiac, Michigan, layering it over the history of federally funded public housing in the city, intertwined with the political economy of the auto industry, in order to reveal an absence overflowing with meaning: the (now invisible) Lakeside Public Housing Complex (1952–2002).

Between 2002 and 2018, the former site of the Pontiac, Michigan, Lakeside Housing Complex served as an illegal dumping ground (see Figure 5.2). Some of the waste was from contracting work: tiles, rebar, planks, lights (see Figure 5.3). Other items, furniture (see Figure 5.4), children's toys, musical instruments (see Figure 5.5), suggested evictions, foreclosures, abandonment. Yet this was an idyllic wasteland. The forest had grown over old foundations (see Figure 5.6). The roads were remarkably quiet, with only a few engine sounds from the nearby city center penetrating the woods. And the entire area nearly surrounded by Crystal Lake (see Figure 5.7). Why was this beautiful space an abandoned wasteland? Perhaps it was contaminated? This chapter does not address the various failed development projects that plagued the Lakeside site between 2002 and 2017.[2] However, we do address the question of contamination. The Lakeside Homes (as the complex was sometimes called during its early years) were built beside Crystal Lake because that site was deemed, from the first, *contaminated*. It may, or may not, have been polluted by chemicals and carcinogens, but social stigma contaminated the site. From its construction in the early 1950s, until demolition, at the turn of the century, the Lakeside Complex occupied stigmatized space.

Stigmatized space is branded space that brands its inhabitants; polluted space that pollutes its inhabitants; and ritually contaminated space that

2 Natalie Broda, "Pontiac Housing Commission accepting all offers for Crystal Lake site," *The Oakland Press*, May 31, 2017.

FIGURE 5.1 Elliott Tower, Oakland University
SOURCE: PHOTOGRAPH BY GRAHAM CASSANO

FIGURE 5.2 Loiterers in Lakeside
SOURCE: PHOTOGRAPH BY GRAHAM CASSANO

FIGURE 5.3 Waste
SOURCE: PHOTOGRAPH BY GRAHAM CASSANO

FIGURE 5.4 Fish
SOURCE: PHOTOGRAPH BY GRAHAM CASSANO

FIGURE 5.5 Music
SOURCE: PHOTOGRAPH BY GRAHAM CASSANO

FIGURE 5.6 Picnic
SOURCE: PHOTOGRAPH BY GRAHAM CASSANO

FIGURE 5.7 Crystal Lake
SOURCE: PHOTOGRAPH BY GRAHAM CASSANO

symbolically contaminates its inhabitants. Erving Goffman defines stigma, first, through etymology.

> The Greeks ... originated the term stigma to refer to bodily signs designed to expose something unusual and bad about the moral status of the signifier. The signs were cut or burnt into the body and advertised that the bearer was a slave, a criminal, or a traitor—a blemished person, ritually polluted, to be avoided, especially in public places.
>
> GOFFMAN 1963: 1

Goffman conceives stigma as an imposition by normative society, a relation of domination in which the dominant community punishes the stigmatized individual for their identity. Stigmas exist in various forms, some visible, others concealed. Some allow for 'passing,' but "abominations of the body" and "physical deformities" often defy concealment. In addition, "there are tribal stigma of race, nation, and religion, these being stigma that can be transmitted through lineages and equally contaminate all members of the family" (Goffman 1963: 4).

In a sense, stigma is deviation from an accepted norm. "At the same time, mere desire to abide by the norm ... is not enough, for in many cases the individual has no immediate control over his level of sustaining the norm. It is a question of the individual's condition, not his will; it is a question of conformance, not compliance" (Goffman 1963: 128). Those unable to conform become others, or strangers, or, worse still, trash. At the extreme end of the spectrum, stigma represents more than mere deviance; it is a pollution, a violation of the sacred, a contagious defilement. Stigma, then, is an imposed and projected identity that attempts to defile the stigmatized and to shame them.

Just as an identity can be stigmatized, so, too, a spatial region. Goffman anticipates this spatial extension when he writes that "urban milieux" sometimes provide a "territorial base" for identity construction, and "within the city, there are full-fledged residential communities, ethnic, racial, or religious, with a high concentration of tribally stigmatized persons ..." (Goffman 1963: 23). Goffman argues there is a relation between space and stigma. But this is a simple, causal relation: Space is stigmatized by its inhabitants' stigma. More recently, Loic Wacquant has called attention to the fact that space itself is productive, that there is an overdetermined and reciprocal relationship between "territorial stigma" and the stigma imposed upon that territory's residents. In his comparative study of Chicago public housing projects and Parisian working class *banlieues*, Wacquant describes the "*powerful stigma attached to residence in the bounded and segregated spaces,* the 'neighborhoods of exile' to which the populations marginalized or condemned to redundancy by the post-Fordist reorganization of the economy and the post-Keynesian reconstruction of the welfare state are increasingly consigned" (Waquant 2008: 169). These locales represent "branded space," "a blemished setting," described by inhabitants and strangers with terms like "dumpster," "or even a 'reservation' " (Waquant 2008: 171). In the United States, this distinct form of spatial segregation, abetted by stigma, allows for "the *demonization of the black city (sub) proletariat* by symbolically severing it from the 'deserving' working class and by making the state policies of urban abandonment and punitive containment that are responsible for its downward slide" (Waquant 2008: 175).

Thus, space has a productive impact upon stigmatized identity, sustaining, reproducing, and often intensifying, the dominant community's pre-existing prejudice. "A *blemish of place* is thus superimposed on the already existing stigmata traditionally associated with poverty and ethnic origin or postcolonial immigrant status, to which it is closely linked but not reducible" (Waquant 2007: 67). The Lakeside Homes produced stigma because they occupied such stigmatized space. But territorial stigma does not simply produce social stigma. Let us return, via Goffman, to the original Greek meaning of the term. "The signs [of stigma] were cut or burnt into the body and advertised that the bearer was a slave, a criminal, or a traitor—a blemished person, ritually polluted, to be avoided, especially in public places." Social stigmata, physical and symbolic boundaries, act like the signs burnt into Greek bodies. They separate stigmatized space from "public places," and thus, the stigmatized from the public. Stigmatized space sets boundaries that designate the stigmatized as the anti-thesis of the public, as anti-citizens, as anti-neighbors (Roediger 1991: 36; Sugrue 1996). Between the 1950s and the 1990s, the Lakeside's invisibility temporarily hid its stigma, and its residents. But by the 1990s, when they became a visible symbol of urban failure, the Lakeside Complex had to be demolished, and its residents, displaced.

This chapter is divided into two parts. First, we examine the history of the Lakeside Housing Complex and the social and physical space the complex occupied. That space was stigmatized before its construction, and territorial stigma shaped local perception of the Lakeside and its residents. In this, as in so much else, the history of the Lakeside reflects the history of public housing throughout the United States. These parallels emerge not only from the stigma imposed upon the Lakeside, but from the manner in which the Lakeside, like public housing all over the US, was systematically underfunded, neglected, and left to physical decay and deterioration. Further, we argue that the same stigma that shaped perceptions of the Lakeside eventually also shaped perceptions of late twentieth century Pontiac. As the city's economy struggled, economic and social difficulties were often attributed to changes in the city's real estate market (especially the relative increase in rental properties) and, more subtly, to changes in Pontiac's racial constituency. The second part of this chapter demonstrates that Pontiac's economy tracked very closely to the vicissitudes of its major employer, General Motors. As GM struggled, so too did the city. However, rather than recognizing the structural forces shaping Pontiac's destiny, political leaders continued to blame the city's residents, and housing patterns, for its economic distress. The consequence of this racialized political vision was Michigan's Emergency Manager law. We argue that the same territorial stigma that depressed Pontiac's economy, and mediated the exploitation of the Black working class, led to the legal disenfranchisement of the city's voters. Emergency Management represented the legal equivalent of a symbolic wall built around Pontiac: the attempt to contain, control, and colonize, a Black-majority city.

2 The Lakeside Housing Complex, 1950–2002

2.1 *The Ban on Public Housing*

In 1886, the property that would become the Lakeside Homes was a sheep farm beside Mud Lake, under the management of William Newton.[3] By the mid-1920s, the area surrounding the site became the center of Pontiac, Michigan's Black community (Woods 1990: 173–198). When Matilda Dodge Wilson owned the property, in 1930, Mud Lake, now rechristened 'Crystal Lake,' remained undeveloped and largely out-of-sight, except from the city's municipal golf course (*McAlpine's Atlas of Oakland County* 1930: 14) (see Figure 5.8).

Racialized preconceptions built into planning and policy constructed Crystal Lake as a site for throwaway housing, and throwaway residents. During the Second World War, city factories, converted to armaments production, recruited Black and white workers from the South in large numbers. These new workers added to an already acute housing crisis (Scherer et al. 1981: 22–23). The land beside the lake became the site of temporary wartime housing—a trailer park for these transplanted workers (see Figures 5.9, 5.10, 5.11) (Archer and Scales 1950). By the time the Lakeside was owned by the Oakland Housing Corporation, in 1947, most of the trailers were being towed out and the City of Pontiac was preparing to develop what would become the Lakeside Housing Complex (*McAlpine's Atlas of Oakland County* 1947: 14). But it was not merely the shortage of quality housing that brought the Lakeside "projects" (as they

3 *The Lake Gems of Oakland County, Published by the Pontiac Gazette,* August, 1886.

FIGURE 5.8 Crystal Lake aerial photograph, c. 1950
SOURCE: COURTESY OF THE OAKLAND COUNTY PIONEER AND HISTORICAL SOCIETY

Looking West into Center of site

FIGURE 5.9 Looking West into center of site, c. 1950
SOURCE: COURTESY OF THE OAKLAND COUNTY PIONEER AND HISTORICAL SOCIETY

FIGURE 5.10 Looking south from center of site, c. 1950
SOURCE: COURTESY OF THE OAKLAND COUNTY PIONEER AND HISTORICAL SOCIETY

FIGURE 5.11 Looking south from southerly end of site, c. 1950
SOURCE: COURTESY OF THE OAKLAND COUNTY PIONEER AND HISTORICAL SOCIETY

came to be known) into being, it was the shortage of housing for Pontiac's African American working class in particular.

The Lakeside site is located just southwest of the center of Pontiac, on a small peninsula. By 1950, the southwest section of the city was largely Black (see Figure 5.12). Thus, from the perspective of the white city government, the Crystal Lake site was necessarily going to be Black, and probably residential. As Archer and Scales put it in their "Appraisal":

> The fact that the area to the North as far as Orchard Lake Avenue and Northeast as far as Saginaw Street is largely occupied by colored people, inclines to the future use of the property by colored people.
>
> ARCHER and SCALES 1950: 5

In the section of their "Appraisal" entitled "Favorable and Unfavorable Conditions," Archer and Scales further emphasize the need for (middle-class) Black residential space.

> As hereinbefore mentioned there is an acute shortage of property open to colored people for use and occupancy. In spite of the removal of legal barriers they are reluctant to invade unfriendly communities. They are reluctant to locate in remote communities open to them. On the other hand, there are many anxious and able to purchase new and modern homes in a new and well located area. This will be that sort of community if and when it is properly developed.
>
> ARCHER and SCALES 1950: 19–20

Although the Supreme Court decision, *Shelley v. Kraemer* (1948), ruled the racially restrictive covenants that blanketed most of "white" Pontiac unenforceable, Archer and Scales make it clear that, as in Detroit, "unfriendly" white Pontiac residents continued to resist African American "invaders" through various informal methods (Scherer et al. 1981; Sugrue 1996; for a discussion of the manner in which city planners and commissioners in Michigan used zoning to preserve "white only" and "black only" urban and suburban spaces, see Freund 2007). Nonetheless, the rapid redevelopment of the auto industry after the war meant that the African American population had the ability to "purchase new and modern homes." Probably in order to appease the fears of a white city government, Archer and Scales promise that the Lakeside site would be precisely "that sort of community," that is, a community of middle-class African Americans. Instead, the city housing commission selected Crystal Lake as the site for Pontiac's first federally funded public housing project (see Figure 5.13).

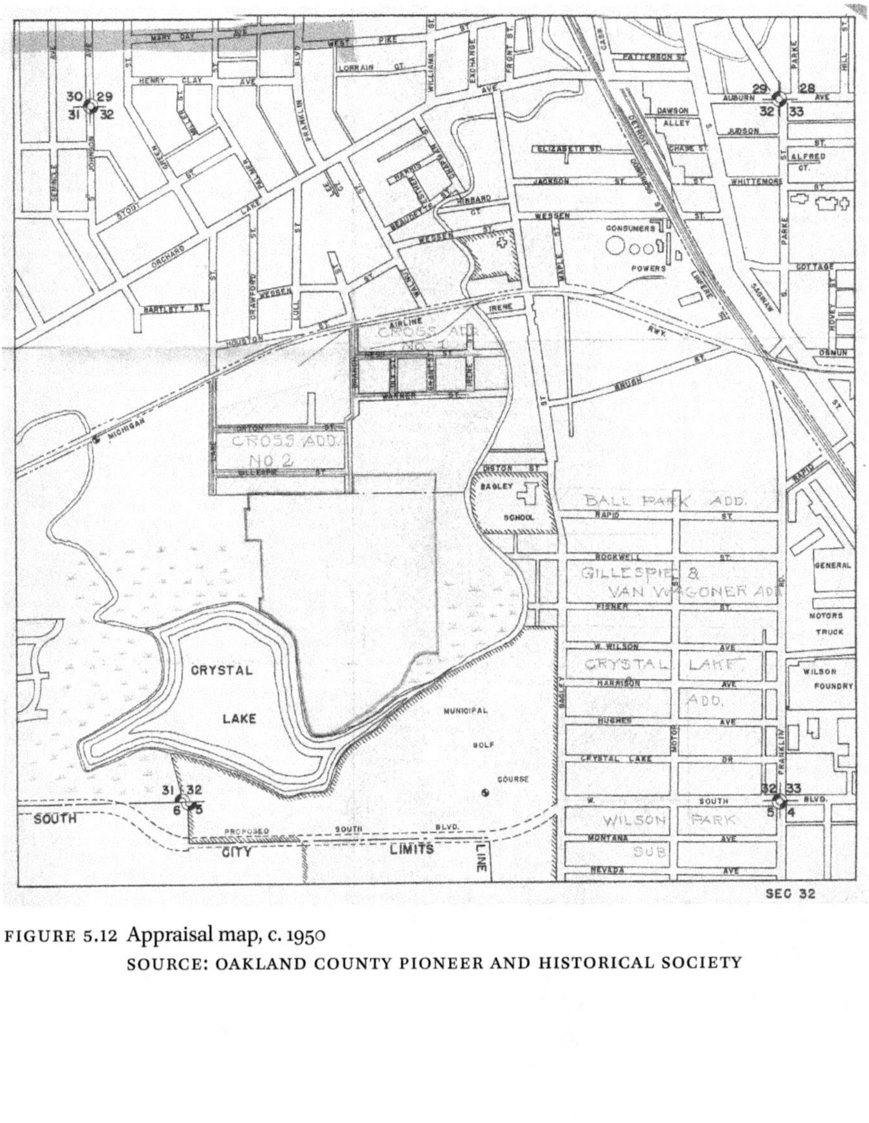

FIGURE 5.12 Appraisal map, c. 1950

SOURCE: OAKLAND COUNTY PIONEER AND HISTORICAL SOCIETY

FIGURE 5.13 The Lakeside Housing Complex, 1963. Oakland County, MI. Property gateway
SOURCE: OAKLAND COUNTY, MI. PROPERTY GATEWAY

Public housing was the last major initiative of the New Deal. Federal funds were first appropriated for public housing in 1937, and a small number of projects were built around the country, including in Detroit. However, the material requirements of the war led to the widespread suspension of new public housing projects until the passage of the Taft-Ellender-Wagner Housing Act of 1949. While the first projects were the result of direct federal intervention and construction in local communities, the constitutionality of the federal government's use of eminent domain came under scrutiny. As a result, the 1949 Housing Act established local housing authorities who would select sites and supervise construction. The federal government would subsidize capital costs through low interest loans and grants, but once the housing units were constructed, all operating and maintenance expenses had to be paid through rents received (Hays 2012: 95–101; Biles 2000: 143–162; Goetz 2013: 25–37). In site selection, the local housing authorities in Michigan followed the directives of bankers, homeowners, the FHA, and city governments, and chose sites that maintained and reproduced the racialized geography already present in these urban spaces. For instance, in their first policy statement in 1943, the Detroit Housing Commission said "that it would 'not change the racial pattern of a neighborhood' in determining the occupancy of public housing units" (Fine 2000: 119).

With subsidies from the Federal government, the Pontiac Housing Commission opened the Lakeside Housing Complex, nearly 400 housing units, in 1952, and promised two more public housing developments. According to Sloan, in spatial terms, the Pontiac Black community in the 1950s and 1960s was "largely invisible to many ... white citizens. This invisibility could be an important factor contributing to the general ignorance of the Negro community on the part of many white community leaders" (Sloan 1967: 97). The entire African American community was isolated from Pontiac's white residents through a systematic spatial apartheid. In this racialized geography, the Lakeside Complex was especially isolated. One road, Gillespie, marked the northern border, and two roads, Lake and Branch, entered the complex from the outside neighborhood. The city planners attempted to locate the second development in a "white" neighborhood. "White residents objected to locating the development at the selected site or at any other site in the white areas of the city" (Sloan 1967: 164). When the city then tried to relocate the development to a site adjacent to the Lakeside Complex, the Black community objected to the continuing segregation of housing. According to Sloan:

> While the controversy regarding an acceptable site continued, white citizens began circulating petitions calling for a referendum of the issue of public housing. Faced with this pressure, the commission in 1955 moved

> to pass ordinance 1560 which prohibited the construction of public housing in [Pontiac].[4] At a later time, the ordinance was amended so as to prohibit even commission discussion of public housing construction.
>
> SLOAN 1967: 165

In order to understand the decision to ban public housing in Pontiac, we need to examine housing politics in Detroit. Detroit had a longer experience with public housing and more projects. Consequently, events in Detroit shaped the way in which white Pontiac residents came to view public housing. As the last great experiment of the New Deal, public housing was attacked by critics from the business community, industry associations, and the Republican right.[5] In 1949, the National Association of Home Builders denounced "subsidized public housing" and opposed the "further invasion of its field by the Government."[6] The Michigan Real Estate Association "were emphatic in their expressed opposition to both rent control and public housing."[7] The Builders Association of Metropolitan Detroit constructed a low-cost demonstration home project in Royal Oak. These single-family homes were an alternative to public housing. George A. Duke, president of the Association, put it this way: "Architecturally attractive, livable, low-cost single homes in good communities that can be bought by any family of average wage-earning capacity is our answer to socialized public housing."[8] Nor were the attacks coming only from industry groups. George A. Isabell, head of the Detroit Housing Commission, and, simultaneously, head of a real estate management firm, told the Free Press, "Too many public housers ... try to solve social problems when their real and only interest should be getting people housed." Outraged that 42 per cent of tenants in the City's public housing were receiving some form of public assistance, he articulated a perception (in 1953) that would continue to plague public housing residents for decades: "Our housing projects are rapidly becoming correctional and welfare shelters."[9]

Even as industry groups and government officials were working to stigmatize public housing and public housing residents, African American citizens in Detroit were increasingly frustrated with the segregation of the city. Based on the *Shelly v. Kraemer* decision, the NAACP protested, and lobbied the Detroit

4 Following the custom in mid-twentieth century community studies, Sloan uses the pseudonym "Lakeland" for Pontiac. However, Scherer et al. (1981) reveals Lakeland's identity.

5 For the national response of industry to public housing, see Goetz 2013: 27–29.

6 Col. Henry H. Burdick, "Builders Score U.S. Intervention," *Detroit Free Press*, February 25, 1949.

7 "Realtors Hit Rent Control," *Detroit Free Press*, September 12, 1952.

8 "Low-Cost Home Project Attracts Large Crowds," *Detroit Free Press*, February 20, 1949.

9 Bud Goodman, "Housing Boss Raps Banks, Scores Lack of Home Loans," *Detroit Free Press*, August 28, 1953.

Housing Commission to desegregate public housing.[10] When the Housing Commission took no action, the NAACP went to court. In 1954, Chief Federal Judge Arthur F. Lederle ordered the desegregation of Detroit's public housing, saying "it is more important to end housing segregation than school segregation. Children spend more time at home than at school."[11] The Detroit Housing Commission appealed Lederle's decision, asking for more time to integrate the public housing facilities. Throughout the 1950s, "[integration] of Detroit's public housing proceeded at a snail's pace" (Fine 2000: 120). Nonetheless, the federal courts ruled for integration and white residents of Pontiac understood that new public housing would be integrated public housing. As Sloan puts it, "It was clear to opponents [of public housing in Pontiac] that since the developments were to be subsidized by the federal government, apartments were to be rented on a non-discriminatory basis. Whites were convinced that this would result either in an all Negro development or an integrated development" (Sloan 1967: 164–165). Indeed, just nine months after Lederle's decision, "a group composed mainly of property owners" circulated a petition in Pontiac to ban further public housing because it "affects property values, discourages home ownership by the tenants and puts a premium on low wages."[12] A month after the initial petition appeared, the signatories bullied the City Commission into passing the ordinance banning additional public housing construction in Pontiac.[13]

2.2 *Stigma*

Despite the reputation imposed upon the projects by her white neighbors, advertising executive Valerie Graves does not remember the 1950s Lakeside as a "correctional and welfare shelter":

> The public housing project was not the urban nightmare that springs to mind when the term "projects" is used. Instead of fatherless welfare-dependent families stereotypically associated with public housing, Lakeside was home to many young nuclear families with working fathers and even stay-at-home mothers. Most of these families comprised recently migrated black Southerners, with a smattering of Mexicans, and even the odd white family.
>
> GRAVES 2016: 19

10 "Racial Policy on Housing Is Attacked," *Detroit Free Press*, January 26, 1950.

11 John Griffith, "City Told to Drop Housing Race Bar," *Detroit Free Press*, June 23, 1954.

12 "Group Seeks Housing Plan," *Detroit Free Press*, March 15, 1955.

13 "City Studies Public Housing Ban, Subdivision Rezoning," *The Pontiac Press*, April 19, 1955; "Pontiac Bans Housing Jobs," *Detroit Free Press*, April 21, 1955.

Graves makes no pretense that the Lakeside was as "idyllic" as it "should have been" (Graves 2016: 19). The lake water was polluted, the constant wear and tear of children had begun to affect the already underfunded upkeep of the grounds, and the playground had its share of bullies. But Graves also remembers her neighbors, Reverend Morris, the Gonzalez family, and others, as hard working, respectable people. Nonetheless, the scent of stigma that already surrounded the Lakeside invaded Graves's understanding of her own life.

Without citing DuBois, Goffman argues that the stigmatized develop a kind of "double consciousness" (Du Bois 1907: 3). Or, in Goffman's words:

> The stigmatized individual tends to hold the same beliefs about identity that we do; this is a pivotal fact. His deepest feelings about what he is may be his sense of being a "normal person," a human being like anyone else, a person, therefore, who deserves a fair chance and a fair break. ... Further, the standards he has incorporated from the wider society equip him to be intimately alive to what others see as his failing, inevitably causing him, if only for moments, to agree that he does indeed fall short of what he ought to be. Shame becomes a central possibility, arising from the individual's perception of one of his own attributes as being a defiling thing to possess, and one he can readily see himself as not possessing.
>
> GOFFMAN 1963: 7

To the extent that the stigmatized understand social norms, they understand that they do not fully conform, whether the reaction be protest, alienation, or shame. Consequently, when a community valorizes whiteness as normative, all racial and ethnic groups are judged by their (arbitrarily determined) proximity to the norm. The stigmatized learn to categorize themselves as beyond the norm (deviant). As Graves puts it:

> In those early days, the charming camouflage of new furniture, a clean house, reliable meals, and a peaceful environment shielded me from a harsher reality. Over time, the realization seeped out of the TV that our family and our neighborhood were somehow lacking, and I began to feel deprived, a sensation that would be with me for many years and later be given names like "underprivileged" and "disadvantaged." When I learned that our side of the lake was called Mud Lake, I felt ashamed and wondered why God hadn't put us on the Crystal Lake side. When I noticed that the people on that side of the lake were white, I wondered why God liked them better than us.
>
> GRAVES 2016: 23

For Graves, the geography of race written into the city of Pontiac became a mirror through which she came to perceive her young self. As that geography made clear, Crystal Lake belonged to the white community. She lived beside Mud Lake. Of course, Crystal Lake and Mud Lake are the same body of water. But this shift to the older name reveals her sense that she was apart, and should, therefore, feel ashamed, despite the sense of home and community she felt in her neighborhood.[14]

In her collective biography of former public housing residents from Baltimore, *The Politics of Public Housing*, nearly all Rhonda Williams's interviewees share Valerie Graves's perception of the stigma imposed upon "the projects." Williams goes further and highlights one of the central forces behind this stigma: the cultural assault on Black mothers. During the 1950s and 1960s, the sociological consensus blamed African American poverty on the absence of Black fathers from households. "The cure: black men must be elevated to their rightful positions as primary providers and thereby free the government of its responsibility" (Williams 2004: 127). This liberal, patriarchal response to poverty both stigmatized Black women and denied them the cultural possibility of independence from men. But, for many women, public housing was a refuge from unhappy or abusive relationships. Rosetta Schofield told Williams: "When I went on welfare and moved in public housing, I had a place for me and my children, a nice, decent, clean place for my children and I to call home. And that meant I didn't have to take no beatings and no kind of abuse from no man out here in order to have a place ..." (Williams 2004: 128). Another interviewee from a "respectable" Black family "felt shame" when, after her divorce, she and her five children moved into public housing. Martha Benton describes her parents' attitude: "They always thought the people there didn't want nothing, didn't care about nothing, wasn't trying to achieve anything, and that it would take away any incentive that I might have ... to try to rise above the situation" (Williams 2004: 133). Still another former resident, and tenant activist, Goldie Baker: "I didn't want to live in public housing because I had already been familiar with the stigma and the label of people in public housing. Lazy, no-good, dumb, ignorant, don't want nothing, want somebody to give them something. ... That was just in my mind" (Williams 2004: 135).

Williams' respondents thus evince self-consciousness about the stigma imposed upon public housing residents. But more than that, they demonstrate the pervasiveness of the stigma across social strata and through social hierarchies.

---

14 Du Bois reports a similar sense of isolation and stigma in his discovery of his "blackness." "Then it dawned upon me with a certain suddenness that I was different from the others; or like, mayhap, in heart and life and longing, but shut out from their world by a vast veil" (Du Bois 1907: 2).

Respectable Black urban residents looked down on the projects and saw their residents as victims of a "culture of poverty" (Sugrue 1996). Indeed, residents themselves seemed to share this cultural explanation of poverty: "Public housing tenants also judged the behavior of other tenants, creating status hierarchies and cliques ... within and among public housing complexes" (Williams 2004: 140). In Baltimore, high-rise public housing had more stigma than the low-rise townhouses. Perhaps more important, some public housing residents maintained self-respect by differentiating themselves from later arrivals. As Williams puts it,

> Among the pioneers—the first tenants in any complex—newcomers provided a visible and tangible explanation for, as well as a way to distance themselves from, disrepute. ... Loubertha Ward distinguished between Lafayette Courts' first tenants and the next generation. "They called us mostly the cream of the crop that was getting first priority to the building, you know. Then there were others [*draws out the word*]. People that moved in weren't scrutinized; just anybody, you know."
>
> WILLIAMS 2004: 132

Williams does not downplay the problems residents encountered in public housing. There were conflicts between neighbors. The close proximity of the community's elderly and young children was a constant source of difficulty. The poor infrastructure made the projects dangerous. And, with the deindustrialization of Baltimore in the 1970s and 1980s, the problems of violent crime that plagued many urban neighborhoods also troubled public housing complexes. But rather than addressing those problems in constructive ways, city officials and housing managers left the infrastructure of the projects to decay, and attempted to forget the residents.

2.3 *Deterioration*

Public housing residents thus recognized the projections imposed upon them by politicians, the housing industry, and white homeowners, and some blamed the decay of infrastructure on the stigma produced by that racism.

> Well when I first moved in it was a country club, okay. Because you had services. See everybody wants to say we became a prison or whatever you want to call it because black people moved in. But you see if they would have gave us the same services as I got when I first moved here, this place would still be looking good, okay? But what happened was black people moved in and the services were gone.
>
> WILLIAMS 2004: 145; see also GOETZ 2013: 39

Like the projects in Baltimore, the Lakeside Housing Complex was built upon previously stigmatized ground. Unlike those Baltimore complexes, however, geography concealed the Lakeside from ready view. This isolation probably accelerated the Lakeside's physical deterioration. But the same physical deterioration that began to impact the Lakeside was happening to public housing projects all over the United States. In fact, deterioration was built into the symbolic space the projects occupied. These buildings were planned for decline. From the beginning, they were intentionally underfunded.

> The prevailing view among conservative critics and among many liberals as well was that the quarters provided by the government should be spartan. ... Congress placed tight limits on per unit prototype costs often setting them well below average construction costs for an area. ... Therefore, these limits often resulted in shoddy construction of such basic elements as doors, windows, plumbing, and heating equipment. ... Widespread negative perceptions of the poor obscured this problem, since the tenants themselves were blamed by the public for the poor condition of the units.
>
> HAYS 2012: 102–103

"Shoddy construction," made possible by the stigma already imposed upon the poor, led to rapid deterioration of some of the most visible features of public housing, producing, in turn, further stigma. Until 1968, the projects had to pay for all maintenance and operating costs through rents and local housing authorities were not allowed to keep potential surplus funds. Any surplus had to be used to pay-down the debt owed to the federal government. The Federal Government imposed income ceilings upon potential renters and evicted any tenant who rose above the ceiling. That meant that only the most economically disadvantaged population remained. All of this was occurring as Pontiac proceeded into the first stages of neighborhood integration. Relatively affluent Blacks moved into "better" neighborhoods as whites left for the Oakland County suburbs, so there was more quality housing stock available for working class Blacks. At the same time, with the Fair Housing Act of 1968, the federal government began to experiment with new forms of housing and mortgage subsidies for lower income families, and the federally funded housing projects of the post-New Deal that continued to exist were considered legacies of the past, hampering new developments (Hays 2012: 110–132; Goetz 2013; Biles 2000).

In 1973, public housing and public housing residents were so stigmatized that they made easy targets for Richard Nixon. Nixon declared a moratorium on federal aid for housing. In announcing this new policy, Nixon's housing secretary, former Michigan governor, George Romney, took particular aim at public housing projects. In doing so, he echoed the words spoken two decades earlier by George Isabell, then head of the Detroit Housing Commission. "The public housing units," Romney said, "began to fill up with welfare families and many who exhibited anti-social behavior. … Gradually, criminal elements, drug addicts, and other problem elements came to dominate the environment of these units" (Hays 2012: 137).

2.4 *Demolition*

By the 1980s, the Lakeside's infrastructure was failing and 36 buildings in the complex had to be demolished.[15]

> Pontiac City Councilman Otis Lawrence looked around the dilapidated community center in disbelief. He was on the Housing Commission and remembered when the center was dedicated in 1953.
>
> "It's a pitiful situation to see this place in the shape it is. It's absolutely deteriorated," he said.
>
> The once-solid glass walls are now bricked in. "When you close it in like this, it's like a big jail," Lawrence said.[16]

As with Valerie Graves, young residents recognized the stigma produced by their community. " 'Because we stay in the projects, they think we're bad kids,' said 12-year-old David Daniel."[17]

Less than a decade later, across Crystal Lake, new, private, housing was constructed.

> When Darryl Keels was 10 years old, he and his friend would stand by the Lakeside Homes in Pontiac—'the projects,' he says, and look across Crystal Lake to the land at the municipal golf course.
>
> 'Man, someday they're going to develop this,' they would say, and dream how they'd live on the golf course. … The first of 185 handsome homes, called the Villages of Crystal Lake, have started going up around the golf course. … At $112,000 to $150,000, nearly every house in this first section of the Villages at Crystal Lake has a beautiful view of the golf course or woods. This would be a great, desirable development anywhere. But in Pontiac it seems amazing … These are not subsidized houses for

15 Lara Mossa, "Housing commission sees 'good things' in Lakeside's wake," *The Oakland Press*, December 10, 2000.

16 Linda Stewart, "Play is Work at the Lakeside," *The Oakland Press/Gazette Edition*, Wednesday, October 3, 1984.

17 Ibid.

> lower-income folks, but middle- to upper-middle-price houses that stand on their own in the free market. ...[18]

The "free market" made the Lakeside's new visibility a problem. As one former resident put it: "The city was not doing their job. ... They were not keeping up the outside of the Lakeside. They just let it run down."[19] Walter Norris, head of the housing commission, emphasized both the decaying infrastructure, and the exterior appearance: "[With] a casual drive by the buildings, one can see they were dilapidated."[20] Norris also acknowledged the housing commission's role in the Lakeside's physical decline.

> Norris, who took over the housing commission in 1998, said upkeep on such a complex is a terrific and costly burden.
>
> "Over the years, there has been a significant amount of deferred maintenance," he said. [21]

Thus, "a combination of decaying physical structure" and so-called "sociological problems" slated the Lakeside for demolition.[22]

By the 1990s, political leaders and the press considered Pontiac's housing "blight" to be a crucial culprit in the city's decline. Pontiac's local newspaper published a Sunday supplement in 1995 called "The Rental Rundown," opening with a picture of low-income housing recently condemned by the city.[23] The focus of the feature is the rise of rental property in Pontiac, and the consequent stigma associated with it. In the first article, the author compares Pontiac's situation with that of the other cities and towns in the majority-white Oakland County. "An aging housing stock combined with a 51 percent level of rental property saddles Pontiac with a burden unique in Oakland County. In contrast, rental units count for about 26 percent of housing county-wide."[24]

For a local politician, this "unique burden" was a specular problem. City Councilman John Bueno told the reporter: "If you drive down a street, you

18 Judy Rose, "This Old City," *Detroit Free Press*, Sunday, October 30, 1994.

19 Lara Mossa, "Relocation Problems Complicate Lakeside's Demolition," *The Oakland Press*, Tuesday, June 27, 2000.

20 Lara Mossa, "City begins demolition of low-income housing," *The Oakland Press*, November 23, 1999.

21 Lara Mossa, "Housing commission sees 'good things' in Lakeside's wake," *The Oakland Press*, December 10, 2000.

22 Ibid.

23 "The Rental Rundown," feature in *The Oakland Press*, Sunday, January 15, 1995.

24 Dan Desmond, "Rental majority contributing to withering sites," *The Oakland Press*, January 15, 1995.

can pick out the rental property from the home owner property." According to both the reporter and the Councilman, this rise of rental "blight" hurts the city "socially [and] economically." Bueno claimed that rental blight makes the city less attractive to family residents. "We're catering to a more transient community than a family community. ... That's the way Pontiac has gone."[25] In cities all over Michigan, the "demolition" of "blight" replaced "urban renewal" as the new watchwords for city planners, politicians, and the press (Highsmith 2015).

During the 1990s, the history of the Lakeside thus continued to reflect national trends. Democratic politicians followed Nixon's lead and continued to stigmatize public housing. "Public housing projects were, according to national leaders 'monuments of hopelessness' [Al Gore] and 'as close to the approach to hell' as one could find in America [Henry Cisneros]" (Goetz 2013: 8). When the National Commission on Severely Distressed Public Housing published its final report in 1992 and designated 86,000 units of public housing unfit for human habitation, it was the death knell for the Lakeside (Hays 2012: 271; Goetz 2013: 62–68). HUD Secretary Cisneros commented, "if anything, ... the analysis of the National Commission on Severely Distressed Public Housing had understated the severity of the problem" (Goetz 2013: 66) The resulting legislation, HOPE VI, shared a name with previous legislation, but provided a powerful new weapon against legacy public housing complexes. "This act enabled the program [of public housing demolition and sales] to proceed more vigorously by eliminating the 'one for one replacement rule' which had compelled local authorities to replace any public housing unit demolished with another comparable one" (Hays 2012: 271–272; Goetz 2013: 64–74). No longer required to replace demolished units with low-income housing, the Pontiac Housing Commission used HOPE VI to eradicate the Lakeside and its memory (Hanlon 2012: 373–388).

Seated behind the controls of a Caterpillar backhoe, Housing Commissioner Norris smiled for the camera as he personally began the demolition of one of the Lakeside buildings.[26] The city promised new housing development on the site. However, in 2017, the Pontiac Housing Commission sold the Lakeside site to the Hantz Group, an industrial urban farming interest based in Detroit. With community volunteers as assistants, Hantz cleared the trash from the property, presumably as preparation for a new, non-residential, use of the land (see Figures 5.14, 5.15). As of July 2020, the grounds of the former Lakeside Housing Complex remained vacant (see Figure 5.16).

---

25 Ibid.

26 Photo: "Walter Norris, executive director of the Pontiac Housing Commission, gets demolition started on a structure in the Lakeside Homes," *The Oakland Press*, June 27, 2000; Diana Dillaber Murray, "Lakeside site to have $130,000 homes," *The Oakland Press*, Saturday, August 21, 2004.

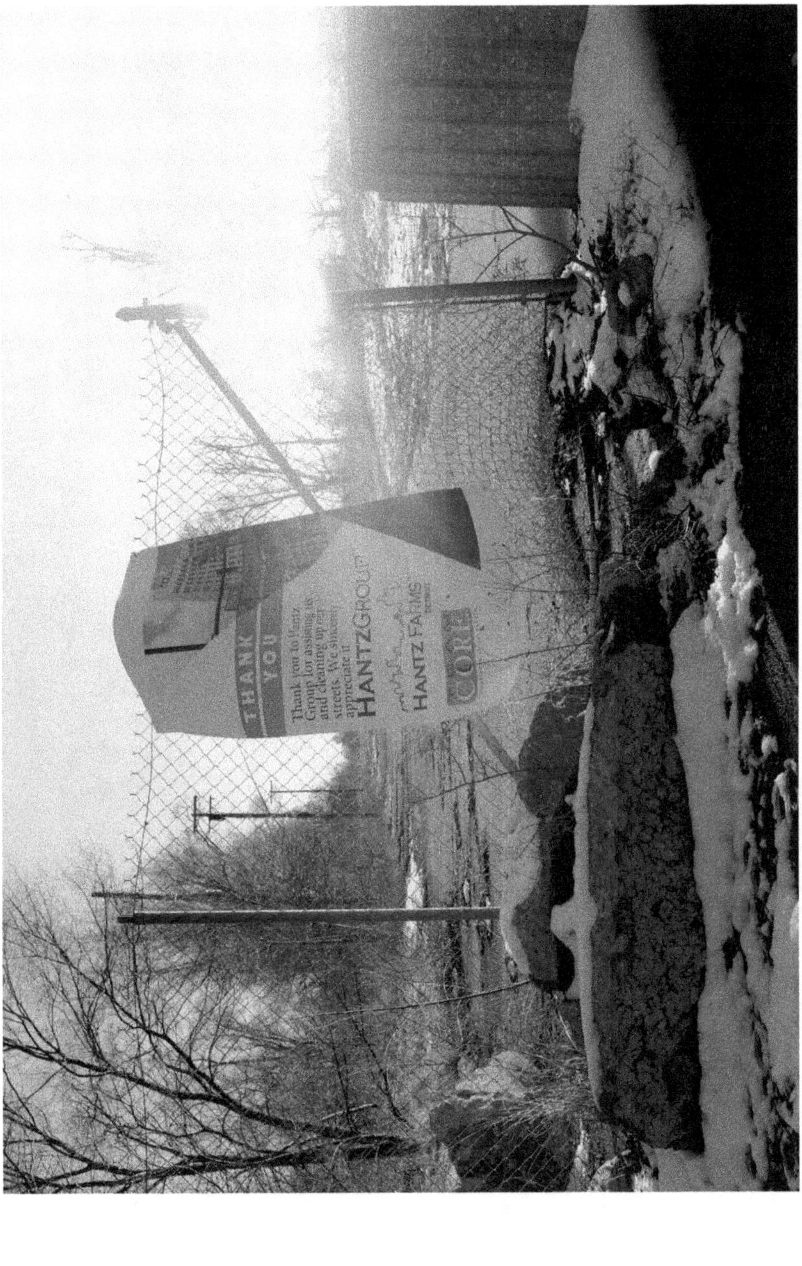

FIGURE 5.14 Thank you
SOURCE: PHOTOGRAPH BY GRAHAM CASSANO

FIGURE 5.15 Lakeside hydrant
SOURCE: DOUBLE EXPOSURE BY GRAHAM CASSANO

FIGURE 5.16 Lakeside summer
SOURCE: DOUBLE EXPOSURE BY GRAHAM CASSANO

3 Contexts: Demographic Change and Deindustrialization

In order to understand the forces that led to the closure of the Lakeside, we need to explore the demographic and economic changes in Pontiac between 1960 and 2000. Thomas Sugrue argues that in postwar Detroit, "blackness and whiteness assumed a spatial definition" (Sugrue 1996: 9). This section of the paper demonstrates, first, the spatial dimensions of race in postwar Pontiac through a series of racial population maps that focus upon the Black and white populations within the city, and, second, discusses the economics of deindustrialization in an industry town. We begin with demographic changes in the Black and white populations of the city between 1960 and 2000.[27]

Figure 5.17 shows the distribution of the Black and white populations in 1960. The total population of Pontiac at the time was 89,820, with 75,810 white residents and 13,802 Black residents. As we've already discussed, the Black population at that time was confined largely to the southwest of the city center, with some significant population centers in the southeast as well.

By 1970, the total population of Pontiac was 92,852, with 69,330 white residents, and 22, 934 Black residents. The southeast neighborhoods of the city were almost entirely Black and as the white population of the city declined, African Americans move into formerly "white" neighborhoods in the northwest and northeast sections of Pontiac (see Figure 5.18).

That trend continued through 1980 (see Figure 5.19), although the north of Pontiac remained predominately white. In 1980, the total population for the city was 85,317, with 52,159 white residents and 29,140 Black residents.

In 1990, the total population of Pontiac was 85,078, with 48,945 white residents, and 30,913 Black residents. By 2000, Pontiac had a total population of 71,552. 30,112 residents were white, while 32,477 were Black. Between 1990 and

27 The geospatial data used in this study were obtained from the Social Explorer database (http://www.socialexplorer.com) using their online mapping interface. Both spatial and tabular census data were collected for the 1960–2000 census years. We included all census tracts that had *any* area fall within the boundaries of the city of Pontiac, Michigan at Social Explorer's default visualization scale. We were interested in collecting data for population and family income coded by race. Although we recognize that this strategy has limitations, we felt it was the best way to account for changing census tracts and city boundaries across time. While Social Explorer was a convenient and powerful exploratory data tool, ArcGIS 10.7.1 was ultimately used to organize and visualize the spatial datasets for cartographic purposes (http://www.esri.com/). These population maps are presented using bivariate graduated symbol/choropleth symbology using Jenks natural breaks classification; hence, the percentage intervals vary for each decade. Historical census tract data in the form of shapefiles were downloaded from the National Historic GIS portal (see Manson, Schroeder, Van Riper, Ruggles 2018; and the State of Michigan GIS Open Data portal).

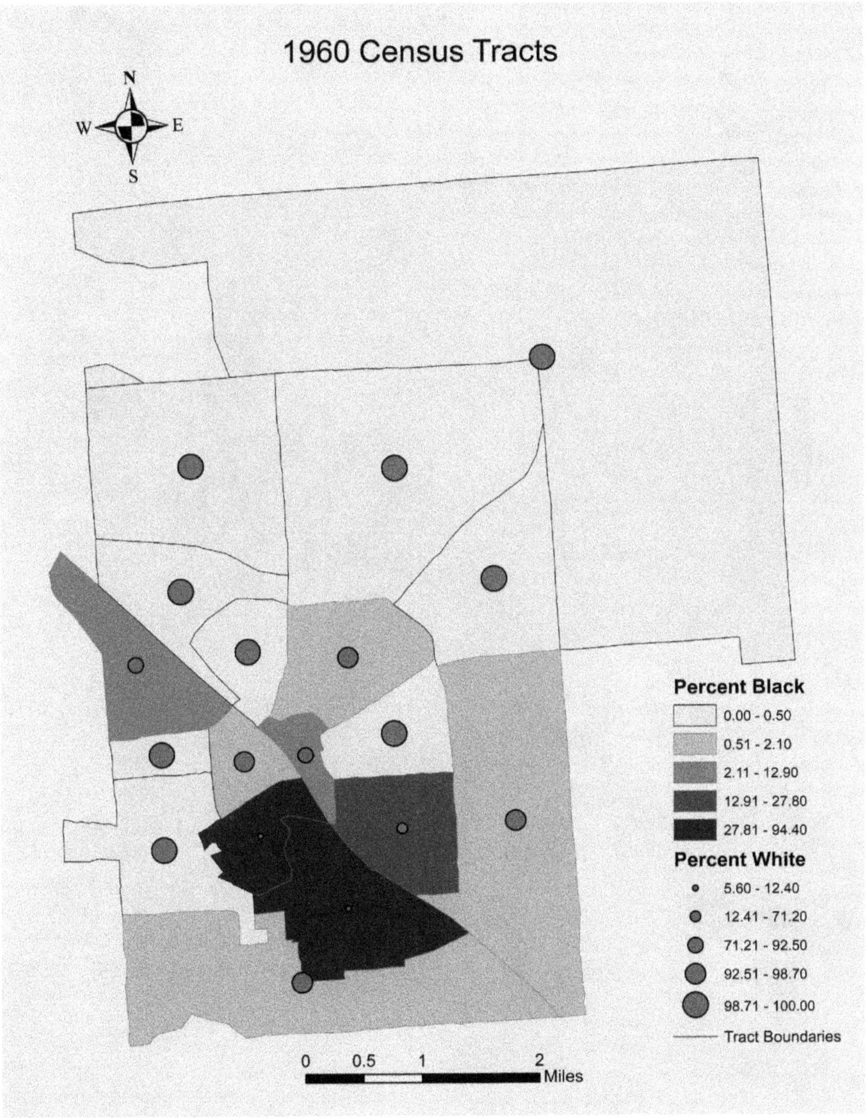

FIGURE 5.17 1960 Census Tracts

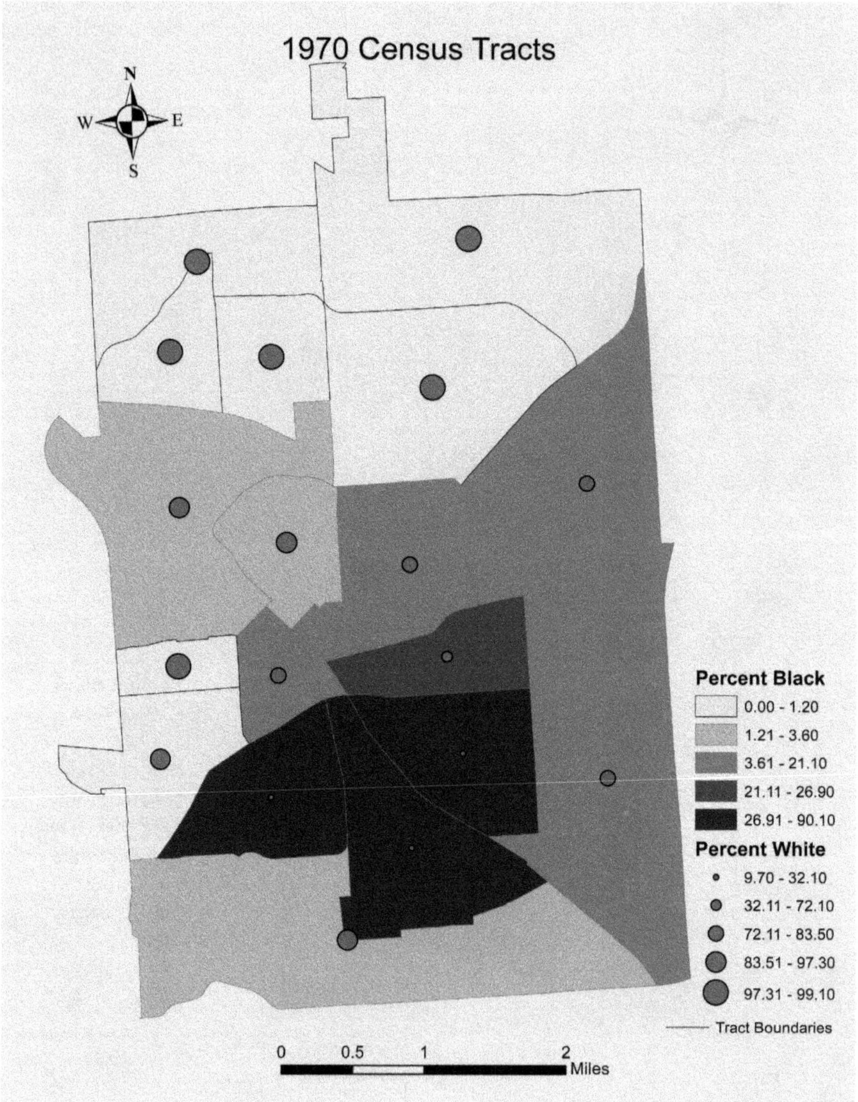

FIGURE 5.18 1970 Census Tracts

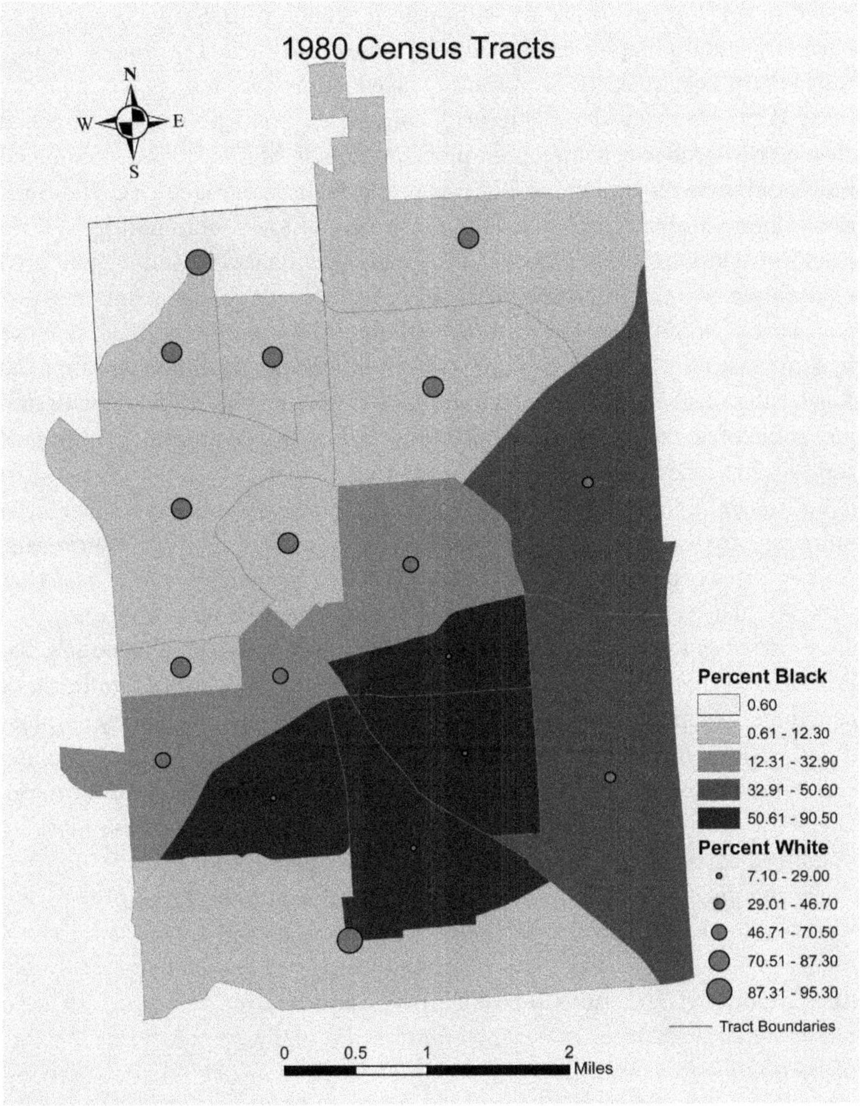

FIGURE 5.19 1980 Census Tracts

2000, several census tracts in the northern section of the city continued to have large white majorities, but African Americans moved into most census tracts in the eastern sections of the city (see Figures 5.20, 5.21).

As Pontiac's racial demographics changed, its political economy tracked closely with the city's major employer, General Motors, which produced mid-sized vehicles under the Pontiac brand in its namesake city. The massive Pontiac Motor complex, on the north side of town, bordered by Walton Boulevard, Joslyn Avenue, Montcalm Avenue, and Baldwin Avenue, consisted of multiple plants, producing parts and assembling vehicles. Pontiac Truck and Coach, popularly referred to as "Yellow Cab," occupied a large expanse in southeast Pontiac, near the intersection of Opdyke Road and Square Lake Road. Numerous additional parts and supplier plants, some affiliated with GM, and some of them independent, also provided industrial employment opportunities for working-class residents of Pontiac.

Although offering the highest wages around for blue-collar employees, the auto industry was notoriously unstable throughout the early post-WWII years. Autoworkers experienced frequent layoffs, often prolonged, and hoped that they would be called back before unemployment pay ran out (Clark 2018). The circumstances were more difficult for African-Americans, who faced job discrimination that often limited them to brutally difficult work in foundries, or as menial sweepers or helpers. There were also far fewer secondary employment options for African Americans during auto layoffs because so many stores and businesses in Pontiac refused to hire Black employees (Sugrue 1996). One African-American autoworker, L.J. Scott, hedged his bets in the 1950s by opening a barbershop while working as much as possible for Pontiac Motor.[28]

During peak operations in the 1950s, Pontiac Motor employed over 10,000 workers, and employment remained strong throughout the 1960s, when low-mileage "muscle cars," like the GTO, were in high demand and kept assembly lines humming. The 1960s brought many additional opportunities in auto plants for African Americans, who comprised roughly 40 percent of the City of Pontiac's population, as Detroit's Big Three automakers filled out second and third shifts with new hires and the Pontiac brand was in hot demand. In contrast, the 1970s were difficult years for Pontiac's autoworkers. Oil crises in 1973 and 1979 reduced demand for gas-guzzling vehicles, and GM's efforts

28 See also L.J. Scott, interview by Daniel Clark, October 27, 2003, in Metropolitan Detroit Autoworkers Oral History Collection, Walter Reuther Library, Archives of Labor and Urban Affairs, Wayne State University.

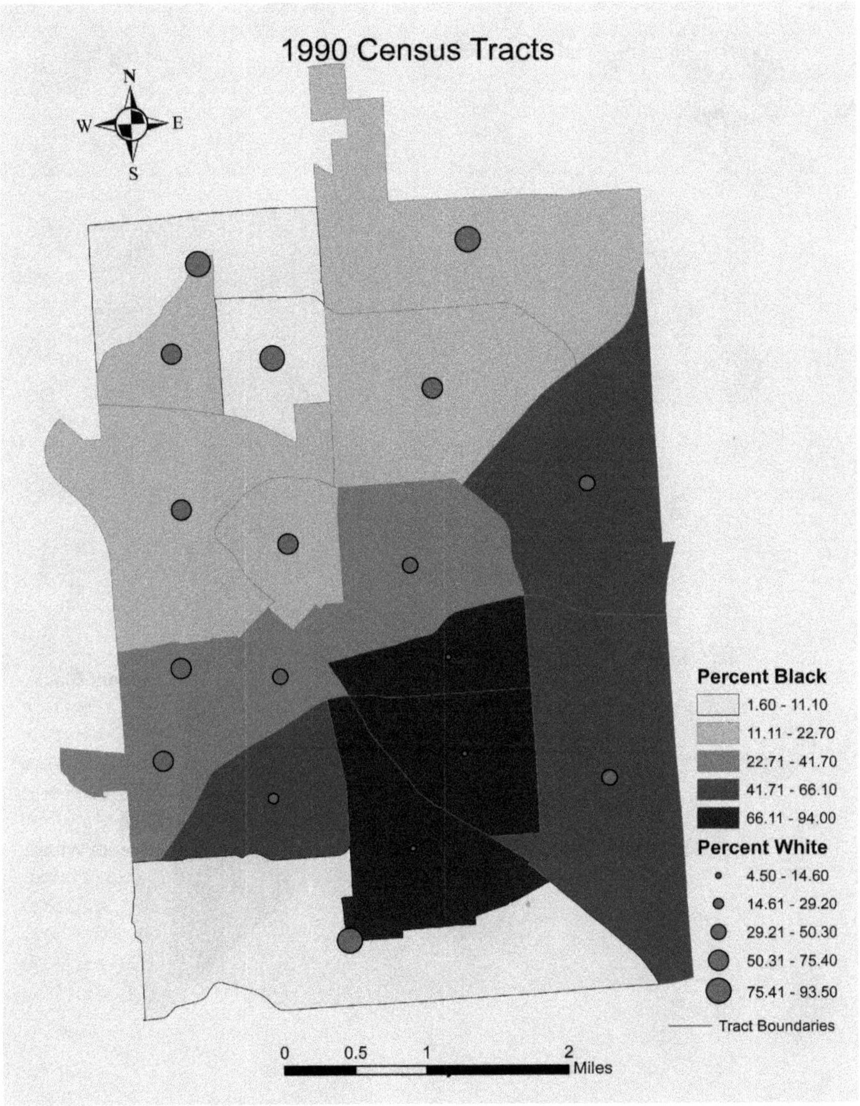

FIGURE 5.20 1990 Census Tracts

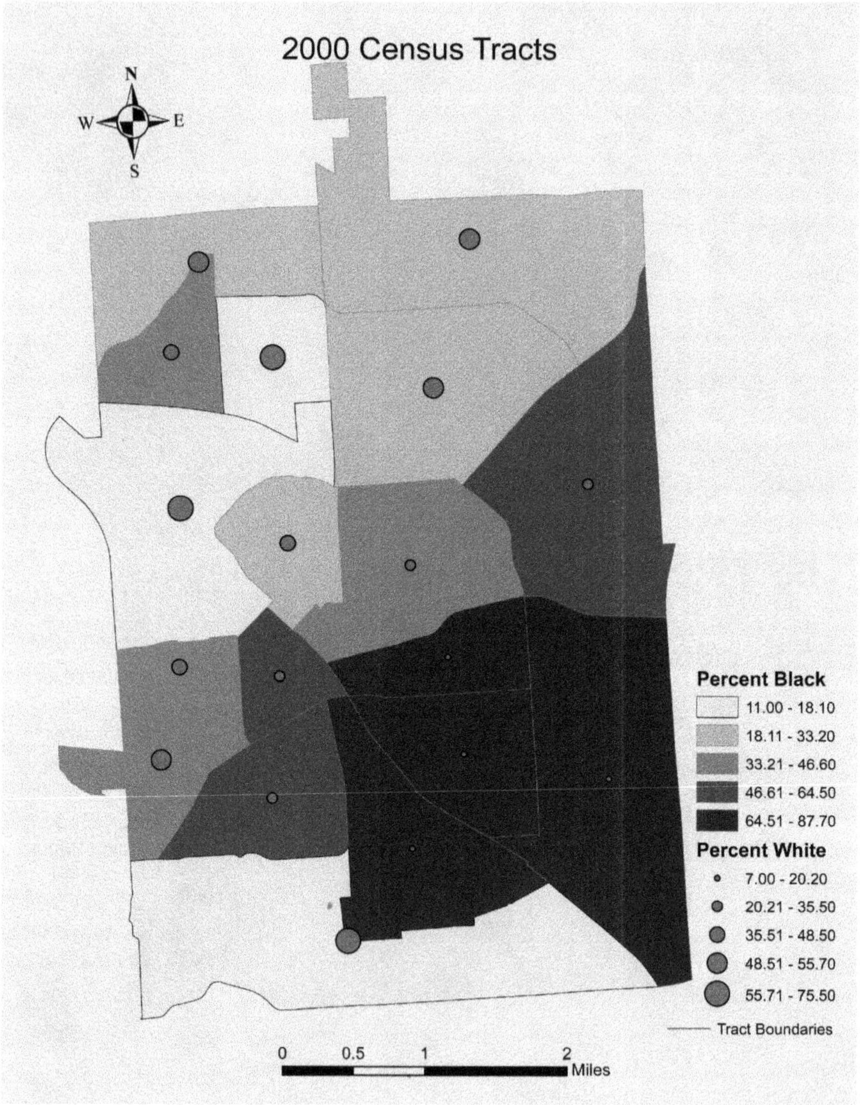

FIGURE 5.21 2000 Census Tracts

to improve efficiency led to a blurring of distinctions between their various brands, limiting the appeal of Pontiacs (Barnard 2004: 392).[29]

The "Reagan Recession" of the early 1980s hammered the City of Pontiac. By October 1982, unemployment reached a staggering 27 percent, heavily concentrated among the city's industrial workers. Layoffs always jeopardized workers' mortgages and car payments, and by the 1980s they also cast doubt on the future. Pontiac Motor (by then called Pontiac Assembly) appeared doomed. It was nearly fifty-five years old, outdated, expensive to heat and light, and unsuitable for retooling to build fuel-efficient cars or for retrofitting to meet current environmental standards. Several thousand workers were still affiliated with the plant, 55 percent of them Pontiac residents, with most of the rest commuting in from fast-growing, almost exclusively white suburbs and townships to the north and west. GM floated plans to abandon Pontiac Assembly and build a new plant, either near the Oakland County Airport, nine miles to the west in suburban Waterford, or four miles to the north, in rural Orion Township. Either plan would jeopardize both the employment prospects for Pontiac residents and the city's tax base. Even in the tough year of 1979, the City of Pontiac had received over $6 million in taxes from GM plants. GM ultimately chose Orion Township, although not all of its residents were grateful, and production began at the new plant in December 1983.[30]

By the fall of 1986, GM announced that in its quest for greater efficiency, it would soon be closing Pontiac Assembly and the Central Foundry Division Plant 6. Together that meant the loss of jobs for at least 3,600 workers, and, the city estimated, a loss of $600,000 to $800,000 in annual tax revenues. In addition, GM's Press Mill #1 was imperiled, with the possible loss of another 3,500 jobs, and Pontiac Truck and Coach would have its production cut by two thirds, with nearly 1,500 layoffs expected. GM had sold its bus operations to Greyhound, which planned to move production out of Pontiac to New Mexico. On the bright side, an assembly plant that had been part of Truck and Coach, now called Pontiac East Assembly, added a second shift of about 1,300 workers to produce highly popular full-sized pickup trucks. More sobering, however, GM had placed great hopes in the Pontiac Fiero as a popular successor to the

29 Paul Lienert, "Fiero!," *Detroit Free Press*, September 18, 1983; Constance C. Prater, "Black Jobs Report Looks Bleak," *Detroit Free Press*, September 6, 1991.

30 Jack Germond and Jules Witcover, "Is it Carr vs. Dunne? Or Carr vs. Reagan?," *Detroit Free Press*, October 13, 1982; Donald Woutat, "Lifting the Burden of Inefficiency," *Detroit Free Press*, September 30, 1980; Louis Cook, "GM is Ready to Build, but Orion Hesitates," *Detroit Free Press*, April 12, 1980; Donald Woutat, "Oakland Site for GM Plant," *Detroit Free Press*, February 1, 1980.

GTO, but the Fiero, introduced in 1983, flopped, and its assembly plant and its 600 remaining Pontiac employees were placed on permanent layoff. The last Fiero rolled off the line in August 1988.[31]

According to GM, the company employed nearly 36,000 people in Pontiac in 1985, a number that shrank to about 26,000 by 1989. The downward trend continued, with Pontiac West small truck assembly to close by 1994 and Pontiac Central medium truck assembly to shut down immediately. GM looked to consolidate operations as it was operating at only 70 percent of capacity and was losing national market share to foreign competitors (down from about 44 percent in the early 1980s to 35 percent in 1991). A Linden, New Jersey plant, the company determined, was better suited to handle all small truck assembly operations.[32]

The impact on Pontiac's African-American community was devastating. With so few manufacturing jobs available, and what remained being fought over by high-seniority GM employees, few opportunities existed for young, Black, would-be autoworkers. Jacquelin Washington, President of the Pontiac Area Urban League, confirmed the bleak economic outlook for the city's 30,000 Black residents. "Pontiac is really hit hard," she said. "We have the highest unemployment rates in Oakland County." The cause was no secret, she insisted. It was the series of plant closings by GM. And there were few viable alternatives: "Pontiac's black labor force is ill-equipped to compete for the high-tech service industry jobs that are gradually replacing factory work."[33]

In late 1991, GM announced that by 1995 it would close 21 plants nationwide and eliminate 74,000 jobs in an effort to reverse losses that had mounted to $7 billion that year. Pontiac West Assembly was already on that chopping block, but most remaining Pontiac plants figured to be in jeopardy. West Assembly workers managed to stay on the job a few extra months because

31 Jeanne May, Maryanne George, and Dawson Bell, "Pontiac, Flint Employees Accept the Bad News," *Detroit Free Press*, November 7, 1986; Helen Fogel, "GM to Shut Down 9 Plants," *Detroit Free Press*, November 7, 1986; John Spelich, "Pontiac is Likely to Lose Bus Work to New Mexico," *Detroit Free Press*, January 22, 1987; Helen Fogel, "Pontiac May Lose GM Truck and 2,500," *Detroit Free Press*, February 12, 1987; John Lippert, "What's Up for Fiero Plant?," *Detroit Free Press*, February 12, 1987.

32 Janet Braunstein and John Lippert, "Pontiac to Lose Small Truck Work," *Detroit Free Press*, April 24, 1990; Greg Gardner, "GM to Close More Plants by '93," *Detroit Free Press*, November 1, 1990; Janet Braunstein, " 'There is No Job Security,' GM Worker Says," *Detroit Free Press*, November 1, 1990; Cecilia Deck and Christopher Cook, "Workers Left Wondering if They'll be the Ones to Go," *Detroit Free Press*, December 19, 1991; Bill Vlasic and Helen Fogel, "UAW Goes to the Mat on Key Issues," *Detroit Free Press*, April 2, 1995; Greg Gardner, "GM, UAW Reach an Agreement," *Detroit Free Press*, April 6, 1995.

33 Constance C. Prater, "Black Jobs Report Bleak," *Detroit Free Press*, September 6, 1991.

of surging sales for the sport utility vehicles they produced, the Chevrolet S-Blazer and the GMC Jimmy. But production was eventually moved both out of the state and out of the country, to Mexico, as planned, and a few hundred West Assembly workers hoped to land positions building pickup trucks on the third shift at East Assembly.[34]

The future of Pontiac, according to middle-class, white observers, depended on people like themselves repopulating the city. About a mile and a half from the shuttered Pontiac West Assembly plant, the Fairways of Crystal Lake subdivision began construction, which created demand for "a trendy area of galleries and restaurants" on Saginaw Street, in the heart of the city. Boosters maintained that GM's new "Centerpoint," a facility designed to house the entire corporation's design and engineering operations, would be the economic generator of the future. Centerpoint was expected to employ up to 18,000 people, mostly in white-collar jobs, with hopes that a number of those newcomers would buy homes in Pontiac in places like the Fairways of Crystal Lake. Centerpoint itself was located directly next to the embattled Pontiac East Assembly plant, replacing razed manufacturing facilities. As one observer noted approvingly, GM "turned 650 acres of rusting, idled assembly plants on the south side into the $750 million Centerpoint Business Campus."[35]

Part of GM's effort to remain competitive involved adopting "lean production" methods, which to workers meant heavy, sped-up workloads, fatigue, and injury. Nearly 4,100 Pontiac East Assembly workers went on strike in April 1997 in hopes of restoring workers who had not been replaced and establishing more reasonable work assignments. Because of so many plant closings in the city, followed by union members with high seniority "bumping" those with low seniority from the jobs, workers in the East Assembly plant were, on average, forty-eight years old and were thus heavily affected by the strenuous workloads yet obviously still in need of employment. To counteract the strike, GM ramped up production of pickup trucks in Oshawa, Ontario and Fort Wayne, Indiana. The company still hoped to build a new line of pickup trucks at East Assembly, but with 30 percent fewer workers than before, and it did not want to hire new

---

34 Greg Gardner, "GM Wields the Ax," *Detroit Free Press*, December 19, 1991; John Lippert, "UAW Insists on Engler's Help," *Detroit Free Press*, January 14, 1992; Greg Gardner, "GM Delays New Blazer, Jimmy," *Detroit Free Press*, July 15, 1993; Keith Naughton, "GM Plants Get New Life as Sales Boom," *Detroit Free Press*, April 17, 1994; Greg Gardner, "UAW Workers Set Strike Deadline," *Detroit Free Press*, March 28, 1995; Greg Gardner, "GM, UAW Reach an Agreement," *Detroit Free Press*, April 6, 1995.

35 Louise Taylor, "GM Boosts Pontiac Future," *Detroit Free Press*, February 20, 1996; Judy Rose, "Boom Times in Pontiac," *Detroit Free Press*, June 28, 1998.

employees now only to lay them off a few months later when the new model run began. Business leaders and their allies demanded that GM hold firm and not hire a single additional worker. GM's productivity, they argued, paled compared with that of its foreign competitors and an excess of workers was a large part of the problem. The following summer a strike at two GM plants in Flint, also over workloads and job security, resulted in suspension of truck assemblies in Pontiac, where workers sympathized with the triggering grievances.[36]

The national narrative among elites emphasized that blue-collar industrial workers had to accept that they were no longer going to be able to claim a living wage and middle-class benefits. During the 1998 strike, experts observed that GM had 58,330 hourly employees in the state of Michigan, fewer than the number of private-sector jobs created every two years in Oakland County. The economy was growing by leaps and bounds all around, but not in the City of Pontiac. As one auto industry reporter noted, the future belonged to "manufacturing technology. Michigan has become one of the world's leading centers for the marriage between manufacturing, computers, design and engineering. That, in turn, is leading to a diversification into plastics, robotics, machine tools and software development—all of which have applications far beyond the auto industry." Strikers in Flint and Pontiac, he maintained, represented "the last gasps of resistance to the relentless demands of manufacturing efficiency."[37]

A few Pontiac auto factories hung on, but East Assembly ceased operations in September 2009, as part of the plant closings and job reductions mandated by the bankruptcy of General Motors in June of that year. About 1,100 former East Assembly workers either transferred to a plant in Ft. Wayne, Indiana, took a buyout from GM that eliminated access to pensions and health care, or just lost their jobs. Pontiac Stamping, which had opened in 1926, stopped operations shortly afterward, with the loss of another 1,100 jobs, and the last truck plant in Pontiac closed in 2012. This cascade of plant closings resulted in a 40 percent loss of tax revenue for the City of Pontiac between 2008 and 2012, and the State of Michigan took control of the city's financial affairs in 2009 with a controversial "emergency manager" appointment. As the need for

36 Alan Adler, "Attrition at Heart of Latest GM Fight," *Detroit Free Press*, April 24, 1997; Alan Adler, "UAW Strike Leads to More Layoffs," *Detroit Free Press*, April 26, 1997; Ted Evanoff, "GM Workers Walk to Add Jobs," *Detroit Free Press*, June 14, 1997; Alan Adler, "Feared GM Shutdown in Low Gear," *Detroit Free Press*, June 18, 1997; Daniel Howes, "A New Quality Process Emerges in GM's Truck Assembly Center," *Detroit News*, January 4, 1998; Ted Evanoff, "60,000 Idled by Strike," *Detroit Free Press*, June 13, 1998.

37 Daniel Howes, "Walkout Begins to Hit Home," *Detroit News*, June 28, 1998; Jon Pepper, "Michigan is on the Cusp of New Industrial Revolution," *Detroit Free Press*, June 28, 1998.

public housing increased, the ability of the City of Pontiac to contribute to the building or maintenance of any such facilities essentially disappeared.[38]

4 After Demolition: Bankruptcy and Emergency Management in Pontiac

The loss of General Motors jobs, and all the ancillary service employment that accompanied those jobs, was, at least in part, responsible for the loss of population. Whatever the causes, throughout the late twentieth century, Pontiac experienced demographic changes that made it a smaller, Blacker, and poorer, city. As the white population of Pontiac declined, and the Black population grew, the same stigma imposed upon the Lakeside expanded, encompassing the city itself. The Lakeside was demolished as part of this war on blight. But the disappearance of one landmark did not end the stigma imposed upon the city. In Pontiac, in Benton Harbor, in Detroit, in Flint, the combination of economic decline, anti-urban state policies, and this persistent stigma, resulted, ultimately, in the disempowerment of local (majority Black) city governments and take-overs by the state through emergency management. Following the bankruptcies and bailouts of the auto industry in Michigan, the Republican governor and legislature imposed Public Act 4. David Fasenfest provides a useful summary of the Act:

> In March 2011, Gov. Rick Snyder signed into law the Local Government and School District Fiscal Accountability Act, also known as Public Act 4, stating: 'For too long in this state, we've avoided making the tough decisions.' PA 4 would now allow the governor and the state to make those 'tough decisions'. The newly revised financial emergency law changed the EFM [Emergency Financial Manager] position to an EM [Emergency Manager], and included some substantial alterations that eased the requirements necessary for the state to place a municipality under state receivership. PA 4 permitted the state to appoint an EM without evidence of fiscal distress. That is, a state takeover of a municipality, which suspends the decision-making authority of a local government's elected

38 Joseph Szczesny, "Workers: Pontiac GM Plant Left to Die," *Oakland Press*, February 15, 2012; Chris Christoff, "Pontiac's Workforce is Cut 86 Percent As Michigan Makes City Obsolete," *Bloomberg*, November 28, 2012, available at https://www.bloomberg.com/news/articles/2012-11-28/pontiac-workforce-cut-86-percent-as-michigan-makes-city-obsolete, accessed on March 10, 2019.

> leaders, could be initiated based on the sole discretion of the governor and other state officials.
>
> PA 4 also upgraded the governing authority of EMs, transferring all governing power of elected officials to the EM, stating that EMs will 'act for and in the place and stead of the governing body and the office of chief administrative officer'. This law further specified that throughout the 'pendency of receivership, the governing body and the chief administrative officer of the local government may not exercise any of the powers of those offices except as may be specifically authorized in writing by the emergency manager and are subject to any conditions required by the emergency manager'. In effect, EMs essentially became a fourth branch of government, one unelected and unaccountable to anyone save the governor who appointed them. The law substantially reduced the governing powers of local officials—or, in many cases, removed those powers altogether.
>
> FASENFEST 2019: 37

Ultimately, seven Michigan cities fell under emergency management: Detroit, Allen Park, Benton Harbor, Ecorse, Flint, Hamtramck, and Pontiac. Six of the seven cities had majority non-white populations. Thus, emergency management had a disproportionate impact on communities of color, with "nearly half of the state's African American population … under emergency [management]" in 2013 (Fasenfest 2019: 38). This disempowering of local government authorities had profound implications for Flint and was one of the major causes of the water contamination in that city (Cassano and Benz 2019). Pontiac did not experience the same health consequences that plagued Flint as a result of emergency management, but Pontiac's infrastructural resources were sold to contractors, private companies, and other municipalities. The city was effectively plundered by the surrounding all-white county.

While it remains a contested question whether the Emergency Management law was racist in intent, it clearly had a racialized impact on Michigan residents. In the same sense, while we do not attempt to prove that Emergency Management was the result of the stigma imposed upon Michigan's Black residents, the financial ills that brought the EM law into existence were, at least in part, a result of racialized, and stigmatized, urban space. Because of a projected and imposed social stigma, Michigan's African Americans continue to be confined to urban centers that have been systematically and intentionally forgotten by the surrounding white communities, with economic consequences for those stigmatized communities. In this paper, we have offered a piece of Pontiac, Michigan's history in order to excavate some of the forces that maintained the racial boundaries of urban and suburban space through processes of projection, stigmatization, and systematic disenfranchisement in civil affairs. In Pontiac, Michigan, as in so much of the United States, spatial segregation is the symbolic emblem of racial division. And space is itself productive, in the sense that it further promotes division by symbolically branding its inhabitants. For Michigan's Black and white population, these materialized symbolic boundaries have produced a racialized political economy that reinforces white wealth by stigmatizing (and plundering) Black communities.

References

Archer, V.K. and Scales, G.L. (1950). "Appraisal: Part of Lot 5 of Assessors Plat No. 83 and Part of Lot 1 of Assessors Plat No. 85 For the City of Pontiac." (Oakland County Pioneer and Historical Society [OCPHS]).

Biles, R. (2000). "Public Housing and the Postwar Urban Renaissance, 1949-1973." In: Bauman, J., Biles, R., and Szylvian, K. *From Tenements to the Taylor Homes: In Search of an Urban Housing Policy in Twentieth Century America*, pp.143–163. University Park, PN: University of Pennsylvania Press.

Barnard, J. (2004). *American Vanguard: The United Auto Workers during the Reuther Years, 1935-1970.* Detroit, MI: Wayne State University Press.

Cassano, G. and Benz. T.A. (2019). "Introduction: Flint and the Racialized Geography of Indifference." *Critical Sociology* 45(1): 25–32.

Clark, D.J. (2018). *Disruption in Detroit: Autoworkers and the Elusive Postwar Boom.* Urbana, IL: University of Illinois Press.

Du Bois, W.E.B. (1907). *The Souls of Black Folk: Essays and Sketches*. 7th ed. Chicago, IL: A.C. McClurg & Co.

Fasenfest, D. (2019). "A Neoliberal Response to an Urban Crisis: Emergency Management in Flint, MI." *Critical Sociology* 45(1): 33–47.

Fine, S. (2000). *Expanding the Frontiers of Civil Rights: Michigan, 1948-1968.* Detroit, MI: Wayne State University Press.

Freund, D. (2007). *Colored Property: State Policy & White Racial Politics in Suburban America.* Chicago, IL: University of Chicago Press.

Goetz, E.G. (2013). *New Deal Ruins: Race, Economic Justice, & Public Housing Policy.* Ithaca, NY: Cornell University Press.

Goffman, E. (1963). *Stigma: Notes on the Management of Spoiled Identity.* New York, NY: Touchstone.

Graves, V. (2016). *Pressure Makes Diamonds: Becoming the Woman I Pretended to Be.* New York, NY: Open Lens.

Hanlon, J. (2012). "Beyond HOPE VI: Demolition/Disposition and the Uncertain Future of Public Housing in the U.S." *Journal of Housing and the Built Environment* 27(3): 373–388.

Hays, R.A. (2012). *The Federal Government & Urban Housing*. 3rd ed. Albany, NY: SUNY Press.

Highsmith, A. (2015). *Demolition Means Progress: Flint, Michigan, and the Fate of the American Metropolis*. Chicago, IL: University of Chicago Press.

Lavin, M. (2014). "If You Want It, You Can Get It Right Here: Space and Drug Use in Strip Clubs." *Humanity and Society* 38(2): 132–157.

McAlpine's Atlas of Oakland County Michigan (1930). (Oakland County Pioneer and Historical Society [OCPHS]).

McAlpine's Atlas of Oakland County Michigan (1947). (Oakland County Pioneer and Historical Society [OCPHS]).

Manson, S.J., Schroeder, D., Van Riper, and Ruggles, S. (2018). IPUMS National Historical Geographic Information System: Version 13.0. Available at: https://www.nhgis.org (consulted March 9, 2019).

Oakland County Michigan Property Gateway: https://gis.oakgov.com/PropertyGateway/Home.mvc, accessed July 1, 2020.

Roediger, D. (1991). *The Wages of Whiteness: Race and the Making of the American Working Class*. Revised ed. New York, NY: Verso.

Scherer, J. et al. (1981). "School-Community Relations in Pontiac, Michigan During the 'Age of Complexity'." Report Prepared for the National Institute of Health. US Department of Education, ERIC: Institute of Education Sciences. Available at: https://files.eric.ed.gov/fulltext/ED227184.pdf (consulted June 29, 2020).

Sloan, E.L. (1967). *Negro and Community Leadership in a Northern City*. Sociology Doctoral Dissertation, Michigan State University.

State of Michigan GIS Open Data Portal. Available at: http://gis-michigan.opendata.arcgis.com (consulted March 9, 2019).

Sugrue, T. (1996). *The Origin of the Urban Crisis*. Princeton, NJ: Princeton University Press.

Wacquant, L. (2007). "Territorial Stigmatization in the Age of Advanced Marginality." *Thesis Eleven* 91(1): 66–77.

Wacquant, L. (2008). *Urban Outcasts: A Comparative Sociology of Advanced Marginality*. New York, NY: Polity.

Williams, R.Y. (2004). *The Politics of Public Housing: Black Women's Struggles Against Urban Inequality*. Oxford: Oxford University Press.

Woods, E. (1990). *Pontiac ... The Making of a U.S. Automobile Capital, 1818-1950*. Pontiac, Michigan. This book was a publication sponsored by the Pontiac business community. (Oakland County Pioneer and Historical Society [OCPHS]).

PART 2

Reaction and Resistance

CHAPTER 6

Technocracy and Populism

Remaking Urban Governance in Post-Democratic Flint

Jacob Lederman

1 Introduction

At an August 2016 public meeting meant to solicit opinions on Flint's new zoning regulations, the assembled public took a sharply contentious turn. For roughly three years, the city planning department, along with outside planning consultants, had gone through a vigorously participatory master planning process meant to reshape the city and decrease its over-extended urban footprint. Some high-vacancy parts of the city would transition to "Green Neighborhoods," with low-maintenance parks, community gardens, and expanded plots of land for existing homes. Others would be converted into "Green Innovation" districts, in which windmills, solar fields, or urban prairies would proliferate. The local state would scale back maintenance and investment in these neighborhoods.

City officials and consultants had presented these thematic districts in tones of win-win consensus. Plans showed low-income neighborhoods with deep social needs as idyllic spaces of community gardens and carefully maintained public spaces.[1] But as a number of scholars have suggested, the incongruence between the trappings of community participation on the one hand, and the lack of power to set the scope and rules of participation on the other, may lead some citizens to view participation as incapable of meaningfully resolving problems (Lee 2014; Dagnino 2008; Holzner 2007). Under some circumstances, then, participation may impede rather than encourage truly democratic forms of decision-making.

Confronted with the official zoning codes that would support the Green Neighborhoods, many residents were shocked. Until this August meeting, multiple years of community engagement had not involved discussion of the hard choices in store for Flint. Neighborhoods that officials represented

1 Portions of this chapter were adapted from Lederman, J. (2019). "The People's Plan?: Participation and Post-Politics in Flint's Master Planning Process." *Critical Sociology* 45(1): 85–101.

as harmoniously "green" would no longer allow single-family dwellings, officially relegating low-density neighborhoods to future decline. In the "Green Innovation" districts, zoning plans called for the elimination of new housing permits. Far from embracing their new access to natural environments, residents voiced a desire for more homes, more residents, and more services. As the assembled officials attempted to maintain order at the city hall meeting, residents forcefully pushed back. An older black resident from the historically disinvested North Side of the city summed up the divergence between the win-win language of planners and the experience of residents. He had no interest in living in a "greener" neighborhood, he said. Instead, he upbraided the assembled officials, while sharing his own experiences of overgrown vegetation, an unsettling dearth of built structures, and the uncomfortable creep of urban nature. Groundhogs had borrowed under his lawn and house, a neighbor complained of rat infestations, and an overgrowth of non-human nature now threatened the livability of his neighborhood. The assembled officials appeared poised to enshrine this situation into law. They did so in the name of "the community," and under the consensual aegis of a green, sustainable, and inclusive city.

In the lead-up to the meeting, officials had carefully managed to avoid zero-sum discussions of city investment decisions, and instead advanced the rhetoric of a singular community interest. In so doing, officials sidelined any discussion of adversarial politics, group interests, or electoral politics, adducing for themselves the welfare of a public deemed universally represented by the plan's consensual vision. Through the emergence of a purportedly a-political set of administrative best practices, excised of party politics and embedded in a singular construction of the social collectivity, these forms of urban governance evidenced a series of conceptual foundations that might well be understood as "populist." Taken as a whole, this process served to naturalize the politics of local austerity by tying land use to technocratic logics and market principles, validated through a carefully constrained process of participation.

2 Populism and Neoliberal Politics

Populism's incubation in contexts characterized by weak party affiliation and appeals to a universal political subject remain a rare point of consensus in a literature otherwise characterized by scholarly dispute and little conceptual clarity (e.g. Jansen 2011). These features of governance, however, increasingly characterize the market-led programs of contemporary urban governance in contexts rarely described as populist. In producing a consensual political discourse rhetorically rooted in the will of "the community," tied to public participation, and foreground by expert administration, scholars have noted how contemporary urban governance has come to embed technocratic logics, while foreclosing upon contentious group claims-making. Examining these changes through Flint, Michigan's master planning process, this chapter suggests the analytical import of populism in techniques of governance tied to consensus. These practices in turn produce a singular legitimate political subject; namely the community, while narrowing the possibilities for community participation to alter market-centric logics in urban governance. If contemporary scholarship often casts technocratic administration as the bedfellow of market rule, it overlooks an important feature of this configuration: Much like the literature on populism, expert authority and technocratic policymaking rely upon a universalistic conception of the community and its interests, adducing for itself the legitimate arbitration of collective interests.

3 Democracy's Unwanted Other

The growing visibility of populist parties and nationalist politics across the globe has reanimated decades-old debates on the nature and theoretical status of populism. While the precise definition of the term persists as a point of contention (Jansen 2011: 77), core features of the historical scholarship remain salient.[2] The decline of strong party affiliation, alongside appeals to universal publics—exemplified by concepts such as "the people"—maintain a privileged position in contemporary scholarship on populism.[3]

2 Much like populism's more famous conceptual bedfellow, nationalism, the term has been notoriously difficult to pin down. It evokes little ideological precision, comprises no shared doctrine or worldview, may be channeled by a charismatic leader or everyday people, and has various historical relationships with formal electoral democracy. For this reason, some of the most insightful commentary on populism seeks to reorient this tendency toward conceptual rigidity. By focusing on *populist mobilization* (Jansen 2012) or populism as a *dimension* present in various moments of political culture (Laclau 2005, following Worsley), contemporary work on the concept have sought to discard normative views of populism as a democratic Other, confined to deficient democracies or authoritarian states. Instead, populism can best be conceptualized as a political strategy, a tactic of mobilization, and a rhetoric underpinning the creation of new hegemonies that transform a prior balance of social and cultural power (Laclau 2005).

3 The lack of robust party institutionalization, however, has been a classic of the populism genre for more than half a century. As Gino Germani (1978) suggests in his canonic text on nationalism and the paradigmatic case of Perón's Argentina, the working-class movement at the heart of Perón's populist government could not find an outlet in the traditionally middle-class democratic parties of the pre-Perón electoral system. The result, he argues, is

Technocratic criteria in urban policy making would, then, appear to represent a stark polarity to the highly politicized form of governance characterizing populism. In fact, a generation of scholarship on urban governance has highlighted the consolidation of a set of technocratic best practices, rooted in market mechanisms, which have transformed cities according to neoliberal priorities and reoriented urban regimes around entrepreneurial strategies aimed at competitively seeking out investment (e.g. Harvey 1989; Hackworth 2007; Lederman 2019). Institutionally, these transformations often rely upon new mechanisms of democratic control that upend the relationship between the practice of politics and the pursuit of urban governance. For example, quasi-public bodies, immune to electoral politics, such as Business Improvement Districts, downtown redevelopment authorities, or park conservancies may shield public decision-making from the participation of the public or electoral politics (Ward 2006; Low 2006; Purcell 2008). Purportedly technical in nature, these novel forms of governance serve to safeguard state and private investment from the vicissitudes of public opinion or democratic input.

These techniques of governance may achieve political-economic aims that crown outside investment supreme in the political life of cities. They also, however, pose theoretical questions that invoke more Foucauldian notions of governance, beyond the crass competitive city strategies that animate them. In circumscribing democratic authority through new forms of participation, these innovations suggest new discursive formation in the Foucauldian sense (Foucault 1984; Hall 2001). That is, they produce a new set of political rhetorics and associated practices that include community participation, while carefully managing this engagement within the technocratic straitjacket of contemporary economic development goals. A technocratic narrowing of policy horizons means that the practice of public participation operates to stymie broad democratic input even as it summons a novel set of practices (such as carefully choreographed public meetings), appeals to knowledge (such as an expert-dominated synthesis of community input), and the elevation of an imprecisely defined notion of community empowerment.

that "... [T]he lack of mass parties with proletarian traditions capable of incorporating the newly formed group of workers meant that the only possible movement—in an extremely limited span of time—had to involve some form of populism" (Germani 1978: 233). In short, Germani, like many of his contemporaries, argued that populism involves the inability of existing parties to incorporate new political subjects into the connective tissue of prior institutional arrangements. This connective tissue constitutes the democratic norms and institutional processes of a party system.

Empirically, some contradictory features of these changes merit additional attention. The circumscribed forms of democratic governance, noted above, are occurring as cities and other governmental bodies tout community participation, citizen engagement, and democratic openness. In fact, community planning demonstrates the civic ideals animating processes of shared governance in cities across the United States. It is impossible to ignore the deeply felt resonance of local participation and the community bonds that congeal in an atmosphere of high-minded civic ritual. Referring to the sacred symbols that connect everyday citizens to an imagined national community of civic virtue and democratic autonomy, Robert Bellah (1967) famously referred to these shared meanings as "American civil religion."

This notion of civic virtue has found resonance in newly dominant urban planning cultures. Movements like the New Urbanism suggested a critique of modernist planning's monumental scales and infrastructure, not only for their lack of attention to environmental issues, but also their anti-democratic and non-deliberative implementation (Berke 2002). As sociologist Michael McQuarrie (2011) has noted in the US context, the urban social movements of the 1960s and 70s, particularly those organized by communities of color seeking more influence in urban redevelopment decisions, augured an increased role for community input. The War on Poverty's "Model City" and "Community Action Program" required "maximum feasible participation" in development decisions, a rhetoric that in part reflected the clarion call of social movements for community control (Lee, McQuarrie, and Walker 2015). The political reformist and social movement impetus for such policies may have dissipated, but the appeal to notions of public participation and consensus endured as features of the professional discourse on urban development and planning (Lederman 2020: Ch. 1).

The siren call to "join the conversation" characterizes processes from urban rezoning, to the drafting of urban charters in cities around the country. Increasingly, however, cities and other public bodies are promoting public participation even while this participation may be in keeping with the needs of powerful interests (Levine 2016). In fact, the organization of community participation itself has become an "engagement industry," tasked with producing lively events that appear to be raucously participatory but may be circumscribed in their decision-making power by the officials, NGOs, or philanthropies that organize them (Lee 2014; 2015).

Citizens may indeed be asked to lend their opinions on a variety of subjects, but scholars have noted the limitations imposed by "rules of the game" that are produced from on high. Baiocchi and Ganuza (2014) refer to this as the "empowerment dimension" of participation. Research on community participation, they insist, has tended to focus on the communicative aspects of these undertakings—the processes, settings, and inter-group dynamics that take place in participatory contexts such town hall style planning meetings or budgeting exercises (e.g. Forester 1999; Umemoto 2001). According Baiocchi and Ganuza, past approaches have missed the empowerment dimensions of such processes, defined as the scope and importance of these forums in decision making. The empowerment dimension includes the regulations, rules, and frameworks for incorporating citizen input into actual policy (2014: 39). By legitimating expert established "rules of the game," insignificant issues may be resolved through deliberative practices, yet structural features of governance remain unchecked by citizen input.

The empirical case here centers upon a master planning process in Flint, Michigan in 2012–2013. The process was paradoxically undertaken during a period of financial emergency management[4] in which electoral politics were deeply constrained, even while city officials touted the development of the master planning as profoundly pluralistic and participatory. This case holds theoretical promise precisely for its extreme display of a range of contemporary patterns of political legitimacy. On the one hand, the politics of austerity at the heart of Flint's economic crisis have been experienced by a range of cities with responses that have typically coalesced around an increased role for market forces in the provision of public goods (Peck 2012). At the same time, the exhaustively participatory ethos of the master plan mirrored contemporary efforts to involve the community through a series of well-funded and consultant-developed engagement tactics.

The case demonstrates how local elites may forge new politics of "populist" legitimacy in order to manage such contradictions. In so doing, this chapter suggests that an appeal to a universal political subject—that is, "the community," promoted a decline in partisan, contentious, or even electoral, politics. At the same time, it demonstrated the emergence of a new kind of populism discursively rooted in a universal conception of "the community."

4 Neoliberalism, Politics, and Populism

Political theorist Chantal Mouffe's *On the Political* (2005) offers one general account of the patterns described above. Written against the "Third Way" politics of traditional social democratic parties at the turn of the 21st century,

4 Flint entered state administration under an emergency management law in 2012.

Mouffe argues that the rise of explicitly a-political and anti-ideological platforms dovetailed with the popularity of "end of history" narratives characteristic of late millennial social theorists. Mouffe has argued that this position is untenable, in that contentious politics tied to group claims is at the heart of any political association. The disappearance of *the political* simply sublimates such politics outside of institutional channels. According to Mouffe, the rise of extremist parties, which paradoxically emerged as Third Way politics flourished, demonstrates this tension.

In expanding upon the way contentious claims making has been replaced by a veneer of consensus in a range of institutional settings, Eric Swyngedouw argues that the current period is characterized by a "post-political" (2014), or "post-democratic" (Swyngedouw 2011; MacLeod 2011) form of governance. Swyngedouw is not suggesting that such a moniker is plausible in the exercise of power. Rather, the post-political refers to elite efforts to naturalize technocratic and market principles in policy, by casting decision-making as the product of expert know-how, unassailable administration norms, and the unequivocal superiority of market solutions. In its ability to assert that there is nothing "political" to be debated, post-politicization, is indeed a highly political undertaking.

These techniques of de-politicization in turn connect post-political frameworks to broader research agendas around the diffusion and mutation of neoliberal ideologies, subjectivities, and governance. In a period of intense inter-urban competition (e.g. McCann 2004), the neoliberal city is an especially instructive site of innovation for elites and government officials, who must promote a "good business climate," while at the same time framing urban spaces as diverse and "green," with lifestyle amenities and a festive public sphere capable of attracting a vaunted creative class of highly educated professionals (Peck 2012; Lederman 2015). Post-politics suggests one of the ways in which these neoliberal logics are made compatible, producing cities that are governed through market-centric criteria, even as officials and boosters promote them as spaces of cultural diversity, social encounter, and pluralism.

If the political is conceived as a means to channel group antagonism into a particular kind of social order (Swyngedouw and Wilson 2011: 11, following Mouffe 2005), win-win conceptions of decision-making rest on claims of consensus that reduce politics to the effective management of pre-existing administrative norms or market needs. In so doing, the post-political insulates decision-making from truly democratic debate, suggesting that concepts such as "best practices" are natural, have no political valence, and are bereft of forms of domination. Concretely, post-political rationales in urban governance imply that public spaces can only be supported through private largesse (Loughran

2014; Newman 2015), that concepts such as urban greening lack political content, and are beneficial to all residents (Checker 2011; Greenberg 2013), and that participatory processes are to be celebrated as consensual, while foreclosing on the possibility of contestation or democratic antagonism (e.g. Cooke and Kothari 2001; Levine 2016; Lee 2015: Ch. 1; Karpowitz et al. 2009).

The proliferation of participatory processes in cities around the country and across the globe assumes unique importance in light of these insights. An emerging body of research suggests that a contradictory process is afoot in the implementation of participatory mechanisms in urban policymaking. While neoliberal reforms have insulated various aspects of governance from open debate—for example, by creating new quasi-public bodies immune to democratic control such as Business Improvement Districts (Ward 2006) or Enterprise Zones (Purcell 2008: 27)—citizens are increasingly exhorted to "join the conversation," provide input, and be an active member of the community. A growing number of cities are adopting forms of shared governance at the same time as these processes are increasingly choreographed to the tune of powerful actors. The professionalization of participation now comprises an "industry" of public engagement (Lee 2015), capable of producing participatory "events" (see also Blakeley 2010; Gotham and Greenberg 2014: Ch. 4), yet lacking the grassroots democratic appeal at the center of historical efforts to include residents in decision-making, particularly in low-income neighborhoods (McQuarrie 2013; Lee et al. 2015: Ch. 1; Huxley 2013).

Participation itself can be situated within a larger transformation in the organization and political representation of cities. A shift in federal urban policy beginning in the 1980s has had a profound impact on how the practice of everyday politics intersects with the pursuit of urban governance. As Pacewitcz (2015) has argued, the move toward federal transfers based upon competitive grant-making rewarded community "partners" rather than partisan activists, empowering civic actors and non-profits that eschewed explicitly political agendas. Whereas Fordist regimes of urban governance relied principally upon federally earmarked discretionary spending, creating strong ideological and deeply sectorial antagonisms among particular constituencies vying for resources—such as business, labor, or the urban poor (Pacewicz 2015; Biles 2011)—the contemporary period has encouraged the language of community partnership. By forcing cities to compete for competitive grants, coupled with the need to attract mobile investment, the partisan "fighters" of the Fordist period have become today's community "partners" (Pacewicz 2015: 827). In order to create flexible relationships with different interest groups capable of winning grants from outside the community, local leaders avoid explicitly political language or contentious group claims making. As a result, funding for local projects increasingly rests upon the active silencing of explicit forms of adversarial politics, while elevating non-government actors who now hold the purse strings in development projects (Marwell 2007; Elwood 2002; Lederman 2019).

In this context, the role and importance of elected officials may be reduced. Urban development is coordinated through unelected officials and planners along with real estate developers or community development corporations (CDCs) and community-based organizations (CBOs) who build new housing or contract social services. The result is the merging of technocratic rationale in terms of city planners and administrators, private interests in terms of developers and consultants, and community input in terms of residents who choose to participate in these processes, often at the behest of grant-funded CBOs. As a result, elected officials become bit players in key urban developments.

Deliberative exercises may vary in their structural relationship to local decision-making, but as Levine (2017) notes, they share a claim to legitimacy based on "community talk." The community, of course, is a slippery concept, as generations of scholars and commentators have pointed out (see Young 2011 [1990], for a prominent critique). In a study of redevelopment projects in low-income neighborhoods in Boston, Levine (2017) describes the ways in which non-profits and developers strategically appeal to the legitimacy of community, while at the same time circumscribing its boundaries in order to build consensus around new development. In a context in which participatory processes occur without precise measurement of just who the community is and what the community "wants," officials "laud the *abstract moral significance* of 'the community,' " and in so doing they "… [c]ircumvent participating community *members* without appearing to do so" (Levine 2017: 3, italics in original). In short, by convening the community to participate, and representing the outcome of such participation to suit particular needs, local non-profits and developers may choose which voices exemplify the collective good, shielding such processes from accusations of extra-local or "inauthentic" interference (Walker 2014). Dissenting voices, from this perspective, can be minimized, cast as particularistic threats to the universal wishes of "the community."

These insights point to a number of empirical puzzles in a context framed by a staggering loss of local political autonomy. Michigan's Emergency Manager (EM) law, Public Act 436, passed in 2012 (following a landmark referendum on a prior EM law, which citizens voted down), represented an exceptional circumscription of local political autonomy (Fasenfest 2019; Fasenfest and Pride 2016). Drafted in the context of the post-2008 financial crisis, and with an eye toward expanding austerity policies, the EM law went far beyond prior forms of state intervention in cities under financial duress. It allowed the EM to break union contracts, fire employees, and sell off assets. The only notable check on the EM's authority was, perhaps unsurprisingly, a restriction on defaulting on financial obligations to bondholders. In this context, how did a master planning process that has won planning awards and outside accolades for democratic engagement balance a technocratic consensus around the need for investment in "viable" neighborhoods with an equity priority in one the country's lowest income communities? How did community participation advance or impede such an undertaking at a time of restricted democratic authority?

5 "Rightsizing" as Dispossession

A critical question for Flint is how to attract investment to a city with a reputation for crime, depopulation, and economic decline. Given a rising public discourse around the issue of inequality, a further challenge is to generate new growth in ways that residents perceive as socially equitable. Private investment in fiscally strapped cities often requires strong state-led incentives (see for example Pacewicz 2012; Peck and Whiteside 2016), including fiscal and infrastructural benefits oriented toward business, requiring local states to earmark or forgo revenue that might otherwise be oriented toward deep social needs. In a period of intense inter-urban competition (Brenner and Theodore 2002), cities are faced with the necessity of producing an economic surplus capable of attracting outside investment through tax abatements, a beautified downtown, or parks and amenities necessary for luring a "creative class" of white-collar professionals. These demands often come at the cost of declining services and public spending in peripheral areas unlikely to draw extra-local investment (e.g. Smith 1982; Squires and Kubrin 2005; Gotham and Greenberg 2013, Ch. 4).

Flint's Master Plan (*Imagine Flint*) represented an innovative blueprint for a smaller city. Having lost half of its peak population of 200,000, Flint has been notable for the extent of its housing abandonment, a drastically shrinking tax base, and a staggering web of costly fixed infrastructure meant for a larger city (Hollander 2010; Highsmith 2015; Schilling and Logan 2008). After years of ill-fated revitalization efforts, including a failed downtown theme park and events center dedicated to the city's history of automobile production ("Autoworld"), *Imagine Flint* made a compelling case for a new start, with a smaller, more sustainable urban footprint. To do so, plan officials sought to incorporate new landscapes such as urban prairies, solar fields, or farms into areas of the city historically constructed for a built environment of residential housing.

The rationale for "right-sizing" (Hummel 2015) was clear. In Flint's poorest neighborhoods with the highest levels of vacancy, tax arrears and foreclosure were common. Municipal officials conceived of these areas as a net loss for city ledgers, with costly infrastructure hardly balanced by meager fiscal revenue. To remove this costly burden, the master plan represented an opportunity to move these areas to fiscally productive uses by converting neighborhoods with high levels of vacancy into either residential areas with more green space and fewer services (Green Residential) or commercial spaces for so-called green industry (Green Innovation).[5]

The areas targeted, however, were not exactly vacant. In line with scholarship on land and property regimes, typically associated with rural studies and "land grabs" in the global South (see Sassen 2014: Ch. 2), right sizing signaled a new technique of dispossession for close to a third of the city's residents. Areas in which city disinvestment in services and infrastructure hastened further residential abandonment could be sold to investors with the hopes of spurring new rounds of growth, breathing fiscal life onto city balance sheets. For residents living in Green or Green Innovation neighborhoods, this represented a significant setback for prior home improvements or mortgage equity, as residential uses were curtailed for the future and municipal disinvestment decreased traditional services. Representing a redistribution of value from impoverished residents to potential green businesses in the future, such "austerity urbanism" (Peck 2012) appeared at odds with the equity priorities outlined by the plan and touted by city officials.

6 Overview of a Master Planning Process

The inauguration of *Imagine Flint* came at a strange time in the city's history. In late 2011, as the master planning process was kicking off, Michigan's Republican Governor, Rick Snyder, placed the city under local government financial emergency, naming an emergency manager (EM) to run the city's finances and government. Simultaneously the *Imagine Flint* plan was emerging to be an exhaustively participatory process aimed at galvanizing citizen buy-in for the creation of a smaller, denser city, representing the first holistic planning process in close to 50 years.

From the start, *Imagine Flint* had to overcome a number of hurdles. Sixty miles away, Detroit's attempt to envision a smaller city had hit serious roadblocks the year before. Detroit residents outside of the greater downtown area voiced hostility toward the mayor's pronouncement that he would "shrink" the

5 Throughout this paper, I refer to these "place types" as originally conceived in *Imagine Flint*. Based on some of the political contention outlined in this chapter, many of these names and zoning criteria have been modified.

city. Early attempts to catalyze community buy-in had been met with rowdy town hall style meetings in which residents denounced a lack of everyday services and safety, shunning a high-minded discussion of a 50-year blueprint for a more sustainable Detroit (Oosting 2010).

Flint's process, on the other hand, sought to encourage resident support and input from the start. Lacking an elected local government with the power to implement policy or financial decisions, *Imagine Flint* rested its claims to legitimacy squarely on the shoulders of community engagement. As the plan itself reads: "Above all, the process was designed and executed to ensure transparency and to build upon the thoughts, ideas, concerns, and aspirations of the people of Flint. ***Imagine Flint*** is the community's plan and the process has ensured a sense of community involvement and authorship, and perhaps most importantly, a stewardship for the new Master Plan." (City of Flint 2013: 5, bold in original).

From the start, *Imagine Flint* relied upon a mix of technical expertise and community participation. The Chicago-based planning consultants Houseal Lavigne crafted the analysis and plan specifics. At the same time, a Steering Committee (SC) was responsible for convening participation and ensuring the clarion voice of "the community" in the consultant-led plan. Yet one problematic premise of community engagement was the selection process for the plan's Steering Committee (SC). The city's appointed Planning Commission (PC) was charged with choosing the 21-person committee with input from the mayor and a city councilperson. A Memorandum of Understanding created for the master plan states that the SC did not have decision-making authority, nor was it a public body, but rather "its role will be to help channel community resources towards the master planning effort and ensure the broadest feasible community ownership of the master planning process" (City of Flint 2011).

To this end the memorandum states that the SC should represent the social makeup of the city of Flint by race, gender, age, and geography to generate broad community support. Yet in a city with 40% of the population below the poverty line, the 21-person committee largely reflected the selection of local elites. From leaders of the city's art museum, to local businesses, to members of local law enforcement, the committee did not reflect the majority of low-income households, despite containing a few "ordinary residents." The majority were leaders or representatives of city institutions; government, religious, academic, and not-for-profits. In line with scholarship on neoliberal transformations in governing structures (Ward 2006; Peck and Tickell 2002), the SC was a quasi-public, non-elected body, immune from democratic control and largely composed of powerful city institutions, despite a genuine sense of high-minded civic duty that members felt and conveyed in participatory exercises. Unencumbered by democratic control, expert knowledge and technical specifications produced by planning consultants and officials shaped the goals of civic engagement. Rather than a democratic check on strictly technocratic logics, the SC reflected a consensus view that the city would have to concentrate efforts on viable neighborhoods near downtown, precisely where many of the institutions represented on the SC were located.

But beyond socio-economic indicators per se, elite representation may take place within marginalized neighborhoods or communities as well. As has been documented in a number of contexts, institutions such as churches or community associations in low-income neighborhoods may nonetheless reflect the interests of a comparatively privileged segment of residents (see Hyra 2006). Absent electoral politics, these seemingly mundane observations take on increased importance. Local institutions representing low-income residents may be organizationally conditioned to adopt the language of partnership as they attempt to gain access to competitive resources. With elected officials having little input into master planning priorities, many local organizations may have correctly perceived that the quasi-public bodies overseeing the master plan were the only game in town. In short, the elevation of community participation over electoral politics helped to advance the technocratic consensus of planners and consultants over the redistributive effects of these plans. The carefully choreographed organization of the body overseeing participation ensured that community input would dovetail with the aspirations of administrators and local stakeholders.

That urban governance often involves the empowerment of voluntary associations to positions of consultative authority is, of course, nothing new (Garcia 2006; Elwood 2002; Rosol 2010; Woolford and Curran 2013). The SC, however, represented an innovation on this form of governance insofar as it operated during a period of abrogated electoral politics, with a purported mission to democratize urban planning, and was infused with the symbolism of local community, rather than specific group claims. The SC's role as a participatory catalyst, working in tandem with the technocratic mission of the city's planners, Planning Commission and an outside consultant shaped the relationship between community input and technocratic decision-making. The SC was meant to be the voice of the community. And yet its empowerment by the PC and the urban planners presiding over the PC's work suggested a gap between a truly generative versus largely consultative community role. Rather than acting as a voice of "the community," it would be confined to responding to the technocratic rationale imbued in the master planning process by planning officials and consultants. From this perspective, it represented a means of channeling community input into the categories of administrative control produced by planners and consultants aimed at shrinking the city's footprint in ways that tended to benefit low-income residents the least.

7 Greenlining the Periphery

On a chilly winter evening in early 2016, Flint's Master Plan Steering Committee gathered in a local library to discuss the implementation of new zoning. Next to a small stand with sandwiches, the members of the committee sat around a large conference table chatting amicably prior to the meeting's start. Comprising the official implementation of land use designations created over the course of a multi-year planning process, the meeting aimed to give technical ballast to master plan neighborhood designations such as Green Innovation, Traditional Neighborhood, or Green Neighborhood. Employed as "place types" during the planning process, these early categories were meant to designate certain neighborhoods as viable for residential uses, while others might be transitioned to the production of renewable energy, urban farms, or simply green spaces requiring little city maintenance. These designations, however, required additional committee work to codify the specifics of density, height, and use restrictions.

On this January evening, the everyday citizens serving on the committee appeared serious about their duties and peppered their meeting with the language of civic officialdom, "calling" the meeting to order and adjournment, and otherwise following the strict requirements of taking minutes and following an official agenda. The group, ranging in age, but with a notable skew toward residents over 50, was racially diverse, though majority white in a city that is majority black. Despite their lack of official authority within the local planning apparatus, these committee members appeared empowered enough to repeatedly question one of Flint's top planners, who attended the meeting to explain the technical rationale of the new codes.

Early on in the meeting, however, a commotion suddenly erupted. A man who appeared to be in his 50s with a long grey braid of hair and a baseball cap entered the room, asking loudly if he was at the proper meeting to contest the new neighborhood designations. As he made his way to a chair designated for the public, he began to explain his purpose and problem. He had heard the *Imagine Flint* Master Plan would turn some neighborhoods into green space; some residents might be denied public services because of such designations and some neighborhoods would be prioritized for development, while others would be left to fend for themselves. He addressed the group angrily, suggesting that nobody would tell him what to do with his land; it was his and he would do whatever he pleased, he said.

But soon after interrupting the proceedings, the committee members calmed him down. Faced with the possibility of chaos in a carefully planned meeting, the members sternly silenced him, arguing that this was not the place to air such grievances and that he had been given two years to voice his concerns during the dozens of public meetings that took place as part of the master planning process. Pressed with the committee members' arguments, the man settled down and agreed to save his comments for the public comments section of the meeting agenda. Unlike the raucously participatory workshops that officials had carefully planned as part of the master plan's development years before, this meeting was meant only for committee members and members of the public wishing to observe.

Though the master plan contained a number of areas of governmental action, including transport, education, and culture, its central role and importance was the alteration of the city's zoning, to transform residential areas with high levels of vacancy or blight into Green or Green Innovation neighborhoods. According to block-level data from the 2010 census at which time *Imaginbe Flint* kicked off, these areas contained 30,210 residents, close to one third of the city's 102,000 residents. By definition these were distressed neighborhoods, with high levels of abandonment and concentrated poverty.

As Figure 6.1 shows, Green Innovation districts tended to be in the city's poorest neighborhoods, representing a form of "greenlining" (Fischer, 2016), not dissimilar to the process of financial redlining characterizing the lack of lending in urban minority neighborhoods in Flint beginning in the 1930s (Highsmith, 2015). Flint's poorest neighborhoods, then, were rezoned in ways that discouraged residents from investing, or new residents from buying, in neighborhoods planned for residential decline.

City planning officials and consultants producing the plan were careful to suggest in public statements that no residents would be forced to leave. According to this perspective, Green Neighborhoods would simply be different than Traditional Neighborhoods. Lot sizes would be larger if residents chose to purchase adjacent parcels that had been abandoned. Urban farming and forestry might coexist with residential uses. On the other hand, such plans appeared to siphon state investment out of these neighborhoods to those prioritized as "viable." As the plan itself reads:

> If future investment and development should occur within a Green Neighborhood, it is possible for these areas to transition to a Traditional Neighborhood, with new homes on vacated lots repairing the neighborhood fabric. However, if a Green Neighborhood cannot be stabilized, and decline and abandonment continues, these areas will transition in the other direction and become Community Open Space or Green Innovation.
>
> CITY OF FLINT 2013: 46

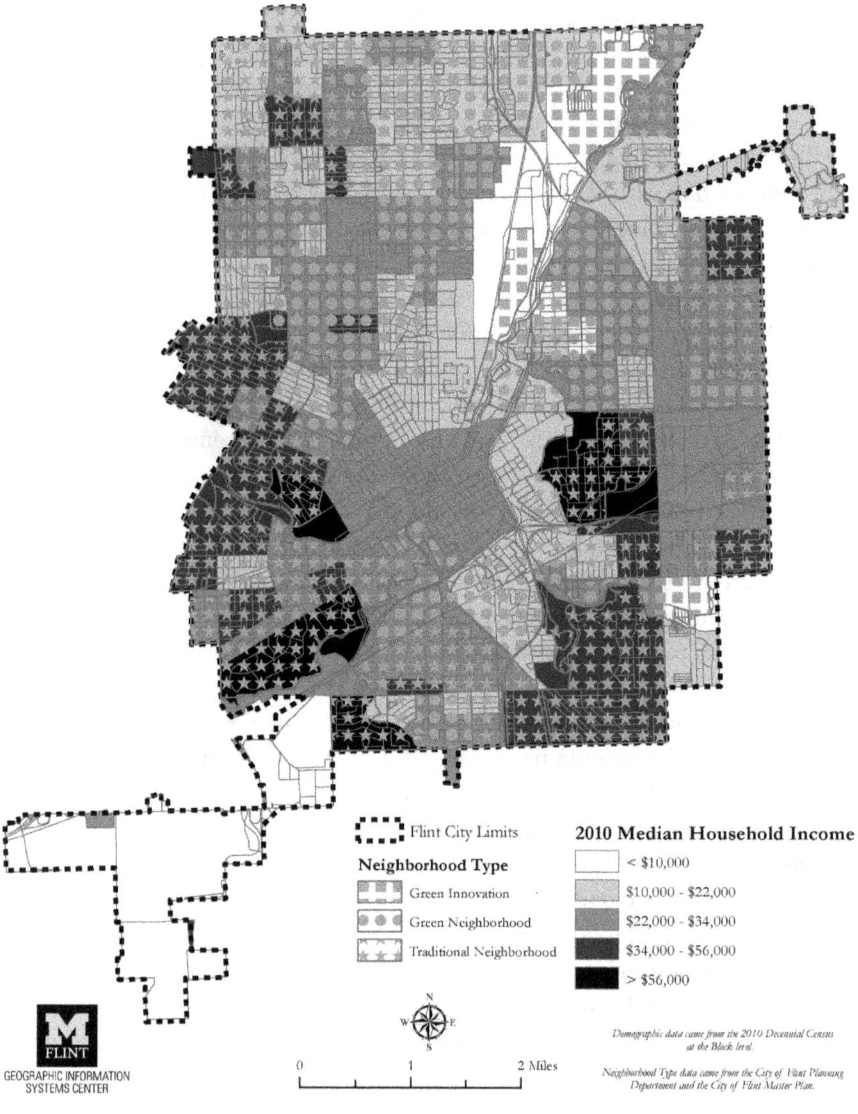

FIGURE 6.1 Flint's Green Innovation Districts
SOURCE: UNIVERSITY OF MICHIGAN-FLINT, GIS CENTER

Though this statement suggests that Green Neighborhoods might remain residential, it also gestures toward the priority of funding those neighborhoods deemed viable in market terms. According to the plan, Green Neighborhoods are "complemented by parks and natural open space areas that are maintained by local residents, community groups, and invested stakeholders" (City of Flint 2013: 46). In other words, residents and community stakeholders are responsible for proving the viability of their neighborhoods in the shadow of state financial retrenchment. In spaces characterized by increased park and green space, the local government will no longer provide traditional maintenance services.

While *Imagine Flint* cast these spaces in the image of urban homesteading, with residents assembling and maintaining multiple adjacent lots, and community groups building gardens and beautifying the natural and built environment, the key structural transformation of these neighborhoods was their lack of city investment. Therefore, some of Flint's poorest and most vulnerable neighborhoods would no longer be prioritized for state support. Rather, they would be expected to organize their own maintenance, attract new investment, and "prove" their viability if they hope to transform themselves into Traditional Neighborhoods.

8 Conflict-Free Zones: Collaboration and Cooptation

Rezoning these districts was an inherently distributional exercise insofar as land use reflects a road map for future state investment, growth priorities, and private development. Yet Flint's planners and the consultants working on *Imagine Flint* framed these decisions through a lens of technocratic know-how that reduced participation to fine-tuning existing decisions based upon indicators of neighborhood health largely informed by market metrics.

In a series of well-attended workshops, Flint planners and consultants took the land use plans directly to the people. Planning officials and Houseal Lavigne convened a number of community planning workshops in which photos and media coverage show a diverse group of residents pouring over tables of maps, workshop guides, and color-coded zoning plans. The central aim of these workshops was to allow residents to collaborate in producing the boundaries of new land use designations, such as Green Innovation or Green Neighborhood. Deliberating around circular tables, residents debated where to place brightly colored dots indicating the new land use designations.

But the most important aspect of this democratic exercise was the structural conditions constraining it. The maps themselves were overlaid with vacancy rates, with high-vacancy neighborhoods shaded in a yellow hue. Participants were instructed that their color-coded dots reflecting Green and Green Innovation neighborhoods were only to be placed in these areas. Residents were limited in the number of spaces they could make Traditional Neighborhoods, but unlimited in their ability to render districts "green."

These rules of the game strongly influenced the outcome. While the ability for residents to maintain Traditional Neighborhoods or create new Mixed Residential (mixed use) areas were limited by the instructions, participants were *required* to rezone much of the city for Green Neighborhood or Green Innovation zoning (see Figure 6.2). The instructions for Green Innovation read: "Minimum of 3. Locate only in mostly vacant areas." The instructions for Green Neighborhood asked for a minimum of 5 with the same criteria for vacancy. These conditions were presented as unquestionable norms, quite literally the incontrovertible background to citizen collaboration in land use designations. Here, then, a process with deeply divergent outcomes for different geographic and social collectivities was presented as apolitical, the process of consensus, stemming from the exigencies of technical know-how.

This performance of participatory planning, then, was deeply constrained by rules set from on high. Such practices highlight Baiocchi and Ganuza's (2014) assertion that analyses of participation must move beyond the interpersonal practices that characterize these forums to examine the rules and regulations that govern them and the ability of participants to change these rules. As Figure 6.3 shows, these strict parameters strongly influenced the outcome of the exercise. The city's color-coded base map showed areas of vacancy and abandonment. Those with higher rates were dubbed "residential blocks in transition," unsuitable to remain Traditional Neighborhoods. Neighborhoods with less vacancy appeared as a default grey area on the map. Participants could only designate grey areas on the map (those without blight) as Traditional Neighborhoods.

These instructions made residents, rather than city officials, accountable for a land use plan that signaled the retrenchment of state investment in Green and Green Innovation neighborhoods. Subsequently, this process of participation was channeled back into the technical plans created by consultants and planning officials. In so doing, the thoroughly political valence of these decisions—that is, an expression of power tied to the distribution of scarce resources, and instantiated in group claims making—was neutralized. Instead, a purportedly technical rationale was crowned supreme as the arbiter of unequal outcomes.

Baiocchi and Ganuza's call to bend the arc of research on participatory governance toward the social production of the "rules of the game" is especially

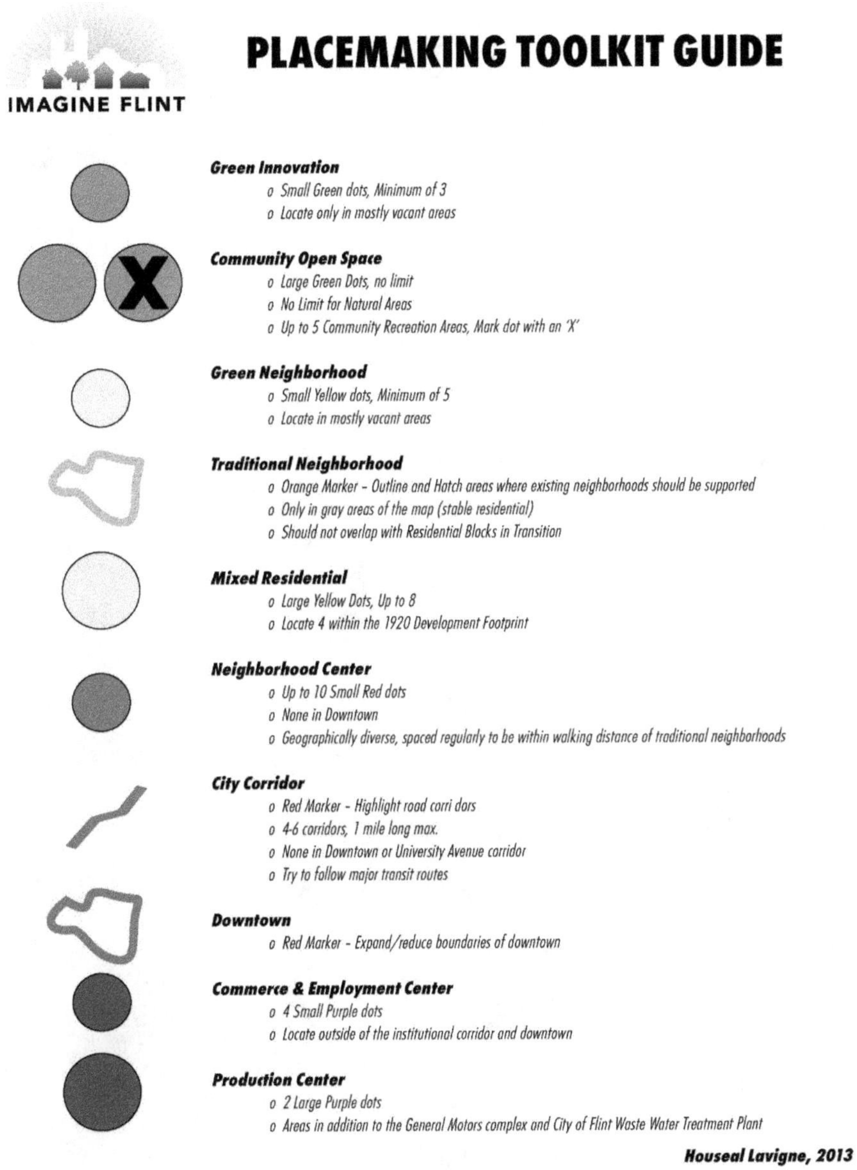
IMAGINE FLINT
PLACEMAKING TOOLKIT GUIDE
Green Innovation
o Small Green dots, Minimum of 3
o Locate only in mostly vacant areas
Community Open Space
o Large Green Dots, no limit
o No Limit for Natural Areas
o Up to 5 Community Recreation Areas, Mark dot with an 'X'
Green Neighborhood
o Small Yellow dots, Minimum of 5
o Locate in mostly vacant areas
Traditional Neighborhood
o Orange Marker - Outline and Hatch areas where existing neighborhoods should be supported
o Only in gray areas of the map (stable residential)
o Should not overlap with Residential Blocks in Transition
Mixed Residential
o Large Yellow Dots, Up to 8
o Locate 4 within the 1920 Development Footprint
Neighborhood Center
o Up to 10 Small Red dots
o None in Downtown
o Geographically diverse, spaced regularly to be within walking distance of traditional neighborhoods
City Corridor
o Red Marker - Highlight road corri dors
o 4-6 corridors, 1 mile long max.
o None in Downtown or University Avenue corridor
o Try to follow major transit routes
Downtown
o Red Marker - Expand/reduce boundaries of downtown
Commerce & Employment Center
o 4 Small Purple dots
o Locate outside of the institutional corridor and downtown
Production Center
o 2 Large Purple dots
o Areas in addition to the General Motors complex and City of Flint Waste Water Treatment Plant
Houseal Lavigne, 2013

FIGURE 6.2 Imagine Flint: Placemaking Toolkit
SOURCE: IMAGINE FLINT MASTER PLAN, AVAILABLE AT: HTTPS://WWW.IMAGINEFLINT.COM/PAGES/PROJECT-LIBRARY

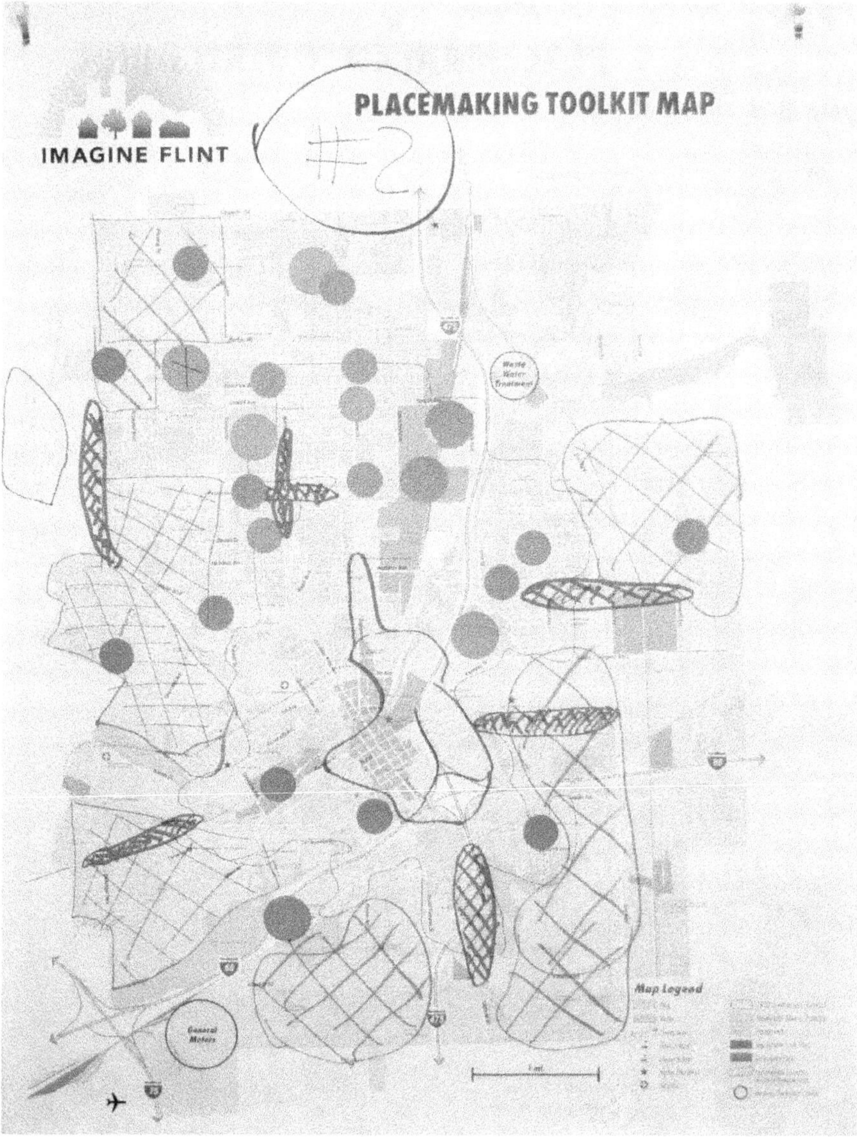

FIGURE 6.3 Imagine Flint: Placemaking Map
SOURCE: MAP COURTESY OF FLINT DEPARTMENT OF PLANNING AND DEVELOPMENT

relevant in this case. Participation operated in a largely performative manner in which consultants and unelected city officials produced the rules, foreclosing on a generative process of resident participation, and instead orienting participation toward the naturalization of existing urban inequalities. Whereas such unequal outcomes are not unique to Flint, the lack of electoral politics within this process suggested that unhappy residents had only themselves to blame.

9 Planning Utopias

Urban inequalities were made invisible in renderings of Flint's Green Innovation and Green Neighborhoods, obscuring the redistribution effects and context of rezoning. In the consultant-produced renderings, the images of these spaces showed residents in well-maintained homes caring for large open plots with neatly arranged urban gardens and greenery. Green Neighborhoods were framed as a consumer choice, with residents able to buy and maintain adjacent plots and live a more pastoral lifestyle within the city limits.

These plans relied upon a class-inflected vision of rural living that departed drastically from the social conditions of Flint's poorest neighborhoods. The renderings framed Green Neighborhoods as a lifestyle, casting proximity to nature not as a threatening assault on the modernist binary between the natural and social worlds, but rather borrowing from contemporary sustainability landscapes tied to images of nature as a luxury amenity (e.g. Checker 2012). Poor and working-class neighborhoods were now framed as bucolic retreats from the city, with gardens and small farms abounding.

This emphasis on lifestyle and leisure departed starkly with the social needs of residents. In short, these images erased urban poverty and deep fiscal neglect. Whereas food production appeared as a new lifestyle in neighborhoods now meant for plentiful community gardens, the objective absence of food economies in Flint's poorest neighborhoods was carefully ignored. This contradiction become clear in contentious community meetings meant to enshrine final zoning rules, such as that held in August 2016 and described in the introduction,

At the center of these dilemmas stood the renderings themselves, which appealed to visual changes in the built and natural environment, yet disavowed the social conditions underpinning these changes. This disavowal signaled another feature of post-political forms of governance; the renderings showed a universal public of middle and upper-income residents who would see these changes in terms of amenities, with gardens, farms and well-maintained homes on generous plots of land. In discussing the scaling back of public services in these neighborhoods, a member of the Steering Committee suggested in an interview that these areas were not being ignored, rather they were simply transforming into a different kind of space. This member raised the fact that in many rural areas residents are simply accustomed to dirt roads and see it as part of a lifestyle of rural living. We had to, in the words of this member, see these areas as simply different, with residents having more access to land, but understanding this implied less services such as street paving.

These visions of the future, however, had clear social implications, visually transforming spaces of neglect and need into scenes of pastoral harmony and social synchronicity with nature. The plans framed these spaces as universally aspirational for all residents living there, elevating the notion of land and local food production for residents who were facing major deficits in health and educational infrastructure and high rates of violent crime. Ignoring the consequences of fiscal retrenchment in Green and Green Innovation neighborhoods, the plan celebrated a form of urban homesteading as a means to overcome the consequences of local austerity.

10 The Centrality of Markets

The reliance on market mechanisms in urban governance has been exhaustively documented as cities privatize services, sell government assets, or scale back social assistance (see Hackworth 2007 for an overview). Flint's planning process, however, emphasized investment in residents, engagement with the community, and an explicit focus on equity as a central axis of the plan's objectives. But how did new land use designations respond to the city's fiscal constraints while addressing the need to gain resident support for redistributing city resources toward those neighborhoods deemed viable in land and real estate markets? In what ways does *Imagine Flint* demonstrate how equity priorities in urban governance must accord with a reliance on market logics?

The process of plan implementation and participation outlined here suggests a consensus of local elites, planners, and urban consultants on the need to scale back state investment in low-income and high-vacancy residential districts. The patterns of local investment and disinvestment suggest that market indicators largely informed this consensus. In short, urban governance in Flint, during a period of limited fiscal resources, required making such decisions not according to a ranking of resident needs, but based on the strength of land and real estate markets (see Akers 2015). With little possibility to spur development based on social priorities or state investment, Flint's plan instantiated markets as the key metric with which to determine planning priorities and thereby social and housing policy for one of the poorest cities in the country.

The Master Plan was undergirded by two assumptions about the local real estate market. First, the plan suggested that state resources should be concentrated in those neighborhoods that could eventually spur market investment. With scant resources available, city officials clearly believed that some neighborhoods would have to be written off in terms of government action. The Green Innovation land use designation suggested that these neighborhoods were too large a drain on city resources to remain residential. From this perspective, the logic of the Master Plan suggested a "salvage what you can" strategy of redevelopment. Strong neighborhoods close to the downtown core where significant improvements in the built environment have taken place over the last 10 years could be saved if resources were channeled in their direction. This required avoiding state spending in neighborhoods far from the downtown with already high rates of vacancy. At the same time, this realist approach to the city's gloomy fiscal situation suggested that Flint's comparatively affluent neighborhoods would receive state support in detriment to some of its poorest.

Real estate markets, of course, are based upon a particular balance of supply and demand. By foreclosing on the building of new residential uses in Green Neighborhoods, particularly those far from the city center, and by hastening the abandonment of high-vacancy neighborhoods by zoning out future residential uses, the Master Plan implied that better positioned neighborhoods could be salvageable through the reduction of the city's housing supply and the allocation of city funds to neighborhoods with market potential. Officials referred to neighborhoods deemed salvageable as "tipping point neighborhoods." This particular conception of neighborhood viability showed preference for real estate markets as the guiding principle for state action. Meeting minutes of a May 7, 2013 Steering Committee meeting show that Flint's outside consultants suggested "[T]here is a need to figure out what are the criteria for tipping point areas and viable neighborhoods, and what is too far gone" in order to "assess neighborhood stability, spreading out of resources, and consolidating resources" (Master Plan Steering Committee 2013).

This same real estate friendly conception of viability was clear in Green Innovation districts. The moving away from residential uses would not leave these neighborhoods vacant per se. Rather, the idea guiding Green Innovation zoning was twofold. On the one hand, the state would save resources in districts no longer requiring fixed capital investment for an overextended residential infrastructure. But the innovation of the plan was to position them for future private investment by symbolically reshaping their categorization by land markets. Fully vacant contiguous plots could once again assume viability in the market by attracting investment requiring large parcels, such as solar panels, wind turbines, or large-scale urban agriculture. Symbolically rendering these areas "blank slates" for new commercial investment, these strategies would be hampered by the existence of continued or new residential uses and the social needs that they encoded in land markets. At the same time, those Green Innovation districts that did not attract green industry could eventually revert to heavy industry uses according to the plan.

Taken together, these principles reflected the common sense of neoliberal governance, in which distributional choices were absent, framed as technocratic dilemmas to be resolved by the salutary presence of functioning markets. Emergency management thereby represented one feature of a longer process of depoliticization, reflected in Flint's culture of community partnership over partisan politics, enervated local government, and reliance on the logic of fiscal austerity. By explicitly privileging balanced budgets over all other criteria of urban success, the EM law explicitly depolarized the inherently political process of fiscal allocation. However, the taken-for-granted status of market conditions as determinants of future social investment represented a similarly post-democratic element of governance as the EM law itself, essential to understanding the local expression of neoliberal crisis.

Paradoxically, many members of the Planning and Steering Committees were critically aware of Flint's history of uneven and racialized development and intent on not repeating it. The development of the master plan, however, produced growth strategies that appeared natural and unproblematic while building upon contemporary planning principles informed by market conditions. Consultants Houseal Lavigne and Flint's top planners carefully directed the democratic process, channeling market principles into the language of inclusive green development and sustainable growth. Importantly, these principles appeared outside the realm of contentious claims making. Across a range of land uses, the guiding principle in assessing the viability of any use appeared strongly influenced by the existing conditions of land markets and the diminutive position of state resources. This common-sense narrative, however, belied the most prominent theme of the plan, that of urban equity and the purportedly open and democratic process through which the plan emerged.

These practices also reflected a larger tension inherent to the constrained tools of urban planning during a period of market rule. When the *Imagine Flint* consultants polled residents about their desired outcomes for the plan, their responses reflected issues of material survival and well-being, not "green" living. Among a list of statements that reflected the top two choices of residents polled, 49% listed "prepare the workforce for today's jobs" as their top choice, while 42% listed "concentrate demolition in high crime areas," the second highest polling statement.[6] The latter statement might appear coherent with officials' desire to "right size" Flint, yet Flint's demolition funding, drawn from federally provisioned Hardest Hit Funds (originally directed toward underwater homeowners and mortgages but later repurposed for demolition), required the city to concentrate demolition only in the least abandoned and most viable neighborhoods.

That residents would be forced to accept green neighborhoods rather than jobs or crime prevention strategies, reflected how contemporary urban planning practices insist that residents produce an account of "what they want to see" in the neighborhood, even while these wishes must cohere to market dictates. In a period of budgetary and structural constraint, city governments cannot provision housing, jobs, or in many cases even education without market mechanisms or competitive grant-funded planning that geographically restricts investment to "mixed use" areas proximate to downtowns.

11 Conclusion

Why would a city under emergency management with an abrogated democratic process explicitly encourage extensive citizen participation in one of its most important and strategic documents? How does the urge to involve the community in decision-making reflect new priorities of urban governance? The paper suggests that such a paradox can be conceived as a coherent strategy for addressing conflicting priorities. On the one hand, the exigencies of official claims to democratic engagement operate during a period in which public discourse on inequality has grown in prominence. On the other, harsh fiscal constraint compels local officials and stakeholders to create the conditions for new market-led investment as the singular remedy to urban decline.

In Flint, the result has been a transformation of the normative boundaries of the public, lauded as democratic, yet narrowly defined as those participating in highly choreographed and non-binding civic rituals. Local stakeholders, outside consultants, and city administrators generated consensus on a set of urban planning best practices deemed conducive to novel forms of growth, suggesting a transferal of authority from elected office holders to non-elected experts. This process then established the conditions under which community participation was pursued. The intertwining of technical expertise and elite

6 See http://www.imagineflint.com/Portals/tempflint/Documents/FlintPowerPoint-0311.pdf.

decision-making, however, predetermined community input by naturalizing technocratic logics in planning policy, while signaling the post-political bent of some participatory processes in US cities.

Scholars have often cast populism in stark opposition to technocratic administration and the market-led programs characteristic of urban governance under neoliberal globalization. But if populism is conceived, in part, as the production of a singular conception of the local or national community, with a monolithic set of interests, contemporary technocratic logics (especially when underpinning participatory processes that empower "the community") likewise evidence this conception. The literature on populism has highlighted the decline of party politics, accompanied by powerful individual leadership that adduces the will of the entire polity for itself. But technocratic and market-centric urban governance demonstrate notably similar logics. A technocratic consensus produced by outside experts, local officials, and powerful stakeholders in Flint suggested that market-centric policies were universal, natural, and in the interest of an ill-defined and all-encompassing "community." In other words, these technocratic logics appealed to the will of a purportedly universal public that might easily be understood as populist.

Such processes may result in clear political-economic trade-offs that disadvantage the least privilege residents, though they also evoke a strongly Foucauldian insight on the nature and workings of power. These are, in other words, *techniques* of governance that ask residents to partake in decision-making unbound by the necessarily political act of group claims-making. Despite a lack of real authority, these processes embed important notions of popular power, brought about by a singular conception of the community and its needs, yet constructed upon taken-for-granted administrative norms, planning criteria, and market needs. In so doing, these anti-political forms of rule inhere seemingly populist ideas. They evoke a universal form of political representation, even as they augur a decline in explicitly "political" framings of urban governance. If populism is said to operate through monolithic representations of the people, so too do processes such as Flint's master plan. This paradoxically occurs despite technocratic attempts to depoliticize governance in ways that cut against the intense politicization that scholars of populism have typically ascribed to the term.

Around the country, powerful actors' elevation of consensual notions of urban governance may diminish the power of everyday citizens to contest technocratic priorities in urban development and redevelopment. In the case of *Imagine Flint* it is not a coincidence that officials, funders, and outside consultants crafted a plan that was deeply shaped by existing market conditions. What is novel, however, is the way in which city officials and elites successfully framed these distributive decisions as the product of unassailable best practices and, importantly, representing the democratic voice of "the community."

Signaling a reconfiguration between the practice of urban governance and the pursuit of everyday politics, local officials and civic elites strove to catalyze new rounds of investment during a period still shaped by the politics of local, state, and federal austerity. To do so, limited local funds were to be channeled into areas with the most market potential, while areas with little market value could be spatially reoriented toward other uses if they could be symbolically rendered "blank slates." Paradoxically, new accumulation strategies tied to assembling contiguous plots for commercial investment through the curtailing of residential uses emerged along with a rhetoric of urban equity. In doing so, market and technocratic logics in urban planning competed alongside increased public discourse around the issue of inequality. The proliferation of participatory language and processes appears to have initially diminished such equity demands by suggesting that the distributional consequences of the master plan were the result of a democratic process of community decision-making. Public participation thus served to insulate local officials from contentious politics, while diminishing the possibility for contentious group claims making around issues of distributional equity.

Such a reliance on market logics in urban planning decisions is not new. What stands out in *Imagine Flint* is the complex system of social meaning that produced, in the words of the master plan itself, "the community's plan" such that the community should take "authorship" over the plan (City of Flint 2013: 5). Echoing Baiocchi and Ganuza (2014), non-elected officials and consultants narrowly framed the empowerment dimension of participation, with participants granted little control over the scope and nature of participation itself. If open and democratic processes indeed took place, and a "populist" rhetoric characterized participation, these processes were a priori shaped according to the concrete economic indicators of land markets and a preexisting technical rationale, which administrators and consultants produced with little input from elected officials or the public.

References

Akers, J. (2015). "Emerging Market City." *Environment and Planning A* 47(9): 1842–1858.

Aylett, A. (2010). "Conflict, Collaboration and Climate Change: Participatory Democracy and Urban Environmental Struggles in Durban, South Africa." *International Journal of Urban and Regional Research* 34(3): 478–495.

Baiocchi, G. and Ganuza, E. (2014). "Participatory Budgeting as if Emancipation Mattered." *Politics & Society* 42(1): 29–50.

Bellah, R. (1967). "Civil Religion in America." *Daedalus* 96(1): 1–21.

Berke, P.R. (2002). "Does Sustainable Development Offer a New Direction for Planning? Challenges for the Twenty-First Century." *Journal of Planning Literature* 17(1): 21–36.

Biles, R. (2011). *The Fate of Cities: Urban America and the Federal Government.* Lawrence, KA: University Press of Kansas.

Blakeley, G. (2010). "Governing Ourselves: Citizen Participation and Governance in Barcelona and Manchester." *International Journal of Urban and Regional Research* 34(1): 130–145.

Brenner, N. and Theodore, N. (2002). "Cities and the Geographies of "Actually Existing Neoliberalism"." *Antipode* 34(3): 349–379.

Calhoun, C., Lee, C., McQuarrie, M., and Walker, E. (2015). *Democratizing Inequalities: Dilemmas of the New Public Participation.* New York, NY: NYU Press.

Checker, M. (2011). "Wiped Out by the "Greenwave": Environmental Gentrification and the Paradoxical Politics of Urban Sustainability." *City & Society* 23(2): 210–229.

City of Flint. (2011). "Memorandum of Understanding. Flint, MI." Available at: http://www.imagineflint.com/Portals/tempflint/Documents/MOU.PDF (consulted June 2, 2016).

City of Flint. (2013) *Imagine Flint: Master Plan for a Sustainable Flint.* Flint, MI.

Cooke, B. and Kothari, U. (2001). *Participation: The New Tyranny?* London: Zed Books.

Dagnino, E. (2008). "Challenges to Participation, Citizenship and Democracy: Perverse Confluence and Displacement of Meanings." In: Bebbington, A., Hickey, S., and Mitlin, D. (eds.). *Can NGOs Make a Difference*?, pp. 55–70. Chicago, IL: University of Chicago Press.

Elwood, S. (2002). "Neighborhood Revitalization Through "Collaboration": Assessing the Implications of Neoliberal Urban Policy at the Grassroots." *GeoJournal* 58(2–3): 121–130.

Fasenfest, D. (2019). "A Neoliberal Response to an Urban Crisis: Emergency Management in Flint, MI." *Critical Sociology* 45(1): 33–47.

Fasenfest, D. and Pride, T. (2016). "Emergency Management in Michigan: Race, Class and the Limits of Liberal Democracy." *Critical Sociology* 42(3): 331–334.

Fischer, E. (2016). "Green-Lined: Demolition, Green Zoning, and Racial Legacies in Flint, Michigan." Master's Thesis, Pratt Institute, NY.

Forester, J. (1999). *The Deliberative Practitioner: Encouraging Participatory Planning Processes.* Cambridge, MA: MIT Press.

Foucault, M. (1984). *The Foucault Reader.* New York, NY: Pantheon.

Fraser, J. and Kick, E. (2014). "Governing Urban Restructuring with City-Building Nonprofits." *Environment and Planning A* 46(6): 1445–1461.

Garcia, M. (2006). "Citizenship Practices and Urban Governance in European Cities." *Urban Studies* 43(4): 745–765.

Germani, G. (1978). *Authoritarianism, Fascism, and National Populism*. New Brunswick, NJ: Transaction Books.

Gotham, K.F. (2014). "Reinforcing Inequalities: The Impact of the CDBG Program on Post-Katrina Rebuilding." *Housing Policy Debate* 24(1): 192–212.

Gotham, K.F. and Greenberg, M. (2014). *Crisis Cities: Disaster and Redevelopment in New York and New Orleans*. New York, NY: Oxford University Press.

Greenberg, M. (2013). "What on Earth is Sustainable?" *Boom: A Journal of California* 3(4): 54–66.

Hall, S. (2001). "Foucault: Power, Knowledge and Discourse." In: Wetherell, M., Taylor, S., and Yates, S.J. (eds.). *Discourse Theory and Practice*, pp. 72–81. London: Sage.

Hackworth, J. (2007). *The Neoliberal City: Governance, Ideology, and Development in American Urbanism*. Ithaca, NY: Cornell University Press.

Harvey, D. (1989). "From Managerialism to Entrepreneurialism: The Transformation in Urban Governance in Late Capitalism." *Geografiska Annaler: Series B, Human Geography* 71(1): 3–17.

Hickey, S. and Mohan, G. (2004). *Participation from Tyranny to Transformation?: Exploring New Approaches to Participation in Development*. London: Zed Books.

Highsmith, A. (2015). *Demolition Means Progress: Flint, Michigan, and the Fate of the American Metropolis*. Chicago, IL: University of Chicago Press.

Hollander, J. (2010). "Moving Toward a Shrinking Cities Metric: Analyzing Land Use Changes Associated with Depopulation in Flint, Michigan." *Cityscape*: 133–151.

Holzner, C. (2007). "The Poverty of Democracy: Neoliberal Reforms and Political Participation of the Poor in Mexico." *Latin American Politics and Society* 49(2): 87–122.

Hummel, D. (2015). "Right-Sizing Cities in the United States: Defining its Strategies." *Journal of Urban Affairs* 37(4): 397–409.

Huxley, M. (2013). "Historicizing Planning, Problematizing Participation." *International Journal of Urban and Regional Research* 37(5): 1527–1541.

Hyra, D. (2006). "Racial Uplift? Intra-Racial Class Conflict and the Economic Revitalization of Harlem and Bronzeville." *City & Community* 5(1): 71–92.

Jansen, R. (2011). "Populist Mobilization: A New Theoretical Approach to Populism." *Social Theory* 29(2): 75–96.

Karpowitz, C., Raphael, C., and Hammond, A. (2009). "Deliberative Democracy and Inequality: Two Cheers for Enclave Deliberation Among the Disempowered." *Politics & Society* 37(4): 576–615.

Laclau, E. (2005). *On Populist Reason*. London: Verso.

Lederman, J. (2015). "Urban Fads and Consensual Fictions: Creative, Sustainable, and Competitive City Policies in Buenos Aires." *City & Community* 14(1): 47–67.

Lederman, J. (2019). "The People's Plan?: Participation and Post-Politics in Flint's Master Planning Process." *Critical Sociology* 45(1): 85–101.

Lederman, J. (2020). *Chasing World-Class Urbanism: Global Policies Versus Everyday Survival in Buenos Aires*. Minneapolis, MN: University of Minnesota Press.

Levine, J. (2016). "The Privatization of Political Representation: Community-Based Organizations as Nonelected Neighborhood Representatives." *American Sociological Review* 81(6): 1251–1275.

Levine, J.R. (2017). "The Paradox of Community Power: Cultural Processes and Elite Authority in Participatory Governance." *Social Forces* 95(3): 1155–1179.

Lee, C. (2014). "Walking the Talk: The Performance of Authenticity in Public Engagement Work." *The Sociological Quarterly* 55(3): 493–513.

Lee, C. (2015). *Do-It-Yourself Democracy. The Rise of Public–engagement Industry.* New York, NY: Oxford University Press.

Lee, C., McQuarrie, M., and Walker, E. (2015). *Democratizing Inequalities: Dilemmas of the New Public Participation.* New York, NY: NYU Press.

Lee, C., McQuarrie, M., and Walker, E. (2015). "Rising participation and declining democracy." In: Lee, C., McQuarrie, M., and Walker, E. (eds.). *Democratizing Inequalities: Dilemmas of the New Public Participation*, pp. 3–23. New York, NY: NYU Press.

Loughran, K. (2014). "Parks for Profit: The High Line, Growth Machines, and the Uneven Development of Urban Public Spaces." *City & Community* 13(1): 49–68.

Low, S.M. (2006). "The Erosion of Public Space and the Public Realm: Paranoia, Surveillance and Privatization in New York City." *City & Society* 18(1): 43–49.

MacLeod, G. (2011). "Urban Politics Reconsidered: Growth Machine to Post-Democratic City?" *Urban Studies* 48(12): 2629–2660.

Marwell, N. (2007). *Bargaining for Brooklyn: Community Organization in the Entrepreneurial City*. Chicago, IL: University of Chicago Press.

Master Plan Steering Committee Minutes. (2013). Available at: http://www.imagineflint.com/Documents/SteeringCommitteeMaterials.aspx.

McCann, E. (2004). " 'Best Places': Interurban Competition, Quality of Life and Popular Media Discourse." *Urban Studies* 41(10): 1909–1929.

McQuarrie, M. (2011). "Nonprofits and the Reconstruction of Urban Governance: Housing Production and Community Development in Cleveland, 1975-2005." In: Clemens, E. and Guthrie, D. (eds.). *Politics and Partnerships: The Role of Voluntary Associations in America's Political Past and Present*, pp. 237–268. Chicago, IL: University of Chicago Press.

McQuarrie, M. (2013). "Community Organizations in the Foreclosure Crisis: The Failure of Neoliberal Civil Society." *Politics & Society* 41(1): 73–101.

Mouffe, C. (2005). *On the Political.* New York, NY: Routledge.

Newman, A. (2015). *Landscape of Discontent: Urban Sustainability in Immigrant Paris.* Minneapolis, MN: University of Minnesota Press.

Oosting, J. (2010). "Detroit will Dump Breakout Sessions for Town Hall Format at Community Meetings to Re-Imagine City." MLive.com. Available at: http://www.mlive.com/news/detroit/index.ssf/2010/09/detroit_will_dump_breakout_ses.html (consulted May 1, 2016).

Ostrander, S. (2013). *Citizenship and Governance in a Changing City: Somerville, MA.* Philadelphia, PA: Temple University Press.

Pacewicz, J. (2012). "Tax Increment Financing, Economic Development Professionals and the Financialization of Urban Politics." *Socio-Economic Review* 12(2): 413–440.

Pacewicz, J. (2015). "Playing the Neoliberal Game: Why Community Leaders Left Party Politics to Partisan Activists." *American Journal of Sociology* 121(3): 826–881.

Peck, J. (2012). "Austerity Urbanism: American Cities Under Extreme Economy." *City* 16(6): 626–655.

Peck, J. and Whiteside, H. (2016). "Financializing Detroit." *Economic Geography* 92(3): 235–268.

Peck, J. and Tickell, A. (2002). "Neoliberalizing Space." *Antipode* 34(3): 380–404.

Purcell, M. (2008). *Recapturing Democracy: Neoliberalization and the Struggle for Alternative Urban Futures*. New York, NY: Routledge.

Rosol, M. (2010). "Public Participation in Post-Fordist Urban Green Space Governance: The Case of Community Gardens in Berlin." *International Journal of Urban and Regional Research* 34(3): 548–563.

Sassen, S. (2014). *Expulsions*. Cambridge, MA: Harvard University Press.

Schilling, J. and Logan, J. (2008). "Greening the Rust Belt: A Green Infrastructure Model for Right Sizing America's Shrinking Cities." *Journal of the American Planning Association* 74(4): 451–466.

Singh, R. (2017). " 'I, the People': A Deflationary Interpretation of Populism, Trump and the United States Constitution." *Economy and Society* 46(1): 20–42.

Smith, N. (1982). "Gentrification and Uneven Development." *Economic Geography* 58(2): 139–155.

Squires, G. and Kubrin, C. (2005). "Privileged Places: Race, Uneven Development and the Geography of Opportunity in Urban America." *Urban Studies* 42(1): 47–68.

Swyngedouw, E. and Wilson, J. (2014). *Post-political and Its Discontents: Spaces of Depoliticisation, Spectres of Radical Politics*. Edinburgh: Edinburgh University Press.

Umemoto, K. (2001). "Walking in Another's Shoes: Epistemological Challenges in Participatory Planning." *Journal of Planning Education and Research* 21(1): 17–31.

Ward, K. (2006). " "Policies in Motion", Urban Management and State Restructuring: The Trans-local Expansion of Business Improvement Districts." *International Journal of Urban and Regional Research* 30(1): 54–75.

Walker, E. (2014). *Grassroots for Hire: Public Affairs Consultants in American Democracy.* Cambridge, UK: Cambridge University Press.

Wilson, J. and Swyngedouw, E. (2014). *The Post-Political and Its Discontents: Spaces of Depoliticization, Spectres of Radical Politics.* Edinburgh: Edinburgh University Press.

Woolford, A. and Curran, A. (2013). "Community Positions, Neoliberal Dispositions: Managing Non-Profit Social Services within the Bureaucratic Field." *Critical Sociology* 39(1): 45–63.

Young, I.M. (2011). *Justice and the Politics of Difference.* Princeton, NJ: Princeton University Press.

CHAPTER 7

Waging Love from Detroit to Flint

Michael Doan, Shea Howell and Ami Harbin

Over the past five years the authors have been working in Detroit with grassroots coalitions resisting emergency management.[1] In this essay, we explore how community groups in Detroit and Flint have advanced common struggles for clean, safe, affordable water as a human right, offering an account of activism that has directly confronted neoliberalism across the state. We analyze how solidarity has been forged through community organizing, interventions into mainstream media portrayals of the water crises, and the articulation of counternarratives that center the experiences, needs, and collective power of those most directly affected. While our rootedness in Detroit leads us to focus primarily on the experiences of activists based there rather than in Flint, we insist throughout that the experiences, resistance, and aspirations of these communities are best understood as interconnected and mutually empowering.

1 Resisting Emergency Management in Michigan

Detroit has provided water to the City of Flint since 1967, the year of the Detroit Rebellion. Within a few years Detroiters had elected Coleman A. Young, one of the first and strongest African American mayors in the United States. Young's election reverberated across the country. Many whites living in the Southeast Michigan region perceived emerging African American political power as a threat and, over the next several decades, abandoned cities for suburbs (Sugrue 2005). During the 1970s, nearly 250,000 jobs left Detroit and the city lost one-fifth of its population. Over the next decade, black unemployment had risen to 34 percent and the Metro Detroit region had the largest income differential between city and suburbs of any major metropolitan area in the country. Oakland and Macomb Counties welcomed whites fleeing from Detroit while Genesee County welcomed scores more from Flint. Suburban, white residents were concerned that their water supply had been left in the hands of a majority

1 The following chapter is an expanded version of the 2019 article by Sharon Howell, Michael D. Doan, and Ami Harbin entitled "Detroit to Flint and Back Again: Solidarity Forever" that was published in *Critical Sociology* 45(1): 63–83.

black city with a steadfast leader. Young famously warned Detroiters not to give up control of the Detroit Water and Sewerage Department (DWSD), as Oakland County Executive L. Brooks Patterson had been attempting to wrest control of Detroit's water system for decades (Cramer 2015).

Emergency management and the Detroit bankruptcy process would eventually provide a convenient means of seizure. Over the past thirty or so years, the State of Michigan has adopted a series of statutes for dealing with municipal fiscal distress by interfering in the affairs of fiscally troubled municipalities. In March 2011, two months after Governor Rick Snyder took office, the Republican-controlled state legislature passed Public Act (PA) 4, replacing Emergency Financial Managers (EFMs) with Emergency Managers (EMs) and significantly extending the scope of an EM's powers. PA 4 not only allows an EM to assume the responsibilities of all local elected officials, but grants them "quasi-judicial powers related to breaking contracts" (Scorsone 2014: 39). The law empowers EMs to modify, terminate, and ban entry into collective bargaining agreements; contract out public services and sell off public assets; and dismiss public officials, set aside minimum staffing requirements, and consolidate or dissolve local departments. PA 4 enables the suspension of a city's charter and strips all local elected officials of their powers, imposing the authority of the state through an EM accountable solely to the governor, effectively stripping city-dwellers of their citizenship rights.

Such political disenfranchisement has disproportionately impacted working-class communities of color, particularly African Americans. Between 2007 and 2013, "51.7 percent of black Michigan residents had been subjected to emergency intervention, while only 2.7 percent of their white counterparts were similarly affected" (Kirkpatrick and Breznau 2016). When Kevyn Orr was appointed as Detroit's EM in 2013, 57 percent of the state's African American population were living without political representation in either their municipality or school district. As residents of Flint, and then Detroit, found themselves under the control of unelected technocrats, forces that had long been stymied by effective African American leadership surfaced to accomplish mutually reinforcing goals. For Flint, emergency management became a vehicle for ending the half-century connection to DWSD amidst plans to shift the water supply to the emerging Karegnondi Water Authority (KWA). For Detroit, emergency management facilitated the establishment of a second regional authority, placing control of Detroit's water system in the hands of the suburban-dominated Great Lakes Water Authority (GLWA). Central to both decisions were the racist perceptions of mostly white suburban officials, who repeatedly cast city-dwellers as incapable of governing and standing in the way of "progress."

Emergency management in Michigan has been resisted at every stage of its development, forcing right-wing legislators to continually refine their efforts. Opposition has included civil disobedience, petition drives, a statewide referendum, public protests, court challenges, public theater, alternative media production, and intense organizing of opposition voices and alternative forms of governance. In the wake of numerous statewide demonstrations, a petition drive carried forward by members of the Stand Up for Democracy (SUD) coalition succeeded in getting PA 4 on a referendum ballot. The law was overturned in November 2012 when 53 percent of Michigan's citizens voted it down. Nevertheless, in a lame-duck session in December of the same year the state legislature passed PA 436, which functions similarly to its widely unpopular predecessor. Appropriations were also written into the new law that shield it from public challenge, effectively making PA 436 referendum-proof.

Efforts to repeal PA 4 were both propelled by and helped inspire challenges to the constitutionality of the law. In early 2011, the Sugar Law Center for Economic and Social Justice filed a suit alleging that PA 4 violated the principle of municipal home rule, violated citizens' right to vote and petition, abolished the separation of executive and judicial powers, and forced local taxpayers to pay the salaries of state-appointed EMs. Since this first suit was rendered pointless when PA 4 was repealed, the attorneys involved filed a second suit against PA 436. Arguing before federal judges, they alleged that PA 436 violated the Voting Rights Act in addition to the US Constitution's First, Thirteenth, and Fourteenth Amendments, as well as its Due Process, Guarantee, and Equal Protection Clauses. In November 2014, a district court judge dismissed most of the charges, leaving the alleged violation of the Equal Protection Clause on the basis of race as the only one left to be tried. Instead of arguing that PA 436 was discriminatory in intent (a burden of proof that is notoriously difficult to meet), the attorneys decided to pursue an appeal via the Sixth Circuit Court of Appeals, only to have it dismissed by unanimous decision in September 2016. Since the US Supreme Court declined to consider the constitutionality of the law in October 2017, the options for mounting constitutional challenges against emergency management have all but been exhausted. As Flint-based scholar-activist Benjamin Pauli points out, though, "the legal battles against PA 4 and PA 436 may have had their most important effects outside a legal context," insofar as they diminished the standing of emergency management in "the court of public opinion," perhaps even helping to "generate *de facto* constraints on the exercise of state power" (Pauli 2019: 114).

2 Emergency Management and Mass Water Shutoffs

In 2013, Governor Snyder declared that the City of Detroit was in a state of "financial emergency." He appointed Kevyn Orr, a bankruptcy attorney, to replace all duly elected officials and govern over the city as its Emergency Manager. After filing for the largest Chapter 9 bankruptcy in US history in July of the same year, Orr listed DWSD as an asset in the bankruptcy proceedings, saying he planned to sell off the water system to reduce the city's debt. In order to make the water department more attractive to buyers, Orr ordered a crackdown on overdue residential water bills in an effort to collect $90.3 million in delinquent fees. Following Orr's order, DWSD signed a two-year, $5.6 million contract with Homrich Wrecking Company, authorizing the private contractor to conduct turnkey disconnections at a rate of between 1,500 and 3,000 homes per week. Homrich was directed to shut off water to all households with a bill of more than $150 or an arrearage of greater than 60 days (Rall 2018). Households were immediately subject to shutoffs without any advance notification or warning. In March 2014, Homrich began carrying out Orr's mass water shutoff campaign, which targeted some 100,000 Detroit residents, or about one sixth of the city's population. Red Homrich trucks with DWSD logos plastered on their doors could be seen creeping up and down neighborhood blocks on a daily basis. Homrich workers strolled from house to house, spraying a bright blue line on each spigot they turned.

Homrich trucks rolled onto Charity Hicks' block early in the morning of May 16, 2014. Already up for the day, Hicks started running from door to door, waking up her neighbors and telling them to fill up their bathtubs, pots, and pans. When Homrich workers arrived at her house she was waiting out on her front lawn. Knowing that she had two more days left to pay her bill, Hicks demanded that the men present an official shutoff order, only to be met with a shrug—all they could produce was a list of addresses. When Hicks refused to let the men turn off her water, the argument evolved into a progressively louder and, eventually, physical confrontation, prompting Hicks to call police to the scene. In a strange, if predictable, reversal, the cops—both white—placed Hicks—a black woman and environmental justice activist known for her fierceness and determination—under arrest, effectively punishing her for taking a stand in defense of her water. As they drove her to the Central Detention Center, the cops threw Hicks' keys and phone out on the front lawn and left her house unlocked. Her husband would later return home to this scene, frightened and confused. It was only after filing a missing person report with the police that he would learn that it was the police who had made her disappear.

For her simple and dignified act of resistance, Hicks was quickly recognized as the "Rosa Parks of the Detroit Water Struggle" (Wiley-Kellermann 2017: 105). Upon her release from jail, she shared her story with fellow activists gathered at St. Peter's Episcopal Church, urging her comrades to "wage love" in the water struggle already intensifying across the city. The phrase quickly caught on and would later be invoked as a way of honoring Hicks in the wake of her tragic passing. Hicks was struck down by a car in a hit-and-run as she waited for a bus in New York City while on her way to speak about the Detroit water crisis at the 2014 Left Forum. After spending the next few weeks in a coma, she joined the ancestors in early July.

As Hicks' example shows, the methods Detroiters have devised to cope with waves of mass water shutoffs reflect a persistence in finding ways to survive with dignity. Some people have simply turned their water back on, a practice that became so widespread that the water department began levying strict fines and permanently shutting off offenders. Others share water from house to house, stringing garden hoses across alleys and through windows. Still others open their homes to share bathing, cooking, and laundry facilities. Prior to the start of the 2018 school year, neighborhood schools opened early and closed late so that children could bathe and wash clothes. Careful to frame these activities in ways that would not further endanger families (as child protective services is authorized to remove children from homes without water), teachers developed tactical responses using school resources to directly support children.

3 Stop the Shutoffs!

Building on methods devised at the neighborhood level, Detroit's water warriors have responded to mass shutoffs with a range of strategies and a diversity of tactics. Some immediately recognized the fight for water access led primarily by black women as the next phase in the long civil rights struggle, seeking structural change through a combination of direct action, courtroom battles, and efforts to push progressive legislation. Other, especially younger activists have been less optimistic about creating meaningful change through the existing political system, which they regard as having long been broken beyond repair. While differing tendencies continue to exist in creative tension, community activists have worked to create a movement that challenges the existing system on all fronts, integrating "both efforts to influence the workings of the current political system and efforts to create independent systems that will supplant that system" (Rall 2018: 119). Specific tactics have included water deliveries to meet immediate needs, acts of civil disobedience, public protests and press conferences, teach-ins and public forums, a people's tribunal, lawsuits, video clips for social media, and documentary films.

The dramatic escalation in shutoffs was initially met with organized resistance in the streets as well as efforts to secure a moratorium through direct action and in the courts. Marches were organized every Friday out front of the downtown DWSD building, where Detroiters could be heard chanting, "Stop the shutoffs!" "Whose water? *Our* water!" and "Water is a human right—fight, fight, fight!" Dubbed "Freedom Fridays," the gatherings invoked the spirit of the "Moral Mondays" movement already underway in North Carolina. Building on the momentum created by these marches, a series of higher profile actions helped draw more media attention to the shutoffs. From July 17 to 21, 2014, the Netroots Nation conference took place at the Cobo Center in downtown Detroit, opening an opportunity for Detroit organizers to amplify the work underway on the ground. The Netroots conference featured panels with frontline activists from Detroit and Flint, including a keynote focused on resisting shutoffs. Upon learning of the public health implications of the shutoffs, National Nurses United (NNU)—the largest union and professional association of registered nurses in the country—called a march through downtown Detroit on July 18 and released a statement declaring a public health emergency in the city. Union members were joined on the streets by hundreds attending the Netroots conference, including actor and water rights activist Mark Ruffalo. In collaboration with Detroit organizers, they created a media spectacle that drew national attention to the situation.

The visibility of the march also created an opening for Detroit activists to engage in a strategically timed act of civil disobedience. While the action involved placing bodies on the gears of the city's shutoff machine to temporarily halt harms, those involved would also challenge the conscience of city officials and residents through the ensuing trial. On July 18, 2014, the group that came to be known as the "Homrich 9" (Marian Kramer, Bill Wiley-Kellermann, Baxter Jones, Joan Smith, Jim Perkinson, Hans Barbe, David Olson, Marianne McGuire, and Kim Redigan) were arrested and charged with disorderly conduct for blocking Homrich trucks from leaving their Detroit base to execute shutoffs. After demanding a jury trial, hoping to tap into "the last vestige of democracy" in a city under dictatorial rule, the defendants faced several delays and motions secretly crafted by law department officials in an attempt to prevent the jury from issuing a verdict (Wiley-Kellermann 2017: 153). The powers that be seemed especially wary of the optics of a jury expressing their collective opinion in response to the necessity defense advanced by the defendants, who claimed that the act of blocking the Homrich trucks, though illegal, was necessary to prevent serious harm. Although the jury was ultimately prevented from expressing their assessment of the evidence, the Homrich 9 were never convicted for their act of safeguarding. After nearly three years of court proceedings that included a highly controversial emergency stay, in July of 2017 Judge Ronald Giles of the 36th District Court dismissed all charges, citing a lack of a speedy trial (Williams 2017).

Several victories could be claimed from the Homrich 9 saga. First, the willingness of this group of ordinary people to openly defy the law in defense of themselves and fellow Detroiters demonstrated the seriousness of the harms the state was inflicting on entire neighborhoods. Their effort to expose and halt state violence underscored the consequences of usurping local democracy, challenging people of conscience to act directly to end the shutoffs. Second, the defendants refused a guilty plea that the state would have been pleased to solicit, mounted a compelling necessity defense, and provoked government officials into interfering with the trial. Had the jury been allowed to issue a verdict, a significant precedent would have been set, perhaps opening the door to further disobedient acts and further undermining the legitimacy of emergency management. Third, as reports of the Homrich 9's action merged with national news stories highlighting the NUN march, city officials were forced to respond with more than words of reassurance. The city instituted a temporary moratorium on shutoffs effective July 21, 2014. Although the moratorium lasted for just over a month, it demonstrated that a small group of Detroiters stripped of their citizenship rights could intervene directly, thwarting the tyranny of emergency management armed only with their bodies and appeals to conscience.

The Homrich 9 saga also strengthened parallel efforts to secure a more lasting moratorium through the courts. On July 21, 2014, activist-lawyer Alice Jennings of the National Conference for Black Lawyers (NCBL), working with a broad coalition of grassroots organizations including the People's Water Board (PWB), We the People of Detroit (WPD), and Detroiters Resisting Emergency Management (D-REM), filed a civil rights case requesting that the bankruptcy court halt the shutoffs for a period of six months. After refusing to grant the moratorium, Judge Steven Rhodes, who was charged with overseeing the bankruptcy process, justified his decision by claiming that, "Detroit cannot afford any revenue slippages" (Lambert 2014). Undeterred, Jennings took the case to the Sixth Circuit in October 2015. After nearly two years on the case, however, federal judges were unwilling to overrule Rhodes' decision, which meant that ending the shutoffs through the courts would be far more difficult than many had hoped.

4 International Connections and United Nations Visit

Back in May 2014, Charity Hicks had attended a conference in Detroit that she and other PWB members organized with Maude Barlow—renowned Canadian water rights activist and co-founder of the Blue Planet Project (BPP) who played a pivotal role in getting the United Nations (UN) to declare a human right to water. Upon hearing Hicks' story, Barlow insisted they draft a report requesting UN support (BPP 2014: 7). In response to the report, the UN Office of the High Commissioner for Human Rights issued a press release stating that Detroit's water rates were relatively high and that widespread poverty made these bills "unaffordable for a significant portion of the population" (OHCHR 2014). "Disconnections due to non-payment are only permissible if it can be shown that the resident is able to pay but is not paying," said Catarina de Albuquerque, Special Rapporteur on the Human Right to Safe Drinking Water and Sanitation. "In other words, when there is genuine inability to pay, human rights simply forbid disconnections." Leilani Farha, Special Rapporteur on the Human Right to Adequate Housing, raised concerns about children being removed from their families by social services. "If these water disconnections disproportionately affect African Americans they may be discriminatory, in violation of treaties the US has ratified," she added (OHCHR 2014).

The UN report was further supported by testimonial evidence gathered at a Town Hall Meeting held at Wayne County Community College on October 19, 2014 (MWRO and PWB 2014; Lewis-Patrick and Cabbil 2014). Nearly 800 people joined the two UN representatives to hear the stories of people experiencing shutoffs, giving Detroiters an opportunity to directly shape the UN response. Detroit native Gregory Price offered the following: "I live in zip code 48204; my block was hit by foreclosures … 2 or 3 people have lost their house for not paying water tax—they have children; they are not receiving any services/ benefits; when they receive 'help' it's a bill too high to pay—that's the payment plan! It's a lose-lose situation; I want to make sure I and my community are heard; if you can do something about it we need your help." Nichole Hill, also of Detroit, recounted how, "The water was cutoff for 8 weeks in 2014; they were steadily cutting off the whole neighborhood so there was nobody to ask for water; the whole block except 3 or 4 homes were cutoff. I have asked to dispute my bill or for a hearing; I was told I could get a hearing time in 2015 possibly; they continue to bill me; they billed me when the water was cut off; it was cutoff again in October despite supposedly being in a payment plan; the bill is over $6,000; they can't explain it; I've paid $3,000 in the last few years" (D-REM 2014).

5 Conflicting Values, Visions, and Narratives

The controversy over Detroit's mass water shutoffs brought into focus two opposing visions of the city, underwritten by conflicting understandings of water and what we owe each other. On the one hand, for Orr, Duggan, and the corporate establishment, water is a commodity to be bought and sold on the market. While it happens to be a good that humans need to survive, water is by no means a right to which we are entitled—like food and shelter, there is no such things as "free" water. For these reasons, access to water is and ought to be conceived as a privilege available only to those with the means to pay. (As one city official succinctly put it: "Go down to the river and get a bucket—*that's* your right"). On the other hand, throughout the city there has been an emerging consensus that water, which is essential to all life, should be seen as a basic human right to be held in the public trust. It is, therefore, the responsibility of local and regional governments to ensure the availability of safe, clean, affordable water for all.

As this growing consensus was channeled into organized resistance and the UN's involvement drew international media attention to what reporters started identifying as "Detroit's water crisis," a new arena of struggle was opened over perceptions of the situation on the ground. Shaping public perceptions was a difficult task for community activists owing to the pervasiveness of deeply entrenched negative attitudes towards Detroit, especially in the wealthier, whiter suburbs. The suburban view is reflected in the comments of Oakland County Executive L. Brooks Patterson, who, in the midst of the city's bankruptcy, gave an interview to the *New Yorker* entitled "Drop Dead, Detroit!" After explaining that he would not allow his children to go into the city for fear of crime, he responded to the question of how Detroit might fix its financial problems by saying, "I made a prediction a long time ago, and it's come to pass. I said, 'What we're gonna do is turn Detroit into an Indian reservation, where we herd all the Indians into the city, build a fence around it, and then throw in the blankets and corn' " (Williams 2014). While these comments ignited a firestorm, they were vintage Patterson, who once said of an African American Councilwoman that he would rather "own a 1947 Buick than own her." Racialized logics of corruption and incompetence have been essential to shifting public assets away from the city, as well as to denying analyses of suburban dispossession and discounting the credibility of their proponents.

Nevertheless, the seriousness of mass water shutoffs, combined with the testimony of people whose lives and communities had been disrupted, sometimes helped make the truth more compelling—or difficult to dismiss—than usual. The struggle over public perceptions of the shutoffs took the form of a struggle between conflicting answers to the following questions: What made the situation in Detroit a "crisis"? What sort of crisis was it? What was the central problem and how had it taken shape? Who was responsible in what ways? How could the problem be resolved? Community activists' claims about the context, causes, and harms of mass water shutoffs consistently challenged the assertions of state and local officials, uncovering myths and exposing lies. Their assessments of who and what was responsible for the crisis also prompted officials to minimize and deny their own culpability and to strategically shield from view the legal frameworks and structures within which they were all operating.

5.1 *The Official Narrative*

The narrative pushed by government officials and mainstream media pundits is that the central problem of Detroit's so-called water "crisis" is residents' refusal to pay their bills. According to this "official narrative," the failure of some residents to make timely payments has forced the water department to raise rates on all residential customers. As a result, more financially responsible residents end up paying more for water than they otherwise would, so these more responsible customers are effectively subsidizing all the delinquent ones.

Mayor Mike Duggan has been one of the chief pushers of this narrative. When it became clear that citizen outrage over the shutoffs was garnering international attention, EM Orr turned over operations of DWSD to Duggan, the then newly elected mayor. Although he had been critical of the way Orr pursued the shutoffs, Duggan defended their necessity, insisting they were justified. When he assumed responsibility for the water department in July 2014, he began claiming that, "When some Detroit residents don't pay their bills, those bills have to be paid by other Detroiters" (AlHajal 2014). By saying this, Duggan is suggesting that it is *unjust* for those who make timely payments to be paying *extra*—an added tax, as it were, to cover the debts of delinquent customers. The unspoken implication is that justice demands these delinquents be punished for harming everyone else. Far from a miscarriage of justice, then, water shutoffs are precisely what justice requires.

Writing in support of the official narrative, Nolan Finley of the *Detroit News* underscores the scandal of residents refusing to pay their bills: "instead of using what resources they have to cover their needs, many water customers instead have chosen to service their wants" he claims, adding that such types continue to splurge cable television and cell phones. "That's what happens when people are conditioned to think someone else is responsible for taking care of them," continues Finley. "In Detroit, the someone else is the half of residents who *do* pay their water bills, and this year were hit with an 11 percent increase that was largely necessary to cover the unpaid bills of scofflaws" (Finley 2014). Interestingly, Finley's "scofflaw" comment went to print just a day after Orr had used the same label in an interview. "Let's find the legitimate need," Orr told *Detroit News* reporters, "but the scofflaws and the people gaming the system, let's either bring them into compliance or not provide them with a free service. That's not fair" (Ferretti and Pardo 2014).

Appeals to fairness aside, Orr has also defended his shutoff campaign on strictly economic grounds. He has argued that clearing delinquent accounts from the water department's books is a matter of "financial necessity" for a utility aiming for solvency in the midst of a steady decline in the city's population and revenues. His decision to balance DWSD's books through the adoption of a tougher debt collection policy was based on "general business principles": the department needed to recoup millions in unpaid bills and customers needed to pay up. Besides, the decision to cut off services to delinquent customers is completely normal: it is a "decision to do what every other regulated utility does in the United States, which is, if you use water you've got to pay for it" (Ferretti and Pardo 2014).

Not only were shutoffs positioned as what justice requires and a financial necessity, but they could also be justified by their anticipated effects. According to Daniel Howes of the *Detroit News*, Orr's shutoff campaign was about initiating a "shift in culture"—away from frivolous spending and dependence on government largess, towards personal responsibility and financial independence. "Residents struggling to pay their water bills are not the central issue," claims Howes. "It's the culture of non-payment that afflicts those with means" (Howes 2014). "By moving to repair what's long been broken, accepted by many and exploited by some," he adds, "the department is leading its own effort to modernize a culture marked by entitlement and abandonment" (2014). Echoing Howes, Finley insists that, "This is not a humanitarian crisis"—let alone a crisis of *any* kind—but simply "a necessary forced reordering of priorities" (Finley 2014).

With Orr, Duggan, and their boosters taking turns in the roles of bad cop, municipal bureaucrats stepped forward to play good cop. By adding nuance that only local knowledge can provide, they worked to strengthen the official narrative. For example, instead of pinning all the blame on delinquent customers, DWSD officials added that these types have historically been enabled by a lack of serious enforcement. "There was no rigid enforcement policy or practice at the water department for years," recalls Bill Johnson, the utility's head spokesperson. "You allow the situation to languish and people think you don't care." But the water department is not solely to blame for its lax enforcement. "Some of it was under pressure from the mayor's office, some of it from

City Council" (quoted in Howes 2014). While DWSD's reluctance to "get serious" may have sent the wrong message, the obvious implication is that it is long past time to implement the more "rigid" debt collective policy that past officials were too permissive to support. Were it not for the intervention of an Emergency Manager, Johnson implies, locally elected officials may never have had the guts to do what justice requires.

Tellers of the official narrative invite us to imagine entitled, "scofflaw" Detroiters talking on iPhones while water flows for free. Meanwhile, their neighbors end up footing the bill one way or another, and everyone's bills keep rising because of this "culture of non-payment." It's only fair that Orr is finally giving these crooks what they deserve *and* forcefully reforming their backward culture. For those who truly deserve help with their bills, the water department has made assistance programs available: "All they need to do is call," Orr assured reporters (Ferretti and Pardo 2014). Since these programs are funded largely through private donations, more generous donors are needed—at least, that is, so long as the bad Detroiters keep causing everyone's water rates to rise, and the good ones keep struggling to afford them. To sum up the official narrative: *no "crisis" here, just a few undisciplined customers adrift in cultural backwardness*. Shutoffs may seem harsh, but nothing less will bring justice and order to the city.

5.2 *Reframing Detroit's Water Crisis*

By way of contrast, community activists have consistently focused on the harm government officials were inflicting on entire neighborhoods by shutting off water. As the UN had confirmed, Orr's ramped-up shutoff campaign was a gross violation of human rights, and this inherently unjust policy had only been made possible under emergency management. Mass shutoffs were also creating a growing public health crisis, as tens of thousands of residents have been rendered unable to wash clothes and dishes, flush toilets, or bathe themselves, children, and elders (see, e.g., Gross 2017, Recchie et al. 2019). As Charity Hicks emphasized, "There are people who can't cook, can't clean, people coming off surgery who can't wash. This is an affront to human dignity" (Lukacs 2014). Her remarks are echoed by seasoned activist Jim Perkinson: "Those of us involved in trying to remediate the situation are discovering homes with kids who can't drink, homes with elders who can't bathe, homes with patients unable to change wound dressings. Some of them have been without access for as long as a year now" (Perkinson 2014). To make matters worse, child protective services has been authorized to remove children from homes without running water. In addition to a matter of water justice, democracy, and public health, then, Detroit's water crisis raises concerns about reproductive justice, particularly given the racial and class dynamics of whose children would be forcefully removed, whose families torn apart and by whom.

As many activists have emphasized, Orr's mass shutoffs were also but the latest episode in a decades-long assault on and attempt to dispossess and displace the Detroit's poorest, predominantly African American residents so that the city could be remade in the images of billionaires, suburban developers, foundations, and far wealthier, mostly white newcomers. The emergency manager law was an important tool in advancing the visions of wealthy elites, wielded skillfully whenever an EM put the interests of bondholders and speculators ahead of the health and well-being of city-dwellers. Emergency management meant that Detroiters were systematically deprived of water *all as a direct result of state policies pursued in support of urban "revitalization."* As with Flint, it was not just *that* Detroiters were harmed or *how badly* they were harmed that needed to be kept in the forefront, but *how, by whom, in accordance with what laws and in support of what private interests*.

While there were plenty of households in arrears when EM Orr came to power, community organizations such as MWRO had been arguing for years that the main problem was the unaffordability of water in a city where 38 percent of residents live in poverty and the unemployment rate is more than twice the national average. The cost of water and drainage in the city has risen by 119 percent over the past decade, and in July of 2014 alone it rose by 8.7 percent. It is not uncommon for water bills for families of four or more to be around $150–200 per month. In a city with an average household income of $28,000 (Smith 2014), this means that some families are forced to set aside 20 percent of their annual income *just for water*. One fifth of the city's roughly 700,000 residents are paying at least four times the Environmental Protection Agency's (EPA) affordability standard for water and sewerage usage, which recommends that residents be charged no more than 2.5 percent of their annual income.

Water is unaffordable in Detroit, not because certain residents refuse to pay up, but because of the decades-long economic evisceration of the city and the harsh realities of grinding poverty (Sugrue 2005). "Detroit was targeted for disinvestment and political repression because it was a center of power for labor and civil rights," notes scholar-activist Scott Kurashige. "The toxic stew of economic dislocation and racial resentment made the region a breeding ground for all varieties of populism" (Kurashige 2017: 4). Congressman John Conyers, the first elected official to take a stand on Detroit's water crisis, points out that water shutoffs are serving as "a form of collective punishment, victimizing families who are behind on their payments not because of 'behavioral payment patterns,' but because of poverty" (quoted in Howell 2014c). "Full discussion of the situation would require deep analysis of the reasons for so much poverty being concentrated in Detroit in the first place, while so much wealth is concentrated in Oakland County next door," notes Perkinson. "It would require telling the story of redlining and racial discrimination in the housing, insurance, and food industries at least," not to mention "the more recent subprime machinations and foreclosures by the banks" (Perkinson 2014).

In the context of capital flight and a rapidly declining tax base, corruption and mismanagement has afflicted Detroit's water department for decades. Contrary to the official narrative, though, it is not city officials who have been in charge of department policy, but federal judges. Between 1977 and 2013, DWSD was under an EPA consent decree because of clean water violations. For most of that time, Federal Judge John Feikens—an open racist and longstanding opponent of integration—held the reigns at DWSD (Wattrick 2011). Through his appointees, union jobs were cut, especially in maintenance and repair, and outsourcing to the private sector became common practice. It was not until March 27, 2013 that US District Judge Sean Cox ordered the return of DWSD to Detroit's EM, ending more than thirty-five years of federal oversight and clearing the way for Orr to begin his mass shutoff campaign.

Under federal oversight, DWSD accumulated more than $1 billion in debt, to the point where 50 percent of its 2014 budget was devoted to servicing debts to major banks. Research conducted by the We the People of Detroit Community Research Collective (WPDCRC) confirmed that the largest sources of DWSD debt were not the unpaid bills of residents, which constituted a tiny fraction of the balance sheet. Instead, $561.1 million in debt resulted from interest rate swaps (a high-stakes financial gamble gone awry—see Kurashige 2017: 55–57), while another $576.9 million resulted from the consequent cancellation of several infrastructure repair projects between 2007 and 2014 (WPDCRC 2016). While Orr claimed that shutting off water to residential customers was necessary to balance the department's books, delinquent *corporate* accounts—some, such as Joe Louis Arena and Palmer Park Golf Course, owing hundreds of thousands of dollars—were not subjected to DWSD's more "rigid" debt collection techniques. Why, then, were Detroit's poorest residents being punished for the failed gambles of department management and the refusal of corporate customers to pay their bills? "When corporations don't pay, there is no mention of the fact and no rebuke," notes Perkinson. "But if poor people of color struggle with bills, then all manner of stereotype and indignant excoriation come rolling to the surface" (Perkinson 2014).

Not only are many Detroiters struggling to pay their bills, but the city as a whole has been disempowered as a result of numerous structural political-economic factors, including state revenue-sharing policy, the emergency manager law, and the nexus of private interests such legislation serves. The denial of local representative democracy is among the chief causes of Detroit's water crisis, since it was EM Orr who made the deeply unpopular decision to initiate mass shutoffs in 2014. But this particularly decree needs to be understood in the context of numerous others: "It has been a brutal year for the people of Detroit," writes long-time community activist Shea Howell, as Detroiters have, "seen long cherished rights and values trampled on in the name of financial necessity" (Howell 2013). "Public lands have been given away. Generous tax breaks have been handed to developers, while elders have seen their pensions taxed and slashed," she continues. "People have been threatened. Many have lost livelihood, home, and health care. Schools have been closed. Classrooms are packed. Political cronies line their pockets while abusing our children in academies designed to deaden imagination, connection, and creativity" (Howell 2013).

Community activists have also drawn attention to the city's location next to the Great Lakes, home to 20 percent of the Earth's surface freshwater. When Orr initiated Chapter 9 proceedings in 2013, the city's water system remained one of its most valuable assets. During his tenure as EM, more than 40 private companies reportedly made bids on DWSD. There were also whispers of creating a regional public-private partnership, yet decision-making processes were rendered non-transparent during the bankruptcy. Writing in 2014, Howell suspected that the water crisis "was orchestrated to make the Detroit Water and Sewerage Department more attractive to buyers," and that Orr's "tougher" debt collection measures were "required to convince suburban powers and private speculators the Detroit water system is a valuable asset" (Howell 2014b; 2014a). These suspicions turned out to be well placed: after indicating his support for the creation of a regional water authority, Orr used the threat of privatization to pressure Macomb and Oakland County into finding an acceptable regional solution, resulting in the creation of the Great Lakes Water Authority (GLWA). The form that regionalization has taken remains an ongoing concern vis-à-vis privatization, particularly because of the under-representation of Detroit in the authority's governance (Howell 2019).

6 Water Affordability vs. Assistance

The shared perspective of numerous organizations in Southeast Michigan that water is a human right and public trust led to the foundation of the People's Water Board (PWB) coalition in 2008, and has since fueled their struggle to develop a water affordability plan as an alternative to the assistance programs offered by DWSD and GLWA. The particular plan endorsed by the PWB, known as the Water Affordability Plan (WAP), assesses the cost for water based on income and ability to pay rather than use. From 2004 to 2005, MWRO, a founding member of the PWB, collaborated with municipal utilities expert Roger Colton and Michigan Legal Services in crafting an income-based water rate structure, which showed that and how DWSD could create a system in which low-income households pay no more than 2.5 percent of their income for water. The WAP was approved by City Council in 2006, due in part to the support of Councilwoman JoAnn Watson. However, after the water department claimed to have the funds to implement the program, these funds suddenly vanished from the budget and the WAP was replaced by the Detroit Residential Water Assistance Plan (DRWAP). DRWAP provides limited assistance to financially struggling households, and only retroactively, once residents have already fallen into shutoff status (Colton 2005).

Beginning with Kwame Kilpatrick, Detroit's mayor from 2002 to 2008, mayors in Detroit have refused to pursue an income-based model for water providence, arguing that the state's legal framework will not support it (Noble and Ferretti 2019). Instead, Mayor Duggan has helped foster two strands of the official narrative: that Detroiters just don't want to pay for water, and that help is there for those with "legitimate" needs. When Orr turned over operations of DWSD to Duggan following the month-long moratorium won by activists in July 2014, Duggan announced a new 10-Point Plan that he said would aid residents behind on their bills, replacing the ineffective DRWAP. Despite the initial fanfare around Duggan's new plan, its effectiveness has since been thoroughly debunked. In its first year, only 300 of the several thousand customers who qualified were able to keep up with scheduled payments (Guyette 2015a; 2015b).

Since assuming the powers of mayor following the limited restoration of home rule at the end of 2014, Duggan has continued Orr's aggressive shutoff policy. While Duggan was busy selling his 10-Point Plan to the press, the water department announced plans to commence another round of shutoffs in the spring of 2015—a campaign that targeted 800 households per day, affecting upwards of 34,000 customers. Duggan's efforts to support low-income households remain grossly inadequate, yet he continues to block the implementation of an affordability program. Despite the continued failure of Detroit's mayors to rally behind it, the affordability plan designed for Detroit has been hailed nationally as a model approach to issues plaguing urban areas struggling to provide water, and has been the starting point for the adoption of similar policies in Philadelphia, and soon in both Baltimore and Chicago.

In September 2014, the Great Lakes Water Authority (GLWA) was created in the course of the bankruptcy proceedings. With GLWA scheduled to commence operations in July 2015, the budget for the newly created regional water authority allocated just $4.5 million (0.5 percent of DWSD's annual revenue) to aiding customers behind on their bills. While this meager sum would have been woefully inadequate to need in Detroit alone, the fact that GLWA's regional service area spanned across several counties was not lost on activist social workers, who contested false claims about the extent of help available, balking at Orr's suggestion that, "All Detroiters need to do is call." Volunteers responding to calls for aid on WPD's Water Rights Hotline (1-844-42-WATER) and at the MWRO office shared countless stories of low-income customers who had dialed numerous numbers recommended to them by water department administrators, only to hear dial tones or notices that funds were temporarily unavailable (D-REM 2014). The existence of such funds depended on pools of money that rapidly dried up when the fluctuating generosity of private donors predictably proved an unreliable supplement to budgeted allocations. Since the water department could afford $5.6 million to hire a private contractor for shutoffs, its unwillingness to devote comparable resources to helping people get out of shutoff status was striking.

The assistance-based models championed by Duggan and others are premised on ignoring the systemic sources of poverty and the fact of limited and, in some cases, fixed incomes that predictably lead to recurring shutoffs. These vicious cycles force families to make dangerous trade-offs between fulfilling basic needs and meeting regular health-related expenses such as food, childcare, energy use (including heating and cooling), and medical care. As community activists have emphasized for more than a decade, a more effective and sustainable way to remedy the situation is to permanently end the shutoffs, refrain from implementing further assistance programs, and devote serious effort to reviewing and adopting some version of the water affordability programs already underway in major cities across the US. Although we are still waiting to see how well these affordability initiatives work out in practice, Detroit's current policies and programs clearly do not work and it is time to explore an alternative rooted in a fundamentally different way of valuing human life.

7 Free the Water!

On November 3, 2014, Detroit natives Antonio Cosme and William Lucka were arrested for allegedly painting "Free the Water" and a large black first on the Highland Park water tower, which stands aloft at the intersection of the I-75 and I-94 highways. Both in their twenties, the duo are members of a

Southwest Detroit-based hip-hop collective called the Raiz Up, which pursues community-building through art, education, and direct action and is actively involved in several grassroots coalitions in the city. On March 15, 2015, several months after being arrested, Lucka and Cosme were formally charged with malicious destruction of property and trespass upon a key facility, despite the fact that the water tower had been out of use for some time. So, in addition to looking at four years in prison and paying thousands of dollars in fines, the two also faced the possibility of being branded as felons, with all of the trappings of the label—forced to "check the box" on employment applications, denied access to public housing, and so forth.

In his coverage of the case in the *Metro Times*, reporter Aaron Robertson posed the question many Detroiters were asking: "Why is a city fresh out of bankruptcy paying its lawyers to prosecute two young artists who, according to their attorney, have no previous criminal records, who are accused of felonies and not misdemeanors, and possibly send them to prison for years?" (Robertson 2016). As Cosme and Lucka were well aware, Mayor Duggan had created a special "graffiti task force" soon after taking office in 2014. Within the first three years of the task force's operation, the city had issued well over 3,000 blight tickets with accompanying fines to owners of residential and commercial buildings that had been subject to "vandalism." If the property owners failed to paint over the graffiti themselves, the city would pay to have it removed before billing the owners upwards of $1,000 for the work.

In the Free the Water case, though, there was more at stake than the contested term "blight" or how the city would align itself with respect to graffiti. After all, the artwork just happened to be a timely political statement about water, and it had been placed strategically along a major commuter route. In response to Robertson's "Why?" question, Cosme characterized the city's response as "political theater." "This is not about justice," added defense attorney Robert Mullen, who represented the pair of young artists in court. "I'm not saying that tagging property that you don't own isn't criminal in some sense, but this water tower case is not about crime; it's about politics" (Robertson 2016). Some noted how the painting put a twist on the Republic of New Afrika's (RNA) call to "Free the Land!"—a black nationalist and secessionist slogan that originated in Detroit in the late 1960s. The painting also poked fun at officials' blanket characterization of activists as demanding "free water," while owning that demand in a way that pushes beyond calls for "affordability," directly challenging the logic of commodification.

The Free the Water case illustrated the willingness of city officials to abuse their powers for the sake of silencing dissent, once again making plain the indefensibility of their shutoff policy. Duggan's administration seemed to be making an example of the two young artists in a desperate attempt to close one of the few remaining windows through which Detroiters could lay claim to public space under conditions of emergency management. As in the case of the Homrich 9, though, the courts proved to be a space not yet completely immune to popular influence. Dozens of friends and comrades packed the courtroom whenever Cosme and Lucka were called to appear for the theater. An art exhibition was organized, press conferences were convened, banners were dropped, and funds were raised to help offset the two defendants' legal fees. Ultimately the pair managed to avoid trials, felony convictions, and jail time. As the final update on the Free the Water Defense Campaign website reports: "Thanks to widespread community support and media coverage, the prosecution agreed to negotiate with Lucka and Antonio. Rather than going to trial, they hammered out an arrangement for 1 year of nonreporting probation and 120 hours of community service each" (Free the Water Defense Campaign 2016).

8 Flint Healing Stories

Against the background of denigrating portrayals of city residents as incompetent, corrupt, and incapable of self-governance, sharing personal stories became a central part of the struggle to draw attention to the crises unfolding in Detroit and Flint. Long before the poisoning of Flint's water supply became a national scandal, Flint and Detroit organizers met regularly to discuss shared concerns over the deprivation of local citizenship rights (Howell 2015c; Howell and Stephens 2015; Guzmán 2016). A few weeks after the switch to the Flint River in April 2014, about 40 activists from Flint, Detroit, Highland Park, and Muskegon gathered as part of a statewide network to strategize. The meeting was hosted by Citizens for Highland Park Public Schools (CHPPS) and MWRO (Unpublished Minutes 2014; Ketchum 2015).

While the discussion focused on the dismantling of local democracy, concerns over the connection between emergency management, rising water rates, and shutoffs also emerged. In her report from Highland Park, Marian Kramer of the Highland Park Human Rights Coalition (HPHRC) characterized outrageously high water bills as a tool to drive people out of their homes and enable the privatization of local water systems. As Kramer pointed out, the state legislature had placed water rates and billing policies under the control of EMs. Alice Jennings of the NCBL emphasized the ability of the state to attach outstanding water bills to property taxes, contributing to the tens of thousands of tax foreclosures already decimating communities throughout the region.

Nayyirah Shariff and Claire McClinton of the Flint Democracy Defense League (FDDL) reported on a press conference where residents appeared with tape over their mouths, having been limited to just 3 minutes each at the end of City Council meetings. Democracy, not water, was their primary concern, though they were fully aware of rising water rates and efforts to cut Flint's ties with DWSD. EM Michael Brown had raised water rates by a stunning 25 percent in the spring of 2012, putting thousands at risk of having their water cut off. In 2014, rates rose by an additional 6.5 percent, bringing the average bill in Flint well over $100 a month. As Pauli notes, "The FDDL realized that popular discontent over water rates and shutoffs, much like discontent over the selling off of public assets, could be a potent source of opposition to emergency management" (Pauli 2019: 125).

Meanwhile, Flint residents started noticing a change in water quality immediately following the switch to the Flint River. They began sharing evidence and testimony on social media pages such as Flint River Water Support Group less than a month after the switch. In response to growing concerns over water-related rashes and illness, the FDDL formed a Water Task Force and, with the help of Detroit activists from WPD, began distributing bottled water in neighborhoods. Over the next few months, while distributing water together in both Detroit and Flint, activists heard dozens of stories of shutoffs, hardships in obtaining drinkable water, as well as diseases and rashes linked to the foul, discolored water flowing from the taps.

As government officials refused to acknowledge Flint residents' complaints for months and months, the emerging coalition accelerated their organizing efforts. In January 2015, they announced a series of public meetings in Flint to develop community-wide strategies, providing a deeply democratic alternative to the officially sponsored, highly paternalistic water forums launched in the same month. While introducing a series of church-based gatherings, Shariff reported that communities were facing plummeting water quality, soaring water rates and the use of police to make arrests for water theft. Flintstones had been receiving boil-water advisories for months, alongside warnings that those in poor health or with compromised immune systems should not consume city water. Chemical treatments were said to be out of balance, yet Flint's EM claimed the water was safe to drink.

Public meetings provided the background for a larger strategy of sharing personal stories to raise awareness and counter the dehumanizing logic of neoliberalism, which casts non-experts as lacking the credibility to speak truthfully about the quality of the water flowing from their taps, let alone about the state of their own health and well-being. This strategy was supported by the Michigan Roundtable for Diversity and Inclusion (MRDI), who organized statewide "Healing Stories" to address race and class-based disparities in the region. Debra Taylor, a Flint native and Detroit activist with WPD, was the main organizer for the first event. "Many people that I know personally there seem to all have at least a $200 water bill per month," she said. "So you've got these extremely high water (bills), and then you're afraid to drink the water" (WCMU 2015).

Over 100 people attended the event. Community activists and leaders from Detroit and Flint served as designated listeners for storytellers hailing from Flint, who worked with Taylor to develop a dramatic way of presenting their experiences: before each person spoke, the others on stage would say in unison, "You have the right to remain silent." The storyteller would then respond, "I waive that right" (Ketchum 2015). Shea Howell, a designated "listener," captured some stories in *The Michigan Citizen*:

> The first woman to step forward said that even her cat won't drink the water out of her tap. She had been taken to the hospital after drinking some soup made for her with tap water. She explained that she had gotten a bill for over $900. "So now I am paying for something I don't drink and paying $150 for bottled water a month. I take a shower and I itch. I was dehydrated from soup. But I am not about to lose my home. I have to choose between property tax and water. I'm 72 years old and getting tired, and my cat only has three or four more lives left."
>
> HOWELL 2015a

Another listener, Councilman Eric Mays, moved the next week to have Flint returned to DWSD, and the Flint City Council voted in favor, 7 to 1. The Council's efforts were immediately rejected by EM Gerald Ambrose, who said: "It is incomprehensible to me that seven members of the Flint City Council would want to send more than $12 million a year to the system serving southeast Michigan." Ambrose claimed definitively that, "Flint water is safe" (Howell 2015a).

Taylor continued as the main organizer of "Healing Stories" efforts while Monica Lewis-Patrick, a fierce water warrior and CEO of WPD, served as host. In July 2015, they held a second event focusing on water, where people were invited to share stories of the illnesses they were developing from consuming contaminated liquids. Reflecting on the importance of this process, McClinton emphasized that, "They were able to tell their stories in a community setting, not alone or in isolation" (Guzmán 2016). The connections established through public storytelling supported ongoing efforts to build relationships and capacities for self-organization among city residents across Southeast Michigan. While delivering thousands of gallons of bottled water door-to-door in Detroit and Flint, Lewis-Patrick observed: "Flint [activists] came down to not only support us and encourage us but also to share their stories of contaminated water." At a meeting in July 2014, McClinton and Shariff arrived in Detroit with water samples. As Taylor pointed out, "It looked like ice tea. They told us it came from their taps. I said, 'Come on, really? This is from your tap?' " (Guzmán 2016). These jugs of poison became symbols of the depth of the disregard for public health embodied in emergency management.

Although concerns about lead in the water dated back as far as February 2015, it would be months before the details of lead and other water-borne contaminants in Flint began to emerge. As local and national media attention continued to focus on Detroit, activists from both cities kept weaving together stories from across the region and beyond. The sharing of these stories from city to city functioned in part as consciousness-raising, helping to overcome the internalization of dominant narratives of victim-blaming (i.e., "it's your own fault if you can't afford to pay for water") and gaslighting (i.e., "there's nothing wrong with the Flint water—residents' perceptions cannot be trusted"). Those sharing their own stories with one another were well positioned to chart the connections between shutting off water and delivering liquid poison. Both resulted from the decisions of EMs, which were made possible by broader statewide efforts to undermine democracy, wrest power from city-dwellers, and escalate the dispossession of low-income, predominantly African American communities.

9 International Social Movements Gathering

From May 29 to 31, 2015, Detroit hosted The International Social Movements Gathering for Affordable Water and Housing (International Social Movements Gathering 2015). The event was organized by a coalition of organizations and spearheaded by Alice Jennings of NCBL and Maureen Taylor of MWRO. 350 people from 47 states and 10 countries attended: residents of Detroit, Highland Park, Flint, and Benton Harbor met with activists from across North, Central and South America, Europe, and First Nations. In addition to film screenings, collective meals, and a water ceremony, conversations focused on sharing experiences from neighborhoods where water access was threatened, along with stories of collective resilience and resistance, proposals for citizen-led policy initiatives, community-based research projects, and organizing and mobilizing in the streets (Howell 2015b).

It was a powerful gathering. Public storytelling played a central role once again, this time as part of broader efforts to forge solidarity between locally-based activists and those visiting from abroad. Conversations focused on the situation in Michigan quickly expanded and deepened as connections were established between water-insecure communities across the US and globally: people enduring droughts in California, families in Appalachia struggling with heavily contaminated water sources, people in Mexico resisting a 22-year effort to privatize local water systems, and communities in Italy resisting attempts by multinational corporations to undermine a referendum that recognized water as a common good. In addition to expanding and strengthening networks of solidarity, the gathering also galvanized resistance in Michigan. The connections between Detroit and Flint were further clarified and emphasized as new relationships were built between organizers from both cities. Melissa Mays stood up in a packed room, held up bottles of brown water and reported:

> We were switched by our Emergency Manager from Detroit water to the Flint River which is disgusting and contaminated ... We have been forced to drink, bathe and cook with contaminated water. As a response ... [w]e are being poisoned. I am sick. I have copper poisoning and lupus, all developed since October. All of my children have been to the doctor for rashes, hair loss, and muscle and bone pain. We are fighting a huge health crisis in Flint ... We have no rights. They don't want us here.
>
> PEOPLE'S TRIBUNE 2015

Against the background of government officials in denial—promising insufficient assistance without addressing the core problem of unaffordability, and "guaranteeing" the safety of water that was obviously toxic—participants spoke countervailing truths in clear, plain language. By fortifying resistance efforts across Southeast Michigan, and situating them in the global context of seizures of water and public infrastructures from low-income communities, the Social Movements Gathering positioned activists well to work as a unified front against attacks on community water security throughout the region.

10 Detroit to Flint Water Justice Journey

Growing out of conversations initiated at the Social Movements Gathering, activists organized a 70-mile, eight-day walk from Detroit to Flint, dubbed the Detroit to Flint Water Justice Journey for Clean and Affordable Water.

Sponsored by the Michigan Coalition for Human Rights (MCHR), PWB, MWRO, and others, the group walked 10 miles per day from July 3 to 10, 2015, stopping in several towns along the way to hold public gatherings, rallies, and conversations (MCHR 2015). The walk began with a spiritual ritual led by indigenous water walkers, convened at the Underground Railroad monument on the Detroit riverfront. From there, the main walkers carried a mixture of water with samples drawn from the Great Lakes and donated by indigenous comrades. Following a send-off rally at the Spirit of Detroit Statue, the first stop was for a Cultural Celebration at Nandi's Knowledge Café in Highland Park, with live drumming, spoken word poetry, a community speak-out, and art-making for people of all ages. Children painted flags with images depicting the significance of water in sustaining all life forms, which were then sewn into a banner to be displayed throughout the walk. Walkers then attended a Town-Hall Meeting and Rally at St. Luke's A.M.E. Church, where people from Highland Park, MI, described how they were facing multiple years of not receiving water bills at all, only to finally receive impossibly high ones, have their water shut off, and face the removal of their children by social services.

Concluding the first day, the Detroit Light Brigade organized an action at dusk in Ferndale, MI, where the message "Clean, Affordable Water Now!" was displayed in lights for all passersby at Woodward Ave. and 9 Mile Rd. to see. Over the following days, the walkers proceeded up Woodward towards Flint, stopping to participate in a service at Birmingham United Church in Bloomfield Hills, MI, a Cross-County Speak-Out at the Baldwin Center in Pontiac, MI, and then on to the cities of Clarkston, Holly, Grand Blanc, and finally, Flint. The journey concluded on July 10, 2015 with a huge rally at Flint City Hall, after which two busses full of people departed for the state capitol in Lansing to deliver a petition demanding safe, affordable water for all.

The Water Justice Journey allowed for conversations among people directly experiencing water shutoffs and exposure to toxic water, who could share how their daily lives had been affected while also speaking to their tremendous capacities to provide care and be cared for by family and neighbors. One woman attended the Flint rally with a jug of brown water drawn from her tap and a fistful of hair that had fallen out after weeks of ingesting the water (Azikiwe 2015). The walk further developed solidarity between Detroit and Flint activists as we built new networks of churches, organizations, and groups along the way. One major goal of the walk was to counter widespread perceptions of Detroit and Flint as disconnected and alone in facing water-related problems. The information packet distributed throughout the walk linked together three major problems: mass water shutoffs, unaffordable water, and toxic, unhealthy, dangerous water. It also highlighted two corresponding demands: (1) implement the 2005 WAP ("Assistance is not Affordability"); and (2) provide clean, healthy water relief to the people of Flint (Samartino 2015). The organizers insisted that water unaffordability and deprivation in Detroit and water contamination in Flint must be understood in relation and rectified together, connected as they are to the same underlying problems: sacrificing the basic needs of people in pursuit of profit, prioritizing private interests over the people's good, and seizing control of land and resources maintained by predominantly African American communities.

11 Grassroots Journalism and Filmmaking

In the face of false, dehumanizing narratives advanced by city and state officials, developing and documenting the story of the impact of mass water shutoffs on the lives of Detroiters became the job of activists, independent filmmakers, and community-based journalists. Community news and radical publications told the story of the shutoffs. Tweets and articles were shared on social media. #WageLove became the preferred hashtag, in memory of beloved Detroit community leader and water rights activist Charity Hicks. Kate Levy, a Detroit activist and videographer, began documenting everyday efforts to organize and resist shutoffs in Detroit. Combining interviews with people who had been disconnected along with city officials and activists, Levy started weaving together a powerful visual narrative of shutoffs and their impacts, as well as direct actions and other forms of resistance. Activists staged viewings of her work throughout the city and suburbs to share the stories of fellow Detroiters. Short clips were shared on social media and mainstream newscasts (Levy 2015a, 2015b, 2015c, 2016a, 2016b; The Raiz Up 2015).

Over the next few months, Levy's filmmaking skills were joined with the investigative reporting of Curt Guyette. A long-time Detroit reporter covering grassroots politics, Guyette was hired by the American Civil Liberties Union (ACLU) to provide a critical perspective on the bankruptcy. By the time the UN convened the Town Hall Meeting in October 2014, Levy and Guyette had compiled a wide array of visual and narrative evidence demonstrating that water shutoffs were happening with complete disregard for the health and well-being of Detroiters and were often conducted in haphazard, patently disrespectful and irresponsible ways (Levy and Guyette 2015c). Levy and Guyette also revealed the Duggan administration's inability to grapple seriously with the underlying problems of poverty, municipal debt, and the financialization of urban governance. They documented the inadequacy of assistance plans, showing that, of the 3,000 people enrolled in Duggan's 10-Point Plan, only 300 were able to meet scheduled payments and stay enrolled for a year (Guyette 2015a, 2015b; Levy and Guyette 2015c). Through their work we met young people defending their neighbors from disconnections by standing on shut-off valves, refusing to move (The Raiz Up 2015); elders living on fixed incomes being forced to return to the water department multiple times with forms to prove their medical needs for water, or gathering rainwater in barrels for cooking and bathing; and mothers organizing entire days around securing bottled water for children (Levy 2015a). These images started to chip away at the legitimacy of EMs, Mayor Duggan, DWSD, and all who defended Detroit's shutoff policy.

Flint community activists such as Claire McClinton, Nayyirah Shariff, Melissa Mays, and LeeAnn Walters played pivotal roles in bringing the Flint water crisis to light, forcing the powers that be to officially acknowledge it as such and return the city to Detroit water in October 2015 (Shariff 2015; Guyette 2016; Guzmán 2016). It was their work, combined with that of Levy and Guyette, that was largely responsible for drawing national attention to the unfolding disaster and its connections with Detroit (Guyette 2015c, 2015d, 2015e; Levy and Guyette 2015a, 2015b, 2015d, 2016). Both the ACLU of Michigan website and Levy's site, www.detroitmindsdying.com were widely circulated, providing up-to-date news and images. Videos produced by Levy and Guyette were also regularly incorporated into reports by independent news outlets such as Democracy Now! and picked up by mainstream pundits such as Rachel Maddow.

12 Press Conference, Teach-In, People's Tribunal

As the region moved closer to launching the GLWA and KWA, a coalition of Detroit and Flint-based organizations orchestrated a series of actions designed to challenge the narratives and policies advanced by state officials, underscore the relationship between the two cities, and further strengthen regional solidarity. The first step was a press conference held at the ACLU offices in Detroit on January 15, 2016 (Levy 2016a). The discussion focused on undermining the idea advanced by Duggan, DWSD Director Gary Brown, and other officials that it was "illegal" to implement water rates adjusted to household income. By convening legal experts from a variety of organizations, the coalition shifted the idea of "criminality" away from those who could not afford to pay for water, or who were turning water back on to meet basic needs, and on to those being paid to turn water off. Attorneys Mark Fancher of NCBL, Julie Hurwitz of the National Lawyers Guild (NLG), Thomas Stephens of D-REM, and Peter

Hammer of the Damon J. Keith Center for Civil Rights presented a series of briefs supporting the legality of an income-based water program. As the briefs made clear, not only is an income-based rate structure legal in Michigan, but it would likely generate more revenue for DWSD while addressing public health concerns raised by mass water shutoffs. "The water affordability plan is not only legal, it is the only right thing to do," said Hurwitz. "It is in the public interest to ensure that not only affordable water but safe water be provided to our community" (Guillen 2016). News accounts of the conference revealed glaring weaknesses in the official narrative and nervous shifting on the part of state officials.

The press conference was followed the next day by a Teach-In emphasizing connections between Detroit and Flint (D-REM 2016a, 2016b, 2016d). Both cities were framed as struggling against EMs whose job it is to balance budgets at the expense of public health and welfare. The Teach-In on Detroit and Flint Water Crises was convened at the Damon J. Keith Center for Civil Rights at Wayne State University on January 16, 2016. A packed house welcomed Flint activists Melissa Mays, Nayyirah Shariff, and Laura Sullivan as they shared news and analysis of the unnatural disaster back home, reminding everyone in the room that the I-75 runs both ways, "from Flint to Detroit and back again." Members of the Homrich 9 invited attendees to consider what it means to engage in civil disobedience under emergency management. As Rev. Bill Wiley-Kellermann of St. Peter's Episcopal Church in Detroit reminded us, "civil disobedience involves breaking an unjust law," such as Jim Crow laws in the South. However, "in a situation where the unjust law is an Emergency Manager law, which takes over the entire structure of governance, the act of civil disobedience needs to be *to become ungovernable.*"

The Teach-In also provided a forum for sharing the work of community-based researchers and modeling the creation of citizen-led policy initiatives. Everyone received a reader filled with stories of collective resistance, analyses of laws and policies, and independent journalism produced by Flint and Detroit activists. After learning about water affordability from Maureen Taylor and Sylvia Orduño of MWRO, participants were among the first to learn of the groundbreaking research conducted by the We the People of Detroit Community Research Collective (WPDCRC). Monica Lewis-Patrick, Emily Kutil, and Gloria Aneb House facilitated a discussion of an ongoing research project the collective had taken on, known at the time as, simply, "The Mapping Project." In August 2016, the results of the project's first phase were unveiled in the same space with the launch of a collaboratively-crafted manuscript, *Mapping the Water Crisis: The Dismantling of African-American Neighborhoods in Detroit: Volume One* (WPDCRC 2016). The statistical evidence gathered throughout the project helped set the stage for the unveiling of the Water is a Human Right Bill Package, which, as State Representative Stephanie Chang explained in her presentation, was a product of decades of dedicated work by a broad-based coalition hailing from Detroit and Flint (Chang and Garrett 2016).

The Teach-In was followed the next week by a People's Tribunal, held in the sanctuary at the Cass Corridor Commons on January 23, 2016 (D-REM 2016c, 2016e). Both events attracted hundreds of people. The People's Tribunal for Violations of the Human Right to Water was a social justice theater project developed by activists to inform the general public concerning the crises that have been created by mass water shutoffs in Detroit, and the criminal negligence that led to the poisoning Flint's water supply. In this trial, the people of Detroit indicted Mayor Duggan (played by Michael Doan), Governor Snyder (Fred Vitale), and EMs Kevin Orr and Darnell Early (who were said to be in their cells) for violations of the human right to clean, safe, affordable water. The indictments were drafted by lawyers for the people, with the role of prosecutor enacted by Attorney William Goodman of the NLG. The witnesses for the people were Detroit's Valerie Jean Blakeley and Debra Taylor, followed by Melissa Mays and Nayyirah Shariff of Flint. The jury was comprised of respected community leaders hailing from both cities, including Claire McClinton, William M. Davis, Elena Herrada, William Copeland, Teresa Kelly, and Rudy Simons.

The trial proceedings were orchestrated as a moral drama featuring testimony from people who had faced shutoffs and exposure to contaminated water. The judge (Wiley-Kellermann) argued that *all* levels of government, including the courts, had either failed us or been rendered powerless under emergency management, "necessitating a People's Tribunal." Drawing a sharp contrast with the judicial system's inability to act on behalf of the people, he offered pointed instructions to the jury: "Ordinarily, judges instruct jurors in a way that actually minimizes, constricts, and constrains their awareness of their own power. I will not do so. Juries are inherently a powerful and authoritative form of direct democracy. I will not hide that fact from you" (D-REM 2016e). Finally, the judge offered these words in closing:

> Mr.'s Snyder, Duggan, (Early, and Orr), you are hereby stripped of your authority to lead or rule the people of Detroit and Michigan. The people are no longer bound to honor you in office. Moreover, you are to be lead in an ignominious spectacle of your failures before the people of Michigan, the people of the nation, and the people of the world. Go. You are no longer over us. Let it be so ordered. *Taps gavel.*
>
> D-REM 2016e

The press conference, Teach-In, and Tribunal were all held as Governor Snyder's failure to respond to the poisoning of Flint's water began to make national headlines. As people across Michigan were waking up to the pivotal role played by EMs in creating the water crises in Flint and Detroit, the Tribunal helped inspire the creation of an Unwanted Poster featuring a mug shot of Snyder, put together by the Beehive Design Collective in collaboration with local activists (D-REM 2016f). Within days the poster could be seen hanging on public buildings from Ann Arbor to Lansing, and from Flint to Detroit. It was also proudly displayed on stage at a reprise of the Tribunal, held at Detroit's Charles H. Wright Museum of African American History on February 16, 2016. Mark Fancher of NCBL joined Monica Lewis-Patrick of WPD and several other activists on a panel. "The issues of race and class are clear," read the flyers for the event, "as no one can imagine affluent, mostly white communities being forced to use contaminated, rash-inducing, lead-poisoned water as is the case in Flint. Likewise, it is no coincidence that massive water shutoffs have been used against an overwhelmingly African American city in the case of Detroit" (Black Bottom Archives 2016). Speaking to a reporter from *The Detroit News*, Lewis-Patrick emphasized that, "It's just as much a danger here [in Detroit] not to have water as having poisoned water." Gloria Aneb House of D-REM clarified the intent of the gathering as follows: "We hope that more and more of us will be mobilized to stand against this" (Hicks 2016).

13 Epilogue: Five Years and Counting

Driving home to Detroit along the I-75, a bumper sticker captures our attention: "Five Years & Counting, Flint is Still Broken." It beggars belief that a city so close to the Great Lakes could still have undrinkable water. How could Flint still be in the midst of a crisis created by the poisoning of its water by policy? How could it be that Detroit continues to violate the human rights of its residents through systematic water deprivation? When could these interrelated crises be declared over, and by whom?

From the perspective of Detroit's water warriors, justice for Detroiters could not be achieved through the declaration of another temporary moratorium, tougher crack-downs on corporate customers, or the implementation of better assistance programs. Nor was the limited restoration of home rule at the end of 2014 enough to ensure that similar crises would not erupt whenever state officials decided to declare another "financial emergency." Since the state created the Michigan Financial Review Commission to ensure that future mayors would remain faithful to the dictates of EMs for the next thirteen years, state receivership in Detroit is not really over, anyway, having "continued by other means" (Kurashige 2017: 70–71). At this point it cannot even be said that *representative* democracy has been restored at the municipal level, let alone deeper forms that would give city-dwellers genuine control over the operations of public utilities.

Despite the claim of state and city officials that there was never a water "crisis" to begin with in Detroit, waves of shutoffs continue as inadequate assistance programs keep failing those struggling to survive poverty. In yet another distressing development, in late August 2018, less than a week before the start of classes, the discovery of water-borne lead contamination in more than fifty of Detroit's public schools led to Detroit's Community School District announcement that drinking water would be shut off in all school buildings. As community activists have emphasized all along, recovery from Detroit's water crisis would have to involve a definitive end to the shutoffs, the adoption of a water affordability program, and the total abolition of emergency management. More broadly, it would require a serious reckoning with a longstanding history of racial and class antagonisms expressed spatially as an urban-suburban conflict over critical infrastructure, resources, and bargaining power. Since there is no previous state of amicable relations to which residents of city and suburbs can be restored, new relations must instead be forged by all those committed to upending the dehumanizing logics of racial capitalism and colonization.

In terms of accountability for Detroit's water crisis, the list of individuals and institutions would need to include everyone involved in creating and maintaining the practice of emergency management, from Governor Snyder on down to the crafters of right-wing policy that meet annually on Mackinac Island. Then there are the media pundits who have either unthinkingly echoed or carefully defended Orr and Duggan's proclamations and justifications of the shutoffs; local elected officials and administrators who, even when stripped of their powers, refused to publicly oppose the shutoffs, wasting their positions of influence; public health officials and researchers who failed to join NUN and others by officially declaring the shutoffs a public health emergency, and to prioritize the health and well-being of Detroiters even when this would have meant risking their political careers; private contractors who continue to make millions by executing shutoffs; and more broadly still, residents of surrounding suburbs who benefit from inequitable rate structures and from having gained greater control over critical infrastructure through emergency management. Without taking account of the broader historical context of the shutoffs, though, Detroit's current situation cannot be adequately understood. Nor can we afford to forget that the actions of individuals and organizations continue to be constrained and enabled by background legal frameworks, such as emergency management. Until the historical, systemic roots of Detroit's water crisis have been addressed, it cannot truly be declared "over."

Five years out, many Flint residents continue to express legitimate concerns that certain water quality issues are not being adequately addressed, that little has been done to fix the overall problem, properly understood, and that what has been done has been carried out largely by state officials and agencies—the very people who caused the crisis in the first place. Official disregard for the health and well-being of Flintstones continues as the officials responsible for creating and maintaining the crisis continue to evade legal accountability. As of April 6, 2018, the state is no longer providing bottled water to Flint residents, leaving many people reliant on point-of-use filters that remain an ongoing health concern, particularly due to the threat of bacterial contamination. While some of the city's pipes have been repaired or replaced, the massive work of laying down new water distribution infrastructure—from municipal service lines to privately owned pipes—is far from complete and sorely lacking in official support.

As in Detroit's case, how and by whom Flint's water crisis is framed matters a great deal to whether and when an "end" could be declared. While state officials have been quick to depict Flint's as strictly a lead-in-water-situation, community activists have been clear from the jump that the crisis is not *only* about lead, but everything else that residents have been forced to endure since the switch to the Flint River. The sources of residents' suffering include the human and property-related harms of lead and other water-borne contaminants; the costs of removing toxic substances and bacteria from the municipal water system; the costs of addressing various illnesses linked to contaminated water, not to mention the heavy psychological toll associated with having one's water poisoned by the very officials one had empowered to safeguard public health, and the profound disruption of daily routines entailed by all of the above.

In connection to the exclusive or excessive focus on lead, Flint's water crisis has often been misrepresented as a water treatment problem—a framing that obscures its inherently political dimensions. Yet as Pauli points out, "If missteps around corrosion control and regulatory failures were at fault, the state could get away with sacrificing some of its low-ranking bureaucrats to popular demands for accountability and placing the rest of the blame on the EPA." Moreover, "because the pipes could be 'healed' through orthophosphate treatment (a notion that became the object of much scorn and ridicule on the ground in Flint), the state could argue that replacing them gradually—or even not at all—would not compromise public health" (Pauli 2019: 60). Depicting the crisis in strictly technical terms has allowed Snyder and Flint's EMs to avoid accountability for their role in creating and maintaining the crisis. While there are undoubtedly systemic dimensions to the problem, Flint activists have emphasized that individual actors, such as Snyder, are squarely to blame, in addition to various government agencies that failed to safeguard public health. Calls to arrest Snyder are not symbolic. They are urgent demands for retributive justice that have yet to be met, underscoring the multifaceted "brokenness" of the existing political system.

Beyond demands for retributive justice, reparations for the harms the state has inflicted on Flint cannot be achieved through the distribution of point-of-use filters, or even the continued provision of free bottled water, important though these measures undoubtedly are in meeting immediate needs. While there may be no reparative gesture adequate to the damage done and the irreplaceable losses suffered, Flint activists have been clear that repairing what state agents and agencies broke would have to involve the replacement of damaged infrastructure, a refund in water bills dating back to April 2014, and full funding to meet the health and education needs of all those exposed to contaminated water. Were a federal disaster to finally be declared in the city (not just an "emergency" of the sort declared by Obama), recovery money and efforts would no longer need to be routed through the state and federal agencies could work directly with communities who have long been active on the ground.

For years Flint and Detroit activists have emphasized that while systematic water poisoning and deprivation are clearly human rights issues, both are deeply local issues too. By insisting that "Flint Lives Matter" and "Whose water? *Our* water!" water warriors have consistently underscored that the questions of *how* and *with whom* recovery efforts are organized is centrally important, not just *whether* some sort of recovery occurs. "What kind of say would residents have over how resources coming into the city were managed?" asks Pauli in Flint's case. "Who would get to decide when Flint had been made 'whole'?" (Pauli 2019: 223). Prioritizing the political self-determination of Flintstones and Detroiters makes the question of local democracy a crucial measure not only of whether each city is being made whole, but how—by and with whom. Contrary to the colonialist logics of state officials, the knowledge and ways of knowing of local people matter. Ongoing water struggles raise the question of to what extent residents of Detroit and Flint are managing to achieve some semblance of *epistemic* self-determination in the wake of rampant state interference into local affairs, and also given the limitations of representative forms of democracy as respecters of the knowledgeable participation of citizens (Doan 2018).

The question of local democracy—whether it can be said to exist, and in what form—links Flint and Detroit together. For Flintstones, the suspension of local representative democracy was chiefly to blame for the water crisis, as the decisions to switch to the Flint River and approve the KWA project would never have been made were it were not the ability of EMs to ignore the opinions of residents and their elected representatives (see Hammer 2016). Nor would local elected officials have implemented Orr's mass water shutoff campaign and sold out Detroiters through the creation of GLWA. Emergency management engenders utter disregard for public health, local knowledge, and popular will. Restoration of local democracy and the abolition of emergency management are preconditions for fixing what has been broken. Yet as Pauli emphasizes—and much the same could be said in Detroit's case—struggles over water and democracy in Flint are not strictly defensive, for water warriors also carry another world in their hearts. The fight for justice in Flint "would not be over until democracy was a reality: not just in the negative sense of freedom from emergency management, but in the positive sense of a community of people empowered to take charge of their water, their infrastructure, their health, their city, and their future" (Pauli 2019: 48). Community activists have enlivened "a more radical democratic vision, one that [seeks] to deepen democracy by building off the popular energies liberated by the crisis, the grassroots associations formed in response to it, and the new political consciousness sparked by it" (6). That vision remains to be realized. The struggle for another world continues.

References

AlHajal, K. (2014). "Detroit Mayor Given Control Over Water Department Amid Shutoff Controversy." *M-Live*. July 29, 2014. Available at: https://www.mlive.com/news/detroit/2014/07/detroit_mayor_given_control_ov.html (consulted July 29, 2019).

Azikiwe, A. (2015). "Detroit to Flint Water March Ends." *Worker's World*. July 18, 2015. Available at: http://www.workers.org/2015/07/18/detroit-to-flint-water-march-ends/#.V7-PK5MrKRs (consulted December 15, 2016).

Black Bottom Archives. (2016). "Water Crimes Tribunal." Available at: http://www.blackbottomarchives.com/calendar/2016/2/16/water-crimes-tribunal (consulted December 15, 2016).

Blue Planet Project (BPP). (2014). "Submission to the Special Rapporteur on the Human Right to Safe Drinking Water and Sanitation Regarding Water Cutoffs in the City of Detroit, Michigan." July 18, 2014. Available at: http://www.blueplanetproject.net/wordpress/wp-content/uploads/Detroit-HRTW-submission-June-18-2014.pdf (consulted December 15, 2016).

Chang, S. and Garrett, L. (2016). "All Michiganders Deserve Clean Water." *Detroit Free Press* February 2, 2016. Available at: http://www.freep.com/story/opinion/contributors/2016/02/02/all-michiganders-deserve-clean-water/79641244/ (consulted December 15, 2016).

Colton, R. (2005). "A Water Affordability Program for the Detroit Water and Sewerage Department (DWSD)." Available at: https://drive.google.com/file/d/0By2p2ytUJwFzRy1VazFhVGlzQTQ/edit (consulted December 15, 2016).

Cramer, J. (2015). "Race, Class, and Social Reproduction in the Urban Present: The Case of the Detroit Water and Sewage System." *Viewpoint Magazine*. October 31, 2015. Available at: https://viewpointmag.com/2015/10/31/race-class-and-social-reproduction-in-the-urban-present-the-case-of-the-detroit-water-and-sewage-system/ (consulted December 15, 2016).

Detroiters Resisting Emergency Management (D-REM). (2014). "Notes from the United Nations Town Hall Meeting at Wayne County Community College in Detroit on 10/19/2014 from 4–6pm." *DREM*. October 20, 2014. Available at: http://www.d-rem.org/notestranscript-from-the-un-town-hall-meeting/ (consulted December 15, 2016).

Detroiters Resisting Emergency Management (D-REM). (2016a). Teach-in on Detroit and Flint Water Crises, January 16th, followed by People's Tribunal, January 23rd—join us! *d-rem*. January 7, 2016. Available at: http://www.d-rem.org/teach-in-on-detroit-and-flint-water-crises-january-16th-followed-by-peoples-tribunal-january-23rd-join-us/ (consulted December 15, 2016).

Detroiters Resisting Emergency Management (D-REM). (2016b). "Teach-in on Detroit and Flint Water Crises." *d-rem*. January. Available at: https://www.scribd.com/doc/295470015/Detroit-and-Flint-Water-Struggles-Readings-and-Resources (consulted December 15, 2016).

Detroiters Resisting Emergency Management (D-REM). (2016c). "New Location for People's Tribunal on Saturday, January 23!" *d-rem*. January 18, 2016. Available at: http://www.d-rem.org/new-location-for-peoples-tribunal-on-saturday-january-23rd/ (consulted December 15, 2016).

Detroiters Resisting Emergency Management (D-REM). (2016d). "January 16 Teach-in on Detroit and Flint Water Crises: Reader, Presentation, and Bill Package." *d-rem*. January 19, 2016. Available at: http://www.d-rem.org/january-16-teach-in-on-detroit-and-flint-water-crises-reader-and-presentation/ (consulted December 15, 2016).

Detroiters Resisting Emergency Management (D-REM). (2016e). "The People's Tribunal on Water Crimes—Judge's Script." *d-rem*. January 28, 2016. Available at: http://www.d-rem.org/the-peoples-tribunal-on-water-crimes-judges-script/ (consulted December 15, 2016).

Detroiters Resisting Emergency Management (D-REM). (2016f). "#ArrestSnyder WANTED poster from Beehive Collective." *d-rem*. February 4, 2016. Available at: http://www.d-rem.org/arrestsnyder-wanted-poster-from-beehive-collective/ (consulted December 15, 2016).

Doan, M.D. (2018). "Resisting Structural Epistemic Injustice." *Feminist Philosophical Quarterly* 4(4): 1–24. Available at: https://ojs.lib.uwo.ca/index.php/fpq/article/view/6230/4987 (consulted July 29, 2019).

Ferretti, C. and Pardo, S. (2014). "Orr Defends City Water Shut-Offs." *The Detroit News*. July 17, 2014. Available at: [broken link] (consulted July 29, 2019).

Finley, N. (2014). "There is No Right to Free Water." *The Detroit News*. July 18, 2014. Available at: http://www.economicpolicyjournal.com/2014/07/there-is-no-right-to-free-water.html (consulted December 15, 2016).

Free the Water Defense Campaign. (2016). "Settlement Negotiated!" *Free the Water Defense Campaign*. October 24, 2016. Available at: https://freethewater313.wordpress.com/2016/10/24/settlement/ (consulted July 29, 2019).

Gross, A. (2017). "Experts See Public Health Crisis in Detroit Water Shutoffs." *Detroit Free Press*. July 26, 2017. Available at: https://www.freep.com/story/news/local/michigan/detroit/2017/07/26/detroit-water-shutoffs/512243001/ (consulted October 22, 2019).

Guillen, J. (2016). "Legal Experts: Detroit Can Reduce Water Rates for the Needy." *Detroit Free Press*. January 15, 2016. Available at: http://www.freep.com/story/news/2016/01/15/legal-experts-detroit-can-reduce-water-rates-needy/78852696/ (consulted December 15, 2016).

Guyette, C. (2015a). "With Detroit's Water Payment Plan a Massive Failure Mayor Duggan Plans Changes." *aclu of Michigan*. April 18, 2015. Available at: http://www.aclumich.org/democracywatch/index.php/entry/with-detroit-s-water-payment-plan-a-massive-failure-mayor-duggan-plans-changes (consulted December 15, 2016).

Guyette, C. (2015b). "Detroit's Water Tug-of-War." *Detroit Metro Times*. June 3, 2015. Available at: http://www.metro-times.com/detroit/detroits-water-tug-of-war/Content?oid=2348110 (consulted December 15, 2016).

Guyette, C. (2015c). "Flint Water Crisis a Bitter Indictment of Dysfunctional Emergency Manager." *The Michigan Chronicle*. October 7, 2015. Available at: http://michronicleonline.com/2015/10/07/flint-water-crisis-a-bitter-indictment-of-dysfunctional-emergency-manager/ (consulted December 15, 2016).

Guyette, C. (2015d). "Flint Water and the No Blame Game." *Michigan Democracy Watch Blog*. October 15, 2015. Available at: http://www.aclumich.org/democracywatch/index.php/entry/flint-water-and-the-no-blame-game (consulted December 15, 2016).

Guyette, C. (2015e). "Flint's State of Emergency is a Sign that Democracy is Working There Again." *The Guardian*. December 16, 2015. Available at: https://www.theguardian.com/commentisfree/2015/dec/16/flint-state-of-emergency-sign-democracy-is-working (consulted December 15, 2016).

Guyette, C. (2015f). "Judge Calls Detroit's Prosecution of Water Shut-Off Protesters a 'Disaster'." *Detroit Metro Times*. December 23, 2015. Available at: http://www.metro-times.com/detroit/judge-calls-detroits-prosecution-of-water-shut-off-protesters-a-disaster/Content?oid=2387489 (consulted December 15, 2016).

Guyette, C. (2016). "Power of the People." *Detroit Metro Times*. February 24, 2016. Available at: http://www.metro-times.com/detroit/power-by-the-people/Content?oid=2397708 (consulted December 15, 2016).

Guzmán, M. (2016). "Water Warriors: How Four Activists Let the World Know About Water Crises in Flint and Detroit." *Sojourners*. May 25, 2016. Available at: https://sojo.net/articles/water-warriors (consulted December 15, 2016).

Hammer, P.J. (2016). "The Flint Water Crisis, KWA, and Strategic-Structural Racism: A Reply to Jeff Wright, Genesee County Drain Commissioner and CEO of Karegnondi Water Authority." Written testimony submitted to the Michigan Civil Rights Commission. December 31, 2016. Available at: https://www.michigan.gov/documents/mdcr/Hammer_Reply_Flint_MCRC_Testimony_123116_552226_7.pdf (consulted October 22, 2019).

Hicks, M. (2016). "Activists Speak Out on Flint, Detroit Water Issues." *The Detroit News*. February 16, 2016. Available at: http://www.detroitnews.com/story/news/local/michigan/2016/02/16/activists-speak-flint-detroit-water-issues/80489336/ (consulted December 15, 2016).

Howell, S. (2013). "Distorted Reality." *The Boggs Blog*. July 15, 2013. Available at: http://boggscenter.org/distorted-reality-by-shea-howell-week-67-of-the-occupation-of-detroit/ (consulted July 29, 2019).

Howell, S. (2014a). "Water, Dispossession, and Resistance." *The Boggs Blog*. June 10, 2014. Available at: http://boggscenter.org/water-dispossession-and-resistance-by-shea-howell-by-shea-howell/ (consulted July 29, 2019).

Howell, S. (2014b). "Water Choices." *The Boggs Blog*. July 4, 2014. Available at: https://conversationsthatyouwillneverfinish.wordpress.com/2014/07/04/water-choices-by-shea-howell-week-65-of-the-occupation/ (consulted July 29, 2019).

Howell, S. (2014c). "Beyond the Bottom Line." *The Boggs Blog*. July 8, 2014. Available at: https://conversationsthatyouwillneverfinish.wordpress.com/2014/07/13/beyond-the-bottom-line-by-shea-howell-week-66-of-the-occupation/ (consulted July 29, 2019).

Howell, S. (2015a). "Flint Water Stories." *d-rem*. March 29, 2015. Available at: http://www.d-rem.org/thinking-for-ourselves-flint-water-stories/ (consulted December 15, 2016).

Howell, S. (2015b). "Gathering Waters." *d-rem*. May 31, 2015. Available at: http://www.d-rem.org/thinking-for-ourselves-gathering-waters/ (consulted December 15, 2016).

Howell, S. (2015c). "Flint and Lead." *The Boggs Blog*. September 7, 2015. Available at: https://conversationsthatyouwillneverfinish.wordpress.com/2015/09/27/flint-and-lead-by-shea-howell/ (consulted December 15, 2016).

Howell, S. (2019). "Resisting Emergency Management." *Liquid Utility*. April 29, 2019. Available at: https://www.e-flux.com/architecture/liquid-utility/262537/resisting-emergency-management/ (consulted July 29, 2019).

Howell, S. and Stephens, T. (2015). "Toxic Twins: Emergency Management and Flint River Water." *People's Tribune*. May. Available at: http://peoplestribune.org/pt-news/2015/05/toxic-twins-emergency-management-and-flint-river-water/ (consulted December 15, 2016).

Howes, D. (2014). "Targeting Water Scofflaws Fair, Long Overdue." *The Detroit News*. July 11, 2014. Available at: http://www.detroitnews.com/article/20140711/BIZ/307100100/1322/BIZ/Targeting-water-scofflaws-fair--long-overdue (consulted December 15, 2016).

International Social Movements Gathering. (2015). "International Social Movements Gathering, May 29–31, 2015 in Detroit, Michigan." Available at: http://www.socialmovementsgathering.info/ (consulted December 15, 2016).

Ketchum, W.E. (2015). "Community Members Share Thoughts, Revelations, and Encouragement at Flint Healing Stories." *M-Live*. March 21, 2015. Available at: http://www.mlive.com/entertainment/flint/index.ssf/2015/03/community_members_share_though.html (consulted December 15, 2016).

Kirkpatrick, O.L. and Breznau, N. (2016). "The (Non)politics of Emergency Political Intervention: the Racial Geography of Urban Crisis Management in Michigan." Mimeo, SMU. Available at: http://papers.ssrn.com/sol3/papers.cfm?abstract_id=2754128 (consulted December 15, 2016).

Kurashige, S. (2017). *The Fifty-Year Rebellion: How the U.S. Political Crisis Began in Detroit*. Oakland, CA: University of California Press.

Lambert, L. (2014). "U.S. Bankruptcy Judge Allows Detroit Water Shutoffs to Continue." *Reuters*. September 29, 2017. Available at: https://www.reuters.com/article/us-usa-detroit-water/u-s-bankruptcy-judge-allows-detroit-water-shutoffs-to-continue-idUSKCN0HO1DS20140929 (consulted July 29, 2019).

Levy, K. (2015a). "Detroit Minds Dying." Available at: http://www.detroitmindsdying.com/ (consulted December 15, 2016).

Levy, K. (2015b). "Disorder in the Court." Available at: https://vimeo.com/149346062 (consulted December 15, 2016).

Levy, K. (2015c). "Bill Wiley-Kellermann's Closing Arguments in District Court—Homrich 9 Trial, December 2015." *d-rem*. December 30, 2015. Available at: http://www.d-rem.org/homrich-9-trial-bill-wylie-kellermans-closing-arguments-in-district-court/ (consulted December 15, 2016).

Levy, K. (2016a). "Watch: January 15 Press Conference on Water Affordability." *d-rem*. January 18, 2016. Available at: http://www.d-rem.org/watch-january-15-press-conference-on-water-affordability/ (consulted December 15, 2016).

Levy, K. (2016b). "Eastside Payment Center, May 2016." *d-rem*. Available at: http://www.d-rem.org/watch-dwsd-assistance-fair-at-eastside-payment-center-23000-shutoffs-on-deck/ (consulted December 15, 2016).

Levy, K. and Guyette, C. (2015a). "Hard to Swallow: Toxic Water Under a Toxic System in Flint." *aclu of Michigan*. June 25, 2015. Available at: https://www.youtube.com/watch?v=L4n9ZeDuhdU (consulted December 15, 2016).

Levy, K. and Guyette, C. (2015b). "Corrosive Impact: Leaded Water & One Flint Family's Toxic Nightmare." *aclu of Michigan*. July 9, 2015. Available at: https://www.youtube.com/watch?v=27K54-lV-Z4 (consulted December 15, 2016).

Levy, K. and Guyette, C. (2015c). "Drops in the Bucket." Available (consulted 15 December, 2016) at: https://www.youtube.com/watch?v=ywzicIRVYoc.

Levy, K. and Guyette, C. (2015d). "Circle of Lies: Dodging Blame for the Flint River Disaster." *aclu of Michigan*. October 29, 2015. Available at: https://www.youtube.com/watch?v=qEWBGE31qCY (consulted December 15, 2016).

Levy, K. and Guyette, C. (2016). "Here's to Flint." *aclu of Michigan*. March 6, 2016. Available at: https://vimeo.com/157922510 (consulted December 15, 2016).

Lewis-Patrick, M. and Cabbil, L. (2014). "On Water Issues, It's Detroit Versus the U.N." *The Detroit News*. November 6, 2014. Available at: http://www.detroitnews.com/story/opinion/2014/11/06/water-issues-detroit-versus-united-nations/18553431/ (consulted December 15, 2016).

Lukacs, M. (2014). "Detroit's Water War: A Tap Shut-Off That Could Impact 300,000 People." *The Guardian*. June 25, 2014. Available at: https://www.theguardian.com/environment/true-north/2014/jun/25/detroits-water-war-a-tap-shut-off-that-could-impact-300000-people (consulted July 29, 2019).

Michigan Coalition for Human Rights (MCHR). (2015). "Join Us as We Walk from Detroit to Flint and Demand Clean, Affordable Water for All!" *mchr*. June 29, 2015. Available at: http://www.mchr.org/2015/06/join-us-as-we-walk-from-detroit-to-flint-and-demand-clean-affordable-water-for-all/ (consulted December 15, 2016).

Michigan Welfare Rights Organization (MWRO) and People's Water Board Coalition (PWB). (2014). "Media Advisory: UN Human Rights Commission Will Hear Michiganders' Testimony." *d-rem*. October 14, 2014. Available at: http://www.d-rem.org/media-advisory/ (consulted December 15, 2016).

Noble, B. and Ferretti, C. (2019). "Detroit Could Be Losing Out on Millions Under Water System Lease." *The Detroit News*. January 14, 2019. Available at: https://www.detroitnews.com/story/news/local/detroit-city/2019/01/14/detroit-losing-out-millions-under-flawed-water-system-lease/2548568002/ (consulted July 29, 2019).

Pauli, B. (2019). *Flint Fights Back: Environmental Justice and Democracy in the Flint Water Crisis*. Cambridge, MA: MIT Press.

People's Tribune (2015). "International Social Movements Gathering on Water and Affordable Housing, Detroit, MI." *People's Tribune*. July. Available at: http://peoplestribune.org/pt-news/2015/06/international-social-movements/ (consulted December 15, 2016).

Perkinson, J. (2014). "Why I Choose to Block Detroit's Water Shutoff Trucks." *Sojourners*. July 21, 2014. Available at: https://sojo.net/articles/why-i-choose-block-detroits-water-shutoff-trucks (consulted July 29, 2019).

Rall, A. (2018). "Community Organizing and the Detroit Water Struggle: Report from the Front Lines." *Journal of Progressive Human Services* 29(2): 103–129.

The Raiz Up. (2015). "In Detroit, Private Demolition Company Shuts Off Water to Pregnant Woman during Ramadan." *The Raiz Up*. Available at: https://vimeo.com/132829920 (consulted December 15, 2016).

Recchie, J., Recchie, A., Powell, J.A., Lyons, L., Hardaway, P., and Ake, W. (2019). *Water Equity and Security in Detroit's Water & Sewer District*. Haas Institute for a Fair and Inclusive Society, University of California, Berkeley: Berkeley, CA. Available at: haasinstitute.berkeley.edu/detroitwaterequity (consulted October 22, 2019).

Robertson, A. (2016). "As the City Zeroes in on Graffiti, Two Detroit Artists Face Possible Prison Time." *Detroit Metro Times*. September 21, 2016. Available at: https://www.metrotimes.com/detroit/as-the-city-zeroes-in-on-graffiti-two-detroit-artists-face-possible-prison-time/Content?oid=2465406 (consulted July 29, 2019).

Samartino, R. (2015). "Water Justice Journey Platform/information Sheet." *pwb*. Available at: https://www.scribd.com/doc/303202449/Water-Justice-Journey-Platform-Information-Sheet (consulted December 15, 2016).

Scorsone, E.A. (2014). *Municipal Fiscal Emergency Laws: Background and Guide to State-Based Approaches (Working Paper 14-21)*. Washington, DC: Mercatus Center, George Mason University.

Shariff, N. (2015). "Lead in Drinking Water: Do Flint Lives Matter?" *People's Tribune*. Available at: http://peoplestribune.org/pt-news/2015/11/lead-in-drinking-water-do-flint-lives-matter/ (consulted December 15, 2016).

Smith, H. (2014). "Four Things You Should Know About Detroit's Water Crisis." *Grist*. Available at: https://grist.org/cities/the-4-things-you-should-know-about-detroits-water-crisis/ (consulted July 29, 2019).

Sugrue, T. (2005). *The Origins of the Urban Crisis: Race and Inequality in Postwar Detroit*. Princeton, NJ: Princeton University Press.

United Nations Office of the High Commissioner for Human Rights (OHCHR). (2014). "Detroit: Disconnecting Water From People Who Cannot Pay—An Affront to Human Rights, say UN experts." *OHCHR*. Available at: http://www.ohchr.org/EN/NewsEvents/Pages/DisplayNews.aspx?NewsID=14777&LangID=E (consulted December 15, 2016).

Unpublished Minutes. (2014). Statewide Anti-EMF Network Meeting, Highland Park, MI, 4 May.

Wattrick, J. (2011). "Despite Remembrances, Judge John Feikens' Legacy is Clouded by Water System Oversight." *M-Live*. May 17, 2011. Available at: https://www.mlive.com/news/detroit/2011/05/despite_remembrances_judge_joh.html (consulted July 29, 2019).

WCMU Public Radio News. (2015). "Flint Grassroots Groups Address Inequity Through Stories." *WCMU*. Available at: http://wcmu.org/news/?p=14276 (consulted December 15, 2016).

We the People of Detroit Community Research Collective (WPDCRC). (2016). *Mapping the Water Crisis: The Dismantling of African-American Neighborhoods in Detroit, Vol. One*. Detroit, MI: Conklin Creative.

Wiley-Kellermann, B. (2017). *Where the Water Goes Around: Beloved Detroit*. Eugene, OR: Cascade Books.

Williams, C. (2017). "Trial Dismissed Against 'Homrich 9' Water Protesters." *The Detroit News*. June 21, 2017. Available at: https://www.detroitnews.com/story/news/local/detroit-city/2017/06/21/homrich-case-dismissed/103087798/ (consulted July 29, 2019).

Williams, P. (2014). "Drop Dead, Detroit!" *The New Yorker*. January 19, 2014. Available at: https://www.newyorker.com/magazine/2014/01/27/drop-dead-detroit (consulted July 29, 2019).

CHAPTER 8

Pure
Bottling Public Thirst
Scarcity, Abundance, and the Exploitation of "Need" in Mid-Michigan
By A.E. Garrison

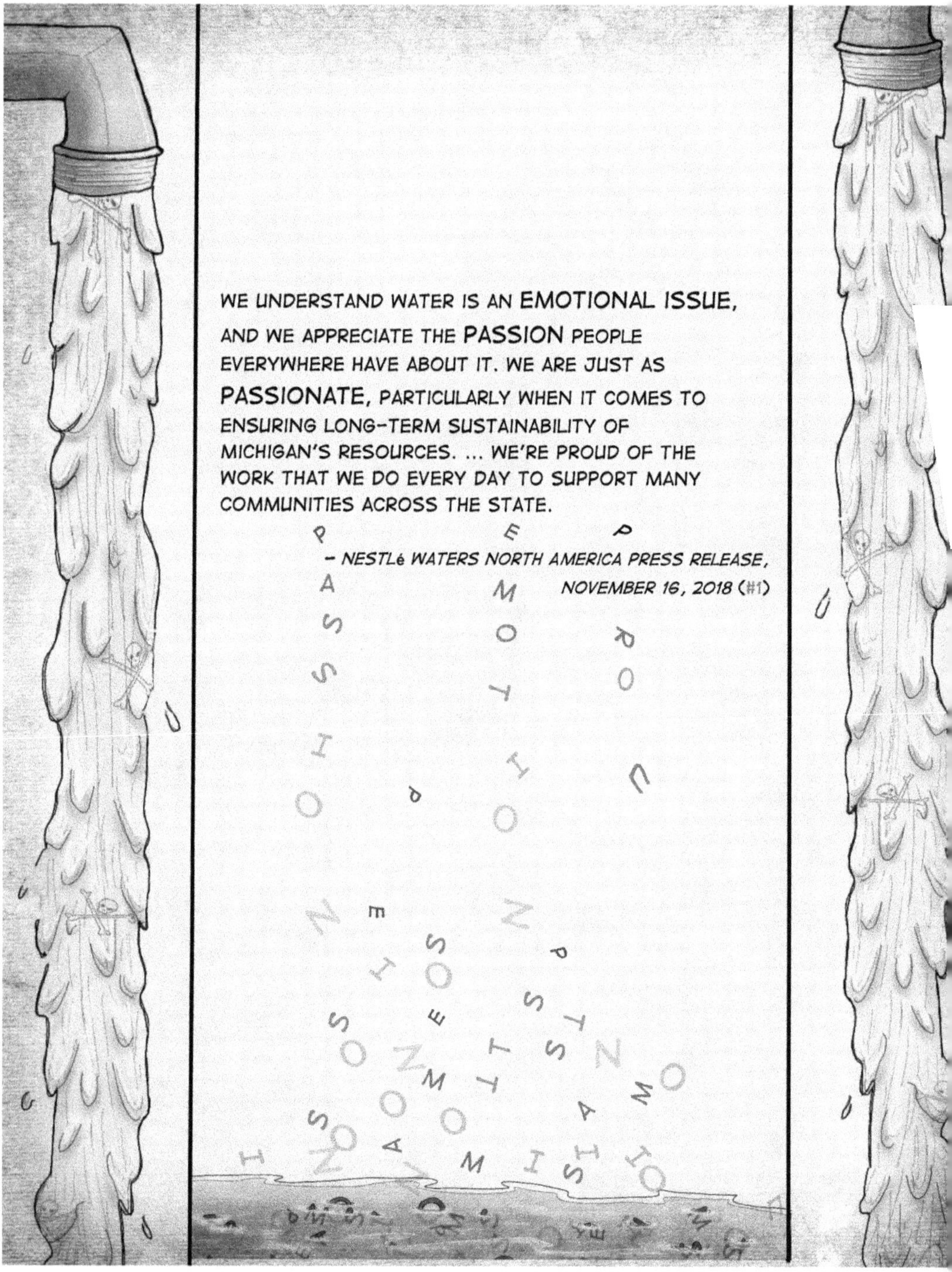
WE UNDERSTAND WATER IS AN EMOTIONAL ISSUE, AND WE APPRECIATE THE PASSION PEOPLE EVERYWHERE HAVE ABOUT IT. WE ARE JUST AS PASSIONATE, PARTICULARLY WHEN IT COMES TO ENSURING LONG-TERM SUSTAINABILITY OF MICHIGAN'S RESOURCES. ... WE'RE PROUD OF THE WORK THAT WE DO EVERY DAY TO SUPPORT MANY COMMUNITIES ACROSS THE STATE.
– NESTLé WATERS NORTH AMERICA PRESS RELEASE, NOVEMBER 16, 2018 (#1)

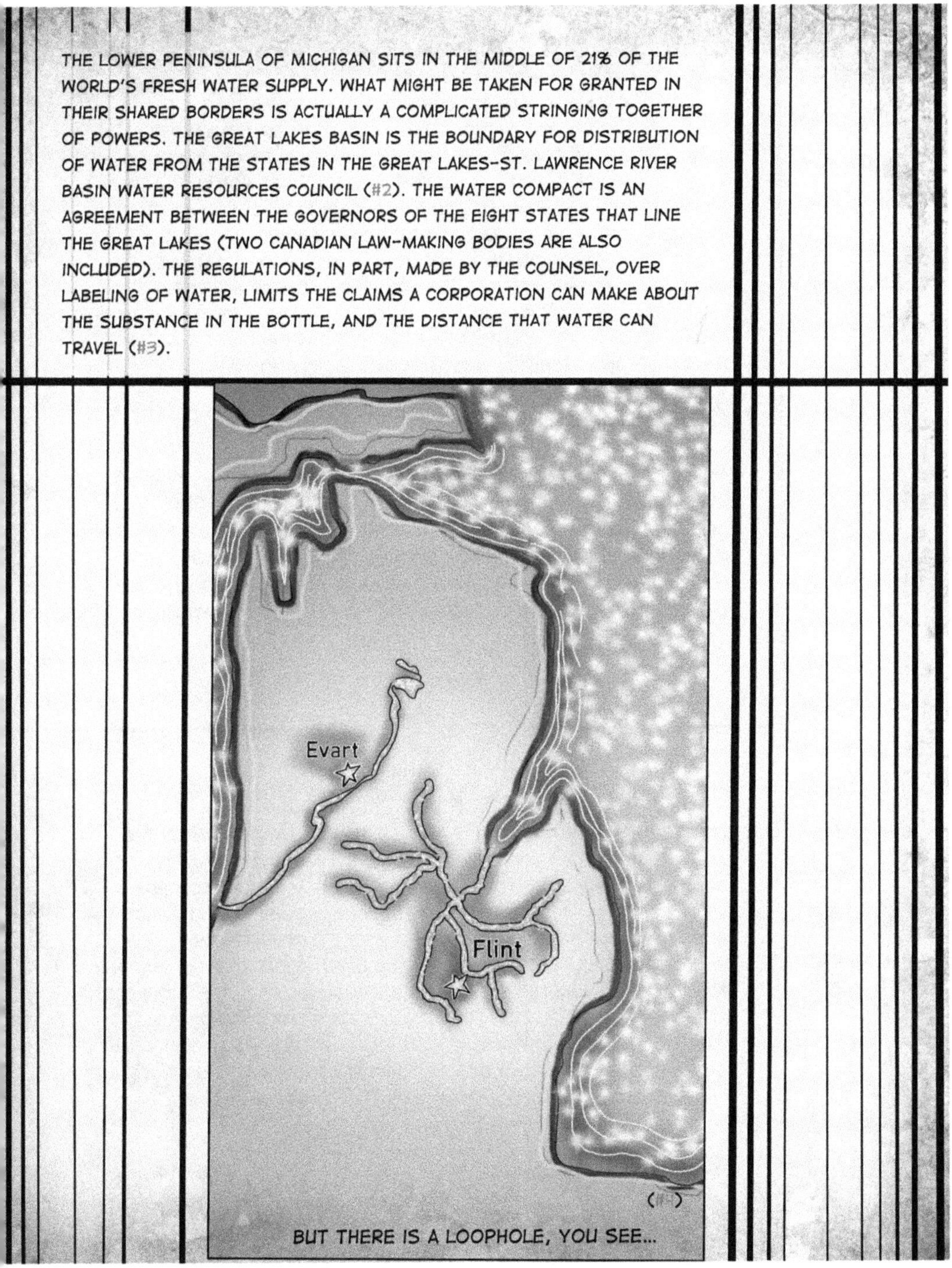
THE LOWER PENINSULA OF MICHIGAN SITS IN THE MIDDLE OF 21% OF THE WORLD'S FRESH WATER SUPPLY. WHAT MIGHT BE TAKEN FOR GRANTED IN THEIR SHARED BORDERS IS ACTUALLY A COMPLICATED STRINGING TOGETHER OF POWERS. THE GREAT LAKES BASIN IS THE BOUNDARY FOR DISTRIBUTION OF WATER FROM THE STATES IN THE GREAT LAKES-ST. LAWRENCE RIVER BASIN WATER RESOURCES COUNCIL (#2). THE WATER COMPACT IS AN AGREEMENT BETWEEN THE GOVERNORS OF THE EIGHT STATES THAT LINE THE GREAT LAKES (TWO CANADIAN LAW-MAKING BODIES ARE ALSO INCLUDED). THE REGULATIONS, IN PART, MADE BY THE COUNSEL, OVER LABELING OF WATER, LIMITS THE CLAIMS A CORPORATION CAN MAKE ABOUT THE SUBSTANCE IN THE BOTTLE, AND THE DISTANCE THAT WATER CAN TRAVEL (#3).
Evart
Flint
BUT THERE IS A LOOPHOLE, YOU SEE...

IN ORDER FOR A WATER DISTRIBUTION COMPANY TO DEFINE THEIR PRODUCTS AS "SPRING" WATERS, THEY MUST BE IN SOME MEASURED PROXIMITY TO THE SOURCE. THE RESEARCH WATER EXTRACTION COMPANIES HAVE DONE REVEALS THAT CONSUMERS WILL PAY MORE FOR WATER FROM A "PURE" SOURCE - SPRING WATER (#5). ACCORDING TO *CRAIN'S DETROIT BUSINESS*, THERE ARE CURRENTLY 50 "LICENSED WATER BOTTLING FACILITIES" IN OPERATION IN MICHIGAN (#6). THESE CORPORATIONS ARE REQUIRED TO SUBMIT APPLICATIONS TO THE STATE, AND BARRING CIRCUMSTANCES THAT WARRANT CONSIDERATION, AND DEPENDING ON THE REQUEST, THE STATE GRANTS THESE PERMITS FOR EXTRACTION WITH LIMITS TO VOLUME AND REQUIREMENTS FOR QUALITY TESTING (#7).

AMONG THESE "LICENSED BOTTLING FACILITIES," IN THE RURAL QUIET OF OSCEOLA COUNTY, NESTLé WATERS NORTH AMERICA (HENCEFORTH "NESTLé") HAS BEEN OPERATING SINCE THE EARLY 2000S (#8). THE RELATIONSHIP BETWEEN THE BEHEMOTH WATER DISTRIBUTOR AND THE PEOPLE LIVING IN THE SURROUNDING AREAS IS A COMPLICATED ONE, AND THE RELATIONSHIP BETWEEN NESTLé AND THE LARGER POPULATION OF MICHIGAN IS EVEN MORE SO.

ISSUES EMERGE WITH NESTLé'S APPLICATION FOR AN INCREASE IN THE AMOUNT OF WATER THEY ARE ALLOWED TO EXTRACT FROM WHAT IS CONSIDERED "PUBLIC WATER SOURCES" IN RURAL MICHIGAN. ACCORDING TO THE GUIDELINES DETERMINED BY THE GREAT LAKES- ST. LAWRENCE RIVER BASIN WATER RESOURCE COUNCIL (2008), EXTRACTIONS/ DIVERSIONS ARE LIMITED BY VOLUME AND USE IS REGULATED SO THAT ANY WATER TAKEN FROM THE BASIN MUST BE RETURNED (#9). THE LOOPHOLE, HOWEVER, ALLOWS FOR THE EXTRACTION AND DISTRIBUTION OF PUBLIC WATER SOURCES IN CONTAINERS LESS THAN 5.7 GALLONS (#10): A LEGAL GATEWAY FOR NESTLé AND OTHERS TO PROFIT FROM WATER SOURCES THEY PAY LITTLE TO ACCESS. THIS IS PART OF THE PROBLEM.

WITH THE SEEMING ABUNDANCE OF PUBLIC WATER SOURCES IN THE MITTEN, WHAT'S THE PROBLEM WITH BOTTLING WATER THAT IS CONSUMABLE IN AN INCREASINGLY TOXIFIED WORLD? IN OTHER WORDS, IF NESTLé AND OTHERS CAN, AS THEY CLAIM, SATISFY THE NECESSARY NEEDS OF THE THIRSTY MULTITUDES, WHAT'S THE HARM? (#11)

ACCORDING TO PETER ANNIN (2018), IN 2018, 780 MILLION OF THE WORLD'S POPULATION EXPERIENCED WATER-STRESS (#12). THIS MEANS THAT 780 MILLION PEOPLE IN THE WORLD DO NOT HAVE ACCESS TO CLEAN DRINKING WATER. "WATER-STRESS" IS DIFFERENT THAN THE CONCEPT OF "SCARCITY." THE UNITED NATIONS STATES "WATER SCARCITY CAN MEAN SCARCITY IN AVAILABILITY DUE TO PHYSICAL SHORTAGE, OR SCARCITY IN ACCESS DUE TO THE *FAILURE OF INSTITUTIONS TO ENSURE A REGULAR SUPPLY OR DUE TO A LACK OF ADEQUATE INFRASTRUCTURE*" (MY EMPHASIS)(#13). BY ALL MEASURES, BY 2025, ANNIN SUGGESTS TWO-THIRDS OF THE WORLD WILL BE IN A STATE OF INSECURE ACCESS TO FRESH WATER (#14).

IN THE UNITED STATES, ACCORDING TO MANY SOURCES, AND PERHAPS SURPRISINGLY, THERE ARE QUITE A FEW REGIONS THAT EXPERIENCE INTERMITTENT TO INCREASINGLY SUSTAINED WATER-STRESS (#15). GIVEN THAT THE ENVIRONMENTAL PROTECTION AGENCY REPORTS SIGNIFICANT VOLUMES OF THE WATER USED IN THE US IS ATTRIBUTED TO LANDSCAPING (30%), THERE REMAINS A QUESTION ABOUT CLAIMS OF ABUNDANCE THAT LIE IN DIRECT CONFLICT WITH THE REALITIES OF ACCESS TO CLEAN DRINKING WATER (#16). IN ADDITION, THE OVERWHELMING POPULARITY OF BOTTLED WATER CONSUMPTION AS A SOURCE OF "CLEAN WATER" HAS CHANGED DEMAND FOR EXTRACTION AND, TO SOME EXTENT, THE "MEANING" OF TAP WATER, OR "PUBLIC WATER" (#17).

TAP WATER IS REGULATED DIFFERENTLY THAN WATER THAT IS BOTTLED AND SOLD TO THE PUBLIC. AND FOR THOSE REGULATIONS TO BE ENFORCED, THERE IS FUNDING TO BE SECURED; BUDGETS TO BE WRITTEN, PROPOSING PROJECTS WITH DETAILED SPENDING PLANS - AND THE WHOLE TICKING OF OPERATIONAL BOXES THAT MAKE REGULATION POSSIBLE. TO SOME EXTENT, THE EVOLUTION OF GOVERNANCE MOVES AT DIFFERENT TEMPOS: "SPECIAL DISTRICTS" (PUBLIC AUTHORITIES) MICRO-MANAGE WHAT HAS BEEN THE RESPONSIBILITY OF CITY AND COUNTY, WHILE THE LARGE MECHANISM OF REVENUE ALLOCATION REMAINS A FIXTURE IN WHAT THE PUBLIC CONSIDERS GOVERNMENT FUNCTION (#18).

THESE LOCAL AUTHORITIES HAVE BEEN OPERATING IN RURAL AND URBAN AREAS FOR MANY DECADES, SPECIALIZING IN MANAGING SPECIFIC FUNCTIONS OF GOVERNMENT, LIKE NATURAL RESOURCE CONSERVATION (#19). MEGAN MULLIN (2009) WRITES THAT "SOMETIMES, IT IS DEVELOPERS WHO PROMOTE SPECIAL DISTRICT FORMATION AS AN ALTERNATIVE TO MUNICIPAL PROVISION OF A FACILITY OR SERVICE" (#20). SHE GOES ON TO SUGGEST THAT "THE LACK OF TRANSPARENCY IN SPECIAL DISTRICT OPERATIONS...CREATES AN OPPORTUNITY FOR PATRONAGE, CORRUPTION, AND RUNAWAY SPENDING" AND THAT "POLITICAL INVISIBILITY PRODUCES A BIAS FAVORING PRIVATE INTEREST WHO INVEST IN LOBBYING SPECIAL DISTRICT OFFICIALS" (#21).

AS A RESULT OF LAWS IN PLACE TO GOVERN/CONTROL WATER EXTRACTION, IT MAKES SENSE THAT "THE PUBLIC" HAS LITTLE KNOWLEDGE OF, AND PERHAPS EQUALLY LITTLE CONCERN FOR HOW THESE REGULATIONS ARE ENFORCED. IT MAKES SENSE THAT, AS LONG AS MUNICIPAL WATER RESOURCES ARE RELIABLE, AVAILABLE, AND "CLEAN," "THE PUBLIC" WOULD BE UNAWARE OF THE QUALITY OF TAP WATER, AND CONCERN THEMSELVES, NOT AT ALL, WITH THE POLITICS OF BOTTLED WATER (#22). THIS IS NOT THE CASE, HOWEVER.

"GOVERNMENT INVISIBILITY", AND THE SEEMING CONTRADICTION TO WHAT WOULD BE DETERMINED AS "JUSTICE," CREATES UNCERTAINTY IN THE PUBLIC PERCEPTION OF GOVERNING BODIES. WHEN THE SYSTEMS IN PLACE FAIL, WHAT IS THE RECOURSE FOR THE PEOPLE SUBJECT TO GOVERNANCE BY THAT SYSTEM? HOW COULD A GOVERNMENT ALLOW ANY OF ITS CITIZENS TO SUFFER, ESPECIALLY WHEN LAWS, POLICIES, RULES, AND REGULATIONS PUT IN PLACE ARE ASSUMED TO PROTECT THE VULNERABLE TAXPAYER (THE PUBLIC) FROM HARM?

A PROXIMITY TO PROBLEMS WITH CLEAN DRINKING WATER AFFECTS THE RELATIONSHIPS PEOPLE HAVE WITH WATER, WITH LAW, WITH GOVERNMENT POLICY AND CORPORATE PRACTICE. EQUALLY, LACK OF AWARENESS REGARDING THE SUFFERING OF OTHERS AS A RESULT OF WATER SCARCITY CANNOT BE BLAMED ON THE INDIVIDUAL WHO OTHERWISE BENEFIT FROM ACCESS TO "CLEAN" WATER SOURCES (#23).

TO ADD TO THE PROBLEM OF CLEAN WATER ACCESS, PEOPLE DO NOT SIMPLY EXPERIENCE SCARCITY AS A MATERIAL DISASTER, BUT THE IMPACTS OF ACCESS TO CLEAN DRINKING WATER EXTEND PAST THE BOUNDARIES OF POLICY AND PRACTICE. C.L. WORKMAN AND H. UREKSOY (2017) ARGUE THAT ACCESS AND "HEALTH" OF A WATER SYSTEM HAS A SIGNIFICANT IMPACT ON PEOPLE'S "PSYCHOSOCIAL HEALTH" (#24). TO SOME EXTENT, THIS MIGHT BE INTUITIVE: OUR ABILITY TO ACCESS CLEAN WATER, AS WE NEED IT IMPACTS THE STRESSES OF OUR EVERYDAY LIVES. AT THE SAME TIME, IF PEOPLE *CAN* TAKE WATER FOR GRANTED, NOT ONLY IS THIS EVIDENCE OF A PARTICULAR "PRIVILEGE," BUT THE LACK OF EXPERIENCE WITH SCARCITY CAN MAKE EMPATHY DIFFICULT.

A CRITIQUE OF "INDIVIDUAL" PRIVILEGE MAKES IT TOO EASY TO FOCUS ON *THE INDIVIDUAL* AS AN AGENT FOR MASSIVE SOCIAL CHANGE. "INDIVIDUALITY," IN THIS WAY, IS A SIGNIFICANT PART OF THE SYSTEMIC FAILURE OF RESPONSIBLE WATER PRACTICE. AT THE SAME TIME, IN MICHIGAN, THE FORCE OF ACCOUNTABILITY WAS SPARKED BY *PEOPLE*, ACTIVELY WORKING TOGETHER TO RAISE PUBLIC AWARENESS ABOUT THE TOXIC WATER FLOWING FROM THEIR FAUCETS AND THE EXPLOITATION OF PUBLIC WATER SOURCES BY NESTLé. THE PEOPLE OF FLINT HAD TO COME TOGETHER TO MAKE THEIR VOICES LOUD ENOUGH FOR PEOPLE TO HEAR THEM. THEY WORKED TO ORGANIZE, JUST AS THE COMMUNITIES IN WEST MICHIGAN (INCLUDING CITIZENS FROM EVART) CAME TOGETHER TO VOICE THEIR CONCERNS AND ANGER WITH THE STATE OF MICHIGAN OVER THEIR HANDLING OF NESTLé'S REQUEST TO INCREASE THE VOLUME OF WATER THEY WERE PERMITTED TO PUMP FROM PUBLIC WATER SOURCES.

ROBERT GLENNON (2007) AND OTHERS NOTE THAT THE INCREASE IN BOTTLED WATER SALES, WHILE CORRELATED WITH A BOURGEOIS DESIRE FOR "HYDRATION ON-THE-GO" (ECHOED BY NESTLé WATERS NORTH AMERICA PUBLIC RELATIONS) IS AN INCREASED LACK OF TRUST FOR THE SAFETY AND REGULATION OF TAP WATER (#25). RAUL PACHECO-VEGA (2019) WRITES:

"WATER UTILITIES ARE OFTEN UNABLE TO PROVIDE HIGH QUALITY DRINKING WATER, MULTINATIONAL CORPORATIONS CAPITALIZE ON THIS FEAR OF THE TAP BY CREATING A SAFER ALTERNATIVE FOR HUMANS TO HYDRATE, AND THE CITIZENS REJECT ANY RISK OF DAMAGE TO THEIR PERSONAL WELLBEING, ENGAGING IN AN INVERTED QUARANTINE PROTECTIVE PROCESS" (#26).

THIS LACK OF TRUST IS PERPETUATED BY DISASTERS LIKE THE LEAD-POISONING, DELIVERED VIA CITY WATER IN FLINT AND THE SLOW CLEAN-UP OF WATER SYSTEMS IN COMMUNITIES THROUGHOUT MICHIGAN (#27). THIS LACK OF TRUST IN PROTECTION AND REGULATION IS ALSO EXACERBATED BY THE STATE OF MICHIGAN'S APPROVAL FOR INCREASED EXTRACTION VOLUMES, DESPITE THEIR OWN FINDINGS OF POTENTIAL ENVIRONMENTAL DISASTER (#28).

THIS LACK OF TRUST ALSO COLLAPSES THE "PUBLIC GOOD" OF MUNICIPAL WATER AS A WORTHY SOURCE OF INVESTMENT AND BENEFITS THOSE CORPORATIONS THAT WOULD PROFIT FROM EXTRACTING "PUBLIC GOOD" FOR THEIR OWN GAINS. THE RESULT...A FURTHER ERODING OF "THE PUBLIC" AS A SITE OF POWER, CHANGE, AND SOCIAL JUSTICE. ANDREW SZASZ'S (2007) "INVERTED QUARANTINE" NOTED BY PACHECO-VEGA AND PRACTICED BY THOSE WHO CAN CHOOSE TO CONSUME BOTTLED WATER IS PART OF THE COLLAPSE OF CONCERN FOR "US," TO CHAMPION THE INDIVIDUAL'S "CHOICE" TO PROTECT THEMSELVES FROM THE DANGERS BROUGHT ON BY "SOCIAL THREAT" (#29).

THE SLOW AND COMPREHENSIVE PUSH OF "INDIVIDUAL RESPONSIBILITY" THAT IS AN UNDERLYING TENET OF NEOLIBERAL IDEOLOGY IS A LURKING SHADOW IN THE STORY OF MICHIGAN. DEINDUSTRIALIZATION LEAVES A SCAR ON THE LANDSCAPE, AND A DEEPER WOUND ON THE HEARTS OF ITS PEOPLE. NESTLE'S CORPORATE MESSAGES SUGGEST THAT IT IS, INDEED, THE CONSUMER THAT WOULD DRIVE THEIR IRRESPONSIBLE EXTRACTION PRACTICES IN RURAL, NORTHWEST MICHIGAN, AND THEIR RESPONSE, THEREFORE, IS ONE OF "PUBLIC SERVICE" (#30). IT IS HERE THAT "CONSUMER" IS TRANSFORMED INTO "THE PUBLIC," AND THE PUBLIC'S NEED IS EXPLOITED.

THERE ARE THREE SECTIONS TO THIS STORY: SCARCITY, ABUNDANCE, AND THE EXPLOITATION OF "NEED." "SCARCITY" SEEKS TO ORGANIZE THE UNFOLDING OF THE ENVIRONMENTAL DISASTER IN FLINT, MICHIGAN. THE LACK OF ACCESS TO CLEAN DRINKING WATER CREATES ACTIONS THAT GIVE RISE TO THE STORIES OF THIS SYSTEMIC FAILURE AND POISONING OF A WHOLE COMMUNITY. THIS TOXICIFICATION MAKES AN OPPORTUNITY FOR ABUNDANCE, WITH A CORPORATION (PRIVATE INTEREST) STEPPING IN, AS THE SERVANTS OF THE PUBLIC HAVE RETREATED; THE ABUNDANCE OF PUBLIC WATER DONATED FOR THE FUTURE OF PROFIT FROM THE AQUIFERS OF MECOSTA AND OSCOLA COUNTIES. THE EXPLOITATION OF NEED TRAVERSES THE STATE OF MICHIGAN AND MAKES ITSELF A HOME IN THE EVERYDAY LIVES OF EVERYDAY PEOPLE MAKING ENDS MEET AS BEST THEY CAN. NESTLé'S RHETORICAL MANEUVERING AROUND WATER POLITICS PROVIDES AN INTERESTING TEMPLATE FOR UNDERSTANDING THE COMPLEXITIES OF RESOURCE CONSUMPTION IN EVERYDAY LIFE - AND THE DISTANCE CORPORATIONS MAINTAIN FROM HUMANITY WITH THEIR COMMUNICATIONS TO "THE PUBLIC."

THE STORY THAT FOLLOWS IS A GRAPHIC TALE OF FAILED TRUST, UNINTERRUPTED PROFIT, AND DEMOCRATIC SUBVERSION; ALL THEMSELVES A PARTICULAR KIND OF "THIRST." THESE ARE NOT NEW ELEMENTS OF ANY NARRATED INTRIGUE, BUT THE COMPLICATION FOR THE SUBJECTS IS DIRE: WHEN THOSE TRUSTED TO "PROTECT" DO NOT, TO WHOM CAN "THE PEOPLE" TURN? AND WHEN WATER IS BOTH A HUMAN NECESSITY AND THE CURRENCY OF EXCHANGE, WHAT IS THE RECOURSE FOR THE THIRSTY AND WANTING?

WE BEGIN WITH **SCARCITY**.

WE BEGIN WITH **FLINT**.

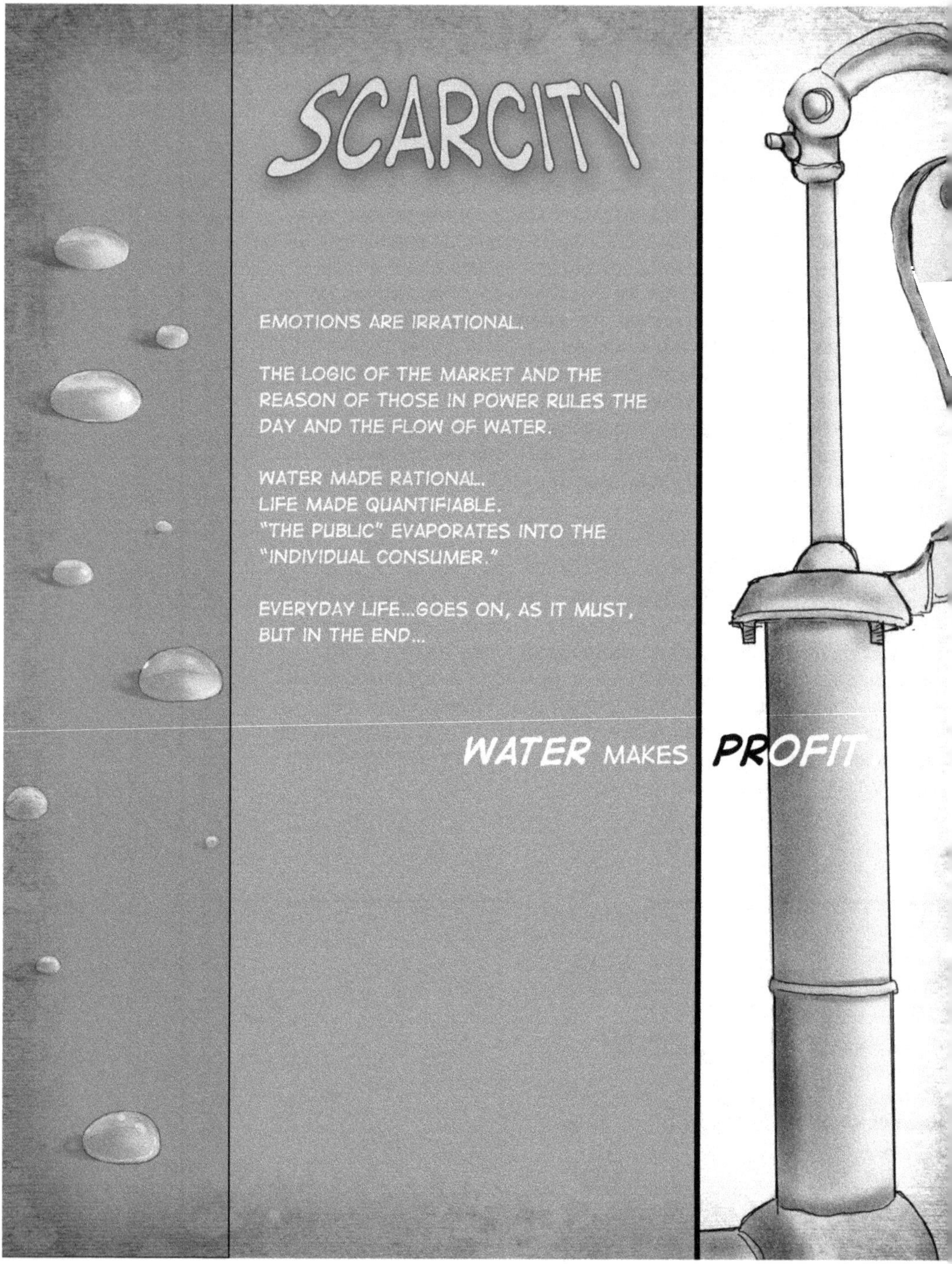
SCARCITY
EMOTIONS ARE IRRATIONAL.
THE LOGIC OF THE MARKET AND THE REASON OF THOSE IN POWER RULES THE DAY AND THE FLOW OF WATER.
WATER MADE RATIONAL.
LIFE MADE QUANTIFIABLE.
"THE PUBLIC" EVAPORATES INTO THE "INDIVIDUAL CONSUMER."
EVERYDAY LIFE...GOES ON, AS IT MUST, BUT IN THE END...
WATER MAKES PROFIT

E...HAVE DONATED APPROXIMATELY 3.2 MILLION BOTTLES OF WATER TO THE CITY OF FLINT" (NESTLé #31)....
FLINT
IN 2014, THE PEOPLE OF FLINT KNEW THEIR WATER WAS POISONOUS - AND TOOK THE NECESSARY STEPS TO INFORM THOSE RESPONSIBLE FOR CORRECTING THE HEAVY CONTAMINATION OF LEAD IN THE CITY'S DRINKING WATER.
THE SWITCH TO THE FLINT RIVER CHANGED THE LIVES OF THE PEOPLE OF FLINT, FOREVER. BATHROOMS ONCE FAMILIAR - ONCE DOTTED WITH PUDDLES FROM THE SHOWER, STILL A ROOM FOR HYGIENE, BUT ITS METHOD LOOKS DIFFERENT...NOT FAMILIAR.
"WATER IS AN EMOTIONAL ISSUE..."
"INSUFFICIENT AND UNSAFE WATER [IS] A STRESS THAT AFFECT[S] MANY DIFFERENT ASPECTS OF PEOPLE'S DAILY LIVES... (#32)" IN WAYS THEY DID NOT IMAGINE. AT ONCE, WITH WATER'S RISKS AND SCARCITY, ITS NECESSITY IS APPARENT.

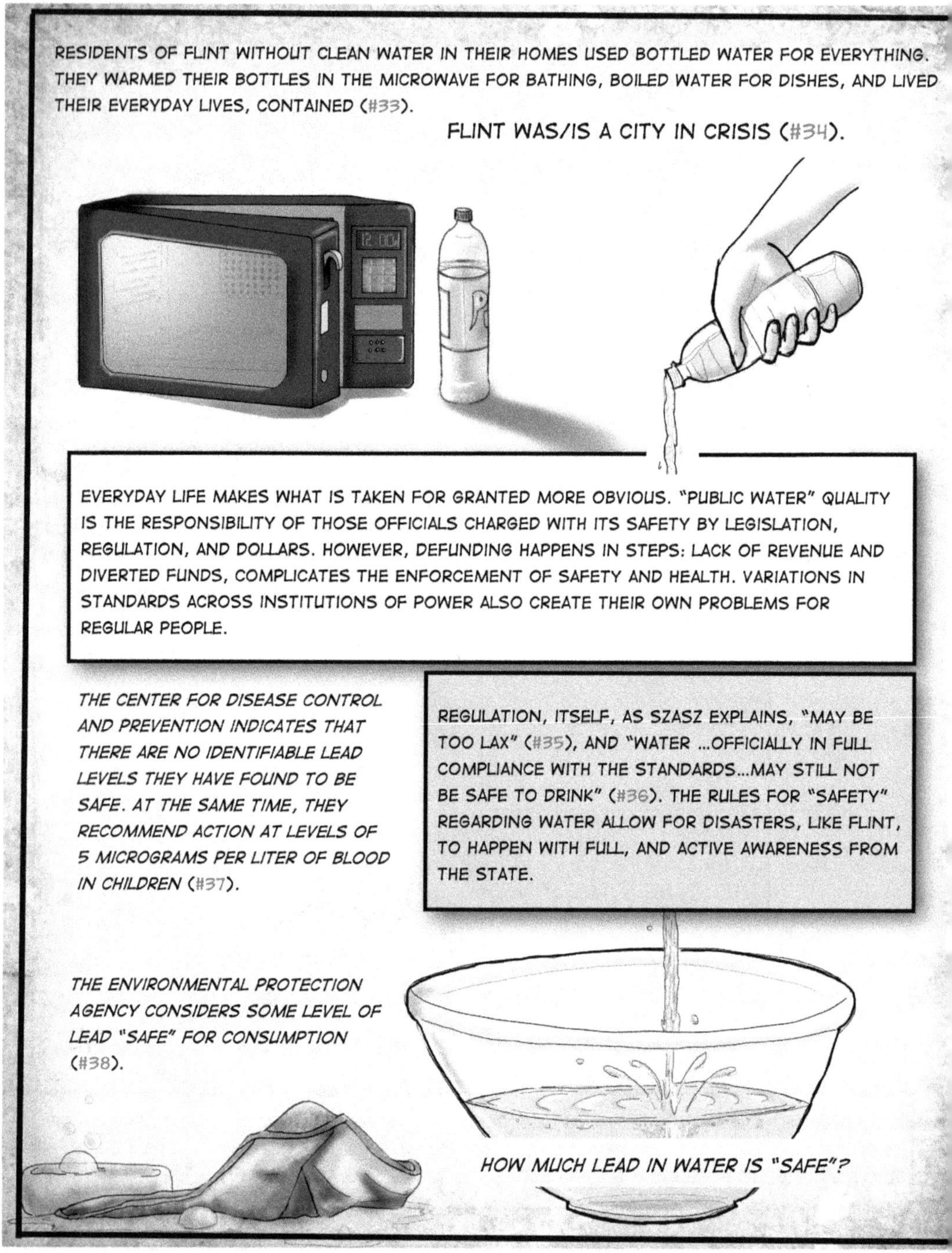
RESIDENTS OF FLINT WITHOUT CLEAN WATER IN THEIR HOMES USED BOTTLED WATER FOR EVERYTHING. THEY WARMED THEIR BOTTLES IN THE MICROWAVE FOR BATHING, BOILED WATER FOR DISHES, AND LIVED THEIR EVERYDAY LIVES, CONTAINED (#33).
FLINT WAS/IS A CITY IN CRISIS (#34).
EVERYDAY LIFE MAKES WHAT IS TAKEN FOR GRANTED MORE OBVIOUS. "PUBLIC WATER" QUALITY IS THE RESPONSIBILITY OF THOSE OFFICIALS CHARGED WITH ITS SAFETY BY LEGISLATION, REGULATION, AND DOLLARS. HOWEVER, DEFUNDING HAPPENS IN STEPS: LACK OF REVENUE AND DIVERTED FUNDS, COMPLICATES THE ENFORCEMENT OF SAFETY AND HEALTH. VARIATIONS IN STANDARDS ACROSS INSTITUTIONS OF POWER ALSO CREATE THEIR OWN PROBLEMS FOR REGULAR PEOPLE.
THE CENTER FOR DISEASE CONTROL AND PREVENTION INDICATES THAT THERE ARE NO IDENTIFIABLE LEAD LEVELS THEY HAVE FOUND TO BE SAFE. AT THE SAME TIME, THEY RECOMMEND ACTION AT LEVELS OF 5 MICROGRAMS PER LITER OF BLOOD IN CHILDREN (#37).
REGULATION, ITSELF, AS SZASZ EXPLAINS, "MAY BE TOO LAX" (#35), AND "WATER ...OFFICIALLY IN FULL COMPLIANCE WITH THE STANDARDS...MAY STILL NOT BE SAFE TO DRINK" (#36). THE RULES FOR "SAFETY" REGARDING WATER ALLOW FOR DISASTERS, LIKE FLINT, TO HAPPEN WITH FULL, AND ACTIVE AWARENESS FROM THE STATE.
THE ENVIRONMENTAL PROTECTION AGENCY CONSIDERS SOME LEVEL OF LEAD "SAFE" FOR CONSUMPTION (#38).
HOW MUCH LEAD IN WATER IS "SAFE"?

THE EMERGENCY MANAGER STRUCTURE, MADE LAW IN 2012 (*PUBLIC ACT 436*), AND APPLIED THROUGHOUT (MOSTLY BLACK, BROWN, AND POOR COMMUNITIES) IN MICHIGAN, ALLOWED THE GOVERNOR TO OPERATE MUNICIPALITIES VICARIOUSLY THROUGH AN EMERGENCY MANAGER (EM)(#39). ACCORDING TO THE LAW, THE APPOINTED EM REPORTS ONLY TO THE GOVERNOR (AND THE LEGISLATURE) (#40). HENCE, THE EM IS MANDATED TO OPERATE DEAF TO THE PEOPLE, BLIND TO THEIR NEEDS, AND MUTE TO RESIST THE WILL OF THE GOVERNOR - BY DESIGN. THE POLITICS OF CRISIS UNFOLDED IN A TECHNOCRATIC APPROACH TO GOVERNANCE.

Technocracy, as defined by Jason Stanley (2016) as a "market-oriented logic that uses technocratic, 'expert'- driven (i.e., the state-appointed emergency manager) decision-making processes" as a mechanism to override democratic processes (unseating representatives elected by the community) (#41).

STANLEY STATES FURTHER: "TECHNOCRATIC THINKING AND LANGUAGE PREVENTED PUBLIC OFFICIALS FROM SEEING THE PERSPECTIVES OF FLINT RESIDENTS COMPLAINING ABOUT THEIR WATER QUALITY, AND WAS THEREFORE...UNREASONABLE (ORIGINAL EMPHASIS)" (#42) IT IS NO COINCIDENCE THAT ALL OF THE APPOINTED EMS, DURING THE SNYDER ADMINISTRATION, WERE CONSIDERED "FINANCIAL EXPERTS" (#43). THE WILL OF THE PEOPLE (THROUGH ELECTION) IS OVERRIDDEN BY THE MANUFACTURING OF "CRISIS"; THE ENGINEERING OF "EMERGENCY" TO BE MANAGED.

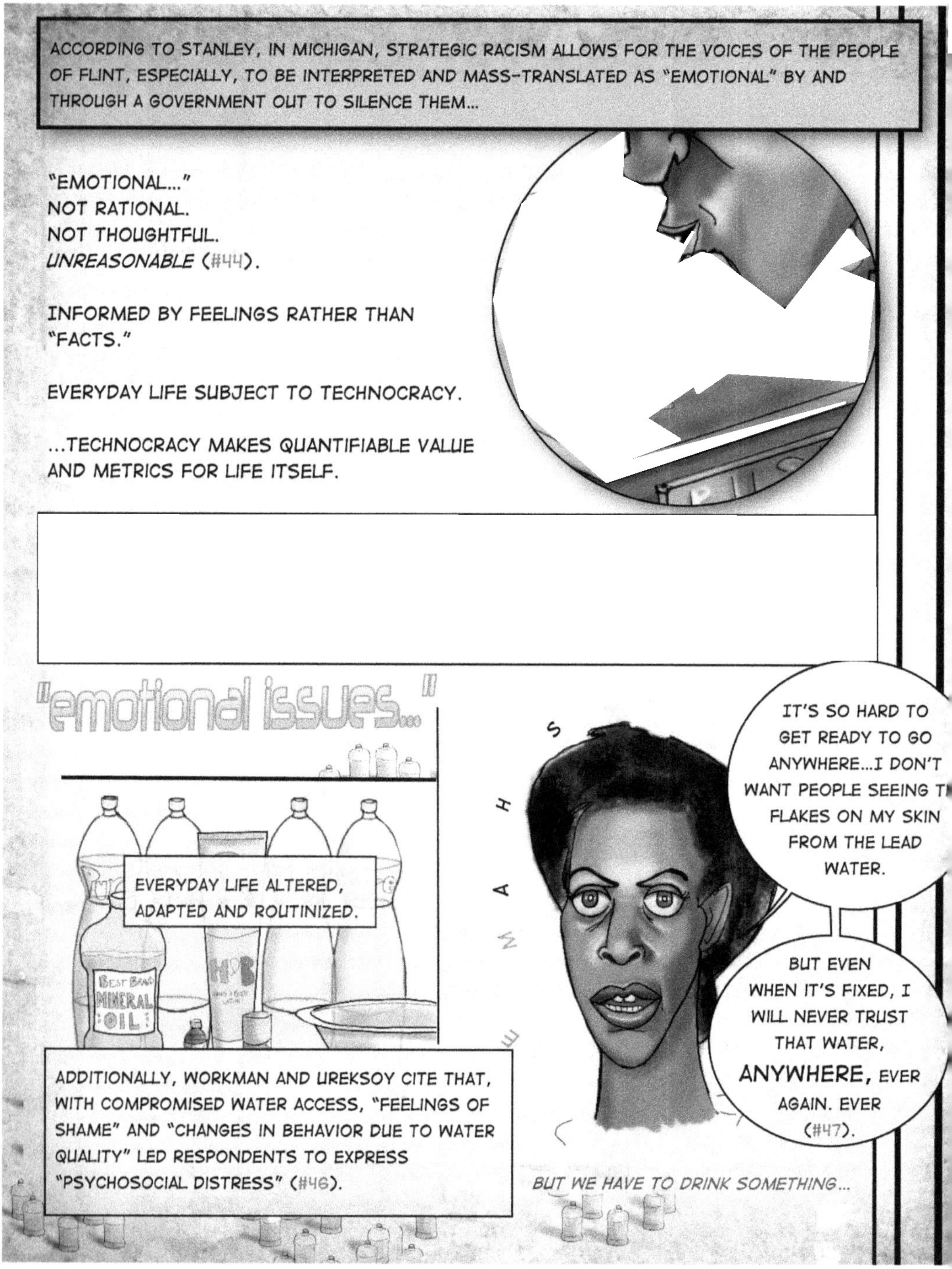
ACCORDING TO STANLEY, IN MICHIGAN, STRATEGIC RACISM ALLOWS FOR THE VOICES OF THE PEOPLE OF FLINT, ESPECIALLY, TO BE INTERPRETED AND MASS-TRANSLATED AS "EMOTIONAL" BY AND THROUGH A GOVERNMENT OUT TO SILENCE THEM...
"EMOTIONAL..."
NOT RATIONAL.
NOT THOUGHTFUL.
UNREASONABLE (#44).
INFORMED BY FEELINGS RATHER THAN "FACTS."
EVERYDAY LIFE SUBJECT TO TECHNOCRACY.
...TECHNOCRACY MAKES QUANTIFIABLE VALUE AND METRICS FOR LIFE ITSELF.
"emotional issues..."
EVERYDAY LIFE ALTERED, ADAPTED AND ROUTINIZED.
BEST BRAND MINERAL OIL
ADDITIONALLY, WORKMAN AND UREKSOY CITE THAT, WITH COMPROMISED WATER ACCESS, "FEELINGS OF SHAME" AND "CHANGES IN BEHAVIOR DUE TO WATER QUALITY" LED RESPONDENTS TO EXPRESS "PSYCHOSOCIAL DISTRESS" (#46).
SHAME
IT'S SO HARD TO GET READY TO GO ANYWHERE...I DON'T WANT PEOPLE SEEING TH FLAKES ON MY SKIN FROM THE LEAD WATER.
BUT EVEN WHEN IT'S FIXED, I WILL NEVER TRUST THAT WATER, ANYWHERE, EVER AGAIN. EVER (#47).
BUT WE HAVE TO DRINK SOMETHING...

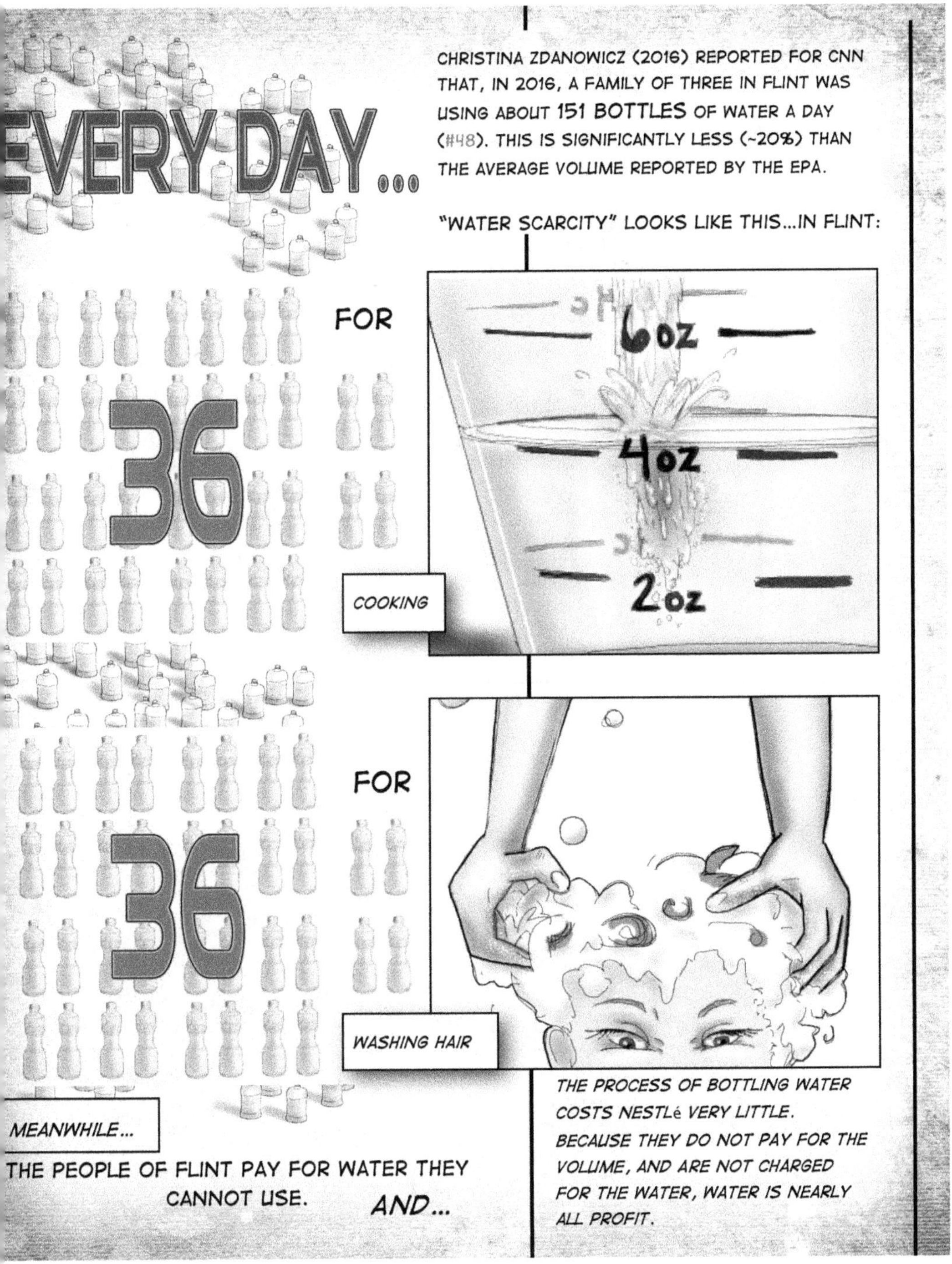
EVERY DAY...
CHRISTINA ZDANOWICZ (2016) REPORTED FOR CNN THAT, IN 2016, A FAMILY OF THREE IN FLINT WAS USING ABOUT 151 BOTTLES OF WATER A DAY (#48). THIS IS SIGNIFICANTLY LESS (~20%) THAN THE AVERAGE VOLUME REPORTED BY THE EPA.
"WATER SCARCITY" LOOKS LIKE THIS...IN FLINT:
FOR
36
6oz
4oz
2oz
COOKING
FOR
36
WASHING HAIR
MEANWHILE...
THE PEOPLE OF FLINT PAY FOR WATER THEY CANNOT USE.
AND...
THE PROCESS OF BOTTLING WATER COSTS NESTLé VERY LITTLE. BECAUSE THEY DO NOT PAY FOR THE VOLUME, AND ARE NOT CHARGED FOR THE WATER, WATER IS NEARLY ALL PROFIT.

THE PEOPLE OF FLINT ARE ENCOURAGED TO TRUST GOVERNMENT OFFICIALS, WHO WOULD ASSURE THEM OF THE QUALITY OF WATER COMING FROM THEIR TAPS.
DRINKING
=
27
ZDANOWICZ NOTES THAT GINA LUSTER, A FLINT RESIDENT AND PARENT, "FEELS LESS LIKE A GOOD PARENT AFTER WATCHING HER DAUGHTER...AND HER NIECE, SUFFER FROM HAIR LOSS AND SKIN RASHES" (#49).
DISHES
=
24
PSYCHO-SOCIAL AND RESPONSES TO SCARCITY CREATE RIPPLES FURTHER INTO THE OPERATIONS OF EVERYDAY LIFE FOR THE FAMILIES. CHILDREN ARE SENT HOME FROM SCHOOL, RATES OF DOMESTIC VIOLENCE INCREASE AND MARRIAGES BREAK APART (#50).
THIS IS CONTEXT...

(TM)
PURE
WATER
OU'VE NEVER TASTED FREEDOM SO
GOOD!
"NOT ONLY DO MULTINATIONAL CORPORATIONS HAVE THE POWER TO EMBED AN IDEA OF PURITY AND HEALTHINESS IN A PACKAGED LIQUID, THEY ARE ALSO ABLE TO MAINTAIN THIS NOTION INGRAINED IN PEOPLE'S MINDS FOR GENERATIONS" ().
BRANDING IS POLITICAL...().

ON TWO SEPARATE OCCASIONS, CEOS OF NESTLé CORPORATION PROVIDED INSIGHTS, PUBLICLY, INTO THEIR PHILOSOPHIES ON "WATER":
IN 2001, WE FILED A PERMIT TO BUILD AND START PUMPING FROM NATURAL SPRING BASINS IN THE WESTERN PART OF MICHIGAN.
SPRINGS ARE LIKE PETROLEUM. YOU CAN ALWAYS BUILD A CHOCOLATE FACTORY. BUT SPRINGS YOU HAVE OR YOU DON'T HAVE (#53).
HELMUT MAUCHER, FORMER CEO
PETER BRABECK-LETMATHE, FORMER CEO
IT IS BEST, IN OTHER WORDS, TO OWN THE SOURCE. AT THE SAME TIME, NESTLé WATERS NORTH AMERIC WORKS TO ASSURE THE PUBLIC THAT "BOTTLED WATER WILL NEVER REPLACE TAP WATER," - BUT THEN, "WE REGULATORY REGIMES COMBINED WITH POORLY REGULATED INDUSTRIES TO CREATE NEW MARKETS FOR PRODUCTS THAT CAN RESPOND TO CONSUMERS' FEARS OF THE TAP" (#54). WEAK REGULATION IS REQUIRED FOR THE ACCESS TO VOLUME AND CONSUMPTION, ALLOWED BY STATE AND LOCAL GOVERNMENTS THAT NESTLé AND OTHER BOTTLERS PROFIT FROM.
HEH. "HUMAN RIGHT."

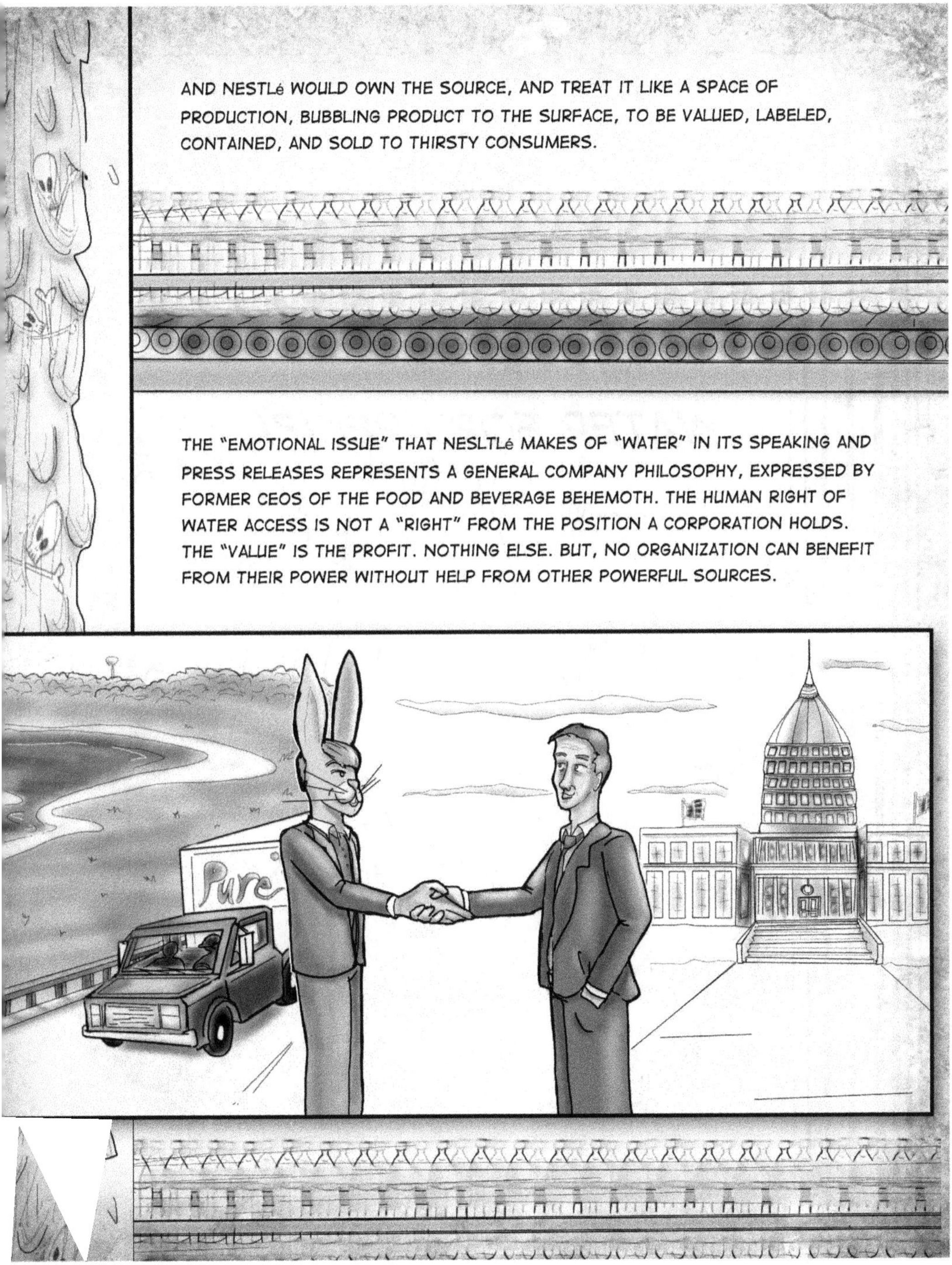
AND NESTLé WOULD OWN THE SOURCE, AND TREAT IT LIKE A SPACE OF PRODUCTION, BUBBLING PRODUCT TO THE SURFACE, TO BE VALUED, LABELED, CONTAINED, AND SOLD TO THIRSTY CONSUMERS.
THE "EMOTIONAL ISSUE" THAT NESLTLé MAKES OF "WATER" IN ITS SPEAKING AND PRESS RELEASES REPRESENTS A GENERAL COMPANY PHILOSOPHY, EXPRESSED BY FORMER CEOS OF THE FOOD AND BEVERAGE BEHEMOTH. THE HUMAN RIGHT OF WATER ACCESS IS NOT A "RIGHT" FROM THE POSITION A CORPORATION HOLDS. THE "VALUE" IS THE PROFIT. NOTHING ELSE. BUT, NO ORGANIZATION CAN BENEFIT FROM THEIR POWER WITHOUT HELP FROM OTHER POWERFUL SOURCES.
Pure

NESTLé'S FRAMING OF WATER AS AN "EMOTIONAL ISSUE," IS AN INTERESTING AND INTENTIONAL POSITING OF WATER AND THE PUBLIC IN MICHIGAN. BY SUGGESTING THAT "PASSION" IS THE DRIVING FORCE OF DISSENT, NESTLé WORKS TO FORCE ITS OWN DEFINITION ("THE FACTS") OF "WATER" AS THE "TRUTH" FOR EVERYONE (#56), IN COLLUSION WITH THOSE WHO WOULD ALSO PROFIT FROM NESTLé'S "TRUTH."
WHEN THIS IS THEIR CORPORATE (IDEOLOGICAL) TRUTH...
WHY WOULD WE GIVE UP ALL THAT MONEY IF WE DON'T HAVE TO...?!
WATER FOR FREE!?!
HA! HA!
HA!
(#57)
"WATER IS...ABOUT CONFLICT.... CONFLICT ABOUT WHO GETS TO CONSUME WATER, WHO GETS TO EXTRACT IT AND COMMODIFY IT, AND WHO IS EXCLUDED FROM ITS CONSUMPTION..."(#58).

FOUR YEARS AFTER THE DISASTER BEGAN, WHEN THE CONTRACT EXPIRED BETWEEN ABSOPURE BOTTLED WATER (OUT OF DETROIT) AND THE STATE OF MICHIGAN, NESTLé PICKED UP DISTRIBUTION TO FLINT RESIDENTS (#59). TESTING DONE BY THE STATE AND OUTSIDE LABORATORIES AS WELL, REVEALED THAT THE TESTED WATER CONTAINED GREATLY REDUCED TOXIC LEVELS OF LEAD (#60). THE STATE DEEMED THE WATER IN MANY FLINT HOMES DRINKABLE. MANY OF THE CITIZENS CONTINUED TO ASK QUESTIONS ABOUT WATER QUALITY, BUT THE STATE'S CONCERN SHIFTED; SCIENCE HAD RELIEVED THEM OF FURTHER ACTION, AND THE PEOPLE STILL DON'T TRUST THE WATER.
NESTLé "VOLUNTEERED" TO DONATE PALETTE UPON PALETTE OF VARIOUS NESTLé BOTTLED WATER BRANDS TO THE CITY OF FLINT WHILE THE CITY'S INFRASTRUCTURE UNDERWENT REPAIRS (#61). THE MAYOR OF FLINT LAUDED THE CORPORATION FOR THEIR INITIATIVE AND CHARITY - ESPECIALLY AFTER THEY EXTENDED THEIR PROMISE INTO THE SUMMER OF 2019 (#62)
WE HAVE TO DRINK SOMETHING...
WE WILL RETURN TO THIS STORY IN A MOMENT...
MEANWHILE, AFTER CLASS DISCUSSION ONE DAY, STUDENTS APPROACHED ME IN DESPAIR:
FAVORITE
WATER
BRAND
WATER
WATER
NESTLé OWNS ICE MOUNTAIN?! WHAT AM I SUPPOSED DRINK NOW? THAT'S MY FAVORITE BRAND!
FAVORITE
E M O T I O N
Brand
water
OUR DISCUSSION OF MICHIGAN WATER HAD COVERED FLINT AND EVART, ENDING WITH NESTLé WATERS NORTH AMERICA. IN 2018, THE AUTHORIZED INCREASE OF WATER TAKEN FROM PUBLIC WATER SOURCES IN OSCEOLA AND MECOSTA COUNTIES, BY THE GLOBAL FOOD AND WATER CORPORATION, RAISED CONCERNS AND QUESTIONS FROM THE PEOPLE OF MICHIGAN.
FROM 250 GALLONS PER MINUTE TO 400 GALLONS PER MINUTE (#63).

WHAT IS A "PUBLIC AQUIFER"?
THERE ARE DIFFERENT WATER SYSTEMS THAT PEOPLE USE. IN A LOT OF RURAL AREAS IN MICHIGAN, PEOPLE HAVE WELLS, YOU KNOW?
THOSE ARE "PUBLIC WATER" SOURCES - ANYONE CAN USE THEM THAT CAN SINK A WELL.
OH YEAH!
IF ANYONE CAN USE THEM, THEN WHAT'S THE PROBLEM WITH NESTLé USING THEM?
I MEAN, I GET THAT THEY TAKE A LOT, BUT...
THE PERMIT'S APPROVAL CAN BE SEEN AS PART OF A LARGER LITICAL STRATEGY...AND ITS NOT NEW!

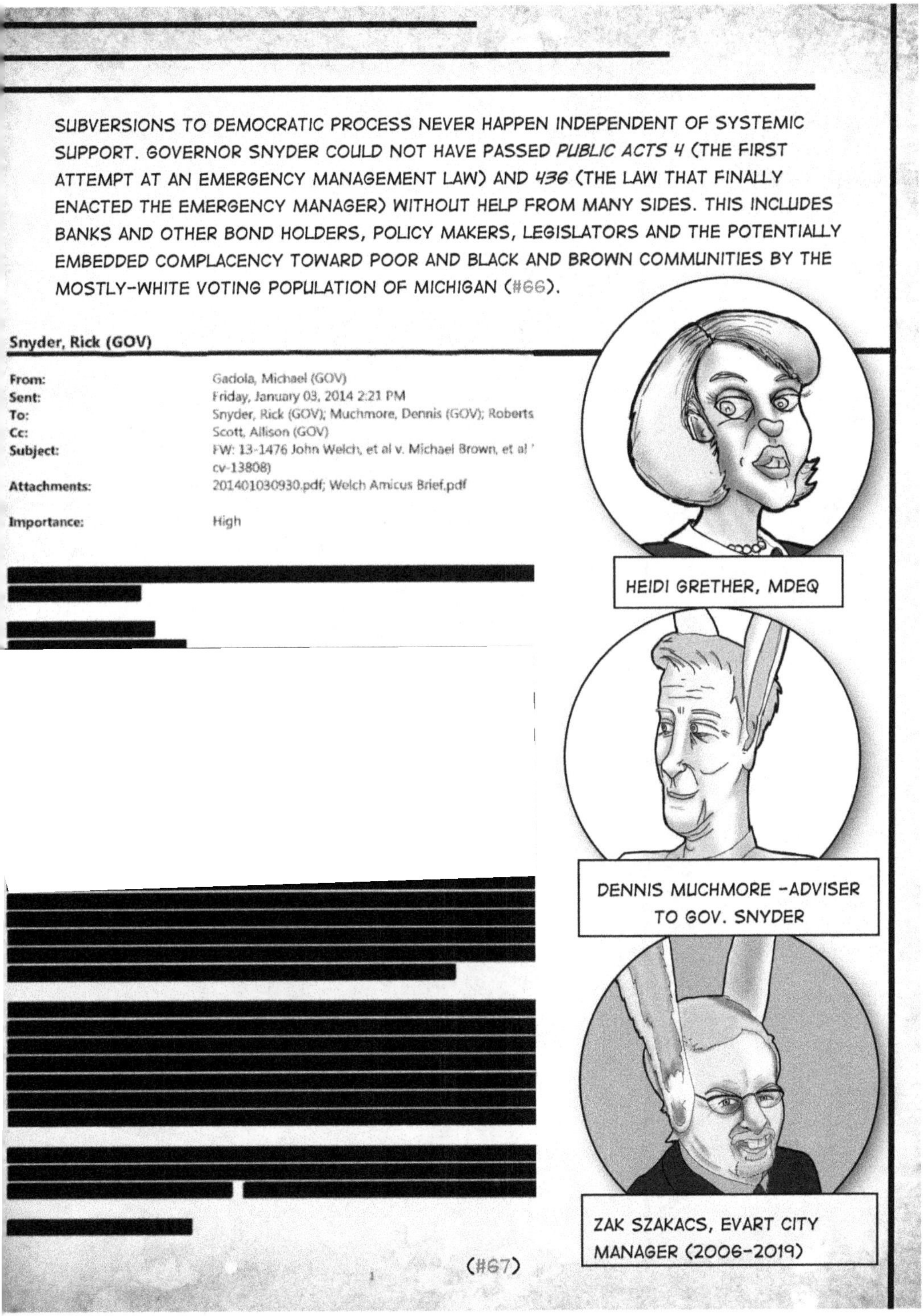

SUBVERSIONS TO DEMOCRATIC PROCESS NEVER HAPPEN INDEPENDENT OF SYSTEMIC SUPPORT. GOVERNOR SNYDER COULD NOT HAVE PASSED *PUBLIC ACTS 4* (THE FIRST ATTEMPT AT AN EMERGENCY MANAGEMENT LAW) AND *436* (THE LAW THAT FINALLY ENACTED THE EMERGENCY MANAGER) WITHOUT HELP FROM MANY SIDES. THIS INCLUDES BANKS AND OTHER BOND HOLDERS, POLICY MAKERS, LEGISLATORS AND THE POTENTIALLY EMBEDDED COMPLACENCY TOWARD POOR AND BLACK AND BROWN COMMUNITIES BY THE MOSTLY-WHITE VOTING POPULATION OF MICHIGAN (#66).
HEIDI GRETHER, MDEQ
DENNIS MUCHMORE -ADVISER TO GOV. SNYDER
ZAK SZAKACS, EVART CITY MANAGER (2006-2019)
(#67)

Snyder, Rick (GOV)

From: Gadola, Michael (GOV)
Sent: Friday, January 03, 2014 2:21 PM
To: Snyder, Rick (GOV); Muchmore, Dennis (GOV); Roberts
Cc: Scott, Allison (GOV)
Subject: FW: 13-1476 John Welch, et al v. Michael Brown, et al ' cv-13808)
Attachments: 201401030930.pdf; Welch Amicus Brief.pdf
Importance: High

[redacted]

[redacted]

[redacted]

[redacted]

[redacted]

[redacted]

1

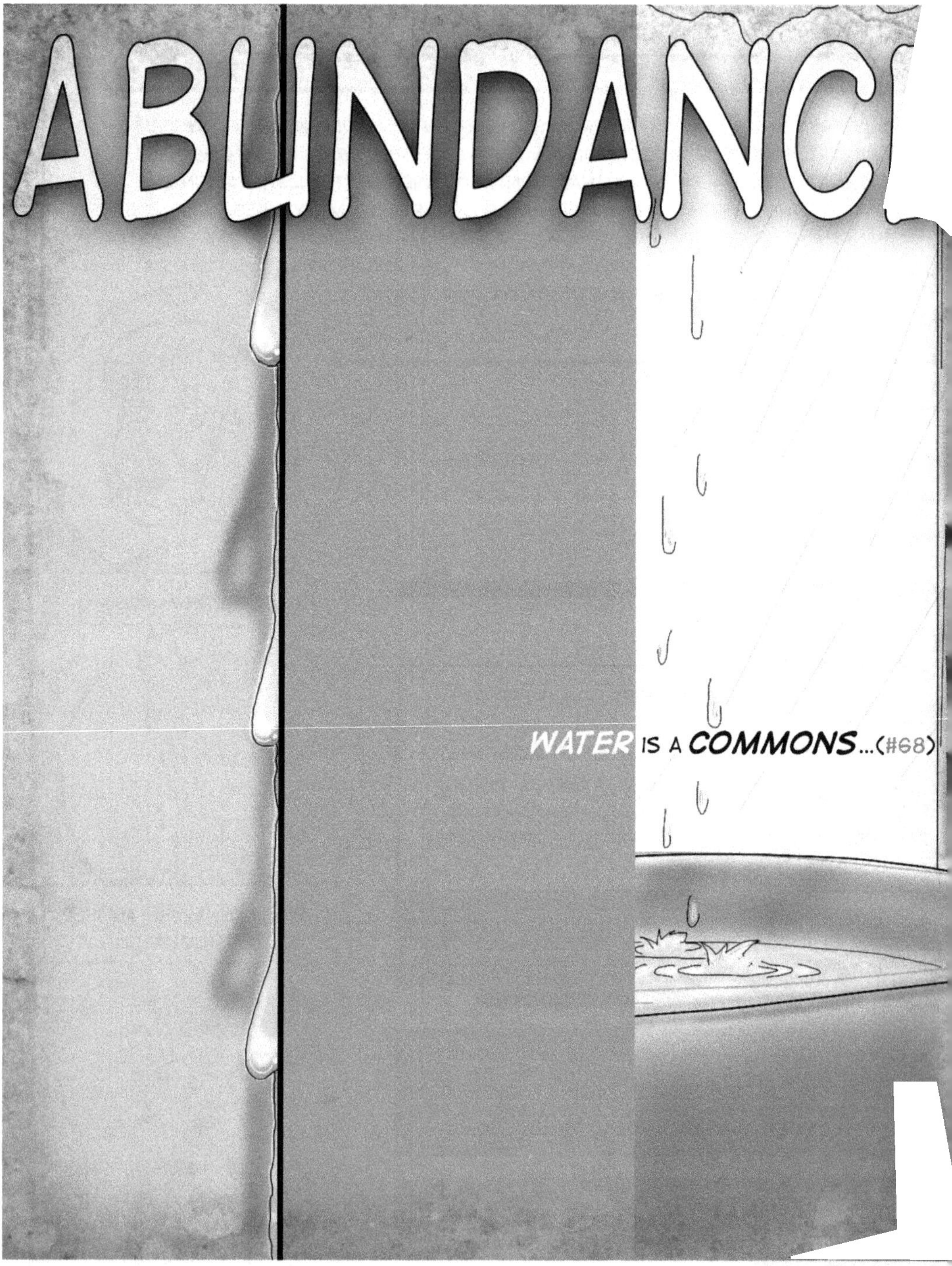
ABUNDANC
WATER IS A COMMONS...(#68)

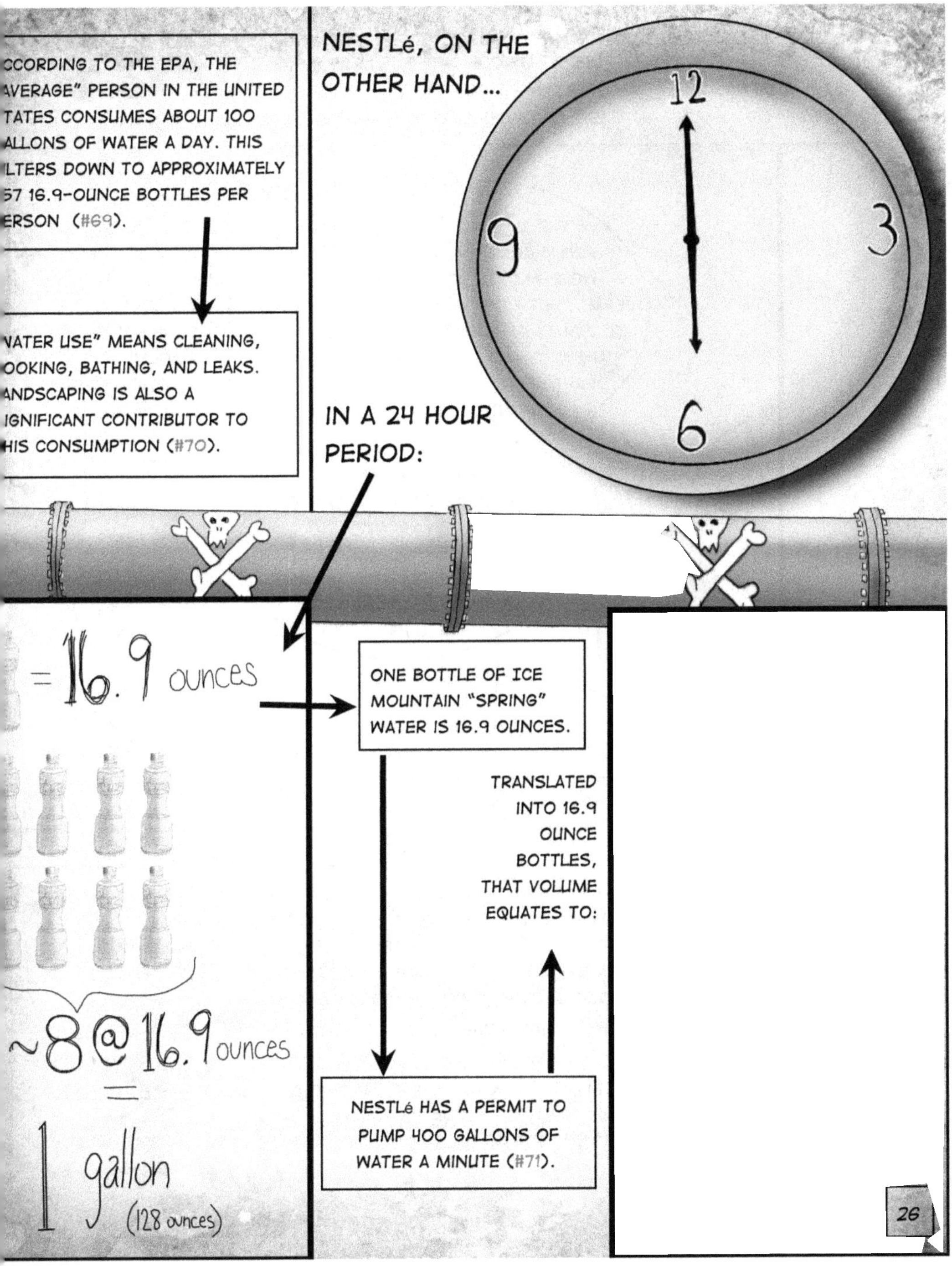
CCORDING TO THE EPA, THE
AVERAGE" PERSON IN THE UNITED
TATES CONSUMES ABOUT 100
ALLONS OF WATER A DAY. THIS
LTERS DOWN TO APPROXIMATELY
57 16.9-OUNCE BOTTLES PER
ERSON (#69).
VATER USE" MEANS CLEANING,
OOKING, BATHING, AND LEAKS.
ANDSCAPING IS ALSO A
IGNIFICANT CONTRIBUTOR TO
HIS CONSUMPTION (#70).
NESTLé, ON THE OTHER HAND...
12
3
6
9
IN A 24 HOUR PERIOD:
= 16.9 ounces
ONE BOTTLE OF ICE MOUNTAIN "SPRING" WATER IS 16.9 OUNCES.
~8 @ 16.9 ounces
=
1 gallon
(128 ounces)
TRANSLATED INTO 16.9 OUNCE BOTTLES, THAT VOLUME EQUATES TO:
NESTLé HAS A PERMIT TO PUMP 400 GALLONS OF WATER A MINUTE (#71).
26

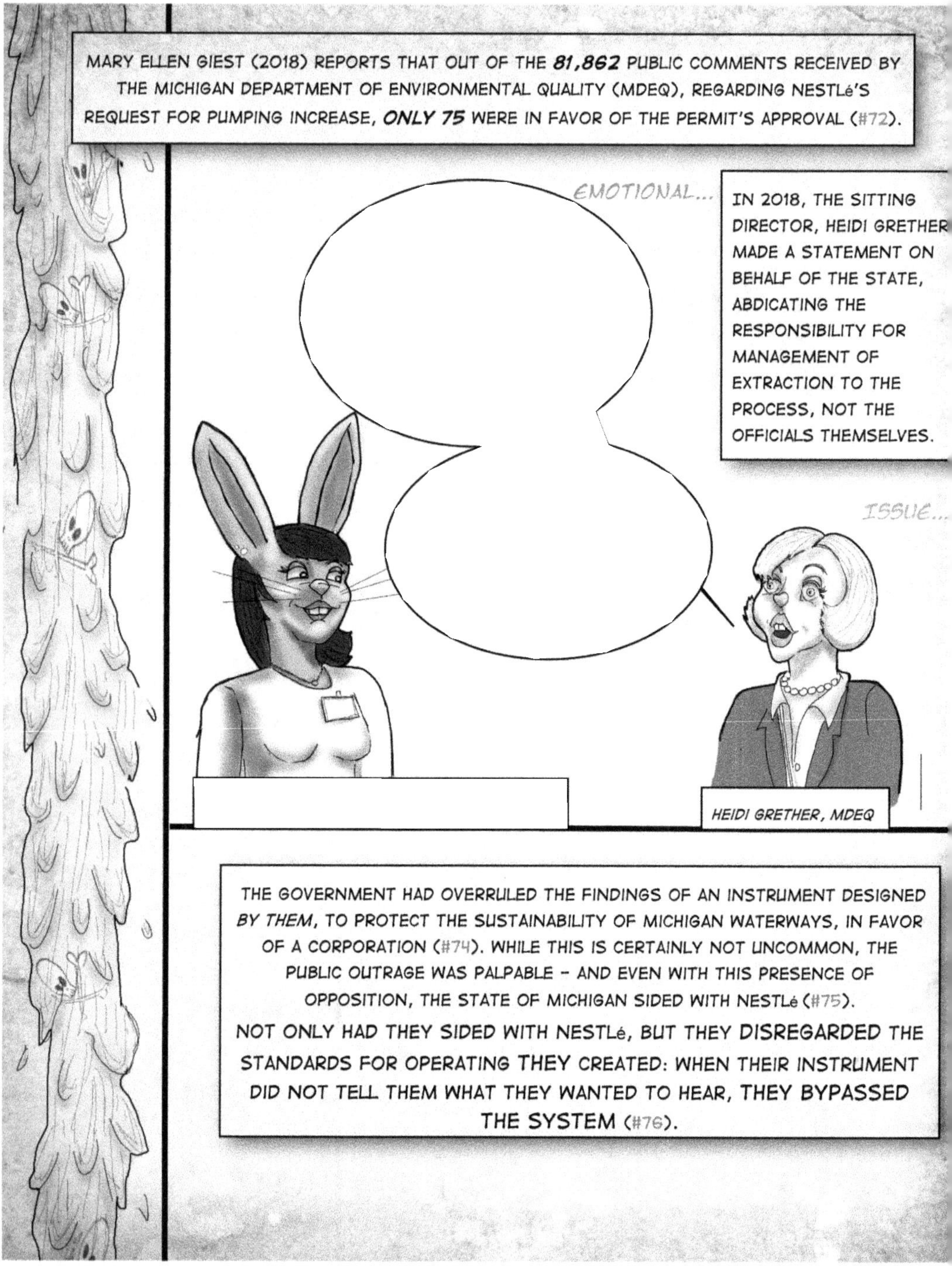
MARY ELLEN GIEST (2018) REPORTS THAT OUT OF THE ***81,862*** PUBLIC COMMENTS RECEIVED BY THE MICHIGAN DEPARTMENT OF ENVIRONMENTAL QUALITY (MDEQ), REGARDING NESTLé'S REQUEST FOR PUMPING INCREASE, ***ONLY 75*** WERE IN FAVOR OF THE PERMIT'S APPROVAL (#72).
EMOTIONAL...
IN 2018, THE SITTING DIRECTOR, HEIDI GRETHER MADE A STATEMENT ON BEHALF OF THE STATE, ABDICATING THE RESPONSIBILITY FOR MANAGEMENT OF EXTRACTION TO THE PROCESS, NOT THE OFFICIALS THEMSELVES.
ISSUE...
HEIDI GRETHER, MDEQ
THE GOVERNMENT HAD OVERRULED THE FINDINGS OF AN INSTRUMENT DESIGNED *BY THEM*, TO PROTECT THE SUSTAINABILITY OF MICHIGAN WATERWAYS, IN FAVOR OF A CORPORATION (#74). WHILE THIS IS CERTAINLY NOT UNCOMMON, THE PUBLIC OUTRAGE WAS PALPABLE - AND EVEN WITH THIS PRESENCE OF OPPOSITION, THE STATE OF MICHIGAN SIDED WITH NESTLé (#75).
NOT ONLY HAD THEY SIDED WITH NESTLé, BUT THEY DISREGARDED THE STANDARDS FOR OPERATING THEY CREATED: WHEN THEIR INSTRUMENT DID NOT TELL THEM WHAT THEY WANTED TO HEAR, THEY BYPASSED THE SYSTEM (#76).

Nestlé
...never
trust
Nestlé
water
anywhere
ever again...
DO NOT ENTER
THE OVERTHROW WAS OBVIOUS...

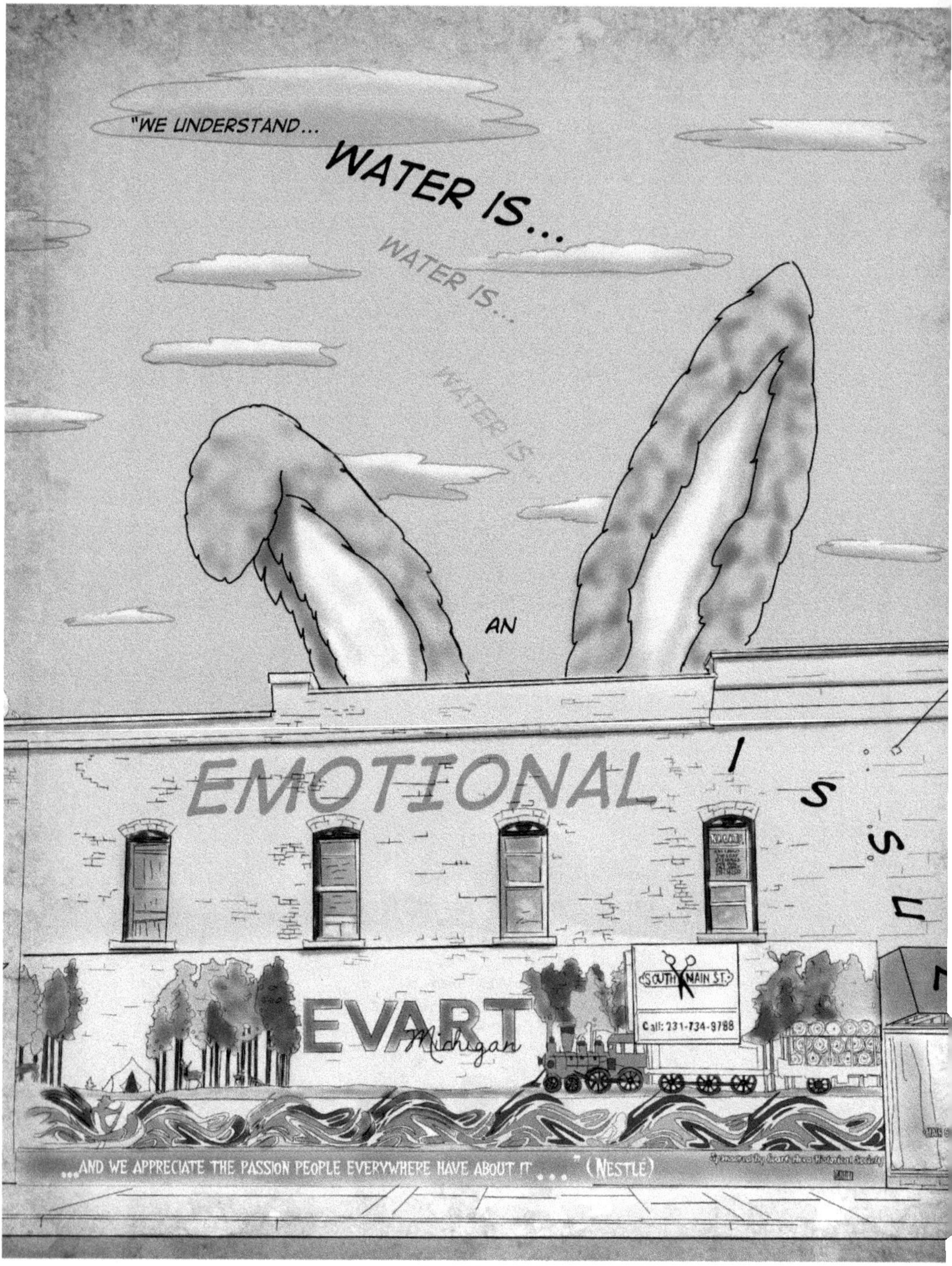
"WE UNDERSTAND...
WATER IS...
WATER IS...
WATER IS...
AN
EMOTIONAL
I
S
S
U
EVART
Michigan
SOUTH MAIN ST.
Call: 231-734-9788
...AND WE APPRECIATE THE PASSION PEOPLE EVERYWHERE HAVE ABOUT IT . . ." (NESTLE)

EVEN AS NESTLé'S CLAIM TO INCREASE VOLUME FROM THE PUBLIC GROUND WATER WAS LEGITIMATED BY THE STATE, THEIR BRAND MEANING WAS IN A PRECARIOUS POSITION.
WHILE THE PEOPLE OF FLINT HAD POISONED WATER (FOR WHICH THEY WERE STILL EXPECTED TO PAY), NESTLé PAID LITTLE TO MAKE PROFIT, SELLING PUBLIC WATER BACK TO THE PEOPLE OF MICHIGAN AND SURROUNDING AREAS (#77).
THE COMPANY RELEASED A SERIES OF ADVERTISEMENTS AND "FACT SHEETS" ABOUT THEIR MICHIGAN OPERATIONS...
DO NOT ENTER
BY CREATING QUESTIONS OR UNCERTAINTIES AROUND THE PROTESTS OF PEOPLE IN THE PUBLIC AROUND NESTLé'S EXTRACTION PRACTICES, NESTLé DIMINISHES THOSE CONCERNS, AND REDUCES THEM TO "EMOTIONAL ISSUES." "PASSION" IS NOT SCIENCE, AND SCIENCE (TECHNOCRACY) IS QUANTIFIABLE PROOF OF "TRUTH" (#79).
PUBLIC WATER SOURCE KEEP OUT!

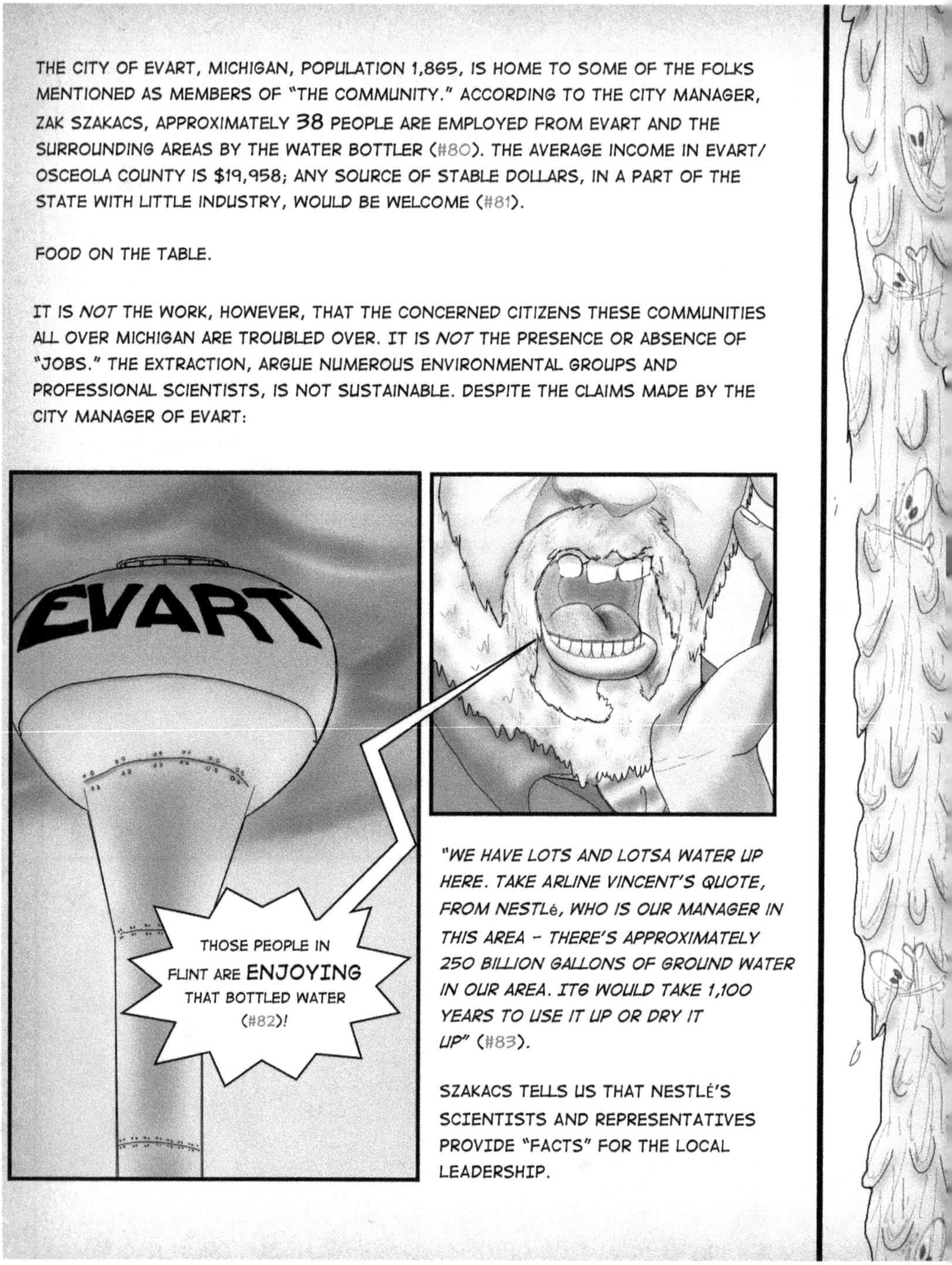
THE CITY OF EVART, MICHIGAN, POPULATION 1,865, IS HOME TO SOME OF THE FOLKS MENTIONED AS MEMBERS OF "THE COMMUNITY." ACCORDING TO THE CITY MANAGER, ZAK SZAKACS, APPROXIMATELY 38 PEOPLE ARE EMPLOYED FROM EVART AND THE SURROUNDING AREAS BY THE WATER BOTTLER (#80). THE AVERAGE INCOME IN EVART/ OSCEOLA COUNTY IS $19,958; ANY SOURCE OF STABLE DOLLARS, IN A PART OF THE STATE WITH LITTLE INDUSTRY, WOULD BE WELCOME (#81).
FOOD ON THE TABLE.
IT IS *NOT* THE WORK, HOWEVER, THAT THE CONCERNED CITIZENS THESE COMMUNITIES ALL OVER MICHIGAN ARE TROUBLED OVER. IT IS *NOT* THE PRESENCE OR ABSENCE OF "JOBS." THE EXTRACTION, ARGUE NUMEROUS ENVIRONMENTAL GROUPS AND PROFESSIONAL SCIENTISTS, IS NOT SUSTAINABLE. DESPITE THE CLAIMS MADE BY THE CITY MANAGER OF EVART:
EVART
THOSE PEOPLE IN FLINT ARE ENJOYING THAT BOTTLED WATER (#82)!
"WE HAVE LOTS AND LOTSA WATER UP HERE. TAKE ARLINE VINCENT'S QUOTE, FROM NESTLé, WHO IS OUR MANAGER IN THIS AREA - THERE'S APPROXIMATELY 250 BILLION GALLONS OF GROUND WATER IN OUR AREA. ITG WOULD TAKE 1,100 YEARS TO USE IT UP OR DRY IT UP" (#83).
SZAKACS TELLS US THAT NESTLÉ'S SCIENTISTS AND REPRESENTATIVES PROVIDE "FACTS" FOR THE LOCAL LEADERSHIP.

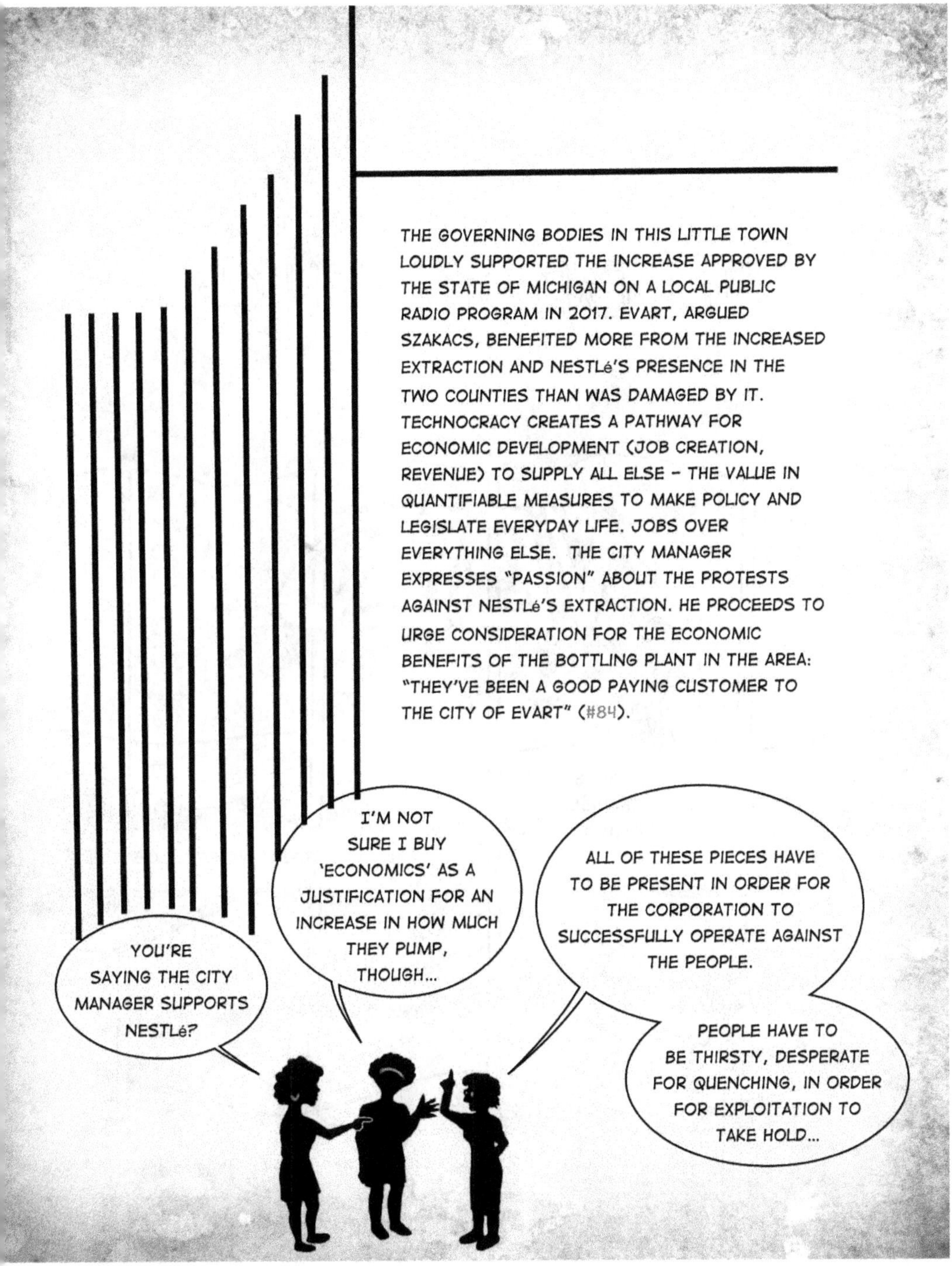
THE GOVERNING BODIES IN THIS LITTLE TOWN LOUDLY SUPPORTED THE INCREASE APPROVED BY THE STATE OF MICHIGAN ON A LOCAL PUBLIC RADIO PROGRAM IN 2017. EVART, ARGUED SZAKACS, BENEFITED MORE FROM THE INCREASED EXTRACTION AND NESTLé'S PRESENCE IN THE TWO COUNTIES THAN WAS DAMAGED BY IT. TECHNOCRACY CREATES A PATHWAY FOR ECONOMIC DEVELOPMENT (JOB CREATION, REVENUE) TO SUPPLY ALL ELSE – THE VALUE IN QUANTIFIABLE MEASURES TO MAKE POLICY AND LEGISLATE EVERYDAY LIFE. JOBS OVER EVERYTHING ELSE. THE CITY MANAGER EXPRESSES "PASSION" ABOUT THE PROTESTS AGAINST NESTLé'S EXTRACTION. HE PROCEEDS TO URGE CONSIDERATION FOR THE ECONOMIC BENEFITS OF THE BOTTLING PLANT IN THE AREA: "THEY'VE BEEN A GOOD PAYING CUSTOMER TO THE CITY OF EVART" (#84).
YOU'RE SAYING THE CITY MANAGER SUPPORTS NESTLé?
I'M NOT SURE I BUY 'ECONOMICS' AS A JUSTIFICATION FOR AN INCREASE IN HOW MUCH THEY PUMP, THOUGH...
ALL OF THESE PIECES HAVE TO BE PRESENT IN ORDER FOR THE CORPORATION TO SUCCESSFULLY OPERATE AGAINST THE PEOPLE.
PEOPLE HAVE TO BE THIRSTY, DESPERATE FOR QUENCHING, IN ORDER FOR EXPLOITATION TO TAKE HOLD...

THE EXPLOITATION OF
NEED
THE EXPLOITATION OF NEED PRESENTS ITSELF THROUGH THE SAME MECHANISMS THAT DELIVER IDEAS OF "FREEDOM" THROUGH CONSUMPTION...
THE ENGINEERING OF CONSENT...
THE ILLUSION OF "CHOICE" CREATED IN NEOLIBERAL SOCIEITIES...
VOTING WITH DOLLARS...INDIVIDUAL RESPONSIBILITY...ETHICAL CONSUMPTION.

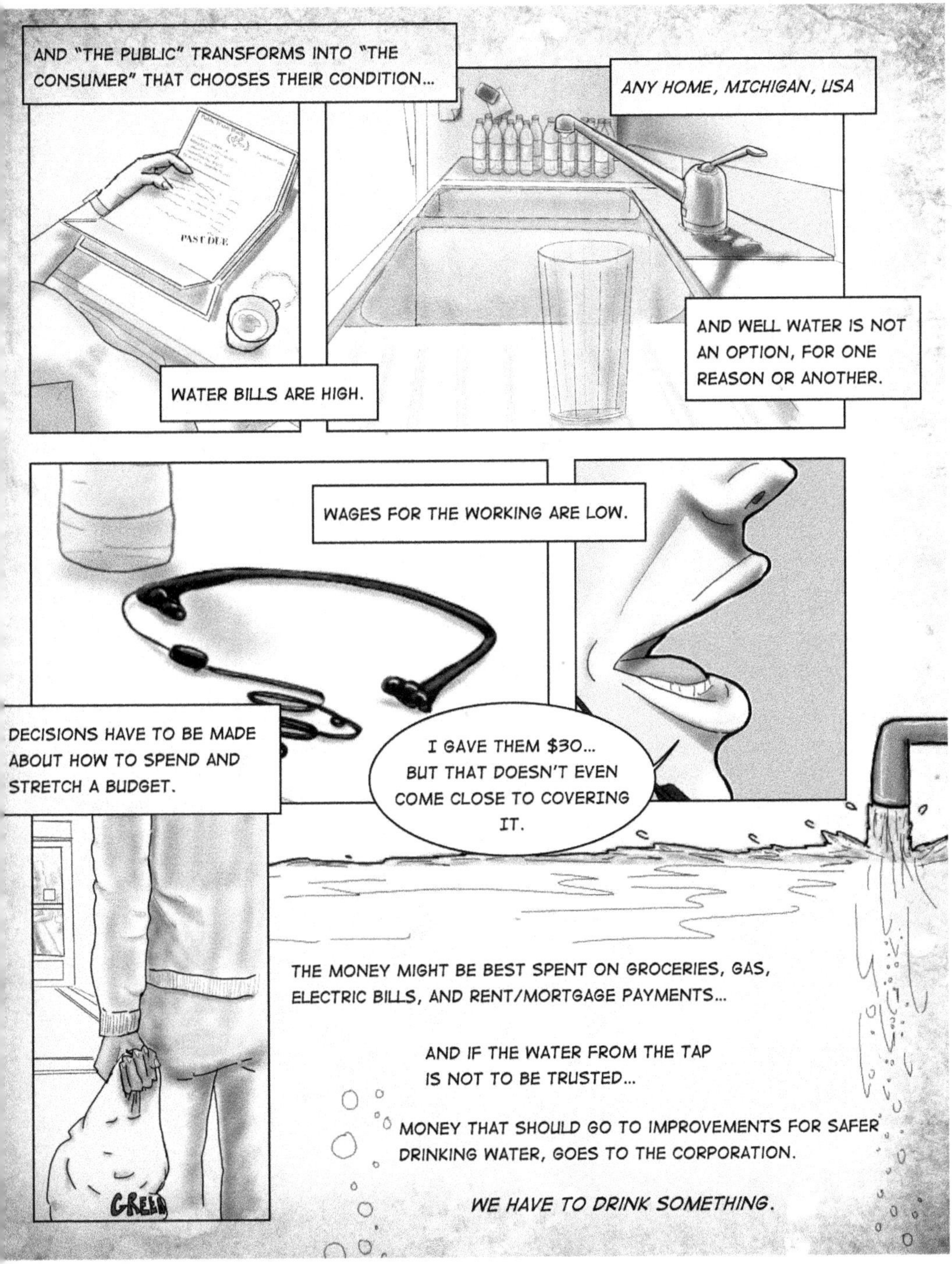
AND "THE PUBLIC" TRANSFORMS INTO "THE CONSUMER" THAT CHOOSES THEIR CONDITION...
ANY HOME, MICHIGAN, USA
PAST DUE
WATER BILLS ARE HIGH.
AND WELL WATER IS NOT AN OPTION, FOR ONE REASON OR ANOTHER.
WAGES FOR THE WORKING ARE LOW.
DECISIONS HAVE TO BE MADE ABOUT HOW TO SPEND AND STRETCH A BUDGET.
I GAVE THEM $30... BUT THAT DOESN'T EVEN COME CLOSE TO COVERING IT.
GREED
THE MONEY MIGHT BE BEST SPENT ON GROCERIES, GAS, ELECTRIC BILLS, AND RENT/MORTGAGE PAYMENTS...
AND IF THE WATER FROM THE TAP IS NOT TO BE TRUSTED...
MONEY THAT SHOULD GO TO IMPROVEMENTS FOR SAFER DRINKING WATER, GOES TO THE CORPORATION.
WE HAVE TO DRINK SOMETHING.

IT SEEMS AS THOUGH THE CORPORATION DOES NOT EVEN NEED TO MAKE AN EFFORT TO MASK THE EXPLOITATION OF NEED THROUGH NEOLIBERAL LEANING IDEOLOGIES.(#85)
EXTRACTION VOLUME IS DRIVEN BY CUSTOMER DEMAND. IF PEOPLE STOP BUYING OUR WATER, WE WON'T NEED TO PUMP AS MUCH FROM THE PUBLIC AQUIFER! (#86)
OFF!
Pure
IT IS THE CUSTOMER THAT DRIVES THE DEMAND THAT REQUIRES THE INCREASED VOLUME EXTRACTION. NESTLé WOULD PUT THE RESPONSIBILITY FOR CONSERVATION ON THE SHOULDERS OF THOSE WHO CANNOT TRUST THE TAP, AND THOSE WHO CAN AFFORD TO "PROTECT" THEMSELVES FROM THE "POISONS" OF PUBLIC WATER.
THE "NEED" FOR BOTTLED WATER IS BORN FROM A FAILURE ON THE PART OF GOVERNING BODIES AND INSTITUTIONAL SYSTEMS. CORPORATIONS DO NOT HAVE THE OBLIGATION TO SHARE THEIR PROFITS WITH THE PEOPLE THAT PAY FOR THEIR PRODUCTS. THEY ONLY *GET*. THEIR "GIVE" IS STILL PROFIT.

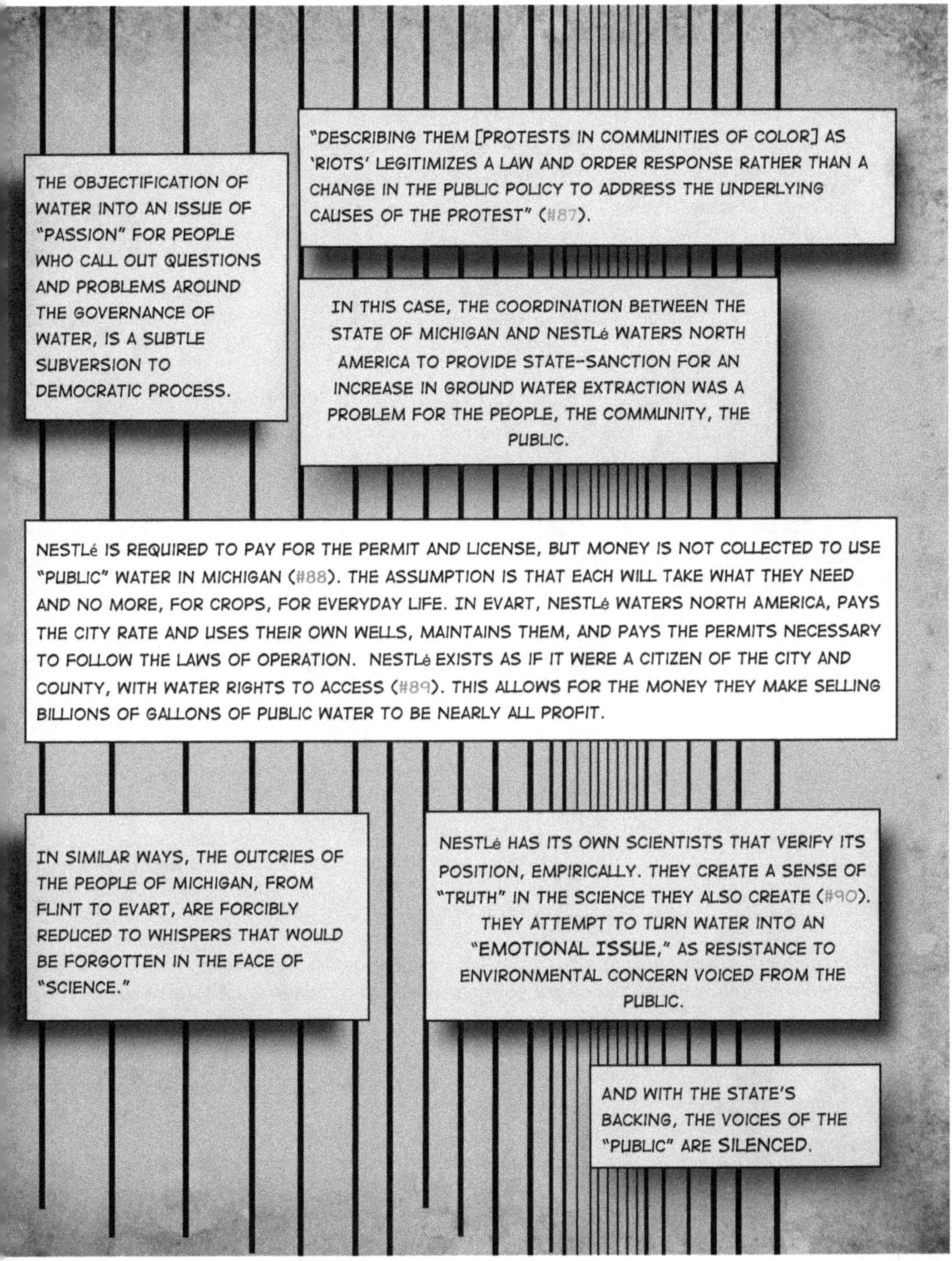
THE OBJECTIFICATION OF WATER INTO AN ISSUE OF "PASSION" FOR PEOPLE WHO CALL OUT QUESTIONS AND PROBLEMS AROUND THE GOVERNANCE OF WATER, IS A SUBTLE SUBVERSION TO DEMOCRATIC PROCESS.
"DESCRIBING THEM [PROTESTS IN COMMUNITIES OF COLOR] AS 'RIOTS' LEGITIMIZES A LAW AND ORDER RESPONSE RATHER THAN A CHANGE IN THE PUBLIC POLICY TO ADDRESS THE UNDERLYING CAUSES OF THE PROTEST" (#87).
IN THIS CASE, THE COORDINATION BETWEEN THE STATE OF MICHIGAN AND NESTLé WATERS NORTH AMERICA TO PROVIDE STATE-SANCTION FOR AN INCREASE IN GROUND WATER EXTRACTION WAS A PROBLEM FOR THE PEOPLE, THE COMMUNITY, THE PUBLIC.
NESTLé IS REQUIRED TO PAY FOR THE PERMIT AND LICENSE, BUT MONEY IS NOT COLLECTED TO USE "PUBLIC" WATER IN MICHIGAN (#88). THE ASSUMPTION IS THAT EACH WILL TAKE WHAT THEY NEED AND NO MORE, FOR CROPS, FOR EVERYDAY LIFE. IN EVART, NESTLé WATERS NORTH AMERICA, PAYS THE CITY RATE AND USES THEIR OWN WELLS, MAINTAINS THEM, AND PAYS THE PERMITS NECESSARY TO FOLLOW THE LAWS OF OPERATION. NESTLé EXISTS AS IF IT WERE A CITIZEN OF THE CITY AND COUNTY, WITH WATER RIGHTS TO ACCESS (#89). THIS ALLOWS FOR THE MONEY THEY MAKE SELLING BILLIONS OF GALLONS OF PUBLIC WATER TO BE NEARLY ALL PROFIT.
IN SIMILAR WAYS, THE OUTCRIES OF THE PEOPLE OF MICHIGAN, FROM FLINT TO EVART, ARE FORCIBLY REDUCED TO WHISPERS THAT WOULD BE FORGOTTEN IN THE FACE OF "SCIENCE."
NESTLé HAS ITS OWN SCIENTISTS THAT VERIFY ITS POSITION, EMPIRICALLY. THEY CREATE A SENSE OF "TRUTH" IN THE SCIENCE THEY ALSO CREATE (#90). THEY ATTEMPT TO TURN WATER INTO AN "EMOTIONAL ISSUE," AS RESISTANCE TO ENVIRONMENTAL CONCERN VOICED FROM THE PUBLIC.
AND WITH THE STATE'S BACKING, THE VOICES OF THE "PUBLIC" ARE SILENCED.

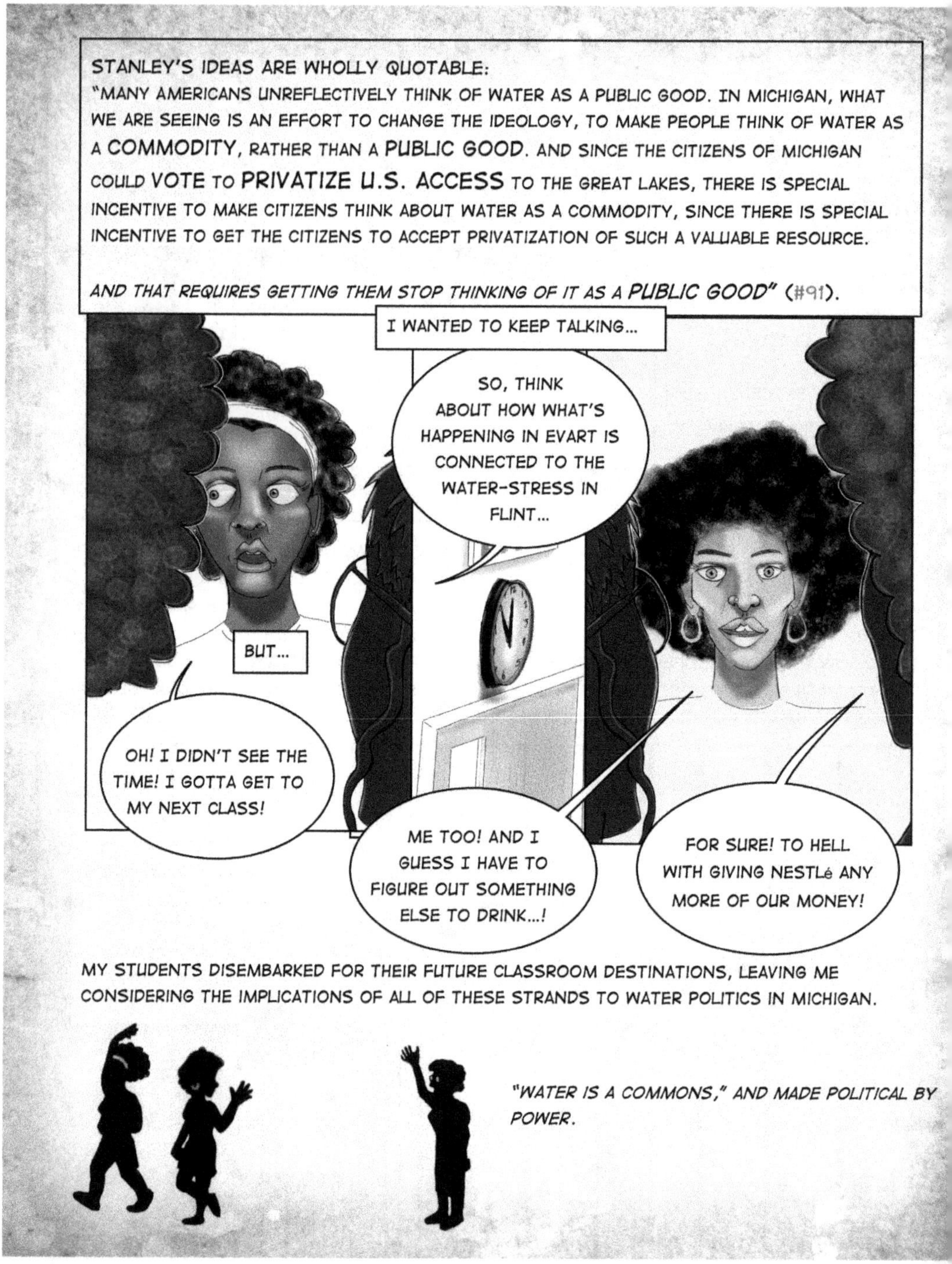
STANLEY'S IDEAS ARE WHOLLY QUOTABLE:
"MANY AMERICANS UNREFLECTIVELY THINK OF WATER AS A PUBLIC GOOD. IN MICHIGAN, WHAT WE ARE SEEING IS AN EFFORT TO CHANGE THE IDEOLOGY, TO MAKE PEOPLE THINK OF WATER AS A COMMODITY, RATHER THAN A PUBLIC GOOD. AND SINCE THE CITIZENS OF MICHIGAN COULD VOTE TO PRIVATIZE U.S. ACCESS TO THE GREAT LAKES, THERE IS SPECIAL INCENTIVE TO MAKE CITIZENS THINK ABOUT WATER AS A COMMODITY, SINCE THERE IS SPECIAL INCENTIVE TO GET THE CITIZENS TO ACCEPT PRIVATIZATION OF SUCH A VALUABLE RESOURCE.
AND THAT REQUIRES GETTING THEM STOP THINKING OF IT AS A PUBLIC GOOD" (#91).
I WANTED TO KEEP TALKING...
SO, THINK ABOUT HOW WHAT'S HAPPENING IN EVART IS CONNECTED TO THE WATER-STRESS IN FLINT...
BUT...
OH! I DIDN'T SEE THE TIME! I GOTTA GET TO MY NEXT CLASS!
ME TOO! AND I GUESS I HAVE TO FIGURE OUT SOMETHING ELSE TO DRINK...!
FOR SURE! TO HELL WITH GIVING NESTLé ANY MORE OF OUR MONEY!
MY STUDENTS DISEMBARKED FOR THEIR FUTURE CLASSROOM DESTINATIONS, LEAVING ME CONSIDERING THE IMPLICATIONS OF ALL OF THESE STRANDS TO WATER POLITICS IN MICHIGAN.
"WATER IS A COMMONS," AND MADE POLITICAL BY POWER.

THERE IS NO CONCLUSION OR END TO THIS STORY. WHILE THIS IS CERTAINLY A FOCUS ON NESTLé WATERS NORTH AMERICA AND ITS PART IN THE PROFITEERING OF PUBLIC WATER, THE PROBLEM IS NOT NESTLé, OR COCA-COLA, OR PEPSI CO. AS PACHECO-VEGA STATES, WHILE WEAKENED REGULATORY AGENCIES FACILITATE THE EXPLOITATION OF PUBLIC GOOD, "GOVERNING WATER IS...ABOUT HARNESSING POWER AND DEALING WITH CONFLICT IN A WAY THAT ENSURES THAT THERE IS EQUITABLE DISTRIBUTION AND ALLOCATION" (#92).

THE THIRSTY KNOW NO BOUNDARIES, BUT THE POWER OF NATIONS TO DEFEND THEIR SUPPLIES ARE DANGEROUS FOR THOSE SEEKING REFUGE FROM THIRST, HUNGER, AND VIOLENCE RELATED TO SCARCITY (#93).

OWNING A SOURCE, HOWEVER, IS A WHOLE OTHER FORM OF "GOVERNANCE," AND WHILE "THE PUBLIC" MIGHT BE COMPELLED TO DEPEND MORE AND MORE ON CORPORATIONS TO SUPPLY NECESSARY GOODS AND SERVICES, THE WAYS IN WHICH CORPORATIONS ARE REGULATED THROWS THE ACCOUNTABILITY OF THEIR DECISIONS AND PRACTICES INTO QUESTION.

IN DECEMBER 2019, NESTLé'S PROPOSAL TO REZONE PARCELS OF LAND ADJACENT TO THEIR WELLHEAD PUMPS IN OSCEOLA COUNTY WAS DENIED BY THE TOWNSHIP COURTS. NESTLé PLANNED TO BUILD INFRASTRUCTURE THAT WOULD ALLOW THEM TO PUMP THE 400 GALLONS A MINUTE THAT WAS APPROVED BY THE STATE IN 2018 (#94).

NESTLé'S CONTENTION, ACCORDING TO GARRETT ELLISON, WITH THE DENIAL OF THE REZONING REQUEST RESTS ON THE COMPANY'S ASSERTION THAT THEIR BOTTLING OF PUBLIC WATER IS AN "ESSENTIAL PUBLIC SERVICE" (#95). THE STATE JUDGE THAT HEARD THE APPEAL ALSO RESISTED NESTLé'S CLAIM THAT, BY DENYING THE CORPORATION ACCESS TO THE LAND, OSCEOLA TOWNSHIP WAS VIOLATING THE *SAFE DRINKING WATER* (1974) AND *NATURAL RESOURCES AND ENVIRONMENTAL PROTECTION ACTS* (1994). ELLISON GOES ON TO REMIND READERS THAT EVEN WITH THE STATE'S APPROVAL OF AN INCREASE IN VOLUME EXTRACTION BY THE BEHEMOTH, AND ALL OF THE SCIENCE REPORTING THAT THE LEVEL OF EXTRACTION APPROVED IS NOT SUSTAINABLE...

NESTLé PUSHES FORWARD ANYWAY, WORKING TO LAY THE BRICKS FOR PROFIT SOLIDLY. WORKING TO OWN THE SOURCE. DRIVEN BY THE PUBLIC'S THIRST EVER CLOSER TO SETTING PRECEDENT FO THE PRIVATIZING OF WATER-SOURCES IN MICHIGAN.

BOTTLED WATER IS THE FUTURE!

ADDITIONALLY, THE "EMOTIONAL ISSUE" MADE OF WATER BY NESTLé DEMONSTRATES A COMMON SYMPTOM OF A NEOLIBERAL CAPITALISM. THE COLLECTIVE RESPONSE TO A THREAT THAT ENDANGERS A DRINKING SUPPLY OR WATER SOURCE CAN BE SILENCED IF MEMBERS OF "THE PUBLIC" CANNOT RELATE TO THE STRUGGLES OF THEIR NEIGHBOR. THE "POLITICAL INDIVIDUAL" IS THE CULMINATION OF POLICY AND PRACTICE THAT ENCOURAGE ISOLATION AND ALIENATION (#96). AND YET, THE IDEA OF THE "INDIVIDUAL" ROMANCES PEOPLE IN PARTS OF US SOCIETY, TO IMAGINE THEIR POWER TO CHANGE LIES SOLELY WITHIN THEM. BOTTLED WATER AS THE CONSUMER SOLUTION TO "LAX REGULATION" COMPLICATES CLEAN WATER ACCESS FOR COMMUNITIES, LIKE FLINT, WHO CANNOT SUSTAIN THE PURCHASING OF BOTTLED WATER WHEN THEY HAVE OTHER EXPENSES, INCLUDING A CITY WATER BILLS FOR WATER THEY CANNOT DRINK. FLINT EXISTS IN SCARCITY. EVART HAS BEEN SO ECONOMICALLY DEVASTATED IN THE PAST DECADES THAT THE MERE PROMISE OF JOBS, NO MATTER HOW FEW, IS LIFE (#97). THIS IS EVART'S OWN EXISTENCE IN SCARCITY, BUT THE ABUNDANCE OF WATER UNDER THE GROUND MAKES EVART ATTRACTIVE TO THE BEWITCHING SPELLS CAST BY NESTLE WATERS NORTH AMERICA-

"THERE IS PLENTY OF WATER..."

BOTTLING WATER...MAKING IT PRIVATE...IS "PUBLIC SERVICE"...

WHAT DO WE DRINK WHEN OUR WELLS ARE POISONED, AND OUR PUBLIC WATER SOURCE IS DANGEROUS?

WE CAN'T LIVE WITHOUT WATER...

AND WE HAVE TO DRINK SOMETHING...

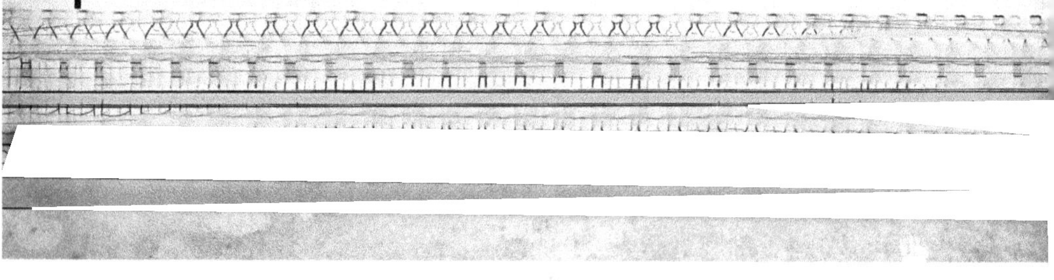

Endnotes

1. Ikonomova 2018.
2. Great Lakes-St. Lawrence River Basin Water Resources Council 2017.
3. Glennon 2009: 46; Great Lakes-St. Lawrence River Basin Sustainable Water Resources Agreement 2017; Szasz 2007: 123.
4. This is an adaptation, of course: not to scale.
5. Glennon 2009: 46.
6. "By the numbers: the business of bottled water." *Crain's Detroit Business*, April 2017, https://www.crainsdetroit.com/article/20170401/NEWS/170339973/by-the-numbers-the-business-of-bottled-water-in-michigan.
7. Michigan Department of Environment, Great Lakes and Energy, 2019. It is important to note here that, at the time of this application, the government agency was named the "Michigan Department of Environmental Quality" (MDEQ). Under Governor Gretchen Whitmer, the name of the agency was changed, in part, as an effort by the state's executive branch to expand the purview of environmental oversight in the state and to create, in some sense, a different agency than the one responsible for the Flint water disaster.
8. Nestlé Waters North America 2019.
9. Great Lakes-St. Lawrence River Basin Sustainable Water Resources Agreement 2017: 7–8.
10. Barrows 2017.
11. Nestlé and the Michigan Department of Environmental Quality both submitted reports that indicated the volume of Nestlé's proposed extraction would not negatively impact the water levels of the areas around the White Pines Spring site.
12. Annin 2018: Location 181.
13. United Nations (n.d.), and United Nations 2014.
14. Annin 2018: Location 181.
15. United Nations 2014.
16. By "question," I only mean that this significant use of water further evidences the "taken-for-grantedness" of water systems in the united states. Excessive use of water for lawns and landscaping demonstrates a privilege of access, a different consideration of water. In my small community, there are a number of apartment "townhouses" with in-ground sprinklers. They spray on in the rain. They are scheduled/timed to turn on everyday. Rain or shine.
17. Glennon 2009: 48; Szasz 2007: 128.
18. Mullin 2009: 1–2.

19. Mullin 2009: 4.
20. Mullin 2009: 6. In the case of Flint, Jeff Wright, the CEO of Karegnondi Water Authority, was also the County Drain Commissioner for Genesee County, where Flint is located. This is not to say that Wright moved to create an opportunity for himself and his company by contributing to the disaster in Flint. It is, however, notable that someone with knowledge of water governance as a county commission official would stand so much to gain from a completion of a water line and initiation of profit, generated by decisions made without a vote from the people of Flint (Taylor 2018). At the time of the Flint disaster, there were also connections between Governor Snyder's Chief-of-Staff, Dennis Muchmore, and the Public Relations consultant and lobbyist for Nestlé, Deborah, being husband and wife. Muchmore suggested, at one point, that Ice Mountain could be donated to church organizations in the poisoned city (Egan, Anderson, and Dolan 2016).
21. Mullin 2009: 7.
22. Stanley 2016: 3.
23. Not having to worry about where potable water comes from, how much is used, and the scarcity of it reflects a socialization around consumption, waste, and globalization. "Water" does not mean the same thing to everyone—it changes meaning depending on the cultural context (See Ashlock 2019; Finnegan 2002; Shiva 2018; and, Slaymaker and Bain 2017). The absence of imperative around conservation or awareness concerning public water access is also a consequence, as Andrew Szasz contends, of ideologies of "individuality" ("inverted Quarantine," Szasz 2007). it is a privilege to isolate and separate from "social threat." Bottled water consumption, by choice, is a particular privilege and device of alienation.
24. Workman and Ureksoy 2017: 52–60.
25. Glennon 2009: 48; Jackman 2016.
26. Pacheco-Vega 2019: 6.
27. Michigan, much like the other states along the Great Lakes system, that fall within the "Rust Belt," have a high rate of environmental disasters related to the late development of the EPA (in relation to the amount of time industry operated without oversight) and the "weak regulatory regimes" that followed its establishment. Michigan has had numerous environmental catastrophes, directly connected to industrial negligence.
28. Duffy and Clark 2017.
29. Szasz 2007: 5.
30. Ellison 2019; Matheny 2019.

31. Nestlé Waters North America (n.d.).
32. Workman and Ureksoy 2017: 56.
33. Taylor 2018.
34. Even with the highly public "safety" of Flint's drinking water, the people do not trust the state to protect them. Even with improvements, many Flint residents cannot trust the tap.
35. Szasz 2007: 117.
36. Szasz 2007: 107.
37. Center for Disease Control and Prevention (n.d.).
38. United States Environmental Protection Agency 2015. This is the agency's information page for the Lead and Copper Rule.
39. Stanley 2016: 13.
40. "Emergency Manager," n.d.
41. Stanley 2016: 4.
42. Stanley 2016: 3.
43. Taylor 2018.
44. Stanley 2016: 3.
45. Taylor 2018: 3:40–4:24.
46. Psychosocial distress can be best described as a response to the ways in which interpersonal and community relationships create an affect in someone or many people's lived experience. Workman and Ureksoy 2017: 53.
47. Taylor 2018: 1:51:44–1:52:20.
48. Zdanowicz 2016.
49. Zdanowicz 2016.
50. Taylor 2018.
51. Pacheco-Vega 2019: 6.
52. Pacheco-Vega 2019: 6.
53. Winter 2017.
54. Pacheco-Vega 2019: 5.
55. Winters 2017.
56. Nestlé Waters North America website 2018.
57. This is author interjection/embellishment. These executives did not make public their disregard for water as a human right explicitly with laughter. Capitalism and technocracy alienate and hinder our abilities to connect with and care about one another (Stanley 2016: 3).
58. Pacheco-Vega 2019: 3.
59. Fonger 2018; Tower 2018.
60. Baptiste 2018.
61. Byrd 2018; Oostling 2019.

62. Moore 2016.
63. Winters 2017; Gray 2018.
64. Szasz 2007: 106.
65. Stanley 2016: 9.
66. Stanley 2016: 5, 12.
67. Bosman, Davey, and Smith 2016.
68. Shiva 2016: xvi.
69. "The average American uses 100 gallons of water a day, according to the U.S. Environmental Protection Agency. That translates to roughly 757 bottles of water, which is way more the 50 water bottles each person in the Luster household is using" (Zdanowicz 2016).
70. Environmental Protection Agency 2018.
71. Tower 2018.
72. Geist (n.d.).
73. Grether 2018.
74. Ellison 2016a.
75. Ellison 2016b.
76. Ellison 2016.
77. Winter 2017.
78. "It is easy to forget, but Nestlé Waters North America, like any company, is made up of people. Here in Michigan, we employ approximately 280 people in the state who care about the environment and the well-being of their local communities, just like you do. They are good people who live, work and raise their families in the same communities where we operate, and for that reason, they are just as passionate as you are about protecting their neighbors and the natural resources of the area." (Nestlé Waters North America website 2018).
79. Foucault 1990.
80. Duffy and Clark 2017: 10:22.
81. United States Census Bureau (n.d.).
82. Duffy and Clark 2017: 7:41–8:01.
83. Duffy and Clark 2017: 8:58–9:30.
84. Duffy and Clark 2017: 9:57–10:45.
85. Ellison 2019.
86. Glenza 2016.
87. Stanley 2016: 7.
88. Gray 2018.
89. Duffy and Clark 2017: 2:08–2:40.
90. Ellison 2017.
91. Stanley 2016: 8.

92. Pacheco-Vega 2019: 3.
93. Shiva 2016: 1–2.
94. Ellison 2019.
95. Matheny 2019.
96. Szasz 2007.
97. Duffy and Clark 2017: 7:41–8:01.

References

Annin, P. (2018). *The Great Lakes Water Wars*. Washington, DC: Island Press.

Ashlock, A. (2019). " 'Years of Neglect' to Blame for Water Crisis in Rural Kentucky, State Rep Says." *Here & Now*. WBUR (Boston, MA). May 31, 2019. Available at: https://www.wbur.org/hereandnow/2019/05/31/kentucky-water-crisis (consulted May 31, 2019).

Baptiste, N. (2018). "Officials Say Flint's Water Is Safe. Residents Say It's Not. Scientists Say It's Complicated." *Mother Jones* (online magazine). Available at: https://www.motherjones.com/environment/2018/04/officials-say-flints-water-is-safe-residents-say-its-not-scientists-say-its-complicated/ (consulted July 23, 2019).

Barrows, M. (2017). "A Great Lakes Water War: Nestlé, the Great Lakes Compact, and the Future of Freshwater." *Freshwater Future* (blog). September 18, 2017. Available at: https://freshwaterfuture.org/policy-memo/a-great-lakes-water-war-nestle-the-great-lakes-compact-and-the-future-of-freshwater/ (consulted December 20, 2019).

Bosman, J., Davey, M., and Smith, M. (2016). "Flint Water Crisis: Emails Released by Gov. Rick Snyder." *New York Times*. January 20, 2016. Available at: https://www.nytimes.com/interactive/2016/01/20/us/document-Emails-Released-By-Michigan-Governor-Rick-Snyder.html (consulted July 20, 2019).

"By the Numbers: The Business of Bottled Water in Michigan." (2017). *Crain's Detroit Business*. April 1, 2017. Available at: https://www.crainsdetroit.com/article/20170401/NEWS/170339973/by-the-numbers-the-business-of-bottled-water-in-michigan (consulted July 14, 2019).

Byrd, A. (2018). "ICYMI: Nestle to Donate Water to Flint." *Colorlines: Race Forward*. May 14, 2018. Available at https://www.colorlines.com/articles/icymi-nestle-donate-water-flint (consulted October 2, 2019).

Center for Disease Control and Prevention. (n.d.). "Health Effects of Lead Exposure." Available at: https://www.cdc.gov/nceh/lead/prevention/health-effects.htm (consulted July 30, 2019).

Duffy, V. and Clark, Z. (2017). "Why a Local Government Official is Defending Nestlé's Water Pumping Plan." *Stateside*. Michigan Radio [FM-digital]. January 13, 2017.

Available from https://www.michiganradio.org/post/why-local-government-official-defending-Nestlé-s-water-pumping-plan (consulted July 12, 2019).

Ehrmann, C. (2019). "Cleanup of Michigan's Largest Superfund Site, Begun in 1998, Could Take 7 More Years." *MLive.com.* May 21, 2019. Available at: https://www.mlive.com/news/saginaw-bay-city/2019/05/cleanup-of-michigans-largest-superfund-site-begun-in-1998-could-take-7-more-years.html (consulted May 22, 2019).

Ellison, G. (2016). "deq Overruled Computer Model that Flunked Nestlé Groundwater Bid." *MLIVE.com.* November 22, 2016. Available at: https://www.mlive.com/news/2016/11/deq_overruled_computer_model_t.html (consulted July 23, 2019).

Ellison, G. (2016a). "More Pumping Could Harm Wetlands, Suggests Nestlé's Own Study." *Milive.com.* April 9, 2016. Available at: https://www.mlive.com/news/2017/04/nestle_evart_wetlands_impact.html (consulted July 23, 2019).

Ellison, G. (2016b). "Nestlé in Michigan: Unpacking the Water Battle Backstory." *MLive.com.* December 26, 2016. Available at: https://www.mlive.com/news/2016/12/Nestlé_water_michigan_backstor.html (consulted May 10, 2019).

Ellison, G. (2019). "Michigan Township Wins Appeal in Nestle Water Zoning Lawsuit." *Mlive.com.* December 3, 2019. Available at: https://www.mlive.com/news/2019/12/michigan-township-wins-appeal-in-nestle-water-zoning-lawsuit.html (consulted December 20, 2019).

Egan, P., Anderson, E., and Dolan, M. (2016). "A Year Ago, Snyder Aide Wanted Bottled Water for Flint." *Detroit Free Press.* February 26, 2016. Available at: https://www.freep.com/story/news/local/michigan/flint-water-crisis/2016/02/26/year-ago-snyder-aide-wanted-bottled-water-flint/80925488/ (consulted July 24, 2019).

"Emergency Manager." (n.d.). Michigan.gov website. Available at: https://www.michigan.gov/documents/snyder/EMF_Fact_Sheet2_347889_7.pdf (consulted July 14, 2019).

Finnegan, W. (2002). "Leasing the Rain." *New Yorker.* April 1, 2002. Available at: https://www.newyorker.com/magazine/2002/04/08/leasing-the-rain (consulted May 26, 2019).

Flint Water Crisis: Emails Released by Gov. Rick Snyder. (2016). *New York Times.* January 20, 2016. Available at: https://www.nytimes.com/interactive/2016/01/20/us/document-Emails-Released-By-Michigan-Governor-Rick-Snyder.html?searchResultPosition=7 (consulted August 12, 2019).

Fonger, R. (2018). "State Spending on Bottled Water in Flint Averaging $22,000 a Day." *MLive.com.* March 12, 2018. Available at: https://www.mlive.com/news/flint/2018/03/states_average_monthly_bottled.html (consulted May 10, 2019).

Foucault, M. (1990). "The Order of Discourse." In Bizell and Herzberg (eds.). *Rhetorical Traditions from the Classical Times to the Present*, pp. 1154–1164. New York, NY: St. Martin's Press.

Geist, M.E. (n.d.). "Another Legal Challenge for Nestlé Water Withdrawal." *Great Lakes Now* website. Available at: https://www.greatlakesnow.org/2018/06/another-legal-challenge-for-Nestlé-water-withdrawal/ (consulted July 4, 2019).

Glennon, R. (2009). *Unquenchable: America's Water Crisis and What to Do About it.* Washington, DC: Island Press.

Glenza, J. (2016). "Michigan Residents Deplore Plan to let Nestlé Pump Water for Next to Nothing." *The Guardian.* November 5, 2016. Available at: https://www.theguardian.com/us-news/2016/nov/05/michigan-nestle-water-extraction-residents (consulted December 20, 2019).

Gray, K. (2018). "Michigan OKs Nestle Permit for Increased Water Withdrawal for Bottled Water Plant." *Detroit Free Press.* April 2, 2018. Available at: https://www.freep.com/story/news/2018/04/02/michigan-oks-nestle-permit-increased-water-withdrawal-bottled-water-plant/479896002/ (consulted July 23, 2019).

Great Lakes Regional Water Use Database. (2017). *2017 BASIN Report.* Available at: https://waterusedata.glc.org/graph.php?type=basin&basin=2&year=2017&units=-gallons (consulted July 20, 2019).

Great Lakes-St. Lawrence River Water Resources Regional Body. (2017). *Agreements.* Available at: http://www.glslregionalbody.org/GLSLRBAgreements.aspx (consulted July 20, 2019).

Grether, H. (2018). "Nestlé Permit Decision is According to Rule of Law." *Lansing State Journal.* April 8, 2018. Available at: https://www.lansingstatejournal.com/story/opinion/contributors/viewpoints/2018/04/08/grether-nestle-permit-decision-according-rule-law/484823002/ (consulted July 23, 2019).

Ikonomova, V. (2018). "Nestlé on Criticism It's 'Exploiting' Flint: 'Water Is an Emotional Issue'." *Deadline Detroit.* November 17, 2018. Available at: http://www.deadlinedetroit.com/articles/21039/Nestlé_on_criticism_it_s_exploiting_flint_water_is_an_emotional_issue (consulted May 10, 2019).

Jackman, M. (2016). "Nestlé's Push to Pump More Water out of Michigan Meets Resistance." *Detroit Metro Times.* December 21, 2016. Available at: https://www.metrotimes.com/detroit/nestles-push-to-pump-more-water-out-of-michigan-meets-resistance/Content?oid=2477720 (consulted July 21, 2019).

Matheny, K. (2019). "State Court of Appeals Rules Against Nestle's Ice Mountain Bottled Water in Zoning Dispute." *Detroit Free Press.* December 3, 2019. Available at: https://www.freep.com/story/news/local/michigan/2019/12/03/nestle-ice-mountain-bottled-water-osceola-court-of-appeals-zoning/2598332001/ (consulted December 29, 2019).

Mecosta County Chamber of Commerce. (n.d.). *Ice Mountain Spring Water.* Available at: https://www.mecostacounty.com/list/member/ice-mountain-spring-water-stanwood-193 (consulted May 18, 2019).

Michigan State Department of Environment, Great Lakes, and Energy. (2019). *Nestlé Waters North America's Submittal of a Permit Application Information Package, under Section 17 of the Michigan Safe Drinking Water Act, 1976 PA 399, as amended.* Available at: https://www.michigan.gov/egle/0,4561,7-135-3313-399187--,00.html (consulted May 13, 2019).

Moore, K. (2016). "Mayor Weaver Announced Bottled Water Donation from Nestle." *City of Flint* (website). May 10, 2016. Available at: https://www.cityofflint.com/2018/05/10/mayor-weaver-announces-bottled-water-donation-from-nestle/ (consulted July 23, 2019).

Mullin, M. (2009). *Governing the Tap: Special District Governance and the New Local Politics of Water.* Cambridge MA: The MIT Press.

Nestlé Waters North America. (2019). "Facts about Nestlé Waters in Michigan." Available at: https://www.Nestlé-watersna.com/en/communities/your-community/michigan/know-the-michigan-ice-mountain-facts (consulted May 10, 2019).

Nestlé Waters North America website. (2018). "Bottled Water Donations to Flint, Michigan." YouTube. November 11, 2018. Available at: https://www.youtube.com/watch?v=REn5QclOcXA (consulted May 10, 2019).

Oostling, J. (2019). "Nestlé Extends Flint Bottled Water Donations." *Detroit News.* April 10, 2019. Available at: https://www.detroitnews.com/story/news/local/michigan/2019/04/10/Nestlé-extends-flint-bottled-water-donations/3426734002/ (consulted June 6, 2019).

Pacheco-Vega, R. (2019). "(Re)theorizing the Politics of Bottled Water: Water Insecurity in the Context of Weak Regulatory Regimes." *Water* 11(4): 658. https://doi.org/10.3390/w11040658.

Shiva, V. (2016). *Water Wars: Privatization, Pollution, and Profit.* Berkeley, CA: North Atlantic Books.

Slaymaker, T. and Bain, R. (2017). "Access to Drinking Water Around the World—In Five Infographics." *The Guardian.* March 17, 2017. Available at: https://www.theguardian.com/global-development-professionals-network/2017/mar/17/access-to-drinking-water-world-six-infographics (consulted May 19, 2019).

Stanley, J. (2016). "The Emergency Manager: Strategic Racism, Technocracy, and the Poisoning of Flint's Children." *The Good Society* 25(1): 1–45.

Szasz, A. (2007). *Shopping Our Way to Safety: How We Changed from Protecting the Environment to Protecting Ourselves.* Minneapolis, MN: University of Minnesota Press.

Taylor, C. (2018). *Nor Any Drop to Drink: Flint's Water Crisis.* Mount Pleasant, MI: Central Michigan University, FILM.

Tower, M. (2018). "Michigan Approves Controversial Nestle Water Pumping Permit." *MLive.com.* April 2, 2018. Available at: https://www.mlive.com/news/grand-rapids/2018/04/state_approves_nestles_controv.html (consulted July 4, 2019).

Winter, C. (2017). "Nestle Makes Billions Bottling Water It Pays Nearly Nothing For." *Bloomberg Businessweek.* September 21, 2017. Available at: https://www.bloomberg.com/news/features/2017-09-21/nestl-makes-billions-bottling-water-it-pays-nearly-nothing-for (consulted May 27, 2019).

Workman, C. and Ureksoy, H. (2017). "Water Insecurity in a Syndemic Context: Understanding the Psycho-Emotional Stress of Water Insecurity in Lesotho, Africa." *Social Science & Medicine* 179(1): 52–60.

United Nations. (2014). "International Decade for Action 'Water for Life' 2005-2015. Focus Areas: Water scarcity." Available at: https://www.un.org/waterforlifedecade/scarcity.shtml (consulted May 16, 2019).

United Nations. (n.d.). Water. "Scarcity." Available at: http://www.unwater.org/water-facts/scarcity/ (consulted May 22, 2019).

United States Census Bureau. (n.d.). "American FactFinder: Community Facts." Available at: https://factfinder.census.gov/faces/nav/jsf/pages/community_facts.xhtml?src=bkmk (consulted July 23, 2019).

United States Environmental Protection Agency. (2015). "Lead and Copper Rule [Policies and Guidance]." *epa.gov*. October 13, 2015. Available at: https://www.epa.gov/dwreginfo/lead-and-copper-rule (consulted July 22, 2019).

United States Environmental Protection Agency. (2017). "How We Use Water [Overviews and Factsheets]." *epa.gov*. January 16, 2017. Available at: https://www.epa.gov/watersense/how-we-use-water (consulted July 4, 2019).

United States Geological Survey. (n.d.). "Per Capita Water Use. Water Questions and Answers. USGS Water Science School." Available at: https://water.usgs.gov/edu/qa-home-percapita.html (consulted May 26, 2019).

U.S. Global Change Research Program. (n.d.). "Water Stress in the U.S." GlobalChange.gov website: https://www.globalchange.gov/browse/multimedia/water-stress-us (consulted July 14, 2019).

Zdanowicz, C. (2016). "Flint Family Uses 151 Bottles of Water Per Day." *CNN*. March 7, 2016. Available at: https://www.cnn.com/2016/03/05/us/flint-family-number-daily-bottles-of-water/index.html (consulted July 15, 2019).

CHAPTER 9

Lead Does (Not) Discriminate

Environmental Racism in Expert and Popular Discourse

Benjamin J. Pauli

When the Flint water crisis became national news toward the end of 2015, commentators were quick to conclude that the racial makeup of the city's population (about 57% African American) helped to explain it. No less an authority than "father" of environmental justice Robert Bullard described the crisis as "the classic case and a poster child for environmental racism" (Krajicek 2016), linking Flint to other communities across the United States with "the wrong complexion for protection" (Bullard 2016b).[1] "Environmental racism" became the term of choice in some quarters to capture both the causes and the effects of the crisis, a tendency that if anything grew stronger after former Governor Rick Snyder emphatically denied the term's relevance (Bixby 2016). Flint's poisoned water became the latest symbol of the vulnerability—indeed, disposability—of people of color in the United States, fitting neatly into the revived national discourse around racial injustice sparked by several high-profile killings of unarmed black men and the rise of the Black Lives Matter movement. Labeling the crisis "environmental racism" not only forced a reckoning with the racial consequences of the economic and political philosophies espoused by neoliberal technocrats like Snyder, but advanced the larger project of awakening the nation from its "colorblind" racial slumber to the reality of racial inequality. Flint showed that there is "racism in the water" in this country, wrote the Center for American Progress, but even more all-suffusingly, that "racism is in the air we breathe, flowing freely into our homes and down the stretch of blocks riddled with liquor stores but begging for a supermarket" (Solomon and Ross 2016).

The framing of the water crisis as "environmental racism" began to take off in earnest in January 2016, when the *New York Times* featured a front-page article by correspondent John Eligon entitled "A Question of Environmental Racism in Flint." (Indeed, it was in response to this article that Governor Snyder issued his denial.) Published just after Snyder's voluntary release of 274 pages

1 For more Bullard on Flint, see Wernick (2016) and Bullard (2016b).

of Flint-related emails, the article noted that they "included no discussion of race," and therefore no explicit evidence of racial animus. But it was "indisputable," wrote Eligon, "that in Flint, the majority of residents are black and many are poor," implying that this was reason enough to raise the specter of racism. When the *Times* editorial board chimed in two months later, after the release of the Flint Water Advisory Task Force's final report on the crisis, it kept the theme alive, highlighting the report's conclusion that the race *and* class of Flint's residents made them more vulnerable to environmental hazards, but again, like Eligon, giving the headline to "racism," which it placed "at the heart of Flint's crisis" (NYT Editorial Board 2016).

January 2016 also happened to be the month that I began what became two-and-a-half years of ethnographic research on water activism in Flint. Given the salience of the environmental racism frame in national coverage of, and commentary on, the water crisis at the time, one of my interests was to explore activists' feelings about the concept. I was already beginning to notice—and the fact only became more and more striking over time—that virtually none of what was being written about Flint and race included references to or citations of actual Flint residents describing their own crisis as "environmental racism." It was possible, of course, that this was mainly a product of the term's unfamiliarity to the average person—it was not difficult, after all, to find residents who saw racial significance in the crisis. Perhaps environmental racism was simply a useful way of summing up effects of the crisis that residents could see plainly with their own eyes, and of gesturing to causal factors (particularly, rampant disregard for people of color) that were equally self-evident to those living the crisis on the ground.

The fact that the term "environmental racism" was being introduced into the national conversation about the crisis mainly from outside the community, however, threw up a red, or at least a yellow, flag for me. As a matter of methodology and as an expression of my personal commitment to capturing and lifting up resident perspectives on the crisis, I was determined to remain as agnostic as possible about which analytical frames were the "right" ones as I focused on listening to, and learning from, resident activists in a prolonged and in-depth way. I was already growing wary of the tendency within academia and beyond to hold up Flint as the ultimate example of *X*, and by the spring of 2016 or so, it was not just "X" but a whole alphabet's worth of issues that Flint was supposed to exemplify. There was nothing inherently wrong with pointing to Flint as evidence of one thing or another, but I noticed that in the rush to fit Flint into pre-established conceptual frameworks and use it to advance agendas (scholarly or otherwise), many accounts of the crisis got key details wrong and engaged in omissions and oversimplifications that severely compromised (in my view) the usefulness of their analyses. Many also brushed right past resident perspectives, or at the most cherry-picked convenient quotes that were then treated as indicative of broader community sentiments.

The environmental racism frame was, at least, usually being put forward not just for analytical purposes, but by people who were clearly incensed by the indignities residents had suffered and who wished to act as allies, of sorts, by helping to crystallize and condemn the community's plight. I was already beginning to discover, however, that even well-meaning frames can have deleterious effects when they fit imperfectly with resident perspectives and are too much under the control of outsiders for their definition and propagation. A notable example, discussed at some length in my book *Flint Fights Back: Environmental Justice and Democracy in the Flint Water Crisis*,[2] is that of "citizen science." Around the same time that "environmental racism" became a go-to term to describe the crisis, the citizen science community was heralding the collaboration between Virginia Tech engineers and Flint activists that helped expose the city's lead contamination as a new "gold standard," exemplifying the use of publicly-oriented science to empower residents of marginalized communities and advance social justice. Activists found themselves being celebrated, all of the sudden, as "citizen scientists," and praised for doing research better than the "experts."

The term "citizen science" was, however, wholly unfamiliar to these activists prior to its introduction by the engineers involved, putting the latter in a privileged position to define and deploy it. While activists were able to make the citizen science frame work for their purposes at first, weaving it into a homegrown, populist discourse of grassroots democratic initiative, it became increasingly problematic as relations with the Virginia Tech team broke down. The engineers began to apply the (ostensibly) honorific "citizen scientist" label far more selectively, to loyal allies who were differentiated from mere "activists," and distinguished (supposedly) by their determination to follow evidence where it led rather than pushing political and personal agendas. Those who failed to live up to the standards of citizen science, as defined by the "experts," were denounced by those same experts as enemies of the truth, dishonest "crybullies" (Roy and Edwards 2019) who were (as Kevin Drum of *Mother Jones* wrote in an article enthusiastically retweeted by members of the Virginia Tech team) "bitter," "angry," "anti-science," and "tribal" (Drum 2019). Despite its veneer of grassroots empowerment, then, the language of "citizen science" revealed itself to be, fundamentally, an expert discourse privileging technical

2 See Pauli (2019: ch. 7).

skills and sensibilities, putting scientific authority figures in positions of control, and treating with contempt those deemed to fall short of external criteria of credibility.

Certainly, it was difficult to imagine the language of environmental racism being used quite so divisively. But the "citizen science" controversy did help to dramatize some of the issues that could arise from disjunctures between outsider frames and narratives controlled by expert types and the sensibilities, needs, and objectives of affected residents. To what extent, I began to wonder, might all the discussion of environmental racism be seen as a kind of expert discourse? Did residents who spoke of "racism" mean the same thing as academics and other interpreters of the crisis when the latter used the term? Could the environmental racism frame be deployed in ways that marginalized, contradicted, or delegitimized certain community perspectives? Could it be used in ways that interfered with community agendas? Could it be a source of conflict and division rather than a boon to the community's struggle? Not all of these questions were fully formulated in my mind in early 2016, but I was, at the very least, on the lookout for incongruities between environmental racism discourse and the views on race I encountered in the community.

Uses of the concept of environmental racism by outside commentators in reference to Flint have tended to share some common features, two of which I highlight here. Firstly, they often treat racism as a concept that can, and even should, be detached from the intentions of individual actors. From this perspective, racially discriminatory outcomes are generated not by present-day, conscious racial animus but by historically accumulated, "structural" features of society and of the human mind (e.g. subconscious, or "implicit" biases that influence cognition surreptitiously). Secondly, they often imply or state outright that Flint is an *obvious* case of environmental racism.[3] They ask us to assume that those who deny it must, presumably, be doing so for some sort of unenlightened, self-interested or ideological reason (à la Snyder, allegedly), without seriously exploring whether there might be defensible reasons for doing so.

In what follows, I draw from my interviews and ethnographic interactions with water activists and other residents[4] to reveal an expert/popular

3 For a prominent example, see Hanna-Attisha (2019).

4 The methodology used to arrive at my conclusions is explained more fully in the Introduction to *Flint Fights Back*. Here I wish simply to make a couple of points about my data, which is gleaned from personal interviews, interviews conducted by others, and ethnographic observations. Firstly, I do not mean to suggest that my sample of resident/activist perspectives is representative of the "community" as a whole, although I do have reason to believe that most of the views described in this chapter were and are widespread in Flint. Secondly, we must

disjuncture around both of these aspects of the environmental racism frame. I found, firstly, that those residents and activists who were apt to racialize the crisis were far less likely or willing than the "experts" to dispense with the phenomenon of conscious racist intent. Popular claims that the crisis was a racial affair often incorporated the belief that decision-makers consciously desired to rid the city of people of color (*not* just that they undervalued black and brown lives in a general way). More generally, residents were very much alive to the possibility that specific acts of intentional discrimination could be pinned on particular people, a possibility sometimes downplayed or marginalized by a focus on "structural" and/or "implicit" factors. I also, however, encountered a competing popular tendency—strong among water activists, in particular—to deemphasize the significance of race altogether, or even treat racialized framings of the crisis with open hostility. Those who adopted this attitude sometimes experienced environmental racism discourse not as a boon to their struggle but as an agenda-driven misrepresentation of it that obscured certain kinds of harm and created or exacerbated divisions within the community.

These two popular tendencies may have pointed in opposite directions, but what interests us here is what they share: both are in tension with expert perspectives on race that have often carried farther than local voices in the discourse around the water crisis. The fact that these latter voices have not been adequately heard, even with all the attention paid to the crisis, should give us pause on three fronts. First of all, their very existence should lead us to question whether "expert" analytical frameworks may have missed something, or multiple somethings, that have led people on the ground to conclusions different from those of people on the outside looking in. This is especially true if we are willing to acknowledge that so-called "laypeople" often possess expertise of their own, borne of intimate acquaintance with the issues that touch their everyday lives. Second, we should consider whether the assumptions and emphases of expert frameworks themselves may be partly to blame for such oversights. Could it be that the analytical tools used by experts actually tolerate

remember that views evolve over time—what someone says in an interview in 2016 may not be the same as what they would say in 2020. In my interactions with residents and activists, I occasionally encountered evidence of unstable and even contradictory views about environmental racism, or at least different responses to environmental racism discourse depending on the context. Consequently, it is not sufficient to pile up quotes as evidence of particular strains of thought within the community—the act of interpretation on the part of the scholar is essential, and, in my view, interpretation is best honed through prolonged ethnographic immersion.

or even encourage certain kinds of blind spots, even as they purport to illuminate? Finally, we should be reminded of the representational power exercised whenever expert analysis takes precedence over popular discourse in characterizations of a complex social phenomenon. Our depictions of the injustice of the Flint water crisis are not just collections of truth claims but interventions into a situation where lives are at stake and where much effort has already been invested by the people affected in developing an understanding of, and story about, what is going on. Representations of injustice have real consequences for real people, and consideration of their effects from the vantage point of those in the thick of the struggle should be as essential as any other consideration in determining when, how, and why we offer them to the world.

1 A (Relatively) Brief Conceptual History of "Environmental Racism"

It is beyond the scope of this chapter to offer a full history of the term "environmental racism," and any attempt to assemble even a summary account is complicated by the fact that the term (like the related term "environmental justice") has been used in a variety of ways, with different definitions sometimes becoming the subject of open disagreement (Holifield 2001). Consequently, I will focus on what I see as most significant about the development and usage of the term for the present discussion, and any generalizations I make should be seen as approximate.

It is generally agreed that the person responsible for inventing and popularizing the term "environmental racism" in the 1980s is Reverend Benjamin Chavis, Jr., a civil rights leader who oversaw the landmark United Church of Christ study *Toxic Waste and Race in the United States of America*, widely seen as the first statistical confirmation of nationwide racial discrimination in toxic waste siting. As Brulle (2000) and others have noted, the existence of racial disparities in environmental quality and toxic exposure was already known to some scholars and activists,[5] but "environmental racism" provided useful conceptual glue whereby pioneering studies of racially-tinged siting decisions (like Robert Bullard's work on waste distribution in Houston)[6] and struggles

5 Brulle (2000: 215–217) usefully traces anticipations of environmental racism discourse back into the 1970s, when people like Nathan Hare (1970) were already raising concerns about how the predominantly white environmental movement was overlooking the environmental issues faced by people of color.

6 Bullard's pioneering 1983 study of solid waste siting in Houston concluded that "institutionalized discrimination through the siting of waste disposal facilities has systematically provided social and economic advantages for whites at the expense of blacks, because whites

against particular polluting facilities and landfills (like the infamous PCB dump in Warren County, North Carolina)[7] were linked to the same, broader phenomenon. The value of the term, then, was at least twofold: it put a name to the burgeoning scholarly effort to document and explain disproportionate environmental burdens endured by people of color, and it offered a common idiom to activists working on locally-rooted issues of contamination who were coming to see themselves as part of the same movement.

Early exponents of the environmental racism frame were especially concerned to demonstrate that race had an effect on siting decisions independently of class. Several studies, including the *Toxic Waste* report, found that the racial makeup of a community was in fact more significant than class demographics in predicting siting locations. While it became conventional to mention race and class in the same breath when characterizing environmentally-disadvantaged populations (as in the many descriptions of Flint as "black" and "poor"), the overall tendency was to foreground race and treat it as the more fundamental variable. Indeed, the environmental justice movement as a whole, especially when its genesis was traced back to Warren County (as opposed to, say, Love Canal) was often depicted as an outgrowth of the civil rights movement, having extended a decades-long struggle against racism into new areas of racial oppression. It was natural enough, then, from this perspective, that people of color, specifically, should be the ones gathering in Washington, DC in 1991 to craft the influential "17 Principles of Environmental Justice."

The increasing popularity of the term "environmental justice" of course raised the question of its relationship to environmental racism. Was environmental justice simply the opposite of environmental racism? Some, at least, implied as much when they began to use the terms "environmental racism" and "environmental injustice" interchangeably (e.g., Cole and Foster 2001: 15). Others, however, preferred environmental justice/injustice for their more inclusive ring, using them to describe a variety of popular struggles against environmental contamination, including in majority white communities.[8] One possibility was to look at environmental racism as one *type* of environmental

do not live around or send their children to schools near landfills" (285–286). He did not use the term "racism" to describe this practice, but did point out that sitings were political decisions and that prior to 1970 Houston had never had a person of color on its city council. Private sitings, he suggested, tended to follow the pattern established by public ones.

7 See Bullard (2000) and McGurty (2009).

8 Laura Pulido (1996b) wrote that the environmental justice movement was "a *multiracial* struggle" but "increasingly, a distinct but prominent submovement is being formed that is limited to people of color" (17).

injustice among others, analogous to "environmental sexism"[9] or "environmental classism." In practice, however, terms like these did not acquire the cachet that environmental racism continued to enjoy with many scholars and activists.

Because of its continued popularity, even as "environmental racism" was supplemented (or, in some cases, supplanted) by the more generic term "environmental justice," it underwent considerable conceptual refinement in the decades subsequent to its coining. It is of some importance to this discussion that from its earliest days, the concept, like the concept of environmental justice, was shaped by a variety of people from different walks of life: academics, national environmental organizations and agencies, as well as people on the ground in affected communities. Neither term, in other words, was ever monopolized by "experts"; as important as academics were to imbuing them with credibility, they always had an aura of advocacy and activism (one reason why some scholars have approached them with skepticism). In 1993, Stella Čapek noted that "environmental justice," as a "conceptual construction, or interpretive 'frame'" was being "fashioned simultaneously from the bottom up (local grass-roots groups discovering a pattern to their grievances) and from the top down (national organizations conveying the term to local groups)," (5) and was becoming prominent in "both popular and academic discourses" (6). Around the same time, Marc Poirier (1994) noted the existence of a "learned discourse" and a "folk discourse" around environmental justice, equity,[10] and racism (EJER), pointing out that "Some of these contemporary articulations of EJER are academic and derivative and have little direct relation with the grassroots of [EJER], or with the folk discourses that make the grassroots organizing and politics possible. Others are much closer to the grassroots, especially where the

9 As Gaard (2010) writes: "Structurally analogous to environmental sexism, environmental racism involves a conceptual association between people of color and nature that marks their dual subordination" (64).

10 I mention the term "environmental equity" only in passing in this chapter, but in some ways its history is instructive for our purposes. After it became the EPA's term of choice in the early 1990s to frame the issue of discriminatory siting, some criticized it for its implication that the issue could be solved through the "equal sharing of risk burdens, not an overall reduction in the burdens themselves." Environmental justice, by contrast, was seen as "a more politically charged term, one that connotes some remedial action to correct an injustice imposed on a specific group of people" (Cutter 1995: 112). The discourse around environmental equity is, perhaps, a better example of an "expert" discourse than environmental racism discourse in that it was embraced and promoted from the top-down, it involved a somewhat technocratic narrowing of the issue at stake, and it was actively contrasted by critics with more popular, and radical, ways of framing and combatting environmental inequality.

individual authors are also involved in some way with specific EJER struggles" (1098).

Notably, although commentators like Čapek and Poirier differentiated between bottom up/top down, local/national, popular/academic, folk/learned uses or definitions of the terms environmental justice and environmental racism, they did not remark on the potential for tensions to arise from these dichotomies. It is worth keeping that potential in mind, however, as we trace the further development of the latter term.

Perhaps the most notable strain within the conceptual evolution of environmental racism was the growing tendency to separate the concept from conscious racist intent. Early definitions of the term suggested that "active racial bias" (Kevin 1997: 125) was behind siting proposals and environmental impact reviews that deleteriously affected communities of color. Chavis's widely-cited 1994 definition, for example, explicitly stated that environmental racism involved the "deliberate" targeting of such communities by would-be polluters, while Bunyan Bryant's 1995 definition used the same language.[11] The underlying claim was that the cultural, political, and economic marginalization of people of color makes it easier to get away with subjecting them to unwanted environmental hazards because majority-minority communities are less able to fight back and less likely than white communities to be taken seriously when they do.

It is significant, however, that the racial bias posited by these definitions does not necessarily imply a conscious desire to cause injury, much less a specifically racial kind of injury. It is possible to see even racialized harms resulting from race-conscious decision-making as byproducts of other motivations. As Daniel Faber (2018) writes, "It is not necessarily anyone's intention to inflict harm upon working-class whites or people of color when siting hazardous operations. The primary goal of capital is instead to seek out the cheap land, favorable zoning laws, less regulation, good infrastructure, and a community less

11 Chavis (1994: xii): "Environmental racism is racial discrimination in environmental policy-making and enforcement of regulations and laws, the *deliberate targeting* of communities of color for toxic waste facilities, the official sanctioning of the presence of life threatening poisons and pollutants for communities of color, and the history of excluding people of color from leadership of the environmental movement" [emphasis mine]. Bryant (1995: 6): "[Environmental racism] is an extension of racism. It refers to those institutional rules, regulations, and policies of government or corporate decisions that *deliberately target* certain communities for least desirable land uses, resulting in the disproportionate exposure of toxic and hazardous waste on communities based upon prescribed biological characteristics. Environmental racism is the unequal protection against toxic and hazardous waste exposure and the systematic exclusion of people of color from decisions affecting their communities" [emphasis mine].

likely to offer opposition" (16). In practice, then, accusations of racism in siting decisions could be met with a whole host of other explanations for those decisions. Further complicating matters, some scholars began to point out that in many cases polluting facilities were actually constructed prior to people of color settling in the communities that were supposedly targeted.

Some tried to keep the argument from intent alive by identifying cases in which minority populations came first and pollution later (for a review, see Mohai and Saha 2015). Concerns began to grow, however, that environmental racism was being defined too narrowly, particularly as legal claims of environmental racism started getting thrown out of court for failure to demonstrate smoking-gun proof of discriminatory intent (see Pulido 2000; Cole and Foster 2001; Holifield 2001). Bullard was the most influential figure during the formative years of the environmental racism concept to stress that intent was not necessary for environmental racism to exist, defining the phenomenon as "any policy, practice, or directive that, intentionally or unintentionally, differentially impacts or disadvantages individuals, groups, or communities based on race or color" (1993b: 6). Making intent optional in this way encouraged broader analysis of the procedures and institutions implicated in environmental decision-making, rather than a hunt for bad actors, and implied that the colorblindness of decision-makers themselves was no guarantee of racially just outcomes.

Picking up from Bullard's work, Laura Pulido (2000) has been especially critical of the "de facto conception" of environmental racism "based on malicious, individual acts" and has led the charge to infuse environmental racism scholarship with a more sophisticated outlook sensitive to the complex and multifaceted ways race and racism operate. In the early 2000s, she began to employ the concept of "white privilege" to encourage a "more structural, less conscious, and more deeply historicized understanding of racism" focused on "the privileges and benefits that accrue to white people by virtue of their whiteness," including environmental "goods" of various kinds. This kind of analysis of racial inequality is "rooted in the past," as Pulido puts it, illuminating the ways in which contemporary choices are made within—and inevitably shaped by—racialized spaces and institutions that have built up over decades.[12] Pulido also invoked the concept of "implicit bias" to draw attention to the calcified prejudices inherited from previous generations that exert subconscious influences

12 As Cole and Foster (2001) put it, "Even if society were to purge itself of racism and become color-blind, and people were to behave purely as rational economic actors in their choices of mobility and residential location, racially segregated space would still persist today absent affirmative efforts to dismantle the vestiges of historical racism" (67).

on behavior in the present, whether or not an individual intends to be "racist" (see Banaji and Greenwald 2013).

The turn toward concepts like "white privilege" and "implicit bias," Pulido (2000) wrote, entailed a deliberate rejection of " 'common sense' assumptions that reflect uncritical, popular understandings of racism," once again implying a divide—or at least the possibility of one—between an expert and a popular discourse around environmental racism. At the very least, the more that historical analysis of social space and institutions, as well as subtle exploration of psychological processes, became necessary to reveal modern-day racism, the more the average person became dependent on experts confirming whether, and for what reasons, any particular phenomenon was "racist." From what I can tell, the implications for those on the "popular" side of being in that rather disempowered position have received very little comment in the literature.

In more recent years, Pulido has grown dissatisfied with the concept of "white privilege" for its implication that whites benefit from racism almost incidentally (as in the well-known "knapsack" metaphor—see McIntosh 1988). After seeking to distance environmental racism from intentionality, she and others have looked for ways to bring the latter back in, though more subtly than before. That subtlety may not be immediately evident in the new term of choice, "white supremacy" (which undoubtedly conjures up images of the overt racism of past eras), but the term is regularly applied to phenomena which, while involving proactive behavior of some kind, are not explicitly racist—attempts to avoid environmental regulations, for example, that have the effect of further disadvantaging minority communities. More broadly, the point is to "emphasize the role of whites in actively producing the system of [white] privilege" through "their participation in a range of social, cultural, and economic processes" (Inwood 2018: 3). The term "racial capitalism"—first developed by the political scientist Cedric Robinson in the 1980s—has brought special emphasis to economic processes, highlighting the ways in which the production of racial inequalities and devaluation of people of color are integrated into supposedly race-neutral market processes and interactions. Relatedly, Wayne State University law professor Peter Hammer (2017) has placed the Flint water crisis at the intersection of "structural racism" and "strategic racism," defining the latter as conscious efforts to exploit vulnerabilities and opportunities with roots in cumulative racial disadvantage. Hammer maintains that anyone who profits economically or politically off the legacy of racism or racial inequality is acting as a "strategic" racist, "regardless of whether the actor has express racist intent" (2). He has argued, provocatively, that some of the key decisions leading up to the Flint water crisis—notably, the financial finagling involved in the construction of the Karegnondi water pipeline to Lake Huron—evidence precisely this kind of strategically racist action.

Actions that are white supremacist or strategically racist in the manner described above are conscious, intentional, and result in racial harms that could and probably should be predicted by those who engage in them, even if they do not go as far as the "deliberate" targeting of minority communities first hypothesized by environmental racism scholars. Still, the actors in question do not, from what we can tell, *mean* to cause racial harm, even if we might be inclined to see them as acting negligently, recklessly, or exploitatively. In other words, while intent has found its way back into environmental racism discourse, directing our attention to the active complicity of present-day actors in perpetuating racial inequality, contemporary accounts of environmental racism do not require—or, necessarily, imply—that racial animus is much of a factor in the present. Those who have applied concepts like white supremacy to the Flint water crisis have generally, like Ranganathan (2016), pushed back against crisis narratives that focus on "individual racist intent" (23), sometimes taking it as their explicit premise that the decision-making process around Flint's water was "color-blind" (Robinson, Shum, and Singh 2018: 315).

2 Racism in the Water?: Expert and Popular Perspectives on Race and the Flint Water Crisis

The historical orientation of contemporary approaches to racial analysis is reflected in a number of accounts of the Flint water crisis that locate its roots deep in the city's past (e.g. Highsmith 2015; Sadler and Highsmith 2016; Stanley 2016; Pulido 2016; Ranganathan 2016; Clark 2017; MCRC 2017; Cassano and Benz 2019). These accounts point to factors like the role of racially restrictive housing covenants, redlining, and educational segregation in shaping Flint's racial geography, fostering latent tensions that erupted into the open during the civil rights era and contributed to the massive white flight the city experienced from the 1960s on. The exodus of white residents—encouraged by the "strategic" racism of opportunistic real estate agents urging them to sell their homes—and the resulting atrophy of Flint's tax base comprised one major strain of the "abandonment" (to use Pulido's language) that the city suffered over the years. A number of commentators have pinpointed racist housing practices in particular as important links in the crisis's causal chain: Clark and Kramer (2017), for example, write that housing discrimination "led to" the water crisis, while Ranganathan (2016) deems "racialized property dispossession" a "major factor underlying the city's financial duress, abandonment, and poisoned infrastructure" (17), with Flint's infamously misguided urban renewal and highway construction projects only compounding the problem.

Depopulation resulting from shifting racial geographies is, however, only one of the "[n]umerous political and economic shifts" that "led to Flint's financial crises" (Pulido 2016: 8). Pulido points out that the city was also abandoned by capital, as General Motors took advantage of the economic liberalization brought about by globalization to move the bulk of its operation away from Michigan's strong labor unions to more lucrative parts of the country and world, resulting in almost total deindustrialization in Flint and massive job loss. Within the logic of racial capitalism, the residents of Flint became a "surplus" population, with their racial devaluation and their economic devaluation being "mutually constituted" (1). The neoliberal state only contributed to the abandonment—and to the general impression that the city was no longer worth investing in—by withdrawing critical financial support in the form of revenue sharing (Stanley 2016; Hammer 2017), leaving Flint largely at the mercy of private financiers. Pulido argues that this state abandonment also extended to environmental protection and enforcement—again, on the premise that a whiter (and wealthier) community would have been more likely to inspire concern in state and federal environmental watchdogs.

Flint's historical trajectory of rapid growth followed by rapid decline created a situation in which its water infrastructure was oversized and underused, increasingly dilapidated, and prohibitively costly to repair given limited resources at the local level. It also created the preconditions for the State of Michigan's declaration of financial emergency in Flint and takeover of the city's government in December 2011. The law that enabled this takeover—Michigan's "emergency manager law"—has also proven ripe for racial analysis. Many have noted its disproportionate impact on minority communities: around 50 percent of Michigan's African American population has at one time or another lived under an emergency manager, compared to 2 percent of its white population, with one study finding that cities with a higher percentage of African Americans are more likely to receive an emergency manager even when controlling for class (Kirkpatrick and Breznau 2016). This conclusion has been taken as evidence that the law's racially-neutral language of "fiscal accountability" is in fact an example of what is sometimes called "symbolic racism," concealing coded assumptions about majority-black communities being especially inept at managing finances and needing paternalistic intervention.

Efforts to trace the racial origins of the water crisis into historical, structural, strategic, and symbolic domains resonated in significant ways with the popular perspectives I encountered in Flint. Certainly, consciousness of Flint's long history of racial injustice fueled the indignation that many residents felt about the crisis, and it was not difficult to find evidence that their palpable sense of abandonment often had a specifically racial character. It was also clear that people were well aware of certain structural disadvantages the city faced, given that its majority-black population was geographically surrounded by—and in many ways politically and economically beholden to—whites with different agendas and interests than the average Flint resident. Additionally, Peter Hammer's analysis of the "strategic" racism behind the Karegnondi pipeline attracted some enthusiastic interest within the activist community, and on multiple occasions I heard activists themselves articulate the idea that the discourse around "fiscal accountability" involved a kind of dog-whistle indictment of African Americans' financial competence and capacity for self-governance. Indeed, popular criticisms of the emergency manager law often played up its racially discriminatory character (one image that circulated on social media portrayed Governor Snyder as a slave-driver lashing majority-black cities across the state into submission), and characterized cities under the law as having reverted to pre-civil rights-era disenfranchisement of African Americans. Pulling some of these threads together, Flint activist Nayyirah Shariff argued that the water crisis was caused by "environmental racism, white supremacy, patriarchal decision-making, capitalism and the belief that needs of a large corporation like General Motors [which got special permission to disconnect from Flint's municipal water system in 2014] are more important than the needs of poor black and brown communities who can't afford to pay $200 a month for water."[13]

When an activist like Shariff described the water crisis in some of the same terms (e.g., "environmental racism," "white supremacy") used by academics and journalists, it understandably gave the impression of strong alignment between expert and popular, outsider and insider perspectives on the crisis. In my experience, however, that degree of concordance was atypical. For one thing, it was unusual (as mentioned earlier) to hear the water activists I knew using this specific terminology (Shariff was the exception rather than the rule). More importantly, there were strong indications that the way the terms were being employed on the expert side clashed, in some respects, with popular sensibilities in Flint itself.

The most instructive point of contact between expert and popular views on race to emerge from the water crisis was the final report of the Michigan Civil Rights Commission (MCRC), *The Flint Water Crisis: Systemic Racism through*

13 Shariff made her remark during testimony at a Congressional environmental justice hearing in Detroit in September 2019. Video is available from: https://www.youtube.com/watch?v=02mWk883O2A.

the Lens of Flint, released in February 2017 and informed by a combination of expert testimony, academic scholarship, and resident comments across three hearings in Flint. The context surrounding the report was significant: two other reports by state-sponsored investigative committees had already come and gone without having convinced residents (by most indications) that the State of Michigan was seriously committed to doing right by the city. While a number of criminal charges had by that time been filed by the Attorney General's office, no official had yet faced any legal consequences for their actions, and with some experts on the scientific side effectively beginning to declare Flint's water back to normal, residents and activists were feeling increasingly desperate for concrete signs of accountability and validation of their sense of the severity of the crisis.

The MCRC framed its hearings to residents as being part of an effort "to determine if any actions resulting in the poisoning of Flint's public water supply abridged your civil rights under state law" (iv). This way of characterizing the investigation raised the obvious hope that specific officials would be charged with specific offenses, particularly racial discrimination of some kind, a hope further kindled by the Commission's "unreserved and undeniable" conclusion that race was "a factor in the Flint Water Crisis" (6). The crux of the matter, however, was what *kind* of factor race was taken to be. The MCRC wrote that its finding was based not on "any particular event," but "on a plethora of events and policies that so racialized the structure of public policy that it systemically produced racially disparate outcomes adversely affecting a community primarily made up of people of color" (6). Just as the report shied away from emphasizing specific events, it declined to assign blame to specific people (rather confusingly suggesting that this was never the Commission's intention, despite its supposed search for civil rights violations):[14] "We are not suggesting," reads the report, "that those making decisions related to this crisis were racists, or meant to treat Flint any differently because it is a community primarily made up by people of color" (2). Taking inspiration from expert testimony, the MCRC argued that a finding of overt and intentional discrimination was not necessary in order to describe the crisis as "environmental racism":

> The Commission believes that finding environmental racism does not require that government's motives be racial, or that government actors be racists. Environmental racism occurs when people of color repeatedly

14 Citing other open investigations into the culpability of specific actors, the MCRC said its report was "not meant to assess blame, but to help ensure that such a crisis does not occur in the future and to address shortcomings that continue to persist over time" (4).

> suffer disproportionate risks and harms from policies and decisions that equally benefit all.
>
> MCRC 2017: 93

Having declined to single out any present-day actions or actors, the Commission instead proposed to "look back much further"—"nearly a century," in fact—at "historical and systemic" "practices, laws and norms" that "fostered and perpetuated separation of race, wealth and opportunity," approaching the crisis as a result of "systemic racism that was built into the foundation and growth of Flint, its industry and the suburban area surrounding it" (2). While the report's ensuing effort to trace Flint's racial history had the effect of making race loom larger within the grand narrative of the crisis, its broad historical brushstrokes touched only lightly upon the fine-grain decision-making comprising the most proximate causes of the crisis (e.g., decisions about water source and treatment). What many in Flint hoped would be an exercise in accountability became, largely, a history lesson, spreading responsibility for the crisis across a vast expanse of space and time and an equally expansive array of actors. Insofar as the MCRC sought to address racial discrimination in the present, it did so—taking its cue from academic scholarship—by way of the concept of "implicit bias." In other words, insofar as racial bias was a factor within the decision-making chain leading up to the crisis, it was exerting a subterranean influence contrary to the conscious intent of the individual decision-maker.

From the perspective of the "expert" literature on environmental racism, the MCRC's adoption of a more historical, "systemic" approach to explaining racial disparity, as well as its invocation of subconscious factors, might be seen as laudable efforts to encourage more sophisticated racial analyses rather than wild goose chases for elusive proof of racist intent. From the perspective of an expectant Flint resident or activist, however, the end consequences of this approach were at the very least anticlimactic. Not only did the report's sweeping historical analysis fail to offer much ammunition to residents making targeted demands for accountability, the recommendations it resulted in fell short in notable respects of the demands coming out of the local activist community at the same time.[15] As the Flint Democracy Defense League's Claire McClinton put it, the report "didn't match the severity of the situation we're in ... I think they talked themselves into being timid" (Karoub 2017).

15 For example, demands for a federal disaster declaration, for total abolition of the emergency manager law, and for charges to be filed against Governor Snyder.

The more fundamental divide, however, between the Commission's perspective and the community's (if I may generalize) was around the question of racial animus. Technically, the MCRC's position on animus was agnostic—as it wrote in a footnote, "We do not find that there was no overt racism, only that to date we have not found evidence to establish it played a role" (20). But by creating a dichotomy between overt racism and implicit bias—as if people are either consciously and openly racist or, as it were, accidentally racist—the Commission's report essentially rendered invisible a fairly sizable genre of popular thinking about race, wherein decision-makers harbor conscious racial prejudices and, in various ways, act on them without admitting it. In my own comments to the MCRC, I suggested that for all intents and purposes it was rather peremptorily jumping to the conclusion that racially discriminatory outcomes were unintended just because incriminating evidence to the contrary was not readily available, overlooking completely the phenomenon of "covert" bias.[16] Just over three months later, an activist journalist recorded an inebriated Genesee County Land Bank official saying the water crisis was caused by "niggers not paying their bills." In Inwood's (2018) reading of this incident, the remark illustrates an attempt to construct "white innocence," whereby whites are exonerated for their role in creating the system in which people of color find it difficult to pay bills and communities of color find it difficult to maintain their infrastructure. Missing totally from the analysis, however, is the significance that the comment had to the scandalized residents of Flint: it was a revelation of—more accurately, *confirmation* of—behind-the-scenes, conscious racism that for all anyone knew was influencing any number of decisions.

The particular official in this case was not directly involved in water matters, but the fact that the remark had come from someone at the Land Bank was full of symbolic significance that cut to the heart of the expert/popular divide. When some residents—quite a few, by my reckoning—described the water crisis as "intentional" (a term employed almost ubiquitously), their point was not just that there were surely some bad apples in powerful positions with covert biases, or that the state had knowingly allowed water of questionable quality to flow through Flint's pipes (even Pulido [2016] calls the poisoning of residents "intentional" on this basis), but that the crisis was part of a *conscious and systematic effort to drive people of color out of the city of Flint.* Implicated in that agenda, according to some popular perceptions, anyway, were institutions like the Land Bank, the largest landholder in Flint; the C.S. Mott Foundation,

16 My comments to the Commission are referenced in Worth-Nelson (2017).

a major influence on the city's "master plan" and on local development schemes; local universities like Kettering (the largest private landowner in Flint) and the University of Michigan-Flint; and the State of Michigan, at least under the Snyder administration.[17] The residents I encountered posited the existence of this agenda with varying degrees of fervor, consistency, and literalness (depending, in part, on whose company they were in), but without understanding its grip on the popular imagination—particularly within Flint's African-American community—we are poorly equipped to understand what "racism" meant to many of the people actually experiencing the crisis.

The MCRC was aware enough that some residents saw the crisis as "genocidal" to feel the need to address the claim in its final report. Without giving residents space to explain the significance they saw in the term, the Commission summarily defined "genocide" as a "deliberate and organized effort targeting the extermination of a (racial/political/cultural) group" (20). This definition not only ignored the nuances of local perspectives, it also ignored the subtler ways in which the term has been employed historically, particularly by African Americans,[18] as well as popular discourses around gentrification (the ostensible objective of the institutions mentioned above) as a kind of genocide. In fact, the MCRC used the bulk of the brief paragraph allotted to the subject to reiterate—twice—the Commission's refrain that it had found no evidence of "deliberate targeting or intent to harm" (20), before moving on.

The consequences of this dismissive—and rather incurious—attitude toward popular, intent-based analyses of the crisis became clear during a particularly dramatic moment in the MCRC's official proceedings. On the day of the final report's release, the Commission held two public meetings to announce its findings—one during the day and one in the evening. I was only able to attend the evening meeting, and the commissioner officiating made it clear that there had been some controversy earlier in the day. Drawing largely from the historian Andrew Highsmith's analysis of the regional factors contributing to Flint's economic and political disempowerment, the MCRC had recommended establishing a form of "regional government" that could correct the

17 These institutions comprised at least some of the "they" referenced by activists like Nakiya Wakes, who told me that "they" wanted "all African Americans up out of Flint" (Pauli 2019: 139). Other examples of this kind of thinking can be found in Chapter 5 of Pauli (2019).

18 Consider the 1951 petition to the United Nations by the Civil Rights Congress, *We Charge Genocide: The Crime of Government against the Negro People*, which built off the UN's more nuanced definition of genocide in applying the concept to the predicament of African Americans.

imbalance between Flint and its suburbs. By all appearances the Commission was not aware of how deeply some residents opposed the idea of regionalization, widely seen as a means of absorbing Flint's mostly-black residents into mostly-white Genesee County and popping their fragile bubble of political power—nor was the Commission aware (apparently) that some residents thought the water crisis would be exploited as an opportunity to do just that. Having faced some popular anger earlier in the day, prior to public comment the presiding commissioner warned the residents who had come out for the evening meeting that he would not tolerate any more "bitching" about regionalization. The expert analysis of Flint's "systemic" challenges, derived mainly from academic scholarship, was to be heard; popular voices fearful that this analysis was flawed or incomplete were to be silent.

If popular racializations of the crisis that accorded a central place to racist intent were one kind of silence within the discourse around environmental racism, there was another silence very evident to me from my position within the activist community: namely, any acknowledgement at all that some Flint residents might have good reason for *not* racializing the crisis, or might even be annoyed, offended, or disadvantaged by outsider attempts to do so. In my interviews and ethnographic interactions, I found that activists were often considerably less eager than outside commentators to frame the crisis as a product of racism. This attitude was usually comprised of one or more of three distinct (but often intertwined) elements: firstly, a belief that describing the crisis as a specifically racial injustice was empirically wrong, secondly, a belief that racial frames obscured, denied, or downplayed harms done to white residents, and thirdly, a belief that emphasizing race was disruptive to movement unity and that activists' objectives were better served by talking about harm in more inclusive ways.

Many of the Flint residents and activists who felt it was wrong to frame the crisis as a "black" issue pointed to the fact that water quality problems had been distributed across the entire city: all were exposed to contamination, all were affected, or at least potentially affected.[19] No particular racial pattern emerged from activists' early attempts to plot out evidence of bad water geographically, nor did one surface in official data or scientific findings on lead or any other contaminant.[20] Claims that the water was "killing all of us," that

19 Cuthbertson et al. (2016) report that some residents they surveyed believed African Americans (and lower-income people) were being harder hit by the crisis, but they offer no data to show how prevalent this sentiment was.

20 With respect to lead, Sadler, LaChance and Hanna-Attisha (2017) found that numerous other variables were more strongly correlated with blood lead than the percentage of black population in a given area, including house age, neighborhood housing condition,

"everyone of every race has been affected," that "lead does not discriminate," were commonplace, and were sometimes explicitly juxtaposed to efforts by outsiders to portray the crisis in racial terms (Pauli 2019: 139–140).

Of course, many depictions of the crisis as an example of environmental racism hinged not so much on the existence of disparate harms within Flint's population as they did on the premise that the city as a whole—a majority-black city—had suffered unusual harm relative to other cities.[21] This empirical claim was usually accompanied by a causal one linking the origins of

---

water age, socioeconomic distress, and vacancy rates, commenting that the minimal correlation they found with race was "encouraging" (765). This conclusion comported with research showing no difference in water lead levels across zip codes (Pieper et al., 2018). As for health effects, Abouk and Adams (2018) found lower birthweights after the switch to the river in children of white mothers, but not in those of black mothers, and Grossman and Slusky (2020) failed to find a notable disparity in fertility rates, concluding that both white and black women suffered negative impacts. A rash study led by the CDC in 2016 did not find striking differences between white and black participants (Unified Coordination Group 2016). I am not aware of any efforts to evaluate disparate racial impact with respect to other contaminants like *Legionella pneumophila* and trihalomethanes.

We should always keep in mind the limitations of these studies and avoid jumping to the conclusion that they offer a comprehensive picture of the quantity and quality of harm done in Flint. I cite them here simply to make the point that the scientific literature on the crisis has not given residents (or others, for that matter) any special reason to believe that residents of color were disproportionately harmed in the ways measured. It is also worth remembering, however, the important concept of "cumulative impact" when assessing harms: even when harms do not appear disproportionate when viewed in isolation, they may interact with other kinds of harm and disadvantage to produce compounding effects. The many barriers faced by Flint's black population must be kept in mind, then, if we are to adequately measure the damage done by the water (though this, of course, makes the damage all the more difficult to add up).

21 We must remember, before adopting this premise as an axiom, that the severity of the harm done in Flint has been the subject of debate (Pauli 2019; 2020), with some on the "expert" side arguing that the water crisis never qualified as a public health emergency at all (Gomez et al. 2018). This perspective was in clear contradiction to the conventional wisdom about the crisis at the "popular" level, but since it was not typical of environmental racism arguments I do not explore it here.

As for how Flint compared to other cities, one of the ripple waves emanating from the crisis was an uptick of water testing across the country, which often led to the discovery of comparable, or worse, contamination in other communities, and which—even more significantly, for our purposes—complicated the notion that racist disregard for a population was a consistent or essential factor in explaining such contamination. For example, in 2019 most of the Michigan cities that were found to be in violation of the federal action level for lead were overwhelmingly white, with the highest result—an astonishing 370 parts per billion at the 90th percentile—found in the 87% white city of Melvindale. The relevant data is available from: https://www.michigan.gov/mileadsafe/0,9490,7-392-92796-500553--,00.html.

the harms in Flint—and the official indifference that exacerbated them—to undervaluation of the city's population. Most residents and activists I knew would not have argued with these claims: the belief that Flint's crisis was especially, or even uniquely, severe and the belief that residents were perceived by officials as disposable were virtually ubiquitous. Where the expert/popular divide appeared, in some cases, was over what explained the latter perception. In my conversations with activists and observations of activist discourse, I found that many activists placed class rather than race at the center of the crisis. Activists told me that the crisis was "more about class than anything," or even "all based on class"—again, sometimes explicitly situating this frame against race-based frames and lamenting that race-oriented analyses like the MCRC's had the effect of marginalizing class (Pauli 2019: 140). Activist rhetoric that seemed a priori to have racial connotations—e.g. denunciations of the crisis as "genocide"—was often applied to the city's poor population rather than its black population, specifically (Pauli 2019: 141). Even activists who told me that racism played a "major" part in the crisis, like Tru Saunders, sometimes suggested that the poverty of residents was just as if not more important, and that perceptions of poor people as being "undesirables" were leading to efforts to push them out Flint and similar cities (personal interview with the author, Flint, MI, June 6, 2017).[22]

22 It goes without saying that race and class are in many ways inextricable, as are the injustices of racism and classism. We are by no means condemned to choose between race *or* class in explaining a social phenomenon, and as already mentioned, many accounts of the water crisis referred to the fact that Flint residents are mostly black *and* (largely) poor, implying that both characteristics factored into the crisis. What is at stake is not a dichotomous choice but a matter of emphasis: if race *and* class are to blame for a crisis, what determines whether we choose to sum up the harm done as "environmental racism"? Is it simply that more people of color are affected than white people (or poor people, for that matter)? Is it necessary to show also that the effects are in some sense "caused" by racist attitudes, behaviors, or institutions (past or present)? Once we enter the complicated and slippery world of causation, where variables abound, what determines whether we conclude that race is a decisive, or even significant, factor in any particular outcome?

As environmental racism scholars have grown more historical and "structural" in orientation, they have relied increasingly on theory and interpretation in arriving at their conclusions. There is nothing inherently wrong with this, of course, but it does mean that the scholar exercises more power in determining which representations of "reality" are to prevail than they might if they were chained to a narrow range of positivistic "facts" (e.g. data on toxic waste siting, or fine-grain decision-making around water treatment). Heavily interpretive methodologies also raise the risk that the scholar's preconceptions will creep into the analysis and overshadow inconvenient data points or other plausible lines of argument—including those that seem compelling from "popular" perspectives. Again, I do not wish to suggest that any of this in any way precludes the development of

In addition to these empirical objections, a big part of the resistance I observed to racial framings of the crisis had to do with the belief that they devalued the suffering of white residents. It is worth remembering that the appearance on the Flint water activist scene of white people who had personally experienced harm from the water was one of the turning points in the formation of the water movement. Prior to that time, as Claire McClinton explained to me, what water activism existed in Flint was largely focused on issues of affordability and accessibility and was led primarily by black activists. From early 2015 on, harms to white bodies, and particularly to white children, like the children of LeeAnne Walters, came to be closely associated with revelations about just how bad Flint's water quality problems were (Walters herself was sometimes described as the "Martin Luther Queen" of the movement). Compelling officials to acknowledge the harm done to white residents was a central part of the movement's struggle, and when I began to speak with Flint's prominent white activists I got the sense that they were having trouble figuring out how this harm was supposed to fit into an "environmental racism" framework. Certainly, any suggestion that white residents were merely collateral damage—the MCRC called them "victims of racism by association" (85)[23]—was totally absent from the way these activists spoke about their own victimhood.

That the feeling of being seen as secondary sufferers could lead to real offense and distress on the part of white residents was illustrated in a particularly vivid example I witnessed in April 2018. A group of activists had just taken a chartered bus to Lansing for an emergency protest after news broke that the State of Michigan was discontinuing Flint's bottled water distribution sites, and we were gathered in an auditorium serving as a staging area. Organizers with the group Michigan United began to lead us through

---

useful expert analyses that advance understanding and contribute to the cause of environmental justice. I only wish to suggest that the combination of power and partiality described above can be cause for concern when the perspectives of those affected by representations are not carefully consulted.

23 Pulido (2016) writes that "some may argue that racism is not relevant in Flint because white people were also hurt. Such logic refuses to grasp how racism operates as an ideological process. Flint is considered disposable by virtue of being predominantly poor and Black. Here, racism is a process that shapes places, and in this case, produces a racially devalued place. Accordingly, the white people who live there, most of whom are poor, are forced to live under circumstances similar to that of Black residents" (8).

In fact, most white residents of Flint are *not* poor, at least not by official measures (the poverty rate of the city as a whole hovers in the low 40th percentile), raising the question of whether poverty can simply be used in this manner to explain whatever racism does not.

a series of chants we were supposed to learn for later on. When they got to the chant "Water is a human right, not just for the rich and white!," one of the white activists—a woman whose distinctively traumatized visage, jugs of brown water, and bundles of lost hair had featured prominently in coverage of the crisis—objected, pain etched into her face and eyes welling with tears. The chant was "so racist," she said, because it implied that people like her were not suffering.[24] Claire McClinton, an African American activist, spoke up sympathetically, pointing out that while the "one percent" was white, the wording of the chant could make it sound like white people in Flint were getting clean water. The language, she suggested, should be changed. "Thank you," the white activist replied, " 'cause I'm poisoned." Another black activist added his support, saying that the crisis was really about "class," while others nodded in agreement. Ultimately, we dropped the chant altogether.

Incidents like these raised the possibility that in some contexts racializations of the crisis could themselves be sources of harm, intensifying feelings of invisibility and marginalization among affected white residents. There were also other reasons, however, for activists to resist language that might undermine the claims these residents were making to victimhood. Part of the reason why certain white activists floated to the top of the water activist scene in 2015, becoming some of the most prominent faces in the water movement, was that it was widely believed they were more likely to be believed and responded to than their black counterparts. As Flint pediatrician Larry Reynolds, an environmental justice leader in the community, put it to me: America "needed a particular face" (146) before it was convinced to take the crisis in Flint seriously. In one notable instance, during public comment after a water panel sponsored by the University of Michigan-Flint, a black resident described an interaction with prominent white activist Melissa Mays, who had been granted a privileged position onstage. He said Mays had asked him why he wasn't more vocal about the water: "I said, no, Melissa, you have to. It's your turn. Because you know the racism in the city ... the white woman must speak up before to

24 Lest this concern seem petty, consider the characterization of the crisis as "the slow poisoning of an entire generation of African-Americans," which Ranganathan (2016: 19) describes as "Flint's predicament." In formulations like these, the substantial harms done to white residents (not to mention other racial groups, like Flint's Latino/a population) are erased from the "predicament" of the city as a whole. While erasures like these may be unintended, their consequences for affected populations are, I would submit, in need of careful consideration.

get the notice of what's going on in this community." When black people like himself had raised concerns, "nobody wanted to hear it."[25]

While we may lament the racist underpinnings of any perceived credibility gap between white and black testimony, we need to recognize this gap as being part of the strategic landscape that movements must confront and, to some extent, work within. If whiteness is in some sense a "resource" that individual white people can use to exert influence and obtain other resources (see, e.g., Lewis 2004), it is potentially a resource at the movement level as well. To put it bluntly: the water movement in Flint was in special need of officially-recognized white victims whose personal stories of harm inspired attention, outrage, and assistance. Anything that seemed to downplay the victimhood of those residents risked robbing the movement of a critical asset.

Another, even more prevalent, reason why activists sometimes deemphasized race, if only for strategic purposes, was because they viewed the subject as a potential threat to unity. One prominent black activist went so far as to call the MCRC's hearings on racism a "trick" to divide the water movement, while another warned that the crisis was being exploited by "race-baiting" figures like Jesse Jackson (a leader of the large "Rebuild Flint" march in February 2016 and a repeat visitor to the city throughout the crisis). These and other activists insisted that the water movement had "no color," a motto included on one of the popular T-shirts that many activists wore to rallies and marches. Some, for a number of months, replaced their usual Facebook photos with pictures of black and white hands intertwining to symbolize the need for cross-racial cooperation.

As a practical matter, cross-racial alliances were crucial to the success of the Coalition for Clean Water, which brought a variety of water groups together in 2015 around a legal injunction and other efforts to force the city off the Flint River. By early 2016, when I got involved in local water activism, the Coalition had effectively dissolved, but it was clear that racial unity was still a priority within the broader movement. Flint Rising, a newly-formed group with ambitions of funneling water relief efforts into long-term community organizing across the city, very deliberately struck a balance of black, white, and (when possible) Latino/a faces in the images it projected in press conferences and media appearances. The Flint Democracy Defense League Water Task Force, another frontline organization, also prided itself on being racially mixed, and more than once I was pulled into a picture to help ensure a critical mass

25 This exchange is available from https://www.youtube.com/watch?t=6020&v=ulowd6DgS-k, beginning at 1:40:20.

of white representation. Activists did, as I have explained elsewhere (Pauli 2019: chapter 8), take advantage of the flood of national attention and sympathy in 2016 to raise up black voices that might otherwise have failed to find an audience, balancing out some of the disproportionate attention given to white activists early on. But this is very different from representing the harms done to black residents as being somehow more fundamental or indicative of the "real" causes of the crisis.

In short, with an affected white population as substantial as Flint's (about 37% of residents), and with white activists proactively putting themselves on the front lines and making critical contributions to the movement, the language of environmental racism was not always, in Flint, the "superb rallying cry" it has sometimes been made out to be (Foreman 1998: 123). If anything, it threatened to make the delicate work of coalition building more complicated and fraught. Poirier (1994), pointing out that organizing rhetorics are shaped by local conditions, asks us to consider the difficulty of an organizer applying a term like environmental racism in Appalachia, but it may be even more important in communities with mixed populations—where collective action depends on racial cooperation—for organizers to devise frames that do not foreground the struggle of any particular race or assign guilt in ways that threaten to undermine movement solidarity.[26]

On strategic grounds, then, Flint activists often had reason to eschew overly-racialized rhetoric and emphasize more inclusive-sounding "collective illness identities" (Brown et al. 2012) in which all victims of the water could readily see themselves. We have already seen that appeals to shared class identity were sometimes used to defuse situations in which race had become uncomfortably salient and to encourage racially cross-cutting solidarities—logically enough, in a city with a high poverty rate and proud tradition of working-class struggle. Even more prominent within activist discourse, however, was language that

26 Activists who had participated in the struggle against Michigan's emergency manager law—a struggle that in many respects informed the water movement in Flint (Pauli 2019)—had already come to appreciate the strategic value of racially-inclusive frames. They were fully aware, of course, of the law's disproportionate effect on African Americans, but they knew that their effort to repeal it depended on convincing people from all parts of Michigan, including predominantly white areas, that it put their communities at risk, too, and that it violated political principles that Americans of all colors were supposed to share. Emergency management, the Flint Democracy Defense League's Bishop Bernadel Jefferson told me, was ultimately a "people" issue, rather than a black issue, per se (personal interview with the author, May 17, 2017). The fact that in 2012 a majority of voters in almost every county in the state voted to repeal the law was taken by Jefferson and other activists as a sign that this message had resonated.

transcended racial and class distinctions entirely. The main slogan of the water movement, "Flint lives matter," reflected activists' sense of sharing a *municipal* identity, informed by the citywide exposure that had taken place and by the belief that the future of the city as a whole was imperiled—by bad water and ruined infrastructure, but also by the erosion of its public sphere and the specter of political disincorporation (one of the many powers granted to emergency managers). To be "from Flint"—a designation activists often proclaimed loudly and proudly—was to share a fundamentally common condition with one's fellow residents whose roots went deeper than whatever differences and divisions cropped up within it.

More inclusive still was the humanistic language activists in Flint picked up from what Barlow (2019) has called the "global water justice movement," an international network of water advocacy groups fighting for water to be recognized as a "human right." The idea that water is a human right found its way into Flint water activism in part through the influence of Detroit activists, who already had deep ties to the movement Barlow describes, and who in 2014 had convinced the United Nations' Special Rapporteur on water to investigate whether local water shutoffs constituted human rights violations. At the very first Flint water rally I went to, it was the Detroit Light Brigade that projected "Water is a Human Right" onto the side of the Genesee County Jail across from Flint City Hall, and subsequent rallies often began with Claire McClinton handing out posters with the same slogan that were left over from Detroit water shutoff protests. The idea was well-established within local activist discourse by the time I arrived and was employed frequently by activists of all racial backgrounds, suggesting that it had broad appeal.

The notion of a "human right" to water, which all are said to possess simply by virtue of being members of the human species, treats the contamination or denial of water as, at root, a violation of human dignity, finding in humans' universal dependence on water a potent symbol of commonality and interconnectivity. Many Flint residents arrived at similar perspectives on water organically. As Reverend Al Harris, one of the African-American leaders of the Coalition for Clean Water, put it: "the beautiful thing is that we found out we're really not separated. If it really was an issue to bring the people together, this was it. Everybody needs water. Black, white, rich, poor, educated, uneducated" (Gringlas 2016). Characterizing the crisis this way meant depicting contaminated water not as a marker of racial difference but as a common thread tying together the experiences, concerns, and needs of residents across all manner of social categories. Using this kind of humanistic language was not, of course, irreconcilable with acknowledging racial (or other) disparities, or even foregrounding them when appropriate. But the consistency with which activists returned to it created a bent in their rhetoric whose contrast with prominent outsider representations of their struggle cannot—or at least should not—be ignored.

3 Conclusion

Relative to many other concepts used widely by academics and other members of the cultural elite, environmental racism has an unusually grassroots pedigree. For many environmental justice advocates, it continues to evoke the image of ordinary people, mostly African-American, lying down in the middle of the road in Warren County to prevent dump trucks from passing with their toxic loads—the first shot in an ongoing, grassroots, organic struggle against the harms done to black and brown bodies and minds by environmental contamination. David Benford (2005) has argued that the original resonance of the term environmental racism for people of color stemmed from its being consistent with the "everyday life experiences of living in a racist society," with the empirically-obvious environmental degradation of minority neighborhoods, and with the "knowledge, folk wisdom, and stories" of residents endeavoring to explain mysterious health symptoms. The term also resonated, Benford suggests, because of its "evocation of feelings and memories of the legacy of intentional racial discrimination, of victimization, of white racism" (40).

In no way do I wish to deny what meaning the term continues to have for people of color (especially) within affected communities. But I do wish to question whether that meaning is always consistent with what those doing the conceptual work on the "expert" side intend. And I also wish to draw attention to instances where the term resonates in a bad way, or not at all. The gaps between what I have called "expert" and "popular" (or "insider" and "outsider") perspectives on race and environmental contamination in Flint are, I believe, instructive in many ways. They offer us valuable opportunities to reflect critically on expert environmental racism discourse and assess whether it is as analytically powerful and complete as it sometimes purports to be. By reminding us of what that discourse does *not* explain—or, in some cases, overlooks or marginalizes—popular perspectives help to reveal that efforts to make the concept of racism more expansive may in other ways, ironically, narrow the field of view.

Insofar as environmental racism discourse has the effect of making popular beliefs about race look unsophisticated, ignorant, self-serving, or irrelevant, other considerations must come into play as well. One of the most important things activists fought for in Flint was to control the "narrative" of the water crisis, and they were extremely touchy about outsiders, well-intentioned or otherwise, using their platforms in academia, the media, and elsewhere to put forward competing narratives, insisting on residents being able to tell their own stories and decide for themselves what the significance of the crisis was. As Nayyirah Shariff put it, what the world needed to hear about was the "lived experience" of residents, not what "experts" and academics had to say about Flint (Author's field notes, Second International Gathering of Social Movements on Water conference, June 9, 2017). Sometimes residents found the concept of racism useful for capturing aspects of that lived experience, but in many cases they did not, and in those instances the insistence of outsiders on racial interpretations of the crisis threatened to deepen residents' feelings of discursive disempowerment rather than lifting up their struggle.

Of course, no one has any right to expect "outsiders" to refrain from analyzing and interpreting a crisis as significant as the one in Flint, or to expect that the fine grain of local perspectives be carefully accounted for in every representation. But I would submit that those "experts" whose work is informed by principles of justice, and especially those who want to be effective advocates and allies, need to be more awake to the possibility that the frames that seem commonsensical and justice-oriented to them might be different from, or even at odds with, those that seem experientially valid and/or strategically advantageous to members of marginalized communities. Understanding how frames will be received by a community, and whether they really serve the community's interests, requires prolonged consideration of the nuances of the "insider's" point of view. Academics (and others) also need to be aware that their voices often have more reach than the voices of those whose social reality they seek to interpret, which can make any incongruities between insider and outsider frames even more consequential. This power differential must be openly acknowledged and carefully navigated to avoid exacerbating the marginalization of community perspectives. I do not at all mean to suggest that racial analyses of the crisis are not useful, or even essential, or that "insider" perspectives that deemphasize or complicate the role of race are innately superior simply because they are found within the community. But I do mean to suggest that those who are committed to social justice have a responsibility to acknowledge, and problematize, the differences between their preferred frames and those that are intuitive and useful to the people for whom environmental injustice is all too close to home.

Acknowledgements

The author would like to thank Yanna Lambrinidou, Vivian Kao, and two anonymous reviewers for their helpful comments on an earlier draft of this chapter.

References

Abouk, R. and Adams, S. (2018). "Birth Outcomes in Flint in the Early Stages of the Water Crisis." *Journal of Public Health Policy* 39(1): 68–85.

Agyeman, J., Bullard, R., and Evans B. (eds.). (2003). *Just Sustainabilities: Development in an Unequal World*. London, UK: Earthscan Publications Limited.

Arbulu, A.V. and Levy, D. (2018). "A One-Year Update on the Recommendations." In: *The Flint Water Crisis: Systemic Racism through the Lens of Flint*. Michigan Civil Rights Commission.

Balibar, É. (2005). "The Construction of Racism." *Actuel Marx* 2(38): 11–28.

Bailey, K.D. (2016). "The Untold Story of Flint: The Assault on Democracy for Poor and Black People." *Black Bottom Archives*. Available at: http://www.blackbottomarchives.com/blackpapersocialjustice/the-untold-story-of-flint-the-assault-on-democracy-for-poor-black-people (consulted February 28, 2016).

Banaji, M.R. and Greenwald, A.G. (2013). *Blindspot: Hidden Biases of Good People*. New York, NY: Bantam Books.

Barlow, M. (2019). *Whose Water Is It, Anyway?: Taking Water Protection into Public Hands*. Toronto: ECW Press.

Benford, R. (2005). "The Half Life of the Environmental Justice Frame: Innovation, Diffusion, and Stagnation." In: Pellow, D.N. and Brulle, R.J. (eds.). *Power, Justice and the Environment: A Critical Appraisal of the Environmental Justice Movement*. Cambridge, MA: MIT Press.

Benz, T.A. (2019). "Toxic Cities: Neoliberalism and Environmental Racism in Flint and Detroit Michigan." *Critical Sociology* 45(1): 49–62.

Berliner, J.V. (2017). "Environmental Injustice/Racism in Flint, Michigan: An Analysis of the Bodily Integrity Claim in Mays v. Snyder as Compared to Other Environmental Justice Cases." *Pace Environmental Law Review* 35(108): 108–134.

Bixby, S. (2016). "Michigan Governor Says Environmental Racism Not to Blame for Flint Water Crisis." *The Guardian*. Available at: https://www.theguardian.com/us-news/2016/jan/22/flint-water-crisis-michigan-governor-says-environmental-racism-not-to-blame (consulted January 22, 2016).

Bolin, B., Grineski S., and Collins, T. (2005). "Geography of Despair: Environmental Racism and the Making of South Phoenix, Arizona, USA." *Human Ecology Review* 12(2): 155–167.

Brewer, J. (2017). "Michigan Blames Flint Water Crisis on Racism, Parts One and Two." *World Socialist* website. Available at: https://www.wsws.org/en/articles/2017/03/03/flin-m03.html (consulted March 3 and 4, 2017).

Brown, P., Morello-Frosch, R., Zavestoski, S., and the Contested Illnesses Research Group (eds.). (2012). *Contested Illnesses: Citizens, Science, and Health Social Movements*. Berkeley, CA: University of California Press.

Brulle, R. (2000). *Agency, Democracy and Nature: The U.S. Environmental Movement from a Critical Theory Perspective.* Cambridge, MA: The MIT Press.

Bryant, B. (ed.). (1995). *Environmental Justice: Issues, Policies, and Solutions.* Washington, DC: Island Press.

Bryant, B. and Mohai, P. (eds.). (1992). *Race and the Incidence of Environmental Hazards: A Time for Discourse.* Boulder, CO: Westview.

Bullard, R.D. (ed.). (1993a). *Confronting Environmental Racism: Voices from the Grassroots.* Boston, MA: South End Press.

Bullard, R.D. (1993b) Environmental Equity: Examining the Evidence of Environmental Racism. *Land Use Forum* 3: 6–11.

Bullard, R.D. (1993c). "The Threat of Environmental Racism." *Natural Resources and Environment* 7 (3): 23–26, 55–56.

Bullard, R.D. (1997). *Unequal Protection: Environmental Justice and Communities of Color.* San Francisco, CA: Sierra Club Books.

Bullard, R.D. (2000). *Dumping in Dixie: Race, Class, and Environmental Quality.* Boulder, CO: Westview Press.

Bullard, R.D. (2016a). "Flint's Water Crisis Is a Blatant Example of Environmental Injustice." *The Conversation.* Available at: https://theconversation.com/flints-water-crisis-is-a-blatant-example-of-environmental-injustice-53553 (consulted January 22, 2016).

Bullard, R.D. (2016b). "Five Questions for Robert Bullard on the Flint Water Crisis and Justice." *YaleEnvironment360.* Available at: https://e360.yale.edu/digest/five_questions_for_robert_bullard_on_the_flint_michigan_water_crisis (consulted February 3, 2016).

Butts, R. and Gasteyer, S. (2011). "More Cost per Drop: Water Rates, Structural Inequality, and Race in the United States—The Case of Michigan." *Environmental Practice* 13(4): 386–395.

Čapek, S.M. (1993). "The 'Environmental Justice' Frame: A Conceptual Discussion and an Application." *Social Problems* 40(1): 5–24.

Carey, M.C. and Lichtenwalter, J. (2019). " 'Flint Can't Get in the Hearing': The Language of Urban Pathology in Coverage of an American Public Health Crisis." *Journal of Communication Inquiry*: 1–22.

Carpenter, Z. (2016). "How the EPA Has Failed to Challenge Environmental Racism in Flint—and Beyond." *The Nation.* Available at: https://www.thenation.com/article/archive/how-the-epa-has-failed-to-challenge-environmental-racism-in-flint-and-beyond/ (consulted January 28, 2016).

Cassano, G. and Benz, T.A. (2019). "Introduction: Flint and the Racialized Geography of Indifference." *Critical Sociology* 45 (1): 25–32.

Chavis, B.F., Jr. (1994). "Preface." In: Bullard, R.D. (ed.). *Unequal Protection: Environmental Justice and Communities of Color*, pp. xi–xii. San Francisco, CA: Sierra Club Books.

Checker, M. (2005). *Polluted Promises: Environmental Racism and the Search for Justice in a Southern Town*. New York, NY: New York University Press.

Clark, A. (2019). "Clean, Affordable Drinking Water is a Racial Issue." *The Washington Post*. Available at: https://www.washingtonpost.com/opinions/2019/09/23/clean-affordable-drinking-water-is-racial-issue/ (consulted September 23, 2019).

Clark, A. and Kramer, J. (2017). " 'An Equal Opportunity Lie': How Housing Discrimination Led to the Flint Water Crisis." *Splinter*. Available at: https://splinternews.com/an-equal-opportunity-lie-how-housing-discrimination-le-1820482045 (consulted December 5, 2017).

Clark, C. (2019). "Race, Austerity and Water Justice in the United States: Fighting for the Human Right to Water in Detroit and Flint, Michigan." In: Sultan, F. and Loftus, A. (eds.). *Water Politics: Governance, Justice and the Right to Water*. New York, NY: Routledge.

Clark, K. (2016). "The Value of Water: The Flint Water Crisis as a Devaluation of Natural Resources, Not a Matter of Racial Justice." *Environmental Justice* 9(4): 99–102.

Cole, L. and Foster, S. (2001). *From the Ground Up: Environmental Racism and the Rise of the Environmental Justice Movement*. New York, NY: New York University Press.

Craven, J. and Tynes, T. (2016). "The Racist Roots of Flint's Water Crisis." *Huffington Post*. Available at: https://www.huffpost.com/entry/racist-roots-of-flints-water-crisis_n_56b12953e4b04f9b57d7b118 (consulted February 3, 2016).

Cuthbertson, C.A., Newkirk, C., Ilardo, J., Loveridge, S., and Skidmore, M. (2016). "Angry, Scared, and Unsure: Mental Health Consequences of Contaminated Water in Flint, Michigan." *Journal of Urban Health: Bulletin of the New York Academy of Medicine* 93(6): 899–908.

Cutter, S.L. (1995). "Race, Class and Environmental Justice." *Progress in Human Geography* 19(1): 111–122.

Dicochea, P.R. (2012). "Discourses of Race and Racism within Environmental Justice Studies: An Eco-racial Intervention." *Ethnicity and Race in a Changing World: A Review Journal* 3(2): 17–28.

Dietz, T., Duan, R., Nalley, J., and Van Witsen, A. (2018). "Social Support for Water Quality: The Influence of Values and Symbolic Racism." *Human Ecology Review* 24(1): 51–70.

Drum, K. (2019). "Marc Edwards Is a Sad Victim of Our Modern Political Era." *Mother Jones*. Available at: https://www.motherjones.com/kevin-drum/2019/01/marc-edwards-is-a-sad-microcosm-of-our-modern-political-era/ (consulted January 20, 2019).

Eligon, J. (2016). "A Question of Environmental Racism in Flint." *The New York Times*. Available at: https://www.nytimes.com/2016/01/22/us/a-question-of-environmental-racism-in-flint.html (consulted January 21, 2016).

Faber, D. (2018). "Global Capitalism, Reactionary Neoliberalism, and the Deepening of Environmental Injustices." *Capitalism Nature Socialism* 29(2): 8–28.

Fasenfest, D. and Pride, T. (2016). "Emergency Management in Michigan: Race, Class and the Limits of Liberal Democracy." *Critical Sociology* 42(3): 331–334.

Fisher, M.R. (1994). "On the Road from Environmental Racism to Environmental Justice." *Villanova Environmental Law Journal* 5: 449–478.

Fisher, M. (1995). "Environmental Racism Claims Brought Under Title vi of the Civil Rights Act." *Environmental Law* 25(2): 285–334.

Food and Water Watch. (2017). *Water Injustice: Economic and Racial Disparities in Access to Safe and Clean Water in the United States*. Washington, DC: Food and Water Watch.

Foreman, C.H., Jr. (1998). *The Promise and Peril of Environmental Justice*. Washington, DC: Brookings Institution Press.

Foster, S. (1993). "Race(ial)Matters: The Quest for Environmental Justice." *Ecology Law Quarterly* 20(4): 721–753.

Gaard, G. (2010). "Women, Water, Energy: An Ecofeminist Approach." In: Brown, P.G. and Schmidt, J.J. (eds.). *Water Ethics: Foundational Readings for Students and Professionals*, Washington, Covelo, London: Island Press.

General Accounting Office. (1983). *Siting of Hazardous Waste Landfills and Their Correlation with Racial and Economic Status of Surrounding Communities*.

Gómez, H.F., Borgialli, D.A., Sharman, M., Shah, K.K., Scolpino, A.J., Oleske, J.M., and Bogden, J.D. (2018). "Blood Lead Levels of Children in Flint, Michigan: 2006–2016." *Journal of Pediatrics* 197: 158–164.

Grimmer, C. (2017). "Racial Microbiopolitics: Flint Lead Poisoning, Detroit Water Shut Offs, and the 'Matter' of Enfleshment." *The Comparatist* 41: 19–40.

Gringlas, S. (2016). "Will the Water Crisis Finally Secure More Than Band-Aids For Flint?" *Belt Magazine*. Available at: https://beltmag.com/will-water-crisis-finally-secure-band-aids-flint/ (consulted June 27, 2016).

Grossman, D.S. and Slusky, D.J.G. (2020). "The Impact of the Flint Water Crisis on Fertility." *Demograph* 56: 2005–2031.

Hammer, P.J. (2017). "The Flint Water Crisis, the Karegnondi Water Authority and Strategic–Structural Racism." *Critical Sociology* 45(1): 103–119.

Hanna-Attisha, M. (2019). "I Helped Expose the Lead Crisis in Flint. Here's What Other Cities Should Do." *The New York Times*. Available at: https://www.nytimes.com/2019/08/27/opinion/lead-water-flint.html (consulted August 27, 2019).

Hare, N. (1970). "Black Ecology." *The Black Scholar* 1(6): 2–8.

Highsmith, A. (2015). *Demolition Means Progress: Flint, Michigan, and the Fate of the American Metropolis*. Chicago, IL: University of Chicago Press.

Highsmith, A. (2016). "Flint's Toxic Water Crisis Was 50 Years in the Making." *Los Angeles Times*.

Holifield, R. (2001). "Defining Environmental Justice and Environmental Racism." *Urban Geography* 22(1): 78–90.

Hurley, A. (1995). *Environmental Inequalities: Class, Race, and Industrial Pollution in Gary, Indiana, 1945–1980*. Chapel Hill, NC: The University of North Carolina Press.

Inwood, J.F.J. (2018). " 'It Is the Innocence which Constitutes the Crime': Political Geographies of White Supremacy, the Construction of White Innocence, and the Flint Water Crisis." *Geography Compass* 12(3): 1–11.

Jackson, D.Z. (2017). "Environmental Justice? Unjust Coverage of the Flint Water Crisis." Shorenstein Center on Media, Politics and Public Policy, July 2017.

Jackson, D.Z. (2018). "The Goldman Prize Missed the Black Heroes of Flint—Just Like the Media Did." *Grist*. Available at: https://grist.org/article/the-goldman-prize-missed-the-black-heroes-of-flint-just-like-the-media-did/ (consulted April 23, 2018).

Kaffer, N. (2017). "It's Time to Speak up about Racism in Flint Water Crisis." *Detroit Free Press*. Available at: https://www.freep.com/story/opinion/columnists/nancy-kaffer/2017/02/20/time-speak-up-racism-flint-water-crisis/98061076/ (consulted February 20, 2017).

Karoub, J. (2017). "Decades of 'Systemic Racism' at Root of Flint Water Crisis, Commission Says." *The Associated Press*. Available at: https://www.thestar.com/news/world/2017/02/17/decades-of-systemic-racism-at-root-of-flint-water-crisis-commission-says.html (consulted February 17, 2017).

Kevin, D. (1997). " 'Environmental Racism' and Locally Undesirable Land Uses: A Critique of Environmental Justice Theories and Remedies." *Villanova Environmental Law Journal* 8: 121–160.

King, S. (2016). "Michigan Gov. Rick Snyder Did Nothing as Flint's Water Crisis Became One of the Worst Cases of Environmental Racism in Modern American History." *New York Daily News*. January 11, 2016.

Kirkpatrick, L.O. and Breznau, N. (2016). "The (Non)Politics of Emergency Political Intervention: The Racial Geography of Urban Crisis Management in Michigan." Available at SSRN: https://ssrn.com/abstract=2754128 or http://dx.doi.org/10.2139/ssrn.2754128.

Kornberg, D. (2016). "The Structural Origins of Territorial Stigma: Water and Racial Politics in Metropolitan Detroit, 1950s-2010s." *International Journal of Urban and Regional Research* 40(2): 263–283.

Krajicek, D.J. (2016). "Flint Is Part of a Pattern: 7 Toxic Assaults on Communities of Color." *Alternet*. Available at: https://www.salon.com/2016/01/26/the_hideous_racial_politics_of_pollution_partner/ (consulted January 26, 2016).

Lee, S.J., Krings, A., Rose, S., Dover, K., Ayoub, J., and Salman, F. (2016). "Racial Inequality and the Implementation of Emergency Manager Laws in Economically Distressed Urban Areas." *Children and Youth Services Review* 70: 1–7.

Lewis, A.E. (2004). " 'What Group?' Studying Whites and Whiteness in the Era of 'Color-Blindness'." *Sociological Theory* 22(4): 623–646.

Lewis, C. (2013). "Does Michigan's Emergency-Manager Law Disenfranchise Black Citizens?" *The Atlantic*. Available at: https://www.theatlantic.com/politics/archive/2013/05/does-michigans-emergency-manager-law-disenfranchise-black-citizens/275639/ (consulted May 9, 2013).

Logan, J. (2018). "Liberty and Environmental Justice for All: An Empirical Approach to Environmental Racism." *Wake Forest Law Review* 53(4): 739–766.

Mascarenhas, M. (2016). "The Flint Water Crisis. A Case of Environmental Injustice or Environmental Racism." Testimony delivered to Michigan Civil Rights Commission. September 8, 2016.

Mascarenhas, M. (2012). *Where the Waters Divide: Neoliberalism, White Privilege, and Environmental Racism in Canada*. Lanham, MD: Lexington Books.

McGurty, E. (2009). *Transforming Environmentalism: Warren County, PCBs, and the Origins of Environmental Justice*. New Brunswick, NJ: Rutgers University Press.

McIntosh, P. (1988). "White Privilege: Unpacking the Invisible Knapsack." Available at: https://www.racialequitytools.org/resourcefiles/mcintosh.pdf.

McKenna, B. (2018). "The Agony of Flint: Poisoned Water, Racism and the Specter of Neoliberal Fascism." *Anthropology Now* 10(3): 45–58.

Meyer, J.M. (2009). "Populism, Paternalism, and the State of Environmentalism in the US." In: Bomberg, E. and Schlosberg, D. (eds.). *Environmentalism in the United States: Changing Conceptions of Activism*, New York, NY: Routledge.

Michigan Civil Rights Commission. (2017). *The Flint Water Crisis: Systemic Racism through the Lens of Flint*. Lansing: State of Michigan.

Mohai, P. and Saha. R. (2007). "Racial Inequality in the Distribution of Hazardous Waste: A National-Level Reassessment." *Social Problems* 54(3): 343–370.

Mohai, P. and Saha, R. (2015). "Which Came First, People or Pollution? A Review of Theory and Evidence from Longitudinal Environmental Justice Studies." *Environmental Research Letters* 10(12): 1–9.

Muhammad, M.E., De Loney, H., Brooks, C.L., Assari, S., Robinson, D., and Caldwell, C.H. (2018). " 'I Think That's All a Lie … I Think It's Genocide': Applying a Critical Race Praxis to Youth Perceptions of Flint Water Contamination." *Ethnicity and Disease* 28: 241–246.

Mutz, K., Bryner, G.C., and Kenney, D.S. (eds.). (2002). *Justice and Natural Resources: Concepts, Strategies, and Applications*. Washington, DC: Island Press.

New York Times Editorial Board. (2016). "The Racism at the Heart of Flint's Crisis." *The New York Times*. March 25, 2016.

Nickels, A.E. and Clark, A.D. (2019). "Framing the Flint Water Crisis: Interrogating Local Nonprofit Sector Responses." *Administrative Theory & Praxis* 41(3): 200–224.

Omi, M. and Winant, H. (2015). *Racial Formation in the United States*. New York, NY: Routledge.

Pauli, B.J. (2019). *Flint Fights Back: Environmental Justice and Democracy in the Flint Water Crisis*. Cambridge, MA: MIT Press.

Pauli, B.J. (2020). "The Flint Water Crisis." WIREs Water.

Pellow, D.N. (2000). "Environmental Inequality Formation: Toward a Theory of Environmental Injustice." *American Behavioral Scientist* 43(4): 581–601.

Pellow, D.N. (2018). *What Is Critical Environmental Justice?* Cambridge, UK and Malden, MA: Polity.

Pellow, D.N. and Brulle, R.J. (eds.). (2005). *Power, Justice and the Environment: A Critical Appraisal of the Environmental Justice Movement*. Cambridge, MA: MIT Press.

Pieper, K.J., Martin, R., Tang, M., Walters, L., Parks, J., Roy, S., Devine, C., Edwards, M.A. (2018). "Evaluating Water Lead Levels During the Flint Water Crisis." *Environmental Science and Technology* 52: 8124–8132.

Poirier, M.R. (1994). "Environmental Justice/Racism/Equity: Can We Talk." *West Virginia Law Review* 96(4): 1083–1107.

Pulido, L. (1996a). "A Critical Review of the Methodology of Environmental Racism Research." *Antipode* 28(2): 142–159.

Pulido, L. (1996b). *Environmentalism and Economic Justice: Two Chicano Struggles in the Southwest*. Tuscon, AZ: The University of Arizona Press.

Pulido, L. (2000). "Rethinking Environmental Racism: White Privilege and Urban Development in Southern California." *Annals of the Association of American Geographers* 90(1): 12–40.

Pulido, L. (2015). "Geographies of Race and Ethnicity I: White Supremacy vs White Privilege in Environmental Racism Research." *Progress in Human Geography* 39(6): 809–817.

Pulido, L. (2016). "Flint, Environmental Racism, and Racial Capitalism." *Capitalism Nature Socialism* 27(3): 1–16.

Pulido, L. (2017). "Geographies of Race and Ethnicity II: Environmental Racism, Racial Capitalism and State-sanctioned Violence." *Progress in Human Geography* 41(4): 524–533.

Ranganathan, M. (2016). "Thinking with Flint: Racial Liberalism and the Roots of an American Water Tragedy." *Capitalism Nature Socialism* 27(3): 17–33.

Robinson, T.M., Shum, G., and Singh, S. (2018). "Politically Unhealthy: Flint's Fight Against Poverty, Environmental Racism, and Dirty Water." *Journal of International Crisis and Risk Communication Research* 1(2): 303–324.

Ross, T. and Solomon, D. (2016). "Flint Isn't the Only Place with Racism in the Water." *The Nation*. Available at: https://www.thenation.com/article/archive/flint-isnt-the-only-place-with-racism-in-the-water/ (consulted February 9, 2016).

Roy, S. and Edwards, M. (2019). "Flint Water Crisis Shows the Danger of a Scientific Dark Age." *CNN.* Available at: https://www.cnn.com/2019/03/14/opinions/flint-water-myths-scientific-dark-age-roy-edwards/index.html (consulted March 21, 2019).

Sadler, R.C. and Highsmith, A.R. (2016). "Rethinking Tiebout: The Contribution of Political Fragmentation and Racial/Economic Segregation to the Flint Water Crisis." *Environmental Justice* 9(5): 143–151.

Sadler, R.C., LaChance, J., and Hanna-Attisha, M. (2017). "Social and Built Environmental Correlates of Predicted Blood Lead Levels in the Flint Water Crisis." *American Journal of Public Health* 107(5): 763–769.

Sandler, R. and Pezzullo, P.C. (eds.). (2007). *Environmental Justice and Environmentalism: The Social Justice Challenge to the Environmental Movement.* Cambridge, MA: MIT Press.

Sandweiss, S. (1998). "The Social Construction of Environmental Justice." In: Camacho, D.E. (ed.). *Environmental Injustices, Political Struggles: Race, Class and the Environment.* Durham, NC: Duke University Press.

Schlosberg, D. (2013). "Theorizing Environmental Justice: The Expanding Sphere of a Discourse." *Environmental Politics* 22(1): 37–55.

Solomon, D. and Ross, T. (2016). "Protecting America from Racism in the Water." Center for American Progress, Available at: https://www.americanprogress.org/issues/race/news/2016/02/03/130524/protecting-america-from-racism-in-the-water/ (consulted February 3, 2016).

Stanley, J. (2016). "The Emergency Manager: Strategic Racism, Technocracy, and the Poisoning of Flint's Children." *The Good Society* 25(1): 1–44.

Sugrue, T.J. (2005). *The Origins of the Urban Crisis: Race and Inequality in Postwar Detroit.* Princeton, NJ: Princeton University Press.

Switzer, D. and Teodoro, M. (2017). "The Color of Drinking Water: Class, Race, Ethnicity, and Safe Drinking Water Act Compliance." *Journal—American Water Works Association* 109(9): 40–45.

Szasz, A. (1994). *EcoPopulism: Toxic waste and the Movement for Environmental Justice.* Minneapolis, MN: University of Minnesota Press.

Sze, J. (2006). *Noxious New York: The Racial Politics of Urban Health and Environmental Justice.* Cambridge, MA: MIT Press.

Taylor, D.E. (2014). *Toxic Communities: Environmental Racism, Industrial Pollution, and Residential Mobility.* New York, NY: New York University Press.

Turner, R.L. and Wu, D.P. (2002). "Environmental Justice and Environmental Racism: An Annotated Bibliography and General Overview, Focusing on U.S. Literature, 1996-2002." Berkeley, CA: Berkeley Workshop on Environmental Politics, Institute of International Studies, University of California, Berkeley.

Unified Coordination Group. (2016). *Flint Rash Investigation: A Report on Findings from Case Interviews, Water Testing, and Dermatologic Screenings for Rashes that*

Developed or Worsened after October 16, 2015. Flint, MI: Agency Unified Coordination Group.

United Church of Christ Commission for Racial Justice. (1987). *Toxic Wastes and Race in the United States: A National Report on the Racial and Socio-Economic Characteristics of Communities with Hazardous Waste Sites*. New York: United Church of Christ.

Vang, M. (2017). "Racial Composition of School District on School Leaders' Responses to State Takeover: A Field Experiment on the Application of Michigan's Emergency Manager Law." *Journal of Educational and Social Research* 7(2): 31–41.

Washington, H.A. (2019). *A Terrible Thing to Waste: Environmental Racism and Its Assault on the American Mind*. New York, Boston, London: Little, Brown Spark.

Washington, S.H. and Pellow, D.N. (2016). "Water Crisis in Flint, Michigan: Interview with David Pellow, Ph.D." *Environmental Justice* 9(2): 53–58.

Wernick, A. (2016). "This Professor Says Flint's Water Crisis Amounts to Environmental Racism." *Public Radio International*. Available at: https://www.pri.org/stories/2016-02-11/professor-says-flints-water-crisis-amounts-environmental-racism (consulted February 11, 2016).

Worth-Nelson, J. (2017). "Longstanding 'Systemic Racism' Implicated in Flint Water Crisis, Civil Rights Commission Asserts." *East Village Magazine*, February 18, 2017.

Yamamoto, E.K. and Lyman, J.W. (2001). "Racializing Environmental Justice." *University of Colorado Law Review* 72: 311–360.

Zimring, C. (2016). *Clean and White: A History of Environmental Racism in the United States*. New York: New York University Press.

AFTERWORD

The Flint Water Crisis, KWA and Strategic-Structural Racism

Written Testimony Submitted to the Michigan Civil Rights Commission Hearings on the Flint Water Crisis

Peter J. Hammer

Flint is a complicated story where race plays out on multiple dimensions.[1] It is a difficult story to tell because many facts suggesting the State's real complicity in the tragedy are still being revealed. That said, three truths about Flint, race, and water are beginning to resonate strongly. The first truth is how the entire Emergency Management regime and governor Snyder's approach to municipal distress and fiscal austerity serves as a morality play about the dangers of structural racism and how conservative notions of knowledge-and-power can drive decisions leading to the poisoning of an entire City. The second truth is the role strategic racism played in motivating actors at the Karegnondi Water Authority (KWA), Treasury, DEQ and various Emergency Managers to disregard the lives of the citizens of Flint in seeking initial approval of the KWA pipeline and how these same players manipulated rules governing bond financing in a way that cemented use of the Flint River as an interim drinking water source as a predicate for financing the distressed City's participation in KWA. The third truth is how the structural racism embedded in the first serves to enable and reinforce the strategic racism embedded in the second.

The hearings of the Michigan Civil Rights Commission are an effort to seek answers about what really happened in Flint and why. The water crisis in Flint needs to be understood from a perspective of strategic and structural racism. These perspectives substantially change how one thinks about the underlying problem of municipal distress, the tool of Emergency Management, initial decisions relating to Flint's participation in KWA, bond financing for the KWA project, the financially driven decision to use the Flint River as an interim

1 This chapter contains the complete written testimony submitted by Peter Hammer to the Michigan Civil Rights Commission for its inquiry into the Flint water contamination crisis. For the original appendix to the testimony and further context, see: https://www.michigan.gov/mdcr/0,4613,7-138-47782_77964---,00.html.

source of drinking water, and the political environment that failed to recognize and respond to the mounting crisis.

1 Flint, Municipal Distress, Emergency Management and Strategic-Structural Racism

1.1 *What Is Structural and Strategic Racism?*

We need to develop more meaningful understandings of how race and racism function in modern America if we want to achieve greater racial equity. The only types of racism most Americans imagine are intentional forms of discrimination. Sadly, intentional discrimination is also about the only type of racism our laws address.

While intentional racism does exist and must be fought, it is not the only type of racism we need to be concerned about. Research in cognitive psychology documents how implicit bias can impact thought and action at an unconscious level. These unconscious biases are created and reinforced by media messages and dominant social narratives about history, politics, power, and the economy. Relatedly, there are significant forms of structural racism. Structural racism consists of the inter-institutional dynamics that produce and reproduce racially disparate outcomes over time (Powell 2012). These racially desperate outcomes occur in areas of health, education, income, transportation, housing, and the environment. Historically, these forces served to perpetuate notions of white supremacy most evident in institutions of slavery and Jim Crow segregation. Today, these same forces continue in different institutional forms to protect and reinforce notions of white privilege. The oppressive and hierarchical nature of these forces, however, remain the same.

Geography plays an important role in understanding structural racism. In this context, we need to be more aware of the spatialization of race and the racialization of space throughout Michigan (Lipsitz 2011). A frame of structural racism helps do this. Theories of structural racism are also useful because they employ systems-based forms of reasoning that can help identify root causes of problems that change over time and better inform future policy actions.

There is another form of racism—Strategic Racism (López 2014). The forces of intentional racism, structural racism, and unconscious biases are strong in American society and can be manipulated for political and economic purposes. Strategic racism is the manipulation of these forces regardless of whether the actor has express racist intent, although the vary act of engaging in strategic racism is itself a form of racist behavior.

This testimony will be framed to explore the answers to a number of important questions. 1) How is the Emergency Manager Law, particularly as imposed after repeal by popular referendum, an illustration of stucturalized racialization? 2) How is the phenomenon of municipal distress in Michigan itself a manifestation of a history of structural racism? 3) How did strategic racism enable decisions regarding Flint's initial participation in KWA? 4) How were rules concerning bond financing manipulated in a manner that committed the use of the Flint River as the interim drinking water source to enable Flint's financing its contribution to KWA? 5) How did the features of Emergency Management, government conflicts of interest, and the embedded nature of structural racism influence the delayed institutional and political response to the emerging crisis?

1.2 *Knowledge, Power, Emergency Management and Race*

At the heart of Emergency Management in Michigan are questions of knowledge-and-power and how knowledge-and-power relates to policy and race. Different groups of people have different sets of information and beliefs (knowledge) and are differentially situated to influence policy (power) (Foucault 1977). As it relates to Emergency Management, Flint is a story about who's knowledge matters; how the information and beliefs of particular groups can pre-determine policy; and how resistant established knowledge-and-power matrices are to change, especially when challenged from below by groups historically marginalize in terms of race, ethnicity, and national origin.

Governor Snyder, based on a conservative set of beliefs about the sources of municipal distress and the types of austerity policies needed to address them (knowledge-and-power) passed an enhanced Emergency Manager Law (PA 4) through a majority republican legislature. The new law displaced local democratic rule and provided an extraordinary set of powers for Emergency Managers to enact unilateral change, with the primary objective of balancing local municipal budgets. This triggered a popular movement to repeal the Emergency Manager Law through the referendum process, by different groups of people, based on a different set of information and beliefs about the role of local government and the proper policy response to municipal distress (knowledge-and-power). Within weeks after repeal, however, the same legislature that adopted the initial Emergency Manager Law, sitting in lame duck session, passed a slightly revised Emergency Manager Law (PA 436) with an appropriations provision, making the new law impossible to repeal by popular referendum.

In essence, the Governor and the republican legislature privileged its conservative set of Emergency Manager policies, with its embedded knowledge-and-power assumptions, over competing visions and ensured that its policy regime would govern events in Flint and elsewhere in Michigan. This unleashed a series of events, now well-known, relating to Emergency Management, democracy, municipal finance, lead, and water.

Matrices of knowledge-and-power relations are real, exerting their own social-political force fields that can determine the outcomes of political disputes, as well as people's lives. Competing matrices of knowledge-and-power can be evidenced in official documents, campaigns, emails, and newspaper accounts. Two reports are particularly helpful in deconstructing the Flint water crisis from a perspective of structural racism. The Flint Water Advisory Task Force Final Report essentially vindicates (ex post) the beliefs and information held by opponents of the Emergency Manager law, who spearheaded the repeal effort.[2] Democracy, checks and balances, and citizen participation all matter in governance. In Flint, that which was feared most was permitted to come into being, while the same blindness that prevented the Governor and Republican legislature from questioning their own information and beliefs in the wake of the successful referendum effort, prevented them and other government officials from recognizing the emerging crisis and taking appropriate remedial actions. What causes this blindness to *external* truths and how is it related to issues of knowledge, power, and structural racism?

The second revealing document is the September 2011 report, Long-Term Crisis and Systemic Failure: Taking the Fiscal Stress of American Cities Seriously: Case Study: City of Flint, by Eric Scorsone and Nicolette Bateson.[3] The Scorsone and Bateson Report was published in the midst of the state's assessment of Flint's alleged financial emergency and only weeks before the appointment of Flint's first Emergency Manager—Michael Brown. Contemporary actors in the Governor's office, at Treasury and the various Emergency Managers can be charged with an awareness of its contents. The Report calls into serious question the basic assumptions of the Emergency Management policy as applied to Flint, even if one accepts the conservative

2 Flint Water Advisory Task Force, FINAL REPORT (March 2016) (Commissioned by the Office of Governor Rick Snyder State of Michigan) (hereinafter "Task Force Report"), available at https://www.michigan.gov/documents/snyder/FWATF_FINAL_REPORT_21March2016_517805_7.pdf.

3 Eric Scorsone and Nicolette Bateson, Long-Term Crisis and Systemic Failure: Taking the Fiscal Stress of American Cities Seriously: Case Study: City of Flint (September 2011) (hereinafter "Scorsone and Bateson") available at https://www.cityofflint.com/wp-content/uploads/Reports/MSUE_FlintStudy2011.pdf.

economic precepts embedded in Emergency Management's internal set of information and beliefs.

It should have been clear to the Governor, the Treasury Department, and the appointed Emergency Managers that there were deep structural problems in the city. As a matter of basic economics, it would not be possible to cut the Flint budget or generate sufficient additional revenue to remedy Flint's fiscal distress. Nevertheless, Emergency Managers in Flint continued on course with "business as usual," without adjustment. What causes this *internal* blindness and how is it related to issues of knowledge, power, and structural racism?

Underlying the interpretation of these documents are streams of recently released emails illustrating how strategic racism can and did manipulate racialized forces in Flint for private gain at critical junctures of the Flint water crisis—the decision to opt for the KWA pipeline and the financially driven decision to use the Flint River as an interim drinking water source in order to circumvent debt limits governing bond financing of the KWA project. Strategic racism manipulates the forces of express and structural racism, while structural racism provides cover for strategic racism. This was sadly illustrated in the delayed institutional and political response to the water crisis and the efforts by the Department of Environmental Quality (DEQ) to obfuscate, deny, and cover up the poisoning of an entire city.

1.3 *Flint from a Perspective of Structural Inequality*

Flint is a shrinking, post-industrial city. Flint's population reached a peak of nearly 200,000 in 1960, only to shrink by more than half today. While Flint is now a majority African-American city with roughly 57% of the population Black and 38% white,[4] the story of when and why people started leaving the city is quite different (Hammer 2016). Flint's white population has been fleeing the city for more than half a century—declining from 162,128 in 1960 to 38,328 in 2010 (Scorsone and Bateson 2011: 4). In contrast, Flint's Black population continued to grow from 1960 (34,521) to 1990 (67,488) and did not start meaningfully to decline until 2010 (57,939) (Scorsone and Bateson 2011: 4). Significantly, when white people left the City, they did not leave the region. The population of Genesee County has remained relatively stable from 1970 to the present. The percentage of the population represented by the City of Flint, however, has fallen dramatically from just over half to less than a quarter in the past 50 years.

4 Task Force Report at 15.

As in most cases of the spatialization of race and the racialization of space, the City of Flint and Genesee County have taken on increasingly different socio-economic characteristics over time, with increased segregation of race, wealth, and opportunity. The population of Genesee County is not just whiter than the city of Flint, it is also wealthier. In 2010, median household income in Flint ($28,384) was 31.7% lower than that of Genesee County ($41,586) (Scorsone and Bateson 2011: 6). Other characteristics of Genesee County facilitate greater spatial segregation and make tighter regional integration—economic and racial—more difficult. Genesee County is another illustration of unplanned urban sprawl. "Genesee County consists of eleven cities and seventeen townships. ... [O]ver half of the county's population is dispersed in townships that cover 87% of the land area. The remaining cities are relatively small" (Scorsone and Bateson 2011: 26). This stimulates substantial inter-governmental competition in terms of taxes, investment, and development, mostly to the disadvantage of Flint.

Flint is also an economic story of job losses associated with deindustrialization and changes in the auto industry, particularly as mediated through General Motors. In this process, there has been substantial spatial relocation of workers holding many of the remaining good paying jobs, while there has been an increased concentration and economic isolation of the poor and jobless of all races, increasingly trapped inside of Flint. The numbers are staggering. "In 1978, over 80,000 Flint-area residents were employed by GM. By 1990, the number of employees decreased to 23,000. It was reported to be as low as 8,000 in 2006" (Scorsone and Bateson 2011: 1). While unemployment statistics notoriously understate the existence of joblessness in urban areas because they fail to capture those who have stopped looking for work, Flint's unemployment rate in 2010 was 23.2%, the highest in the State (Scorsone and Bateson 2011: 6).

Distressed economic systems can be tipped into downward spirals. In 1990, 30.6% of Flint residents lived below the poverty line (Scorsone and Bateson 2011: 6). By 2009, it was 34.9%. By 2016, it was over 40%, constituting the second highest rate in the country (Lurie 2016). With concentrated poverty comes increased social and economic isolation. In an insightful article, Stephen Henderson and Kristi Tanner examine "How job loss and isolation help keep Flint poor" (Henderson and Tanner 2016). With increased regional job sprawl, nearly "half of the working population [in Flint] travels 25 miles or more to work each day" (Henderson and Tanner 2016). This is in a city where nearly one in five residents do not have access to a car and the City's public transportation systems serves the urban core with little access to suburban spaces. Isolation brings mounting physical, mental, and emotional stress, where access to basic services, even groceries, can become daily challenges.

In the end, these are structural problems that need structural solutions. Henderson and Tanner conclude: "In Flint, lead poisoning in the water supply has generated a wealth of attention. But when we talk about what to do in that city, the conversation needs to focus on the complex web of policy dynamics that create dramatic job loss and economic isolation. It needs to address decisions that, for more than a generation, have driven urban areas into economic chasms that almost seem designed to nurture and trap poverty, and to destroy opportunity and hope" (Henderson and Tanner 2016). The only element expressly missing from this analysis is the role of race in these processes, but Flint is and must be understood as a dramatic illustration of structural racism.

1.4 *Municipal Distress as Evidence of a History of Structural Racism*

What are the causes of financial health and municipal distress? Distress at the household level is deeply interconnected with distress at the municipal level. The three primary sources of municipal revenue in Flint are property taxes, income taxes, and state revenue sharing. Between fiscal year 2006 and the planned fiscal year 2012, there were dramatic reductions in each revenue category. Property tax revenue fell 33% from $12.5 million to $8.3 million, a sign of a collapsing real estate market (Scorsone and Bateson 2011: 50). Income tax revenue fell 39% from $19.7 million to $12 million, a sign of a collapsing jobs market (Scorsone and Bateson 2011: 50). State revenue sharing fell a dramatic 61% from $20 million to $7.9 million, a sign of the state's abandonment of it older urban areas (Scorsone and Bateson 2011: 50). This reflects a deep structural crisis.

Property tax revenues are inherently unstable in a city that has lost half its population and the majority of its manufacturing base. Problems in the real estate market translate into problems in municipal tax revenue. In Flint, many houses are simply being abandoned and increasing amounts of land lay vacant. "The rate of housing abandonment in the City of Flint presents numerous long-term structural budget issues. Housing vacancy has increased from 8.2% in 1990 to 21.1% in 2010" (Scorsone and Bateson 2011: 4). Abandoned houses not only translate into falling property tax revenue, but into increased costs for the city, including "increased municipal maintenance, police patrol, fire protection, and other costs to preserve health and human safety concerns" (Scorsone and Bateson 2011: 5). The city is in a double bind.

One response to falling property values and falling property tax revenues might be to increase taxes to increase revenues. The first problem with this is that it has already been done. Flint has the fifth highest property taxes in the state (Scorsone and Bateson 2011: 12). The second problem is that increasing taxes further could actually make things worse. Sadly, competitive regional dynamics punish distressed cities that raise taxes. "When competing for residents within Genesee County, the City of Flint is further disadvantaged by a high homestead tax rate ... The City of Flint homeowner will pay, on average, 28% more than County residents in the nine other largest communities" (Scorsone and Bateson 2011: 12). It is not possible to tax oneself out of a structural deficit. Similar observations could be made about trying to increase income tax revenue.

Scorsone and Bateson conducted an analysis to see what it would take for the City of Flint to return to levels of property and income tax revenue comparable to fiscal year 2006, the last time that the city ran a budget surplus. What would it take to generate an additional $4.2 million in property tax revenue? "[N]ew investments in taxable property of $525 million with an assessed value of $262.5 million would be needed in order to generate $4.2 million in revenue. In other words, the additional taxable value needed equates to almost eleven times the current assessed value of the City's single largest taxpayer, General Motors. Similarly, new projects equal to almost four times the assessed value for all of the ten largest taxpayers would be needed to return revenues to the fiscal year 2006 level" (2011: 53–54). These estimates suggest the tremendous depth of the structural challenges facing Flint in 2011.

Similar disturbing results flow from the analysis of the investments in job growth needed to reverse the $7.6 reduction in income tax revenue. The authors conclude that "40,000 new taxpayers would be needed to return income tax revenue to the FY 2006 level" (54). Relative to the anemic employment picture in Flint, this is a staggering number. "To put the estimate of 40,000 into perspective, that amount exceeds the total number of employees at the City's ten largest employers combined" (Scorsone and Bateson 2011: 55).

What was the State's response to Flint's structural financial problems? Between 2006, the last year Flint ran a budget surplus and planned FY 2012, on the eve of it being placed under an Emergency Manager under PL 4, state revenue sharing fell 61% from $20 million to $7.9 million (Scorsone and Bateson 2011: 50). *The inference is clear. The primary, non-structural reason Flint was in financial distress was the direct result of state revenue sharing policy. This fact does not get the public attention it deserves. The State of Michigan created the very financial distress in Flint and other cities that it then used to supposedly justified the need for Emergency Managers.*

One lesson is important. You cannot simply cut your way out of this type of financial hole. Between 2000 and 2010, the City of Flint implemented many cost cutting measures, including a workforce reduction of over 50% (Scorsone and Bateson 2011: 14). But the dynamics driving personnel and other costs are complicated. "Despite reduced staffing levels, the City of Flint's expenditures have continued to increase. This is symptomatic of a structural budget deficit" (Scorsone and Bateson 2011: 18).

An Emergency Financial Manager (Ed Kurtz) was appointed in Flint in May 2002 and stayed in place till January 2004, leaving the city with a budget surplus. By June 2008, however, the city was in deficit again. The conclusion that the dominant conservative political narrative draws from this (knowledge-and-power) is that poor, predominately African-American cities cannot govern themselves. Scorsone and Bateson draw a different conclusion, "Ultimately, however, if cities with chronic fiscal stress are suffering from structural challenges beyond their control, improved management will only be able to cure a limited number of problems" (9–10). The authors state in their Executive Summary: "While the city can do some things to manage its financial stress, the revenue structure does not provide a means to solve the fiscal stress. Long-term problems will require long-term solutions at both the state and local level" (i). In this environment, imposing cuts on top of cuts actually threatens the economic viability of the entire system. "City services and infrastructure maintenance have suffered. Attracting and retaining taxpayers is dependent on providing reliable service and high value for the high rate of taxes paid" (i).

One cannot destroy a village in order to save it. Just a few weeks after the Report was published, Michael Brown was appointed Flint's first Emergency Manager. It is fair to charge him and the other Emergency Managers with knowledge of the contents of this Report and to judge them in terms of whether and how they addressed Flint's underlying structural challenges.

1.5 *Emergency Management and Structural Racism*

One might think that a characteristic of good management, emergency or otherwise, is consistent, coherent leadership. Emergency Management in Flint has had none of these attributes. The State ushered in a revolving door of Emergency Managers.[5] It is difficult to keep them all straight. Ed Kurtz served as Flint's Emergency *Financial* Manager under PA 72 of 1990 from May 2002 to 2004. On November 20, 2011, Michael Brown was appointed Flint's first Emergency Manager under PA 4. In August 2012, Ed Kurtz again became Emergency Financial Manager when PA 4 was suspended in light of the certification of the ballot initiative and Michael Brown was not eligible to serve under PA 72. Kurtz was subsequently named Emergency Manager under the newly enacted PA 436. When Kurtz stepped down in June 2013, Michael Brown was reappointed as Emergency Manager under PA 436. Barely four months

5 Task Force Report at 39.

later, Darnell Earley replaced Brown as Emergency Manager in October 2013. Finally, Jerry Ambrose replaced Earley in January 2015. Ambrose left the position in April 2015, when control over the city's finances was assigned to a city administrator under the supervision of a Receivership Transition Advisory Board. All totaled, Flint was served by four different Emergency Managers, serving at five different times.

The sets of knowledge-and-power relations in which Emergency Management is situated are not well suited to address the multilayered causes of municipal distress. Many of these structural considerations lie outside the Emergency Managers mandate and set of constrained tools. Instead, Emergency Managers operate within a narrow accounting frame with the specific charge of balancing the budget, regardless of social cost, believing that policies of fiscal austerity alone will breathe life into historically distressed communities. Moreover, these actions are undertaken in an environment that completely displaces democracy and civil society.

The actions of Flint's Emergency Managers are consistent with this template. In December 2011, shortly after assuming authority, Michael Brown laid off "several high-ranking City Hall appointees and eliminated pay for the mayor and city council (which he later partially restored)" (Longley 2012). The following week, he eliminated the position of Ombudsman and the Civil Service Commission. Contrary to the lessons that you cannot cut your way out of a structural deficit, as part of the FY 2013 budget, he sent 100 additional layoff notices to city employees, this in a city that had already reduced its workforce by more than half between 2000–2010 (Scorsone and Bateson 2011: 14).

The following year, Emergency Manager Ed Kurtz submitted a "balanced" budget for FY 2014. This was not necessarily an event to celebrate. As reported in Bloomberg News: "After firing 20 percent of its workers, doubling water rates and outsourcing trash collection, Flint, Michigan, has a balanced budget. It's also approaching the point at which it can't function as a city" (Niquette 2013). Even the Emergency Manager noted that this was not a sustainable process. "Without reliable revenue to replace dwindling property and income taxes and state funding, the birthplace of General Motors Co. won't be able to support its citizens, even if its books are square, Kurtz said" (Niquette 2013).

Kurtz deserves some credit for understanding the limits of his tools, the social costs of his austerity policies and the profound dilemma he faced. Deeper cuts could quicken the city's downward spiral, potentially making it unviable as a social, political, and economic entity. "We can't just keep putting it on the backs of the people who live in the city. Pretty soon, we won't have anybody left to tax" (Niquette 2013). Kurtz warned of mounting structural deficits in coming years if things continue as is. He also cautioned that further personnel cuts could not be made without them coming out of public safety (Carmody 2013). Police and fire were next on the chopping block.

Without similar nuance, but with a clear budget cutting mandate, Emergency Manager Darnell Earley was committed to submitting a "balanced" FY 2015 budget in the face of increasing structural pressures by making deeper and deeper cuts. Earley did exactly what Kurtz warned against, cutting into the core of public safety. Police and fire represent half of all city employees and, according to Earley, constituted the "single biggest stress" on the budget, "The city's police and fire departments would lose 36 police officer positions and 19 firefighter jobs under a new $55-million budget" (Fonger 2014a). In addition, water and sewer rates would increase an additional 6.5 percent in Earley's budget. Increasing water and sewer rates, along with other fees for basic services such as garbage, had become a staple of Emergency Management revenue seeking. During Flint's time under Emergency Management, water rates in the City more than doubled.

Emergency Management can be a cruel and misguided tool. Flint was in municipal distress as a consequence of decades of structural racism, deindustrialization, white flight, economic deprivation, and isolation. Rather than addressing these root issues, Emergency Management displaced democratic institutions and further marginalized citizen participation and the role of civil society. In addition, Emergency Managers imposed progressive budget cuts, weakening core city services and turning Flint into one of the latest "minimal cities" (Anderson 2014). A city made vulnerable as a result of structural racism was made even more vulnerable through Emergency Management and fiscal austerity.

2 KWA, DEQ, Treasury, Emergency Managers, and Strategic Racism

Strategic racism is the conscious manipulation of the forces of intentional racism, structural racism, and unconscious bias for personal or political gain. In examining the Flint water tragedy, some simple questions can help identify the existence of strategic racism. Were decisions made in the best interests of Flint residents? Were the people of Flint treated as ends in themselves or simply as instrumental means to further the objectives of others? Were decisions consistent with or deviations from the standard cost benefit analysis that is supposed to characterize Emergency Management under the direct supervision of the Department of Treasury? Would the same events be possible in a wealthy, predominately white community?

As more documents come to light, what emerges in Flint is a troubling story of strategic racism as it relates to 1) the initial decision for Flint to participate in

KWA and 2) the financially driven decision to use the Flint River as an interim drinking water source, in part, because the KWA commitment obligated the City to a multi-million dollar upgrade of its Water Treatment Plant (WTP) it could not afford and, in part, to manipulate bond finance rules to secure financing for Flint's share of KWA construction costs. Nowhere in this story are the interests of Flint residents afforded pride of place. Instead, the City and its residents are manipulated as means to the predetermined ends of others.

The reaction of most thoughtful observers is that things just do not seem right when they study KWA's role in Flint, particularly at a time of financial distress. This was the assessment of the Flint Water Advisory Task Force Final Report. The Task Force called for a further investigation of KWA by an independent outside authority, specifically noting the following:

- State and local officials repeatedly characterized Genesee County and Flint leadership, including Flint's emergency managers, as *adamant in their promotion of KWA* and desire for independence from DWSD.
- Several firms, each with ties to the respective and effectively competing parties, issued conflicting studies as to the merit of KWA. Independent review was requested of MDEQ, an agency ill-equipped to render judgments regarding economic feasibility.
- Contracting related to Flint's water purchase commitments and to use of the Flint WTP on an interim basis were effected through action of Flint's emergency managers.[6]

Sometimes, where there is smoke, there is fire. Strategic Racism in the approval of KWA, the decision to use the Flint River as an interim source of drinking water, and the delayed enforcement response in light of the mounting crisis are all deeply interconnected. Shortly after the Release of the Flint Water Advisory Task Force Final Report, the State Attorney General announced a series of criminal indictments relating to the Flint Water Crisis. The names of the first three individuals facing criminal charges will play key roles in the KWA saga explored here—Stephen Busch (DEQ), Michael Prysby (DEQ) and Michael Glasgow (WTP). "Messrs. Busch and Prysby were each charged with three felony counts, including for allegedly misleading federal environmental

6 Task Force Report at 59 (emphasis added). The influence that KWA and Genesee County Drain Commissioner Jeff Wright exercised was undeniable. They got exactly what they wanted from Flint City Officials, Emergency Managers and State Officials at DEQ and Treasury. The more difficult question to answer is the source of that influence. $300 million in KWA contracts is a substantial amount of money to control and hand out. Contractors are known to establish and maintain relationships with politicians through campaign contributions. Politicians, in turn, can help channel contributions to others public officials to expand their own sphere of influence. Whether KWA's influence is just an extreme and tragic illustration of politics as usual or whether there is something more at work is still unanswered.

officials and tampering with evidence related to lead testing of Flint's water. *Mr. Prysby faces an additional felony count for authorizing the operation of the Flint water-treatment plant when he allegedly knew it couldn't provide safe drinking water*" (Maher 2016). The story begins, however, with the decision to approve Flint's participation in the KWA pipeline.

2.1 *The Decision to Approve Flint's Participation in KWA*

There is another name in the email trails central to the KWA story—John C. O'Malia. John O'Malia is a professional engineer coordinating much of the engineering and political work for KWA. From the beginning, one senses an inappropriately close relationship between those associated with KWA, officials in the City of Flint and employees of DEQ. On November 11, 2011, John O'Malia sent an email to Liane Shekter Smith (DEQ) concerning "Revised Memo Regarding KWA." The message read: "See attached. John O'Brien [of DEQ] made a few changes. Any question[s] let me know." It then added, "[t]he incumbent Flint Mayor was reelected so good news. Thanks for your help." Signed, "John O'."[7] Liane Shekter Smith forwarded the message to Mike Prysby (DEQ), Jon Bloemker (DEQ), Kelly Green (DEQ), and Laura Verona (DEQ), with copies to Mark Joseph (DEQ), Lonnie Lee (DEQ) and Pat Cook (DEQ).

On January 5, 2012, John O'Malia sent New Year's greetings and a recapitulation of end of the year KWA discussions with DEQ to Liane Shekter Smith (DEQ) and Karen Teeples, concerning "Updated Status on GCDC/KWA:" "See attached. More later as development happens. Any question[s] let me know. Happy New year to you and staff. John O'."[8] The following is a reproduction of the entire attached memorandum.

MEMORANDUM
TO: Liane Shekter Smith, John O'Brien, and David Jansen
FROM: John C. O'Malia, P.E.
DATE: January 3, 2012
RE: KWA Status
It was good to talk to you regarding the status of KWA at the end of the year.

---

7 Governor Snyder has released batches of emails and related documents. In citing to these documents, I will provide sufficient detail in the text for the reader to understand the context and provide a citation to the file name and page number in the file where the document can be found. For example, the email from John C. O'Malia can be found in the file "DEQ11" on page 1362 of the 2147 page document—(DEQ11 1362/2147) (brackets in original). The website containing the file can be found on one of the Governor's Press Releases, *Gov. Rick Snyder releases departmental emails produced regarding Flint water crisis* (12 February 2016), available at http://www.michigan.gov/snyder/0,4668,7-277-57577_57657-376716--,00.html.

8 (DEQ12 578/2200) (GCDC is the Genesee County Drain Commission headed by Jeff Wright).

I am confirming our conversations as follows.

1. Mayor Walling, the incumbent, was re-elected. He is very much in favor of the KWA project and sits as Chairman of the KWA Board.
2. The Emergency Manager [EM], Mike Brown, was appointed by Governor Snyder. EM Brown formerly served as interim mayor of the City of Flint. He has expressed support for the KWA project.
3. EM has given powers back to Mayor and Council to make the decision on KWA as a precaution if the EM court challenge holds up. This will enable the Mayor and Council to approve the KWA agreement and not be challenged in court!
4. Expect Flint to approve KWA agreement January or February of 2012.
5. Would expect a meeting with MDEQ end of January or in February.

Will keep you posted on events as they develop. Look forward to working with you and staff Happy New Year

Smith forwarded the message and attachment to Mike Prysby (DEQ), Jon Bloemker (DEQ), Kelly Hoffman (DEQ) and Kristina Donaldson (DEQ), with copies to Jeanette Noechel (DEQ), Bethel Skinker (DEQ), Lonnie Lee (DEQ) and Pat Cook (DEQ).[9]

---

9 Id. (exclamation mark in original). At every turn of the Flint story when there is an intersection between engineering and politics involving DEQ, the City of Flint and KWA, John C. O'Malia is there. He is convening meetings, setting agendas and making phone calls. On Wednesday, March 14, 2012, he sent another email to Liane Shekter Smith (DEQ) concerning "Meeting with MDEQ March 20,21,22 or 26." The message reads: "Liane-Flint wishes to meet with you et al on any day listed above. GCDC will also be in attendance. We wish to discuss the option for Flint City to Blend with DWSD water? Also, if they are allowed to blend what improvements, in the interim, until the KWA project is fully online [say 3 years]. Also, blending for 3 years and improving the Flint water plant, as a 365 day facility, using Flint River water, and they not join KWA? Other items for sure but in substance these are the main topics. We suggest at 1ish meeting. Mike Brown [EM] and his staff to present, GCDC in attendance and myself. Suggest Mike be in attendance, Brock, Benzie and maybe Brent as water quality and withdrawal maybe issues in play. If the Flint WTP is to be a 365 facility, using Flint river water, is there going to be a NPDES [withdrawal/dilution] issue at the downstream WWTP due to WTP withdrawal? Flint withdrawal rate to be 20MGD max. day. Your thoughts. I called today and left a message with your assistant regarding this meeting. Also called Mike as it appeared your number had changed. Have not heard from Mike. Let me know what is best for you and staff. It appears, if Flint does not go with KWA, that GCDC and customers will go alone. John" (DEQ1 3821/4581) (brackets in original).

Later that year, on December 13, 2012, Jon Bloemker (DEQ) sent a message to Stephen Ashford (DEQ), Mike Prysby (DEQ), Stephen Busch (DEQ) and Liane Shekter Smith (DEQ) concerning "Genesee County Drain Commission—KWA." The message summarized yet another call from O'Malia covering topics from engineering, to the political intent of Flint

While the timing did not go as predicted, within weeks of the appointment of Mike Brown as Flint's Emergency Manager, the O'Malia memo outlined the specific decision points and sequence of events that would ultimately lead to Flint's participation in KWA and the poisoning of an entire City, with the involvement and complicity of a wide range of DEQ employees supposedly charged with protecting Flint's public safety. The O'Malia memo is not an outsider trying to lobby or influence decisions of government, but the recapitulation and summary of outcomes and planned decisions between KWA and those at DEQ.[10]

The Flint story is complicated. Flint had been buying finished water from DWSD as a wholesale customer since 1967. This water was ready for residential use and required no additional treatment. Flint also has a Water Treatment Plant (WTP) that was constructed in 1954 and is now used as an emergency backup system that could process water directly from the Flint River. The WTP was started only four times a year for testing. The plant was in need of substantial repairs and updates even as an emergency backup system. It would need much more work if it were to process water on a fulltime basis.[11]

Updating the WTP would cost a substantial amount of money, money the distressed City of Flint did not have. A July 2011 study commissioned by the City

---

to proceed with KWA to the role of Treasury, to the latest news on interest rates for bond financing. (DEQ11 1527/2147). O'Malia is back at it again on January 22, 2013, sending a message to Mike Prysby (DEQ) with copies to David Jansen and Elgar Brown concerning "KWA meeting": "Thanks Mike and you are correct Wed meeting at 1:30PM your office. John and Dave plus Elgar. The agenda is to meet Steve, generally go over the project i.e. KWA report dated 2009, discuss who is in and who maybe out, current status in terms of the intake bidding, preparation of preliminary design by Wade Trim, projected timeline for letting more engineering design contracts, projected start up of the project and financing (bonding) update. Important to discuss the current status of Flint City and DWSD as well. Probably take several hours. John O' " (DEQ1 3813/4581). This meeting took place months before Flint's approval of the KWA project.

10 Nor is this an isolated incidence. There are other examples where DEQ employees seem to revel in having inside political information. (Email from Mike Prysby (DEQ) to Richard Benzie (DEQ), RE: Genesee County & Flint (13 June 2012) ("Genesee County has mentioned to me verbally several times that they will proceed with KWA with or without Flint. They also indicated that the project could be scaled down. As far as I am aware the county has not gone public with this ... since this could be one of their trump cards they're not wanting to play prematurely (if they need to) depending on the long-term alternative Flint commits to.")) (DEQ12 857/2299) (ellipses in original). We will learn later that Flint's involvement in KWA and the quantity of water that Flint would commit to purchase would be critical to issues such as the diameter of pipes and the total capacity (and profitability) of the entire KWA system.

11 Officials in Flint demonstrated a strong attachment to the WTP. This fact was noted and exploited by others. In a June 13, 2012, message from Richard Benzie (DEQ) to Michelle

from Rowe Engineering estimated total cost of upgrades at over $61 million.[12] The December 2013 price tag for more limited work to make the plant operational was somehow placed by Rowe at $25 million.[13] It was also clear that the pre-existing debt burden and strapped financial condition of the City rendered certain past WTP repairs impossible. The January 2013 MDEQ Flint Water System—Water Distribution report indicates that DEQ had identified necessary upgrades and repairs to pumping stations and that construction permits were issued, but "these projects did not proceed due to the city's current bond debt."[14] The City was not in a position to borrow money to improve its existing water system.

This was most dramatically illustrated in May 2012, when the city turned down projects to improve its water infrastructure, even though half of the loans would be forgiven. A May, 24, 2012, message from Rick Freeman of the City of Flint to Valorie White (DEQ) explains: "This email is to inform you that the City of Flint has decided not pursue DWRF funding for Project No. 7310-01 for Fiscal Year 2012. Due to the current financial situation that exists in Flint, it is believed that it would not be feasible to pursue the bonding necessary to complete these projects."[15] Mike Prysby's reply was not very sympathetic: "All this work ... down the drain ... again."[16] Richard Benzie (DEQ) explains some of the reasoning behind Flint's decision. "[T]he city has declined a DWRF loan next year for distribution system improvements even though it was being proffered with 50% loan forgiveness due to the city's disadvantaged status. The acting city manager said he just couldn't ask residents to go further in debt even if it is only for half the cost of the project. He said that when your pockets are empty, further debt is irresponsible."[17]

Lee with copies to Linda Hills and Mike Prysby (DEQ) concerning "Flint Needs," Benzie muses over what would ultimately tempt Flint to join KWA. He settles on Flint's WTP. "Like me, the county believes the city will not be able to resist the opportunity to operate their water treatment plant on more than a standby basis that this project [KWA] will offer." (DEQ1 4042/4581) (brackets added). In behavioral economics, there is a phenomenon known as the "endowment effect," where people can irrationally value more highly something already in their possession. This factor can be and apparently was being manipulated to make the KWA raw water deal more attractive that it really was.

12 Rowe Engineering, Analysis of the Flint River as a Permanent Water Supply for the City of Flint. (July 2011) (prepared for the City of Flint) (DEQ2 746/3795).

13 Rowe Professional Service Company, City of Flint Water Reliability Study: Distribution System. (December 2013) at 10, available at http://www.michigan.gov/documents/snyder/Rowe_2013_Reliablity_Study_compressed_515343_7.pdf.

14 (DEQ2 504/3795).

15 (DEQ1 3659/4581).

16 Id. (ellipses in original).

17 (DEQ1 4042/4581).

Somehow, however, Flint officials believed that resources could be found for KWA. In a May 7, 2012, letter from Howard Croft, Director of Flint's Infrastructure and Development, to Michael Prysby (DEQ), Croft wrote: "The City of Flint is pleased to be a partner in the [KWA] process and we pledge to offer our assets to support the development. We appreciate your technical support as we develop our components of the project."[18] For some reason, debt for the costly KWA project was not "irresponsible."

In 2012, Flint was considering three options for its future supply of drinking water. First, continue to source treated water from DWSD, as it had done since 1967. Second, reduce purchases from DWSD and supplement the difference by blending DWSD treated water with water drawn from the Flint River and treated at an upgraded Flint WTP. Third, switch from treated DWSD water and purchase raw (untreated) water from the recently formed KWA and treat the raw KWA water at an upgraded Flint WTP. The KWA pipeline that would transport the raw water to Flint did not exist in 2012 and was nothing more than a stack of blueprints at the time of these discussions.

In 2009, KWA received a permit to pump an incredible 85 MGD from Lake Huron and transmit it though a yet to be constructed pipeline that would run parallel to that of DWSD. The initial granting of the KWA permit was not uncontroversial. Wayne State University Law School Professor Nick Schroeck wrote: "The economic assumptions behind and the potential environmental impacts of the proposed Genesee withdrawal render the proposal flawed, at best, and a cynical ploy, at worst. We don't need to drive another wedge between Detroit and the rest of the region. We should seek to improve upon the efficiency and conservation measures of the water delivery system that we already have rather than spending vast sums of public dollars on projects that are completely unnecessary"(Schroek 2009). A broad alliance of environmental groups opposed granting the KWA permit.[19]

The primary beneficiaries of raw water are agricultural and some manufacturing processes. The largest political entity in KWA's service area with the least to gain from raw water was arguably the City of Flint. Yet, Flint was said to be essential to the viability of the KWA vision and Flint was supposed to pay 30% of the expected costs. No one asked what should have been obvious questions.

---

18 (DEQ12 856/2299) (brackets in original).

19 Letter from Alliance for the Great Lakes—National Wildlife Federation—Michigan Environmental Council—Tip of the Mitt Watershed Council—The Ohio Environmental Council—Great Lakes Environmental Law Center—Indiana Wildlife Federation to Mr. Brant O. Fisher, Water Withdrawal and Contamination Investigation Unit, Drinking Water and Environmental Health Section, Water Bureau, MDEQ (July 15, 2009), available at http://www.greatlakeslaw.org/files/genessee-final-comments.pdf.

How would the financially distressed city under Emergency Management pay for its $85 million share of the conservatively estimated $285 million project? Given all of Flint's immediate needs, was this the most important issue for the Emergency Manager to address? Whose agenda was the KWA project really serving?

Regardless of the answer to these questions, the January 3, 2012, O'Malia Memo reported that the KWA project was essentially a done deal in Flint. Mr. O'Malia's name comes up again in a December 13, 2012, email revealing additional behind the scenes conversations between KWA and DEQ Staff. Jon Bloemker (DEQ) reports the contents of phone conversation he had earlier that day with O'Malia in correspondence to his colleagues Stephen Ashford (DEQ), Mik Prysby (DEQ) and Stephen Busch (DEQ), with a copy to Liane Shekter Smith (DEQ) concerning "Genesee County Drain Commission—KWA." "The city of Flint has provisionally accepted the offer to join the KWA. The city's approval is subject to the subsequent approval by the Department of Treasury. The state's approval (or possible hearings leading to the approval) is expected in January. There may be some opposition by DWSD about Flint participating in the project."[20]

In theory, for the Emergency Manager and for Treasury, decision making is supposed to be about the economics, not politics. Treasury commissioned the engineering firm of Tucker, Young, Jackson Tull (TYJT) to assess Flint's three options for drinking water.[21] TYJT gave a preliminary assessment of its findings in a presentation on December 21, 2012. The February 2013 final report was critical of many of the cost assumptions underlying the KWA proposal and warned of potential cost overruns as high as $85 million, with Flint holding the bag for 30% of any additional expenses, potentially as much as $25 million.[22] After weighting all options, TYJT concluded that the option of staying with DWSD and blending DWSD water with water drawn from Flint River was the cheapest alternative. The Report suggested that a "new" fourth Imlay City option of building a parallel DWSD pipeline that could function as a backup supply, making the Flint WTP unnecessary, while spreading the capital costs through the entire DWSD rate base, might be the cheapest option of all.

Apparently, this was not the answer that the Emergency Manger and other KWA backers in Flint wanted to hear. It is worth recalling how the Task

20 (DEQ11 1527/2147).

21 Tucker, Young and Jackson Tull. City of Flint Water Supply Assesment. (February 2013) (Submittal to State of Michigan, Department of Treasury) (hereinafter "TYJT Report").

22 Id. at 15.

Force Report described KWA backers, including the Emergency Manager, as "adamant" in their KWA support.[23] Soon after TYJT's December 21, 2012, negative assessment, Ed Kurtz commissioned a counter-study to undermine the TYJT analysis, not by a new independent entity, but by Rowe Engineering.[24] The Task Force also noted the potential conflicts of interest of the engineering firms called upon to assess the feasibility of KWA.[25] Not surprisingly, the Rowe analysis was favorable to the KWA proposal. The resulting duel of alleged experts resulted in a substantial muddying of the technical waters.

At this point, Emergency Manager Kurtz started to strategically remove options from the table. A February 15, 2013, memo "Updated Flint Water System Status Assessment" prepared by Eric Cline (Treasury) reports the results of a January 10, 2013, meeting with Emergency Manager Kurtz.[26] TYJT has costed out a number of alternatives, many of them demonstrably cheaper than KWA. At the meeting, Kurtz eliminated all of the cheaper options from consideration—WTP employing the Flint River (which was the cheapest), all of the options blending DWSD water with treated Flint River water, and the DWSD Imlay City option—many of which had previously been proposed and advocated by himself or his predecessor. After removing all the cheaper options, KWA was determined to be the cheapest.

At this juncture, a page from the original O'Malia playbook comes back into play. Points 1 and 2 of the January memo stressed the pre-existing support of the Mayor and Emergency Manager for the KWA pipeline. Point 3 envisioned a strategic role for the Flint City Council: "EM has given powers back to Mayor and Council to make the decision on KWA as a precaution if the EM court challenge holds up. This will enable the Mayor and Council to approve the KWA agreement and not be challenged in court!"[27] On March 25, 2013, the City Council was indeed asked to approve the KWA option.

From viewing the video tape of the City Council vote on the KWA, it is clear that council members were not provided with all the information needed to

---

23 Task Force Report at 59.

24 Cover letter from James E. Redding, Vice President Engineering of Rowe Professional Service Company to Emergency Manager Edward Kurtz (January 7, 2013) (attaching copy of *Review of TYJT December 21, 2012 Presentation City of Flint Water Supply Assessment*, Prepared by Rowe Professional Services Company) (DEQ2 873/3795).

25 Task Force Report at 59.

26 (Treasury 705/7871). Emails and documents from the Treasury file are contained in a different release of documents. Press Release: *Gov. Rick Snyder releases additional batches of departmental emails and documents regarding Flint water crisis* (June 21, 2016), available at http://www.michigan.gov/snyder/0,4668,7-277-57577_57657-387125--,00.html.

27 (DEQ12 578/2200) (exclamation point in original).

make an informed decision.[28] For example, Council was not formally provided with copies of the TYJT Report that was critical of KWA. One Council member learned about the Report from the media and tracked it down on his own. The public expressed substantial anger over high water bills, without a clear differentiation between DWSD's role in providing Flint treated water at a wholesale price and the City of Flint's role in setting retail rates. Under Emergency Management, Flint water rates doubled, but public anger was often being misdirected at DWSD and not the Emergency Managers and used in support of the KWA proposal.

Tellingly, there was no discussion by Council of how the distressed city would finance the multi-million-dollar project, nor an appreciation on how existing city debt limits had prevented basic repairs and updates to the WTP in the past. In the end, the Council voted to join KWA on a 7–1 vote, but amended the proposal to contract for only 16 MGD and not the 18 MGD originally proposed by the Emergency Manager. Council anticipated that any future shortfalls could be made up for by blending water from the Flint River or purchasing, at cost, additional excess water from KWA.

Council made the decision to contract for only 16 MGD to save the distressed City money. The volume reduction could save the City some $2 million a year in charges. Significantly, however, if Flint reduced its purchases from 18 MGD to 16 MGD, it would trigger a reengineering of the entire KWA pipeline to use a smaller diameter pipe. This, in turn, would reduce the overall capacity of the pipeline to the detriment of KWA supporters. The smaller diameter pipe, however, would also reduce total construction costs, with 30% of these saving redounding the benefit of Flint.

The video of the Council deliberation also demonstrated some confusion, suspicion and consternation on the part of Council as to why on this one issue, amongst all issues, the democratically disempowered Council was being asked to make a decision. If one believes the O'Malia Memo, the City Council vote on KWA was a strategic ploy with no legal effect unless the Emergency Manager law was held invalid. As such, the Council vote was not an exercise of democracy, but an insurance policy for KWA.

To illustrate the meaninglessness of the Council vote, Emergency Manager Kurtz proceeded to contract with KWA not at the Council approved quantity of 16 MGD, but with Kurt's own original proposal of 18 MGD.[29] Looking after

28 Flint City Council Meeting (March 25, 2013), available at https://www.youtube.com/watch?v=U3gbZ8hZ_KI&index=8&list=PLom4-mJ5N8tY1oN8aYUc8j-LtaslW-4vR.

29 Edward L. Kurtz, Resolution to Purchase Capacity from Karegnondi Water Authority, City of Flint Office of the Emergency Manager (March 29, 2013) (page 135 of 274), available at http://somcsprod2govm001.usgovcloudapp.net/files/snyder%20emails.pdf.

the best interests of KWA, the diameter of the pipe would not be reduced, but Kurtz's decision would ensure higher costs to the City of Flint in the short and the long run.

In truth, the final decision was not the Emergency Manager's to make. The final decision belonged to Treasury and Treasury alone. After Kurtz recommended the KWA option, Treasurer Andy Dillon instructed DWSD to submit a final counter offer. On April 15, 2013, DWSD sent a detailed proposal with several options. Kurtz rejected the offer, almost upon receipt. At this point, Treasury exhibited very little leadership and made few efforts to conduct further authoritative or independent assessments of the competing proposals. Instead, Treasury turned to DEQ for advice, but as the Task Force Report notes, DEQ was "an agency ill-equipped to render judgments regarding economic feasibility."[30] Tellingly, these are the same DEQ officials that according to the O'Malia Memo, were treating the KWA project as a done deal as early as 2012. The decision was supposed to be about economics and not politics, but it was much more about politics than economics.

This fact was not lost on the participants. In an April 14, 2013 email from William Creal (DEQ) to Director Dan Wyant (DEQ), Creal reported that "Sue McCormick discussed this with me Friday before our wastewater meeting. She is not happy but intends to make an offer that should keep Flint and Genessee county in the DWSD system, but she recognizes that politics will probably not make this happen."[31] Abdicating his responsibility as the ultimate decision maker, Treasurer Dillion was not looking for the most defensible economic proposal for Flint residents. In an April 15, 2013, email to Dan Wyant, Dillion stated that his concern now was only making sure that Flint Emergency Manager's "expected rejection is made in good faith."[32]

DWSD made a fairly dramatic counter offer. In an April 16, 2013 email to Andy Dillon and others, Jim Fausone summarizes the DWSD offer: "Folks—This proposal saves Flint./Genessee essentially 50% TODAY and 20% when compared to KWA over 30 years. If the decision is about economics or engineering, I don't see how F/G proceeds with KWA."[33] Following this email thread within Treasury and the Governor's office is revealing. Kurtz did indeed reject the DWSD offer, almost out of hand. An April 17, 2013, email from the Governor's Chief of Staff Dennis Muchmore (GOV) to Dillon states: "So, if the last DWSD proposal saves so much money, why are we moving ahead with KWA? I take it

30 Flint Water Advisory Task Force at 59.

31 (DEQ11 2124/2147).

32 (DEQ11 2126/2147).

33 (Treasury 421/7971).

that Flint doesn't trust them and is just fed up? Does Kurtz have his head on straight here?" Dillon responded the same day: "That is the $64,000 question. DEQ is firm that KWA is better. Are they an honest broker?"[34]

On April 24, Mr. Dillon received an email from TYJT President George Karmo assessing DSWD's subsequent final, final revised proposal. "We have reviewed DWSD's final offer to Flint/Genesee County of April 24, 2013 and find it responsive to Flint's concerns and their water demand requirements."[35] Among other considerations, the DWSD option was attractive because it provided Flint a workable alternative to obtain financing that the distressed City would find difficult to obtain elsewhere. "Since Flint is unable to cost-effectively bond capital, the cost of financing could be easily obtained by DWSD."[36] Twice rejecting the TYJY analysis he had contracted for, Dillon ultimately accepted the recommendation of Emergency Manager Kurtz. No one explained how Flint would finance the KWA option.

It is difficult to excuse Treasury's failure to exercise separate, independent judgment in this matter. About the only redeeming feature of the Emergency Management is the potential for the State to step in and mitigate the negative effects of intra-regional and inter-regional conflicts. This factor was noted in the February 2013 TYJT Report: "KWA supply option appears to run counter to the Treasury's Competitive Grant Assistance Program (Formerly EVIP Grant). This program has been put in place to allow for communities to consolidate their services and save money. Two existing customers of DWSD (Flint and Genesee County) ... separating to from another water system is in contradiction to the program."[37]

Much of the public blame for the Flint Water Crisis has rested on DEQ, but Treasury is equally blameworthy. The Emergency Management law established a draconian regime, eliminating the normal checks and balances of democratic processes. The only system of accountability over the Emergency Management system rested with the Governor and the Department of Treasury. At the time the KWA approval was made, Treasury was overseeing Emergency Managers in both Flint and Detroit, yet Treasury failed to actively reconcile the conflict and acquiesced in a decision by the Flint Emergency Manager that inflicted substantial economic damage to Detroit and set Flint up for a public health, economic, and environmental disaster. Treasury was the ultimate decision maker and Treasury cannot escape ultimate responsibility for the crisis.

---

34 (Treasury 420/7971).

35 (DEQ12 8/2299).

36 Id.

37 TYJT Report at 20.

The decision of Flint to participate in KWA was publicly announced on May 1, 2013. Construction on the KWA pipeline began on June 1, 2013.

2.2 *Flint's Financing of KWA and the Use of the Flint River for Drinking Water*

In all the assessments of the alleged cost effectiveness of KWA, one important issue went almost entirely unaddressed. How was the financially distressed city of Flint going to pay for this major $85 million project? We know that debt limits prevented past repairs and upgrades to the WTP. We also know that in a June 25, 2012, email from Mike Prysby (DEQ) to Ben Hall (DEQ) providing a briefing in preparation for Director Wyant's visit to the Flint WTP, Prysby writes: "The city is very aware of the need to commit to a new source of drinking water; however, given their current financial situation, it does not appear that the city can move forward towards establishing any binding commitments."[38] We know that the comparatively greater ability of DWSD to obtain financing for projects was a factor making some of the DWSD alternatives more attractive. We also know that in addition to paying $85 million for the KWA pipeline, Flint independently had to pay to upgrade its WTP and to maintain and repair an aging water infrastructure; itself a multi-million dollar obligation. It seems incredible that the project pushed by two EMs and approved by the Department of Treasury did not require these issues to be resolved before KWA approval was given.

2.2.1 The Decision to Use the Flint River

Surprisingly, there is yet no clear answer to the questions of *who* made the decision to use the Flint River as the interim source of drinking water or *when* the decision was made. In reconstructing events, the first thing to make clear is that the DWSD April 17, 2013, one-year termination notice plays no legitimate role in the story. The letter had no implications for Flint's ability to access DWSD water on April 18, 2014, and everybody knew it. Claims to the contrary are completely pretextual. In a June 26, 2012, letter to Roger Fraser (Treasury), Howard D Croft, Director of Flint's Infrastructure and Development, wrote: "In recent years our 40 year contract to purchase treated drinking water from the Detroit Water and Sewer Department [DWSD] has expired but Flint continues to purchase water from DWSD without a signed contract or agreement."[39]

---

38 (DEQ12 518/ 2299).

39 (Treasury 82/7971). Efforts to suggest that Flint officials (in reality Treasury officials such as the various Emergency Managers) did not understand this only speaks to the condescension those actors hold for the residents of Flint. An example can be found in Brad

Similarly, Genesee County continued to receive water from DWSD in May 2014, even though they failed to negotiate a contract. The decision to use the Flint River for drinking water bares no direct relationship to the conduct of DWSD.

Instead, the decision to use the Flint River and the question of how to finance necessary improvements to the WTP were driven by financial concerns, implicating the frames of structural racism and fiscal austerity. Long before the KWA proposal was at center stage, Emergency Managers were looking at the Flint River for drinking water simply to save money. The preliminary draft of the very first "Flint Deficit Elimination Action Plan" prepared by Michael Brown and dated February 13, 2012, states: "Consideration is being given to utilizing the Flint River and Flint's water treatment plant as a short term alternative to water purchase from Detroit. Preliminary indications are that this alternative may cost significantly less than the net $11 million spent annually by the City on water purchase. If so, this would allow for funds to upgrade the plant, provide funds to enable a concentrated effort on reducing water leakage, and make debt service payments on the Financial Stabilization Bonds."[40] This is the cruel economic reasoning of fiscal austerity. This analysis became the predicate for considering the 100% Flint River option and the various "blending" water alternatives discussed earlier. In 2012, however, use of the Flint River for drinking water was rejected because of safety concerns (Guyette 2016).

June 2013 was a pivotal month. Significantly, after Kurtz strategically took the 100% Flint River option and the various blending alternatives off the table for consideration at the January 10, 2013, meeting to tilt the scales in favor of KWA, he was writing Detroit Emergency Manager Kevin Orr on June 7, 2013, proposing new "blending" options for DWSD for the interim construction period for the KWA pipeline.[41] On June 19, 2013, Kurtz sent a letter to Edward Koryzno at the State Office of Fiscal Responsibility providing Treasury an update on his plans for the Flint River. "Due to contractual relations with the DWSD, Flint is investigating the possibility of placing the Flint Water Plant (FWP) into operation using the Flint River as a primary drinking water source for approximately

---

Wurfel's (DEQ) January 28, 2015, email to Terry A. Stanton (Treasury), Sara Wurfel (GOV), David Murray (GOV), Ken Silfven (GOV), Dan Wyant (DEQ) and Maggie Datema (DEQ) establishing "DEQ Flint Backgrounder/talking points:" "Following the formal approval of Flint into the KWA, DWSD sent Flint a letter saying their contract was thereby terminated (early 2013). According to our folks, Genesee County has been using DWSD water without a contract since May 2014. But Flint took the letter to imply a water cutoff, and promptly turned to DEQ with a proposal to use the Flint River (their historic backup system)." (Treasury 4509/7971).

40 (Treasury1 43/7971).

41 (Treasury 1058/7071).

two years and then converting to KWA delivered lake water when available."[42] On June 26, Kurtz entered into a sole source contract with Lockwood, Andrews and Newman (LAN) "for assistance in placing the Flint Water Plant into operation using the Flint River as a primary drinking water source for approximately two years and then convening to KWA delivered lake water."[43]

The June 30, 2013, "City of Flint Financial and Operating Plan—FY 2013—Third Update," suggests, that despite substantial consideration being given to the river, other options were still being explored. "The City is currently exploring its options for water service between May 2014 and the full operation of the KWA pipeline. High consideration is being given to utilizing the Flint River, and/or blending River and DWSD water. The City of Flint is also considering contracting with DWSD to be the back-up water source for the City."[44]

A January 13, 2015, document prepared by the Flint Department of Public Works and addressed to City of Flint Residents concerning "Water Questions" reports the contents of a critical meeting on the issue. "On June 29th, 2013, following many preliminary discussions on how the City would fill the interim gap, a formal, all day meeting was held at the Flint Water Plant with all interested parties including City of Flint Officials (COF), representatives from the Genesee County Drain Commissioners Office (GCDC), the Michigan Department of Environmental Quality (DEQ), and the design engineers from the previous plant upgrade Lockwood, Andrews, and Newman (LAN)."[45]

It is worth reproducing at length what was discussed at that meeting:

> The purpose and agenda of the meeting was to determine the feasibility of the following items:
>
> 1. Using the Flint River as a Water Source
> 2. The ability to perform the necessary upgrades to the Treatment Plant
> 3. The ability to perform quality control
> 4. The ability for Flint to provide water to Genesee County
> 5. The ability to meet an April/May 2014 timeline
> 6. Development of a cost analysis
>
> The conversation was guided with focus on the engineering, regulatory, and quality aspects of each item listed. The resulting determinations were made.

42 (Treasury 1064/7071).
43 (Treasury 5556/7071).
44 (Treasury 7024/7971).
45 (Treasury 4404/7971).

> 1. Yes, the Flint River would be more difficult to treat but is viable as a source.
> 2. Yes, it was possible to engineer and construct the upgrades needed for the treatment process.
> 3. Yes, with support from LAN engineering which works with several water systems around the state, quality control could be addressed.
> 4. No, the Flint treatment plant would not have the capacity needed to treat and distribute sufficient water to meet the documented needs of Flint and Genesee County.
> 5. Possible, it was determined that many obstacles needed to be overcome but completion by the April/May 2014 target was reachable.
> 6. Next steps from the meeting were for LAN to present the City with a proposal that would include engineering, procurement, and construction needs for the project along with cost estimates.
>
> As a result of extensive evaluation, discussions with the professional engineers, and consulting the state regulators, *the Department of Public Works along with the Finance Department recommended utilizing the Flint River as a temporary water source while waiting for the KWA to come online.* The plan to accomplish this was accompanied with a construction timeline, a needs analysis for resources, and an FY 14 spending plan to complete the project.[46]

In the end, these decisions were being made in the shadow of the legacy of structural racism and the dictates of fiscal austerity. In truth, the financially distressed city had few alternatives, given the need to make a multi-million-dollar investment in the WTP, as part of its KWA commitment.

At this very critical point, the game of Emergency Manager musical chairs continued. Kurtz resigned and ended his term in June 2013. Michael Brown was back as Emergency Manager in July 2013. Brown was gone in October 2013, and Darnell Earley was Emergency Manager in November 2013.

On November 14, 2013, Flint Financial Director Jerry Ambrose sent new Emergency Manager Darnell Earley a memorandum outlining the justification for a "change order" to the LAN contract. The earlier LAN work was now described as a feasibility study that had found use of the Flint River feasible, but on a "temporary basis only."[47] No explanation is provided as to why the river was safe at all, or, if safe, not safe on a permanent basis or only safe now on a

46 (T1 4404/7971) (emphasis added).

47 (Treasury 1303/7971).

temporary basis. The change order would authorize LAN to develop "a proposal for conducting final design work, construction engineering, and necessary regulatory submittals associated with the expansion of the Water Treatment Plant." No permits had yet been sought, but the memo reports: "We have been working with MDEQ to be assured that the course of action being pursued is consistent with their expectations. Most recently (this morning), we met with MDEQ representatives and reviewed the proposed course of action. While formal approval cannot be given until detailed working drawings are presented, the representatives indicated their conceptual approval."[48] In November, however, the clock was ticking fast. A separate memo supporting a separate contract for "Electrical Distribution Upgrade for the Water Treatment Plant" notes that "accomplishing that within the April 17, 2014 deadline will require expediting the upgrades necessary for the WTP to receive raw water."[49] Each of these contracts that exceeded $50,000 independently had to be approved by Treasury.

Even as investments were being made in upgrading the WTP, there was still public ambiguity about the Emergency Manager's true intentions for using the River as the source of interim drinking water. Similar upgrades at the WTP would be needed to treat raw water whether that water would come from the Flint River or the KWA. In July 2013, at the same time internal documents were suggesting a final commitment to the Flint River, officials were making conflicting public statements.

> "The engineering work they're looking at involves potentially using the river on a continuing basis," said Steve Busch, a district supervisor with the Michigan Department of Environmental Quality. "I think it's yet to be determined if they would use (the Flint River) as a primary source."
>
> City Spokesman Jason Lorenz said Flint would like to work out an agreement with Detroit to provide water for Flint until KWA's pipeline is built "We still believe that going with Detroit for the next two years (while the KWA pipeline is built) is the best option," said Flint Spokesman Jason Lorenz. "We already had to make these upgrades ahead of KWA."
>
> ADAMS 2013

As late as January 2014, City Council President Scott Kincaid was saying publicly that no definitive decision had been made. "In July, city officials said they

48 Id.
49 (Treasury 1306/7971).

still were trying to figure out whether they would renegotiate a temporary deal with Detroit while the KWA pipeline was built. Kincaid said a decision about where the city will get its water during the KWA construction hasn't been finalized" (Adams 2014). We also know that negotiations with DWSD over continued use of treated water continued until March 2014.[50]

Some conclusions can be drawn. The documents reveal that consideration of the use of the Flint River for drinking water had nothing to do with public safety, but had everything to do with saving money. Treasury and the Emergency Managers had committed the City to the KWA project, which required multi-million dollar improvements in the WTP, without providing the means to finance that investment. The City had been unable to raise capital in the past for necessary expenditures. How would it get the money to pay the millions needed to prepare the WTP for the KWA project? About the only available source of financing was the $12 million being paid to DWSD for treated water. This stack of money was a substantial temptation, but a temptation based in desperation and rooted in the structural racism embedded in Flint's municipal distress, the fiscal austerity politics wrought by Emergency Management and the strategic decision foisted upon it to participate in KWA.

2.2.2 Flint's Financing the $85 Million for KWA Pipeline Construction

If Flint could not raise the necessary fund to make basic improvements in the WTP, how was it going to finance the $85 million needed to pay for its share of the KWA pipeline construction? With the State approval of Flint's participation in KWA, attention belatedly turned to how the City of Flint would finance its obligation. Ironically, many of these overtures were made to DEQ and not Treasury. On July 19, 2013, Bradley Comment, Vice President of Government Affairs for Kindsvatter, Dalling and Associates, Inc., a firm that promotes itself as Michigan's Premier Association Management and Lobbying Professionals, emailed DEQ to try and set up an appointment with Director Wyant: "I am hoping that we can meet with Director and the person that oversees the DWRF regarding the KWA waterline project. Any chance we can get a meeting in the near future?"[51]

On September 4, 2013, attorney and lobbyist Manny Lentine sent an email with a "schedule request" to see DEQ Director Wyant. "Rick Johnson and I would like to visit with Director Dan to talk about Karegnondi Water Authority and some

50 Letter from Darnell Earley, Flint EM, to Sue McCormick, DWSD (March 7, 2014), available at http://mediad.publicbroadcasting.net/p/michigan/files/201512/earlely_letter.pdf?_ga=1.224901786.1036207224.1446746452.

51 (DEQ12 718/2299).

recent meetings we have been in with Genesee County Drain Commissioner Jeff Wright concerning funding options since the County pulled back on its intended bond offering. Need 30 minutes or whatever you can offer. It will only be Rick and I and we simply want to update Dan and sound out a thought."[52] There is no indication as to what the "thought" was.

As the message circulated within DEQ, it engendered some commentary. On September 18, 2013, Stephen Busch (DEQ) sent a message to a number of DEQ colleagues explaining that "The Director asked me about this about a week and a half ago during our drive to Monroe, and I briefly discussed it with Dave Jansen at the AWWA Section Meeting last week. ... Dave indicated that he previously had discussions about DWRF funding with Jeff Wright, indicating to him that it is not a viable option, particularly given the time constraints for construction."[53] Kelly Hoffman (DEQ) replied to Stephen Busch (DEQ), "I did have a meeting about a year or so ago with the Director and Jeff Wright, and I believe Liane regarding KWA and funding. Jeff Wright does understand that DWRF is not an option for the intake and pipeline construction."[54]

There would be no simple or easy resolution to the question of how Flint would pay for its participation in KWA. The challenge was obvious. Flint was in financial distress and was constrained by law in terms of the amount of debt it could hold. The clearest extant explanation of the problem can be found in a March 18, 2014, email from then Miller Canfield attorney Dan Massaron to Gerald Ambrose with copies to Emergency Manager Darnell Earley and others. Massaron explains: "As you know, the City of Flint has lived through a dramatic decline in property values and state revenue sharing. These declines have dramatically reduced its debt capacity under the Home Rule City Act."[55] However, there is a loophole in the form of an Administrative Consent Order (ACO). "[I]f the KWA project is done to comply with an ACO, the debt associated with the project would not 'count' toward the City's debt limit."[56]

The problem, as of March 18, and the reason for the email, was that the desired ACO had not been finalized and the administrative delay was jeopardizing KWA's ability to go to the bond market. Calling the ACO a "condition precedent," Massaron stated that "we cannot continue with the transaction without the ACO."[57] This would put a stop to the KWA construction. "If there

52 (DEQ11 1651/2147).
53 (DEQ12 538/2299).
54 (DEQ11 1934/2147).
55 (Treasury 2613/7971).
56 Id.
57 Id.

is much more of a delay, the KWA will have expended its initial resources and be forced to stop construction and the project will be delayed for at least one construction cycle. Assuming the ratings come in as planned, the City needs the ACO in place by the end of the week."[58]

That same day, Ambrose forwarded Massaron's email to Wayne Workman (Treasury) and Edward Koryzno (Treasury), with copies to Darnell Earley and Richard Cline (Treasury). "We greatly appreciate the call made after our last meeting to DEQ by Eric Cline regarding the pending ACO. It has moved along, but still in process. Any additional assistance you can give would be greatly appreciated. As you can see from Dave Massaron's email, formal approval of the ACO is required in order for the bond sale to proceed."[59] On March 19, 2014, Workman instructed a colleague to "get a call into the Director to push this through."[60] The ACO was signed and finalized the next day on March 20, 2014.

This was not a typical ACO. While it seems like Treasury was playing a key role in helping obtain KWA financing, Treasury had no jurisdiction to initiate an ACO for the Flint WTP. That was the job of the DEQ. Flint-KWA started fishing for an ACO at DEQ as early as December 2013. Nicole Zacharda (DEQ) sent an email to William Creal (DEQ) on December 19, 2013, reporting the contents of a call the previous day from Michael Robinson, a Warner Norcross attorney who handled environmental issues for the City of Flint. "Yesterday I received a call from Mike Robinson ... seeking what I'd characterize as a 'sweetheart' ACO intended to ease the City's ability to access bond funding for their possible new water intake from Lake Huron."[61] This was not the first time DEQ had been approached on this issue. "Mr. Robinson and Dept. of Treasury officials have already been communicating with Steve [Busch] about an Order of some sort in light of Flint's financial situation."[62]

Rather than using an ACO as a tool to fix an existing regulatory violation, Flint-KWA-Treasury-DEQ started searching for a regulatory violation to justify an ACO, in order to bootstrap financing for the KWA, which was completely unrelated to the underlying regulatory violation justifying the ACO. After ping-ponging around different DEQ departments, the "violation" ultimately settled upon was a relatively minor and inexpensive problem with a lagoon at the Flint WTP's lime sludge facility. The key for determining the scope of potential bond financing that Flint could seek pursuant to the ACO, while circumventing

58 Id.
59 (Treasury 2612/7971).
60 Id.
61 (DEQ1 3666/4591).
62 Id.

its state-imposed debt limit, was the language defining the "Statement of Purpose."

Flint environmental attorney Mike Robinson reemerges in the story. On February 10, 2014, he sends an email to Steve Busch (DEQ) concerning "ACO:" "Steve, I checked with the City's bond counsel, here is the Language that we MUST include in the consent order so that the City can move forward on this."[63] The language the bond lawyers wanted was as follows: "The Respondent plans to use the Flint River as a temporary source of untreated water supply until KWA water is available. The Respondent must undertake the KWA public improvement project or other public improvement projects to continue to use the Flint River, such as additional water treatment plant public improvements, source water protection public improvements and public improvements to obtain back-up water supply, in order to comply with Act 399."[64] This last critical sentence was included almost verbatim in the final ACO.

If there was a point of no return in the tangled process leading to the use of the Flint River as the interim source of drinking water, this was it. The use of an ACO predicated on problems with the WTP in order to finance the KWA pipeline effectively obligated the City to use the Flint River as the interim source of drinking water during KWA construction. This legal commitment was strategically driven by the need to manipulate rules governing the bond market, not considerations of public safety. The Emergency Managers, KWA, DEQ and Treasury were all intimately involved. There would be no turning back. Earlier that month, while the ACO and bond details were being worked out, Emergency Manager Darnell Earley sent a letter to DWSD head Sue McCormick rejecting a number of DWSD offers to continue to sell Flint water after the April 17, 2014, termination of the pre-existing arrangement.[65] The die was cast.

The final ACO includes a truly Orwellian re-write of Flint's water history. According to the ACO, rather than Flint Emergency Managers and Treasury opting for KWA and rejecting numerous long-term DWSD proposals (leading to the one year contractual DWSD notice of termination), the ACO blames DWSD's notice of termination as the reason Flint was forced to opt for KWA (and ultimately rely on the Flint River as a source of drinking water). "The Respondent has chosen to use the WTP to supply water to its customers and discontinue using the Detroit Water and Sewerage Department (DWSD) after receiving

63 (DEQ3 4057/4719) (emphasis in original).

64 Id.

65 Letter from Darnell Earley, Flint EM, to Sue McCormick, DWSD (March 7, 2014). Available at: http://mediad.publicbroadcasting.net/p/michigan/files/201512/earlely_letter.pdf?_ga=1.224901786.1036207224.1446746452.

a notice of termination of services from DWSD. In order for the Respondent to continue to use of the WTP, Respondent must undertake the KWA public improvement project."[66]

The language and logic of the ACO was ultimately embedded in the documents underwriting Flint's bond financing for KWA construction. The Official Statement of the Karegnondi Water Authority Counties of Genesee, Lapeer and Sanilac State of Michigan $220,500,000, Water Supply Bonds (Karegnondi Water Pipeline) Series 2014A incorporates the same false narrative as the ACO.

> On April 17, 2013, DWSD notified Flint that it was terminating its contract with Flint for the supply of water in one (1) year as required by the contract. As a result, no later than April 17, 2014, Flint intends to begin withdrawing water from the Flint River, treat the water in its water treatment plant and then make such treated water available to the customers of the Flint System until the [KWA] System is completed and operational. After the notification from DWSD, Flint sought another source of water and determined to use its water treatment plant to provide water to its customers. In order to do so it negotiated an administrative consent order with MDEQ that permitted the temporary use of the Flint River (the "ACO"). The ACO requires Flint to either undertake a public improvement project to connect to the System or undertake other public improvements to continue to use the Flint River. In order to comply with the ACO, Flint has determined that connecting to the [KWA] System is the most cost effective means to obtain untreated water and to comply with the ACO.[67]

Ironically, the very same document reports facts relating to Genesee County that contradict the claim that the lack of a contract with DWSD somehow forced Flint to use the River.

> In January, 2014, the County Agency entered into contract negotiations with DWSD to secure a water supply directly from DWSD for the customers of the Genesee System without using Flint as a pass through, until the [KWA] System has been completed and is operational. DWSD representatives have indicated that in the event that an agreement cannot be

66 Michigan Department of Environmental Quality, Office of Waste Management and Radiological Protection, In the Matter of the Administrative Proceeding against City of Flint, doing business at 5200 Bray Road, Genesee Township, Genesee County, Michigan (March 20, 2014) (OWMRP Order No. 115-01-14) (hereinafter "ACO").

67 (Treasury 2655/7971) (brackets added).

> reached with the County Agency during these negotiations, DWSD will continue to supply water to the County Agency via Flint without a contract in place.[68]

The only real difference between Flint and Genesee County is money. Genesee County could afford safe water from DWSD, Flint could not.

Equally troubling, there are serious inconsistencies in the stance of DEQ-KWA-Emergency Managers when it comes to the safety of using water from the Flint River as a source of drinking water over time. In 2012, DEQ rejected early proposals for the continuous use of the Flint River as a permanent alternative (Guyette 2016). In 2013, in order to prevail in their advocacy of the KWA option, Flint Emergency Mangers, DEQ and KWA had to be critical of the Flint River being used in any capacity. They were critical of any of the proposed "blending" options with DWSD (found to be the lowest cost option in the TYJT study). Finally, they were critical of the Flint River as a supplemental alternative when the City Council approved a 16 MGD contract with KWA rather than the Emergency Manager's proposed 18 MGD option (a decision that would have reduced the diameter of the KWA pipe and it ultimate aggregate carrying capacity).

In January 2013, when Treasury was reviewing Emergency Manager Kurtz recommendation of the KWA option, Mike Prysby (DEQ) raised concerns about the quality and safety of the Flint River in conversations with Randy Byrne at Treasury.[69] Similarly, on March 26, 2013, Stephen Busch sent an email to Director Wyant highly critical of the TYJT Report and raising the specter of serious health concerns associated with the Flint River, including "an increased microbial risk to public health;" "increased risk of disinfection by-product (carcinogen) exposure to public health;" "additional regulatory requirements under the Michigan Safe Drinking Water Act;" and "significant enhancements to treatment at the Flint WTP."[70]

This all changed in 2014 after the KWA pipeline was approved and use of the Flint River was necessary to secure Flint's bond financing. Now that KWA had been approved, fulltime use of the Flint River was fine with DEQ, the Emergency Managers, KWA, Treasury and others.

Still, one senses some apprehension, even by bond counsel, over the use of the Flint River as the interim source of drinking water. One draft of the ACO

68 Id. (brackets added).

69 (DEQ2 732/3795).

70 (DEQ3 3647/4719).

would have required Flint to switch to an alternative drinking water source within 5 years. "After five years [the City of Flint] COF must undertake a public improvement project to receive water from KWA or some source other than the Flint River in order to continue to use its water treatment plant."[71] This proposal was rejected by Steve Busch (DEQ): "Long term we all know it would be best for the City to use a better source than the river, but I don't want it to be forced by an order."[72] After health problems started to become clear in January 2015, Richard Benzie who earlier spoke about how Flint's attachment to its WTP would lead it ultimately to join KWA stated, "I can't say the city wouldn't be better off to not have switched to the River."[73]

Despite all of the efforts of KWA-DEQ-Treasury to ensure that Flint would be able to finance its part of KWA pipeline construction, no comparable effort was made to secure additional finances to help Flint get the WTP up and running at a level where it would be safe. Flint was left to fend for itself within the legacy of structural racism and the constraints of Emergency Management. In a March 3, 2015, Memo to Wayne Workman (Treasury), Emergency Manager Ambrose explains that the work at the WTP was largely self-financed out of savings from the funds not paid to DWSD. Flint did not have the money to afford both safe water and to make the upgrades to the WTP required by its commitment to KWA. The decision to use the Flint River "offered an immediate cost savings opportunity which translated into the ability to upgrade the Water Treatment Plant without having to seek financing."[74]

It is still unclear what scope of work actually took place at WTP before switching to the Flint River as a full time drinking water source. Part of the opacity is due to the failure of the firm Lockwood, Andrews and Newman (LAN) to cooperate with the Flint Water Advisory Task Force in its investigation.[75] This is a critical line of inquiry that deserves more attention. There is substantial reason for concern. Recently, LAN was charged in a civil law suit by the Michigan Attorney General for "negligence" and creating a "public nuisance" in relationship to its work at the WTP (Kennedy 2016). In addition to what structural work was or was not done, there is the critical issue of the failure to implement basic corrosion control measures. "The obvious question that MDEQ, along with the City and its consultants, should have asked was: 'What will happen without corrosion control treatment?' Similarly, they could

71 (DEQ1 3688/4581) (brackets added).
72 Id.
73 (DEQ1 4343/4581).
74 (Treasury 4720/7971).
75 Task Force Report at 3.

have asked why a less corrosive source of water (Lake Huron water) would be required to have corrosion control treatment, but not the more corrosive Flint River source. In Flint, the more corrosive water source ultimately destroyed the protective scaling on pipes and plumbing that orthophosphate addition had provided through the water supplied by DWSD."[76] This is a critical element in the State's suit against LAN and Violia (Michigan v. Violia 2016).

Some indication of how little was done at the WTP is reflected in how little was spent. Recall that in 2009 Rowe Engineering estimated it would take \$61 million before the Flint River could become the fulltime drinking water source.[77] In 2011, LAN did an analysis suggesting that work on the WTP would cost \$69 million in capital improvements (Michigan v. Violia 2016: paragraph 25). Even when scaled down by Rowe in December 2013 when work on the plant was being done, the estimate was \$25 million for the job.[78] According to LAN's 2013 proposal, "the estimated construction cost to prepare the water plant for continuous operation using Flint River water for the interim period is on the order of \$33 to \$34 million" (Michigan v. Violia 2016: paragraph 30). By November 14, 2014, however, LAN had scaled down the estimate to \$7–10 million.[79] In the end, apparently \$8 million was spent on the WTP before it started distributing water from the Flint River.[80] It is likely that this amount was spent, not because that was the amount required for safe use of the WTP, but that was the highest amount Flint could self-finance from diverted DSDW dollars.

Furthermore, it is not clear how much candor and objectivity can be expected of Flint Emergency Mangers, DEQ staff and Treasury staff concerning the capacity of the WTP or the safety of the Flint River after negotiating the ACO committing them to use the river as an interim drinking water source for financial reasons. They are clearly responsible for the decision and it was made for financial reasons, regardless of public health concerns.

76 Task Force at 28.

77 Rowe Engineering, Analysis of the Flint River as a Permanent Water Supply for the City of Flint. (July 2011) (prepared for the City of Flint) (DEQ2 746/3795).

78 Rowe Professional Service Company, City of Flint Water Reliability Study: Distribution System. (December 2013) at 10. Available at: http://www.michigan.gov/documents/snyder/Rowe_2013_Reliablity_Study_compressed_515343_7.pdf.

79 (Treasury 1303/7971).

80 Memo from Tom Saxton (Treasury) to Wayne Workman (Treasury), concerning "City of Flint Water Rates (February 11, 2015) ("The \$8M capital costs to upgrade the Water Treatment Plant was made to be able to treat both river water and KWA water. This upgrade has been funded with the cost reduction in operating costs achieved by not buying water from DWSD during the interim period.") (Treasury 4267/7971).

What we do know is that WTP employees did not think that they were ready for full time use of the Flint River on the eve of termination of the DWSD contract. On April 16, 2014, Michael Glasgow, a laboratory and water quality supervisor for the Flint WTP, reached out to Adam Rosenthal of the MDEQ's ODWMA because he had concerns about starting up the WTP for full-time use. He wrote that he expected "changes to our Water Quality Monitoring parameters, and possibly our DBP and lead & copper monitoring plan."[81] He went on to say that "[a]ny information would be greatly appreciated, because it looks as if we will be starting the plant up tomorrow and are *being pushed to start distributing water as soon as possible.*"[82]

The next morning, Glasgow sent Rosenthal, along with Mike Prysby and Stephen Busch, another email after receiving the revised MDEQ monitoring schedule, which had "dramatic changes."[83] Glasgow explained that he was "reluctant before," and after reviewing the new monitoring schedule, did "not anticipate giving the OK to begin sending water out anytime soon."[84] The email continued, "If water is distributed from this plant in the next couple weeks, it will be against my direction. I need time to adequately train additional staff and to update our monitoring plans before I will feel we are ready."[85] Unfortunately, it is clear that the final decision was not in Glasgow's hands. In closing, Glasgow stated, "I will reiterate [my opinion] to management above, but they seem to have their own agenda ... *I have people above me making plans to distribute water ASAP.*"[86]

It should be remembered that one of the felony counts in the indictment against Michael Prysby was "for authorizing the operation of the Flint water-treatment plant when he allegedly knew it couldn't provide safe drinking water" (Maher 2016). On April 25, 2014, Flint officially began using the Flint River as its primary water source. Almost immediately, Flint residents began complaining about the quality of the new drinking water source.

Flint is the only DWSD customer in Genesee Country that did not negotiate contracts with DWSD for the interim supply of treated drinking water pending the construction of the KWA pipeline. On June 12, 2014, Emergency Manager Earley finalized the sale of a 9-mile section of water pipeline, which was previously used to connect Flint to the DWSD system, to Genesee County

81 (DEQ4 7105/7579).
82 Id. (emphasis added).
83 (DEQ4 7103/7579).
84 Id.
85 Id.
86 Id. (emphasis added).

for $3.9 million (Fonger 2014b). Ironically, Genesee County would begin utilizing the pipeline as it implemented its new service with DWSD (Fonger 2014b).

When one recalls our criteria for strategic racism, it is easy to see how they apply in Flint. The decisions made by KWA, the Emergency Managers, DEQ, Treasury and others were not made in the best interest of the residents of Flint. There was a clear agenda on the parts of these actors to pursue the KWA pipeline, regardless of the needs and priorities of Flint. The residents of Flint were instrumentally used as means to be manipulated and not as ends in themselves. Decision making in DEQ and Treasury was not consistent and objective. DEQ flip-flopped on the question of the safely of the Flint River, depending on the strategic need to advocate for the KWA pipeline. To the extent that Emergency Management is supposed to be about the rigorous application of economic rules, the various Emergency Managers and Treasury failed in this role. Ultimate decisions regarding approval of the KWA pipeline were made for political, not economic reasons. All of this took place against the backdrop of the structural racism that defines the Flint economic crisis, the displacement of democracy and the express disempowerment of Flint residents. It is difficult to imagine the same sequence of events unfolding in Ann Arbor or Bloomfield Hills (two affluent, majority white cities in Michigan).

By its very nature, structural racism, intentional discrimination, and unconscious bias create vulnerability on the part of effected populations. This vulnerability was consciously exploited to the detriment of the residents of Flint.

3 The Perfect Storm of Strategic and Structural Racism: Conflicts, Complicity, Indifference and the Lack of an Appropriate Political Response

The lack of response to the mounting crisis in Flint reveals disturbing truths about Structural and Strategic Racism in America. The Flint Water Advisory Task Force Final Report highlights the dangers of Emergency Management and Structural Racism. To this foundation, needs to be added the troubling consequences of Strategic Racism.

3.1 *Flint, Emergency Management and Structural Racism*

Flint residents had knowledge of the water crisis almost immediately upon the switch to the Flint River, but they lacked the power to influence the decision making of the Emergency Managers, Treasury, DEQ or the Governor. This knowledge was real and visceral, flowing from the color, smell, taste and detrimental effects of the water on exposed skin. In a prosperous, predominately white community, complaints of residents based on this knowledge alone would have forced change, because this knowledge would have been combined with the power necessary to demand action (knowledge-and-power).

Residents of Flint lacked this power. Power lay first in the hands of the Emergency Manager, who had just made the decision to support the KWA pipeline and to use the Flint River as an interim source of drinking water. Emergency Managers do not have to listen to residents, because they are not popularly (re)elected. They report to Treasury and to the Governor. Treasury officials are unlikely to be predisposed to grant the complaints of people in cities like Flint much credibility. The whole premise of Emergency Management is that people like the residents of Flint cannot govern themselves. Of course, Treasury would believe, Flint residents are going to complain about many aspects of the strong medicine required to put their cities back in order. These residents do not have to be taken seriously.

The Task Force Report mounts a persuasive critique of the Emergency Management regime that resonates strongly with the teachings of Structural Racism, as well as with the Knowledge-and-Power claims of opponents of Emergency Management who led the successful referendum process to repeal PA 4. The Task Force identifies three structural failings. First, Emergence Management removes the necessary checks and balances inherent in a functioning democracy.[87] Second, Emergency Management creates a balanced-budget-accounting framework that biases decision making in favor of fiscal austerity over competing social needs. This frame inevitably leads to financial decisions that can threaten public safety.[88] Finally, Emergency Management

87 "The Flint water crisis occurred when state-appointed emergency managers replaced local representative decision-making in Flint, removing the checks and balances and public accountability that come with public decision-making." Task Force Report at 1; "The emergency manager structure made it extremely difficult for Flint citizens to alter or check decision-making on preparations for use of Flint River water, or to receive responses to concerns about subsequent water quality issues." Task Force Report at 8.

88 "[T]his failure must force us to review the EM law and the general approach to financial problems. Government approaches to cities in fiscal distress must balance fiscal responsibility with the equally important need to address quality of life, economic development, and infrastructure maintenance and provision." Task Force Report at 40; "EMs are asked to ensure the protection of the public health and safety and yet are not provided adequate tools and resources to achieve this objective. EMs are empowered to effect cost-cutting measures such as the ability to terminate contracts and restructure budgets. However, they are given little or no priority access to state or federal resources or assistance in undertaking the complex activities of running a municipality. Other states take different approaches that may do a better job of balancing the need for fiscal discipline with the

fails to build in the necessary non-financial sources of expertise needed to govern a city across its full range of human and social concerns.[89]

In sum, Emergency Management creates a dynamic where bad decisions that threaten public safety are almost guaranteed to occur, and when they take place, there is no ready mechanism to identify and correct them. The Task Force proceeds to frame these structural problems in terms of environmental (in)justice.[90] Environmental justice has both a procedural and a substantive component. Procedurally, environmental justice requires the ability of all people to participate in decision making regardless of race, color, national origin or income. Second, decisions must be substantively fair and non-discriminatory. By definition, Emergency Management violates the process criteria. In substance, it violated the second criterion. The Flint water crisis created a public health catastrophe that disproportionately affected people of color and other historically marginalized communities. The Task Force concludes: "The Flint water crisis is a clear case of environmental injustice."[91]

Language matters. The notion of environmental justice is a good first step, but it is important to move from environmental justice to environmental racism to structural racism to fully understand what happened in Flint. Structural racism connects the dots of the racialized history that constitutes the root cause of municipal distress, the financial misdiagnosis behind the Emergency Management regime and the manner in which the entire apparatus of Emergency Management and the policies of fiscal austerity will disproportionately target disadvantaged communities of color. "Emergency Management is a racially blind and fiscally flawed response."[92] It is at this already highly racialized point that the structural failings inherent in Emergency Management (the

---

need to provide basic public services, especially when scientific, health, and/or engineering expertise is involved. Task Force Report at 42; "Michigan's Emergency Manager Law and related practices can be improved to better ensure that protection of public health and safety is not compromised in the name of financial urgency." Task Force Report at 41.

89 "Emergency managers charged with financial reform often do not have, nor are they supported by, the necessary expertise to manage non-financial aspects of municipal government." Task Force Report at 8; Recommendation: "Ensure proper support and expertise for emergency managers to effectively manage the many governmental functions of a city. Decisions on matters potentially affecting public health and safety, for example, should be informed by subject matter experts identified and/or provided by the state." Task Force Report at 12.

90 Task Force Report at 54.

91 Id. at 55.

92 Peter J. Hammer, *The Flint Water Crisis: History, Housing and Spatial-Structural Racism*, Testimony before Michigan Civil Rights Commission Hearing on Flint Water Crisis, slide 36 (July 14, 2016).

absence of checks and balances, a financial accounting bias that threatens public safety and the lack of social decision making expertise) take hold and create the environment where tragedies like the Flint water crisis unfold.

In reality, human tragedies, great and small, are inseparable from the machinery of Emergency Management. Flint is just the most extreme example. Flint now serves as a morality play illustrating all that is wrong with Emergency Management. It would be inexcusable if substantial reform or wholesale repeal of the Emergency Manger law does not take place in the wake of the Flint crisis.[93]

3.2 *Strategic Racism and the Failure to Respond to the Flint Water Crisis*

Sadly, the frame of structural racism does not go far enough to fully explaining the tragedy in Flint. The reality of strategic racism adds an additional layer of intent and complicity to the story. These dynamics change substantially how the inexcusably slow response to the emerging crisis needs to be understood and explained.

The Task Force tells the story of the events in Flint without the full benefit of knowledge of the role DEQ played in manufacturing an ACO to facilitate the City's bond financing for the KWA pipeline and how these actions legally committed the City to use of the Flint River as its interim drinking water source. In this manner, the Task Force knew the "what" without completely understanding the "why" of DEQ's misconduct. The Task Force states: "With the City of Flint under emergency management, the Flint Water Department rushed unprepared into full-time operation of the Flint Water Treatment Plant, drawing water from a highly corrosive source without the use of corrosion control."[94] The Task Force did not know the role that arranging KWA financing and the timing of the bond offering played in this decision and how financial concerns trumped any consideration of public safety. The decision to use the Flint River was financially driven and began on a time table to meet the needs of the bond market, not the public safety needs of the residents of Flint.

93 "Review Michigan's Emergency Manager Law (PA 436) and its implementation, and identify measures to compensate for the loss of the checks and balances that are provided by representative government." Task Force Report at 11; "Consider alternatives to the current EM approach—for example, a structured way to engage locally elected officials on key decisions; an Ombudsman function in state government to ensure that local concerns are a factor in decisions made by the EM; and/or a means of appealing EM decisions to another body." Task Force Report at 42.

94 Task Force Report at 1.

The Task Force tries to explain decisions at DEQ largely in terms of gross incompetence and cultural shortcomings. The Report's findings are reproduced here at length.

F-1. MDEQ bears primary responsibility for the water contamination in Flint.

F-2. MDEQ, specifically its ODWMA, suffers from cultural shortcomings that prevent it from adequately serving and protecting the public health of Michigan residents.

F-3. MDEQ misinterpreted the LCR and misapplied its requirements. As a result, lead-in-water levels were under-reported and many residents' exposure to high lead levels was prolonged for months. Specifically:
- MDEQ's misinterpretation of the LCR and lack of due caution resulted in the decision not to require corrosion control upon the switch to the Flint River but, rather, to begin two consecutive 6-month water quality monitoring periods.
- MDEQ failed to promptly require corrosion control even after the initial 6-month monitoring period results were received and 90th percentile lead sampling results were at 6 ppb, which would have disqualified Flint from being exempted from having to have corrosion control treatment—even under MDEQ's flawed interpretation.
- MDEQ's guidance to Flint on LCR compliance sampling techniques (calling for pre-flushing, use of small mouthed bottles, etc.), while possibly technically permissible, was not designed to detect risks to public health. MDEQ failed to take adequate steps to correct Flint water operations staff's inaccurate LCR sampling.
- MDEQ ODWMA advised Flint Utilities Department personnel to make sure the rest of the water samples in the second 6-month monitoring period were clean, since the samples they had already submitted exceeded EPA's action level for lead.
- MDEQ conveniently, and without adequate investigation, excluded LeeAnne Walters's water quality test results for purposes of determining whether Flint sampling results exceeded EPA's action level.

F-4. MDEQ waited months before accepting EPA's offer to engage its lead (Pb) experts to help address the Flint water situation and, at times, MDEQ staff were dismissive and unresponsive.

F-5. MDEQ failed to move swiftly to investigate, either on its own or in tandem with MDHHS, the possibility that the Flint water system was contributing to an unusually high number of Legionellosis cases in Flint.

MDEQ caused this crisis to happen. Moreover, when confronted with evidence of its failures, MDEQ responded publicly through formal communications with a degree of intransigence and belligerence that has no place in government. These failures are not diminished, nor should focus on them be deflected, by the fact that other parties contributed to the disastrous decisions or the prolonging of their consequences.[95]

While this list of failings may be the product of incompetence or indifference as suggested by the Task Force, within the frame of Strategic Racism, the actions of DEQ take on even more troubling connotations. When the Task Force findings are juxtaposed to the facts pertaining to the O'Malia memo, DEQ's role in promoting the KWA pipeline in the first place, it's enabling Flint's bond financing for the KWA by bootstrapping a "sweetheart" ACO that committed the City to using the Flint River and its subsequent regulatory approval of the use of the Flint River as an interim drinking water source, DEQ's conduct takes on much more sinister overtones.

DEQ appears to have adopted a strategy to "run out the clock" in terms of environmental oversight, believing that all would be forgotten once the KWA pipeline was constructed and the River was no longer in play. For example, DEQ's flawed interpretation of the Lead Copper Rule (LCR) ensured that its regulatory oversight would be defined by inaction not action. DEQ started a process in July 2014 that would require no further steps until July 2015, at the earliest.

But, DEQ could not control facts on the ground. By August 2014, there were boil water advisories because of E-Coli bacteria in the water. In September, there was another boil water advisory do to Coliform bacteria. On October 13, 2014, General Motors announced that it would stop using Flint River water at its Flint Engine Operations facility due to corrosion concerns. Even members of the Governor's executive staff called for a switch back to DWSD. In an October 14, 2014, email to Valerie Brader (GOV), Dennis Muchmore (GOV), Jarrod Agen (GOV), and Elizabeth Clement (GOV) concerning "Flint water," Michael Gadola in the Governor's office writes: "[T]o anyone who grew up in Flint as I did, the

95 Id. at 28–29.

notion that I would be getting my drinking water from the Flint River is downright scary. Too bad the EM didn't ask me what I thought, though I'm sure he heard it from plenty of others. My Mom is a City resident. Nice to know she's drinking water with elevated chlorine levels and fecal coliform. I agree with Valerie. They should try to get back on the Detroit system as a stopgap ASAP before this thing gets too far out of control."[96]

Incredibly, it took just one day for DEQ to beat back the panic. An October 15, 2014, memo from Emergency Manager Darnell Earley to Wayne Workman (Treasury) provides a summary of a conference call held that day. The governmental consensus was clear. There were no serious health problems in Flint. "The DEQ has been supportive of the decision for Flint to move to use of the Flint River as a water source. The DEQ receives regular reports from the City's continuous water quality monitoring. They have agreed that the water being produced for distribution is safe. Flint needs the DEQ to make an unequivocal statement that the Flint River water is safe for drinking and all other uses."[97] This is just one of many examples of DEQ engaging in block and tackle strategies to deny, obscure, and cover up aspects of the emerging public health crisis.

On January 1, 2015, DEQ started the second of its six-month monitoring period under its inactive interpretation of the Lead Copper Rules.[98] To address concerns of elevated bacteria, officials at the WTP increased levels of chlorine and other disinfectants. As a byproduct of excessive levels of disinfectants, trihalomethanes (THM), a potential carcinogen, was now present in the water. On January 2, 2015, the City mailed a notice to all residents that the City was in violation of the Safe Water Drinking Act.[99] It would not be publicly known till much later, but the WTP had failed to implement any corrosion control measures when it switched to the Flint River. The immediate consequence was substantial discoloration of the water and attendant issues of odor and taste (the more deadly and not publicly known consequences would be lead poisoning).

The combination of these failings—bacteria, boil advisories, THM, discoloration, rashes and odor—was producing stronger and stronger public outcries. This was not lost on State officials. On January 23, 2015, Snyder Administration's Special Projects Manager Ari Adler raised concerns about Flint with Communications Director Jarrod Agen: "This is a public relations

96 (Treasury 3428/7971).

97 (Treasury 3459/7971).

98 *Flint crisis timeline Part 2: January 2015-June 2015*, BRIDGE (March 1, 2016) (hereinafter "Flint Crisis Timeline Part 2"). Available at: http://bridgemi.com/2016/03/flint-crisis-timeline-part-2/.

99 Id.

crisis—because of a real or perceived problem is irrelevant—waiting to explode nationally. If Flint had been hit with a natural disaster that affected its water system, the state would be stepping in to provide bottled water or other assistance. What can we do given the current circumstances?"[100]

The state action that came was not aimed at the obvious public safety concerns. In February 2015, the Governor announced grants to cities, including Flint, to improve water, public safety and appraisal issues. Flint would receive $2 million support for its aging water infrastructure to addresses "waste management, leak detection and pipe assessment."[101] A briefing memo for the Governor's grant announcement stated that a "key thing to remember is that once the city connects to the new KWA system in 2016, this issue [of THM in the water] will fade in the rearview."[102] The State's strategy was still about holding tight and letting the storm pass.

Other evidence of the State's running out the clock strategy came in its response to the THM issue. On February 27, 2015, LAN released its "Operational Evaluation Report City of Flint Trihalomethane Formation Concern." In addressing the problem there was a stated bias in favor of not making any changes that would be structural in nature. "Considering that the Flint River is being used as the water source only until the KWA supply is available (expected late 2016), options to address high THM formation that require new construction or extensive time to implement are not preferred."[103] The State believed that problems would go away on their own, once there was a new water supply. These health issues did not have to be taken that seriously, especially in a city like Flint.

Behind the scenes, the looming threats to public safety were growing even more ominous. County and State officials were aware of a serious outbreak of Legionaries' disease in Flint, information that would be withheld from the public for over 9 months.[104] On February 26, 2015, DEQ was aware of testing of lead levels at LeeAnne Walter's home that were off the charts dangerous.[105] She had two children under the age of three living in the house at the time.

In early February 2015, senior officials inside the Governor's Office were once again calling for a return to DWSD. Snyder Chief of Staff Dennis Muchmore

100 Id.
101 Id.
102 (DEQ2 3310/3795).
103 (Treasury 4374/7971).
104 Flint Crisis Timeline Part 2.
105 Id.

wrote on February 5th: "Since we're in charge, we can hardly ignore the people of Flint. After all, if GM refuses to use the water in their plant and our own agencies are warning people not to drink it … we look pretty stupid hiding behind some financial statement."[106] Muchmore's protestations continued into March. An email entitled "Contaminated Drink Water in Flint" and exploring potential civil rights action based on theories of environmental racism was sent to Mayor Dan Walling, who forwarded it to Emergency Manager Gerald Ambrose, who forwarded it to Kelly Rossman-McKinney at the firm of Truscott Rossman, who forwarded it to Dennis Muchmore, with the statement "I'm concerned about the implications that this may have racial overtones. Ugh."[107]

Muchmore forwarded the email to Elizabeth Clement (GOV), Thomas Saxton (Treasury), Wayne Workman (Treasury), Jarrod Agen (GOV) and Harvey Hollins (GOV) with the following:

> Might want to get Jarrod and Terry Stanton on this as well as Harvey. Otherwise it will get out of hand. It's in the city's long term interest to make the KWA work and we can make the river water safe, but we need to work with the ministers this week to help them out. It's tough for everyday people to listen to financial issues and water mumbo jumbo when all they see is problems. You can't expect the ministers to hold the tide on this problem.
>
> How about cutting a deal with Ice Mountain or Bill Young and buying some water for the people for a time? $250K buys a lot of drinking water and we could distribute it through the churches while we continue to make the water even safer.
>
> If we procrastinate much longer in doing something direct we'll have real trouble.[108]

Wayne Workman responded: "If this does happen, we need to figure who would hand out the water. It should not be the City. It would undercut every point they are making. It probably should also be reserved for people who can't afford to buy water."[109]

While the October 2014 panic was beaten back by DEQ assurances that the water was safe, the panic of early 2015 would be beaten back almost strictly

106 (Treasury 4212/7971) (ellipses added).
107 (Treasury 4733/7971).
108 Id.
109 Id.

out of financial concerns. On March 3, 2015, Emergency Manager Ambrose strongly opposed any move away from the Flint River strictly on cost grounds. "The oft-repeated suggestion that the City should return to DWSD, even for a short period of time, would, in my judgment, have extremely negative financial consequences to the water system, and consequently to the rate payers. By the most conservative estimates, such a move would increase costs by at least $12 million annually, with that amount achieved only by eliminating virtually all budgeted improvements in the system. … the only recourse within the City's control would be to increase revenues significantly. And in my judgment, that would come from raising rates for water by 30% or more."[110]

On March 23, 2015, the Flint City Council voted 7–1 "to do all thing necessary" to return Flint back to the safe water of DWSD (Fonger 2015). Citing cost concerns, Emergency Manager Jerry Ambrose called such a demand "incomprehensible." The City Council's vote carried no legal weight. Recalling the O'Malia play book, the City Council would be permitted to vote on the decision to approve the KWA pipeline as a legal insurance policy in case of a successful court challenge to the Emergency Manager law, but they would not be given the authority to decide to move back to DWSD, even on a temporary basis, because of safety concerns.

It is important to recall the first sentence of Denise Muchmore's February 5, 2015, email: "*Since we're in charge we can hardly ignore the people of Flint.*" On Feb 18, 2015, he wrote in another email that "[t]his train is leaving and we'll be holding the bag if we don't work out a deal on DWSD for Flint."[111] One way to solve this dilemma, if one lacked the political will to actually help the people of Flint, would be to make arrangements so the State would no longer be "in charge." In the face of a mounting public health and environmental crisis, Treasury did not want to be left "holding the bag." In April 2015, Treasury somehow decided that Flint was no longer facing a financial emergency, even though it still had more than a nearly $8 million accumulated general fund deficit. In an act that would be the envy of David Copperfield, Treasury simply made the Emergency Manager in Flint disappear.

It is important to note the fiscal hypocrisy. The State's panic over the growing water crisis was beaten back upon the realization that Flint lacked the financial ability to pay for clean DWSD water—a cost that would be approximately $12 million a year. It was only by cannibalizing the money formerly paid for clean water that Flint was able to afford upgrades to the WTP in preparation for its commitment

110 (Treasury 4720/7971).

111 (Treasury 4324/7971).

to KWA. If the cost of clean water was put back on the books, Flint would have a deficit of over $20 million, an amount higher than when the "financial emergency" was originally declared. Furthermore, Treasury made no effort to project and include the costs that would be needed to remedy the human toll of the water crisis or to repair the damage to the water infrastructure in its economic analysis. Some estimates put the cost of repairing damaged infrastructure alone at $1.5 billion.[112] Flint was facing far greater fiscal challenges when the so-called emergency was declared over, than when the stated emergency was originally declared.

But Flint was not out of the woods yet. Flint had to enter into an Emergency Loan Agreement with the Michigan's Local Emergency Financial Assistance Loan Board to formally bring an end to Emergency Management. The fine print of the loan shows how tightly bound Flint-Treasury-KWA-DEQ had legally become to the continued use of the Flint River. The state Emergency Loan "effectively precluded a return to DWSD water, as Flint citizens and local officials were demanding without prior state approval."[113] The Agreement also prevented Flint from terminating its participation in KWA before the system became operational and from reducing its already high water rates without state approval.[114] Remarkably, the Resolution submitted to City Council to approve the agreement "contained no information regarding the DWSD and water rates conditions contained in the emergency loan."[115]

This is another area requiring more detailed investigation. The investigation will likely find that the logic of the ACO tying the regulatory violation at the WTP to the financing of the KWA pipeline to the use of the Flint River as an interim source of drinking water are all deeply embedded in the terms of the bond finance agreements as well. When Treasury drafted the terms of the Emergency Loan Agreement, it would have transposed the legal commitments of the ACO and the bond financing into the Emergency Loan Agreement. As such, Flint found itself in a position where it could not legally stop using the Flint River, or return to the safe water of DWSD, or decrease its water rates, or terminate its involvement in KWA, all because the City was bound to finance its participation in a pipeline that better served the interests of others.

The Emergency Loan Agreement was signed on April 29, 2015. Two days before, Miguel Del Toral of the EPA sent an email to EPA colleagues "stating that Pat Cook/MDEQ has confirmed the Flint WTP has no corrosion control

---

112 (Treasury 6237/7971).

113 Task Force at 7.

114 Emergency Loan Agreement at 5 (April 29, 2015). Available at: http://www.eclectablog.com/wp-content/uploads/2016/03/Emergency-Loan-Agreement-Flint-4292015.pdf.

115 Task Force at 41 n. 55.

treatment (CCT), which is 'very concerning given the likelihood of lead service lines in the city.'"[116] That same day, Del Toral visited the home of LeeAnne Walters to inspect plumbing and deliver sampling bottles. Meanwhile, "Pat Cook and Stephen Busch/MDEQ exchange emails complaining about Del Toral/EPA's questions on corrosion control treatment."[117] On June 24, 2015, Miguel Del Toral submitted his Interim Report: High Lead Levels in Flint, Michigan.[118] On August 27, 2015, Virginia Tech professor Marc Edwards released his first set of findings showing elevated lead levels in Flint.[119] On September 24, 2015, Dr. Hanna-Attisha presented the findings of her analysis "reporting that the proportion of children with elevated blood lead levels has increased since the switch to the Flint River water source in April 2014."[120] On October, 16, 2015, Flint stopped using the Flint River for drinking water and switched back to DWSD.

The cost of the transition back to DWSD was $12 million—$6 million from the State, $4 million from the Mott Foundation and $2 million from the City. This is approximately the same amount of money Flint payed for water before the approval of the KWA pipeline.

4 Conclusion

Nothing about what happened in Flint was accidental. Flint needs to be understood as a morality play illustrating the dangers of Emergency Management and fiscal austerity. Flint needs to stand as a profound multi-generational testimony to the dangers of strategic-structural racism in the same manner as the Tuskegee tragedy forever shames medical science.

The list of individuals and agencies contributing to the Flint water crisis is long. *But for* our county's failure to understand the root cause of municipal distress in the context of structural racism, the Flint tragedy would never have occurred. *But for* the Governor's insistence on Emergency Management and the policies of fiscal austerity, the Flint tragedy would never have occurred. *But for* the displacement of democracy and the marginalization of the voices of its residents, the Flint Tragedy would never have occurred. *But for* the many acts of strategic racism by KWA, DEQ, Treasury and the various Emergency

116 Task Force at 19.
117 Id.
118 Id. at 20.
119 Id.
120 Id. at 21.

Managers exploiting the vulnerability of an entire city, the Flint tragedy would never have occurred.

We need a deeper awareness of the reality of multiple forms of racism at work in this country and how they interact to make better policy decisions moving forward. The problem is not a lack of knowledge. The people of the State of Michigan viscerally understood the dangers of Emergency Management and collectively opposed it. The people in Flint understood the insanity of using the Flint River as a source of drinking water and had immediate, firsthand knowledge of how dangerous and inappropriate the water was for human consumption when it began flowing in April 2014. Engineers understand the basic chemistry of corrosion control and the relatively simple measures that can be taken to mitigate its ruinous effects. Physicians understand the permanent debilitating effects of lead on the human brain, especially for children.

The problem is not a lack of knowledge. The problem is the often willful blindness of people in positions of privilege and authority (knowledge-and-power) to the needs, perspectives and interests of others, particularly when the "other" is from a community that differs from their own in terms of race or class or ethnicity. The problem is that the information and beliefs held by people in authority often reinforce that blindness and permit the unquestioned projection of policies and programs on others, even when it is clear that those policies are inappropriate or have harmful consequences. The problem is that vulnerable populations are often subject to exploitation that strategically manipulates the very vulnerability created by express racism, structural racism, and unconscious bias, and yet this exploitation finds ready shelter in the very forces it exploits.

The Michigan Civil Rights Commission is undertaking important work. This is the only forum constitutionally charged with examining this tragedy from a perspective of civil right and racial justice. This is Flint's last best chance to have the real truth be told.

References

Adams, D. (2014). "Flint Spends $4 Million on Water Plant in Last Eight Months." *MLive*. January 4, 2014. Available at: http://www.mlive.com/news/flint/index.ssf/2014/01/flint_spends_4_million_on_wate.html.

Adams, D. (2013). "Flint to Spend $171,000 for Engineering to Treat Flint River Water While KWA Pipeline is Built." *MLive*. July 8, 2013. Available at: http://www.mlive.com/news/flint/index.ssf/2013/07/flint_to_spend_171000_for_engi.html.

Anderson, M.W. (2014). "The New Minimal Cities." *Yale Law Journal* 123(5): 1118–1625. Available at: http://www.yalelawjournal.org/article/the-new-minimal-cities.

Carmody, S. (2013). "Flint's Budget Balanced, but Multimillion-Dollar Deficits Loom. *MLive*. May 20, 2013. Available at: http://michiganradio.org/post/flints-budget-balanced-multimillion-dollar-deficits-loom#stream/0.

Flint Water Advisory Task Force (TFR). (2016). "Final Report (March)." Commissioned by the Office of Governor Rick Snyder State of Michigan. Available at: https://www.michigan.gov/documents/snyder/FWATF_FINAL_REPORT_21March2016_517805_7.pdf.

Fonger, R. (2014a). "Flint Emergency Manager's Budget Proposal Would Cut 36 Cops, 19 Firefighters." *MLive*. April 30, 2014. Available at: http://www.mlive.com/news/flint/index.ssf/2014/04/new_flint_budget_proposal_woul.html.

Fonger, R. (2014b). "Emergency Manager Accepts $3.9 Million Genesee County Offer to Buy Flint-Owned Pipeline." *MLive*. June 12, 2014. Available at: http://www.mlive.com/news/flint/index.ssf/2014/06/emergency_manager_accepts_39_m.html.

Fonger, R. (2015). "Emergency Manager Calls City Council's Flint River Vote 'Incomprehensible'." *MLive*. March 24, 2015. Available at: http://www.mlive.com/news/flint/index.ssf/2015/03/flint_emergency_manager_calls.html.

Foucault, M. (1977). *Discipline and Punish: The Birth of the Prison*. New York, NY: Random House.

Guyette, C. (2016). "Exclusive: Gov. Rick Snyder's Men Originally Rejected Using Flint's Toxic River." *The Daily Beast*. January 24, 2016. Available at: https://www.thedailybeast.com/exclusive-gov-rick-snyders-men-originally-rejected-using-flints-toxic-river.

Hammer, Peter J. (2016). *The Flint Water Crisis: History, Housing and Spatial-Structural Racism*, Slides and Testimony before Michigan Civil Rights Commission Hearing on Flint Water Crisis. July 14, 2016. Available at: https://www.michigan.gov/mdcr/0,4613,7-138-47782_77964---,00.html.

Henderson, S. and Tanner, K. (2016). "How Job Loss and Isolation Help Keep Flint Poor." *Detroit Free Press*. February 21, 2016. Available at: http://www.freep.com/story/opinion/columnists/stephen-henderson/2016/02/20/how-job-loss-and-isolation-help-keep-flint-poor/80199226/.

Kennedy, M. (2016). " "They Made It Worse": Michigan Sues 2 Companies Over Flint Crisis." *National Public Radio*. June 22, 2016. Available at: http://www.npr.org/sections/thetwo-way/2016/06/22/483083095/they-made-it-worse-michigan-files-suit-against-2-companies-over-flint-crisis.

Lipsitz, George. (2011). *How Racism Takes Place*. Philadelphia, pa: Temple University Press.

Longley, K. (2012). "Flint Emergency: Timeline of State Takeover." *MLive*. December 1, 2012. Available at: http://www.mlive.com/news/flint/index.ssf/2012/12/flint_emergency_timeline_of_st_1.html.

López, Ian Haney. (2014). *Dog Whistle Politics: How Coded Racial Appeals Have Reinvented Racism and Wrecked the Middle Class*. Oxford: Oxford University Press.

Lurie, J. (2016). "While Lead Flowed Through the Pipes, Flint Residents Paid America's Most Expensive Water Bills." *Mother Jones*. February 17, 2016. Available at: http://www.motherjones.com/environment/2016/02/while-lead-flowed-through-taps-flint-had-most-expensive-water-nation.

Maher, K. (2016). "Three Officials Criminally Charged Over Flint Water Crisis." *Wall Street Journal*. April 20, 2016. Available at: http://www.wsj.com/articles/three-officials-to-face-criminal-charges-over-flint-water-crisis-1461166410.

Michigan v. Violia. (2016). (Complaint for Damages and Request for a Jury Trial) (Case No. 16-16107175-NM). June 22.

Niquette, M. (2013). "Flint Balances Books at Cost of Services Citizens Need." *Bloomberg News*. March 26, 2016. Available at: http://www.bloomberg.com/news/articles/2013-03-27/flint-balances-books-at-cost-of-services-citizens-need.

Powell, J.A. (2012). *Racing to Justice: Transforming our Conceptions of Self and Other to Build an Inclusive Society*. Bloomington, IN: Indiana University Press.

Schroeck, N. (2009). "Genesee County's Proposed Lake Huron Water Withdrawal Would Drain Public Resources and Undermine Regional Cooperation." *Great Lakes Law*. July 16, 2009. Available at: http://www.greatlakeslaw.org/blog/2009/07/genesee-countys-proposed-lake-huron-water-withdrawal-would-drain-public-resources-and-undermine-regi.html.

Scorsone, E. and Bateson, N. (2011). *Long-Term Crisis and Systemic Failure: Taking the Fiscal Stress of American Cities Seriously: Case Study: City of Flint*. September. Available at: https://www.cityofflint.com/wp-content/uploads/Reports/MSUE_FlintStudy2011.pdf.

Index

Note: Page numbers with t refer to tables. Page numbers with f refer to figures.

www.ingramcontent.com/pod-product-compliance
Lightning Source LLC
Chambersburg PA
CBHW070858030426
42336CB00014BA/2249
9781642597912